PEOPLE OF THE EARTH

An Indian couple eating, painted by John White in the late sixteenth century. Thomas Hariot wrote of the Indians "They are verye sober in their eating and trinkinge, and consequently verye longe lived because they doe not oppress nature. . . . I would to God we would followe their exemple."

FIFTH EDITION

PEOPLE OF THE EARTH

An Introduction to World Prehistory

Brian M. Fagan

University of California, *Santa Barbara*

Little, Brown and Company   BOSTON   TORONTO

Library of Congress Cataloging in Publication Data

Fagan, Brian M.
    People of the earth.

    Includes bibliographies and index.
    1. Man, Prehistoric. 2. Civilization, Ancient.
I. Title.
GN740.F33 1985   930   85-4565
ISBN 0-316-27322-8

Library of Congress Catalog Card No. 85–4565

ISBN 0-316-27322-8

9 8 7 6 5 4 3 2 1

ALP

Published simultaneously in Canada
by Little, Brown & Company (Canada) Limited

Printed in the United States of America

COVER

Photo is of a fragment from a large Chibcha burial urn. This sculptured head is said to represent the goddess Bachue, who is also often modeled in smaller figurines. Reprinted courtesy of Museum of the American Indian, Heye Foundation, New York.

CREDITS

Frontispiece: Reproduced by courtesy of the Trustees of the British Museum.

CHAPTER 1

Photo Essay Credits
Page 6: *top left,* courtesy of the Center for American Archaeology, Kampsville Archaeological Center; *middle left,* courtesy of Stuart Streuever; *bottom left,* courtesy of the Colonial Williamsburg Foundation; *bottom right,* courtesy of the Department of Anthropology, Northwestern University/photo by Dell Baston.
Page 7: *top left,* photo by W. Swalling/UCLA; *top right,* courtesy of University Museum, University of Pennsylvania/photo by Nicholas Hartman; *bottom left,* courtesy of University Museum, University of Pennsylvania/photo by George Bass; *bottom right,* photo by D. C. Oschner, copyright © UCLA Institute of Archaeology. Moai Documentation Project, Easter Island 1984. Jo Anne Van Tillburg, Director; David C. Ochsner, project photographer.

Figure 1.3: From *Invitation to Archaeology* by James Deetz. Copyright © 1967 by James Deetz. Reprinted by permission of Doubleday & Company, Inc. *Figure 1.4:* Left: Earthwatch; right: Courtesy of the Society of Antiquaries of London. *Figure 1.5:* From *Invitation to Archaeology* by James Deetz. Copyright © 1967 by James Deetz. Reprinted by permission of Doubleday & Company, Inc.

(Credits continued on page 532)

TO

* All the dozens of archaeologists and students who have read and used this book in its various editions and sent me their comments and criticisms. This is the only way I can thank them all and expose them for what they are — honest and unmerciful critics. I am deeply grateful.

* All the people at Little, Brown who have worked on this manuscript and invariably managed to produce an attractive book out of it. I am grateful for their cheerful help, and above all for their friendship, which is much cherished.

* And, lastly, and as usual, to our cats, who disapprove of authors in general and my writing efforts in particular. Their contribution was to tread on the manuscript — with muddy paws, of course.

To the Reader

People of the Earth is an attempt at a straightforward narrative of human history from the origins of humankind up to the beginnings of literate civilization. To make the book accessible to those who have not previously studied archaeology, I keep technical terms to a minimum and define them where they do occur.

Anyone who takes on a task having the magnitude of a world prehistory must make several difficult decisions. One such decision was to gloss over many heated archaeological controversies and sometimes to give only one side of an academic argument. But the Bibliography of Archaeology at the back of the book is designed to lead you into the more technical literature and the morass of agreement and disagreement that characterizes world prehistory.

The structure of *People of the Earth* is comparatively straightforward. Part 1 deals with general principles of archaeology, theoretical views of the past, and the climatic background. The remainder of the book is devoted to the story of human prehistory. Chronological tables are provided at the beginning of most chapters, putting cultural names, sites, dates, and other subdivisions of prehistory into a framework. Key dates and terms appear in the margins to give you a sense of chronological direction throughout the text. I would draw your special attention to the Note on the Calibration of Radiocarbon Dates, which appears on page 500. This is fundamental to your understanding of the chronology of world prehistory.

All measurements are given in both metric and nonmetric units. Metric equivalents are used as the primary unit except in the case of miles/kilometers. More readers conceive of long distances in miles, so it seemed logical to use them first.

To the Instructor

With this edition, *People of the Earth* has been in print for more than a decade, a decade that has seen momentous changes in our understanding of world prehistory. Like archaeology, this book has undergone radical change over the past ten years. Somewhat to my surprise, I find myself preparing a fifth edition of a volume that is used as a text in courses as varied as archaeology, physical anthropology and archaeology, world history, and, of course, world prehistory. *People* is used in Australia, in New Zealand, at European universities, and even in Africa. I find myself corresponding with users thousands of miles away and learning about archaeological research that I otherwise would never have discovered. The book now represents not only my own archaeological experience, but the insights, advice, and research of hundreds of instructors, research archaeologists, and thousands of students. I am also flattered to meet occasional colleagues who remember reading *People* as a first undergraduate text — and it got them interested in archaeology. All of this makes the monotonous task of revision a unique opportunity to look at the world of archaeology on the broadest possible canvas.

Like its predecessors, the fifth edition aims to communicate the work of scientific archaeologists to the broadest possible audience. There are still some people who believe that modern archaeology is all an elaborate fol de rol and a hoax. Archaeologists are under attack from religious fundamentalists who believe that the scriptures offer the only true account of human history as well as from those who believe with the same religious fervor that their theories about the settlement of the Americas or the origins of civilization are the only possible truth. This book is an account based on scientific research, not religious belief or wild speculation. Its purpose is to provide the student with a straightforward account of human prehistory from the earliest times up to the advent of literate civilization. As such, *People* provides an answer to the critics of our discipline, for its pages show that we know much more about human prehistory than our critics suspect, or want to believe. What this book does *not* attempt is a frontal attack on either creationists or diffusionists. Not only is this a fruitless pastime, for you cannot shake people's sincerely held beliefs, but also I believe that instructors should tailor-make their courses to their audiences. All *People* can do is provide some theoretical background and basic data as a framework for teaching. It is up to you to defend archaeology against its critics, however ignorant they may be. To my mind, one of the best defenses is a well taught undergraduate course based on good data. And this is what *People* attempts to provide.

I have revised about 40 percent of the book for this edition, with the greatest changes coming in the first two parts. I have recast the beginning of Chapter 1 to make it of more general appeal, made major changes in the "approaches" chapter, and completely rewritten the background on the Pleistocene, as sea-core researches have revolutionized our knowledge of the Ice Age. The chapters on early human evolution have been rewritten to reflect an explosion of new data and ideas, especially on the evolution of human behavior. I have also taken account of new fossil finds. Throughout the book I have updated and refined the text and illustrations, changing chronologies here, adding new sites there, and updating references throughout. There are exciting new finds relating to the Bering Land Bridge and new insights into pre-Clovis sites. These have been added to this edition, as well as a recasting of the European prehistory chapters. The previous edition saw a major rewrite of the chapters on the early civilizations. These revisions have stood the test of time well. Some of the latest research in areas such as Mexico or Sumer is so detailed that it has little impact on a basic text such as this, except, perhaps, in the addition of a reference, a few sentences, or a brief paragraph. The publication of many highly important pieces of research, foreshadowed in preliminary reports cited in earlier editions, has been noted.

There is no question that the basic formula for *People* has worked well. Almost all users have supported the broad geographic coverage of this book, so this remains a feature of the fifth edition. All too often, we teach students about the Americas, Europe, and the Near East, and forget that insights from less well-known areas can often illuminate problems nearer to home. One only has to look at the research on early Australian Aboriginal adaptive patterns or living archaeology in the Kalahari desert in South Africa to get the point. If I have sometimes skimped on detailed coverage of well-known areas, I am unrepentant. It is well worth it in the interests of balanced coverage.

Anyone writing a book on world prehistory is poised on the horns of a sharp-pointed academic dilemma. Should one write a book that is heavy on theory, perhaps encased in a specific theoretical framework? Or is it better to compile a basic culture-history of the world with relatively little emphasis on theory? Most reviewers and colleagues seem to feel we have achieved a realistic balance. *People* is written without an overriding theoretical framework, and with plenty of descriptive passages, in the knowledge that different instructors use the book in different ways, each bringing his or her theoretical bias to the material. If there is a pervasive theoretical theme for the book, it is the gradual progress of humankind as a member of the world ecological community. If there are three overriding developments in world prehistory in recent decades, they are a massive expansion of field research to all parts of the world, the widespread adoption of scientific and quantitative methods, and a much greater concern with theoretical models. *People* navigates between these developments with sedulous care, and tries to avoid excesses of scientific and theoretical bias. Presently, archaeologists seem intoxicated with science, sometimes to the extent that they forget they are studying human beings with all their complex motivations and thought processes. Perhaps the greatest message of world prehistory is not that we humans are different, but that our behavior is so strikingly similar. You only have to compare the archaeological record from Mexico and Egypt to see what I mean. And this is a theme which I feel should pervade our world prehistory courses, a theme far more important than the latest nuances of archaeological theory or excavation technique.

Everyone working with students who are new to archaeology has to balance strict scientific accuracy and terminological precision against the dangers of misinformation and overstatement. I have tried to avoid a catalog and have deliberately erred on the side of overstatement. After all, the objective in a first course is to introduce students to a fascinating and complex subject. Overstatement is more likely to stick in their minds and can always be qualified at a more advanced level. The complexities of academic debate will be left to more specialized syntheses and to advanced courses. The important truth the student should learn early is that science deals not with absolute truth, but with successive approximations of the truth.

Undoubtedly the biggest problem in preparing this book is the huge flood of literature that now surrounds world prehistory. It is impossible for me, or anyone, to keep pace with all the material from every corner of the world. Like most archaeologists, I am not a linguistic genius. Unlike Heinrich Schliemann, who mastered at least eight languages, and Arthur Evans, who spoke a minimum of six, my expertise is limited to English and French with a smattering of German and Swahili. Thus, my reading has necessarily been selective, especially in regions like central Europe, where a knowledge of German is essential. In these and other areas, I have had to rely heavily on secondary and tertiary sources. For these reasons, I have undoubtedly missed some key references and misled readers with some wrong information. I hope that you will update readers from your own knowledge, and, if you find oversights, drop me a line to tell me about them. I am deeply grateful to those of you who have taken the time to send me reprints, corrections, or information on references. Your efforts are valuable and deeply appreciated. It is now almost a full-time job to keep up with world prehistory, because the days of the specialist and the subspecialist are truly with us. I would like to thank the dozens of colleagues and friends, as well as students, who have taken the trouble to provide feedback, update information, and research materials over the years.

As always, the new edition has benefited greatly from the detailed criticisms and frank advice of dozens of colleagues. I owe a particular debt to Dr. Peter White of the University of Sydney, New South Wales, for his critique of the first three chapters. Professors Don D. Fowler, University of Nevada, Reno; Norman Hammond, Rutgers the State University of New Jersey; Donald A. Proulx, University of Massachusetts, Amherst; and William A. Turnbaugh, University of Rhode Island, kindly provided insightful reviews of the text during revision. I am deeply grateful to them all.

Lastly, a word of thanks to Billie Ingram, Hazel Wright, and Rachel Parks of the production staff at Little, Brown. They have made the revision of this book a (comparative) pleasure; I can but dedicate this book to them.

CONTENTS

Chapter Two

Approaches to World Prehistory

Chapter Three

The Pleistocene Epoch

Chapter Thirteen

New World Agriculture

279

PART FIVE

OLD WORLD CIVILIZATIONS

307

Chapter Fourteen

The Development of Civilization

308

PEOPLE OF THE EARTH

PART ONE

PREHISTORY

"We are concerned here with methodical digging for
systematic information, not with the upturning of earth in a
hunt for the bones of saints and giants or the armory of
heroes, or just plainly for treasure."
–Sir Mortimer Wheeler

Part One contains the essential background about the study of archaeology
needed for any examination of human prehistory. We make no attempt to give a
comprehensive summary of all the methods and theoretical approaches used
by archaeologists. Rather, Part One touches some of the high points and basic
principles behind archaeologists' excavations and laboratory research. Our
narrative is, in the final analysis, based on the systematic application of these
principles. Chapter Three gives some all-important background on the great
climatic changes that form the backdrop to human prehistory.

Chapter One

Archaeology

PREVIEW

✣ The systematic study of world prehistory began in the late nineteenth century as anthropologists began to study human diversity. At the same time biologists and social scientists were exploring the implications of biological and social evolution.

✣ Archaeology is the study of past human societies and is an integral part of anthropology. Archaeologists have four objectives: the construction of culture history, the reconstruction of past lifeways, the study of processes of cultural change, and the understanding of the archaeological record through analogy and experiment.

✣ Culture is a theoretical concept formulated by anthropologists to define the adaptive systems unique to humanity, for culture is the means by which we humans adapt to the challenges of the world's diverse environments.

✣ A culture is a complex system, a set of interacting variables that serve to maintain the population in equilibrium with its environment. No cultural system is ever static. It is always changing in ways that can be studied in the archaeological record.

✣ The archaeological record is the data amassed from archaeological survey and excavation. Preservation factors play an important part in the amount of information that can be obtained from the archaeological record.

✣ Every archaeological find has a context in space and time, be it an artifact, a site, or food remains. The study of patterns of artifacts in space depends on the Law of Association, the notion that an object is contemporary with the other objects found in the same archaeological level.

✣ Relative chronology is based on the Law of Superposition, which holds that the lowest occupation level on a site is older than those that have accumulated on top of it. Chronometric chronology involves dates in years and is developed by a number of methods: potassium argon dating, radiocarbon dating, dendrochronology, and cross-dating using objects of known age.

✣ Archaeological survey and excavation are carried out using carefully formulated research designs. Excavation methods vary with the type of site being investigated.

✣ Archaeologists have developed sophisticated classification methods to describe artifacts and other finds; the classifications provide the basis for theorizing about archaeological cultures and for studying cultural process (the mechanisms by which cultures change).

INTRODUCTION

The two men paused in front of the sealed doorway bearing the seals of the long-dead pharoah. They had waited six long years, from 1917 to 1922, for this moment. Silently, Howard Carter pried a hole through the ancient plaster. Hot air rushed out of the small cavity and massaged his face. Carter shone a flashlight through the hole and peered into the tomb. Gold objects swam in front of his eyes and he was struck dumb with amazement.

Lord Carnarvon moved impatiently behind him as Carter remained silent.

"What do you see?" he asked, hoarse with excitement.

"Wonderful things," whispered Carter as he stepped back from the doorway.

The door was soon broken down. In a daze of wonderment, the discoverers wandered through the antechamber of Tutankhamun's tomb. They fingered golden funerary beds, admired beautifully inlaid chests, and examined the pharoah's chariots stacked against the wall. Gold was everywhere — on wooden statues, inlaid on thrones and boxes, in jewelry, even on children's stools. Soon Tutankhamun was known as the golden pharoah, and archaeology as the domain of buried treasure and royal sepulchers.

Gold, silver, lost civilizations, unsolved mysteries, grinning skeletons . . . all are part of the romantic world of archaeology in most people's minds. Archaeologists seem like romantic adventurers, digging pyramids and finding long-forgotten inscriptions in remote places. Like Indiana Jones of movie fame, we come across as students of sunken continents and great migrations, as experts on epic journeys and powerful civilizations. A century ago, many archaeologists were indeed adventurers. Today, however, archaeology has become a complex and demanding scientific pastime that studies over 3 million years of human existence. On the face of it, modern scientific archaeology may seem dull and highly technical, but the fascination of great adventure has been replaced by all the excitement of the detective story. Fictional detectives take a handful of clues and solve apparently insoluble murders. Archaeologists take a multitude of small and apparently trivial archaeological finds and use them to answer basic questions about ancient societies.

Even as late as the 1870s, you could go out digging in the Near East and find a long-lost civilization. German businessman-turned-archaeologist Heinrich Schliemann was convinced that Homer's Troy had actually existed. Armed with a copy of the *Iliad*, he went out to Turkey and cut great trenches into the ancient mounds at Hissarlik. Schliemann found the remains of nine cities stratified one above the other and announced that the seventh was Homer's Troy (Ceram, 1953; Daniel, 1981). His discoveries caused an international sensation. So did Frenchman Emil de Sarzec when he unearthed the Sumerians in desolate southern Mesopotamia, a civilization that soon turned out to be one of the earliest in the world, and the society where the Flood legend in Genesis probably originated (Fagan, 1979).

The twentieth century has seen archaeology turn from a casual treasure hunt into a science. There have been dramatic discoveries by the dozens — Tutankhamun's tomb in 1922, the royal cemetery at Ur of the Chaldees in Iraq in 1928, the spectacular early human fossils discovered by the Leakey family in East Africa during the last quarter century, and, in the 1980s, magnificent royal burials in China and Guatemala. While these finds have stirred the popular imagination, archaeologists have been engaged on a less conspicuous but just as fascinating adventure of discovery — through 3 million years of prehistoric times.

In the 1840s, most scientists assumed that humankind was only a few thousand years old, perhaps no more than the 6000 years allowed for by the biblical account of the Creation in Genesis (Grayson, 1983). By the late nineteenth century, archaeologists believed that the first human beings had lived on earth some tens of thousands of years ago, perhaps as much as 100,000 years before the present. Modern scientific archaeology, with its elaborate dating methods and close ties to the natural sciences, has drawn back the curtains on a much longer prehistoric stage. Thanks to radiocarbon and potassium argon dating techniques, we know that the first humans emerged in East Africa at least 3 million years ago. For more than one and a half million years, our early ancestors lived on wild vegetable foods and by scavenging meat from predator kills. Then, about 1.5 million years ago, the first true humans emerged, hunters and gatherers who spread from the savanna regions of Africa into more temperate latitudes. These larger-brained people were apparently capable of articulate speech and gave way some 400,000 years ago to the immediate ancestors of modern human beings, *Homo sapiens.*

For most of the past 3 million years, the pace of human biological and cultural evolution was glacially slow at best, but about 40,000 years ago, the evolutionary pace quickened with the emergence of the first fully modern people. *Homo sapiens sapiens* settled in all parts of the world, in the extremes of arctic and tropical climates. Modern people crossed into the New World from Siberia, settled in the deserts of Australia, and developed the first artistic traditions. Far from being only big game hunters, many of them specialized in gathering wild vegetable foods, in fishing, or in collecting shellfish. And, more than 10,000 years ago, some of them began to cultivate the soil and domesticate sheep, goats, and other animals — a true revolution in human existence.

The new economies took off like wildfire. It took only 8000 years for most of the world to turn to food production. Agriculture and stock raising were well established throughout the Near East by 7500 B.C. and had spread to Europe a millennium later. The Chinese were cultivating by 6000 B.C., the New Guinea highlanders at about the same time. Only in game-rich Africa and isolated Australasia did hunter-gatherer economies survive into recent times. Much of sub-Saharan Africa started growing crops and herding about only 2000 years ago. The early Americans took to food production by the mid-sixth millennium B.C., domesticating wild cereal grasses and beans, as well as root crops like the sweet potato. Food production was probably the most significant watershed in human prehistory, for it enabled the development of much more complex societies, and, ultimately, our own industrial civilization.

We live in cities with populations in the millions. Yet, only 10,000 years ago, most humans lived in tiny camps or small, sedentary villages. The inexorable cultural forces of the agricultural revolution soon led to the emergence of literate, urban civilizations, first in Mesopotamia and Egypt, then in the Indus Valley, the Aegean, and the Far East. The great civilizations of the Americas subsisted on maize and bean cultivation — the Olmec and Maya of Mesoamerica, the coastal and highland civilizations of Peru. And, in the Old World, small-scale city-states and valley civilizations were followed by the imperial civilizations of Persia, Greece, and Rome, civilizations that linked many diverse cultures into much larger hegemonies. While the preindustrial civilizations relied on abundant cheap manpower for their prosperity, the industrial civilization of today evolved from a preindustrial base, propelled to ever greater technological complexity by the use of fossil fuels, the advances of science, and the industrial revolution.

The fascinating chronicle of world prehistory has been written from the testimony of millions of chipped stones, animal bone fragments, and potsherds, from Sumerian clay tablets, pollen grains from Scandinavian bogs, and from ancient Peruvian textiles. Archaeology is, as more than one author has reminded us, the science of rubbish (Fagan, 1985). The data may seem trivial, but the results are not. World prehistory is of vital concern to everyone, for it records the collective cultural heritage of all humankind.

Scientific archaeology developed out of treasure hunting. It is a process of careful research design, site survey, excavation, laboratory analysis, and interpretation. In fact, it is no coincidence that the first scientific excavations were conducted by a retired British general and German archaeologists who came from a strongly military cultural tradition. It was they who imposed the first discipline on archaeological excavation, a discipline that continues to this day. To most people, archaeology *is* excavation — trenches, careful troweling and shoveling, and the clearance of burials with paint brushes and dental picks. However, as the accompanying picture essay shows, modern archaeology is far more, involving everything from walking the countryside to sophisticated remote-sensing techniques and many months of quiet laboratory analysis. Archaeology is a complicated form of teamwork, involving not only experts but also volunteers from every walk of life. Many college students go on an excavation as part of their learning experience. If you are lucky, you will find an unusual artifact or help the archaeologists interpret a complicated sequence of long-collapsed buildings. You can spend your spare hours sorting shellfish and bone fragments from Indian shell middens, become an expert on a particular prehistoric pottery, or operate a computer pro-

Above, left. A general view of excavations at the Koster site, near Kampsville, Illinois. Excavated levels are covered with a plastic sheet to protect them against the weather.

Left. A student excavator cleaning a human burial dating from about 5000 years ago. Brushes and dental picks are normally used for this delicate work. The bones are cleaned, then photographed and recorded before being lifted from the grave.

Below, left. An exemplary excavation of an eighteenth-century kitchen at colonial Williamsburg, Virginia. Large tree roots had damaged the north foundation. Behind it lies the H-shaped foundation for the chimney.

Below. Students at the Koster site surveying the area that has been excavated.

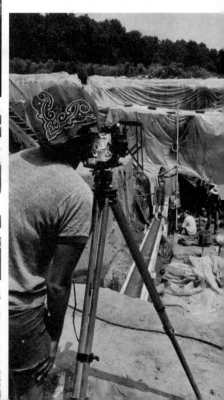

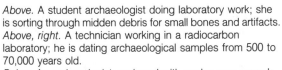

Above. A student archaeologist doing laboratory work; she is sorting through midden debris for small bones and artifacts.
Above, right. A technician working in a radiocarbon laboratory; he is dating archaeological samples from 500 to 70,000 years old.
Below. An archaeologist equipped with scuba gear records features of a Bronze Age shipwreck from Cape Gelidonya, Turkey, dating to about 1200 B.C.
Below, right. Field crew at work measuring prehistoric Easter Island statue for the Rock Art Archive of the Institute of Archaeology, Los Angeles, California.

gram that holds the data from months of field work. Your work may seem trivial, sometimes even dull, but the results are another tiny part of the great jigsaw of world prehistory. None of our attempts to explain the rise of civilization, or the origins of humanity, would mean anything unless they were based on scientifically recovered archaeological data.

People of the Earth takes you on a 2-million-year journey through prehistory, from the very earliest times up to the emergence of the first urban civilizations. However, we begin by explaining some of the basic principles, methods, and theories of archaeology so that you will be better equipped both to understand prehistory and to participate in archaeology yourself as a volunteer if you so desire. Good luck with your adventures in the past!

WHY STUDY WORLD PREHISTORY?

Before starting our journey, we deal with another fundamental point. Why study world prehistory at all? Some people believe that any form of archaeology is a harmless luxury, a low priority in a world beset by inflation, famine, and geopolitics. Why look to the past, they ask, when all our energies should be devoted to preparing for an uncertain future? How can one look at the future, though, without an understanding of the past and, above all, of our own behavior? Whether or not we like it, we live with the legacy of the recent and remote past. Our civilization derives many of its most cherished institutions from Classical Greece, while city life was developed between the Euphrates and Tigris rivers in Iraq more than 5000 years ago. Famine, slavery, warfare, and poverty are nothing new; they were familiar phenomena to the Ancient Egyptians, the Chinese, and the Sumerians. In reality, we live with the consequences of decisions and actions that were enacted centuries or even millenia ago. The study of prehistory gives us a balanced perspective on our behavior and on our responses to pressing problems that are not new, even though they threaten us on a larger scale.

Western civilization has a written chronicle that extends back to Sumerian times, more than 5000 years ago. However, many of the world's societies have very limited historical records, known to us only through scattered folk memories or archaeological excavations. The Aztec people of Mexico first came into contact with the Spanish in 1519. Within a few years their civilization was in ruins, their written chronicles burned by zealous missionaries. As a result, our knowledge of Aztec history is a patchwork of incomplete data from dozens of sources, yet a knowledge of this history is vital not only for fostering a sense of identity among the surviving Aztec people and for nation building in Mexico but also to our understanding of the ways in which the pre-Columbians solved the problems of living (Fagan, 1984a). It is no coincidence that many African nations have active archaeological programs, designed to reconstruct a national history from a morass of obscure tribal histories and excavations at archaeological sites. Likewise, many American Indian groups have become involved in archaeological research (Kirk, 1975). In prehistoric times, most societies were concerned with living in equilibrium with their environment, with existing in a world that was assumed to have been the same in the past and that would remain unchanged in the future. Today industrial civilization, with its concern with cultural roots and cultural identity, dominates the world, and so there are compelling reasons for every society to have at least some sense of its cultural origins. In many cases, archaeology provides the only way of doing so.

We live in a biologically and culturally diverse world, a world that is shrinking rapidly in this age of the jetliner, the satellite, and instant communications. Even half a century ago the world was a large place. Today the world, in all its bewildering diversity, comes right into our living rooms. We can contact Peru within seconds and watch wars on the other side of the world as they are being fought. Confronting this diversity often is an uncomfortable experience, especially since we tend to perceive the differences between various societies as much greater than they really are. By looking back over the long millennia of prehistory we obtain a quite different perspective of a world in which people have worked out solutions to extremely challenging problems with brilliant success, problems such as food shortages, rapidly growing populations, and catastrophic environmental changes. Very often the solutions of various societies, although they are separated by thousands of miles, have been remarkably similar: the advent of writing, the development of cities, or the formation of a state-organized society. What is striking is not the diversity of humankind but the remarkably similar ways in which we respond to external challenges. Societies may wax and wane, civilizations rise and fall, but something new always arises in their place. To look back at prehistory is to acquire a faith in humanity's ability to innovate and respond to changing circumstances. We are surrounded by doomsday prophets, by people who forecast the imminent demise of civilization, of humanity itself. Any serious student of prehistory can have no doubt that humankind will rise to the challenges of the twentieth century. We shall survive.

A final compelling reason to study world prehistory is simply for the fun of it. We can look back at an extraordinary landscape of biological and cultural evolution, at our very origins among the nonhuman primates, at the first migrants to the New World more than 25,000 years ago, and at remarkable civilizations as widely separated as Peru and the Indus Valley. We are surrounded by awesome ruins that have survived the centuries to enlighten our own age: the pyramids of Gizeh erected more than 4500 years ago, the brooding stone circles of Stonehenge in southern Britain, and the vast plazas and temples of the ancient city of Teotihuacán, Mexico. Most of us contrive to visit at least one major archaeological site during our lifetimes, to marvel at the achievements of our predecessors on this planet. An understanding of world prehistory enables us not only to better appreciate these monuments but also to recognize them for what they are, an integral part of the cultural heritage of all humanity.

In the pages that follow the prehistory of humankind from the earliest times is recounted, using scientifically collected data from all over the world. This account is founded on the basic assumption that the theory of biological evolution and natural selection provides a viable framework for the study of world prehistory.

ANTHROPOLOGY

Anthropology

Anthropology encompasses the whole range of human cultures, both Western and non-Western (Pelto, 1966; Penniman, 1965). As the study of humanity, anthropology is a holistic discipline that uses comparative methods to study the variations in economic, political, religious, and other institutions and customs throughout every human society. Anthropologists are interested in comparisons between different cultures, and in biological and cultural evolution. The comparative and evolutionary aspects of anthropology make it unique among the social sciences.

Archaeology

Archaeology is the study of the lives and cultures of ancient peoples. Archaeologists study and interpret the material evidence of past human activity. The archaeologist is a special type of anthropologist who has three main objectives: the study of culture history, a reconstruction of past lifeways, and an explanation of cultural process. Then there is a fourth objective: interpretation of the archaeological record by observing the processes that created it, and by using controlled experiments and analogies from present-day societies. There are many types of archaeologists, each having distinctive objectives, methods, techniques, and theoretical approaches. *Classical archaeologists* study Greek and Roman civilization; *historical archaeologists* study relatively recent sites such as Colonial American towns or medieval cities. *Anthropological archaeologists* (prehistorians) are concerned with sites of all ages, but they tend to concentrate their research efforts primarily on prehistoric settlements. *Paleoanthropologists* study the earliest human cultures of all.

Physical anthropology

Physical anthropologists study the emergence and later evolution of humankind and the reasons why human populations vary one from another (Weiss and Mann, 1985). Early human evolution is documented by fossil human and prehuman remains found in archaeological sites and geological levels. Physical anthropologists are deeply involved in modern human biology, trying to find out why different human populations have adapted physically to widely differing natural environments. *Primatologists* are physical anthropologists who are experts on ape and monkey behavior. Their work provides information relevant to the study of early human behavior.

History

History is the study of our past through written records; such records extend back only 5000 years. *Prehistory*, the millennia before documentary history, goes back at least 2 million years.

HUMAN CULTURE

Culture is a term we will use again and again in these pages (Kroeber and Kluckhohn, 1952). Anthropologists study human cultures and all of us live within a culture. Most cultural descriptions can be qualified by one or more labels, such as "middle-class," "American," "mountain-dwelling," or "Masai." This qualification often becomes associated in our minds with certain behavior patterns or features that are typical of the culture so labeled. One such attribute for "middle-class Americans," for example, might be the hamburger. Culture

Culture is a concept developed by anthropologists to describe the distinctive adaptive system used by human beings (Jochim, 1981). Culture is our primary means of adapting to our environment. Until the emergence of humanity, all animals adapted to their environments through biological evolution. If an animal was well adapted to its environment, it prospered. If it was not, it either evolved into a new species, moved away, or became extinct. The forces of biological evolution gave the polar bear a thick coat and layers of fat to protect it from the arctic cold, but Eskimos, the human occupants of the Arctic, do not possess layers of fur. They wear warm clothing and make snow houses to protect themselves from the environment. Their tools and dwellings are part of their culture — their adaptive system that coincides with the polar bear's fur.

Ordinarily, when animals die their experience dies with them. However, with humans, once biological evolution had led to the development of speech, they were able to communicate their feelings and experiences from one generation to the next. They could share ideas, which in turn became behavior patterns that were repeated again and again. We see abundant traces of this throughout prehistory, when the same types of tools and sites are found, almost unchanged, over millennia of prehistory. A good example of this phenomenon is the stone hand ax, a multipurpose tool that remained in use for more than one million years (Figure 5.3a, p. 119).

Human beings use the symbolic system of language to transmit ideas and their culture. Culture is learned by intentional teaching as well as trial and error and simple imitation. Since people share ideas by teaching, the same artifacts and behavior continue from one generation to the next. Culture is an ongoing phenomenon that changes gradually over time.

It follows that the diversity of human languages has served to accentuate the differences between cultures, simply because people cannot understand one another.

Unlike biological adaptation, culture is nongenetic and it provides a much quicker way to share ideas that enable people to cope with their environment. It is the adaptive nature of culture that allows archaeologists to assume that artifacts found in archaelogical sites are patterned adaptations to the environment.

A culture is a complex system, a set of interacting variables — tools, Cultural system burial customs, ways of getting food, religious beliefs, social organization, and so on — that function to maintain a community in a state of equilibrium with its environment. When one element in the system changes, say hunting practices as a result of a prolonged drought, then reacting adjustments will occur in many other elements, so that the system stays in a state as closely approximating the original system as possible. It follows that no cultural system is ever static. It is always changing in big and small ways, some of which can be studied in archaeological sites.

Archaeologists tend to think of culture as possessing three components:

The individual's own version of his or her culture, the diversified individual behavior that makes up the myriad strains of a culture.

Shared culture, where elements of a culture are shared by everyone. These can include cultural activities like human sacrifice or ritualized warfare, or any shared human activity, as well as the body of rules and prescriptions that go to make up the sum whole of the culture.

Cultural system, the system of behavior in which every individual *participates*. You not only share it with other members of society, you participate in the cultural system as well. Both sharing and participation, however, could not take place without language as a vehicle of communication.

Culture, then, can be viewed as either a blend of shared traits or as a system that permits a society to interact with its environment. In order to accomplish more than merely working out chronological sequences, however, the archaeologist has to view culture as a complex set of interacting components. Unless the processes that actually operate the system are carefully defined, these components would remain static, which is why archaeologists are deeply concerned with what is called "cultural process," the processes by which human societies changed in the past.

Cultural changes take place through time, most being gradual and cumulative. Inventions and design improvements result in dozens of minor alterations in the ways people live. Generally, culture evolution was gradual in prehistoric times, although there are cases of sudden change, such as the Roman conquest of Gaul. Dramatic cultural modification can result from the diffusion from neighboring areas of a new idea or invention, such as the plow (Chapter Two). Culture change is proceeding at a dizzying pace in our own society, to the extent that we have problems adjusting to constant social change.

The cumulative effects of long-term culture change are easily seen. A comparison of the simple flaked stone tools of the earliest humans and the sophisticated contents of the Egyptian pharaoh Tutankhamun's tomb will help one to understand the power of cumulative change over thousands of years.

Modern archaeology swirls with controversy about the goals of research. Earlier archaeologists often were content just to collect and classify their finds into long sequences of human cultures. They described changing cultures but made no effort to explain *why* change took place and *what* changes meant. Today's archaeologist is concerned with explanation as well as description of ancient cultures, with processes of cultural change through time. The term *process* is used in archaeology to refer to mechanisms by which cultures change. These processes are studied by looking at variables in cultural systems that could lead to cultural change (Chapter Two). Then there is the archaeological record itself. Just trying to understand how it came into being is a far less obvious process than might be apparent (Binford, 1983).

THE ARCHAEOLOGICAL RECORD

Archaeologists study human cultures of the past and have to be content, for the most part, with the surviving, more durable evidence of prehistoric culture (Deetz, 1967). Any excavator is like a detective piecing together events from fragmentary clues.

What we can find out about the past is severely limited by soil conditions. Stone and baked clay are among the most lasting substances, surviving under almost all conditions. Wood, bone, leather, and metals are much less durable and seldom remain for the archaeologist to find. In the Arctic, however, whole sites have been found frozen, preserving highly perishable wooden tools or, in Siberia, complete carcasses of extinct mammoths (Clark, 1965). Waterlogged bogs in Denmark have preserved long-dead victims of human sacrifice, and wooden tools survive well there too. Everyone has heard of the remarkable tomb of Egyptian pharaoh Tutankhamun, whose astonishing treasure survived almost intact in the dry climate of the Nile Valley for more than 3000 years (Romer, 1981). Still, in most archaeological sites only a few durable materials survive, and reconstructing the past from these finds often is a difficult riddle to solve.

The *archaeological record* is the data amassed from survey and excavation; we might think of it as the archival raw materials of world prehistory.

Archaeological record

The inevitable result of having only durable remains to study is that many prehistoric cultures are interpreted solely on the basis of such imperishable tools as stone axes or clay potsherds. The only way archaeologists can combat this emphasis on the durable and material elements of a culture is by meticulous study of sites where preservation conditions are outstanding; through careful examination of the arrangement of artifacts in the soil, archaeologists may discover a clue about the activities or social status of the artifacts' owners.

Until recently, most archaeologists simply accepted the limitations of the archaeological record without question. They made little effort to understand the ways in which the record was formed. Consider for a moment, a newly abandoned hunter-gatherer campsite in the Illinois Valley of the Midwest. The inhabitants leave collapsing houses, newly extinguished hearths, broken-up bones, acorn husks, and all manner of domestic debris as well as worn-out artifacts behind them. The years pass. Rain and wind destroy the houses and they become a scatter of foundation stones and postholes. The acorn husks and bones decay and vanish, leaving no trace behind them. Soon the site is covered with dense woodland and grass, soils accumulate, and there are no surface traces of the site left. Once buried, the surviving structures, hearths, and artifacts undergo still further change as a result of processes resulting from the distinctive soil chemistry on the site. Hundreds, if not thousands, of years later some archaeologists come along and dig up the site. All that they will unearth are the surviving remnants of generations of decay processes. These processes vary from site to site and are little understood.

Some of the most interesting recent research in archaeology has focused on these processes, and on the problems of interpreting the archaeological record. Such studies assume that the archaeological record is the result of lengthy decay processes and that the only way we can interpret it is with reference to modern conditions. This approach argues that the archaeological record is in the process of formation all around us and that it is impossible to interpret the past without observations of the present (Binford, 1981, 1983). A whole new body of "middle range" archaeological theory is slowly being developed to aid in interpreting the archaeological record, a theory based on research into modern hunter-gatherer and peasant societies, as well as on decay processes (for a summary, see Binford, 1983).

Middle range theory

Since middle range theory is very much in its infancy, most archaeologists still rely heavily on sites where preservation conditions are exceptional and on the assistance of scholars from other disciplines. Botanists and zoologists can identify seeds and bone fragments from ancient living sites to reconstruct prehistoric diets. Geologists study lake beds, gravels, and caves for their many tools from early millennia. Paleontologists and paleobotanists specialize in the evolution of mammals and plants, studying bones from extinct animals and pollens from long-vanished plants. They help reconstruct ancient climates, which have fluctuated greatly through our long history. Chemists and physicists employ radioactive methods of dating for volcanic rocks and organic substances such as bone and charcoal. These techniques have produced a rough chronological framework for more than 2 million years of human life. Modern archaeology is truly a multidisciplinary team effort, depending on scientists from many fields of inquiry. In one afternoon, an excavator may call on a glass expert, an authority on seashells, an earthworm specialist, and a soil scientist. Each has a piece to fit into the archaeological puzzle.

ARTIFACTS, SITES, AND CONTEXT

World prehistory is recorded in thousands of archaeological sites and artifacts, each of which has a precise place in space and time, that is, in its context. Some understanding of the ways in which archaeologists study the dimensions of space and time is essential to an understanding of prehistory (Dunnell, 1971).

Archaeological context is the culturally significant location of a find spot of any object found in an archaeological site (Fagan, 1985). *Cultural context* is a subcategory that represents the position of an object; was it found in a pit, in a room, on a surface? Metric data are used to define the position of the object uniquely. The time component of the context is the date of the object in years or its position in the layers of an archaeological site relative to other artifacts and layers. The time and space context of an archaeological find provides the basis for building up long sequences of archaeological sites in time and space.

An *artifact* is "anything which exhibits any physical attributes that can be assumed to be the results of human activity" (Dunnell, 1971). The term *artifact* covers every form of archaeological find — from stone axes to clay pots, butchered animal bones, and manifestations of human behavior found in archaeological sites.

Archaeological sites are places where traces of ancient human activity are to be found. The Great Pyramid of Gizeh is an archaeological site; so is a tiny scatter of hunter-gatherer artifacts found on the surface of the Utah desert. There are millions of sites in the world, many still undiscovered. They are limited in number and variety only by preservation conditions and the activities of the people who lived on them. Some, like the early bone caches at Olduvai Gorge, Tanzania, were used for only short periods of time (M. D. Leakey, 1971). Others, like the great Mesopotamian city mounds or *tells*, like Ur of the Chaldees, were occupied for thousands of years (Lloyd, 1963; Woolley, 1954). Archaeological sites often are classified according to the activities that took place upon them — living sites, kill sites, burial sites, religious sites, art sites, and so on. Many archaeological sites contain evidence for different activities: those of individual households, of entire communities, perhaps even of a single craftsperson like a potter, whose artifacts lie in a pattern as they were abandoned.

SPACE

The archaeological context of space can run from a simple spatial relationship between two artifacts to the distance between several households, or even to the relationships between an entire regional network of communities (Flannery, 1976). Context in space is closely tied to cultural behavior. Archaeologists infer behavior from artifacts and their associations, from the patterning (spatial arrangement) of tools around, say, an abandoned bison carcass. A single projectile head dug up out of context at this particular site would allow you nothing more than the reasonable inference that it was part of a weapon. However, the patterning of many such weapon heads in association with the butchered remains of the bison can tell us much about how the animal was killed and cut up. The relationships between the carcass and the tools in the ground are our primary source of information on human behavior there.

The *Law of Association* is based on the principle that an object is contemporary with the other objects found in the precise archaeological level in which it is found (Figure 1.1). The study of space is the study of associations between artifacts within their archaeological cultures. It also involves the study of the distribution of human settlements against a background of the ancient environment in which they flourished.

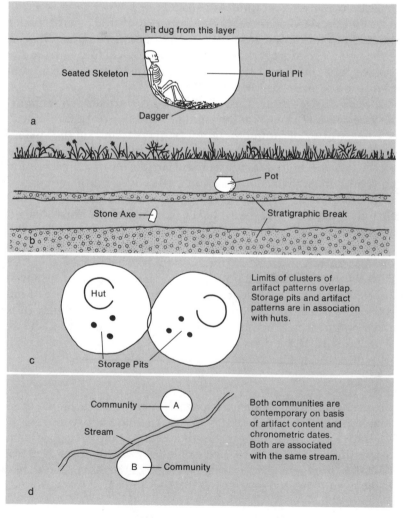

Figure 1.1 The Law of Association. (a) a skeleton associated with a single dagger; (b) a pot and a stone ax, separated by a stratigraphic break, which are not in association; (c) two contemporary household clusters associated with one another; (d) an association of two communities that are contemporary.

TIME

World prehistory extends through at least 3 million years of gradually accelerating cultural change. The measurement of this enormous time scale has been a preoccupation of archaeologists for years.

Relative Chronology

At the end of the eighteenth century, people began to realize that the earth's rocks were stratified, or laid down in layers, one after another. The notion of geological stratification was soon applied to archaeological sites and is now a cornerstone of *relative chronology*, the correlation of prehistoric sites or cultures with one another by their relative age.

Stratification is based on the *Law of Superposition*, which says that the lowest occupation level on a site is older than those accumulated on top of it. The principle can be readily understood by placing a book on a flat surface. Then place a second book on top of the first. Obviously, the first book was put on the table earlier than the second that lies upon it. Unless you took a stopwatch and timed the exact interval in minutes and seconds between the time you placed the first and second books on the surface, you have no idea how much time separated the two events. All you know is that the second book was placed on the first at a *relatively later* moment. Figure 1.2 illustrates the principle of superposition in archaeological practice. Superposition

Superpositions are established by careful excavation and observation of archaeological layers. These layers are excavated with great care, and the artifacts associated with them are carefully studied relative to the stratigraphy of the site. We have stated that artifact styles change slowly through time. Every artifact style, however elaborate or simple, has a period of maximum popularity. This can be a few short months in the case of a dress fashion or tens of thousands of years for a stone tool type. By careful study of artifacts such as pottery found in the successive layers of several archaeological sites in a single region, it is possible to develop a relative chronology of changing artifact styles that is based on the assumption that the period of maximum popularity of a particular pottery type, or series, is the one when it is most frequently found (see Figure 1.3). By using these plots of artifact frequencies, one can develop a relative chronology that later can be used to place isolated sites into the sequence on the basis of their artifact content. This type of ordered or *seriated* relative chronology is not expressed in years unless it can be checked by some dating method that provides dates in years (Deetz, 1967; Marquardt, 1978). Seriation

These ordered sequences of sites and layers can be expanded very effectively by a technique known as *cross-dating*. This requires a well-studied sequence of different artifacts whose development through time has been established by excavation, seriation of the artifacts, and stratigraphic observations. In the Tehuacán Valley in Mexico, Richard Mac- Cross-dating

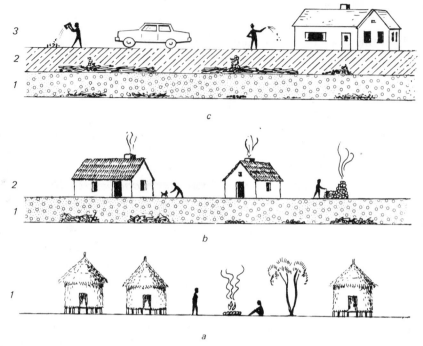

Figure 1.2 Superposition and stratigraphy. (a) A farming village built on virgin subsoil. After a time, the village is abandoned and the huts fall into disrepair. Their ruins are covered by accumulating soil and vegetation. (b) After an interval, a second village is built on the same site, with different architectural styles. This in turn is abandoned; the houses collapse into piles of rubble and are covered by accumulating soil. (c) Twentieth-century people park their cars on top of both village sites and drop litter and coins which, when uncovered, reveal to the archaeologist that the top layer is modern.

An archaeologist digging this site would find that the modern layer is underlain by two prehistoric occupation levels, that square houses were in use in the upper of the two, which is the later (Law of Superposition), and that round huts are stratigraphically earlier than square ones here. Therefore, village 1 is earlier than village 2, but when either was occupied or how many years separate village 1 from 2 cannot be known without further data.

Neish was able to assign a relative date to isolated settlements by careful analysis of their pottery (MacNeish, 1970). He counted the different vessel forms and decorative motifs at each site, then simply placed them in chronological order by matching the percentages of forms and motifs at undated sites with those in a dated sequence nearby. For example, a site with 60 percent red painted bowls is dated to 150 B.C., so it is a reasonable supposition that an undated settlement with the same proportion of similar vessels (and, of course, comparable percentages of other features) is of approximately the same date. Cross-dating like this has been used over wide areas of Mexico to compare sites in different valleys and environments.

Another type of cross-dating has proved useful in European and later American sites. The early civilizations of the Near East traded extensively

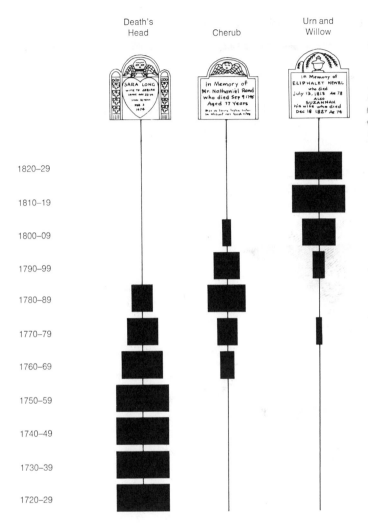

Figure 1.3 Seriation. The changing styles of New England gravestones from Stoneham, Massachusetts, between 1720 and 1829, seriated in three different styles. Notice how each style rises to a peak of maximum popularity and then declines as another comes into fashion.

with the Minoan and Mycenaean civilizations of Greece and Crete as well as with Barbarian Europe (Childe, 1958; C. Renfrew, 1972). They exchanged luxuries such as semiprecious stones and ornaments with the illiterate Europeans for copper, salt, and other raw materials. Some of these luxuries can be dated very precisely in their home countries, so much so that their discovery on an archaeological site in central Europe enables one to say that the level in which the dated foreign object was found dates to the time of the import or later. Since the date of the artifact is known at source, the settlement in which it is found can be relatively dated to a period contemporary with, or younger than, the exotic object of known age. For instance, a Roman coin of 55 B.C. found in an undated French village would date that settlement to a date no earlier than 55 B.C.

Chronometric (Absolute) Chronology

Chronometric dates are dates in calendar years. Prehistoric chronologies cover long periods of time, millennia and centuries as opposed to days or minutes. Some idea of the scale of prehistoric time can be gained by piling up one hundred quarters. If the whole pile represents the entire time that humans and their culture have been on earth, the length of time covered by historical records would equal considerably less than the thickness of one quarter.

How do we date the past in years? Numerous chronometric dating techniques have been tried over the years, but only a few have survived the test of continual use (Table 1.1) (Michels, 1973; Taylor and Meighan, 1978).

Table 1.1 Methods of dating in prehistory.

Date	Method	Major events
Modern times (after A.D. 1)	Historical documents; dendrochronology; imported objects most useful	European settlement of New World; Roman Empire
2,500 B.C.		Origins of cities
		Origins of agriculture
	Radiocarbon dating (organic materials)	First Americans
		Homo sapiens sapiens
70,000 B.C.	Obsidian hydration	*Homo sapiens neanderthalensis*
500,000 B.C.		*Homo erectus*
	Potassium argon dating (volcanic materials)	*Homo* *Australopithecus*
5,000,000 B.C.		

These conventions have been used in the tables throughout this book:

——————— A continuous line means that the chronology is firmly established.

—————▶ A line terminating in an arrow means the time span continues beyond the arrow.

—————| A line terminating with a horizontal bar means the limit of chronology is firmly established.

············ A broken line means the chronology is doubtful.

?Escale A question mark beside the name of a site means its date is not firmly established.

Potassium argon dating

TIME SPAN: From the origins of humankind down to approximately 400,000 years ago.

PRINCIPLES: Potassium (K) is an abundant element in the earth's crust and is present in nearly every mineral. Potassium in its natural form contains only a small proportion of radioactive ^{40}K atoms. For every one hundred ^{40}K atoms that decay, 11 percent become argon 40, an inactive gas that can easily escape from its material by diffusion when lava and other igneous rocks are formed. As volcanic rock forms by crystallization, the argon 40 concentration drops to almost nothing, but the process of ^{40}K decay continues, and 11 percent of every one hundred ^{40}K atoms will become argon 40. Thus it is possible, using a spectrometer, to measure the concentration of argon 40 that has accumulated since the volcanic rock formed.

APPLICATIONS: We are fortunate that many of the world's earliest archaeological sites occur in volcanically active areas. Human tools are found in direct association with cooled lava fragments from contemporary eruptions. Potassium argon has been used to date Olduvai Gorge and other famous early sites (Chapter Four) (Dalrymple and Lamphere, 1970).

Radiocarbon dating (C14)

TIME SPAN: Approximately 70,000 years ago to A.D. 1500.

PRINCIPLES: The radiocarbon (C14) dating method, developed by physicists J. R. Arnold and W. F. Libby in 1949, puts to use the knowledge that living organisms build up their own organic matter by photosynthesis and by using atmospheric carbon dioxide. The percentage of radiocarbon in the organism is equal to that in the atmosphere. When the organism dies, the carbon 14 (C14) atoms begin to disintegrate at a known rate. It is possible then to calculate the age of an organic object by measuring the amount of C14 left in the sample. The initial quantity in a sample is low, so that the limit of detectability is soon reached, although efforts are being made to extend the limit beyond 70,000 years (Grootes, 1978).

Radiocarbon dating is most effective for sites dating between 50,000 and 2000 years before the present (B.P.). Dates can be taken from many types of organic material, including charcoal, shell, wood, or hair. When a date is received from a C14 dating laboratory, it bears a statistical plus or minus factor; for example, 3621 ± 180 years (180 years represents one standard deviation), meaning that chances are two out of three that the reading is between the span of 3441 and 3801. If we double the deviation, chances are nineteen out of twenty that the span (3261 to 3981) is correct. Most dates in the book are derived from C14 dated samples and should be recognized for what they are — statistical approximations (Fagan, 1985; Sharer and Ashmore, 1980).

CALIBRATION: Radiocarbon dating was at first hailed as the solution to the archaeologist's dating problems. Later research has shown this enthusiasm to be a little too optimistic (C. Renfrew, 1971). Unfortunately, the rate at which C14 is produced in the atmosphere has fluctuated considerably because of changes in the strength of the earth's magnetic field and alterations in solar activity. By working with tree-ring chronologies from the long-lived California bristlecone pine, a number of C14 laboratories have agreed on correction tables for C14 dates between approximately 6500 B.C. and A.D. 1950. The discrepancies between radiocarbon and calibrated dates differ widely, but a typical adjustment is that for 10 B.C. $\pm$ 30, which has a calibrated interval of 145 B.C. to A.D. 210. We use the agreed correction tables in this book (J. Klein et al., 1982).

APPLICATIONS: Radiocarbon dating has been used to establish most of the chronologies described in this book for sites dating to between about 70,000 B.C. and A.D. 1500. It has been used to date early agriculture in both the New and Old Worlds, the beginnings of metallurgy, and the first settlement of the Americas. Without C14 dates, world prehistory would be almost entirely undated.

Obsidian hydration

TIME SPAN: Recent times to about 800,000 years ago.

PRINCIPLES: Obsidian is a natural glass substance often formed by volcanic activity. It has long been prized by humankind for its sharp edges and excellent qualities for toolmaking. A new dating method makes use of the fact that a freshly made surface of obsidian will absorb water from its surroundings, which forms a measurable hydration layer that increases with the passage of time. Thus, the depth of hydration on the fractured surface of a stone tool represents the time since the artifact was manufactured or used. Hydration is observed with the aid of microscopically thin sections of obsidian from artifacts that are ground down to about .003 in. The thickness of the layer is measured through the microscope in units of microns. Although there are still some problems with such unknown variables as temperature changes and their effects on hydration, the method holds great promise for the future.

APPLICATIONS: Obsidian hydration is a useful way of ordering large numbers of artifacts in relative series, simply by using their micron readings as they increase with age. It can also be used for dating sites, provided one has some other form of chronology, like tree rings, to check the results. Some of the world's earliest sites have yielded obsidian and the method has been tried experimentally with settlements as early as 780,000 years ago. Once the bugs are worked out, obsidian hydration may be more useful than radiocarbon dating.

Dendrochronology

TIME SPAN: Present day to sites dating to 59 B.C. in the American Southwest.

PRINCIPLES: Many years ago Dr. A. E. Douglass of the University of Arizona used the annual growth rings of trees in the southwestern United States to develop a nonarchaeological chronology for this area that extends back 8200 years (Bannister and Robinson, 1975). Douglass used the sequoia and other slow-growing trees to develop a long master series of annual rings that he used to date fragments of wooden beams found in Indian pueblos. By using cycles of rings from dry and wet series of years, he was able to set up an archaeological chronology for the Southwest that extends back to 59 B.C. Tree rings produce a highly accurate chronology, for the long sequence of annual growth is connected to present-day trees. Dendrochronology is most effective in areas like the Southwest where there is marked seasonal tree growth.

APPLICATIONS: The chronology of Southwestern archaeology described in Chapter Thirteen is developed from dendrochronology. Tree rings have been used to date Roman sites in Germany and even the oak boards that formed the backings for paintings by old Dutch masters (Baillie, 1982)!

Historical records (present day to 5000 years ago) Historical records can be used to date the past only as far back as the beginnings of writing and written records. The Sumerian King Lists of Mesopotamia are some of the first attempts to record past events (Kramer, 1963). Many areas of the world, such as New Guinea or tropical Africa, entered the realms of recorded history only in the last century, while continual historical documentation began in the Americas with Christopher Columbus.

Experimental methods A number of newly developed dating methods promise to amplify both potassium argon and radiocarbon techniques. *Fission track dating* uses the principle that minerals and natural glasses contain uranium atoms that decay by spontaneous fission (Fagan, 1985; Fleischer 1975). The decay rate can be measured in volcanic rocks and has been used to date some samples from Olduvai Gorge. Fission track dating may have applications for sites between a million and 100,000 years old.

Amino acid racemization may emerge as a method for dating fossil bones between 100,000 and 5000 years old. Racemization dating is based on the fact that the amino acids, which make collagen in bones, slowly change their character. The rate of change can be measured, a technique that has been used with interesting results on early American Indian skeletons in California; some specimens have been dated as early as 40,000 years (Chapter Seven) (Bada and Helfman, 1975; Goodman, 1980). However, the method is considered by some experts to be unreliable.

Thermoluminescence dating involves measuring the radioactive properties of baked clay vessels. Sudden and violent heating of the vessel allows the scientist to study stored energy and radioactive impurities in the clay. Thermoluminescence may one day provide a means of dating clay vessels as old as 10,000 years, but the method is still under development (Aitken, 1977).

None of these experimental methods has yet played a major part in the development of the chronology of world prehistory.

However effective and accurate a chronometric method, it is useless unless the dated sample — be it a fragment of a wooden beam, a handful of charcoal, or a lump of cooled lava — is interpreted correctly. For instance, a lump of lava associated with an early stone tool does not date the tool, it dates the moment at which the lava cooled. It is up to the archaeologist to establish that the tool is contemporary with the lava. Beams may be used years after their parent tree was cut down, or buildings burned down centuries after they were built. All these factors have to be taken into account when interpreting chronometric dates.

ARCHAEOLOGICAL SURVEY AND EXCAVATION

How do archaeologists find sites? Many large sites, such as the pyramids of Gizeh in Egypt or Teotihuacán in Mexico, have been known for centuries. Evidence for less conspicuous sites may be accidentally exposed by water or wind erosion, earthquakes, and other natural phenomena. Burrowing animals may bring bones or stone tools to the surface on ancient settlements. Farmers plow up thousands of finds. Road makers and land developers move massive quantities of earth and destroy sites wholesale. Treasure hunters and collectors have done irreparable damage to many more locations.

Most archaeological sites are discovered as a result of careful field survey and thorough examination of the countryside for both conspicuous and inconspicuous traces of the past (Crawford, 1953; Schiffer and House, 1977). A survey can cover a single city lot or an entire river basin, a reconnaissance that could extend over several years. The theoretical ideal is to locate all sites in the survey area, but this is impossible, for many sites leave few traces above ground and the best that one can hope for is a sample of what is in the area. The most intensive surveys are made on foot, with field workers spaced out at regular intervals so that as little as possible is missed. Surface finds from newly discovered sites can provide clues about the identity of the occupants, although even scientifically collected surface finds are no substitute for excavation.

Originally, archaeologists looked for individual sites, which they then excavated on a large scale. Today, the environmental context of a site is often as important as the settlement itself, so much so that regional surveys of prehistoric sites and their settlement patterns are as important as

Settlement patterns

excavation. *Settlement patterns* are distributions of prehistoric occupation on the landscape. Establishing such patterns requires a large investment of time and money. It took William Sanders and his colleagues a decade to survey the evolving settlement pattern in the Basin of Mexico over the millennia that preceded the emergence of Aztec civilization in the fifteenth century A.D. (Sanders, Parsons, and Santley, 1979). They relied heavily on remote-sensing methods, among them aerial photography. This approach has long been used to plot more conspicuous sites, an approach that works well with large prehistoric agricultural systems, Roman road networks, and other large-scale archaeological phenomena. In recent years, archaeologists have turned to infrared film, side-scan radar, satellite imagery, and three-dimensional radar to help them with regional surveys. Remote-sensing methods will come into increasing use in future years, partly because they are cost-effective when surveying large areas and also because excavation will become increasingly selective as more and more sites are destroyed by industrial development.

Excavation

Archaeological excavation has developed from a form of treasure hunting into an exact and precise discipline. The fundamental premise of excavation is that all digging is destruction, even that done by the experts. The archaeologist's primary responsibility, therefore, is to record a site for posterity as it is dug because there are no second chances.

Every excavation is undertaken to answer specific questions, according to a formal *research design* that is worked out beforehand. The research design can ask questions about the chronology of the site, the layout of the settlement it contains, or about changing artifact styles within the levels to be excavated (Binford, 1964; Mueller, 1975). By meticulous digging and careful sampling of the archaeological deposits, the excavator implements his research design and digs up and records the data that are used to test the hypotheses developed as part of that research design. Most archaeologists distinguish between two basic excavation methods (Figure 1.4) (Barker, 1983; Joukowsky, 1981; Wheeler, 1954):

Research design

1. *Area or horizontal excavation,* in which the objective is to uncover large areas of ground in search of houses or entire settlement layouts. This type of digging is on a relatively large scale and is designed to uncover household and other activities that are normally discoverable only by digging over an extensive area.

Area excavation

2. *Vertical excavation,* designed to uncover stratigraphic information or a sequence of occupation layers on a small scale. This type of excavation often is practiced when chronology or artifact samples are a primary concern.

Vertical excavation

The numerous archaeological sites described in this book fall into several broad categories, each of which presents special excavation problems. The most common are *living sites*, the places where people have lived and carried out a multitude of activities.

Living sites

Much of our knowledge of the earliest hunters and gatherers is found by excavating abandoned living sites. They favored lakeside camps or convenient rock overhangs for protection from predators and the weather, availability of abundant water, and ready access to herds of game and vegetable foods. Olduvai Gorge in Tanzania is renowned for its prehistoric sites, small lakeside bone caches used by early humans for a few days or weeks before they moved on in their constant search for game, vegetable foods, and fish (see Figure 4.12, p. 98) (M. Leakey, 1971).

Fortunately for archaeologists, these people abandoned food bones and tools where they were dropped. Crude windbreaks were left and

Figure 1.4 Area (horizontal) and vertical excavations. Although archaeologists excavate in many ways and sometimes use sampling techniques, there is a basic distinction between area (photo at left) and vertical (photo at right) methods.

Left: An area excavation of a stone circle at Strichen, Scotland, is designed to expose large segments of ground on a site so that buildings, all other structures, and even the layout of the entire settlement can be traced over a much larger area than would be uncovered in a vertical excavation. Area excavation is widely used when budget is not a problem and the archaeologist is looking for settlement patterns.

Right: A vertical excavation of Maiden Castle, Dorset, England, shows how a narrow trench is cut through successive layers of an earth rampart. Notice that only a small portion of the layers in the trench walls has been exposed by the vertical cutting. The objective of this excavation was to obtain information on the sequence of layers on the outer edge of the earthwork and in the ditch that originally lay on its exterior side. Only a narrow trench was needed to record layers, the finds from them, and the dating evidence.

might be burned down by the next brush fire or blown away by the wind. In Olduvai, the gently rising waters of a prehistoric lake slowly covered the bone caches and preserved them for posterity with the tools lying where they were dropped. Other people lived by the banks of large rivers. Their tools are found in profusion in river gravels that were subsequently jumbled and re-sorted by floodwater, leaving a confused mass of tools, not undisturbed living floors, for the archaeologist to uncover (Oakley, 1964).

Caves already occupied more than half a million years ago were reoccupied again and again as people returned to preferred spots. Many natural caves and rock shelters contain deep occupation deposits that can be removed by meticulous excavation with a dental pick, trowel, and brush. The sequence of occupation layers can be uncovered almost undisturbed from the day of abandonment (Jennings, 1957; Movius, 1977).

In contrast, farmers usually live in larger settlements than hunters, for they are tied to their herds and gardens and move less often. Higher population densities and more lasting settlements left more conspicuous archaeological sites from later millennia of human history. In the Near East and many parts of the New World, farming sites were occupied time after time over several thousand years, forming deep mounds of refuse, house foundations, and other occupation debris. These *tells* require large excavations and extensive earthmoving if anything is to be understood about how towns and settlements were laid out.

Tells

Kill sites are places where hunter-gatherers killed large mammals, then camped around the carcass for several days as they butchered their prey. The most famous kill sites are in the Great Plains, where entire bison herds have been found trapped in narrow defiles where they were driven to their death (see Figure 7.5, p. 180) (Wheat, 1972). The stone projectile heads, scraping tools, and butchering artifacts used by the hunters have been found around the carcasses. *Ceremonial sites* may or may not be part of a living site (Weaver, 1981). Mesopotamian temples formed the focus of a city, while Maya ceremonial centers, such as Tikal in Guatemala, were an integral part of a scattered settlement pattern of towns and villages in the countryside (Figure 21.9, p. 457). Some structures, such as the pyramids of Egypt or Stonehenge in England (Figures 16.3, p. 355 and 19.6, p. 417) (Chippendale, 1983; Edwards, 1973), were isolated sites that served the religious needs of a king or of a wider community around them.

Kill sites

Ceremonial sites

Burial sites can yield important data from periods later than 70,000 years ago, the time when the first deliberate burials were made (J. Anderson, 1969; Brothwell, 1965). Skeletons and their accompanying grave goods give us a rather one-sided view of the past — funerary rites (Figure 16.5, p. 358). Among the most famous prehistoric burials are those of the royal kings deposited at Ur of the Chaldees in Mesopotamia during the second millennium B.C. (Chapter Fifteen) (Woolley, 1934), as well as the Shang graves in China, where charioteers and many retainers accompanied the royal dead (Figure 20.5, p. 433) (Chang, 1980). The celebrated mounds of Pazyryk in Siberia show us other spectacular burial customs (Chapter Six) (Rudenko, 1970). Important people were buried with their chariots and steeds, the later wearing elaborate harness trappings preserved by ice that formed when water entered the tombs and froze.

Burial sites

STUDYING THE FINDS

Archaeological finds take many forms. They may include fragmentary bones from game or domesticated animals (Binford, 1981). Vegetable foods such as edible nuts or cultivated seeds sometimes are found in archaeological sites where preservation conditions are good. Pottery, stone implements, iron artifacts, and, occasionally, bone and wooden tools all build up a picture of early technical achievements.

Archaeologists have developed elaborate classification systems that set down certain criteria for their finds. They also apply sophisticated analytic techniques for both classifying and comparing human artifacts (Watson, LeBlanc, and Redman, 1984). They use collections of stone tools, pottery, or other artifacts like swords and brooches for studying human culture and its development. Whatever the classificatory techniques used, however, the objective of analyzing bones, pottery, and other material remains is the study of prehistoric culture and of cultural change in the past. We classify the remains into arbitrary groups either by their shape or design or by their use, the latter a difficult task (Figure 1.5). We fit them together to form a picture of a human culture.

From time to time we shall refer to archaeological groupings like the Acheulian culture or the Magdalenian culture, which consist of the material remains of human culture preserved at a specific space and time at several sites; these finds are the concrete expressions of the common social traditions that bind a culture. When we speak of the Magdalenian

Archaeological culture   culture, we mean the *archaeological culture representing a prehistoric*

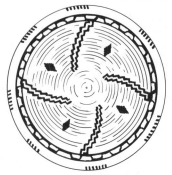

Figure 1.5 Inference from an artifact. This Chumash Indian parching tray from Southern California shows how inferences can be made from an archaeological find. Clearly, the range of inferences that can be made from artifacts alone is limited, especially when the find has no context in a site.

Context

The archaeological context of the tray is defined by its position in a site and what it is associated with, level, square, etc.; its relationship to other features, such as houses, is also recorded. Unless this information is known, the tray is an isolated specimen devoid of a cultural context or even a date. Context cannot be inferred from an artifact alone.

Construction and materials

The tray was made of reed, its red-brown color determined by the reed, known from modern observations to be the best material available. The steplike decoration on the tray was dictated by sewing and weaving techniques of basketry. The diamond patterns were probably added as a personal touch by the craftsman who made it. The shape and decoration of the tray are repeated in many others that have been found and are evidently part of a well-established Chumash basketry tradition. More information about an artifact's construction and materials can be learned than about any other category of inference.

Function

The flat round shape of the tray is determined by its function, for such trays were used to roast seeds by tossing them with embers in the tray. The function of a tray normally cannot be inferred from its shape, but identical modern versions have been found that are used for parching. We employ the technique of analogy, inferring that the archaeological find had the same function as the modern tray.

Behavior

The parching tray reveals something about the cooking techniques of the Chumash, but again only by analogy.

social system, defined in a context of time and space, which has come down to us in the form of tools or other durable objects. The description "Magdalenian" is quite arbitrary, derived from the cave site at La Madeleine, France, where the tools of the culture were first discovered. Such labels as Magdalenian are devised by archaeologists for their convenience.

The geographic extent or content of any archaeological culture is also defined somewhat arbitrarily but as precisely as possible, so that an archaeological word has an exact implication for other scholars. Much of the archaeological data summarized in this book consists of carefully compiled chronological sequences of archaeological cultures often extending over thousands of prehistoric years. The workings of archaeological research compare one collection of artifacts with assemblages from different layers in the same sites or other sites near or far away from the original find. Our record of human activity consists of innumerable classified and cataloged archaeological finds whose relationships determined much of the story of human culture that follows in these pages.

EXPLANATION AND INTERPRETATION

Anthropological archaeology is much more than inference and induction from the archaeological record, for our ultimate aim is to explain the past, not simply describe it. Until recently, most archaeologists concentrated on descriptions of sites and artifacts. They accumulated the minute chronological and spatial frameworks of archaeological data that provide a basis for observing *how* particular cultures changed and evolved through prehistoric times. Many scholars felt constrained by poor preservation conditions from making inferences about anything other than the material remains of ancient human behavior. They were unable to explain *why* the cultures they had studied had changed.

Recent years have seen a rapid change in archaeological approaches. Computers have become commonplace, more and more scientific methods have been applied to raw archaeological data, and there has been an explosion of field research all over the world. There has also been a theoretical revolution, one that places major emphasis on explaining the past and on exploring the processes by which human cultures changed through prehistoric times. Using both advanced data collection methods and new theoretical models, some archaeologists of the 1980s are seeking to apply theories of anthropology to archaeological evidence to arrive at new laws of cultural process. Others are primarily interested in the history of culture, viewing each society as a unique phenomenon (Binford, 1983; Redman, 1973). In recent years, the archaeological record itself has received greater attention. How were sites formed, and what decay processes have been at work over the centuries, even millennia, that separate the archaeological site from the present? A whole new body of archaeological theory is being developed to explore these links between past and present. In Chapter Two we explore these and other approaches to world prehistory.

GUIDE TO FURTHER READING

Binford, Lewis R. *In Pursuit of the Past*. New York: Thames and Hudson, 1983.
A personal account of developing ideas in archaeology that is a marvelous introduction to archaeological reasoning. You may not agree with everything Binford says, but he makes you think!

Ceram, C. W. *Gods, Graves and Scholars*. New York: Knopf, 1953.
This probably is the best-known book on archaeology ever written. A classic account of early archaeologists and the discovery of the early civilizations written for a popular audience.

Fagan, Brian M. *Archaeology: A Brief Introduction* (2d ed.). Boston: Little, Brown, 1982.
A widely ranging brief introduction, with major coverage of subsistence and settlement patterns.

Fagan, Brian M. *In the Beginning* (5th ed.). Boston: Little, Brown, 1985.
A comprehensive survey of method and theory in archaeology that covers everything from stratigraphy to cultural resource management.

Sharer, Robert J., and Ashmore, Wendy. *Fundamentals of Archaeology*. Menlo Park, Calif.: Cummings, 1980.
Another detailed introduction to anthropological archaeology that is especially strong on American examples. Excellent bibliography.

Chapter Two

Approaches to World Prehistory

PREVIEW

✤ Although biological evolution resulted in the emergence of humankind, cultural evolution assumed the dominant role in our prehistory. It became humankind's unique means of adapting to the natural environment.

✤ Early archaeologists confronted with the problem of classifying and dating the past were at a loss until Christian Jurgensen Thomsen developed the Three Age subdivision for prehistory. This scheme was verified by excavation and widely adopted during the nineteenth century.

✤ The social scientist Herbert Spencer developed the notion of social evolution. Along with Edward Tylor and Lewis Morgan, Spencer believed in unilinear cultural evolution, under which all humankind progressed from a state of simple savagery to civilization.

✤ Later scholars showed that these schemes were too simplistic when tested against data from archaeological excavations. We describe the basic cultural processes — invention, diffusion, and migration — and give examples of their application.

✤ Franz Boas and V. Gordon Childe fostered detailed studies of sites, peoples, and artifacts that placed scientific archaeology on a new footing. Boas collected minute details of dozens of societies. Childe believed in cultural evolution in which technology played a major role. He ignored the importance of environmental adaptation in world prehistory.

✤ Anthropologists Julian Steward and Leslie White played an important role in showing cultural evolution to be a major cornerstone of world prehistory. Steward demonstrated that all human cultures interacted with their natural environments and stressed the importance of constantly changing adaptations. Leslie White conceived of cultures as complex systems whose various parts interacted with each other and with the natural environment.

✤ From these researches developed two concepts, those of cultural ecology and of multilinear cultural evolution, both based on the notion that each human culture evolved independently and as a result of changing adaptations to its ever-changing environment.

✤ Ethnoarchaeology, the study of modern hunter-gatherer and agricultural societies, has become an important factor in interpreting world prehistory. From it, we basically derive general theories about the relationship between human behavior and archaeological debris.

- Elman Service, Morton Fried, and Marshall Sahlins developed four stages of sociopolitical evolution, which are widely used to classify groups: bands, tribes, chiefdoms, and state-organized societies.
- Middle range theory is a body of theory that is being developed to bridge the gap between the static evidence of the archaeological record and the dynamic adaptations of modern societies.
- The past quarter century has seen a trend toward rigorous scientific methods in archaeology, methods that use models based on the principles of general systems theory. We use the example of early agriculture in highland Mexico to illustrate applications of systems models.
- Our narrative of world prehistory is based on gradual, multilinear cultural evolution and on increasingly effective adaptations to the natural environment that have led to the dangerous overexploitation of resources commonplace today.

The theory of evolution and natural selection provides an explanation for the biological evolution of humankind. We modern people do differ from our predecessors; we have adapted successfully to the world's many environments as a result of our superior intelligence, gradually acquired during biological evolution (Campbell, 1982). The evolutionary process of *adaptive radiation,* whereby animal species branch off from a common ancestral form, has led to an order of primates, and a family of *Hominidae,* of which modern people *(Homo sapiens* — the wise human being) are only one member and the sole survivors. Space restrictions prevent us from describing the basic principles of biological evolution here; the interested reader is referred to the many standard textbooks on the subject (Campbell, 1985; Weiss and Mann, 1985).

Humankind is unique in its use of culture as a means of adapting to the natural environment, and our culture has evolved to great levels of complexity since the appearance of the first human beings more than 3 million years ago. The study of world prehistory is the study of not only biological evolution, but also primarily of cultural evolution and the ways in which people have adapted to their natural environment. The cultural diversity of humankind is truly amazing and extremely difficult to explain. Ever since scholars first began to study world prehistory, they have tried to explain this diversity and to account for its origins and for the reasons why some societies achieved a much greater cultural complexity than others. Why, for instance, did the Australian aborigines never take up agriculture but develop a highly complex social life? Why did their contemporaries, the Ancient Egyptians, enjoy a literate civilization that lasted for thousands of years? The explanations for cultural diversity must come from anthropological archaeology, the primary source of data on early human history.

In Chapter One we described the four basic objectives of anthropological archaeology:

- Constructing culture history, a descriptive process that involves studying archaeological sites and artifacts in time and space
- Studying ancient lifeways, ways in which people adapted to and exploited their natural environment
- Studying cultural process, how human cultures have changed in the past, and explaining these changes
- Interpreting the archaeological record with reference to the processes that created it (Chapter One) — site formation processes.

Much of the prehistory recounted in these pages is basic culture history, based on hundreds of sites, cultural sequences, and millions of individual artifacts. These culture histories from all areas of the world have been constructed using the basic principles mentioned in Chapter One. Culture history alone, however, does not serve to explain culture change, nor does it provide information on the ways in which people have adapted to or exploited the natural environment. It is only in recent years that archaeologists have attacked the complex problems of reconstructing past lifeways and studying cultural process, with the aid of digital computers, sophisticated statistical methods, and enormous new bodies of excavated data from all over the world (Binford, 1983; Fagan, 1985).

Today's theoretical models and methodology for studying world prehistory cannot be considered in isolation from earlier attempts at explaining past lifeways and culture change. Our approaches to the past are cumulative in the sense that they are based on the contributions of many earlier scholars who were working with inadequate data and much less sophisticated methods than are available in the 1980s. The debt we owe our predecessors is enormous.

ACCOUNTING FOR CULTURAL DEVELOPMENT

The excavators of the early eighteenth century dug into burial mounds and ancient settlements with such frenzy that they acquired an enormous mass of miscellaneous artifacts that defied classification into any semblance of chronological order. This horrendous jumble made no sense at all until Christian Jurgensen Thomsen, curator of Denmark's National Museum in Copenhagen, rearranged the prehistoric galleries of the museum in 1807. Boldly he laid out the exhibits to represent three great ages of prehistoric time: a Stone Age, when metals were unknown, a Bronze Age, and an Iron Age. Thomsen worked strictly with tools, each of his three ages in fact representing a stage of technological development in prehistoric times. His Three Age system soon was adopted widely throughout Europe, and the broad labels still are used as convenient terms today (Daniel, 1981; Grayson, 1983).

Thomsen concerned himself with how the level of technology affected

Three Ages

the evolution of cultures. The essential validity of his Three Age theory of cultural development was proved not long after he proposed it by excavations all over Europe. These early nineteenth-century digs raised a whole new set of questions about the Three Ages. The Three Age system implied that all humankind has passed through comparable broad stages of technological development, but what about economic development? In 1838 another Dane, zoologist Sven Nilsson, invented an economic model for the past, arguing that humankind had developed through a series of stages — from a state of savagery, to one of herder-agriculturalist, and on to a final phase, civilization. He based his economic model on both archaeological and anthropological observations. Nilsson's model was not in conflict with Thomsen's theory; it merely addressed a different aspect of the fact of evolution. What Nilsson did was to concentrate not on technology but on how in different societies lifeways always seemed to change in the same direction.

Economic model

Both the Thomsen and Nilsson models were developed at a time of intense interest in human origins and progress. Pioneer social scientists like Herbert Spencer (1820–1903) began to develop theories of human progress that hailed Victorian civilization as the pinnacle of human achievement, a state to which all humankind aspired (Spencer, 1855). Spencer, indeed, was the first person to use the famous Darwinian expression *survival of the fittest*, but only in a social context. Both the Three Age system and Nilsson's ideas implied that all humankind had passed through comparable broad stages of technological and economic development. It was logical for Herbert Spencer and others to think of prehistory as an extension of biological evolution. Scientists now asked whether human culture evolved just as our bodies had.

Spencer's cultural evolution

CULTURAL EVOLUTIONISTS

It was almost inevitable that anthropologists developed the notion of *cultural evolution*, the concept that human societies evolved from simple hunter-gatherers to complex civilizations, but along a single evolutionary line so that, theoretically, every society could achieve the highest pinnacle of civilization. This form of cultural evolution was considered subject to the same laws as biological evolution. Two anthropologists, Edward Tylor and Lewis Morgan, had a strong influence on the development of an evolutionary approach to world prehistory.

Edward Tylor

Sir Edward Tylor (1832–1917) was a gentleman of leisure who became interested in anthropology as a result of a visit to Mexico in the 1850s (Hatch, 1973). He devoted the rest of his life to the study of non-Western societies and their institutions. Tylor was the first person to attempt a chronicle of the full extent of human diversity. He argued that the cultures of humankind were governed by laws of evolutionary change somewhat similar to those in biological evolution. Human beings, said Tylor, had behaved in a common-sense and rational way since the earliest times. This rational behavior had led to cultural evolution over time, during which processes of selection, like those of natural selection in biological evolution, had made human institutions more efficient and more complex. Tylor was an ardent believer in human progress and argued that the institutions of Western civilization had their origins in those of what he called "ruder" peoples.

Tylor's evolutionist view of human society was, of course, far too simple to reflect reality, and his beliefs that some human races had greater intellectual and moral powers than others are no longer accepted. He went as far as to propose three broad stages of human development: savagery, barbarism, and civilization. Few societies occupied the civilization rung of Tylor's ladder. Despite his prejudices, this fine scholar made two lasting methodological contributions to anthropological archaeology: (1) He studied prehistoric cultures by examining surviving peoples at the same broad level of development; *ethnographic analogy* has become one of the cornerstones of modern archaeology. (2) He developed a technique for sampling the culture of dozens of different peoples, a method that developed into the *comparative method* of study, which is used extensively by anthropological archaeologists today.

Lewis Morgan and Karl Marx

Lewis Morgan (1818–1881) was a pioneer American anthropologist and ardent social evolutionist who thought that social evolution occurred as a result of human societies adapting to the stresses of their various environments (Harris, 1968). Morgan identified no fewer than seven stages of social evolution in his classic book *Ancient Society* (1877). His "Lower Status of Savagery" was a stage of simple food gathering, while the ultimate rung of his evolutionary ladder was "Civilization," which he considered to be attained when a society developed writing. Both Tylor and Morgan believed that all human societies had passed through evolutionary stages on their way to civilization, but neither of their schemes could stand up against the actual complexity of human cultural diversity revealed by later field workers.

One famous thinker who followed Lewis Morgan's conception of cultural evolution was Karl Marx (1818–1883). He used Morgan's seven stages of cultural evolution but built on them, arguing that each stage was brought on by economic factors. Changes in material production, and also in the control of the means of production, were *the* forces that determined social, political, and legal aspects of society. Marx's historical materialism regarded economic developments as the prime movers of social evolution. The most lasting contribution of these and other pioneer evolutionists was this basic assumption: human cultures have, in general, proceeded from the simple to the complex.

INVENTION, DIFFUSION, AND MIGRATION

Spencer, Tylor, and Morgan believed in human progress, in universal schemes of cultural evolution that were soon shown to have little substance in reality. Even before Tylor started work on his universal schemes, the Danish archaeologist J. J. A. Worsaae had pondered the ways in which cultures changed (Worsaae, 1849). How, for example, did humankind acquire bronze weapons? Did one people invent metal tools and then spread their innovation to other parts of the world? Or did metallurgy come into being in many areas? Worsaae raised one of the fundamental questions of archaeology: By what processes did culture change take place? Did it result from the invention of the same idea in many different places, through gradual parallel evolutions? Or did it result from the diffusion of ideas, or from actual migrations of people carrying new cultures with them? The study of prehistoric culture change is still concerned with these basic questions, albeit in a much more sophisticated form.

Primary cultural processes

The refinement of research methods used by the pioneer evolutionists enabled scientists to study what were soon recognized as *primary cultural processes* in prehistory: invention, diffusion, and migration. Both the comparative method and ethnographic analogy played an important part in the refinement of the study of these processes (Trigger, 1968).

Invention

Invention involves creating a new idea and transforming it — in archaeological contexts — into an artifact or other tangible innovation that has survived. An invention implies either modifying an old idea or series of ideas or creating a completely new concept. It can be made by accident or by intentional research. Inventions are adopted by others if they are useful; if sufficiently important, they spread rapidly. The transistor, for example, is in almost universal use because it is an effective advance in electronic technology.

There is a tendency to think of inventions as dramatic discoveries, the products of a moment of inspiration. In practice, though, most inventions in prehistory were the result of prolonged experimentation, a logical extension of the use and refinement of an existing technology or else a response to changes in the surrounding environment.

People once searched for the site where the first solitary genius planted grain and invented agriculture. Today's archaeologists are still investigating the origins of food production, but they are finding dozens of major and minor changes in peoples' lifeways that cumulatively resulted in a shift from hunting and gathering to agriculture and animal domestication. The toolkits and subsistence activities that archaeologists have found shown evidence of changes over a long period. In the Tehuacán Valley of Mexico, for example, people experimented for thousands of years with maize cultivation, and their toolkits reflect an increasing dependence on cereal agriculture (MacNeish, 1970), but the old hunter-gatherer tools and practices still appear in the archaeological record long after maize cultivation had become commonplace.

Culture change is cumulative — that is, people learn the behavior patterns of their society. Inevitably some minor differences in learned behavior will appear from generation to generation; minor in themselves, they do accumulate over a long time, especially among isolated populations. This snowballing effect of slow-moving cultural evolution can be detected in dozens of prehistoric societies, among them the coastal people of Peru, who relied heavily on fishing and maritime resources and gradually developed complex societies based largely on fishing and gathering (Moseley, 1975a).

Diffusion

Diffusion is the label for those processes by which new ideas or cultural traits spread from one person to another or from one group to another, often over long distances. These ideas are socially transmitted from individual to individual and ultimately from group to group, but the physical movement of many people is not involved. Instances of diffusion are legion in prehistory, cases in which ideas or technologies have spread widely from their place of origin. A classic modern example of diffusion is tobacco smoking, a favorite pleasure of the North American Indians adopted by Elizabethan colonists in the fifteenth century. Within a few generations, tens of thousands of Europeans were smoking pipes and enjoying the calming effect of American tobacco. Tobacco smoking soon reached every corner of the Old World, carried there not by thousands of people migrating from American to Europe, but by small numbers of seamen and traveling merchants, by word of mouth, and though the human habit of adopting new, fashionable ideas. Smoking became socially acceptable and remains so to this day in many societies (although not necessarily in ours). There are numerous examples of the diffusion of religious beliefs in prehistory, transmitted through trading contacts and simply by the spread of ideas.

Migration

Migration involves the movement of a people and is based on a deliberate decision to enter new areas and leave the old. English settlers moved to North America, taking their own culture with them; the Spanish occupied Mexico. Such population movements result not only in the diffusion of ideas, but in mass shifts of people and in social and cultural changes over a wide front. Migration implies a complete, or at least an almost complete, transformation in culture. Perhaps the classic instance of migration in prehistory is that of the Polynesians; they settled the remote islands of the Pacific in consequence of deliberate explorations of the open ocean by their skilled navigators (Bellwood, 1978; Jennings, 1979). These superb seamen learned the lore of the heavens and made long-distance voyages of discovery, whereby they found such remote islands as Hawaii and Easter Island. In most cases, they returned safely to their homelands with detailed sailing directions to the new islands that could be followed by later colonists. No one knows why the Polynesians set out on voyages to the unknown. Perhaps population pressure and political considerations played their part. Undoubtedly, many long voyages of exploration were undertaken simply because the navigators were curious to learn what lay over the horizon.

Boas on data

The early students of diffusion and migration often carried their ideas to ridiculous extremes, claiming, for example, that all civilization originated among the Ancient Egyptians and then spread all over the globe in a series of great voyaging adventures. Soon the experts reacted violently against these simplistic ideas with much more sophisticated research projects. One such expert was Franz Boas (1858–1942), an anthropologist of German birth who immigrated to the United States and became a professor at Columbia University. Boas attacked those who sought general comparisons between non-Western societies; he helped to establish anthropology as a form of science, applying more precise methods of the collection and classification of minute details of human cultures, especially those of North America. He and his students sought explanations of the past based on meticulous studies of individual artifacts and customs. Boas instilled respect for the notion that data should not be subordinated to elaborate theoretical schemes. The myriad data provided by Boas and others gave great emphasis to the use of the comparative method and ethnographic analogy in archaeology (Hatch, 1973).

THE COMPARATIVE METHOD

Artifact comparisons were used by pioneer anthropologists like Morgan and Tylor, as well as by early European prehistorians like J. J. A. Worsaae and Oscar Montelius in the nineteenth century (Daniel, 1981). But the real proponent of the method was anthropologist Franz Boas, who devoted a long career to studying and comparing hundreds of American Indian societies. His preoccupation with the minute details of artifacts (as well as other, less tangible aspects of human society) strongly influenced archaeologists of the 1930s and 1940s. Even today, archaeologists spend a great deal of time in comparative studies of artifacts, settlement patterns, and art styles in different archaeological cultures. The comparative method in archaeology is closely tied to the classification and analysis of artifacts such as pottery and stone tools. Much of what we know of the prehistory of Bronze Age Europe is based on the study of swords, brooches, and pins, for example. Archaeologists of the American Southwest rely heavily on changing styles and distributions of painted pottery to construct the culture history of the region. Until the advent of radiocarbon dating in the 1950s, European archaeologists made great use of comparative studies of pottery and metal artifacts to refine their cross-datings of cultures far from the Mediterranean civilizations in which such artifacts had their origin.

Perhaps one of the best-known experts on the comparative method was an Australian-born archaeologist named Vere Gordon Childe (1892–1957) (Childe, 1958; Trigger, 1980). Childe was a brilliant linguist who made his life's work the study of the diffusion of civilization throughout prehistoric Europe. He became familiar with even the most trivial sites and artifact assemblages, and with obscure central European journals that few English-speaking archaeologists read. He used his encyclopedic knowledge to develop a thesis that Europe was a province of the Near East, an area that had received agriculture, metallurgy, and other major inventions by diffusion from the East. He traced these traits from one end of Europe to the other by comparing cultural sequences and artifact distributions from area to area. Childe combined cultural evolution and diffusionist ideas into unexpected notions of human prehistory. He believed, for instance, that farming was introduced into Europe from the Near East; local cultures developed their own distinctive economies and social institutions in later millennia, he thought.

Childe's aim was to distill from archaeological remains "a pre-literate substitute for conventional history with cultures instead of statesmen as actors and migrations instead of battles" (Childe, 1942). He drew together approaches to the past from various schools, including the Marxists (he was a self-professed Marxist). He was convinced that humanity had made rational, intelligent progress from its earliest development. Gordon Childe was a brilliant and articulate popular writer whose syntheses of prehistoric times were — and still are — widely read by generations of archaeologists as well as the general public. His methods influence archaeologists to this day, although his comparative studies are slowly being replaced by much more sophisticated studies based on far more data than was available to him. He also worked before the advent of radiocarbon dating, which outdated much of this work. These new studies allow for one major variable that Childe downplayed — the natural environment. One cannot blame him for ignoring environmental factors: the necessary scientific methods for reconstructing prehistoric environments have been developed only in recent decades.

Childe on cultures

American archaeologists adopted the comparative method as a result of Boas's work and developed their own elaborate classification systems for New World prehistory that correlated local cultural sequences over thousands of miles (Willey and Sabloff, 1980). Between 1930 and 1960, they constructed hundreds upon hundreds of local sequences of culture history based on pottery styles and other artifacts. Their concern was with classification and chronology rather than the explanation of culture change or reconstruction of past lifeways. Once again, the natural environment and any notion of cultural adaptation entered but little into archaeological research.

To say that Childe and his American contemporaries ignored the environment as a factor in human history in no way detracts from their valuable contribution to archaeology. They provided the raw data that have enabled archaeologists of the 1960s and 1970s to attempt much more ambitious researches into past lifeways and cultural process.

PREHISTORIC LIFEWAYS

Childe, Boas, and their contemporaries were concerned for the most part with artifacts and structures, with material remains of human behavior. They paid relatively little attention to prehistoric lifeways, the ways in which people made their living in early times. Although Danish archaeologists were identifying animal bones from coastal shell mounds in the 1840s, and California scholars examined seasonality using bird bones in the San Francisco area middens during the 1920s (Fagan, 1985), it was not until the 1950s that people began to take prehistoric lifeways seriously. The British prehistorian Grahame Clark applied pollen analysis to a 10,000-year-old hunter-gatherer site in northeast Britain in the late 1940s with spectacular results. By using both pollens and fragmentary red deer antlers from the camp, he showed that Star Carr was occupied during the spring and summer months (J. D. G. Clark, 1954). The preservation conditions at the swampy site were so good that he was able to recover other evidence of prehistoric lifeways, too, including a canoe paddle, rolls of birch bark, and the remains of a brush platform built out toward the water's edge. At about the same time, University of Chicago archaeologist Robert Braidwood led a multidisciplinary research team to the Near East on a broad-based study of the origins of agriculture. He excavated the 8000-year-old farming village of Jarmo in the Zagros foothills of Iraq, while zoologists studied domestic animal bones and, geologists studied the evidence for recent climatic change in the area (Braidwood and Braidwood, 1983). These studies were the forerunners of the much more sophisticated multidisciplinary researches done today.

Currently, there are many different avenues of research that provide information on hunting and gathering practices, and on agriculture, pastoralism, and even long-distance trade. Here are some major lines of evidence:

Artifacts such as axes, plow shares, and digging sticks, to say nothing of stone spear points, provide evidence for subsistence activities. The discovery of a plow share, for example, implies a more complex set of tools for cultivation, which penetrate deeper into the ground and can be used on a much wider range of soils, as happened in prehistoric Europe after 2200 b.c. But the evidence for hunting, gathering, and food production that comes from tools is necessarily limited. Very often, the food remains themselves provide more precise insights.

Settlement data, in the form of house foundations, temple ruins, and the surviving traces of complete camps, villages, towns, or cities, tells us much about the changing ways in which people have exploited their ever-changing environment. Archaeologists working in the Valley of Mexico have shown how the prehistoric population distributions changed in response to the growth of the Aztec Empire and later as a result of the Spanish Conquest (Sanders, Parsons, and Santley, 1979).

Rock paintings and other art objects can sometimes provide information on ancient subsistence. Witness Figure 8.2 (p. 196), which shows a San hunter from southern Africa with his toolkit. Sometimes such evidence can also be used to interpret the function of incomplete artifacts found in archaeological deposits nearby (J. D. Clark, 1959).

Indirect evidence of subsistence activities comes from several sources, not only from geological studies but also from surprisingly esoteric sources. For example, we can learn much of the subsistence ecology of the early hominids at Olduvai Gorge by examining the cut marks on the broken animal bones associated with their tools (Potts, 1984). These marks show that the hominids concentrated on meat and marrow-rich bones. It seems possible that our earliest ancestors competed with predators for much of their game meat, scavenging it from carnivore kills in hasty forays. They were opportunistic foragers rather than true hunters such as were found among later humans. Fossil pollens from prehistoric swamps not only tell us much about ancient natural vegetation but also reveal abrupt changes in tree cover resulting from forest clearance by early farming communities. Prehistoric farmers in Denmark and northern Germany, for example, burnt off and cleared forests for their fields 6000 years ago. As the forests were cleared, characteristic cultivation weeds that infest newly planted wheat fields appear in the pollen diagrams for the first time. Both pollen analysis (palynology) and zooarchaeology (the study of ancient animal bones) enable one to look at the constantly changing relationship between a human cultural system and its environment, as well as at the ways in which people made their living. And, as time went on, both archaeologists and anthropologists began to look more closely at this very subject, called cultural ecology, which we discuss on the following pages. They found, for example, that there was a quantum jump in the number of archaeological sites in the Valley of Mexico once the Aztecs developed a distinctive form of swamp agriculture that doubled maize productivity over thousands of acres of hitherto unexploited land. By the time of the Spanish Conquest, the Indians were occupying every acre of potentially cultivable land in the area. This was in sharp contrast to earlier times when far more selective, usually nonirrigation, agriculture was practiced.

Food remains, such as animal bones or seeds, provide direct evidence for types of food eaten and, by sophisticated analyses, can provide insights into overall dietary pattern as well. The remains of domestic animals or game can be identified by such parts as teeth, jaws, horns, and sometimes the articular ends of limb bones. Not only can one establish the proportion of the diet which each type of animal supplied but also, in some cases, invaluable data on butchery practices, the ages at which animals were killed (determinable by study of the teeth), and even the seasons at which the site was occupied. When Joe Ben Wheat excavated the 8000-year-old Olsen-Chubbock bison kill in Colorado, he found the bones of sixteen calves only a few days old. He concluded from known data about bison breeding seasons that the kill took place in late May or early June (Wheat, 1972).

Seeds are much harder to come by than animal bones and are often recovered using a flotation method: the soil is passed through water so that the fine seeds float on the surface (Hole, Flannery, and Neely, 1969). Dry caves in the United States and Mexico have yielded tens of thousands of once-edible seeds. Those from caves in the Tehuacán Valley in Mexico have shown how the inhabitants scheduled their gathering of wild plants with great care. The seeds yield an excellent chronicle of their early experiments with maize and other crops (MacNeish, 1978; J. Renfrew, 1973).

Food remains can come in many other forms, too. Fish and bird bones are highly informative and often provide evidence of specialist hunter-gatherer activities. Human feces can be subjected to detailed analysis and provide a fascinating insight into the diet of a site's inhabitants (Bryant, 1974). The ultimate objective of studying food remains is to understand the minutest details of a prehistoric society's adaptation to its environment.

THE CONCEPT OF CULTURAL ECOLOGY

The ecological crisis that confronts humanity is now so much of our basic thinking that the notion that humans adapt to their natural environment seems obvious. But ecological interpretations of world prehistory are a surprisingly new concept, partly because it is only recently that researchers have developed methods for studying ancient environments. At first they started by using isolated techniques, studying animal bones or using pollen analysis. Then, in the 1950s and 1960s, a new body of ecological theory emerged, theory that owed much to the basic concepts of systems theory in the natural and physical sciences.

Steward on environment

It was the American anthropologist Julian Steward who first developed the notion that human cultures were adaptations to the subsistence and ecological requirements of a locality. Steward saw this adaptation as constantly changing. "No culture," he wrote, "has ever achieved an adaptation to its environment which has remained unchanged over any length of time" (Steward, 1970). This viewpoint contrasted sharply with that of many archaeologists of the time, who felt that human cultures were built by accumulation of cultural traits through diffusion and not as responses to ecological factors.

White on equilibrium

Another famous anthropologist, Leslie White, argued that human culture was made up of many structurally different parts that interacted; they reacted to one another within an overall cultural system (White, 1949). He pointed out that cultures can change in response to changes in the environment, that one part of a cultural system could not change without triggering change in other segments. There was a relationship between a human cultural system and its natural environment, and the system was constantly adjusting to environmental changes. Steward and White assumed that successful adaptive patterns continued in use and acted as an important stabilizing influence over a long period of time. From their work has developed a new recognition of the importance of cultural evolution in prehistory, not the cultural evolution of Tylor and Morgan, which implied that some human races were superior to others, but evolution based on many and increasingly complex adaptations to the natural environment. The study of the total way in which human populations adapt to and transform their environments is called *cultural ecology.*

Archaeologists who study cultural ecology are primarily interested in human cultures as systems interacting with other systems: other human cultures, the biotic community (other living things around them), and the physical environment. They are concerned not only with cultural evolution but also with reconstructing ancient environments and ways in which past cultures made their living (Fagan, 1985; Hole and Heizer, 1973).

Cultural ecology

At this point, we should look more closely at environment and archaeology.

ENVIRONMENTAL ARCHAEOLOGY

The ultimate goal of environmental archaeology is to understand the relationships between human cultures and their environments, which involves, among other things, defining the characteristics and processes of the biophysical environment. This environment is the matrix for studying the human ecosystem, the interaction between human cultures and their natural surroundings. Archaeological sites, or distributions of them, are part of the human exosystem (Butzer, 1982).

Human societies are a segment of the *biosphere*, which encompasses all the earth's living organisms interacting with the physical environment. The biosphere is organized both vertically and horizontally. Vertically, genes and cells are found at the base; organisms, populations, and communities occur above them. Horizontally, the community, all the biological populations in a given area, functions together with the nonliving environment, in a biome.

Biosphere

Biomes are the largest terrestrial communities, major biotic landscapes on earth in which distinctive plant and animal groups live in harmony together. *Habitats* are the areas within a biome where different populations and communities flourish, each with hundreds of individual *sites*, specific locales each with their own immediate settings. There are often transition zones between different habitats, and frequently are areas of considerable importance to human communities exploiting specific resources such as certain game or vegetable foods. These are known as *ecotones*.

Biomes

Habitats

Sites

Ecotones

Ecology is a study of functional relationships rather than genetic or phylogenetic ones. This is reflected in the concept of the ecological *niche*, the tertiary space occupied by an organism, its functional role in the community, and how it is constrained by other species and external factors.

Ecology

Niche

Every ecosystem is maintained by the regulation of trophic levels (vertical food chains) and by patterns of energy flow (Figure 2.1). The complexities of even modern ecosystems make them difficult to study

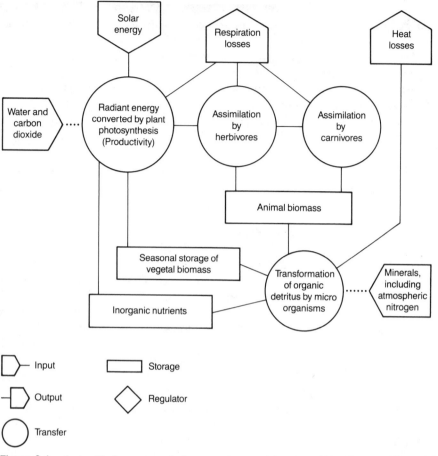

Figure 2.1. A simplified energy cycle for an environmental system. (After Butzer, 1982)

empirically; prehistoric ones are impossible to reconstruct. Yet the broad conceptual framework of the ecosystem serves as a very useful research tool for archaeologists.

Human ecosystems differ from biological ecosystems in many ways. Information, technology, and social organization all play much greater roles. Human beings, both as individuals and as groups, have unique capacities for matching resources with specific objectives. They not only think objectively about such matching but also transform the natural environment to meet their objectives. As Figure 2.2 shows, value systems and goal orientation are important to human ecosystems, as are group attitudes and decision-making institutions, especially in more complex societies. Any attempts to reconstruct prehistoric environments must take account of not only environmental resources and constraints but also of the ways in which humans utilized resources and intervened in the environment and changed it.

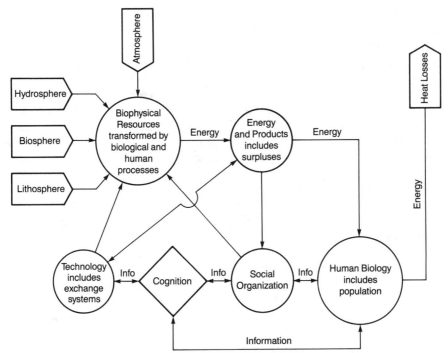

Figure 2.2 A much simplified energy cycle for a human ecosystem. This does not include provisions for storage of food and other resources. (After Butzer, 1982)

GEOARCHAEOLOGY

Geoarchaeology, archaeological research using the methods and concepts of the earth sciences, is a cornerstone of environmental reconstruction (Butzer, 1982). Until recently, geoarchaeology was little more than a battery of scientific techniques used for such things as radiocarbon dating and pollen analysis. But as archaeologists have concentrated more and more on environmental matters, and on the study of changing human settlement distributions over long periods of time, they have come to appreciate the great importance of an integrated approach to environmental reconstruction. The new geoarchaeology fills this role (Butzer, 1982).

Geoarchaeology

Ideally, and whatever their expertise, geoarchaeologists should be members of a multidisciplinary research team. They should work alongside the excavators in the field, collecting pollen and soil, and dating samples; recording stratigraphic profiles; relating the site to its landscape by topographic survey; and so on. Working closely with survey archaeologists, geoarchaeologists can locate sites on the natural landscape with the aid of air photographs, satellite images, and other remote-sensing devices. They can examine geological exposures and study the stratigraphic and sedimentary history of the entire region in a wider context vis-à-vis the sites found within it. Back in the laboratory, they can analyze maps and soil samples. Studying the sediments in the site, they can work out the microstratigraphy of the site down to the centimeter relative to that of the surrounding area. (Figure 2.3). They can also analyze site deposits for such properties as pH and organic content, and so on, to establish the effects of human activity on the sedimentary sequence at the site. The ultimate objective is to establish the ecological and spatial frameworks for the prehistoric data that emerge from archaeological excavations and surveys.

This approach has been tried with success in many places, including the Nile Valley, where Karl Butzer (1981) has argued that the Ancient Egyptians constantly modified their state and economic structure to overcome external and internal crises, while maintaining the same basic adaptation to a floodplain environment for millennia.

Geoarchaeology is definitely not geology, since it deals not only with sediments but with human activity as well. People are geomorphic agents, just as the wind is. Accidentally or deliberately, they carry inorganic and organic materials to their homes. They remove rubbish, make tools, build houses, abandon tools. All these mineral and organic materials are subjected to all manner of mechanical and biochemical processes during and after the time the site is occupied. The controlling geomorphic system at a site, whatever its size, is made up not only of natural elements but of a vital cultural component as well. So the geoarchaeologist is involved with archaeological investigations from the very beginning, and is concerned not only with the formation of sites, and with the changes they underwent during occupation, but also with what happened to them after abandonment.

Site formation processes

Thus, geoarchaeologists are deeply involved in the study of what are called *site formation processes* (Schiffer, 1983). These are the processes by which an abandoned prehistoric site is transformed into the archaeological record, the pattern of artifacts, food remains, and so on, that archaeologists investigate today, in the 1980s. Site formation processes are still imperfectly understood, because archaeologists have only just begun to look at this type of environmental archaeology, the environment in which a site decayed after abandonment. Wind, earthworms, cattle trampling, even human feet can shift the position of artifacts, erode and deposit soil, and cause artifacts and food remains to disappear or even change shape. Geoarchaeologists use sedimentation studies, soil samples, and chemical analyses to study site formation processes.

Environmental archaeology involves, then, not only the study of ancient environments but also an examination of the highly localized environmental context in which the archaeological record of a site or area is created.

We return to geoarchaeology in Chapter Three, when we consider the environmental background to world prehistory.

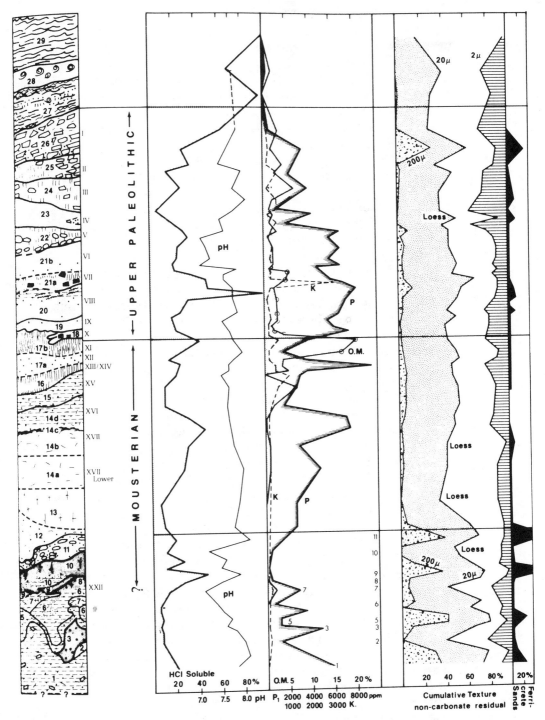

Figure 2.3 The complexities of microstratigraphy. A composite archaeosedimentary profile for Cueva Morin, a Paleolithic cave in northern Spain. The different sedimentary classes form the vertical columns; the actual stratigraphic layers appear at the left. (After Butzer, 1982)

ANALOGY AND EXPERIMENT

One obvious way to interpret the archaeological record is to compare prehistoric societies with living peoples, and archaeologists have been doing this for more than a century. A geologist named W. J. Sollas believed, for example, that the Eskimos of the Arctic were living examples of Stone Age hunter-gatherers who flourished in southwestern France toward the end of the Ice Age. These reindeer hunters lived in the Dordogne Valley when Europe had an arctic climate. Thus, he argued, one could make direct comparisons between the Eskimo society and that of arctic hunter-gatherers in prehistory. Such analogies at the society level were commonly used by archaeologists as late as the 1930s. When A. V. Kidder used direct-historical analogy in the southwestern United States, he excavated the great middens at Pecos pueblo, New Mexico, and worked back directly from the modern known to the prehistoric unknown, as far as artifact interpretation was concerned (Kidder, 1927). Given the long continuity of Indian culture in this area, the approach was fundamentally sound. Unfortunately, however, this direct and comprehensive way of comparing prehistoric and modern society is simply too elementary, because there are far too many uncontrollable variables and too great a time depth between present and past.

The modern attitude toward analogy is far more rigorous. During the past quarter century, archaeologists have refocused analogy in much more specific terms. They approach it in the context of a carefully defined problem, such as the function of an artifact, ways in which garbage was discarded, and so on. Here again there are serious problems, because the earlier the site the more likely it is that site formation processes and other variables have affected the patterning of artifacts, food remains, and other phenomena in the ground.

Artifact analogies

Many archaeologists have turned to highly specific artifact analogies and have made exact replicas of prehistoric tools and weapons that they then tested under controlled conditions. Jeffrey Flennikan of Washington State University learned how to make Paleo-Indian projectile heads, which he tested in deer hunts. John Coles of Cambridge University fabricated exact copies of European Bronze Age shields and swords, which were tested one against the other, showing that such weaponry was highly effective (Coles, 1973). Another fashionable form of experimental archaeology has been to build prehistoric settlements, then find volunteers to live in them for months on end, acting out the ancient lifeway as closely as possible. Such experiments are informative, and, when conducted under carefully controlled and specific circumstances, they are of great value. Artifact by artifact, even dwelling by dwelling, it is sometimes possible to make useful analogies about the ancient use of specific artifacts.

Modern archaeology still grapples with another problem, that of deciding the role of an artifact in prehistoric society. Since this "functionalist" approach considers an artifact as an integral part of the larger society of which it is part, it should be possible to establish its role in it. Such an analogy involves selecting a modern society that most closely resembles the archaeological culture in subsistence, technology, and environment — and those least removed from it in time for select analogies. But even this apparently reasonable approach has serious objections. For example, we might want to know about the role of sandal making among the Great Basin Indians of 6000 years ago. Were sandals produced by men, women, individuals, or groups? If we consider sandal making an aspect of technology, we might turn to the ethnographic literature on San hunter-gatherers from southern Africa in which sandals were sometimes features. Since women normally carry out domestic tasks among the San, one might argue that sandal making was a domestic task in the Great Basin and was done by women. However, even closer to home, the Pueblo Indians of the Southwest consider weaving a man's work, a task carried out in special ceremonial rooms, as it has been for centuries. Did the Great Basin people have a similar tradition of men carrying out domestic tasks? We do not know. No matter which analogical choice we make, we probably would not have much confidence in our choice.

Artifact analogies are now realized to have somewhat limited value. Controlled experiments with prehistoric artifacts, ancient agricultural methods, and early technology are more precise forms of analogy that lead logically into broader attempts to use modern hunter-gatherer or farming societies as a way of interpreting the past. This is ethnoarchaeology, sometimes called "living archaeology."

ETHNOARCHAEOLOGY

Ethnoarchaeology is a form of ethnography with a strongly materialist bias (Gould, 1978). It is not just a mass of observed data on human behavior, the sort of simple, isolated analogy that Sollas made. It is the study of dynamic processes in the modern world. For example, the South African anatomist Raymond Dart claimed that the australopithecines, who lived in southern Africa more than a million years ago, made bone tools by twisting, fracturing, and hammering animal bone fragments. This, he claimed, was the first human culture, evolved long before people used stone artifacts. Biologist C. K. Brain tested Dart's hypothesis against a set of controlled observations on modern hyena dens. He was able to show that the bone accumulations in australopithecine caves had been created by predators, not hominids (Brain, 1981; Dart, 1957).

The most famous ethnoarchaeological studies have been carried out among hunter-gatherers: the San of the Kalahari Desert in southern Africa and the Nunamiut Eskimo caribou hunters of Alaska. The San research began when anthropologist Richard Lee undertook a long-term study of !Kung hunter-gatherers. He collected a mass of data on hunting and gathering, including residence patterns, that were of potentially vital use to archaeologists working on prehistoric hunter-gatherer bands.

Ethnoarchaeology

Then an archaeologist accompanied the research team and made detailed studies of butchery techniques as well as plans of abandoned settlements of known, historical age. John Yellan's (1977) research yielded a treasure trove of data on house and camp arrangements, hearth locations, population densities, and bone refuse. For example, he points out that a San camp develops through conscious acts, such as the construction of windbreaks and hearths, as well as through such incidental deeds as the discarding of refuse and manufacturing debris (Figure 2.4). Yellan recognized communal areas, open spaces where dancing and distribution of food took place. Then there were family hearths for food processing and cooking. These, and other activity areas leave different tracks in the archaeological record.

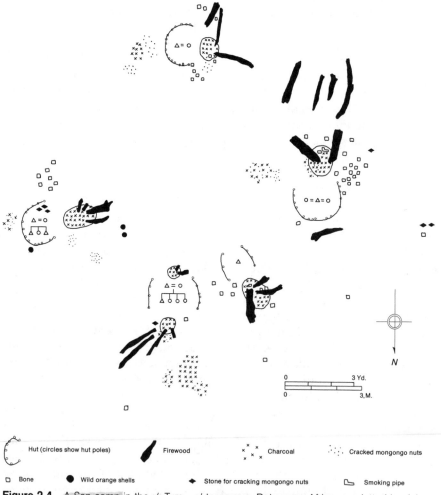

Figure 2.4 A San camp in the ≠ Tum = / toa grove, Botswana, Africa, as plotted by John Yellen to show the layout of activity areas and artifacts. (After Lee and DeVore)

Lewis Binford's Nunamiut research concentrated on the food procurement systems of a group of caribou hunters (1978). In a carefully designed piece of research, he wanted to find out as much as he could about their hunting and food-processing systems, and did so by studying the animal bones that resulted from the chase. He studied not only seasonal hunting but also the storage systems that carried them from one year to the next — fresh meat is available only two months a year. By close study of the Nunamiuts' annual round, as well as their butchery and storage strategies, Binford was able to develop indices that measured the way the Eskimo used different caribou body parts and utilized their primary food resource. The Nunamiut research provided a mass of empirical data on human exploitation of animals and also showed just how local many cultural adaptations are. Thus, argued Binford, many of the artifact differences recognized in the archaeological record are, in fact, reflections of highly localized adaptations to the environment.

Ethnoarchaeology has profoundly affected the ways in which archaeologists study prehistoric hunter-gatherer societies. But how does one integrate the results of such studies into the study of archaeology? A new body of archaeological theory is emerging that seeks to bridge the static past and the dynamic present.

MIDDLE RANGE THEORY

Middle range theory originated as a concept in sociology, a body of theory designed as a link between general theories of social systems and low-order empirical generalizations (Raab and Goodyear, 1984). Lewis Binford began to think about such linking theory in archaeology during his Nunamiut researches. He began to use the term middle range theory in archaeology soon afterward, but in a specific way, as a potentially accurate means of identifying and measuring specified properties in past cultural systems (Binford, 1978, 1981). This new body of theory is based on the assumption that the archaeological record is a contemporary, static phenomenon, formed not only by human behavior but also by all manner of natural and humanly caused factors that buried artifacts, destroyed sites, rebuilt other settlements on them, covered them with wind-blown sand, and so on. These processes create the archaeological record — the phenomena that the archaeologist finds in the ground today. They provide the critical link between long-extinct, dynamic human behavior in the past and the static material properties common in both past and present — the artifacts we examine, pots that were used in the past, and similar types of vessels still used today. What middle range theory tries to do is to treat the relationship between statics and dynamics, between human behavior and its material derivatives. Some people call this "actualistic" theory, because it studies the coincidence of both statics and dynamics in cultural systems in the only time frame in which it can be achieved — in the present.

Middle range theory

Middle range theory is still a new concept in archaeology and one that has raised considerable controversy. For instance, Lewis Binford considers the archaeological record static and material, containing no direct information on the relationship between human behavior and material culture. Others disagree and argue that it does (Schiffer, 1976). Just how much genuine middle range theory has yet been generated is still arguable, but it is certainly of value when studying the wear on the working edges of prehistoric stone tools, and in examining site formation processes. This narrow focus is likely to change in future years, since ethnoarchaeology and experimental archaeology provide unique opportunities for archaeologists to gather data for interpreting artifact patternings in the archaeological record and to integrate both statics and dynamics (for a critique, see Raab and Goodyear, 1984).

Living archaeology has opened up new interpretative vistas in world prehistory, vistas that have direct application to broader problems of studying multilinear cultural evolution.

MULTILINEAR CULTURAL EVOLUTION

The work of Leslie White and Julian Steward resulted in the emergence of a new school of evolutionary thought, one with no pat formulas and more variables. The Victorian evolutionists had thought in terms of a single line of cultural evolution, from simple hunter-gatherers to civilization. Elman Service, Morton Fried, and Marshall Sahlins argued that this unilinear (one-line) process was far too simplistic and that each human culture pursues its own individual evolutionary course, a course determined by the long-term success of its adaptation, via technology and social institutions, to its natural environment (Sahlins and Service, 1960). This concept of *multilinear* (multiple-line) evolution now is widely accepted by students of world prehistory.

Some societies achieve a broad measure of equilibrium with their environment in which adaptive changes consist of little more than some refinements in technology and the fine tuning of organizational structures.

Growth cycles

Other societies become involved in cycles of growth that are triggered by environmental change or from within society. If these changes involve either greater food supplies or population growth, there can be accelerated growth resulting from the need to feed more people or the deployment of an enlarged food surplus. Continued growth can place additional strains on society, triggering technological changes, adjustments to social organization, or alterations in the belief system that provides the integrative force for society.

Every society has its growth limits imposed by the environment and available technology, and some environments have more potential for growth than others. Certain types of sociopolitical organization, such as centralized control of specialized labor, are more efficient than others. The emergence of food production in Mesoamerica (Central America) and the beginnings of urban civilization there are both cases of societies having entered on a major growth cycle after centuries of relatively slow cultural evolution in the same regions. Adaptive changes have triggered technological innovation that has led to increased food supplies and higher population densities. Our own society is embarking on such a growth cycle today — with open-ended and dangerous consequences.

This sophisticated concept of multilinear cultural evolution led Service, Fried, and others to develop four broad stages of societal complexity that were of great importance in prehistory, stages that are implicit throughout this book (Service, 1962):

Stages of society

Bands are associations of families that may not exceed twenty-five to sixty people. These bands are knit together by close social ties; they were the dominant form of social organization for most hunter-gatherers from the earliest times up to the origins of food production.

Tribes are clusters of bands that are linked by clans into tribes. A clan is a group of people linked by common ancestral ties, ties that cut across the narrow frontiers of bands and serve as unifying links between widely scattered communities. Clans are important because they are a form of social linkage that give people a sense of common identity with a wider world than their own immediate family and relatives. They are much more of a kin than political unit, and, as such, are not used as one of the major stages of social evolution in themselves.

Chiefdoms develop among some tribes, societies in which clan groups assume a ranking within society. One clan may achieve dominance because its members have extraordinary religious or organizational powers. The leaders of this clan may become chieftains who act as social instruments for the control and redistribution of goods and services within the tribe as a whole. Chiefdoms, such as those found among the Hopewell people of the Midwest some 1500 years ago, are a transitional stage between the tribe and the state societies of the earliest civilizations.

State-organized societies develop from chiefdoms and are governed by a full-fledged ruling class and a hierarchy of social classes below them that include such diverse groups as specialist craftspeople, merchants, peasants, and even slaves. State-organized societies of the past were first ruled by priest-bureaucrats, then gradually came under the rule of secular kings who sometimes became despotic monarchs, often with alleged divine powers. This type of social organization was typical of the early literate civilizations and was the forerunner of the Classical civilizations of Greece and Rome.

The theory of multilinear cultural evolution assumes that similar developments can occur in different cultures in broadly similar environments separated by thousands of miles. Both the Ancient Egyptians and the Maya of Mesoamerica, for example, lived in highly complex societies organized into rigid social classes of nobles and commoners, built spectacular temples, and used a form of writing. In these senses their cultural developments were similar, but even a superficial glance at each society reveals striking differences between them. The Egyptians relied on irrigation agriculture based on seasonal flooding of the Nile and lived in a predictable environment. They never engaged in human sacrifice. The Maya's lowland rain-forest environment could yield ample crops only if cultivated by a variety of techniques. The gods were seen as hostile and were appeased by human blood. The startling differences between these two societies can be explained by studying them as highly complex, ever-changing systems that interacted constantly with their local environments. Modern archaeology uses the notion of societal stages not to propose simple schemes of cultural evolution but to study the dynamics of growth within a culture and the complex mechanisms that led to cultural evolution.

CULTURAL PROCESS, SYSTEMS, AND EVOLUTION

In recent decades not only has a mass of new information become available to archaeologists but also new and much more complex methods of studying cultural process have been developed. At the heart of the new methodology is an insistence that archaeological research be based on deductive research. This type of inquiry is based on formal research designs and testable hypotheses, which are then compared against data collected in the field.

Systems theory

Multilinear cultural evolution is the vital integrative force that brings together systems theory and cultural ecology into a closely knit, highly flexible way of studying and explaining cultural process (Sanders and Webster, 1978). When systems theory first came into fashion in archaeology during the 1960s, it was regarded as the solution to all theoretical problems. Kent Flannery (1968a) studied early agriculture in Mexico's southern highlands. He discovered that between 8000 and 2000 B.C. the highland peoples relied on five basic food sources — deer, rabbits, maguey, tree legumes, and prickly pears — for their sustenance. By careful predicting of the seasons of each food, they could schedule their hunting and gathering at periods of abundance and before animals gained access to the ripe plants. Flannery assumed that the southern highlands and their inhabitants were part of a large open environmental system consisting of many subsystems — economic, botanical, social, and so on — that interacted with one another. Then something happened to jolt the food procurement system toward the deliberate growing of wild grasses. Flannery's excavations at dry sites dating to between 5000 and 2000 B.C. showed wild maize cobs slowly increasing in size and other signs of genetic change. He suggested that the people began to experiment with the deliberate planting of maize and other grasses, intentionally expanding the areas where they would grow. After a long period of time, these intentional deviations in the food procurement system caused the importance of wild grass collecting to increase at the expense of other collecting activities until it became the dominant one. Eventually, the Indians created a self-perpetuating food procurement system, with its own vital scheduling demands of planting and harvesting that competed with earlier systems and won out because it was more durable. By 2000 B.C., the highly nutritious bean and corn staple diet of the highland peoples was well established.

Flannery's Mexican research dramatizes the importance of looking at cultural change in the context of the interrelationships between many different variables. There is no one prime agent of cultural evolution, but rather a whole series of important variables, all with complex interrelationships. When we seek to explain the major and minor events of prehistory, we consider the ways in which change took place, the processes and mechanisms (cultural evolution, experimentation), and the socioeconomic stresses (population pressure, game scarcity, and so on) that trigger these mechanisms (Flannery, 1972).

The problem is that testing such multicausal models is a difficult task, involving rigorous methodologies for identifying the variables in the archaeological record, as well as comparative studies of these variables in regions where a particular development (say, the emergence of civilization) occurred and where it did not, and also in societies that flourished immediately before its development (Redman, 1978). Flannery's systems approach has been criticized by some scholars for its heavy reliance on cultural evolution (Sanders and Webster, 1978). They point out that environmental stimuli are probably far more important than the universal, evolutionary processes of multilinear evolutionists.

CURRENT DIRECTIONS

Evolutionary theory has yet to be explored systematically in archaeology. Flannery's methods are still fundamentally based on the anthropologists' notions of cultural evolution, a view that tends to emphasize variability in human culture as a whole at the expense of individual human actions and decisions. Just how important was the individual in prehistory, as opposed to biological, cultural, and environmental forces? Much current archaeological research is trying to move us closer to understanding the frameworks within which cultural process took place. Some of the exciting new directions of this research include:

Structural Archaeology and the Individual

Some archaeologists believe that there is much more to human culture than functions and activities. Behind all activities of any society, ancient or modern, are the logic and coherence that have to be understood in their own terms (Hodder, 1982). This "structure" of prehistoric society is defined as "the codes and rules according to which observed sets of interrelations are produced," the set of rules or "code," as it were, that can be likened to those in chess or Trivial Pursuit. They are followed as people go about the business of survival, adaptation, and making a living.

Structural archaeology is an attempt to get at objects as they were perceived by their original owners, at the symbolism of burial rites, and ultimately at the reasons why societies remain static, change, collapse, and so on. Structural archaeology is in its infancy, since few areas provide the enormous quantities of archaeological data that are needed to trace and observe the subtle changes in artifact patterning over time.

Cultural Evolution and Sociobiology

Some of the understanding of cultural process will come from the theories and research of modern evolutionary biology, a new and exciting area of inquiry. In many ways, the biologist and the archaeologist are facing the same problem: How do forms, whether living or cultural, emerge and stabilize? There are two dramatically contrasting viewpoints of human behavior that bear on this question. One, espoused by most anthropologists, is that the greater part of human behavior is not constrained by genetics but is produced by our unique culture. In contrast, the sociobiologists (Wilson, 1977) believe that cultural expression is a flimsy blanket for compelling genetic imperatives. Wilson believes that human behavior is in part explained by a form of genetic determinism. In other words, our actions are much more genetically directed than we might think. The debate between the sociobiologists and anthropologists rages on, and generates much emotion on both sides. Has the direction of human evolution stripped us of all genetically directed behavior? Or has our incredible adaptability, so richly documented by archaeology, caused our culture to reign supreme over the forces of biological evolution? We do not yet know.

After more than a century of theorizing about world prehistory, we are slowly groping toward a general theory that is capable of generating scientific explanations within a historical framework. So far we have failed to generate such general theory: the problems are too fundamental, the research still too inadequate. Clearly, some of our insights will come not from archaeology but from the new biology of the 1980s and 1990s.

Site Formation Processes and Living Archaeology

Despite thousands of excavations all over the world, we still know almost nothing about how the archaeological record was formed. What geological forces covered the bones and artifacts at Olduvai Gorge, Tanzania? How can we account for the distributions of different body parts in bone assemblages? How did California Indians open shellfish? Do the fragmentary shells in the archaeological record actually reflect similar techniques to those used in historical times, or have the shells been modified by later human activity? A whole body of new research, into site formation processes and into "taphonomy," the study of how animal bones are transformed into fossils, is throwing new light on the past. For instance, recent tool wear and taphonomic researches at Olduvai Gorge have shown that the famous "living floors" there may in fact be caches of bones left by scavenging hominids (Potts, 1984).

As we move toward general theory, we will need far more empirical studies of variability within human cultures. This will be derived not only from excavations, archaeological surveys, and laboratory analyses, but also from living archaeology and from controlled experiments that range from burning down houses to Stone Age technology and prehistoric cultivation methods.

Our knowledge of world prehistory grows ever more complex every day, but our understanding of it is still grossly inadequate. Although we can discern some regularities, the general relationships and processes that have led to them remain little understood. This is where living archaeology and empirical studies of site formation processes come in, and they will undoubtedly assume much greater importance in the future.

The Finite Archaeological Record and Remote Sensing

The days of uncontrolled archaeological excavations are long gone. Yet the destruction of archaeological sites proceeds at a breathtaking pace. Land developers, deep-plowing farm machinery, and strip mining have destroyed thousands of unique sites; collectors and unscientific archaeologists have destroyed thousands more. Since the archaeological record is being destroyed faster than it can be conserved, archaeologists are more and more avoiding destructive excavation where at all possible and turning to side-scan radar, satellite imagery, and other sophisticated remote-sensing devices to study the past without digging. Remote sensing enables us to look at ancient landscapes, and peoples' imprints upon them, and through computerized data bases to begin to predict densities of archaeological sites in different landscapes. As the number of undisturbed archaeological sites dwindles, we can expect all forms of remote sensing to assume much greater importance than conventional excavation.

Examining a satellite photograph of the earth or flying from Los Angeles to New York makes you realize one fundamental truth about world prehistory, which serves as a good starting point for the next chapters. Of all the millions of animals on earth, we are the only ones who have so relentlessly and universally transformed the face of the globe. We have done both bad and good, and we have at times caused lasting damage to the earth, damage that prompts some people to predict that the end of human existence is near. But we are also the only ones of a myriad of living creatures who have evolved the intellectual powers to guide our own destiny. It is this capacity that enables us to ask the question, "Why are we here?" This book cannot do much to answer that question, but it can give you an understanding of some of the complex processes in human prehistory that have led us to master and transform the earth.

GUIDE TO FURTHER READING

Binford, Lewis R. *In Pursuit of the Past*. New York and London: Thames and Hudson, 1983.
A basic account of processual archaeology, with lengthy discussions of ethnoarchaeology and middle range theory.

Butzer, Karl. *Archaeology as Human Ecology*. Cambridge: Cambridge University Press, 1982.
A basic account of cultural ecology and environmental archaeology from a geological perspective.

Daniel, Glyn E. *A Short History of Archaeology*. London: Thames and Hudson, 1981.
A brief summary of the major events and trends in archaeology since Classical times. Tends to be weak on recent developments.

Fagan, Brian M. *In the Beginning* (5th ed.). Boston: Little, Brown, 1985.
The early chapters of this textbook cover major theoretical developments.

Harris, Marvin. *The Rise of Anthropological Theory*. New York: Thomas Crowell, 1968.
A magnificent, if occasionally polemical, survey of theory in anthropology that covers many personalities mentioned in this chapter.

Salmon, M. *The Philosophy of Archaeology*. New York: Academic Press, 1982.
A thoughtful book on the basic philosophies behind archaeology and its relationships to other intellectual disciplines.

Watson, Patty Jo, LeBlanc, Steven, and Redman, Charles. *Archaeological Explanation*. New York: Academic Press, 1984.
A description of the basic principles of processual archaeology, widely used by serious students.

Chapter Three

The Pleistocene Epoch

PREVIEW

❊ The later part of the Cenozoic, the age of mammals, was a period of rapidly changing and often intensely cold climate. These changes reached a peak during the Quaternary, the most recent period of earth history, which began about 1.7 million years ago. The Pleistocene or great Ice Age forms most of the Quaternary until about 10,000 years ago.

❊ The Quaternary is important because it is the only geological epoch contemporary with human activity. Its deposits offer unique opportunities for studying ancient environments and dating prehistoric human cultures.

❊ The Quaternary was once studied by means of glacial deposits and other land formations, as well as high levels. But deep sea cores provide the most accurate and comprehensive chronicle of climatic change during the past 3 million years. These changes are mirrored by sequences of vegetation changes obtained from fossil pollens in waterlogged deposits on land.

❊ Geologists divide the Quaternary into Early, Middle, and Late subdivisions for their own convenience, and date the beginning of the era to about 1.7 million years ago.

❊ While the Early Quaternary saw rapid cooling, its fauna still include Pliocene animals. The Middle Quaternary began about 700,000 years ago and included two major glacial periods: Elster and Saale, separated by short interglacials between 515,000 and 315,000 years ago.

❊ The Late Quaternary began with the Eemian interglacial in 127,000 B.C. The climate cooled down rapidly after 115,000 and reached a cold climax about 18,000 years ago.

❊ Postglacial times (the Holocene) began about 10,000 years ago. The climate reached a warm climax about 7000 years ago, and the global climate is now cooling.

The later part of the Cenozoic — the age of mammals — was, and still is, a period of rapidly changing and often intensely cold climate. These changes culminated during the Quaternary, the most recent period of earth history, which began about 1.7 million years ago. This period is sometimes called the "Age of Humanity," for it was during that time that human beings first populated most of the globe. This chapter describes some of the major climatic and environmental changes that have taken place during the Quaternary, changes that were the climatic backdrop for some of the most important stages in human evolution.

For most of geological time, the world's climate was warmer and more homogeneous than it is today. As long ago as the Miocene epoch (Table 3.1), land began to uplift in many places and mountains began to form, continuing through the Pliocene into recent time (Butzer, 1974; Flint, 1971). During the Oligocene, some 38 million years ago, the first signs of glacial cooling appeared, with the formation of a belt of pack ice around Antarctica. This was followed by a major drop in world temperatures between 14 and 11 million years ago. As temperatures lowered, glaciers formed on high ground in high latitudes. About 3.2 million years ago, large ice sheets formed on the northern continents, locking up enough water to lower world sea levels by about 130 ft (40 m). Then, about 2.5 million years ago, glaciation intensified still more and the earth entered its present period of constantly fluctuating climate.

THE GREAT ICE AGE

The Quaternary (or Pleistocene) era had constant fluctuations between warm and intensely cold global climates. Climates as warm or warmer than that of today were rare during the Quaternary. Called *interglacials*, they lasted only about 10,000 years each. The cold, *glacial* periods between them were not uniformly cold but fluctuated constantly between milder phases, called *interstadials*, and millennia of intense cold. Not that the interstadials were warm, far from it. They were merely slightly less frigid.

During Pleistocene times, climatic change repeatedly displaced plants and animals from their original habitats (Kurtén, 1968, 1980; Martin and Wright, 1967). When a glacial period began, plants and animals usually fared better in lower altitudes and warmer latitudes. Populations of animals spread slowly toward more hospitable areas, mixing with populations that already lived in the new areas and creating new communities with new combinations of organisms. This repeated mixing surely affected the directions of evolution in many forms. No one knows exactly how many species of mammals emerged during the Pleistocene, although Björn Kurtén has estimated that no fewer than 113 of the mammal species now living in Europe and adjacent Asia appeared during the last 3 million years.

The Pleistocene is important because it is the only geological epoch contemporary with human activity. People lived and hunted over much of the terrain covered by its ice sheets and dwelt in arctic steppe zones during the more temperate interglacials. Stone Age humans killed many types of animals for food, animals whose butchered bones often are

Table 3.1 Geological epochs from more than 60 million years ago. The curve demonstrates lasting temperature changes on earth since the late Miocene; the dotted line indicates lack of data. Notice that the general trend is toward cooler temperatures with fluctuations (Pleistocene temperatures are shown in Table 3.2).

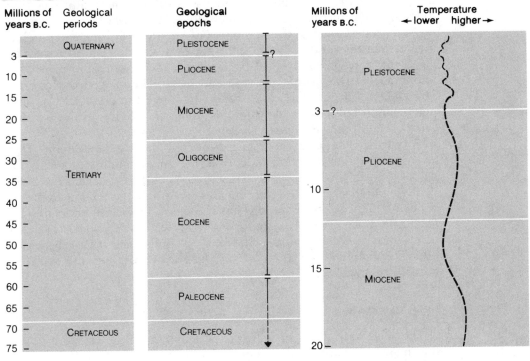

found in river gravels and other Pleistocene deposits in the Old World. Early hunters preyed on animals now extinct, whose carcasses sometimes sank into lake mud or washed into river backwaters, burying the skeletons for archaeologists to find thousands of years later.

With these fossils and careful study of geological deposits, a complex chronological record of the Pleistocene has been assembled. Some Pleistocene sites, for example, can be dated very roughly by examining the fossilized teeth of elephants, for elephants changed radically during each glacial and interglacial period; each species of this animal has a tooth pattern that distinguishes it from earlier and later forms (Oakley, 1964). Numerous branches of science — botany, zoology, geomorphology (the study of landforms), and nuclear physics — have helped build up the story of the Pleistocene epoch we shall outline here.

STUDYING THE QUATERNARY

In the late nineteenth century, two Austrian geologists, A. Penck and E. Brückner, studied the glacial deposits in four northern Alpine valleys

(Penck and Brückner, 1909). They identified at least four major Pleisto-cene glacial periods — Günz, Mindel, Riss, and Würm — which were named after Alpine valleys. These, they said, designated times when the ice sheets of the mountains extended into much lower altitudes than today. At the same time, vast ice sheets flowed southward from Scandina-via and arctic Canada, covering much of northern Europe and much of the northeastern and midwestern United States. Penck and Brückner ar-gued that these glaciations were separated from each other by prolonged interglacials, when sea levels rose and the world enjoyed warmer and often drier climates (Table 3.2). When the longest interglacial was at its height, such animals as the hippopotamus were living in the Somme, Thames, and other European rivers.

For years, Quaternary geologists accepted the Austrian scheme. They relied on river gravels, glacial deposits, and other crude geological indi-cators to study the Pleistocene. They thought of the Quaternary as being divided into three, perhaps four, major glaciations. But the inevitable ad-vance of science and technology has changed all this and shown that the Quaternary was far more complicated than was once suspected (a valu-able summary can be found in Street, 1980). Today, scientists rely heavily on evidence of climatic change from deep sea cores to examine ancient climatic change.

Deep Sea Cores

The science of oceanography relies heavily on deep sea core borers that bring up columns of sediment from the ocean floor (Butzer and Isaac, 1976). Chemical and paleontological studies of these cores have provided a wealth of information on Ice Age climates. Thousands of tiny marine fossils have come from the cores. These planktonic foraminifera are small animals that once lived close to the ocean's surface. The com-position of their shells reflects the seawater around them in life and gives us a record of the ratio of the two oxygen isotopes, ^{16}O and ^{18}O, in surface ocean water. Despite some possible contaminating factors, this ratio clearly reflects the total volume of seawater locked up in glacial ice at the time. By paleomagnetic-dating the cores, the paleontologists obtain a time scale for the entire Ice Age.

One advantage of sea cores is that you can confirm the climatic fluctu-ations by using several different lines of evidence. For example, you can analyze the changing frequencies of foraminifera and other groups of marine microfossils in the cores. By using statistical techniques, and as-suming that relationships between different species and sea conditions have not changed, climatologists have been able to turn these frequen-cies into numerical estimates of sea-surface temperature and ocean sa-linity over the past few hundred thousand years (CLIMAP, 1976).

Sea cores have produced a highly complex picture of Quaternary cli-mate. Early Quaternary cores show that the climatic fluctuations be-tween warm and cold were relatively minor until about 800,000 years

Table 3.2 Old World geological events, climatic changes, and chronology during the Pleistocene (highly simplified), with approximate dates.

Temperature ← lower higher →	Date (B.C.)	Periods	Epochs	Subdivisions	European glacials/interglacials	North American glacials/interglacials	Human evolution	Prehistory	Three Age System
									IRON AGE
								Cities, agriculture Settlement of New World	BRONZE AGE
							Homo sapiens sapiens		NEOLITHIC
	8,000 —	QUATERNARY	HOLOCENE	HOLOCENE	HOLOCENE	HOLOCENE			
	75,000 —		PLEISTOCENE	UPPER PLEISTOCENE	WEICHSEL (Würm)	WISCONSIN		Hunter-gatherers	PALEOLITHIC
	?130,000 —				EEM	SANGAMON			
	?200,000 —				SAALE (RISS)	ILLINOIAN	Homo sapiens		
	?400,000 —			MIDDLE PLEISTOCENE	HOLSTEIN	YARMOUTH	Homo erectus		
	?700,000 —			LOWER PLEISTOCENE (Villafranchian)	ELSTER (MINDEL)	KANSAN	Early hominids and Australopithecus		
					Uncertain sequence of geological events	Uncertain sequence of geological events			
	?1,800,000 —	TERTIARY	PLIOCENE						

Uncertain climatic sequence →

Note for the advanced reader and the instructor: Throughout this book I have used the glacial terminology applied to northern Europe in discussing the successive glaciations and interglacial periods in the Old World. This system follows Karl Butzer's definitive synthesis, *Environment and Archaeology*, 3rd ed. (Chicago: Aldine, 1974). Many still use the Alpine names preferred in earlier literature, but I have chosen to reduce confusion and recognize that not everyone will agree. For the newcomers, here are the equivalent names:

Alpine terms:	Würm	Riss	Mindel
Northern European terms:	Weichsel	Saale	Elster

*Data are from Flint, 1971. The chronology of earlier glacial periods is controversial. Terms are greatly simplified and there are many local labels.

ago. Since then, periods of intense cold have recurred about every 100,000 years, with minor oscillations about 20,000 and 40,000 years apart. Many scientists believe that these changes are triggered by long-term astronomical changes, especially in the earth's orbit around the sun (Covey, 1984), which affect the seasonal and north-south variations of solar radiation received by the earth. Of course there are other factors, too, such as variations in the amount of volcanic dust in the atmosphere (Gribben, 1978).

Land Observations

The geological record on land is much less complete than that from the ocean floor, partly because the ever-present forces of erosion, deposition, and earthquake movement are constantly changing the earth's surface (Bowen, 1978). The fragmentary deposits that do survive are extremely difficult to date either stratigraphically, or in years, except in volcanic areas where potassium argon dating can be used. Penck and Brückner's classic Alpine glacial sequence is now considered far too simplistic for general use, so geologists rely on two other forms of deposits for much more accurate correlations:

Loess deposits

Loess deposits are deep layers of wind-blown dust that were laid down during dry, arctic steppe conditions during glacial periods. Strong winds blowing out from the ice caps carried loess over enormous distances, dropping it in thick belts that mantle much of China, central Europe, and parts of North America. When the climate warmed up, these loess layers carried woodland or grassland, which formed rich soils that show up clearly in geological exposures, and they were often covered by later deposits of glacial dust. The loesses can be dated by paleomagnetic techniques and confirm what we already know from oxygen isotope sea core analyses: that the climate has fluctuated constantly between warm and cold for at least 1.8 million years.

Pollen analysis

Pollen analysis (palynology) has long been used to study vegetational changes over long periods of time, using sample cores taken from lake deposits and peat bogs. One lake core in northern Greece provides a vegetational sequence that goes back more than 600,000 years (Turekian, 1971). This finding can be correlated with deep sea cores. Pollen analysis came into its own in the last 130,000 years, when many more core sequences survived.

Quaternary geologists are experimenting with all kinds of new techniques, and many of them are doing isotopic analyses on such phenomena as cave stalagmites, ice cores, tree rings, and soil sediments.

Animal remains

Animal remains have long been used to make crude correlations of Quaternary climatic changes. For example, the fossilized teeth of elephants provide an interesting chronicle of dramatic changes in elephant populations during the Ice Age, although these changes are of a very general nature. Since many mammals are relatively insensitive to rapid climatic change and can flourish in a wide range of climatic regimens, only the most general impression of a Quaternary climate can come from such data. Studies of tiny mammals like rats and mice, however, can often provide a relatively sensitive picture of Quaternary environments such as those at the famous early hominid sites at Olduvai Gorge, Tanzania, in East Africa.

THE EARLY QUATERNARY

The beginning of the Quaternary is a purely arbitrary geological boundary defined by geologists for sake of convenience (Table 3.2). International agreements have used Italian marine sediments about 1.7 million years old to define the earliest boundary. By this time, great mountain chains had formed in the Alps, Himalayas, and elsewhere. Land masses had been uplifted; there was less connection between northern and southern areas, lessening the heat exchange between those latitudes and causing greater temperature differences between them. Marine temperatures cooled gradually during the Pliocene. By 3 million years or so ago, northern latitudes, still warmer than today, were much cooler than they had been 70 million years before. A cooling of the northern seas 3 million years ago can be detected from finds of marine deposits in northern Europe and North America that show temperate, northern mollusks replacing warmer species.

The terms *Early, Middle,* and *Late Quaternary* (or *Pleistocene)* break the epoch into large subdivisions according to their fossils and climatic changes. The Early Quaternary normally includes surviving Pliocene animal fossils, as well as wild horses, cattle, elephants, and camels, all of which appear for the first time in the Quaternary.

The Early Quaternary is still very imperfectly known. However, it is known from sea cores that climatic fluctuations between warmer and colder regimens were still relatively minor (Kurtén, 1968). It lasted about a million years, up to about 700,000 years ago, when the present phase of the earth's magnetic polarity began. Many Early Quaternary fossil beds come from Africa, where early hominids hunted both large mammals and smaller animals. This was the critically important period of time when *Homo erectus* evolved and human populations moved out of Africa into Asia and Europe.

MIDDLE QUATERNARY

There have been at least eight glacial and interglacial cycles during the past 700,000 years, a period sometimes called the Brunhes epoch (Table 3.2) The seesaw pattern of sea core changes suggests that although ice sheets formed gradually, deglaciation took place with great rapidity, during phases that geologists call "terminations," which corresponded with major sea level rises that flooded low-lying coastal areas. Lesser rises took place during interstadials. Street (1980) estimates that glaciers covered a full one-third of the earth's land surface during glacial maxima, while they were about as extensive as today during interglacials. Thus, during interglacials sea levels were within 18 to 30 ft (5 to 10 m) of present shorelines.

The fluctuations in ice sheets were mirrored by major vegetational changes away from the ice sheets. Treeless arctic steppe and tundra covered much of Europe and North America during cold periods but gave way to temperate forests during interglacials. Much less is known about changes in tropical latitudes, although it is thought that the southern fringes of the Sahara Desert expanded dramatically during cold periods: high percentages of wind-blown desert sand have been found in sea cores taken off West Africa.

In earlier editions of this book, I used a long-established sequence of glacial episodes and interglacials to subdivide both the Middle and Late Quaternary. Although many details of these periods have been modified by sea core research, it is still worth summarizing the major episodes (Table 3.2).

The best glacial deposits in Europe come from northern Germany and are named after three rivers: the Elster, Saale, and the Weichsel.

Elster 525,000 B.P.

The *Elster* glaciation reached its height about 525,000 years ago. Ice covered much of central Britain, the Low Countries, and central Europe as far east as the Ural Mountains. The Alpine ice extended northward and local glaciers sat on the Pyrenees and the Caucasus, so that much of Europe between latitudes 40 and 50° N was arctic plains country, with severe winters in the Mediterranean. The North American equivalent was the Kansan ice sheet that extended southward from three ice caps near the sixtieth parallel in Canada. Its southern limits were Seattle, St. Louis, and New York. At that time as much as 33 percent of the earth's surface was covered with ice, and sea levels were about 650 ft (197 m) below their present heights.

The succeeding interglacials brought much more temperate conditions, at times milder than today's in northern latitudes (Figure 3.1). It was during this period that human settlement of temperate latitudes really took hold, as small bands of hunters exploited the rich game populations of European river valleys (Chapter Five). The oscillations between warmer and colder weather, which are chronicled in Table 3.2, show a surprising regularity, with peaks of more temperate conditions between about 515,000 and 315,000, with, however, colder incidents breaking up the warmer climate.

Saale 180,000 to 127,000 B.P.

The *Saale* glaciation coincides with the Illinoian in North America. In places, the Saale was fully as intense as the Elster, with an arctic climate persisting over much of the neighboring parts of Europe, which were marked by extensive loess deposits. But it was relatively short-lived, from about 180,000 to 127,000.

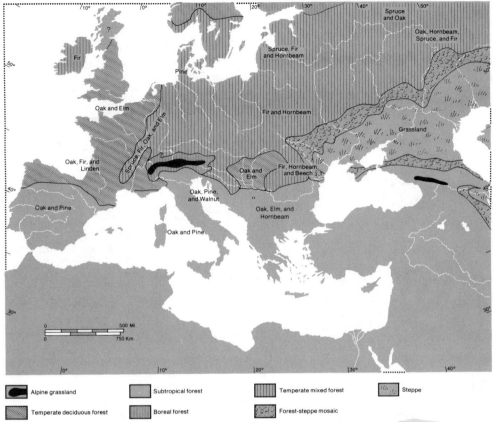

| ██████ | Alpine grassland | ▓▓▓▓ | Subtropical forest | ▌▌▌▌ | Temperate mixed forest | ░░░ | Steppe |
| ▓▓▓▓ | Temperate deciduous forest | ░░░░ | Boreal forest | ∴∴∴ | Forest-steppe mosaic | | |

Figure 3.1 Generalized distribution of vegetation in Europe during the height of the Holstein interglacial. (After Butzer, 1974)

LATE QUATERNARY

The Late Quaternary began with a major warming trend and a rapid rise of sea levels about 127,000 years ago. An important datum point in Quaternary chronology, it is often called *Termination II*. This *Eemian* interglacial lasted a mere 10,000 years, but global temperatures were between 1 and 3° C warmer than today. The sea rose about 20 ft (6 m) above its present level, ice sheets were much reduced, and temperate forest covered much of Eurasia and North America.

Eemian
**127,000 to
117,000 B.P.**

But change was afoot. By 115,000 years ago, the North American ice sheets were expanding again and sea levels had already fallen an estimated 230 ft (70 m). Forests gave way to open grassland and scrub or steppe. Only two brief warmer episodes, about 105,000 and 82,000 years ago, interrupted the cooling, but from 75,000 years ago, glacial conditions persisted. This was the *Weichsel* (Wisconsin in North America) glaciation that lasted until about 10,000 years ago (Figure 3.2; Table 3.3).

Weichsel
**115,000 to
10,000 B.P.**

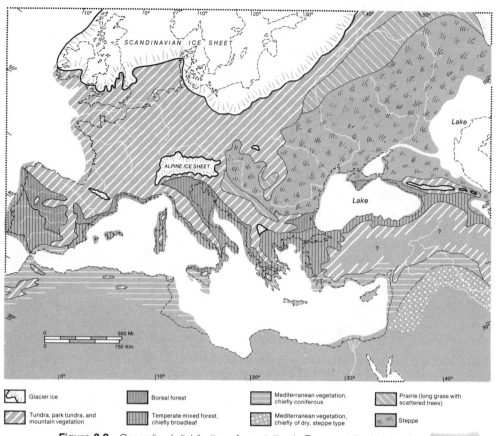

Figure 3.2 Generalized distribution of vegetation in Europe at the height of the Weichsel glaciation. Land areas were larger than today's. Notice, too, the extent of the ice sheet. (After Butzer, 1974)

The Weichsel glaciation is much better known than its predecessors and formed the backdrop for some of the most important developments in human prehistory: the final emergence of *Homo sapiens,* the Neanderthals, and the first human settlements in the Americas. The Scandinavian and North American ice sheets reached their maximum extent about 18,000 years ago, when the sea levels dropped at least 425 ft (130 m) below present shorelines. This drop led to the exposure of huge continental shelves, especially in southeast Asia. The Bering Strait between Siberia and Alaska became dry land and a refuge for humans and large mammals during the height of the last glaciation (Hopkins et al, 1982).

The bitterly cold Weichsel climate effectively blocked off huge areas of the world for human settlement. The North American ice sheet extended as far south as 39° N, the Scandinavian to 52° N. Snowlines on most mountains were lowered by as much as 3300 ft (over 1000 m). Barren

Table 3.3 The Weichsel glaciation in Europe. (After Butzer, 1974)

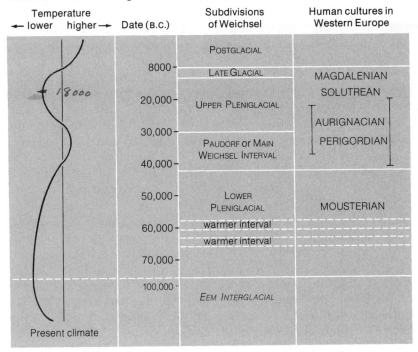

Temperature ← lower higher →	Date (B.C.)	Subdivisions of Weichsel	Human cultures in Western Europe
		POSTGLACIAL	
	8000	LATE GLACIAL	MAGDALENIAN
			SOLUTREAN
18000	20,000	UPPER PLENIGLACIAL	
			AURIGNACIAN
	30,000		PERIGORDIAN
		PAUDORF or MAIN WEICHSEL INTERVAL	
	40,000		
	50,000	LOWER PLENIGLACIAL	MOUSTERIAN
	60,000	warmer interval	
		warmer interval	
	70,000		
	100,000	EEM INTERGLACIAL	

Present climate

polar deserts covered the dry, northern latitudes of Siberia and Alaska on both shores of the Bering Strait. The European and North American climate was harsh, dry, and windy. World temperatures fell by as much as 60° F near the ice sheets, between 37 and 48° F in the tropics. Lower sea levels and cooler ocean temperatures resulted in lower rainfall and less atmospheric moisture transport.

The world's vegetation was very different during the Weichsel period. Treeless tundra vegetation extended south of the ice sheets, giving way to a wide belt of continental, cold steppe that extended from the Low Countries into China and from Siberia to the Mediterranean. The steppe was much narrower in North America, soon giving way to coniferous forest farther south. Huge zones of desert occupied more than half the earth's surface between latitudes 30° N and S, but some of today's desert areas like the American Southwest, the northern Sahara, and the southern African deserts were more hospitable, supporting scrub, grassland, and shallow lakes. The rain forests of tropical Africa and Asia gave way to open woodland and grassland; coral reefs and mangrove swamps contracted drastically as a result of cooler temperatures. However, despite the harsh world climate, humankind managed to survive and flourish in this very different world.

POSTGLACIAL TIMES

The world climate remained extremely cold for about 4000 to 8000 years after the Weichsel maximum. Then the ice sheets began to retreat, at times very rapidly — the Bering Strait, which was dry land as late as 15,000 years ago, was ocean again by 10,000. The onset of postglacial warming (sometimes called the Holocene) was determined by many factors and fluctuated widely in different areas, among them proximity to the ice sheets that surrounded the North Atlantic. But the decisive warming took place shortly before 9300 years ago. By that time sea levels were rising rapidly, especially in areas like Scandinavia, where the earth's crust was depressed by the massive weight of retreating ice sheets. The North Sea was flooded, and Britain was separated from the continent by approximately 6000 B.C. Pollen cores from Scandinavian and North American swamps have chronicled the dramatic changes in temperature vegetation that accompanied the warming trend, with steppe and tundra giving way in rapid succession to birch forests, then dense temperate oak woodland.

Perhaps the climatic changes in warmer latitudes were even more important for humanity. Some scientists believe that wild cereals and legumes migrated into the Near East about 11,000 years ago, as the present-day Mediterranean-type climate became reestablished at the end of the Weichsel glaciation. Periods of increased rainfall between 12,500 and 5000 years ago led to the expansion of equatorial forests far beyond their present limits, and to much wetter conditions in the Sahara and Arabia, which supported grassland and scrub, and, eventually, cattle herders. But by 5000 years ago, desiccation had set in, areas like the American Southwest and Sahara were much more inhospitable, and, perhaps, changing climatic conditions accelerated the extinction of Quaternary big game in North America and other areas.

Paleoclimatologists believe that our present interglacial reached its peak several thousand years ago, in North America some 7000 years ago, when deciduous forest reached its northern limits. It has been retreating since, as have the woodlands that once covered most of England, Scotland, and Wales. The world's climate appears to be getting colder again, as evidenced by the mountain glaciers and snowfields that have grown in many parts of the world. More important, tropical deserts have expanded in the past 5000 years. But, especially in tropical and humid areas, human activity has played a more important role in changing the world's climate and vegetation than have natural processes. We can only guess at what climatic regimens will confront our descendents.

This broad framework of Quaternary climate is only general backdrop for human prehistory. In most cases, however, the archaeologist is more concerned with local environmental conditions, with the specifics of the ecological adaptations made by our ancestors. In the pages that follow, we look at human populations strictly in their own improvements, using pollen analysis and other sophisticated scientific technologies to reconstruct not only human cultures but also the microenvironments in which they flourished.

GUIDE TO FURTHER READING

Bowen, David Q. *Quaternary Geology*. Oxford: Oxford University Press, 1978.
 An admirable general account of the study of the Quaternary in easily intelligible language.

Butzer, Karl. *Environment and Archaeology*. Chicago: Aldine, 1974.
 A highly technical account of the geological and environmental complexities of the Pleistocene.

Flint, R. F. *Glacial and Quaternary Geology*. New York: Wiley, 1971.
 The classic college textbook on the Ice Age. Although much outdated, it is still a primary source on basic glacial geology.

PART TWO

THE FIRST HUMANS
(c. 4 million to 40,000 B.C.)

"The art of fabricating arms, of preparing aliments, of
procuring the utensils requisite for this preparation, of preserving these aliments as provision against the seasons in
which it was impossible to procure a fresh supply of them —
these arts, confined to the most simple wants, were the first
fruits of a continued union, and the first features that
distinguished human society from the society observable in
many species of beasts."
— Marquis de Condorcet

We describe the origins of humankind, and the early evolution of human
culture from the first toolmakers up to the emergence of modern humanity.

Chronological Table A

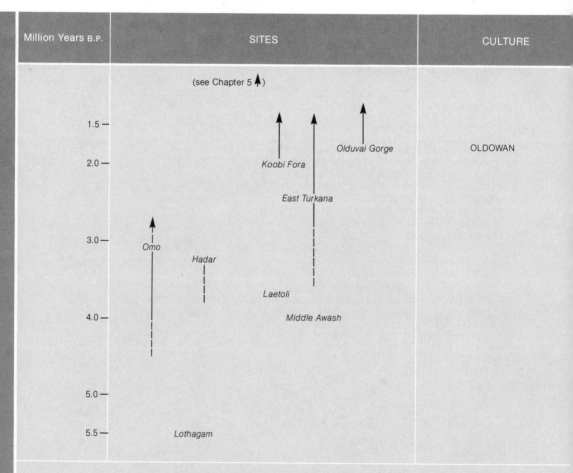

Million Years B.P.	SITES	CULTURE
	(see Chapter 5 ⬆)	
1.5 —	Olduvai Gorge	OLDOWAN
2.0 —	Koobi Fora	
	East Turkana	
3.0 —	Omo Hadar	
	Laetoli	
4.0 —	Middle Awash	
5.0 —		
5.5 —	Lothagam	

Note: In chronological tables in this book, cultures are indicated by all capital letters, sites by italic.

A chronological table appears at the beginning of most chapters, which covers the sites and cultures mentioned in the narrative. These sites and cultures, and their dates, are also listed in the margins opposite the place where they are mentioned. *Only sites and cultures listed in the margins are in the tables.*

In addition to being keyed to the text, the chronological tables are labeled A, B, C, and are cross-referenced at the beginning of the chapter. They form an interlocking sequence; the beginning and end of each chart are keyed to earlier and later chapters.

The following key is used throughout the tables:

———————	A continuous line means that the chronology is firmly established.
———————▶	A line terminating in an arrow means the time span continues beyond the arrow.
———————⊣	A line terminating with a horizontal bar means the limit of chronology is firmly established.
– – – – – – –	A broken line means the chronology is doubtful.
? *Omo*	A question mark beside a site name means its date is not firmly established.
Omo	A name in italics is an archaeological site, normally named after the locality at which it occurs.
ACHEULIAN	A name in capital letters is an archaeological culture, usually named after a type site which in turn is labeled after a geographical location. For instance, the Acheulian culture is named after the French town of St. Acheul, near which many Acheulian sites are found.

Chapter Four

Human Origins: The Emergence of "Handy Person"
(4 million to 1.5 million B.C.)

PREVIEW

✿ The hominids appear to have separated from the nonhuman primates some 5 million years ago.

✿ Upright walking hominids were living in East Africa at least 3.5, maybe 4, million years ago.

✿ At least three hominid forms were living in East Africa 2 million years ago.

✿ Critical developments in the emergence of humanity were a change to an erect bipedal posture, enlargement of brain size, and toolmaking. Major behavioral changes and the development of some form of a more sophisticated communication system were part of the process of constant interaction and feedback between different evolutionary forces.

✿ The earliest stone tools are currently dated to approximately 2 million years ago. They were made of simple flaking techniques that lasted unchanged for at least a million years. This tool tradition is called the Oldowan, after the much-studied Oldowan culture that used it.

✿ The earliest humans used home bases that were less transitory than those of apes. Their living sites, scatters of artifacts, animal bones, and other debris have been excavated at Koobi Fora and Olduvai Gorge in East Africa. Our earliest ancestors seem to have been foragers, who lived on the vegetable foods, fish, and rodents that they collected. They were opportunists who scavenged meat from the carcasses of carnivore kills, perhaps doing some hunting on their own account. Their social organization may have more closely resembled that of chimpanzees and baboons than modern hunter-gatherers.

Chronological Table A

Primates

Nineteenth-century scientists pointed out that our closest living relatives were apes such as the chimpanzee and the gorilla. All of us are members of the order of primates, which are placental mammals, most of them tree-living, with two suborders: anthropods (apes, humans, and monkeys) and prosimians (lemurs, tarsiers, and other "pre-monkeys") (Huxley, 1863). The research of more than a century has shown that the many similarities in behavior and physical characteristics between the hominids (primates of the family *Hominidae,* which includes modern humans, earlier human subspecies, and their direct ancestors) and these closest living primate relatives can be explained by identical characteristics that each group inherited millions of years ago from a common ancestor. (For an overview of human development covered in Part Two, see Table 4.1.)

Hominids

THEORIES ON THE ORIGINS OF THE HUMAN LINE

The great Victorian zoologist Thomas Huxley spelled out his own opinion about the divergences between humans and apes in his classic *Man's Place in Nature* (1863): "The structural differences which separate man from the gorilla and chimpanzee are not so great as those which separate the gorilla from the lower apes." Huxley realized, though, that the gap

Table 4.1 Human development: 10 million to 8000 B.C.

Date (B.C.)	Technology[a]	Economy[a]	Brain changes[a]	Body changes[a]
8,000–	Bows and arrows	Food production		
18,000–				
29,000–	Art in Europe			
38,000–	Mounted tools		Fully developed brain and speech	Modern humanity
200,000–				First *Homo sapiens* forms
250,000–	Fire in use		Premodern speech	
500,000–			Rapid brain expansion	
2,000,000–	Stone toolmaking	Hunting and gathering	Reorganization of brain and slow expansion	Bipedalism is perfected— change in forelimbs
				Bipedalism begins (?)
10,000,000–				

3.5 → 4 my

[a] The developments on this table appeared at the period indicated by their placement. They are assumed to continue until being either replaced or refined.

that separates humans from the higher apes is a gap between parallel lines, not a gap between locations along a single line. The gap measures divergent evolution from a common ancestor.

The question is, When did humankind separate from the nonhuman primates? Experts disagree violently when asked this question.

Aegyptopithecus, Dryopithecus, and Ramapithecus

Some 30 to 35 million years ago, large bands of small, fruit-eating primates known to paleontologists as *Aegyptopithecus* trooped through the lush, wet forests of the Nile Valley. These small creatures were no larger than a fox and weighed no more than 9 to 10 pounds. Elwyn Simons (1984) has found their jaws and skulls near the Fayum Depression west of the Nile. The bones bear some resemblance to later primates in East Africa dating to the Miocene epoch, which lasted from 23.5 to 5.2 million years ago. It was in Africa that apes and humans diverged from the monkeys, but no one knows when this divergence took place. Was *Aegyptopithecus* the basic primate stock from which the great apes and humans radiated, or did the separation take place during the Miocene?

Seventeen million years ago the world looked very different from today. Continental drift linked Africa and Arabia with Europe and Asia. Hitherto they had been separated by sea. New mountain ranges like the Alps formed, and the climate became cooler as atmospheric and ocean circulation patterns changed. As a result, previously separated animal species came into contact via the new land bridges that led them into new habitats.

Several species of apes, some of which are now extinct, were already flourishing in Africa at the beginning of the Miocene, including a tree-dwelling, baboon-sized fruit eater known to paleontologists as *Proconsul africanus*. This was an unspecialized primate, which many believe was ancestral to a wide range of later apes and, ultimately, humans.

Once the continents were joined, the African hominids spread into the rest of the Old World and many new species evolved. They are known from teeth and jaw finds in Africa, Turkey, Europe, and Asia. David Pilbeam (1984a) has identified two broad groups of Middle and Late Miocene primates:

> The dryopithecines, a family of hominids whose distribution seems to coincide with the range of the great tropical forest belt that ringed the earth at the beginning of the Miocene. They seem to have resembled monkeys more closely than modern apes, but also seem to foreshadow the orang-utan, chimpanzee, and other modern apes. Unfortunately, no one has ever found the intermediate fossils between *Dryopithecus* and the modern ape. The ape fossil record is completely blank from approximately 8 million years ago to modern times.
>
> The ramapithecines who are named after a fossil primate called *Ra-*

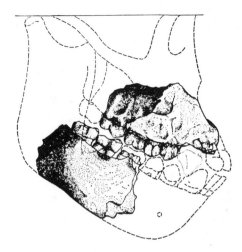

Figure 4.1 Composite reconstruction of the face of *Ramapithecus* from the Siwalik Hills, India, partly based on teeth from Kenya; it is highly tentative.

mapithecus (*Rama,* a Hindu god; *pithecus* from the Greek for apes) (see Figure 4.1). The first jaw was found in India in 1932; additional jaws and teeth have subsequently come not only from India but also from Pakistan and elsewhere in the Old World from Africa to China. Ramapithecine fossils dated to between 18 and 11 million years ago, remains that came from a very small primate, no larger than a medium-sized dog and weighing about 30 pounds. Originally Pilbeam argued that *Ramapithecus* was the possible ancestor of the earliest known hominids like *Australopithecus* from East Africa. He even hypothesized that the ramapithecines walked upright, on two feet. But ten years of field work in the Siwalik Hills of Pakistan has yielded many more fossils, and convinced Pilbeam that *Ramapithecus* was purely an ape, a primate whose only living representative is the orang-utan. (Pilbeam, 1984b).

While most paleontologists agree that apes and humans separated from monkeys at least 20 million years ago, many originally believed that apes and humans diverged *before Ramapithecus* appeared, that is to say, in the Early Miocene, or even earlier. But with *Ramapithecus* out of the way, a much shorter chronology becomes likely, a chronology that fits well with the findings of the molecular biologists (Figure 4.2).

Unfortunately, a vast chronological gap lies between *Ramapithecus* and the earliest hominidae, the australopithecines, which date to approximately 4 million years. Don Johanson and Maitland Edey (1981) refer to this gap rather picturesquely as a "black hole" in our knowledge of early human evolution. In a sense they are right, because no fossils have yet been found to fill the gap between the last of the Miocene primates and the magnificent fossil finds of the Late Pliocene and Early Pleistocene. We have to rely on molecular biology to track the elusive moment of divergence between apes and humans.

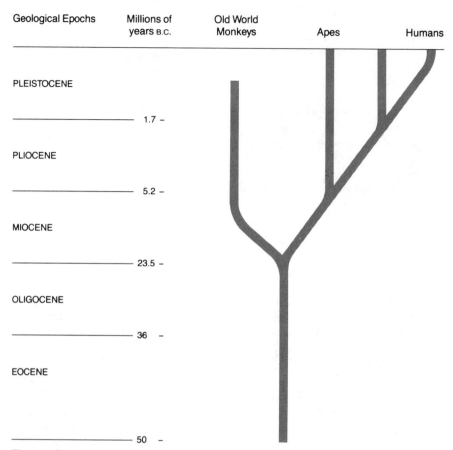

Geological Epochs	Millions of years B.C.	Old World Monkeys	Apes	Humans

PLEISTOCENE

———————— 1.7 –

PLIOCENE

———————— 5.2 –

MIOCENE

———————— 23.5 –

OLIGOCENE

———————— 36 –

EOCENE

———————— 50 –

Figure 4.2 A much simplified version of how Old World monkeys, apes, and humans evolved. For later human evolution, see Figure 4.10.

Molecular Biology and Human Evolution

Some years ago, two biochemists, Vincent Sarich and Alan Wilson, developed a means of dating primate evolution. They believe that the albumin protein substances found in primate blood has evolved at a constant rate (Sarich, 1971). Thus the difference between the albumins of any pair of primates can be used to calculate the time that has elapsed since they separated.

Sarich and Wilson have shown that the albumins of apes and humans are more similar than those of monkeys and humans. Thus, they argue, apes and humans have a more recent common ancestry. They estimate that apes and Old World monkeys diverged approximately 23 million years ago, the gibbon and humankind only 8 million years or so ago, and that the chimpanzee, gorilla, and humans last shared a common ancestor 4 to 5 million years ago. The apparent separation of apes and humans is so recent that statistically reliable numbers of differences have not yet accumulated.

Sarich's work has been criticized because it deals with only one protein. Another biochemist, Morris Goodman, investigated similarities between different primates using antibodies and antigens and comparative analysis plates. He argues that evolution is slowing down in the higher primates, and is far less specific about the date when apes and humans diverged.

A 9-million-year gap separates the most recent ramapithecines from the first hominids of 5 million years ago. Fossil-bearing beds dating from this period are extremely rare and are little studied. More's the pity, for this was a period of considerable environmental change. As recently as 5.5 million years ago, the Mediterranean basin dried up when it became separated from the Atlantic. This must have had major effects on the climate and ecology of Africa, as well as influencing the evolution of many species. That such evolution took place seems certain. During this critical period the African savannah, with its lands of residual forests and extensive grassland plains, was densely populated by many mammal species as well as specialized tree dwellers and other primates. Both the chimpanzee and the gorilla evolved in the forests, surviving from earlier times. On savannah plains other primates were flourishing in small bands, probably walking upright, and, conceivably, making tools. No fossil remains of these creatures have been found, so that we do not know when primates first achieved the bipedal (two-footed) posture that is the outstanding human physical feature. Only future fossil discoveries will resolve the question.

THE EVOLUTION OF HUMAN BEHAVIOR

More nonsense has been put forth about the evolution of human behavior than about almost any other aspect of human history. But times have changed. Paleoanthropology has now become a highly sophisticated, multidisciplinary science. It is no longer a simple alliance between fossil hunters and geologists. It is a systematic inquiry not into unanswerable questions like "What are the links between two-footed posture and tool-making?" but into specific, testable ones. For instance, "What are the energy requirements of bipedalism?" Three researchers have studied the foraging habits of orang-utans, who eat mainly tree fruit, and chimpanzees, who feed off the same food but from more dispersed sources. Does an ape, faced with more diverse food resources, forage more efficiently by walking on four limbs or two? The researchers found that bipedalism is not very efficient compared with a four-limb gait at high speed but compares very favorably at slow speeds on a forest fringe, which is the sort of environment where the first hominids evolved. It may, therefore, have arisen as an energetic strategy for foraging for widespread food sources. Studies of tooth wear, of limb proportions in monkeys, of skeletal anatomy, all have their place in the study of the evolution of human behavior. All are used not to generate idle speculations but answers to testable questions. The discussion of behavioral evolution that follows is based on many such studies (Tanner, 1981).

Adaptations in Posture

The American anthropologist Sherwood L. Washburn has long argued that the close relationship between humans and the African apes makes it likely that our ancestors walked on four feet, with both hands and feet adapted to grasping (Washburn and Moore, 1980). This quadrupedal posture remained in use for a long time. Washburn goes on to suggest that the early apes (a group that included our ancestors) evolved an arboreal (tree-living) adaptation, climbing in trees to feed on fruit as well as on ground-growing foods. Adaptations in their anatomy followed, modifying chests, shoulders, elbows, and wrists to allow swinging from branch to branch, climbing, hanging, and reaching for food, as well as other new behaviors. Unfortunately, we lack the fossil bones that would tell us when these changes took place.

An upright posture and two-footed gait are the most characteristic human physical features, probably gained from modified behavior patterns among the early apes. An upright posture is vital, for it frees the hands for other purposes. We can picture the modified behaviors from analogous actions by the modern African ape. The chimpanzees, ably studied by Jane Goodall, use objects for play and display, carry them in their hands, and use sticks to fish for termites (Figure 4.3) (Goodall, 1973). They take leaves for cleaning the body and sipping water and actually improve their sticks slightly with their teeth, if need be, when searching for termites. Monkeys do none of these things. Chimpanzees have, in fact, inherited behavior patterns far closer to our own than to those of any monkey.

The Washburn theory argues that the chimpanzee and the gorilla get around by knuckle-walking, a specialized way of moving in which the backs of the fingers are placed on the ground and act as main weight-bearing surfaces (Figure 4.4). Jane Goodall finds that chimpanzees knuckle-walk for long distances. But this posture is not commonly used by humans; it is seen only with football linemen or runners at the starting position (Goodall, 1973). With longer arms, like those that ancestral hominids might have had, that posture would have been easier to assume. Knuckle-walking may be an intermediate stage between the ape's arboreal adaptation and the human bipedal posture (Washburn, 1967).

Bipedal posture

Chimpanzees — as knuckle-walking, object-using apes — have been seen to prey on other primates and small antelopes. The change from knuckle-walking to bipedalism *may* have resulted from more frequent object use and more hunting and scavenging; both these behaviors could have led to greater use of bipedalism and of the anatomy making it possible (Napier, 1980; Tuttle, 1969, 1972). The success of the whole behavior pattern led to the evolution of primates with the human attribute of

Figure 4.3 Chimpanzee using a stick as a tool to fish for insects.

upright posture, as well as the characteristic hunting and gathering and toolmaking patterns that went with it.

The Lovejoy Hypothesis

The evolutionary changes that have separated humans from their nearest living relatives, the African apes, have centered around three complex systems (Isaac, Glynn Ll., 1981):

The Locomotor System The development of upright bipedal posture and potentially greater dexterity

The Brain-Culture System The evolution of language, technology, and the intricate social and cultural dealings that involve such phenomena as interdependence and reciprocal expectations and obligations

The Socioreproductive System The suppression of estrus, the concealment of ovulation, and the development of tendencies to form long-term pair bonds, so that males become involved in supporting their mates and their offspring.

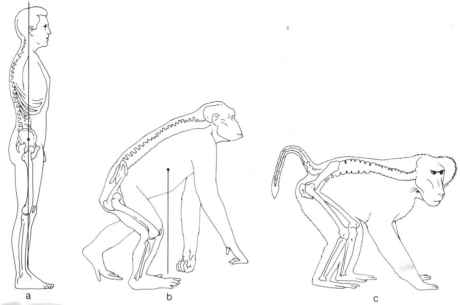

Figure 4.4 Bipedalism and quadrupedalism. (a) Human bipedal posture. The center of gravity of the body lies just behind the midpoint of the hip joint and in front of the knee joint, so that both hip and knee are extended when standing, conserving energy. (b) A knuckle-walking chimpanzee. The body's center of gravity lies in the middle of the area bounded by legs and arms. When the ape walks bipedally, its center of gravity moves from side to side and up and down. The human center of gravity is displaced much less, making walking much more efficient. (After Zihlman, 1967) (c) A baboon. Baboons are quadrupedal and adapted to living on the ground.

For decades, archaeologists and paleontologists have concentrated on the evolution of the first two systems, simply because the fossil evidence is available, although it is fragmentary. Now, anatomist Owen Lovejoy (1981, 1984) has focused attention on the socioreproductive system (see also Lancaster and Whitten, 1980). He believes that the hominids learned to walk on two feet in the forests, not out on the savannah where they lived later. He thinks the reasons they assumed an upright posture were partly sexual and partly social. Hominids contrast dramatically with apes in many behavioral respects. They not only walk upright, but they also enjoy continuous sexuality, while apes are sexually active only during estrus. They care for several infants at one time, while apes wean only one sibling before breeding another. Hominid females are less mobile than apes, who move around constantly to acquire food. Hominids form pair bonds, mate with each other for long periods of time, and develop nuclear families. They share food, tend to create home bases, and their brains continue to enlarge. Eventually, they use tools much more extensively and make them on an everyday basis, but didn't until long after bipedal posture was the hominid means of locomotion. The hominid society was one in which pair bonding produced more incentives toward social harmony, a society in which the females could afford to be less mobile, and in which the bipedal posture was important because it freed the hands for carrying food, infants, and for performing other activities, with a higher survival value than simply running away from danger. Over a period of millions of years, argues Lovejoy, the bipedal hominids developed a new way of living, not through any dramatic discoveries, but simply because thousands of small adaptive shifts in their behavior reinforced one another in cumulative ways. By the time humans moved out on the savannah, they had been walking upright for hundreds of thousands, even millions, of years. They moved out into open country not because they started to walk upright but because the forests were shrinking at a period of increasing aridity and also because there were many more hominids. By this time, the food- and object-carrying hominids could move safely into open country, taking their young with them in their arms.

The Lovejoy hypothesis suffers from the major objection that it ignores archaeological evidence (Isaac, 1981). Archaeological data collected at Koobi Fora, Olduvai Gorge, and other sites (described on pp. 102–105; see Figure 4.5) shows that tools, meat, and food transport were very important factors in hominid life at an early stage, factors that Lovejoy tends to ignore when he discounts the role of toolmaking until approximately 2 million years ago.

In practice, there are a number of experts from divergent academic disciplines hypothesizing about a complex, basic problem, one that can be solved only by close collaboration between anatomists, archaeologists, paleontologists, and, above all, ecologists, who can tell us much about the distribution of food classes in different tropical environments today and about the way in which the earliest hominids may have adapted to forest and savannah.

Certainly, the relative abundance of hominid fossils in East African savannah environments after 3 million years ago strongly suggests that they had moved far from the forests by the Lower Pleistocene. At first, the bipedal hominids used tools just about as much as the nonhuman primates do today, but they had one advantage — a much greater ability to hold, carry, and throw things. There was a period between approximately 4 million and 1.5 million years ago when toolmaking changed from being unimportant to being a critical factor in human development, the moment when culture became an overriding adaptive mechanism in human life. Bipedalism itself is known from the Hadar area of Ethiopia in contexts almost 4 million years old (p. 93).

Cooperation, Hunting, Scavenging, and Gathering

Animal behavior specialist George Schaller says it might be more productive to compare hominids with carnivores such as lions or wild dogs living on the African savannah than with primates (Schaller, 1971, 1972). Lions, hyenas, and wild dogs hunt in groups and share their food, engag-

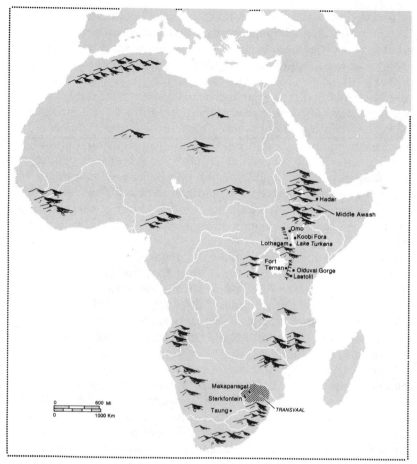

Figure 4.5 Archaeological sites in Africa mentioned in this chapter.

ing in a form of cooperative hunting that has several advantages. Animals that cooperate are more successful at killing, can prey on large animals, and, by eating most of the kill at one time, waste less food. A solitary hunter is obliged either to protect the food he does not consume immediately after the kill or to hunt again when he is hungry. Group hunting allows some members of the pride or pack to guard the young while others hunt and bring back food. When they return, they regurgitate some of their kill for the rest of the group.

Social life of nonhuman primates is structured by hierarchies of dominance, a pattern that has been radically altered among humans, who, when they began systematic hunting, had to cooperate far more closely than their nonhuman, predominantly vegetarian relatives did.

This account of human cooperative behavior is challenged by several anthropologists. Some argue that hypotheses on the origins of culture wrongly make males the architects of all evolutionary change. Theories on the origins of human behavior advanced by Washburn and others have also been attacked because they do not adequately explain the trend toward smaller hominid teeth, which one would not expect if the major element of early humans' diets were, in fact, large animals. Clifford Jolly, in particular, talks of a lengthy period when "basal" hominids — immediate ancestors to humans — were predominantly, if not exclusively, seed eaters (Jolly, 1970). Through much of the Lower Pleistocene, he says, the earliest hominids subsisted on grass seeds and other vegetable foods that must be gathered by agile hands and accurately coordinated eyes and hands. These are, states Jolly, an essential preadaptation for even a medium-sized animal to be able to gather enough seeds to support itself. With these preadaptations, the early hominids would have faced little competition in the exploitation of a concentrated, high-energy food. Jolly believes there were no major advances needed for such hominids in social organization, intelligence, culture, or communication over those attributable to some living nonhuman primates. It was not until much later that evolving hominids became more involved in hunting, when projectiles and fire began to be important in human culture.

Gathering

Hunting

Were the first humans hunters at all? Some microscopic archaeological evidence from very early archaeological sites at Olduvai Gorge in East Africa suggests that scavenging, that is to say the culling of meat from predator kills, may have been much more important. Pat Shipman (1984) and others have examined dozens of broken animal bones from these two localities, peering at minute but distinctive cut marks resulting from such activities as butchery, disarticulation of carcasses, and skin removal. They made high-fidelity replicas of bone marks, then examined them under a scanning electron microscope, comparing the results with those obtained from a 2300-year-old agricultural settlement in Kenya, where the inhabitants were actively engaged in disarticulation, butchery, and other activities. They found that 90 percent of the 2300-year-old bones showed cut marks resulting from the disjointing of carcasses, but only 45 percent of those from Olduvai showed the same phenomenon. This was likewise true with butchery marks, those made when removing meat from bones. In contrast, about 75 percent of both the Olduvai and 2300-year-old bones showed the characteristic marks left by skin and tendon removal, which were especially visible on the lower limb bones since they had little meat on them.

Scavenging

Both disarticulation and butchery were surprisingly uncommon at Olduvai, so it seems doubtful the hominids were butchering and disjointing large animals and carrying them back to base. They seem to have obtained meat without cutting up too many carcasses. It is possible that they got it by scavenging it from predator kills. A tantalizing clue came from thirteen Olduvai bones, where both carnivore and humanly made markings were present. In eight instances, the human bones *overlay* carnivore marks, as if the humans had scavenged the bones from carcasses that had already been killed by lions or other predators.

If the first humans obtained their meat supplies from scavenging, they were acquiring it in a cheap but high-risk way, since predator kills were much rarer than living herds. They needed an efficient way to locate them, for even a tree-climbing, bipedal hominid could not rival a vulture with its overhead view of the landscape. Once a kill was located, they would have to chase off the killers, a formidable task with lions or leopards. Perhaps, like jackals, a band of hominids would charge in, throwing stones and grunting loudly, seize what they could, and leave the kill to its owners. Meat-covered bones were certainly available, since the saber-toothed tigers that abounded on the savanna had admirable teeth for slashing but were poor bone crushers.

Scavenging is successful only when combined with other sources of food. The first humans may have hunted some smaller mammals on their own account, running down antelope and driving them into swamps. But undoubtedly a great deal of their diet came from wild vegetable foods, especially fruit, which abounded for much of the year in the open savannah.

Jolly model of human behavior

The Jolly model of human behavior has significant implications for male and female roles in human evolution. Kay Martin and Barbara Voorhies, writing on the position of women at the species level, follow anthropologist Ralph Linton in replacing the familiar model (a community organization based on a single male) with a social arrangement putting adult females at the head of their own matricentric units (Voorhies and Martin, 1975). These individuals are mainly involved with "reproduction, infant care, and socialization, and the gathering of sufficient seeds or vegetable products for themselves and their dependent young." The adult males have no special attachments to the units of mother and child, adhering merely to the unit of their birth. In other words, all adults foraged for themselves in a community structure that may have survived almost unchanged for thousands of years.

What happened, though, when hunting became more important? Jolly argues that the increased importance of hunting led to the beginnings of food sharing, specialized tools, and new ideas on economic cooperation — and from these to kinship systems. Martin and Voorhies disagree and feel that these developments were foreshadowed in the matricentric family. Food sharing was part of the bond between mother and child. When males started hunting, they logically shared the meat with those who shared other food with them. Sexual division of labor may have begun in the extended, matricentric family rather than with the rise of hunting. Marriage and kinship ties may have developed because of strengthened cooperation by exchange of mating partners and the ultimate development of kinship and marriage.

The Development of Language

We humans are unique in having a spoken, symbolic language that enables us to communicate our most intimate feelings to one another. No other animals have anything remotely approaching human speech. Even our closest living relatives, the chimpanzees, communicate with no more than gestures and many more voice sounds in the wild, while other apes use sounds only to communicate territorial information. However, chimpanzees seem to have a natural talent for learning symbolic language under controlled conditions. A famous chimpanzee named Washoe was trained to communicate with humans, using no less than 175 sign language gestures similar to those of the American Sign Language (Gardner and Gardner, 1969). After more than a year Washoe could associate particular signs with specific activities, such as eating and drinking. Another chimpanzee named Sarah was taught to read and write with plastic symbols and acquired a vocabulary of 130 different words, to the extent that she obeyed sequences of written instructions given with the symbols (Premack and Premack, 1972). The research continues, but there is no evidence that chimpanzees can combine visual symbols to create new meanings or use syntax. Sequences of signs produced by trained chimpanzees may have a superficial resemblance to the first multiword sentences produced by children, but beyond the stage of learning isolated symbols, an ape's language learning is severely restricted (Terrace et al., 1979).

Washoe the chimp

Clearly, articulate speech was an important threshold in human evolution, because it opened up whole new vistas of cooperative behavior and unlimited potential for the enrichment of human life. When did hominids abandon grunts for speech? There are only two potential lines of research, one using *endocasts*, natural casts of the interior of the brain case. Dean Falk (1984) has studied the convolutions of early hominid endocasts and found that those of the early australopithecines are apelike. But the brain cell of Skull 1470 (see p. 97) is about 300 cc larger, and the frontal lobe of its endocast is more humanlike, especially in the Broca's area, the left hemisphere of the brain where speech control is located.

Endocasts

The endocast research is much more generalized than the detailed anatomical studies of the position of the voice box, the larynx, using both comparative anatomy and actual fossils to study differences between apes and humans. Laitman (1984) poses the two fundamental questions:

What was the anatomy of our ancestors' vocal cords?
How does it compare to that of modern humans?

The second line of research has been done by Laitman and others who studied the *position* of the larynx in a wide variety of mammals including humans. They found that all mammals except adult humans have a larynx that is high in the neck, a position that enables the larynx to lock into the air space at the back of the nasal cavity. Although this allows animals like monkeys and cats to breathe and swallow at the same time, it limits the sounds they can produce. The pharynx — the air cavity part of the food pathway — can produce sounds, but animals use their mouths to modify sounds, since they are anatomically incapable of producing the range of sounds needed for articulate speech.

Until they are about eighteen months to two years old, human children's larynxes are situated high in the neck, more like those of other mammals. Then, at about two years of age, the larynx begins to descend into the neck, ending up between the fourth and seventh neck vertebrae. How and why is still a mystery, but the change completely alters the way in which the infant breathes, speaks, and swallows. Adult humans cannot separate breathing and swallowing, so people can suffocate when food lodges in an airway. However, an enlarged pharyngeal chamber above the vocal cords enables them to modify the sounds they emit in an infinite variety of ways, which is the key to human speech.

Can one tell the position of the larynx from fossil skeletons? Fortunately, the shape of the base of the skull is highly informative. Most mammals have flat-based skulls and high larynxes, but humans have an arched skull base associated with their low larynx. Using sophisticated statistical analyses, Laitman and his colleagues ran tests on as many complete fossil skulls as possible. They found that the australopithecines of one to 4 million years ago had flat skull bases and high larynxes, while those of *Homo erectus*, dating to about 1.5 million years and later, show somewhat more curvature, suggesting that the larynx was beginning to descend to its modern position. It is only about 300,000 years ago that the skull base finally assumed a modern curvature, which would allow for fully articulate speech to evolve.

So it seems that language was a relatively late development but one of vital importance. The real value of language, apart from the stimulation it gives brain development, is that we can convey subtle feelings and nuances far beyond the power of grunts or gestures to communicate. We may assume that the first humans had more to communicate with than nonhuman primates, but it appears that articulate speech was a more recent stimulus to biological and cultural evolution.

THE FOSSIL EVIDENCE FOR HUMAN EVOLUTION

For working purposes, we can correlate the emergence of the first human beings with the appearance in the archaeological record of:

- People with erect posture and enlarged brain size
- Living sites that represent more lasting bases than the sleeping places of apes
- Systematically manufactured artifacts
- Evidence for a cultural system which acts as an adaptive device

With these attributes in mind, we will now examine the archaeological and fossil evidence for human evolution. This evidence is fragmentary at best and a veritable battleground between paleoanthropological titans. The controversies are aired within the arid pages of scientific journals, in popular magazines, even on television talk shows. We can but navigate cautiously between the various schools of thought.

Australopithecus

The best-known fossil candidate as a direct ancestor for humankind is *Australopithecus africanus* (Latin for southern ape of Africa), a primate first identified in 1924 by Raymond Dart, an anatomist at the University of Witwatersrand, South Africa (Dart, 1925; Pfeiffer, 1978; Rak, 1983) (Figure 4.6). Subsequently, a more robust form also was discovered and named *Australopithecus robustus* to distinguish it from the lighter, gracile *A. africanus* form (Figure 4.7; and see also Table 4.3, p. 101) (Rak, 1983; Tobias, 1967).

Although dozens of australopithecine fragments have been recovered in Southern Africa, the sites are all undated by potassium argon because there are no lava flows nearby. Only the animal bones from the site provide a rough framework for dating most South African australopithecines to between 3 million and 800,000 years ago; the robust forms may be somewhat later.

Figure 4.6 *Australopithecus africanus* from Sterkfontein, South Africa. *A. africanus* was probably 107 to 127 cm (42 to 50 in) tall; the females, weighing 18 to 27 kg (40 to 60 lb), were somewhat lighter than the males. The posture was fully upright, with the spinal curvature that places the trunk over the pelvis for balanced walking. (Apes do not have this curvature, nor are their legs proportionately as long as those of *Australopithecus*.) The foot was small, with a well-developed big toe. *Australopithecus* looked remarkably human, but with an apelike snout that was, however, less prominent than the ape's. The canines were small, and the incisors were vertical in the jaw, whereas the ape's slope outward. A flat nose was combined with a well-developed forehead, and the brow ridges were much less prominent than those of his modern tree-living relatives. The brain had an average size of about 450 cc, much smaller than that of a modern human male (1450 cc) and slightly larger than that of the chimpanzee (400 cc).

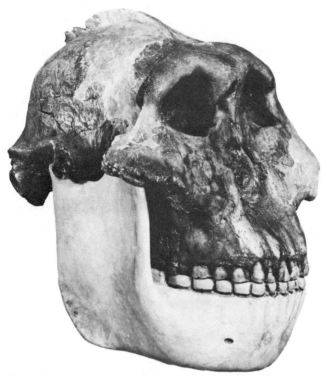

Figure 4.7 A robust australopithecine from Olduvai Gorge, Tanzania. The robust australopithecine was both larger and heavier than the *africanus* forms, with a more barrel-like trunk. The biggest contrasts were in the facial appearance and in the teeth. *Australopithecus robustus* had a low forehead and a prominent bony ridge on the crest of the skull, which supported massive chewing muscles. Its brain was slightly larger than the *A. africanus* form, and *A. robustus* had relatively well-developed cheek teeth as well as larger molars.

For decades, paleontologists believed that *Australopithecus africanus* was descended from *Ramapithecus* and that it was the direct ancestor of humankind. However, recent discoveries from Ethiopia, Kenya, and Tanzania have shown that the evolution of humanity was much more complicated.

Early Hominids in East Africa

We now describe the major sites and fossil discoveries that document the origins of humankind in East Africa. The chronological relationship of these sites are described in Chronological Table A.

Middle Awash, Afar, Ethiopia A University of California, Berkeley, research team has discovered a fragment from the upper femur (thigh bone) of a hominid who walked upright, as well as some cranial pieces from the top right side of the skull of a similar creature. The deposits containing the bones are potassium-argon dated to between 3.9 and 4.1 million years ago. The Middle Awash skull fragments reveal a hominid with practically no forehead, and brow ridges intermediate between those of apes and humans. Paleontologist Timothy White has identified the remains of *Australopithecus afarensis,* the name given to early hominid remains from Hadar to the north, described below. Future researchers are likely to yield many more fossil finds in this remote and inhospitable but archaeologically incredibly rich area.

Hadar (Johanson and Edey, 1981; Johanson and White, 1979; Kalb et al., 1984). When Maurice Taieb and Don Johanson discovered a remarkably complete skeleton of a small primate at Hadar on the Awash river in northern Ethiopia, they named it Lucy (Figure 4.8). Lucy was only 3.5 to 4 feet tall and nineteen to twenty-one years old. Nearby, they found the remains of at least thirteen individuals, males, females, and children. Potassium argon dates for Hadar range between 3.0 and 3.75 million years ago. The Hadar hominid fossils all are from a single species of hominid, despite great variations in size. Some individuals stood 5 feet tall and probably weighed approximately 150 pounds, a far cry from the small, slender Lucy. These small creatures, however, were powerful, heavily muscled individuals, thought to be as strong as chimpanzees. All were fully bipedal, with arms slightly longer for their size than the arms of humans. They had humanlike hands, except that their fingers were slightly more curved. The Hadar hominids had brains approximating the size of chimpanzee brains, ape-shaped heads, and forward-thrusting jaws. There is no evidence that they made tools. The question of questions was, and still is: What were the Hadar hominids? Were they the direct ancestors of humanity, the descendants of *Ramapithecus,* or the predecessors of *Australopithecus?* Intense controversy surrounds this issue. Johanson and White (1979) believe the Hadar hominids are a species of primitive australopithecine, which they have labeled *Australopithecus afarensis.*

> Hadar
> **3.0 to 3.75 million years ago**

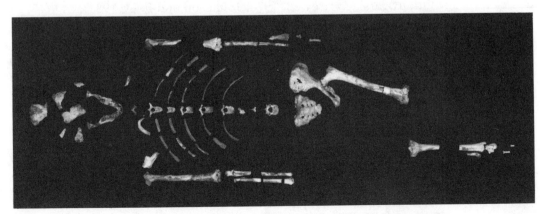

Figure 4.8 "Lucy," a fragmentary Australopithecine from the Hadar, Ethiopia.

Laetoli Broadly contemporary with Hadar are the fossil-bearing beds at Laetoli in northern Tanzania, excavated by Mary Leakey and potassium argon dated to 3.59 to 3.75 million years ago. They have yielded not only the bones of extinct animals but also the incomplete jaws and teeth of at least thirteen hominids (M. D. Leakey, 1976, 1978). The Laetoli hominids share many similarities with those from Hadar, so much so that Johanson believes they are the same species. But the most remarkable finds came from the buried bed of a seasonal river where thin layers of fine volcanic ash once formed a pathway for animals traveling to water holes. The hardened surface of the ash, dated to more than 3.59 million years ago, bore the footprints of elephants, rhinoceroses, giraffes, a saber-toothed tiger, and many species of antelope. Mary Leakey also identified a trail of prints of a fairly large bipedal primate, which, she estimated, stood nearly 4 feet tall (Figure 4.9). "The tracks," she wrote, "indicate a rolling and probably slow-moving gait, with the hips swiveling at each step, as opposed to the free-striding gait of modern man." Unfortunately, no traces of the bones of this primate have come from the excavations so far.

These important finds make it certain that by at least 3.75 million years ago, or perhaps even earlier, some primates were walking upright on two feet. However, their brain size was still little more than 400 cc.

Hadar and Laetoli apart, dozens of australopithecines have come from East Africa in recent years (Figure 4.10).

Lothagam The earliest australopithecine fossil yet discovered is a solitary jaw found on the western shores of Lake Turkana, which has been potassium argon dated to 5.5 million years.

Omo In the late 1960s an American-French-Kenyan expedition found the teeth and lower jawbones of both gracile and robust australopithecines as well as possible traces of a more advanced hominid in late Pliocene and Lower Pleistocene fossil-bearing beds in the Omo Valley near the Kenya-Ethiopia border. These finds were dated to between 3.7 and 1.8 million years ago (Howell, 1974; Johanson and Edey, 1981).

East Turkana Lake Turkana lies in remote and hot northern Kenya, which today supports little more than desert scrub. In recent years, Richard Leakey and Glynn Isaac have been working on the eastern side of the lake, searching for early hominids (Isaac and McCown, 1976; R. Leakey and Lewin, 1977). They have located a thousand square miles of Pliocene and Lower Pleistocene fossil-bearing sediments. The hominids include both australopithecines and specimens of individuals with unmistakably enlarged brains, including the famous Skull 1470 (Figure 4.11), which has a brain capacity of 775 cc, far larger than that of *Australopithecus*. This specimen, with jutting face like an *Australopithecus* but the brain size of a human, is thought to date to approximately 1.8 million years ago. The East Turkana finds include another skull, almost complete, of a hom-

Laetoli
3.6 million years ago

Lothagam
5.5 million B.C.

Omo
3.7 million B.C.

East Turkana
3 to 1.5 million B.C.

Figure 4.9 Pliocene hominid footprints from Laetoli, Tanzania.

inid that is clearly from the genus *Homo,* dated to approximately 1.5 million years ago, and contemporary with australopithecines.

Olduvai Gorge Olduvai Gorge is one of the world's most famous archaeological sites and is closely associated with Louis and Mary Leakey (L. S. B. Leakey, 1951; M. D. Leakey, 1971). The gorge is a spectacular rift in the great Serengeti Plains of northern Tanzania. Earth movements have exposed hundreds of meters of lake beds belonging to a long dried-up Pleistocene lake. In 1959 Mary Leakey found the almost complete skull of a robust australopithecine, *Australopithecus boisei* (see Figure 4.7), on a living floor in Bed I, the lowest of the four lake bed series in the gorge

Olduvai Gorge
**2 million to 500,000
B.C.**

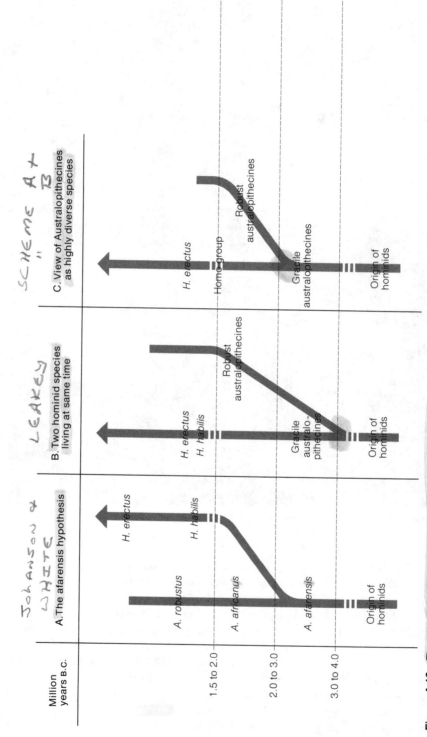

Figure 4.10 Three tentative hypotheses of early hominid evolution.

THE FIRST HUMANS

Figure 4.11 A tentative reconstruction of Skull 1470 from East Turkana. Provisionally identified as *Homo*, this cranium is remarkable for its large brain capacity and rounded back part of the skull.

(Figure 4.12). Later, a more gracile hominid came from a level slightly lower than that of the original robust skull. Fortunately, fragments of lava were in the Olduvai floors, usable for potassium argon dating. The living floor upon which the Leakeys' first skull was found has been dated to approximately 1.75 million years ago. The earliest occupation levels at Olduvai date to approximately 2 million years ago (Table 4.2).

Homo Habilis

By 2 million years ago, there were not only two main australopithecine species in East Africa but also other hominids with much larger brains. A few hominid specimens from Koobi Fora in Kenya and from Olduvai Gorge have cranial capacities between 650 and 800 cc. These larger-brained hominids are generally assumed to represent the first appearance of the genus *Homo* and are known to paleoanthropologists as *Homo habilis*, the Latin for "handy person," a toolmaker.

If you were to encounter *Homo habilis* 2 million years ago, you would have seen little to distinguish the new hominid from *Australopithecus*. Both were of similar height and weight, about 1.3 m (4 ft 3 in) tall and about 40 kg (88 lb). Both were bipedal, but *Homo habilis* would have

Figure 4.12 Olduvai Gorge, Tanzania, with Mary Leakey in the foreground.

looked less apelike around the face and skull. The head was higher and rounder, the face less protruding. Some of the most significant anatomical differences involve the teeth. The molars were narrower, the premolars smaller, while the incisors were larger and more spadelike, as if they were used for slicing. However, microscopic teeth wear studies have shown that both *Australopithecus* and *Homo habilis* were predominantly fruit eaters, so there does not seem to have been a major shift in diet between the two forms.

The first *Homo habilis* fragments, which came from Bed I at Olduvai Gorge in the early 1960s, consisted of some skull and postcranial fragments of a larger-brained hominid. Then Richard Leakey found the famous Skull 1470 at Koobi Fora, a large-brained, round-headed cranium that confirmed the existence of *Homo habilis* in no uncertain terms. Thigh and limb bones from the same site and from Olduvai confirm that *Homo habilis* walked upright. The hand bones were somewhat more curved and robust than those of modern humans. This was a powerful grasping hand, more like that of chimpanzees and gorillas than humans, a hand ideal for climbing trees. An opposable thumb allowed both powerful gripping and precise manipulation of fine objects. With the latter capacity, *Homo habilis* could have made complex tools. Although the highly flexible and muscular fingers were those of a primate

Table 4.2 Highly schematic chronology of Olduvai Gorge, Tanzania, with positions of fossils and tools.

Date (B.C.)		
	Bed IV	Acheulian hand axes
Not less than 700,000	Bed III	Acheulian hand axes
Not less than 1,000,000	Bed II	Acheulian hand axes *Homo erectus*
		Homo habilis finds
1,750,000	Bed I	Oldowan chopper tools
1,800,000		*Australopithecus boisei* *Homo habilis* Stone structure
c. 2,200,000		Volcanic lava

[a]Broken line shows a possible break in the sequence.

that spent most of its days walking upright on the ground, it could have readily climbed trees in times of danger, to pick fruit, and to sleep at night.

There can be no reasonable doubt that *Homo habilis* was a toolmaker. But why should tools be needed? It seems possible that sharp flakes and stones allowed the first humans to grab occasional opportunities to scavenge meat, using sharp cutting edges to gain access to red meat at short notice. In this and many other respects *Homo habilis* was light years ahead of the australopithecines.

From Hominids to Homo

How did *Homo habilis* evolve? The question generates arguments so fiery that no two specialists can agree on the answer, and no unified system of human evolution satisfies every school of thought (Johanson and Edey, 1981; Leakey and Lewin, 1977; Lewin, 1984).

Table 4.3 summarizes the fossil evidence. There are two groups of hominids in East and South Africa after 4 million years ago. Two of them are australopithecines, and the third is *Homo*, with a larger brain capacity and more modern limb bones. Fourth, there are the Hadar and Laetoli fossils, dating to between 3 and 4 million years ago. Figure 4.10 gives a tentative time scale for the various major fossil finds.

There are three major hypotheses for early human evolution. Scheme A in Figure 4.10, espoused by Don Johanson and physical anthropologist Tim White, places *Australopithecus afarensis* as ancestral to the later australopithecines on the one hand and the *Homo* line on the other. Under this scenario, *Homo* was a late development. Scheme B, supported by the Leakey family, holds that a common ancestor of *Homo* and *Australopithecus* diverged fairly early, well before *Australopithecus afarensis* appeared. Scheme C combines A and B and argues that *Australopithecus afarensis* was ancestral to the gracile australopithecine, *A. africanus*. Then *africanus* gave rise to both the *Homo* and robust australopithecine lines.

It should be stressed that, for all the controversies, all these evolutionary schemes are tentative interpretations at best, based on the thinnest of paleontological evidence. Human evolution was a highly complex process, and there remain several blanks in the fossil record, among them the periods between 8 and 4 million B.C. and the critical period between 3 and 2.5 million B.C., when both the australopithecines and humanity branched out on their evolutionary own.

Despite the different interpretations of data, several points seem well established:

1. The australopithecines were a long-lived and highly successful adaptation to the African tropical savannah and perhaps elsewhere. (Nearly all the australopithecine fossils have thus far been discovered in Africa, but that is not to say they may not be found in other regions.) Then, ap-

Table 4.3 Four tentative groups of East and South African hominids, much simplified for this book.

	Robust group	Gracile group	Homo group	Hadar/Laetoli group
Brain size	500-550 cc	450-550 cc	650-775 cc	Comparable to a chimpanzee *400 c.c.*
Teeth	Very large back teeth; relatively small front teeth	Large front and back teeth	Variable; generally smaller than robust and gracile forms	Small back teeth; large front teeth
Limbs	Some elements of limb bones differ from those of modern humans		Lower limbs more modern in morphology than robust and gracile forms	Bipedal; arms slightly longer than Homo sapiens'
Species and sites	*Australopithecus robustus* South Africa: Swartkrans, Kromdraai *Australopithecus boisei* East Africa: Olduvai, East Turkana, Omo	*Australopithecus africanus* South Africa: Taung, Sterkfontein, Makapansgat East Africa: Omo?, East Turkana	*Homo* East Africa: Olduvai and East Turkana South Africa: Sterkfontein	*Australopithecus afarensis* East Africa: Hadar and Laetoli
	East Africa: c. 2,000,000 to c. 1,000,000 B.C. South Africa: no reliable dates	East Africa: c.3,000,000 to c. 1,500,000 B.C. South Africa: no reliable dates	East Africa: c. 2,000,000 to c. 1,500,000 B.C.	East Africa: c. 4,000,000 to c. 3,000,000 B.C.

proximately a million years ago, they suddenly disappear from the archaeological record. The early dates for *Australopithecus* in Omo show that these creatures flourished for at least 3.5 million years.

2. Robust australopithecines are not found earlier than 2.5 million years ago. Although this gap may reflect a lack of discoveries, it may in fact be because the robust species were an evolutionary development from the much older gracile *Australopithecus* form, one that did not occur until approximately 3 to 2.5 million years ago.

3. There is a good evidence for at least two australopithecine groups living alongside each other in East Africa for a considerable period of time. The robust lineage seems to have developed such a distinctive ecological and behavioral specialization that it survived alongside *Homo* for at least 2 million years.

4. The ancestral hominid population was probably a gracile primate, perhaps resembling *Australopithecus africanus*.

5. At issue is the date at which *Homo* and *Australopithecus africanus* diverged, the former with larger brains and more complex societies that depended increasingly heavily on a new element — their own culture.

6. Human culture, in the form of stone implements, can be traced back to approximately 2 million years ago, maybe more, in East Turkana.

HOME BASES

Is there any archaeological evidence for the first humans' home bases? Did they in fact have such bases at all in the sense that later hunter-gatherers developed regular campsites?

The only archaeological evidence for possible bases comes from East Turkana and Olduvai Gorge, where a number of concentrations of bones and stone tools have been excavated with meticulous care. To date, no such concentrations have been found with the South African australopithecines, or with the Omo or Laetoli hominids, or with the finds from west of Lake Turkana.

Koobi Fora

Koobi Fora
1.8 million B.C.

Some of the earliest humanly manufactured tools in the world come from the Koobi Fora area of East Turkana in northern Kenya (Isaac and Harris, 1978). Several localities have been excavated, among them a dry streambed where a group of hominids found the carcass of a hippopotamus. They gathered round and butchered the carcass with small stone knives, crudely flaked choppers, and pebble hammers. The deposits in which these stones and the flaked debris from them are found are so fine-grained that they contain no stones larger than a pea. Thus, every lump of rock there was carried in by the hominids to make tools at the carcass. The hominids visited the locality at least 1.8 million years ago.

We do not know whether they killed the hippopotamus. In all likelihood, they simply cut up the carcass of a dead animal and scavenged the meat.

Site FxJj50 (the designation comes from the site recording system at Koobi Fora) is located in an ancient watercourse, a place where the hominids could find shade from the blazing sun, a site close to water and to abundant supplies of stone for toolmaking (Bunn et al., 1980) (Figure 4.13). The site consists of a cluster of stone artifacts: choppers, crude scrapers, battered cobbles, and sharp-edged flakes. Approximately 2100 bones representing at least twenty vertebrates, mainly antelope, are associated with the tools, some of them bearing carnivore chewing marks. But there are clear signs that the bones were smashed and cut by hominids, for reconstructed fragments show signs of hammer blows and fine linear grooves that can result only from cutting bone with stone working edges. The excavators noted the lack of articular ends of bones, a characteristic of bone accumulations resulting from carnivore kills. Could the hominids simply have chased away lions and other predators, then moved in on the fresh kill? We do not know, but there is a strong possibility that successful hunting played a relatively limited part in hominid life at this early date.

Another site also consisted of a scatter of stone tools and broken animal bones, these from several antelope and larger mammals. The scatter lay on the surface of a dry stream bed where water could still be easily obtained by digging in the sand. The banks of the watercourse were prob-

Figure 4.13 Excavation at site FxJj50, Kenya.

ably shaded by dense stands of trees that provided both shelter and plant foods. Perhaps, too, the people who left the tools and bones climbed into these same trees at night. The site was so sheltered that even minuscule stone chips were still in place, unaffected by the strong winds that sweep over the area; the leaves, too, left impressions in the deposits there. The nearest source of toolmaking stone is two miles from the site, so the inhabitants must have carried in their tools, and, in all probability, portions of the several animals whose bones accumulated at the site. This type of behavior — the carrying in of food to a home base — is fundamentally different from that of the nonhuman primates.

Olduvai Gorge

Zinjanthropus

Much of our present knowledge about the lifeways of the earliest hominids comes from Olduvai Gorge, where Mary Leakey plotted and recorded sites in Bed I at the base of the gorge (M. D. Leakey, 1971). The *Zinjanthropus* at Olduvai was found to be 1239 ft square, consisting of more than 4000 artifacts and bones (see Figure 4.12). Many artifacts and bones were concentrated in an area some 15 ft across. A pile of shattered bones and rocks lay a short distance away, the bones perhaps piled in heaps as the marrow was extracted from them. A barer, arc-shaped area between these bone heaps and the pile of more complete fragments remains unexplained. Mary Leakey wonders whether it was the site of a crude windbreak of branches, since the area lies in the path of today's prevailing winds.

Were locations like the *Zinjanthropus* floor actual home bases? Until recently, most scholars assumed they were campsites, much like those of modern hunter-gatherers. In making these interpretations, everyone relied heavily on the important research into modern San hunter-gatherers in South Africa, assuming that Richard Lee's work would provide insights into our earliest ancestors. The assumption may be wrong, inasmuch as more detailed examination of the bone fragments and taphonomic studies have revealed a somewhat different picture of Olduvai life.

Recent researches have approached the Olduvai locations from several angles (Potts, 1984). Careful examination of the bones revealed that many of them had lain on the surface for considerable periods of time, perhaps as long as 4 to 6, even 10, years, to judge from weathering patterns on modern East African bones. The bones of many different animals are found in the assemblages, and the remains of carcasses are from a very ecologically diverse set of animals. Limb bones predominate on the "floors," as if these isolated bones were repeatedly carried to the site. Furthermore, the stone tools found on the Olduvai surfaces were all imported there from raw material sources located at some distance away.

What is one to make of this pattern of meat and marrow-rich bones concentrated in a small area with stone tools? The percentage of carnivore bones is somewhat higher than the natural environment would suggest, about 3 percent in the Olduvai assemblages, as opposed to 1 percent for the local environment today (in one case the figure was as high as 21 percent). Was there then intense ecological competition for game meat between hominids and other carnivores? It seems possible that the presence of carnivores restricted the activities of hominids at Olduvai. They may have grabbed meat-rich bones from carnivore kills, then taken them to a place where they had a collection of stone tools. There they could have hastily cut off meat and extracted marrow before abandoning the fresh bones for the carnivores hovering nearby. The Olduvai sites may not have been safe from carnivores, and without fire or domesticated dogs, *Homo habilis* probably had to rely on opportunistic foraging. As we have already noted, many of the Olduvai bones bear both carnivore teeth marks and stone tool cuts, perhaps a reflection of competition for game meat. It is also worth noting that one hominid bone found at Olduvai had been knawed by carnivores.

So the Olduvai home bases may, in fact, be bone caches used again and again over considerable periods of time. It was not until much later that humans organized their own campsites, where fire protected them from unwelcome visitors.

OLDOWAN CULTURE

For many years the Leakeys had found crudely chipped stones in the long-buried lake beds at Olduvai. Similar artifacts came from the *Zinjanthropus* floor and from floors associated with more gracile fossils. *Oldowan* tools, named by Leakey after Olduvai Gorge, are nothing much to look at (Figure 4.14). They are broken pebbles and flakes, mostly the latter. Some Oldowan tools are so crude that only an expert can tell them from a naturally fractured rock, and the experts often disagree. All the Oldowan choppers and flakes strike one as extremely practical implements; many are so individual in design that they seem haphazard artifacts, not standardized in the way that later Stone Age tools were. Classifying them is very difficult, for they do not fall into distinct types. The tools cannot be described as primitive, since many display a sophisticated understanding of stone's potential uses in toolmaking. Although Oldowan stone tools are easily confused with naturally fractured stones when found in river gravels or away from sealed occupation sites, we now know that the Olduvai hominids were adept stone toolmakers, using angular flakes and lumps of lava to make weapons, scrapers, and cutting tools. The tools themselves probably were used for cutting skin too tough for teeth to cut. In all probability, the hominids made extensive use of simple and untrimmed flakes for widely differing activities. The earliest human toolkit probably could perform all the basic tasks of tropical, nonagricultural hunter-gatherers, whatever their primary means of subsistence.

Oldowan
**2 million to 1
million B.C. or later**

Figure 4.14 Early stone technology. The principles of fracturing stone were fully understood by early stoneworkers, who used them to make simple but very effective artifacts. Certain types of flinty rock fracture in a distinctive way, as illustrated below. Early stoneworkers used a heavy hammerstone to remove edge flakes or struck lumps of rock against anvils to produce the same effect. Oldowan choppers were frequently made by removing a few flakes from lava lumps to form jagged working edges. Such artifacts have been shown by modern experiments to be remarkably effective for dismembering and butchering game. Perhaps it is small wonder that this simple stone technology was so long-lasting.

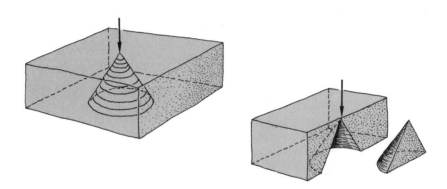

When a blow is struck on flinty rock, a cone of percussion is formed by shock waves rippling through the stone. A flake is formed (right) when the block (or core) is hit at the edge, and the stone fractures along the edge of the ripple.

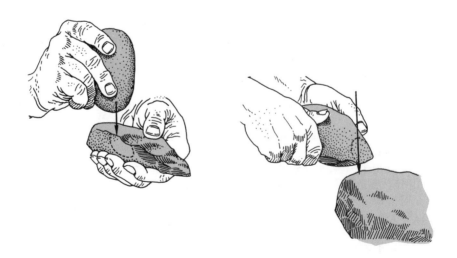

Using a hammerstone (left) and anvil (right).

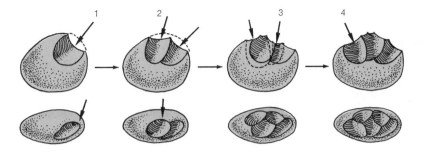

Making a chopping tool. First, sharp blows are struck near the natural edge of a pebble to remove flakes. The pebble is then turned over, and more blows are struck on the ridges formed by the scars of the earlier flakes. A chopping tool with a strong, jagged working edge results.

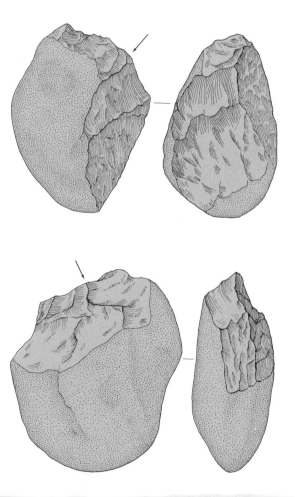

Two Oldowan chopping tools from Olduvai Gorge. Arrows show working edges. Front and side views (three-fifths actual size).

THE EARLY ADAPTIVE PATTERN

The few early living sites that have been excavated show that the first phase of human evolution involved shifts in the basic patterns of subsistence and locomotion, as well as new ingredients — food sharing and toolmaking. These led to enhanced communication, information exchange, and economic and social insight, as well as cunning and restraint. Human anatomy was augmented with tools. Culture became an inseparable part of humanity.

Opportunism

Archaeologist Glynn Isaac believes that opportunism is a hallmark of humankind — a restless process, like mutation and natural selection (Isaac, 1978). The normal pressures of ecological competition were able to transform the versatile behavior of the ancestral primates into the new and distinctive early hominid pattern. The change required feedback between cultural subsystems, such as hunting and sharing food. Weapons and tools made it possible to scavenge and butcher larger and larger animals. Vegetable foods were a staple in the diet, protection against food shortages. Foraging provided stability, and it may also have led to division of labor between men and women. Skin bags, bark trays, and perhaps baskets were useful in collecting food; sharing and manufacturing them encouraged the division of labor. The savannah was an ideal and vacant ecological niche for hominids who lived on scavenging, hunting, and foraging combined.

By a million years ago, the hominid lines had been pruned to the extent that one lineage, *Homo*, remained. Judging from the abundance of finds from East Turkana, the hominids of 2 million years ago appear to have been about as common as baboons are in the savannah today (Lewin, 1984). The microwear patterns on the tooth surfaces of *Australopithecus* and *Homo habilis* show that both creatures flourished on a diet very similar to that of chimpanzees. But this microwear pattern can be produced by all kinds of different combinations of vegetable and meat foods, so much so that the two species may have been ecologically separated from one another by their different dietary preferences. Otherwise it would not have been possible for them to share the same area for very long, but this is purely intelligent speculation. The archaeological deposits in which both fossils and artifacts are found are simply too coarse-grained to dissect even fairly major climatic and ecological changes.

The only clue to this separation may lie in *Homo habilis* appearing at about the same time as the first stone tools. These artifacts must have been connected with new ways of getting and processing foods, even with entirely new forms of diet altogether. *Homo habilis* had a much larger brain, a development that was probably associated with an increase in economic and social complexity, and perhaps food sharing as well.

What sort of social organization did *Homo habilis* enjoy? However much we look at contemporary nonhuman primates, we cannot be sure. Most primates are intensely social and live in groups where the mother-infant relationship forms a central bond. The period of infant-mother dependency found in, say, chimpanzees, was probably lengthened considerably with *Homo habilis*. The larger brain size would mean that infants were born with much smaller heads than adults, at an earlier stage of mental maturity. This biological reality would have had a major impact on social organization and daily habits.

Baboons and chimpanzees live in groups that range from about a dozen individuals up to troops of a hundred or so. They occupy a relatively small territory, one with sufficient vegetable resources to support a considerable population density, which contrasts sharply with the average hunter-gatherer band, typically a closely knit group of about twenty-five people or several families. The kind of systematic hunting such people engage in requires much larger territories and permits much lower densities per square mile. The few home bases that have been excavated suggest that *Homo habilis* tended to live in bands that were much closer to those of modern hunter-gatherers. However, it would be a mistake to assume that they lived in hunter-gatherer bands. In all probability their social organization resembled more closely that of chimpanzees and baboons.

Chimpanzees and baboons live in a world created in their brains by the integration of senses of sight, sound, smell, and touch. The more complex the inputs and their neural processing, the more complex the inner world built by the brain. It may well be that this increase in complexity is what underlies the cumulative increase in brain size that is such a distinctive feature of mammalian evolution, from amphibians to reptiles, then through mammals to humans. The world of *Homo habilis* was much less predictable and more demanding than that of even *Australopithecus*. What was it that was more complex? Why do we have to be so intelligent? Not in hunting animals or gathering food but in our social interactions with other people. The increased complexity of our social interactions is likely to have had a powerful force in the evolution of the human brain. For *Homo habilis*, the adoption of a wider-based diet with a food-sharing social group would have placed much more acute demands on one's ability to cope with the complex and unpredictable. And the brilliant technological, artistic, and expressive skills of humankind may well be a consequence of the fact that our early ancestors had to be more and more socially adept.

GUIDE TO FURTHER READING

Campbell, Bernard. *Humankind Emerging* (4th ed.). Boston: Little, Brown, 1985. A vivid description of the processes of human evolution for the beginning student. Exceptionally well written.

Johanson, Donald C., and Edey, Maitland A. *Lucy: The Beginnings of Humankind*. New York: Simon and Schuster, 1981.

A well-written, racy account of the Hadar hominids that ranges widely over the major controversies of paleoanthropology. Superb descriptions of the research process and of dating methods.

Lewin, Roger. *Human Evolution*. Oxford: Blackwell Scientific Publications, 1984.
A lucid, multidisciplinary account of human origins full of provocative ideas.

Tanner, Nancy. *On Becoming Human*. London: Cambridge University Press, 1981.
A brilliant essay on human origins and male/female roles.

Weiss, Mark, and Mann, Alan. *Human Biology and Behavior* (4th ed.). Boston: Little, Brown, 1985.
A standard undergraduate text that presents the biological background to human evolution. Excellent graphics.

Chronological Table B

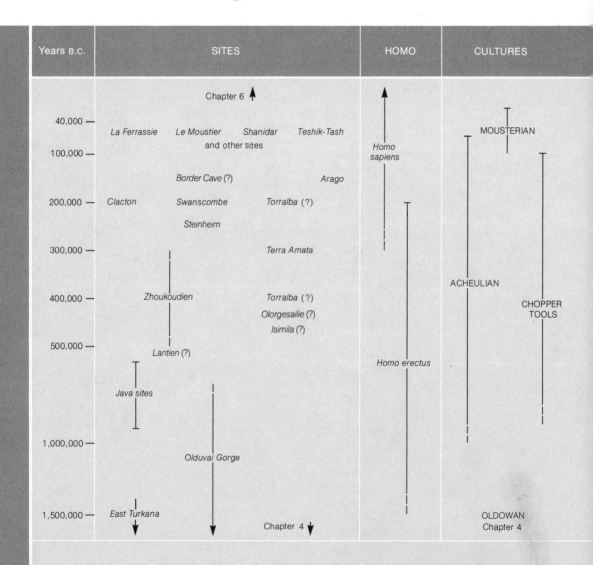

Years B.C.	SITES	HOMO	CULTURES
	Chapter 6 ↑	↑	
40,000 —	La Ferrassie Le Moustier Shanidar Teshik-Tash		MOUSTERIAN
100,000 —	and other sites	Homo sapiens	
	Border Cave (?) Arago		
200,000 —	Clacton Swanscombe Torralba (?)		
	Steinheim		
300,000 —	Terra Amata		ACHEULIAN
400,000 —	Zhoukoudien Torralba (?)		CHOPPER TOOLS
	Olorgesailie (?)		
	Isimila (?)		
500,000 —	Lantien (?)	Homo erectus	
	Java sites		
1,000,000 —			
	Olduvai Gorge		
1,500,000 —	East Turkana		OLDOWAN
	↓ Chapter 4 ↓		Chapter 4

Chapter Five

Toward Modern Humanity

(1.5 million to 40,000 B.C.)

PREVIEW

- Approximately 1.5 million years ago, the first indisputable humans came into existence; they can be recognized in the archaeological record and have been classified by paleontologists as *Homo erectus.*
- *Homo erectus* apparently was the first hominid to adapt to environments as diverse as tropical-forest, temperate, and near-arctic climates. These hominids had enlarged brains, improved communication skills, more elaborate culture, and larger home bases.
- The technology of *Homo erectus* was based on relatively simple stoneworking techniques that produced two major traditions: the hand ax and the chopper. Hand ax sites are confined mostly to southern and temperate latitudes, while chopper tools were favored in Asia and perhaps in northern Europe as well.
- *Homo erectus* relied heavily on big-game hunting and cooperative game drives and used fire. The Terra Amata and Torralba sites show how people butchered big game and returned to the same localities year after year when favored foods were in season. These hominids practiced basic patterns of hunting and gathering that persisted for hundreds of thousands of years.
- The earliest *Homo sapiens* finds date to approximately 300,000 to 250,000 B.C.; these were the predecessors of modern human beings, *Homo sapiens sapiens,* who did not appear until approximately 40,000 years ago.
- The early *sapiens* populations, including the Neanderthals, used a distinctive Middle Paleolithic technology, called Mousterian, that spread far over temperate and tropical latitudes of the world. Its regional variations were based on a wider variety of specialized tools than ever made before, including spearheads and scrapers. The more elaborate Mousterian toolkit may signify that Neanderthal populations made more diverse adaptations than those of earlier times.

It would be a mistake to think of human evolution in terms of neat ladders of progression from one form to the next improved form. With only a handful of fossils to work with, and those fragmentary at best, there has been a tendency even for experts to think in linear terms. However, since human evolution has probably followed the pattern of other animal groups, we are likely to find more rather than fewer species in our ancestry. Instead of a ladder, one should think of a bush, with different branches representing new species that all became extinct, except for the one surviving form — *Homo sapiens*. We are a rarity in nature in that we are all from one species (Lewin, 1984).

In Chapter Four, we noted how opportunism and adaptability were hallmarks of the first hominids, both in terms of diet and ecological exploitation. The australopithecines were not as adaptable as some of their other hominid contemporaries. They lived at a time when baboons and other competitive primates were evolving rapidly, and they probably became extinct as a result of competitive exclusion. We must now examine their successors and those of *Homo*, humans who were capable of a far more complex and varied lifeway than their predecessors. These were hominids who used fire, made systematically manufactured rather than opportunistic tools, developed seasonal home bases, and were the first to settle outside Africa.

HOMO ERECTUS

*Homo erectus*1.5 million to ?200,000 B.C.

Lake Turkana 1.5 to 1.6 million years B.P.

Homo erectus first arose about 1.5 to 1.6 million years ago. The earliest unquestioned specimen comes from East Turkana in Kenya, a skull dated to between 1.5 and 1.6 million years ago (Figure 5.1) (Leakey and Lewin, 1977). This fossil, with its massive brow ridges, enlarged brain size, and high forehead, is morphologically very close to later examples of *Homo erectus* dating to a million years ago and earlier.

Richard Leakey and anatomist Alan Walker have recently discovered the virtually complete skeleton of a twelve-year-old *Homo erectus* boy on the western shores of the same lake, dating to about the same time period. The footprints of hippopotamuses and other animals nearby suggest that the decomposing corpse was trampled to pieces after death. From the neck down, the boy's bones are remarkably modern looking. But the skull and jawbone are more primitive looking, with brow ridges and a brain capacity perhaps as high as 700 to 800 cc, about half the modern size. The skeleton shows that the boy stood about 5 ft 6 in. tall, taller than many modern twelve-year-olds. This new Turkana find tends to confirm many scientists' view that different parts of the body evolved at different rates, the body achieving fully modern form long before the head.

Chronological Table B

Java **900,000 to 600,000 B.P.**

These finds date to much earlier than the classic finds of *Homo erectus*, which were made as early as 1891. A Dutch doctor named Eugene Dubois found the skullcap of an apelike human in the gravels of the Solo river near Trinil in central Java (Pfeiffer, 1978). When, a year later at the same site, he found an upper limb bone that displayed many human features, he named his discovery *Pithecanthropus erectus* ("apeman who walks upright"). A vicious outcry greeted his announcement; Dubois was

Figure 5.1 Skull KNM-ER3733, East Turkana, Kenya.

accused of heresy and his findings dismissed with contempt. Then, in 1928, a Canadian anatomist named Davidson Black announced the discovery of human teeth at Zhoukoudien cave near Beijing (Weidenreich, 1946). A year later, Chinese archaeologist W. C. P'ei recovered a complete skullcap from the same cave; it closely resembled Dubois's Java finds. The human remains were associated with stone tools, crude bone artifacts, and the bones of hundreds of animals. A Dutch physical anthropologist, G. H. R. von Koenigswald, discovered more fossils in Java, examined the Chinese and Japanese remains, and described a new human form: *Homo erectus* (Figure 5.2) (Symons and Cybulski, 1981).

Zhoukoudien **500,000 to 300,000 B.P.**

Homo erectus is known to have lived over a wide area of the Old World. Louis Leakey found a skullcap of *Homo erectus* in the upper levels of Bed II at Olduvai Gorge (Lewin, 1984). This specimen came from levels dating to approximately a million years ago. In contrast, the Chinese finds are now estimated to date to between 500,000 and 350,000 years ago, while new *Homo erectus* finds from the Trinil area of Java have been potassium argon dated to between 900,000 and 600,000 years ago (Weiss and Mann, 1985). *Homo erectus* fossils have come to light in Morocco and Algeria and in Hungary and western Germany. None of the European

Olduvai Gorge **1,000,000 B.P.**

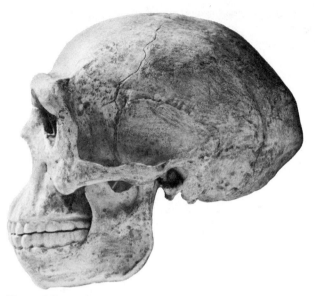

Figure 5.2 A plaster cast of *Homo erectus* from Zhoukoudien, China. The skull bones of *Homo erectus* show that these hominids had a brain capacity between 775 and 1300 cc, showing much variation. It is probable that their vision was excellent and that they were capable of extensive thought. The *H. erectus* skull is more rounded than that of earlier hominids; it also has conspicuous brow ridges and a sloping forehead. With a massive jaw, much thicker skull bones, and teeth with cusp patterns somewhat similar to those of *Australopithecus africanus* and modern humans, *H. erectus* had limbs and hips fully adapted to an upright posture. It stood over 5 ft 6 in with hands fully capable of precision gripping and many kinds of toolmaking.

finds can be dated, but probably belong to approximately 500,000 years ago. Further, although fossil remains of *Homo erectus* are rarely encountered, their distinctive toolkit of stone axes and choppers is relatively commonplace and tells us much about their distribution and adaptations.

WHERE AND HOW *HOMO ERECTUS* LIVED

During *Homo erectus'* long history, humanity adapted to a far wider range of environments, ranging from tropical savannahs in East Africa to forested Javanese valleys, temperate climates in North Africa and Europe, and the harsh winters of China and northern Europe. *Homo erectus* was certainly capable of a far more complex and varied lifeway than previous hominids, and with such a wide distribution, it is hardly surprising that some variations in *Homo erectus* populations appear. For example, some had more robust skulls than others, while it is said that the Zhoukoudien skulls display a gradual increase in brain capacity from about 900 cc in 600,000-year-old specimens to about 1100 cc in 200,000-year-old individuals. In any case, *Homo erectus* was far more "human" than *Homo habilis*, a habitual biped, who had probably lost the thick hair covering that is characteristic of nonhuman primates. Unfortunately, we are unlikely ever to know when we lost our dense facial hair, because soft parts are never preserved. But it seems possible that this occurred when the dramatic enlargement of hominid brains recycled the developmental "clock" — perhaps with *Homo habilis* (Lewin, 1984). In any case, *Homo erectus* certainly had abundant sweat glands and, presumably, in common with most tropical primates, relatively dark skin.

With the exception of some unconfirmed dates from Southeast Asia, all *Homo erectus* fossils more than a million years old come from Africa. Thus, it may be that hominids were confined to Africa until the more resourceful, more adaptable, and more carnivorous big game hunter *Homo erectus* became capable of exploiting cooler, more demanding climates. This is mere speculation, since the picture was undoubtedly more complex. But *Homo erectus* had one powerful adaptive weapon at his disposal — fire. The earliest evidence of fire in the archaeological record, which comes from Chesowanja in Kenya, consists of some burned clay fragments found with stone tools and animal bones. Unfortunately, this is a disputed find, but there is no doubt at all that *Homo erectus* used fire as early as 600,000 years ago. Hearths up to 1.8 m (6 ft) thick come from Zhoukoudien, China.

Use of fire

By half a million years ago, *Homo erectus* hunted big game and gathered wild vegetable foods on a scale that their predecessors would never have contemplated. The basic patterns of hunting and gathering that persisted through millennia into modern times were already well developed by 500,000 years ago.

THE HAND AX TRADITION

The Oldowan industry of simple choppers, crude scrapers, and flakes lasted for more than a million years. If one looks over several Oldowan toolkits of different ages, then examines much later tools made by *Homo erectus*, one is struck by a powerful sense of technological continuity. The earliest stone tools were made with a few blows of a crude hammerstone. (Table 5.1). Many of them were then used to sharpen sticks and other wooden artifacts. The Oldowan survives unchanged through the long millennia of Bed I at Olduvai and into overlying Bed II, where the first traces of *Homo erectus* are found. But about 1.5 million years ago, the Acheulian industry appears, an industry characterized by a new artifact: the stone hand ax. But the age-old Oldowan tool forms persist, crude choppers that were still being made as late as 200,000 years ago in China.

Oldowan industry
**2 million to later
than 1 million B.P.**

The Acheulian was but a modest advance over the Oldowan, for one still has a strong impression that all artifacts were opportunistic, rather casually made to respond to specific challenges. It is only much later, after about 150,000 years ago, that one acquires a stronger sense of sty-

Table 5.1 Classic technological stages of the Old Stone Age.

Approximate Dates B.C.	Stage	Technology	General Trends
After 8,000	No formal term	Trend to smaller tools (Figure 6.7), associated with wide use of bow and arrow.	
?40,000 to 8,000	UPPER PALEOLITHIC	Pressure flaking first used. Blade technology and many specialized artifacts (Figure 6.3). More reliance on bone tools.	Increasing use of composite tools (i.e. wood and stone, bone and stone)
?150,000 to 40,000	MIDDLE PALEOLITHIC	"Disc" and "Levallois" prepared core technologies. Flakes used to make composite artifacts and some specialized tools (Figure 5.13).	Increasingly efficient use of raw materials relative to working edges
Earliest times to ?150,000	LOWER PALEOLITHIC	Simple technology based on use of stone against stone, or bone or wood against stone. Choppers and hand axes are commonplace (Figure 5.4).	

The terms *Paleolithic* or *Old Stone Age* are purely convenient labels, without specific time frames. We use them in this book just for convenience in describing a general level of technological achievement. It is inevitable that stone technologies dominate the definitions of the stages, because technologies centered on tools of other materials cannot have been as well preserved. The table is cross-referenced to figures that illustrate each technology.

listic order, of technological traditions that were applied to a wide range of stone artifacts.

The hand ax is one of the most common exhibits in the world's museums (Figure 5.3). It has been found over a vast area of the Old World, in all shapes and sizes, from crude tear-shaped forms, to ovals, tongue-shaped axes, and occasional finely pointed specimens that were evidently made with considerable care (Figure 5.4). Unlike the crude scrapers and choppers of the Oldowan, the Acheulian hand ax was an artifact with converging edges, whose edges met at a point. The maker had to envisage the shape of the artifact, which was to be produced from a mere lump of stone, then fashion it not with opportunistic blows but with carefully directed hammer blows. Acheulian hand axes come in every size, from small, elegant oval types a few inches long to heavy axes more than a foot long and weighing 5 pounds or more. They must have been a versatile, thoroughly practical artifact to have survived in use so long.

What exactly were hand axes used for? Almost certainly they were held in the hand rather than being hafted on the end of a wooden shaft. They were simply too cumbersome for that, and, in any case, hafted tools probably did not come into use until much later. Conventional wisdom has it

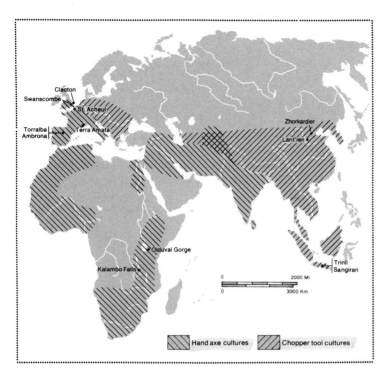

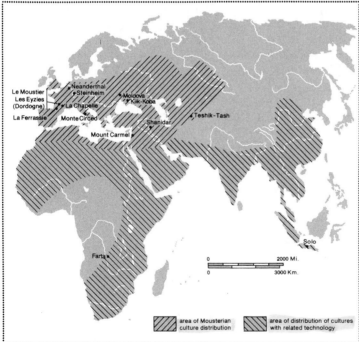

Figure 5.3 (a) Distribution of hand ax and chopper traditions, also showing location of sites mentioned in first half of this chapter. (b) Distribution of Neanderthal cultures, with locations of sites mentioned in text.

Figure 5.4 Lower Paleolithic hand ax technology. Acheulian tool technology first appeared more than a million years ago. Although the Acheulians used wooden tools such as the spear and the club, few examples have been preserved. Their stone tools are much better known and include the ubiquitous hand ax and numerous flake tools. The earliest Acheulian hand axes were crudely flaked with jagged edges but functional points. It is thought that their development was the logical extension of the chopping tool, since they had two cutting edges instead of one. Simple hammerstone techniques were used to make early hand axes. Later examples were much more finely made, with delicate, straight edges and flatter cross sections. A bone hammer was used to strike off the shallow flakes that adorn the margins of these tools (bottom). A widely found variant is the cleaver, a butchering tool with a single, unfinished edge that has proved effective for skinning and dismembering game under experimental conditions. Later hand axes and cleavers are found in a wide variety of forms and lasted in some areas until as late as some 60,000 years ago.

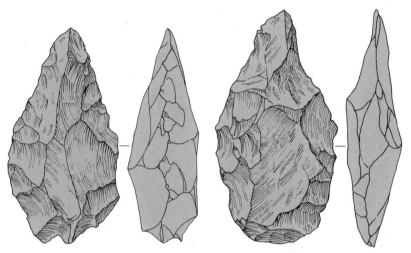

Two early hand axes from Bed II, Olduvai Gorge, Tanzania. Front and side views (three-quarters actual size).

Using an animal bone to make a hand ax.

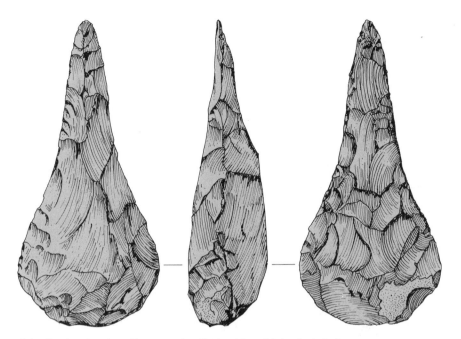

Acheulian hand ax from Swanscombe, England (one-third actual size).

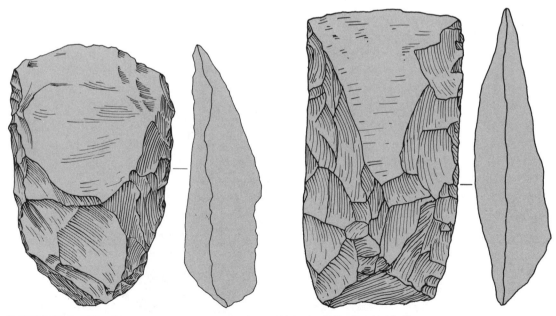

Two Acheulian cleavers, from Baia Farta, Angola (left) and Kalambo Falls, Zambia (both one-half actual size).

that they were multipurpose artifacts, used for grubbing up roots, wood-working, scraping skins, and especially for skinning and butchering large and small game. There is no question that they were highly effective butchery tools. Many archaeologists have tried not only cutting up antelope carcasses but also slicing through hippopotamus and elephant hide as well — with great success. In some ways, the hand ax was ideal for this purpose, because it could be sharpened again and again, and when it became a useless lump of stone, it could then be recycled into flake tools. But you can achieve effective butchery with simple flakes as well, and a number of people have wondered whether the hand ax, which took longer to make, was not used for other purposes.

Eileen O'Brien (1984) has argued that the hand ax was in fact a form of primitive discus. She points out that hand axes are most common on sites near water courses and other places where big game customarily gathered, whereas they are much less common on sites away from such areas. Could they have been projectiles instead? She obtained a weighted fiberglass cast of a Kenyan hand ax that was nearly a foot long and weighed 4 pounds, 3 ounces. An expert discus thrower picked up the hand ax, held it by the butt, and put the point alongside his forearm (Figure 5.5). Then he hurled it again and again in an overarm, sidearm action. The hand ax spun horizontally on its way, then suddenly changed its orientation in midair and nearly always fell to the ground on its edge or point. The average throw carried almost 100 ft, with an accuracy of about 2 yd left or right of the throw line. Could, then, the hand ax with its streamlined shape have been a far more effective projectile than the balls and stones that were the only weapons the first hominids had to protect themselves

Figure 5.5 An expert discus thrower holds a hand ax replica before hurling it as a projectile.

against predators and other enemies? Their only other — suicidal — alternative was hand-to-hand combat with their adversary. But with the discuslike hand ax, one could hunt big game from a relatively safe distance with lethal accuracy and defend oneself with drastically enhanced efficiency. Is it a coincidence that big-game hunting became a significant human activity just as *Homo erectus* developed a new tool that perhaps could be thrown? The thought is a tantalizing one.

Hand axes appear suddenly at Olduvai; they are made of larger rocks than those used for Oldowan choppers (L. S. B. Leakey, 1951; M. D. Leakey, 1971). Their origins in the Oldowan technology are unquestionable, however, for the earliest hand axes are crudely shaped, jagged-edged artifacts that are obvious developments of the chopper. The serpentine edges of the early hand axes in Bed II at Olduvai give way to more advanced artifacts in later levels of the gorge. The hand ax edges become straighter, often flaked with a bone hammer that gave a flatter profile to the ax. The bases are carefully rounded and finished.

In contrast to the earlier Oldowan, the Lower Paleolithic technology of *Homo erectus* varied greatly throughout its duration, reaching considerable heights of delicate artistry (Figure 5.4, p. 120; Table 5.1, p. 118). In addition to hand axes, the new technology resulted in scrapers and other artifacts for woodworking, skinning, and other purposes. But hand axes remain the most characteristic artifact of many *Homo erectus* populations.

The hand ax technology associated with *Homo erectus* is known as the Acheulian, after the French town of St. Acheul. *Acheulian* is a term that covers many different cultural adaptations, for hand axes have been found over an enormous area of the Old World (Figure 5.3, p. 119) Fine specimens are scattered in the gravels of the Somme and the Thames rivers in northern Europe, in North African quarries and ancient Sahara lake beds, and in sub-Saharan Africa from the Nile Valley to the Cape of Good Hope. Acheulian tools are common in some parts of India, as well as in Arabia and the Near East as far as the southern shores of the Caspian Sea and perhaps even further north. They are rare east of the Rhine and in the Far East, where chopping tools were commonly used until comparatively recent times (Butzer and Isaac, 1975; Clark, 1970; Howell and Clark, 1963). No one has been able to explain why hand axes have this restricted distribution. Were such multipurpose tools used only in big-game hunting camps? Was their use restricted by the availability of flint and other suitable raw materials? Did environmental conditions affect the hunters' choice of toolkits? Or were they used as projectiles in areas where big game abounded? We do not know.

Acheulian culture
1,000,000 to 60,000 B.C.

THE CHOPPING TOOL TRADITION

By no means did all *Homo erectus* populations rely on hand axes. The bands who lived at Zhoukoudien, China, made their tools from quartzite

Zhoukoudien
460,000 to 230,000 B.P.

and relied heavily on choppers with jagged edges (Fig. 5.6) (Chang, 1977; Institute of Vertebrate Paleontology, 1981; Rukang and Shenglong, 1983). The Zhoukoudien cave was occupied over an immensely long time, from about 460,000 to 230,000 years ago. As time went on, *Homo erectus* used smaller and smaller tools and employed slightly more sophisticated techniques to make them. The inhabitants hunted at least sixty species of animals including elephants, bears, deer, and many small rodents. They built large fires from the very earliest millennia the cave was occupied, presumably for both warmth and protection.

Choppers were favored over hand axes in southeast Asia and apparently in parts of central Europe and Britain as well. Sites containing hundreds of choppers, flakes, and cores but no hand axes have been found in eastern England. The Clacton site near London, dating to approximately 200,000 years ago, yielded the point of a wooden spear as well (Figure 5.7) (Singer, 1973).

Many of the simple tools used by the Asians and Europeans resemble the Oldowan artifacts of the first toolmakers. Such similarities can be explained as merely the logical result of flaking a pebble to produce a jagged edge and sharp flakes. But did toolmaking originate in Africa, and in Europe and Asia as well, before the evolution of *Homo erectus*? Or were chopping tools carried into cooler latitudes by early, more adaptable *Homo erectus* populations before the hand ax was developed? No hominid fossils earlier than *Homo erectus* have yet been found in Europe or Asia, and, if such people did settle in temperate latitudes, there are few signs of their artifacts. One can perhaps best describe the chopper sites of Britain and Europe as specialized adaptations which are still imperfectly understood. There is a sameness about the tools of *Homo erectus* that is both depressing and remarkable. Acheulian hand axes from as far apart as Olduvai Gorge, the Thames Valley, and the Indian peninsula are simi-

200,000 B.P.

Figure 5.6 A crude chopping tool from Zhoukoudien, China. Front and side views (one-half actual size).

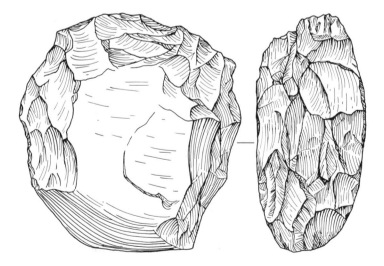

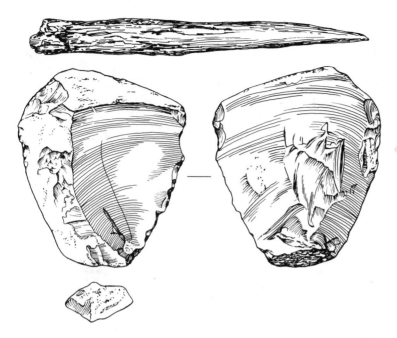

Figure 5.7 At top, a wooden spearhead from Clacton, England, from the Lower Paleolithic (approximately one-eighth actual size). Below, views of a flake from Clacton-on-Sea. The upper surface is shown at left, the flake (lower) surface on the right. The striking platform is at the base (one-third actual size).

lar in shape — the same is true of many other large and small artifacts possessed by *Homo erectus*. Most surviving Acheulian tools are made of stone and give us an extremely limited view of subsistence activities, ecological adaptations, or diet. It is quite possible that different Acheulian bands had ecological adaptations and social and cultural specializations that varied far more than their surviving artifacts suggest (Isaac, 1978). In the Acheulian culture, the long millennia of apparent equilibrium must be thought of in the context of the more rudimentary brain and economic adaptations of *Homo erectus*.

EARLY HUNTING AND GATHERING

Big-game hunting was of more than passing importance to many *Homo erectus* bands, as is witnessed by two remarkable Acheulian butchery sites at Torralba and Ambrona, northeast of Madrid (Howell, 1966). The Acheulians probably lived in this deep, swampy valley either 200,000 or 400,000 years ago (the date is disputed). Torralba yielded most of the left side of a large elephant that had been cut up into small pieces, while Ambrona contained the remains of thirty to thirty-five dismembered elephants. Concentrations of broken food bones were found all over the site, and the skulls of the elephants had been broken open to get at the marrow. In one place, the elephant bones had been laid in a line, perhaps to form stepping stones in the swamp where the elephants had been dispatched (Figure 5.8). Both kill sites were littered with crude hand axes, cleavers, scrapers, and cutting tools.

Big-game hunting

Torralba **400,000 or 200,000 B.P.**

Figure 5.8 From Torralba, Spain, a remarkable linear arrangement of elephant tusks and leg bones that was probably laid out by those who butchered the animals in Stone Age times.

The elephant bones at both sites were buried in clays that were once treacherous marsh. We can imagine the hunters watching the valley floors where the elephants roamed. At a strategic moment several bands would gather quietly, set brush fires, and drive the unsuspecting beasts into the swamps where they could be killed and butchered at leisure.

Gathering wild vegetable foods such as nuts, berries, and seeds was undoubtedly important, although next to nothing survives in archaeological sites. Within their territory the hunters knew the habits of every animal and the characteristics of many edible vegetable foods and medicinal plants; they were familiar with the inconspicuous landmarks and strategic features. From sites like Terra Amata near Nice in France, we know that they returned to the same locality year after year at favored seasons in search of specific foods.

Terra Amata was excavated by Henry de Lumley and included a series of oval huts that once stood on the shores of the Mediterranean at a time of cool and arid climate, some 300,000 years ago (Lumley, 1969; Villa, 1983). He found that the huts consisted of shallow hollows 8 to 15 m (26 to 50 ft) long and 4 to 6 m (13 to 20 ft) wide, with an entrance at one end (Figure 5.9). When he cleared the hollows, he uncovered a series of posts approximately 7 cm (3 in) in diameter that had once formed the walls. The bases of the posts were reinforced with lines of stones. The roof was supported by center posts, and some huts had a hearth in the center. The excavators recovered the bones of wild oxen, stags, and elephants, as well as those of small rodents. There were even imprints of skins once laid on the floors. De Lumley records that the inhabitants never cleaned out their huts. They lived among butchered bones, discarded stone tools, even their own feces. The feces yielded numerous fragments of nuts and seeds that had flourished in the late spring and early summer. De Lumley concluded that Terra Amata was a seasonal camp, occupied by the same band of hunter-gatherers who returned to the same locale year after year in search of vegetable foods and shellfish, another common find in the settlement (for a critique and discussion, see Villa, 1983).

Terra Amata and Torralba show that fire had become an important tool, already in use at Zhoukoudien 500,000 years ago, and in Africa perhaps much earlier. The very earliest humans must have been familiar with the hungry flames of brush fires caused by lightning or volcanic eruptions (Oakley, 1955). Grass fires destroy old vegetation, and game grazes happily on the green shoots that spring up through the blackened soil a few weeks later. This easy familiarity with natural fires may have led *Homo erectus* to keep fires alive, kindling wood from a brushfire or flames from a seepage of natural gas. As people moved into less hospita-

Figure 5.9 Reconstruction of a hut at Terra Amata, France.

ble environments, they needed fire constantly — to keep them warm at night, to protect them from nocturnal predators, to give them light, and to help them with game drives.

Improvements in language and modes of communication are thought to have been a distinctive feature of *Homo erectus's* style of life. With improved language skills and more advanced technology, it became possible for people to achieve better cooperation in gathering activities, in storage of food supplies, and in the chase. Unlike the nonhuman primates, who strongly emphasize individual economic success, Middle Pleistocene hunter-gatherers depended on cooperative activity by every individual in the band. The economic unit was the group; the secret of individual success was group success. Perhaps individual ownership of property was unimportant, since neither individuals or groups as a whole had tangible possessions of significance. People got along well with one another as individuals, as families, and as entire groups. The hunter-gatherers who followed *Home erectus* did not necessarily inherit this advantage.

HOMO SAPIENS EMERGES

When did *Homo sapiens sapiens*, modern humans, originate? The question remains one of the great controversies of paleoanthropology. Most people now believe that *Homo erectus* evolved into *Homo sapiens*, but there are few fossil remains to document this vital transition. Except for a small, overall increase in brain size, *Homo erectus* remained remarkably stable in evolutionary terms for more than a million years, until less than half a million years ago. We do not know when the transition began, nor how it took place. Some people believe it began as early as 400,000 years ago, others a much more recent date, in the neighborhood of 200,000 years.

A handful of human fossils suggest that the shift to an archaic form of *Homo sapiens* was under way by 250,000 years ago. A skull from Petralona, Greece, dates to between 300,000 and 400,000, while the Arago Cave in the French Pyrenees has yielded a skull and several jaws that seem anatomically intermediate between *Home erectus* and *Homo sapiens*. They date to around 250,000 (Campbell, 1985). Swanscombe, a quarry in the Thames River gravels east of London, has yielded the back and sides of a 200- to 250,000-year-old skull associated with hundreds of beautifully made hand axes. Unfortunately the face is missing, but the brain size is considerably larger than that of *Homo erectus* (Ovey, 1964; Roe, 1981). There are several other skulls, like Steinheim in Germany, which suggest that the transition to *Homo sapiens neanderthalis* (the Neanderthals) was completed by 100,000 years ago.

There were no Neanderthals in Africa, but some scientists believe that modern humans evolved there, then spread to the rest of the world via the Near East. Part of a modern form of human skullcap came from the

Border Cave in South Africa and has been dated to 115,000 years. By no means everyone accepts the Border Cave date, but it does highlight the two contrasting hypotheses about the emergence of modern humans:

"The replacement model" believes that modern humans evolved in a single isolated population, which then spread throughout the Old World. The newcomers replaced earlier populations through competition or out-and-out confrontation.

In contrast, the "local continuity model" argues that various populations of archaic *Homo sapiens* populated the Old World by 100,000 years ago. Each evolved independently into fully modern people.

In all probability, both models are too simplistic. The transition from *Homo erectus* to *Homo sapiens* and from archaic to fully modern *Homo sapiens* was a very complicated interaction of the many evolutionary processes that come into play when a single species evolves rapidly. It probably combined elements from both models, and other processes as well. Whatever hypothesis finally emerges from the present confusion, it will have to take account of one indisputable fact: modern humanity displays a remarkable genetic and morphological homogeneity.

The Neanderthals

These so-called early *Homo sapiens* finds are modern looking compared with a primitive skull found at Neanderthal in West Germany in 1856, a discovery that caused a sensation at the time and still generates academic debate today (Huxley, 1863). Despite Neanderthal's primitive appearance, the remains postdate *Homo erectus* by more than 150,000 years. In the century since the first Neanderthal skull was found, substantial numbers of Neanderthal individuals have been unearthed, most of them in western Europe, as well as contemporary human fossils from the Near East, Africa, and Asia. The Neanderthal people are now recognized as *Homo sapiens neanderthalensis*, a subspecies of *Homo sapiens* (Figure 5.10)

Neanderthals first appeared during the Eem interglacial, but they were not widespread. Large Neanderthal sites have been found in the Dordogne area, France, where deep river valleys and vast limestone cliffs offered abundant shelter during the Weichsel glaciation. One site is the cave of Le Moustier near Les Eyzies (Bordes, 1968). The Neanderthal skeletons found in French caves look like anatomical anachronisms, with massive brow ridges and squat bodies (Figure 5.11). They walked upright and as nimbly as modern humans. They stood just over 153 cm (5 ft) high, and their forearms were relatively short compared with modern people. This "classic" variety of Neanderthal is confined to western Europe and is more noticeably different from *Homo sapiens* than its contemporary populations found elsewhere, especially around the shores of the Mediterranean and in Asia (Figure 5.3, p. 119). We find much variability among Neanderthals, who most often display less extreme features than

Neanderthals
?100,000 to 35,000
B.C.

Le Moustier
?70,000 B.C.

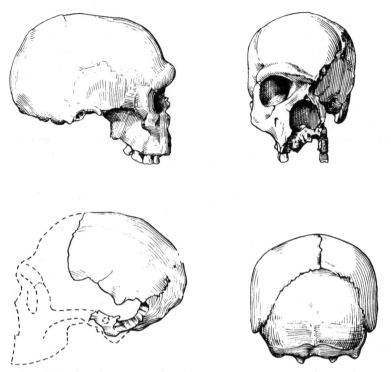

Figure 5.10 The Steinheim (top) and Swanscombe (bottom) skulls (one-fourth actual size). The Swanscombe skull is shown with a tentative reconstruction of the missing parts.

the classic variety of western France. This variability shows in less extreme brow ridges and other cranial features. It is well demonstrated at the Mount Carmel sites of et-Tabūn and es-Skhūl in Israel as well as at Krapina in central Europe (Trinkhaus and Howells, 1979).

Theories about *Homo Sapiens*

The *Homo sapiens neanderthalensis* from the Eem interglacial are the earliest fossils of *Homo sapiens* that are not archaic forms. The first completely modern humans, with high foreheads, no brow ridges, and entirely contemporary features appear in the archaeological record approximately 35,000 years ago and are classified as *Homo sapiens sapiens*. The morphological differences apparent between many Neanderthals and modern *Homo sapiens* are startling. How do these heavily built, beetle-browed people fit into the picture of human evolution? The great French physical anthropologist Marcellin Boule believed, in the 1930s, that the classic Neanderthals were clumsy, shambling people, so specialized that they became extinct while other populations provided the evolutionary basis for modern humans (Figure 5.12) (Boule and Vallois, 1957). Eric Trinkhaus and William Howells (1979) have recently re-

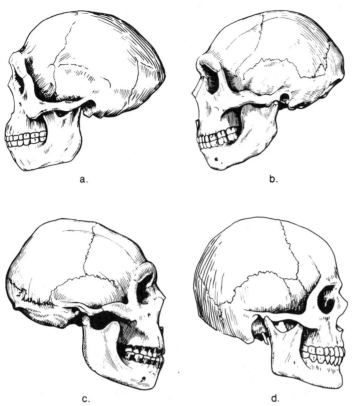

Figure 5.11 Comparisons of four fossil skulls and jaws. (a) The reconstructed *Homo erectus* skull has prominent brow ridges, a bun-shaped rear to the cranium, and a retreating chin. (b) A "classic" Neanderthal skull found at Monte Circeo, Italy, still has well-marked brow ridges and a bun-shaped cranium, but an increased brain capacity. The skull is lower and flatter than those of modern humans, and the jaw is chinless. (c) The Shanidar Neanderthal from Iraq is a less extreme example, with a higher forehead, somewhat reduced brow ridges, and a much more rounded skull. (d) Modern skull with well-rounded contours, no brow ridges, high forehead, and a well-marked chin.

viewed Neanderthal populations from all over Europe and the Near East and point out that their anatomical pattern took approximately fifty millennia from 100,000 years ago to evolve, then stabilized for another fifty before changing rapidly to essentially modern human anatomy within a brief period of 5000 years approximately 40,000 years ago. They point out that Boule was mistaken, partly because his definitive studies were made on an elderly individual suffering from arthritis and partly because much more skeletal material is now available. The Neanderthals had the same posture, manual abilities, and range and characteristics of movement as modern people. They differed from us in having massive limb bones, often somewhat bowed in the thigh and forearm, features that reflect the Neanderthals' greater muscular power. For their height, the Neanderthals were bulky, heavily muscled people, and their brain capacity

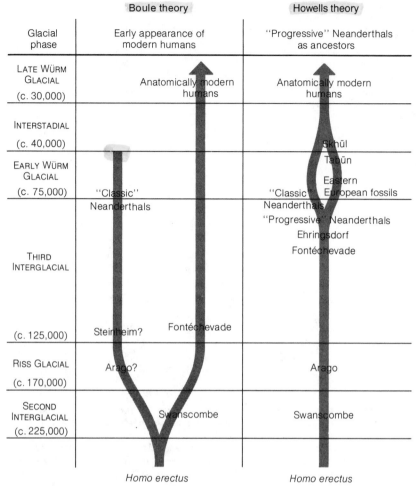

Glacial phase	**Boule theory** Early appearance of modern humans	**Howells theory** "Progressive" Neanderthals as ancestors
LATE WÜRM GLACIAL (c. 30,000)	Anatomically modern humans	Anatomically modern humans
INTERSTADIAL (c. 40,000)		Skhūl
EARLY WÜRM GLACIAL (c. 75,000)	"Classic" Neanderthals	Tabūn Eastern European fossils "Classic" Neanderthals "Progressive" Neanderthals Ehringsdorf Fontéchevade
THIRD INTERGLACIAL (c. 125,000)	Steinheim? Fontéchevade	
RISS GLACIAL (c. 170,000)	Arago?	Arago
SECOND INTERGLACIAL (c. 225,000)	Swanscombe	Swanscombe
	Homo erectus	*Homo erectus*

Figure 5.12   Alternative hypotheses of the evolution of *Homo sapiens:* on the left, the Boule theory; on the right, the Howells theory. A third theory, which sees the classic Neanderthals as direct ancestors of modern humanity, is omitted here because few people now subscribe to it.

was slightly larger than that of modern humans, not because of greater intelligence but because of heavier musculature. Their antecedents are in the *Homo erectus* group, from which they inherited their heavy build, an adaptation so successful that it has lasted for more than 100,000 years.

Why did they suddenly disappear with the coming of *Homo sapiens sapiens?* There are two major viewpoints. The first purports that modern people evolved in one homeland and then spread into other parts of the world, wiping out Neanderthal populations on the way by confrontation or competition. This hypothesis suffers from the weakness that no one has yet found a site where the killed skeletons of Neanderthals have been found in association with the tools of modern humans, nor is there any evidence of a homeland for the first modern populations. Furthermore, populations of modern, although not European, form occupied Australia and sub-Saharan Africa as early as 40,000 years ago, while Neanderthals were still flourishing in the north.

A second hypothesis argues that the Neanderthals evolved directly and at once into the anatomically modern people of the Upper Paleolithic. Again, we are hampered by lack of fossil evidence. Some Neanderthal populations, notably those from the Mount Carmel caves of Israel (Howells, 1957a, b) and from Czechoslovakia (Trinkhaus and Howells, 1979), show great anatomical variation, to the extent that some of them are almost identical to modern *Homo sapiens*. However, the true transitional forms still elude the archaeologist's spade. In evolutionary terms, it seems most likely that some populations of modern *Homo sapiens* evolved in relative isolation, perhaps in Europe and the Near East. Still, we do not know what selective forces favored the modern physique over the Neanderthal one. Some people have argued for climatic change, but the Weichsel glaciation reached its height after the emergence of modern people. Ecological change also has been cited, but the Neanderthals and their successors hunted the same animals and gathered the same foods. Upper Paleolithic technology is different from that of the Neanderthals but not extremely different, for the new tools have few advantages over their predecessors in terms of hunting and gathering. Perhaps there appeared a threshold in human subsistence patterns that can be detected only in tool technology, a threshold that made the bulky Neanderthal physique unnecessary and inefficient in terms of its food requirements. Perhaps, too, the new toolkits and associated behavioral changes gave significant adaptive advantage to Upper Paleolithic people. One thing is certain: Between approximately 40,000 and 35,000 years ago, there was a quantum jump in the complexity of human society, including the advent of much more elaborate social and ritual practices and the emergence of flourishing art styles. It may have been these changes that had a significant influence on the biological evolution of the Neanderthals.

HOMO SAPIENS ADAPTS

Although many details of the biological evolution of early *Homo sapiens* remain unresolved, we know a great deal about the many and diverse adaptations of these people. Their distinctive hunter-gatherer culture, which continued in the basic hominid tradition, is known from hundreds of sites in Africa, Asia, and Europe. The Neanderthals' *Mousterian* technology (named after the Le Moustier rock shelter in southwest France) was far more complex and sophisticated than its Acheulian predecessor, with many regional variations (Trinkhaus, 1983a). Many of the Neanderthals' artifacts were made for specific purposes (Figure 5.13). Like their *erectus* predecessors, the early *Homo sapiens* bands occupied large territories which they probably exploited on a seasonal round, returning to

Mousterian culture
?100,000 to 40,000
B.C. (Chapter 6)

Figure 5.13 Middle Paleolithic tools. Middle Paleolithic stone technology was based on more sophisticated concepts than those of earlier times. Now artifacts of many types were *composite* form—they were made from several different parts. A wooden spear might have a stone tip; a flint scraper, a bone handle. Unfortunately, we know almost nothing about bone and wood tools used.

The points, scrapers, and other stone tools were often manufactured by careful preparation of the core from which they were struck. Prepared cores were carefully flaked to enable the toolmaker to strike off large flakes of predetermined size. One form used was a Levallois core. The stoneworker would shape a lump of flint into an inverted bun-shaped core (often compared to an inverted tortoise shell). The flat upper surface would be struck at one end, the resulting flake forming the only product from the core. Another form was the disc core, a prepared core from which several flakes of predetermined size and shape were removed. The core gradually became smaller, until it resembled a flat disc. Disc cores were often used to produce points and scrapers.

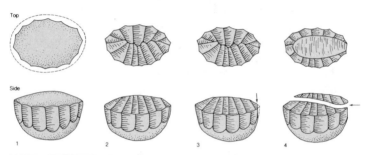

Making a Levallois core: (1) the edges of a suitable stone are trimmed; (2) then the top surface is trimmed; (3) a striking platform is made, the point where the flake will originate, by trimming to form a straight edge on the side; (4) a flake is struck from the core, and the flake removed.

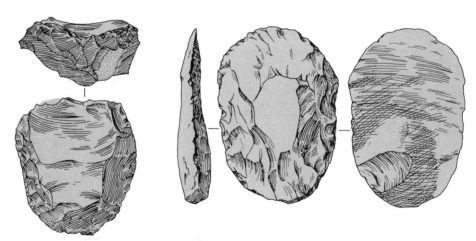

A Levallois core from the Thames valley, England (left), with the top of the core (bottom), shown from above and the end view shown above it. A typical Levallois flake is shown at the right: upper surface (center), lower (flake) surface (right), cross section (left). Both artifacts are one-third actual size.

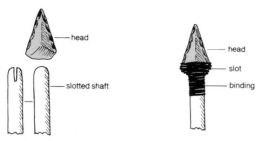

Stone-tipped Mousterian spear (a hypothetical example). The spear was made by attaching a pointed stone head to a wooden handle to form the projectile. The head probably fitted into a slot in the wooden shaft and was fixed to it with resin or beeswax; a binding was added to the end of the shaft.

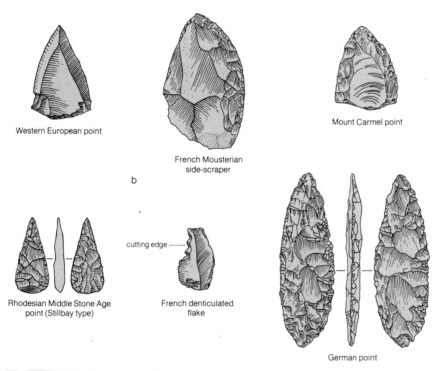

Western European point

French Mousterian
side-scraper

b

Mount Carmel point

Rhodesian Middle Stone Age
point (Stillbay type)

cutting edge

French denticulated
flake

German point

Typical artifacts, all approximately one-half actual size.

the same locations year after year when game migrated or vegetables came into season. The Neanderthals were skilled hunters who were not afraid to pursue large game animals like the mammoth as well as reindeer and wild horses. They also caught birds and fish. It appears that many western European bands lived in caves and rock shelters during much of the year as a protection against arctic cold. During the summer months they may have fanned out over the tundra plains, living in temporary tented encampments. African hunter-gatherers developed woodworking toolkits for use in dense rain forests as well as on open savannah.

Mousterian Technology

Mousterian technology differs radically from earlier toolmaking traditions, both in its techniques and complexity. The Neanderthals were the first to use:

Prepared core techniques, notably the Levallois and disc core methods of producing flake blanks of standard size for reworking into specific tools (Figure 5.13)

Composite tools, artifacts made of more than one component — for example, a spear point, the spear shaft, and the binding that secured the head to the shaft, making a spear

For the most part, Mousterian artifacts were made of flakes, the most characteristic artifacts being points and scraping tools. The edges of both points and scrapers were sharpened by fine trimming, the removal of small, steplike chips from the edge of the implement. These artifacts, almost universally distributed in Middle Paleolithic sites, were used in the chase, in woodworking, and in preparing skins.

The complexity of Mousterian technology is striking. This is well illustrated by the French sites, which have yielded a great diversity of Mousterian artifacts and toolkits. Some levels include hand axes; others, notched flakes, perhaps used for stripping meat for drying or pressing fibrous plants. Subdivisions of Mousterian technology have been identified by the prevalence of specific tool types. The French archaeologist François Bordes identified five traditions which he says represent the work of five distinct bands who were living in one territory at the same time (Bordes, 1968).

Not everyone agrees with Bordes. British archaeologist Paul Mellars hypothesizes that Mousterian technology evolved slowly through time and that the variations in toolkits were the result of slow cultural change with various tools (such as the side scraper or hand ax) in fashion at different times. This, he feels, is a more likely explanation than ethnic differences or different activities (Mellars, 1979). In contrast, Sally and Lewis Binford argue that Bordes's traditions reflect various distinct activities carried out within the same cultural system at different times of the year (Binford and Binford, 1966). In all probability, there is some truth in all these hypotheses. People were developing tools for different activities far more quickly than ever before, perhaps at a time of increasing social complexity. For the first time, diversity in lifeway was possible.

Figure 5.3 (p. 119) shows the distribution of Mousterian and related cultures in the Old World. Although Middle Paleolithic technology is referred to by many regional labels, the basic technological devices differed little from one area to another.

THE ORIGINS OF BURIAL AND RELIGIOUS BELIEF

Although the Neanderthals were still hunter-gatherers and the world's population still small, life was gradually becoming more complex. We find the first signs of religious ideology, of a preoccupation with the life hereafter. Many Neanderthals were buried by their companions. Neanderthal burials have been recovered from the deposits of rock shelters and caves as well as from open campsites. Single burials are the most common, normally accompanied by flint implements, food offerings, or even cooked game meat (evidenced by charred bones). One band of Siberian mountain goat hunters lived at Teshik-Tash in the western foothills of the Himalayas. They buried one of their children in a shallow pit, surrounding the child's body with six pairs of wild goat horns (Klein, 1969).

Burials at Teshik-Tash

Another remarkable single burial came from Shanidar cave in the Zagros Mountains of Iraq (Trinkhaus, 1983b). There a thirty-year-old man (born, incidentally, with a useless right arm) was crushed by a rockfall from the roof of the cave. He was buried in a shallow pit. Other single graves from France and central Europe were covered with red ochre powder.

Shanidar

One rock shelter, La Ferrassie near Les Eyzies in France, yielded the remains of two adult Neanderthals and four children buried close together in a campsite (Peyrony, 1934). Group sepulchres occur at other sites, too, more signs that the Neanderthals, like most living hunter-gatherers, believed in life after death. They may also have had beliefs that coincided with deliberate burial, but details will always remain hypothetical.

La Ferrassie

Some glimmers of insight into Neanderthal beliefs may come from their remarkable bear cults. The Neanderthals were skillful hunters who were not afraid to go after cave bears, which were about the size of Alaskan brown bears and weighed perhaps up to three-quarters of a ton. Like some modern northern hunters, the Neanderthals had a bear cult, known to us from bear skulls that were deliberately buried with ceremony. The most remarkable find was at Regourdou in southern France, where a rectangular pit lined with stones held the skulls of at least twenty cave bears (Howell, 1974). The burial pit was covered with a huge stone

Rituals at Regourdou

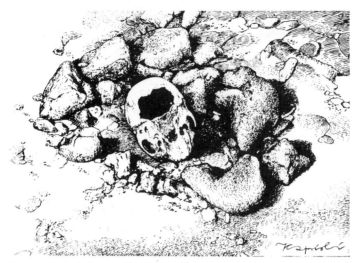

Figure 5.14 In the Guattari Cave of Monte Circeo, a human skull was found lying base upward in the center of a ring of stones. The condition of the skull, as well as other artifacts in the cave, gives evidence of a sacrificial murder.

slab. Nearby lay the entire skeleton of one of the bears. It seems likely that the cave bear became an integral part of these hunters' mythology, an object of reverence and an animal with a special place in the world.

Monte Circeo

Evidence of an even more remarkable ritual appeared in the depths of the Guattari Cave at Monte Circeo, 60 mi south of Rome. A Neanderthal skull was found in an isolated inner chamber surrounded by a circle of stones (Blanc, 1961). The base of the skull lay upward, mutilated in such a way that the brain could be reached. The right side of the skull was smashed in by violent blows. Near the circle of stones lay three piles of bones, from red deer, cattle, and pigs (Figure 5.14). Although ingenious explanations for this curious ritual have been proposed, we shall never know why this sacrificial victim was killed and beheaded outside the cave, his head then laid out as the centerpiece of an important ritual. Like the bear cult, cannibalism and other hunting rituals appear to have been part of human life and subsistence. We find in Neanderthals and their culture the first roots of our own complicated beliefs, societies, and religious sense.

GUIDE TO FURTHER READING

Bordes, François. *The Old Stone Age*. New York: McGraw-Hill, 1968.
A simple manual on the Paleolithic period that covers basic tool types and technologies. Invaluable for the beginning student.

Constable, George. *The Neanderthals*. New York: Time-Life Books, 1973.
A volume in the Time-Life Emergence of Man series that covers the major

THE FIRST HUMANS

controversies and discoveries surrounding the Neanderthals up to the early 1970s. Very well illustrated.

Leakey, Richard, and Lewin, Roger. *Origins*. New York: Dutton, 1977.
A vivid, if somewhat controversial, account of Lower Paleolithic life, emphasizing East African discoveries.

Pfeiffer, John. *The Emergence of Man* (3rd ed.). New York: Harper & Row, 1978.
An articulate and complete account of early human evolution that focuses on behavior and culture as well as fossils.

PART THREE

HUNTER-GATHERERS
(40,000 B.C. to Modern Times)

"There is a passion for hunting something deeply implanted in the human breast."
– Charles Dickens, *Pickwick Papers,* 1836–37, Chapter 10

In this section we describe numerous cultural adaptations by hunter-gatherers and the first settlement of Australia and the New World.

Chronological Table C

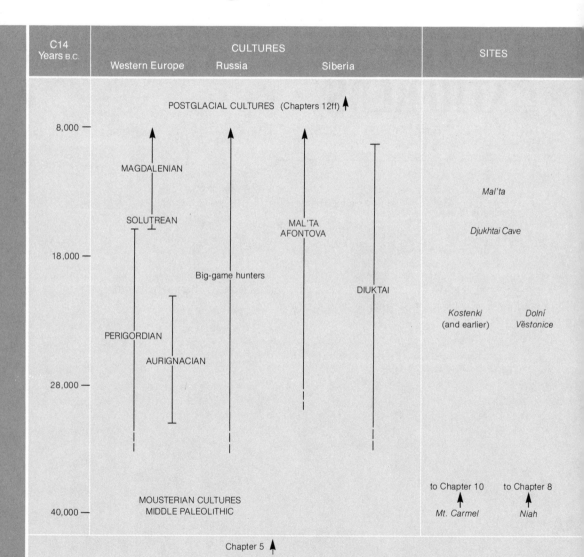

C14 Years B.C.	CULTURES			SITES
	Western Europe	Russia	Siberia	

POSTGLACIAL CULTURES (Chapters 12ff)

8,000 —

MAGDALENIAN

Mal'ta

SOLUTREAN · MAL'TA AFONTOVA

Djukhtai Cave

18,000 —

Big-game hunters

DIUKTAI

Kostenki (and earlier) · *Dolní Věstonice*

PERIGORDIAN

AURIGNACIAN

28,000 —

to Chapter 10 · to Chapter 8

MOUSTERIAN CULTURES
MIDDLE PALEOLITHIC

40,000 —

Mt. Carmel · *Niah*

Chapter 5

Chapter Six

Europeans and Northern Asians
(40,000 to 8000 B.C.)

PREVIEW

❦ The emergence of *Homo sapiens sapiens* saw the development of many and diverse hunter-gatherer adaptations to the world's environments. The more specialized hunter-gatherer societies that flourished after 40,000 B.C. developed more elaborate toolkits; these toolkits contained regularly shaped, parallel-sided stone blades as well as bone and antler implements. This technology is named Upper Paleolithic.

❦ Western Europe was the home of some of the richest Upper Paleolithic cultures, of peoples adapted to an arctic environment in which hunting reindeer and other migratory game was important. These people lived in rock shelters and caves for much of the year and developed a magnificent art tradition of bone artifacts and decorated cave walls. They flourished from approximately 35,000 B.C. until the end of the Weichsel glaciation approximately 8000 years ago. When the ice sheets retreated, these Europeans turned to more specialized hunting and gathering in which fishing and fowling played an important part.

❦ Upper Paleolithic peoples of the Russian plains developed a distinctive mammoth and big-game hunting tradition adapted to the harsh climate. After 25,000 B.C. they lived in large dwellings of skins and mammoth bones.

❦ The earliest settlement of Siberia and northeast Asia is still undated, but people are thought to have settled there by 30,000 years ago. Most archeologists agree that the first Americans came from this cultural background, but the evidence is incomplete.

In the final analysis, the long millennia of prehistory have seen human-kind become ever more efficient at extracting energy from its environment. The first hominids branched out into unfamiliar environments that took them away from an almost total dependence on forest fruit. *Homo habilis* was a scavenger as well as a collector, perhaps even an occasional hunter, a lifeway that further deepened the scope of our predecessors' lives. *Homo erectus* was an active big game hunter, who relied heavily on a cooperating social group for success in the chase. Once they

Chronological table C

143

became serious hunters, people could tap rich supplies of energy-rich meat, as well as vegetable foods. But hunters were, at first, yet another carnivore in a world well populated by successful carnivores. The transition to the new lifeway must have been slow, at times painful, and may have occurred in several stages. There can be little doubt that increased efficiency as a carnivore played an important role in the emergence of both archaic *Homo sapiens* and modern *Homo sapiens sapiens*. It may even be that this vital transition altered the relationships between humans and the natural environment. This chapter chronicles some of these changes and looks at the vigorous hunter-gatherer cultures that flourished in the northern parts of the Old World between 40,000 and 8000 B.C. (Figure 6.1 shows sites in Chapters Six and Eight) (Lewin, 1984).

INCREASED EFFICIENCY

Is there any evidence for humanity becoming a more efficient carnivore after 40,000 years ago, when *Homo sapiens sapiens* first emerged? Some fascinating indications come from coastal caves in South Africa, among

Figure 6.1 Map showing archaeological sites mentioned in this chapter and Chapter Eight.

them Klasies River Mouth and Nelson Bay (R. Klein, 1979). Klein found that the people who inhabited these caves lived not only off vegetable foods but off game and marine resources as well. Klasies River was occupied between about 130,000 and 75,000 years ago, then abandoned until about 5000 years ago. The early inhabitants collected limpets and also pursued seals and penguins. But they took few fish; they preferred game on the hoof, especially such docile animals as the eland and bastard hartebeest. They did kill some more formidable beasts like the buffalo, black wildebeest, and roan antelope but in much smaller numbers, and some of the meat was perhaps scavenged. Interestingly, the bones of these individual species came from either very old or young individuals, which is the sort of age pattern found with predator kills. Only the eland and bastard hartebeest were taken at all ages. Klein believes that they may have been driven into traps or over cliffs.

The Nelson Bay Cave was occupied by modern *Homo sapiens* populations after 15,000 years ago. Again, eland and bastard hartebeest were common, taken at all ages, perhaps using game drives. But the Nelson Bay folk took bush pits and warthogs, much fiercer and more formidable prey. Not only that, they used nets and fish hooks to catch a wide range of ocean fish. They also lived off flying sea birds like cormorants. One could argue, of course, that the Klasies River people simply preferred game on the hoof, but the relative abundance of wild pigs strongly suggests that the Nelson Bay hunters were much more expert and capable of exploiting a far wider range of game. They may have used the bow and arrow, although there is as yet no evidence of this from Nelson's Bay. While the eland lives in widely dispersed herds, other antelope do not and would have been much more vulnerable to efficient hunting. Klein notes that several large mammal species became extinct 12,000 to 10,000 years ago, an event that cannot be accounted for by environmental changes alone. It seems possible that *Homo sapiens* was the destroyer, altering for the first time the delicate ecological balance between humans and their natural environment. One should note that there were large-scale big game extinctions in North America, too, only a few millennia after hunter-gatherer populations expanded rapidly.

In some parts of the world, the changeover from archaic to modern *Homo sapiens* was a rapid, even dramatic, one. Fifty thousand years ago, the Mousterian culture flourished over much of the Old World. Then, around 40,000 years ago, a sharp biological and technological break appeared throughout western and central Europe. So radical a change was not found anywhere else in the world at that time, but biological change does not necessarily coincide with technological innovation. The biological break was the first appearance of *Homo sapiens sapiens*, the technological break was the appearance of numerous specialized tools for the chase, for bone and woodworking, and for many other activities. These toolkits played an important part in hunter-gatherers' increased ability to influence their environment, and in a sharp rise in the efficiency of their lifeway. It is during the past 40,000 years, and especially during the past 15,000, that specialized hunting and gathering developed in many parts of the world (Bailey, 1983).

SPECIALIZED HUNTING AND GATHERING

"Specialized" hunting and gathering implies concentration on a limited number of natural resources to the exclusion of many others. Examples of specialized hunter-gatherers are the Plains Indians of North America, who concentrated on the buffalo, and the Pacific Northwest coast peoples, expert fisherfolk, who were able to acquire large food surpluses by exploiting seasonal salmon runs and other fish species.

Many specialized hunter-gatherers concentrated heavily on wild vegetable foods. In fact, gathering has always been of major importance to hunter-gatherers. Kay Martin and Barbara Voorhies (1975), who studied ninety hunting and gathering societies, found that 75% of them relied more heavily on collecting than on hunting. Only a quarter were predominantly hunters. The importance of gathering has been dramatized by Richard Lee's researches among the present-day !Kung San of the Kalahari Desert in South Africa (Lee, 1979). He found that the !Kung live in an inhospitable, dry woodland environment where game is now rare. They gather the nutritious mangetti nut as a primary food all year round. The remaining vegetable foods are selected from at least eighty-five edible species known to the !Kung, of which only eight are major foods (Figure 6.2). All of them are seasonal favorites, one is a root that provides water at times of the year when people have to venture far afield in search of food, away from water supplies. So plentiful are edible vegetable foods that the !Kung San have two choices when favorite species become exhausted: eat less desirable foods near home, or walk farther, perhaps shifting their camp. Long before the least desirable foods are eaten, the people have moved to a new site.

Few hunters and gatherers are left, and it is difficult to know whether the !Kung life of relative security and leisure is typical of most prehistoric hunter-gatherers. We can be sure that some groups, such as the reindeer hunters of southwestern France 15,000 years ago, were far better off in terms of potential food sources than other groups living in less favorable environments. What is revealing, however, is the efficient way in which the !Kung relate to their environment, for this is surely typical of all *Homo sapiens sapiens* hunter-gatherer societies, probably to an even greater extent than in earlier millennia. The !Kung know their environment intimately, and they know what to expect from it. They can gather their food when they need it and do not have to store it for days. This subsistence strategy is a conservative adaptation, based on plants and animals that come back naturally year after year. Hunter-gatherers tend to put in a constant amount of work, unlike the agriculturalists' sharply seasonal activity of planting and harvest. One of the most striking features of the hunter-gatherer lifeway wherever it can still be observed is its

Figure 6.2 !Kung women gathering food.

flexibility, both in food gathering and in a social organization normally based on the small band and the nuclear family. Perhaps it was this flexibility and resulting built-in insurance against lean years that made hunting and gathering the most lasting of all human lifeways.

NEANDERTHALS AND *HOMO SAPIENS SAPIENS*

The sudden disappearance of the Neanderthals and their replacement by modern humans has sparked some of the most vigorous controversies in archaeology — and some scintillating, if speculative, popular novels. How did the Neanderthals become extinct? Were they attacked and killed by more anatomically advanced newcomers? Did they themselves evolve into *Homo sapiens sapiens?* It is hardly surprising that the fossil record gives us no clues. While some of the more pronounced facial features of the classic Neanderthals like their brow ridges do begin to recede in some later populations, this is far from a conclusive sign that the one population gave way to the other. And the first *Homo sapiens sapiens* populations, like the famous Cro-Magnon people of southwestern France, while robustly built, show no anatomical signs that can be called transitional from the Neanderthals (Figure 6.3). Their robustness still lies within the range of variation of modern populations, albeit at the robust end. It seems most likely that *Homo sapiens sapiens* replaced *Homo neanderthalis* rather than evolving from them (Ronen, 1982).

Homo sapiens sapiens may have evolved from early *Homo sapiens*, and ultimately from *Homo erectus*, by phyletic change and by hybridization from earlier populations that displayed considerable variation. Many of

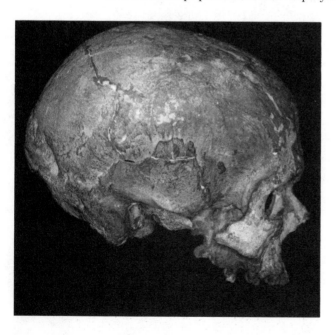

Figure 6.3 *Homo sapiens sapiens* from Cro-Magnon rock shelter, Les Eyzies, France, dating to between 35,000 and 40,000 years ago. (Courtesy of Milford Wolpoff)

the predecessors of *Homo sapiens* displayed only moderately developed brow ridges and well-rounded skullcaps, so that they are virtually indistinguishable from their modern descendants. This variation in skull form is well documented in the caves of Mount Carmel, Israel (Garrod and Bate, 1937; Ronen, 1982), and also by an isolated specimen of *Homo sapiens sapiens* from the Niah Cave in Borneo which was carbon dated to at least 40,000 B.C.

UPPER PALEOLITHIC TECHNOLOGY

The final chapter of human biological evolution was accompanied by considerable technological changes, which were not as drastic as those separating, say, the Acheulian and the Mousterian, but which, nevertheless increased the number of tools in the human toolkit very dramatically. The Acheulians used but a couple dozen simple artifacts, the Mousterians only a few more. The Upper Paleolithic hunter-gatherers developed over a hundred different identifiable tools, many of them, like harpoons, sinew-straighteners, and graving devices, with highly specialized uses.

The final chapter of this biological evolution was accompanied by major technological changes that, in their way, were as radical as the emergence of the humans who made them. These cultural changes are still imperfectly documented, except in the great caves and rock shelters of the Near East such as et-Tabūn and Mugharet el-Wad at Mount Carmel, Israel, and at Shanidar in Iraq. These sites were visited almost continuously by hunter-gatherer bands from Mousterian times more than 70,000 years ago right up to modern times. The Mousterian levels at these sites contain tens of thousands of carefully retouched points and side scrapers, as well as the bones of large deer and wild cattle (Marks, 1983). These layers are covered by further occupation levels containing different toolkits that gradually replace earlier artifact forms and technologies. In these, the long, parallel-sided blades that were the first stage in making stone tools were removed from cylindrical flint cores with a punch and a hammer-stone (Figure 6.4). Some blades were up to 15.2 cc (6 in) long; the tools made from them varied greatly, many of them designed for specific tasks and, in later millennia, mounted in handles.

Upper Paleolithic technology, summarized in Figure 6.4, flourished during the later millennia of the Weichsel glaciation, from approximately 35,000 years ago. Among its major innovations were:

The use of punchstruck blades.

Much greater reliance on composite tools, that is to say, one tool *joined* (hafted) to another artifact such as stone-tipped spears, harpoons, and spear-throwers (Table 6.1). The bow and arrow was the culminating innovation, one that appeared late in the Weichsel.

The use of a much wider range of toolmaking materials, including antler and bone.

Figure 6.4 Upper Paleolithic tools. The stoneworking technology required for Upper Paleolithic tools was based on punchstruck blades. Various methods were used to strike off the blades, using a handheld or chest-impelled punch to produce parallel-sided blades to make tools. The punch allows intense pressure to be applied to a single point on the top of the core and channels the direction of the shock waves. Parallel-sided blades were made into a variety of tools, among them burins and scrapers, which were typical of all stages of the Upper Paleolithic. Burins were used for grooving wood, bone, and particularly antlers, which were made into spears and harpoon points. The chisel ends of burins were formed by taking an oblique or longitudinal flake off the end of a blade. Burins also were used to engrave figures. End scrapers were used on wood and bone as well as skins.

Upper Paleolithic technology was based to a great extent on composite tools, of which the stone elements were only a part. Some blade tools were used by themselves, however, for the blade offered a convenient and standardized way of making many fairly specialized artifacts. See also Table 6.1.

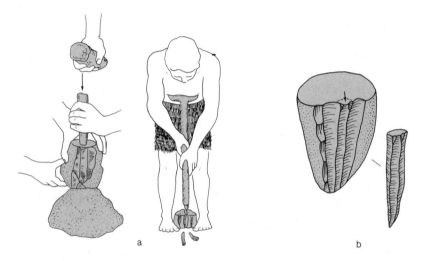

(a) Two punch techniques and (b) a typical product, a core and a blade struck from it. The dotted line and arrow show the point where the next blade will be struck off from the core.

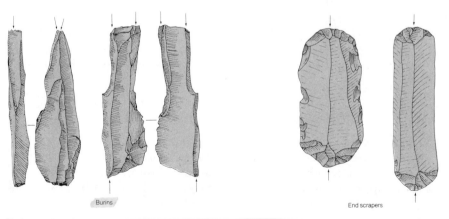

Burins

End scrapers

Burins and end scrapers. Arrows indicate the chisel ends of burins and the scraping edges of the end scrapers.

Skin, horns, hair, and other by-products from game went into housing, clothes, lighting, and coloring. Skins were sewn together with threads; weaving and plaiting were done probably for the first time. Flexible sewn materials make a tent a far more effective shelter than the crude and chilly windbreak of grass or branches. Skin boats for pursuing large sea mammals and deep-sea fish are another innovation made by sewing.

The result of these innovations was a dramatic explosion in diversity of cultures and toolkits, most of them fine tuned to local needs. We cannot possibly describe the full richness of hunter-gatherer peoples who flourished in all parts of the globe after 33,000 B.C., so our narrative concentrates on these major developments:

> The hunter-gatherer cultures that flourished in southwest France during the period 33,000 to 8000 B.C. These cultures are of particular importance because of their arctic adaptation to the last cold snap of the Weichsel glaciation and because of their remarkable artistic traditions.
>
> The big-game hunting cultures that developed on the West Russian plains and Siberia.
>
> The early settlement of the arctic latitudes of northeast Asia from which the first settlement of the New World may have developed.
>
> The first human settlement of the Americas and the cultural traditions that stemmed from it.
>
> The early history of surviving hunter-gatherers in tropical latitudes, especially the Australians and the San peoples of Southern Africa.

EUROPEAN HUNTER-GATHERERS: 33,000 to 8000 B.C.

The emergence of the new Upper Paleolithic technologies is partially documented in the great caves of Mount Carmel in the relatively benign climate of the Near East (Garrod and Bate, 1937; Ronen, 1982). For thousands of years after 40,000 B.C. the inhabitants of this area hunted gazelle and other mammals and practiced a way of life that changed little for over 25,000 years. As their hunting and gathering became more and more specialized, their toolkits became smaller and more locally adaptive to the gathering of cereal grasses or to the intensive hunting of a single animal. We will examine the later prehistory of the Near East in much more detail in Parts Four and Five; here in Part Three, we are concerned with the flowering of the hunter-gatherer culture, which took place most dramatically in northern latitudes. The dramatic fluctuations in northern areas of Weichsel climate, from arctic cold to periods of more temperate weather and then back to bitter cold, caused human societies to make constant changes in their adaptations to what was a rich and diverse natural environment for hunter-gatherers.

Between 35,000 and 8000 B.C., the caves and rock shelters of southwestern France and northern Spain housed some of the most elaborate

Later levels of Mt. Carmel **40,000 to 8000 B.C.**

Table 6.1 Much simplified table showing the Upper Paleolithic cultural traditions of western Europe from 40,000 to 8000 B.C.

The most commonly accepted scheme, that of French archeologists, has two parallel cultural traditions, the Perigordian and Aurignacian, flourishing in western Europe between approximately 30,000 and 23,000 B.C. The Perigordian possessed a technology that produced dozens of backed knife blades, while the Aurignacian favored scrapers and sharpened blades. The Perigordian gave way to the Aurignacian for a considerable period before the former returned to prominence after 23,000 B.C.

The Solutrean is characterized by beautifully made lanceheads that were executed by pressure flaking flint blades. No one knows why these artifacts came into fashion, but they must have fulfilled some specific need, and, like so many innovations, must have enjoyed a brief period of popularity before the Magdalenians began to rely more heavily on bone and antler tools.

It should be noted that all Upper Paleolithic cultures in this area relied heavily on blade technology and on scrapers, burins, and other simple blade artifacts that were common to all cultures.

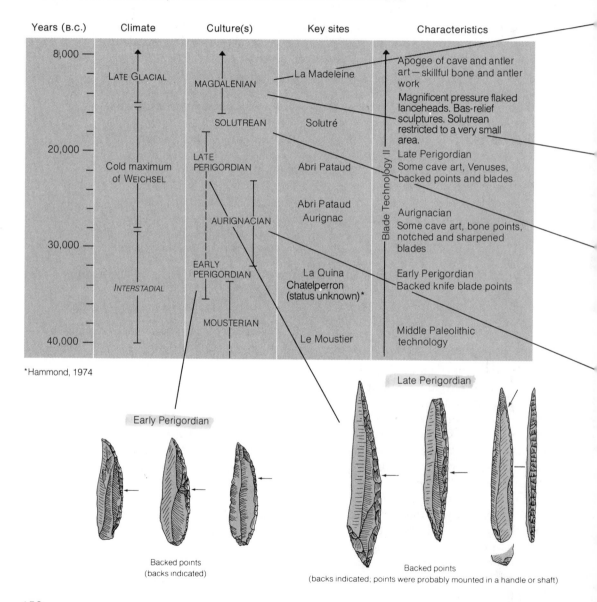

Years (B.C.)	Climate	Culture(s)	Key sites	Characteristics
8,000	LATE GLACIAL	MAGDALENIAN	La Madeleine	Apogee of cave and antler art — skillful bone and antler work
		SOLUTREAN	Solutré	Magnificent pressure flaked lanceheads. Bas-relief sculptures. Solutrean restricted to a very small area.
20,000	Cold maximum of WEICHSEL	LATE PERIGORDIAN	Abri Pataud	Late Perigordian Some cave art, Venuses, backed points and blades
			Abri Pataud Aurignac	Aurignacian Some cave art, bone points, notched and sharpened blades
30,000		AURIGNACIAN		
	INTERSTADIAL	EARLY PERIGORDIAN	La Quina Chatelperron (status unknown)*	Early Perigordian Backed knife blade points
40,000		MOUSTERIAN	Le Moustier	Middle Paleolithic technology

(Blade Technology II — vertical label along right side of table)

*Hammond, 1974

Early Perigordian

Backed points
(backs indicated)

Late Perigordian

Backed points
(backs indicated; points were probably mounted in a handle or shaft)

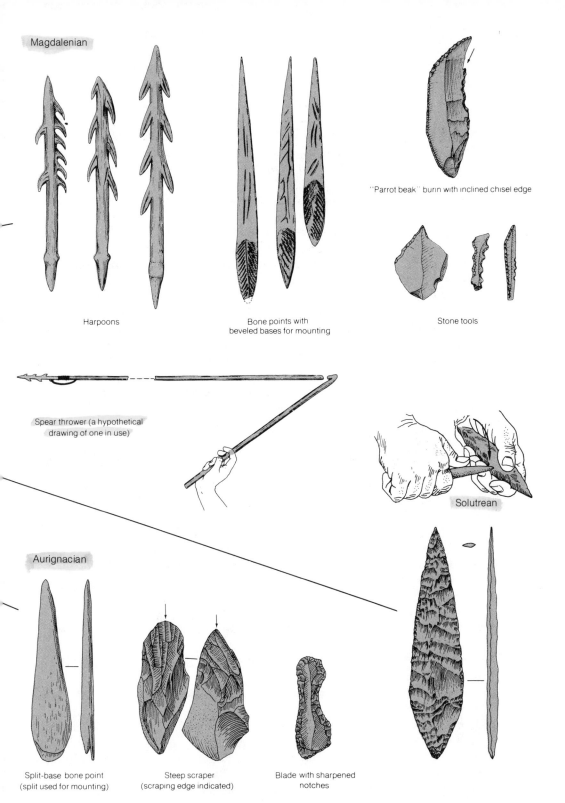

Magdalenian

Harpoons

Bone points with
beveled bases for mounting

"Parrot beak" burin with inclined chisel edge

Stone tools

Spear thrower (a hypothetical
drawing of one in use)

Solutrean

Aurignacian

Split-base bone point
(split used for mounting)

Steep scraper
(scraping edge indicated)

Blade with sharpened
notches

hunter-gatherer cultures the world has ever seen (Laville et al., 1980). These caves contain the remains of people who were modern in appearance, robust, tall, with small faces, high-domed foreheads, and few of the primitive features of the Neanderthals (Figure 6.3). The earliest Upper Paleolithic horizons in French caves immediately overlie Mousterian levels in which Neanderthal fossils have been discovered. With the appearance of *Homo sapiens*, new toolkits based on blade technology came into fashion, with a proliferation of tool types that is highly confusing to the nonspecialist (Table 6.1) (Bordes, 1968). Table 5.1 (p. 118) shows where this phase of technology fits into the overall development. Inevitably, the subject is controversial, for the same arguments surround the various technological changes as those that applied to Mousterian artifacts: are the different tool traditions, changing technologies, and evolving cultures truly a reflection of different peoples, or of different specialized activities? No one knows for sure.

French Upper Paleolithic **35,000 to 8000 B.C.**

The first Upper Paleolithic cave occupations were fleeting, but above the evidence for these brief stays are dense layers of living debris which show that later people lived in the caves and rock shelters more or less continuously for thousands of years. Many of the French caves are located in the sides of deep, sheltered river valleys that provided welcome haven from the bitter winds of the tundra to the north and east. The Dordogne, Vezère, and other rivers were rich in fish which could be caught with lines fitted with bone hooks and gorges. Bottom fish could be trapped in shallow pools and speared with barbed weapons. The hunters engraved salmon from the Dordogne on their weapons. Even more important than fish and seasonal vegetable foods were herds of reindeer that passed through the river valleys during their annual migrations. Many of the hunters followed the migrating reindeer and probably moved out into open country during the summer with the herds; there they lived in tented camps that are represented rarely in the archaeological record. Reindeer were pursued with spears, harpoons, clubs, and throwing sticks. They were probably dispatched in large numbers in cooperative game drives (Burch, 1972). The spear-thrower was a useful invention, for it allowed the hunters to stalk game less closely and to hurl a spear a much longer distance (Table 6.1). They used it to pursue such formidable beasts as wild ox, the woolly rhinoceros, and the mammoth. Sometimes, especially in periods of slightly milder climate, the wild horse was a primary source of meat. However, the hunters did not concentrate on big game alone. They also trapped arctic foxes, beavers, birds, and other small animals.

Magdalenian **15,000 to 8000 B.C.**

The zenith of these cultures was reached after 15,000 B.C. with the evolution of the Magdalenian culture (Table 6.1). The Magdalenians achieved a higher population density in parts of western Europe than any of their predecessors. They occupied groups of rock shelters that extended along the base of cliffs along the larger rivers, often moving to open camps on the riverbanks at favored seasons of the year (Capitan and Peyrony, 1928). Some bands may have exploited shellfish and other maritime resources on the Atlantic and Mediterranean coasts on a seasonal basis. These remarkable Stone Age artisans developed an astonishing artistry with bone and antler that played a far more important role in their culture than mere personal adornment or art for art's sake.

UPPER PALEOLITHIC ART

These hunter-gatherers of the Magdalenian culture, and their immediate predecessors, developed one of the first of the world's artistic traditions, a tradition painted and engraved on the walls of caves and rock shelters and repeated on hundreds of small artifacts and bone and antler fragments (Pfeiffer, 1982).

The earliest art objects are a series of female figurines with pendulous breasts and well-marked sexual characteristics (Figure 6.5) (Grasiosi, 1960; Leroi-Gourhan, 1965; Maringer and Bandi, 1953). Some people think such figures are fertility symbols, although other explanations have been advanced. These female figurines are found from Russia in the east to the Dordogne in the west, most of them in cave deposits dating to approximately 23,000 B.C. Sometimes called "Venus" figurines, few have

Venus figurines

Figure 6.5 Paleolithic art. Venus figurines from Brassempouy, France (left) and from Dolní Věstonice, Czechoslovakia.

facial features, although the hair often is depicted. They seem to be associated with a relatively short-lived religious cult that spread over a wide area of what is now temperate Europe.

No one knows when the first cave paintings were made, but the earliest engravings and paintings are distinctive in their crude depiction of animals. The same cave walls were covered again and again with depictions of wild horses, bulls, reindeer, and many other animals. Many of the animals were painted with long, distorted necks and thick bodies, as if the artists were unaware of perspective (Figure 6.6). The paintings also include squiggles, spaghettilike patterns, and tentlike symbols. Lascaux, the most famous rock art site in France, dates to the earlier period (Windels, 1965). A Great Hall of the Bulls features four immense wild bulls, drawn in thick, black lines, with some of the body details filled in. Horses, deer, a small bear, and a strange unicornlike beast prance with the great bulls in a fantastic display of blacks, browns, reds, and yellows that truly brings the animals to life in a flickering light. It is hard to believe that the paintings are at least 15,000 years old.

The earliest tradition reaches its height with an explosion of antler- and bonework after 15,000 B.C. The hunters engraved their harpoons, spear points, spear-throwers, and other artifacts with naturalistic engravings, fine carvings of wild animals, and elaborate schematic patterns. Even fine eye details and hair texture were shown by delicate graving strokes. But the Magdalenians are most famous for their beautiful rock art, paintings and engravings deep in the caves of northern Spain and southwestern France. At Altamira, in northern Spain, you walk deep into the hillside to enter a low-ceilinged chamber where the painters left fine renderings of bison in red and black (Figure 6.7) (Breuil, 1908). By painting and engraving the animals around natural bulges in the rock, the artists managed to convey a sense of relief and life to the animals. At cave after cave, the hunters left jumbled frenzies of large and small game and animals, hand impressions, dots, and signs, many of which must have had religious significance. An enormous and highly speculative literature concerns itself with the motives behind this remarkable art (Conkey, 1981). Originally, Henri Breuil and other experts (Breuil, 1952) argued that the caves were sacred places where the hunters gathered in rituals and sympathetic magic that would ensure the fertility of game and the success of the hunt. Even the signs on the cave walls were interpreted as traps and snares (Grasiosi, 1960). Today we know a great deal more about symbolic behavior and the art that goes with it, and much more about how hunter-gatherer societies function. The latest cave art research concentrated not only on the art itself, but on the contexts in which it appears. French prehistorian André Leroi-Gourhan argued in 1965 that the art was not random, but was part of a system of meanings, part of an expression of a world view that organized Upper Paleolithic life (Leroi-Gourhan, 1965). By counting the associations of subjects and clusters of motifs, Leroi-Gourhan found that certain themes, among them female figures, appeared in rock shelters and better-lit

Cave art
?29,000 B.C.

Altamira

Figure 6.6 A giant stag from Lascaux, France. An example of the Perigordian style.

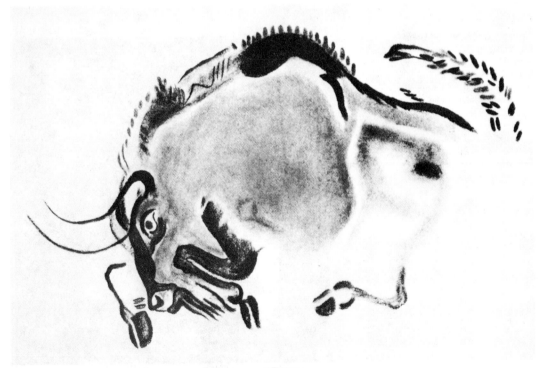

Figure 6.7 A bison in a polychrome cave painting at Altamira, Spain.

locales, while others frequented dark caverns. There are differences in the distribution of art, too. Bison, for instance, dominate north Spanish cave walls, but they rarely occur on portable objects. Perhaps the social contexts of wall and portable art were different (see Ucko and Rosenfeld, 1907; Hammond, 1974).

Alexander Marshack (1972, 1975) has carried out detailed micropho-tographic studies of Paleolithic art and shown that many of the visual forms are ecologically and seasonally related. Rather than concentrating on the naturalistic pictures of animals, he has studied the hundreds of **Nonnaturalistic pieces** nonnaturalistic pieces, with their patterns of lines, notches, dots, and groupings of marks (Figure 6.8). On some pieces, the marks were made with different tools at different times. These pieces, which Marshack named "time-factorial" objects, were used, he believes, as sequential no-tations of events and phenomena, predecessors of calendars. Marshack has examined hundreds of specimens stretching back as far as the Lower Paleolithic. He found duplicated designs, systematic groups of dots and notches that were either counting tallies or the beginnings, he felt, of a writing system; but, he suggests, they differed from later, more formal writing systems that could be read by everyone: the Magdalenian and ear-lier notations were for the engraver alone to read, even if he explained them to others on occasion. To formulate such a notation system re-quired thought and theoretical abstractions far more advanced than

Figure 6.8 Engraved bone (21 cm long) from La Marche, France, which was intensively studied by Marshack. The close-up shot shows tiny marks separated in two groups, each engraved by a different point, with a different type of stroke. (© Alexander Marshack, 1972)

those hitherto attributed to hunter-gatherers of this age. Of course, Marshack's ideas are controversial, but they are the type of ground-breaking research that produces exciting new interpretations and insights into Stone Age life.

Today, we know that many hunter-gatherer groups use ritual and art, creating and manipulating visual forms to structure and give meaning to their existence. Many ethnographic studies have shown how symmetry and other artistic principles may underlie the designs of many art traditions and characterize every aspect of daily life from social relationships to village planning. The people may use relatively few symbols to communicate meanings. Very often it is the context of the symbols that reveals the meaning. For the Upper Paleolithic artists, there were clearly continuities between animal and human life and with their social world. Thus, their art was a symbolic depiction of these continuities. The artists did not choose just any wall or piece of antler or bone for their drawings; nor did they select just any animal or geometric form to depict. Their selections were deliberate, symbolic acts that provide clues to the significance of the world's earliest artistic tradition (for an extended discussion, see Conkey, 1981).

The glorious artistic traditions of the Upper Paleolithic lasted until the Weichsel ice sheets began to retreat in approximately 10,000 B.C. As the climate warmed up, the great herds of reindeer, horses, and bison retreated north or vanished forever, to be replaced by smaller forest game. The successors of the Magdalenians turned more and more to lakeside dwelling and to a life among forests and along seashores. The artistic traditions cherished by their arctic predecessors withered with the passing of big-game hunting in favor of more specialized hunting and gathering (J. G. D. Clark, 1954, 1975, 1979).

RUSSIA AND SIBERIA

The vast, undulating plains of western Russia and central Europe as far east as the Ural Mountains were a much less hospitable environment for hunter-gatherers than the deep, well-watered valleys of the West. There were no convenient caves or rock shelters. For warmth and shelter, the inhabitants of the plains had to create artificial dwellings with their own tools and raw materials.

Only a few rivers dissect the west Russian plains, among them the Don and Dneipr. It is no coincidence that ancient river terraces are the most common locations for Stone Age hunting settlements, often promontories overlooking the river, where the hunters could spy on the movements of the herds of arctic elephant (mammoth), woolly rhinoceros, and wild horse that flourished in the valleys (Dolukhanov, 1982). At the height of the last glaciation, this area was a treeless periglacial landscape, a meadow steppe in warmer interstadials. It was a very inhospitable environment but one where hunter-gatherer societies flourished for thousands of years. Winter temperatures may have averaged −30 to −40° F, summer maxima rarely reaching 64°.

Soviet archaeologists have found traces of human settlements on these plains going back into Mousterian times. But the most spectacular Upper Paleolithic finds date to the period between 18,000 and 14,000 years ago, when scattered hunter-gatherer bands lived in what were often spectacular mammoth bone structures. The Mezhirich site overlooks the Dneipr River southeast of Kiev, a 15,000-year-old settlement of five houses, covering an area of some 110,000 sq ft (Kornietz and Sofler, 1984). Each house was about 4 to 7 m (13 to 22 ft) across and up to 850 sq ft in area. Foundation walls of massive mammoth bones supported an intricate framework of smaller limb bones, vertebrae, and other parts, sometimes arranged in fine herringbone patterns. The roof was supported by uprights that were stuck into holes broken through large mammoth bones, and the entire structure was almost certainly covered with elephant hide. Hearths and work areas lay inside the houses, which seem to have been occupied over long periods of time. More hearths and deep storage pits that kept meat refrigerated in the permafrost soil lay between the houses.

Mezhirich
13,000 B.C.

The Mezhirich dwellings are thought to have housed about fifty people, each dwelling taking ten men about five or six days to complete, a considerable investment of effort. Since mammoth bone dwellings found at other locations are less elaborate, it may be that this settlement was of unusual importance. The inhabitants hunted not only mammoth but also other large mammals, as well as taking river fish and birds. Judging by the evidence from several sites, they pursued mammoth in autumn and winter, reindeer in spring and early summer, fur-bearing animals in winter, and water fowl in summer (Dolukhanov, 1982). So many mammoth bones were used in house construction that the people may have scavenged them from carcasses on the plains in addition to using their own kills. Soviet archaeologists report that seashells from between 400 and 500 mi away came from the Mezhirich houses, while amber, a stone thought by many prehistoric peoples to have magic qualities, was traded in from 100 mi away.

Mezhirich is far from unique. The famous Kostenki sites on the Don River have yielded large, irregular dwellings partially scooped out of the earth (Figure 6.9) (R. Klein, 1969; McBurney, 1976). The floor plans are so irregular that it is difficult to be sure what the house plan was. In some cases, several circular structures up to 4.6 m (15 ft) in diameter were built together in a huge depression with a row of hearths down the middle. Bands of considerable size must have congregated in these tented areas.

Soviet Central Asia

To the east of the western plains stretches Soviet Central Asia, a vast area of continental territory that covers not only northern Afghanistan but the arid Turan depression and the Central Asian highlands. The archaeology of this area is still little known, although research has made rapid strides in recent years (Ranov and Davis, 1979). There are numer-

Figure 6.9 The plan of a long house (top) from Kostenki IV, USSR, and a reconstruction based on the finds at Push Kari. The latter was nearly 12 m long by 3.7 m wide (40 ft by 12 ft) and stood in a shallow depression.

ous Mousterian sites dating to the early part of the Weichsel glaciation, as they do in the west, displaying different toolkit variations that probably reflect different seasonal activities. It is not yet known when the transition to the Upper Paleolithic took place, but there is a possibility that it occurred somewhat later than in the west, for early Upper Paleolithic sites are few and far between.

The Upper Paleolithic of Soviet Central Asia is known from a late Weichsel culture that is widespread in caves, rock shelters, and open sites, but is still not well known. The Shugnou site southwest of the city of Samarkand lies at an altitude of 2000 m (6700 ft), one of the highest Upper Paleolithic sites in the world. Soviet archaeologists found five occupation layers in a site above a mountain river, yielding evidence of big-game hunting, of horses, wild oxen, wild sheep, and goats, dating to at least 15,000 to 20,000 years ago. Pollen grains suggest that weather conditions were somewhat cooler and wetter than today. The hunter-gatherer population of Central Asia may have been sparse for thousands of years, perhaps owing to unfavorable climate conditions, but this is pure conjecture. Population densities rose at the end of the Pleistocene, and human settlement expanded into higher elevations.

Mammoth skins, bones, sinews, and marrow were valuable to the Soviet Central Asian peoples for many purposes. Bone was especially important for fuel; burned mammoth bones have come from Kostenki and other sites. House frames, digging tools, pins, needles, and many small tools were made from the bones of the hunters' prey. Wood was naturally less important in the treeless environment of the steppe. In this difficult environment, we would expect an economy based at least in part on lumbering beasts whose carcasses could support many hungry mouths and fuel fires. The technology of the plains made much use of fire for warmth and for hardening the tips of spears. Indeed, fire was vital in the human armory as people moved outward to the arctic frontiers of the Paleolithic world.

Soviet Central Asia is an area that was subjected to cultural influences from both the flake and blade traditions of the west and from the chopper-chopping tools of the Far East. Consequently, her stone tools frequently are based on stone cobbles and were simple, highly effective artifacts that rarely achieved the sophistication or artistry of western traditions. The same amalgam of cultural traditions filtered into Siberia in far eastern Asia.

Siberia

Remote from Atlantic and Pacific weather patterns, Siberia is dry country with harsh, dry winters and short, hot summers. Treeless plains predominate in the far north and extend to the shores of the Arctic Ocean. Rainfall was so sparse during the Weichsel glaciation that the great ice sheets of the west never formed in Siberia. Herds of gregarious mammoths grazed on the tundra and on the edges of the river valleys where small bands of hunter-gatherers weathered the long winters. The archaeology of this enormous area and of northeast Asia is still little known, despite long-term excavation campaigns by Soviet archaeologists in recent years (Bryan, 1978; Chard, 1974; Klein, 1971; Muller-Beck, 1982). Nonetheless, Siberia and northeast Asia are of vital importance, for they were the staging areas from which the first settlement of the Americas took place, across the Bering Straits. A number of key issues confront anyone working in this area:

What was the date of the first human settlement of the far northeast?
Was there a pre-*sapiens* population in Siberia before 33,000 B.C.?
What technological and cultural traits are found in the Far East that can be identified in the New World?

Soviet archaeologists have identified two different Upper Paleolithic cultural traditions in Siberia and northeast Asia. These are known as the Mal'ta-Afontova, a tradition associated with simple, edge-trimmed tools;

and the Dyuktai, associated with stone knives and spear points which are flaked on both surfaces.

The Dyuktai tradition is found mostly east of the Yenesei Basin and has its roots in Middle Paleolithic technology. The earliest Dyuktai sites are found on the Aldan River and have been dated to approximately 33,000 to 31,000 B.C. (Mochanov, 1978). Dyuktai Cave itself adds to the picture of a long-lived hunting and gathering culture that lived on mammoth, woolly rhinoceros, bison, and some smaller animals. By at least 16,000 B.C., the Dyuktai people were making spear points that were carefully flaked on both sides, as well as using large pebbles that may have served as butchery tools (Figure 6.10). The effective exploitation of this area de-

Dyuktai tradition
?35,000 to
9000 B.C.

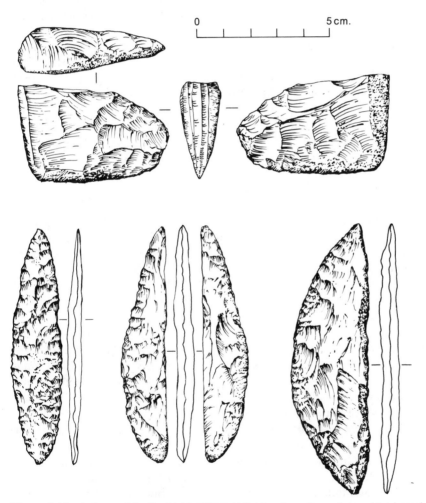

Figure 6.10 Artifacts of the Dyuktai tradition. At the top, four views of a wedge-shaped core, used to make tiny blades. At the bottom, three bifacially flaked projective heads. The wedge-shaped core is a characteristic artifact that is found on both sides of the Bering Strait in contexts of approximately 8000 B.C. It is, of course, a by-product of the production of fine microblades.

pended on a successful adaptation to the open tundra and on the special skills of big-game hunting. As in the west, the plains people would have had to range widely over a huge territory in search of their prey, camping near the kills for a few days and returning to favored spots year after year when the prey were plentiful.

Most Soviet experts believe that the Dyuktai cultural tradition evolved from earlier hunter-gatherer cultures of *Homo erectus* and early *Homo sapiens.* There is no reason to doubt that the same evolutionary pressures existed among isolated Asian human populations as occurred in the western parts of the Old World. Few sites yet document this evolutionary model, but it seems likely that the first human settlement of the tundra took place when *Homo sapiens* managed to adapt successfully to the arctic plains and the specialized lifeway that went with big-game hunting there.

Mal'ta-Afontova tradition
earlier than 20,000 B.C. to 8000 B.C. and later

The Mal'ta-Afontova tradition is best known from the Yenesei Valley and the Lake Baikal region. The Mal'ta site itself was occupied by people who lived in long houses and hunted both arctic and plains game (Gerasimov, 1958). Their tools include Upper Paleolithic scrapers and burins, as well as edge-trimmed points and scraping tools that are obvious survivals from earlier, Middle Paleolithic traditions. The Mal'ta people were expert boneworkers who carved female and bird figurines (Figure 6.11). The Mal'ta-Afontova tradition has been radiocarbon dated to as early as 18,900 ± 300 B.C. in the Yenesei Valley, and Mal'ta itself has been carbon dated to approximately 12,500 B.C.

Approximately 11,000 years ago, at the end of the Weichsel glaciation, the mammoth hunters of the Aldan were replaced by Mal'ta-Afontova peoples from the south, who had already adapted successfully to a more broadly based hunter-gatherer economy that flourished in the relatively warmer climate of postglacial times. By that time, Stone Age hunter-gatherers had long since settled in the New World, carrying with them the basics of cultural traditions that had been evolving for millennia in northeast Asia.

To identify these very earliest cultural traditions in the Americas has so far proved almost impossible (but see Cotter, 1981; Morlan and Cinq-Mars, 1982). There are many possibilities, for there were probably almost continuous contacts across the Bering Strait after the first settlements were established on the Alaskan shore, and sporadic contacts between the Kamchatka Peninsula and Japan and the Aleutian islands are beyond doubt. Japan, for example, was not isolated from the Asian mainland for most of the Pleistocene and there is evidence of continuous human settlement of the archipelago from at least 28,000 years ago, probably even earlier (Ikawa-Smith, 1978). The sophisticated Japanese blade tools and projectile heads flaked on both surfaces have been compared to somewhat similar artifacts in the Americas, although few definite conclusions have yet been drawn.

Japan
28,000 to 8000 B.C.

The technology of the Asian hunter-gatherers evolved over a long period of time; in the far northeast, this technology depended on crudely

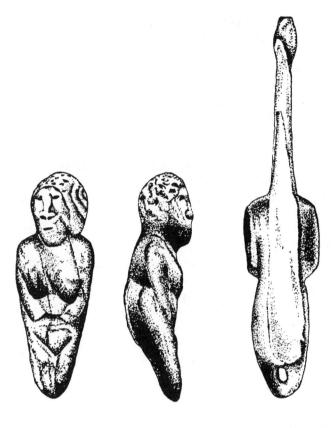

flaked stone pebbles and some small blade artifacts, a toolkit well adapted to the forest environment of the region. In the coastal zones of the Arctic Ocean and the Bering Strait, people were developing adaptations in 8000 B.C. that were eventually to be perpetuated by the rich Eskimo, Aleut, Chukchi, and Koryak hunter-gatherer cultures that survived into modern times; these extended finally over the northern latitudes of the New World as far east as Greenland and the Atlantic coast.

Bering Strait
8000 B.C. (Chapter Seven)

EARLY SETTLEMENT OF JAPAN

During the cold phases of the Pleistocene, Japan often was connected to the mainland, and so it was possible for hunter-gatherers to settle there. Thus far no signs of *Homo erectus* or of hand axes (recently unearthed in South Korea, Nelson, 1982) have come from the islands. No one knows exactly when humans first settled in Japan. It may have been as early as 100,000 B.C. or as late as 30,000. Ikawa-Smith (1980) believes that a date of 50,000 B.C. is a reasonable estimate. Traces of human settlement before 30,000 B.C. are as elusive as they are in the Americas. Few sites are regarded as definitely of human origin, except for the lowermost levels of

Early settlement
?50,000 B.C.

Fukui Cave in northern Kyushu which yielded two bifacial tools and several flakes, radiocarbon dated to older than 29,000 B.C. (Aikens and Higuchi, 1981).

11,000 B.C. The later Stone Age cultures of Japan are characterized by a wide variety of blade tools, including projectile points and scrapers. By 11,000 B.C., the Japanese were making use of small microblades. The climate was warmer, sea levels were rising, and the landmass area available to the hunter-gatherers shrank considerably. Many people settled by coastlines and lake shores and began exploiting a wide range of land and maritime resources in a very diverse series of environments over islands that have approximately the same north-south distribution as the East Coast of the United States, with accompanying climatic differences. They also started making clay vessels, some of the earliest pottery in the world. Archaeologists have always believed that ceramics were associated with agriculture, but the Japanese Jomon people were still hunting, gathering, and collecting shellfish when they first made clay vessels in 10,500 B.C. or so. Jomon pots undoubtedly were used for cooking, for many of them show signs of having been placed in a fire. They probably were used for steaming open shellfish and for making vegetable foods palatable for human consumption. No one knows if the Japanese invented pottery or whether they learned of the new manufacture from people of the mainland to the west, but pottery is found in tenth millennium contexts in southern China.

GUIDE TO FURTHER READING

Bordes, François. *The Old Stone Age*. New York: McGraw-Hill, 1968.
   A basic manual on Stone Age artifacts with a strong emphasis on Western Europe. Excellent illustrations of tool forms.

Chard, Chester S. *Northeast Asia in Prehistory*. Madison: University of Wisconsin Press, 1974.
   A useful synthesis of Siberian archaeology for beginners.

Clark, J. G. D. *Mesolithic Prelude*. Edinburgh: Edinburgh University Press, 1979.
   Clark is the world's authority on this little-known period of prehistory, and this is his latest summary.

Clarke, David. *Mesolithic Europe: The Economic Basis*. Cambridge: Cambridge University Press, 1976.
   A fundamental work on past-glacial adaptations.

Grasiosi, Paolo. *Palaeolithic Art*. New York: Abrams, 1960.
   A superb compendium of Paleolithic cave and mobile art with a clear text that is a joy to read. More descriptive than analytical.

Klein, Richard. *Man and Culture in the Late Pleistocene*. San Francisco: Chandler, 1969.
   The archaeology of Western Russia described for the advanced student. Particularly good on mammoth hunters.

Leroi-Gourhan, A. *The Dawn of European Art: An Introduction to Paleolithic Cave Painting*. Cambridge: Cambridge University Press, 1984.
An introduction that gives a useful summary of major sites and fresh theories on the art.

Pfeiffer, John. *The Creative Explosion*. New York: Harper & Row, 1982.
A wide ranging, popular treatment of early cave art for the general reader.

Chronological Table D

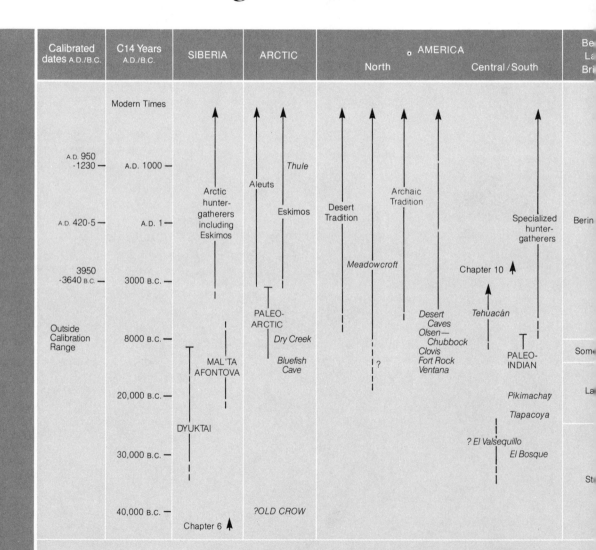

Calibrated dates A.D./B.C.	C14 Years A.D./B.C.	SIBERIA	ARCTIC	AMERICA		Be La Bri
				North	Central/South	
	Modern Times					
A.D. 950 -1230 —	A.D. 1000 —	Arctic hunter-gatherers including Eskimos	Thule / Aleuts / Eskimos	Desert Tradition	Archaic Tradition	Specialized hunter-gatherers
A.D. 420-5 —	A.D. 1 —					Berin
3950 -3640 B.C. —	3000 B.C. —		PALEO-ARCTIC	Meadowcroft	Chapter 10 / Desert Caves Olsen—Chubbock Clovis Fort Rock Ventana	Chapter 10 / Tehuacán
Outside Calibration Range	8000 B.C. —		Dry Creek / Bluefish Cave	?	PALEO-INDIAN	Som
	20,000 B.C. —	MAL'TA AFONTOVA			Pikimachay / Tlapacoya	La
	30,000 B.C. —	DYUKTAI			? El Valsequillo / El Bosque	St
	40,000 B.C. —	Chapter 6	?OLD CROW			

Chapter Seven

The First Americans

PREVIEW

- The earliest human settlement of the New World is now generally agreed to have taken place across the Bering Strait during the Weichsel glaciation. During the coldest phases of that glaciation, a land bridge known as Beringia connected Alaska and Asia. It is known to have existed from 23,000 to 12,000 B.C. and to have vanished altogether in approximately 8,000 B.C.
- Few traces of very early human settlement have come to light in the Americas; the earliest in Alaska may be the Old Crow site, perhaps dating to as early as 38,000 B.C.
- People were hunting big game in Mexico by 20,000 B.C. and may have been living at Meadowcroft rock shelter in the Ohio Valley by 18,000 B.C. Pikimachay Cave in the Andes was occupied at about the same time.
- These little-known cultural traditions developed into specialized Paleo-Indian hunter-gatherer cultures that are best known from their 8000 B.C. kill sites on the North American plains. After 7000 B.C., other specialized hunter-gatherer cultures developed in many parts of the Americas. Prominent among these cultures are the Desert and Archaic traditions of North America. Many varieties of hunter-gatherer adaptation, often involving precise scheduling of gathering activities, developed in Central and South America during the same period. It was among some of these specialized groups that early American agriculture began.
- The hunter-gatherer cultures of the Aleutian Islands and the Arctic developed from earlier cultural traditions based on sea mammal hunting and fishing. Eskimo and Aleut culture can be recognized in the archaeological record at least 3000, perhaps 4000 years ago.

Ever since the Americas were first colonized, people have speculated about where the pre-Columbian populations of the Western Hemisphere came from (Wauchope, 1972). Canaanites, Celts, Chinese, Egyptians, Phoenicians, and even the Ten Lost Tribes of Israel have been proposed as ancestors of the native Americans (Willey and Sabloff, 1974). By the

Chronological Table D

early nineteenth century, field research and museum work had begun to replace the wild speculations of earlier scholars. People began to dig in Indian mounds. Spanish and American explorers rescued the temples of Mesoamerica from the rain forest.

A wise and sober scholar named Samuel Haven summarized myths and legends about pre-Columbian Indian beginnings in 1856 (Haven, 1856). He concluded that the New World was initially settled from across the Bering Strait, designating the earliest Americans as northeastern Asiatics who migrated into North America at an unknown date. (See Figure 7.1 for sites mentioned in this chapter.) Most archaeologists now agree with Haven that the first Americans set foot in the New World by way of the Bering Strait. The Bering route is accepted because at times the strait formed a land bridge between Asia and Alaska during the Wisconsin (equivalent to Weichsel) glaciation (Figure 7.2, p. 172).

ICE SHEETS AND LAND BRIDGES

Human settlement in Siberia and northeastern Asia intensified during the Weichsel glaciation (see Chapter Six). Few traces of earlier hunter-gatherers exist in Siberia; indeed, it has been argued that not until the technology of shelter and clothing was sufficiently advanced to cope with the climatic extremes of Siberia were people able to settle the arctic tundra.

Small bands of hunter-gatherers were living in Siberia and northeastern Asia during the last Weichsel cold snap, when sea levels were as much as 100 m (330 ft) lower than today — so low that a land bridge stood where the Bering Strait now separates Asia and Alaska. (Sea level drops when quantities of ocean water are frozen into continental ice sheets.) The low-lying plain was a highway for such Asian mammals as the caribou and the mammoth, as well as for people, who presumably ventured eastward toward Alaska in pursuit of game. The Pacific coastal plain was much expanded by lower sea levels, enabling movement farther south as well (Figure 7.2).

The Bering Strait was dry land between approximately 50,000 and 40,000 years ago and again from 23,000 to 12,000 B.C. Great ice sheets covered much of North America during the later phases of the Wisconsin glaciation, extending in a formidable barrier from the Atlantic to the Pacific and making any southward movement by man or beast almost impossible. Southerly corridors through the ice were clear for only a few thousand years before and after the glacial maximum. Just how large the ice sheets were during various periods of the Wisconsin is a burning controversy, however. Since the Bering Land Bridge was submerged approximately 10,000 years ago, the only way people could reach the Western Hemisphere has been by water; aboriginal societies developed in almost complete isolation until ships filled with European colonists and missionaries arrived (Hopkins, 1967).

Bering Land Bridge

Figure 7.1 Prehistoric hunter-gatherers in the New World. Sites mentioned in the text are indicated, as well as the limits of ice sheets during the last glaciation. (For the Bering Land Bridge, see Figure 7.2.) The diagonally hatched areas show the distribution of specialized hunter-gatherers after 5000 B.C.

The dry shelf between Asia and the New World formed by the low sea levels of the last glaciation is often called Beringia. It was a continuation of the Siberian steppe-tundra, which probably abounded in herds of large grazing animals. The tundra extended like a peninsula from Asia eastward to the vast ice sheets that covered North America (see Figure 7.2). We know from deep sea cores that Beringia was a dry plain, with brief warm summers, long winters, and continual winds. At first glance, it

Beringia
50,000 to 40,000 B.C. and 23,000 to 12,000 B.C.

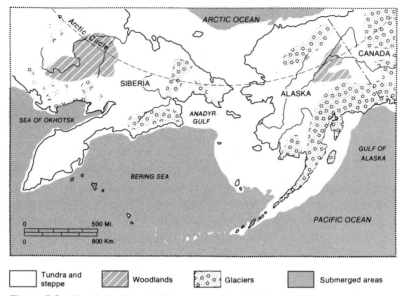

Figure 7.2 The Bering Land Bridge as reconstructed by the latest research.

would seem like a most inhospitable place for human settlement, especially at the height of a glaciation. But the land bridge plains gave way to many marshy areas, where lush meadows provided ample summer fodder for large grass-eating mammals like the mammoth, as well as for wild horses, musk oxen, and other arctic species. The Upper Pleistocene fauna of this general area include many species that are intolerant of deep snow, although they may have flourished in the dry environment, moving from one grazing ground to another as the snow thawed during the summer. Judging from modern arctic environments, the density of game may never have been high, but it may have been up to three and a half times that of today, partly because of a much greater abundance of willow shrub, a shrub that is thought to have provided as much as 50 percent of mammoth diet. This was no land teeming in milk and honey but a very savage climate indeed. Nevertheless, it may have been capable of supporting a human population of between fifteen and twenty-five people per 1000 sq km, a figure roughly equivalent to that for modern Eskimos living off the land and sea alone (for a fascinating set of essays on Beringia, see Hopkins et al., 1982).

The Bering Strait was submerged sometime between 13,000 and 11,000 B.C., but the coastline of Alaska was still up to 60 mi offshore in about 8000 B.C.

With such a harsh environment and extensive glaciation, it is hardly surprising that much of Canada was not occupied until approximately 6000 B.C., and that traces of the earliest peoples to cross into the New World are sparse. Intense controversy surrounds the origins of human settlement in the Americas (Bryan, 1978; Shutler, 1983):

How long ago did humans settle in the Americas?

What toolkit did they bring with them?

Are there cultural connections between American and Asian sites of the time of first settlement?

ALASKA

The obvious place to look for traces of early settlement is in Alaska, where field research is, unfortunately, very difficult because of the remote terrain and severe climate (Dumond, 1977; Morlan, 1983).

The oldest archaeological remains found in North America may come from the eroding deposits of the Old Crow Flats in the Yukon Territory near the border between Alaska and Canada (Morlan, 1983). The area has yielded a number of fossil mammal bones, of which a hundred or so are claimed to have been made into artifacts and hundreds more altered for casual use (Morlan, 1983). Several of these bones have been radiocarbon dated to between 23,000 and 27,000 B.C. Unfortunately, none of the artifacts or altered bones have been found in their original contexts. All of them are from redeposited levels — geological horizons consisting of materials that have been shifted by water action, erosion, or some other natural force from their original position. By careful geological observation, Richard Morlan and his colleagues have tried to establish the date of the bones through relative chronology and suspect that they may be as old as 38,000 B.C. However, these scientists are quick to admit that their dating is insecure and must await the discovery of artifacts in precise association with geological levels, and, if possible, charcoal for radiocarbon dating.

> Old Crow
> ?38,000 B.C.

The first Americans are a shadowy presence in Alaska, known only from a handful of worked bone specimens, perhaps dating to at least 25,000 B.C. It is hardly surprising, therefore, to find American remains only in small numbers, because the Bering Land Bridge was open for very long periods after the emergence of *Homo sapiens* in the Old World and the gradual colonization of the Russian plains and Siberia. As Morlan says, it is rather "like looking for a needle in a haystack (and a frozen one at that)."

The earliest relatively well-dated occupation of Alaska dates to around 13,000 B.C., but there are few dated sites. The *Paleoarctic tradition* covers a scatter of sites that have yielded microblades, wedge-shaped cores, and some leaf-shaped bifacially flaked points. Human occupation at Bluefish Cave southwest of Old Crow has been radiocarbon dated to about 13,500 B.C. and later. The Dry Creek site near Fairbanks has been radiocarbon dated to approximately 9000 B.C. (Powers and Hamilton, 1978). The most famous locality, however, is the 8000 B.C. Akmak site at Onion Portage, which lies in a river valley that has been a migration route for caribou ever since the earliest human settlement in the region (Anderson, 1970).

> Paleoarctic tradition
> 13,000 to
> ?4000 B.C.

> Bluefish Cave
> 13,500 B.C.
> Dry Creek
> 9000 B.C.

> Akmak
> 8000 B.C.

This site consists of little more than a scatter of characteristic tools that once lay by a shelter long since eroded away.

Some archaeologists believe that there are some connections between the Dyuktai artifacts of northeast Asia (Chapter Six) and those of the Paleoarctic tradition, but it would be unwise to pursue these analogies too far until many more sites have been dug on both sides of the Bering Strait. Some of the stoneworking techniques practiced by the Paleoarctic people are similar to those used in Japan between approximately 12,000 and 8000 B.C. Again, it would be easy to read a great deal into these parallels; but in fact their very existence has hardly been established, and that from only a mere scatter of sites (Ikawa-Smith, 1978).

We still lack precise answers to the questions posed at the beginning of this section, but we can say that:

People *may have settled* in Alaska by 38,000 B.C., although the evidence is still highly uncertain.

The first well-attested human settlement is dated to approximately 13,000 B.C. or a few millennia earlier.

There are some technological parallels between Paleoarctic artifacts of approximately 10,000 B.C. and those of contemporary Asia.

Beringia provided an environment suitable for regular contact between Asia and the New World until as late as 8000 B.C.

There remains one fundamental question. Why did humans settle in the New World at all? Was it some inner urge of the spirit that caused the first Americans to endure the harsh climate of the Bering Land Bridge? Or was there some more prosaic reason?

Two great population dispersals occurred during prehistory, the first when *Homo erectus* emerged from the tropics about a million years ago. The second took place after the emergence of *Homo sapiens sapiens* between 35,000 and 40,000 years ago (Lewin, 1984), when the first human populations crossed from the Old World into the New and when Australia was inhabited for the first time. The exact dates of this later dispersal are still highly uncertain but seem to have occurred soon after modern people appeared. The explanation for these sudden dispersals seems to lie mostly in the fact that humans tended to behave as other animals did. Rather than responding to an inborn restlessness, the first Americans were probably behaving in the same way as other animal predators. They spent their days tracking the game herds that formed an important part of their subsistence, and when Siberian game herds moved onto the Bering Land Bridge during the coldest millennia of the last glaciation, their human predators followed.

THE EARLIEST SETTLEMENT OF MORE SOUTHERLY LATITUDES

Exactly the same archaeological problem — lack of sites — arises when we turn our attention to the earliest settlement of the vast continents south of the great ice sheets (Dincauze, 1983; MacNeish, 1979). Until fairly recently most archaeologists believed that the first settlement took place approximately 13,000 years ago, after the retreat of the ice sheets when access from Alaska became possible. Now that more is known of the distribution of Pleistocene ice sheets and about American cultures of the period, there is agreement that the first settlement must have taken place earlier. The American hunter-gatherer cultures of 11,000 B.C. are simply too distinctive for them to have any links with contemporary Asian peoples. The distinctive features of early American toolkits probably resulted from isolation, which occurred after a much earlier initial settlement from the Arctic that took place at a time when access from north to south was possible and there were no intervening groups to hinder progress southward. There are so few sites documenting this settlement that almost nothing is known of the settlers (Hammond, 1980; Stanford, 1983).

Meadowcroft rock shelter southwest of Pittsburgh was used as a home base for hunting, gathering, and food processing from at least 12,000 years ago, and perhaps as early as 17,000 B.C. (Adovasio, 1984; Adovasio et al., 1981). The earliest levels of the site contain a relatively sophisticated blade technology which produced delicately flaked knives, small bifaces, most of them made of small river pebbles. Later levels of Meadowcroft contain typical Paleo-Indian and Archaic artifacts, but excavators are convinced that the lowest horizons are the prototype technology for the fine projectile heads and other artifacts made after 8000 B.C. To date, Meadowcroft is one of the very few North American sites that contain relatively indisputable evidence for human occupation before 11,000 B.C. (Adovasio, 1984; for discussion of problems, see Stanford, 1983).

A lancelike point found in a level dating to approximately 10,000 B.C. at Meadowcroft is similar to other such points found in the base levels of Fort Rock Cave in Oregon, Ventana Cave in Arizona, and some locations in Texas. However, virtually nothing is known of the lifeway or technology of these people, discovered as they invariably are at the base of deep cave sites (MacNeish, 1979). There are numerous reports of humanly struck tools in caves, river gravels, and lakebeds, but almost inevitably there are doubts about the stratigraphy and dating of the finds. Although there have been claims of human occupation of Santa Rosa Island off the southern California coast dating to earlier than 40,000 years ago, these are almost certainly redistributed finds. Then there are claimed amino-acid racemization dates of 48,000 to 70,000 years ago for a group of eleven skeletons from Sunnyvale and Del Mar in southern California. These have recently been more reliably dated at between 9000 and 6300 B.C.

The evidence for early settlement in Mesoamerica is just as incomplete (MacNeish and Nelhen-Terner, 1983). Perhaps the earliest find is El Bosque in Nicaragua, a cave containing bones of extinct animals and some possible human artifacts more than 25,000 years old. Then there

North America; Meadowcroft **?17,000 to 8000 B.C. and later**

Fort Rock **10,000 B.C.**

Ventana

Central and South America

El Bosque

El Valsequillo
23,900 to 35,000
B.P.

are the El Valsequillo finds, unifacial implements and extinct animals found in deposits that may date back to between about 23,900 and more than 35,000 years. In both instances, the excavated evidence is thin at best. The Tlapacoya sites near Mexico City, which have yielded some crudely flaked stone associated with the bones of extinct animals, have been dated to between approximately 22,000 and 20,000 B.C. (Mirambell, 1978).

Tlapacoya
22,000 to
20,000 B.C.

Human occupation between 15,000–20,000 and 10,000 years ago is much better documented from a number of locations, some near Mexico City, where projectile points (Figure 7.3) have been found in association with mammoth bones. There are several projectile point traditions that remained in fashion for considerable periods of time.

South America has yielded a similar scatter of possible early sites, the most celebrated being Pickimachay Cave in the Peruvian Andes, where Richard MacNeish found possible simple cores and retouched flakes in a level dated to 18,250 ± 1050 B.C. (Bryan, 1983; MacNeish, 1983). But by far the most important location yet discovered is the Monte Verde site in southern Chile (Dillehey, 1984). Located in a small river valley, the 11,000 to 10,500 B.C. streamside settlement is covered by a peat bog, so that not only stone and bone survive but wooden artifacts as well. Thus far only a portion of the site has been excavated, revealing two parallel rows of rectangular houses, joined by connecting walls. The skin-covered houses were 3 to 4 m (9 to 13 ft) square, with log and crude plank foundations and a wooden framework. Clay-lined hearths, wooden mortars, and large quantities of vegetable foods were found in these houses. A short distance away lay a wishbone-shaped structure associated with chewed bolo plant leaves (used today to make a form of medicinal tea), mastodon bones, and other work debris. This may have been a work area. The Monte Verde people exploited a very wide range of vegetable foods, including wild potatoes; they also hunted small game and perhaps mammals like extinct camels and mastodons (it is possible that they scavenged such meat, however). Monte Verde was located in a forest, with abundant vegetable foods all year-round. The site was almost certainly a long-term campsite. What is fascinating is that 90 percent of the stone artifacts are crude river pebbles. It is clear that wood was the most important raw

Pickimachay Cave
18,000 B.C.

Monte Verde
11,000 to
10,500 B.C.

Figure 7.3 Points found with mammoths in Mexico. The length of the middle point is 8.1 cm (approximately 3 in).

material. It was certainly used for spears, digging sticks, and for hafting stone scrapers, three of which survived in their wooden handles. Sites yielding simple flaked stone artifacts like those from Monte Verde have been found elsewhere in South America, as far south as Patagonia, but this is the first time that anyone has been able to flesh out the stones with more complete discoveries.

The Monte Verde investigations are still in progress, although they show that early American society may well have been much more sophisticated than had been realized. It is an open forest site, whereas other locations like Pickimachay and Meadowcroft are located in more open country. The site shows just how scanty the archaeological record of the first Americans is, and just how little we are likely to find out about them until more waterlogged sites come to light.

We know so little about the first settlers south of the ice sheets that it is still impossible to say how the first settlement took place. Paul Martin (1973) argued that the first Americans were big-game hunters who spread rapidly through the New World in pursuit of migrating herds. They moved so fast that they colonized both North and South America in a few thousand years. There are numerous objections to this bold hypothesis, the major one being the great diversity of environments between the ice sheets and Tierra del Fuego. It probably took many millennia for the first Americans to learn how to adapt to the many temperate, tropical, and desert environments in the New World.

The Paleo-Indians

Toward the end of the Wisconsin glaciation, the High Plains area east of the Rockies lay immediately to the south of the ice sheets. The plains offer a very diverse range of environments and support a variety of protein-rich grasses and shrubs that once supported a browsing and grazing mammalian fauna, which in turn provided subsistence for a small number of hunter-gatherers (Frison, 1978). However, life was not easy for the bands, as they had to respond to different distributions of animals and plants each year, conditions which depended on rainfall, snowfall runoff from mountain peaks, and so on. The realities of the climate meant that the people had to collect dried meat and vegetable foods in the summer months and store them against the bitter winter. Each family group probably moved at least fifty to one hundred times a year, tending to visit the same campsites year after year, taking all their belongings with them. Archaeologically, they left very little behind them, and so the evidence for prehistoric occupation of the plains normally is limited to remains of large bison kills and scatters of broken flakes and projectile points.

In the plains areas where big-game hunters flourished, numerous varieties of hunting cultures began to appear. They can be distinguished by the styles of their projectile heads, which include Clovis, Eden, Folsom, Plainview, and Scottsbluff (Frison, 1978; Haynes, 1982). Projectile heads are found over an enormous area of North America, from Nova Scotia to northern Mexico, as well as in South America, from Venezuela to Chile. All of them are grouped together under the label *Paleo-Indian tradition*. Most Paleo-Indian sites occur in more temperate latitudes, but as the Pleistocene ice sheets retreated northward, bands of people moved with the big game into more northern latitudes and also toward the Atlantic and Pacific coasts.

For much of their livelihood, many plains bands relied on big-game drives and communal hunting. Both the bison and the mammoth were formidable prey for hunters equipped only with spears. Twelve thousand years ago, the plains also supported herds of camels and horses. Occasional kill sites, with mammoth bones associated with stone projectile points, are found scattered over the plains. The Clovis site in New Mexico is one of the most famous, for it has yielded not only the remains of mammoths but also a distinctive form of projectile head known as a Clovis point, which was used by hunters in the chase. Clovis points were carefully flaked on both sides and then given a "fluted," grooved base for hafting the point on a shaft (Figure 7.4). At the Colby site in north central Wyoming, two stacked piles of mammoth bones represent the remains of at least six animals, five of them immature beasts. A Clovis point lay under one of the bone piles, and so it seems certain Colby was a kill site. Frison (1978) speculates that a mammoth herd once lived in the neighborhood and was preyed upon by a band of hunters, who brought down young beasts as they approached the arroyo where the site lies. Unable to

Figure 7.4 Points from Plains cultures (all actual size). Arrows show fluted bases.

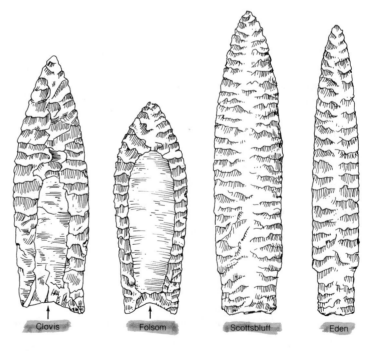

Clovis   Folsom   Scottsbluff   Eden

negotiate the gulley, the wounded animal lay down for the hunters to dispatch at leisure. Killing young animals is a different proposition from killing mature beasts, and, of course, the long-term implications of such selective culling on mammoth populations could be profound.

The Folsom projectile point (Figure 7.4) is a commonplace find on the plains, but few kill sites are known. An individual hunter could, perhaps, kill a solitary bison, but in most cases the hunters cooperated in the chase. They would encircle a few beasts or, more often, stampede a herd into a swamp or a narrow defile. In some cases, they would drive the frightened animals over a cliff or into dune areas. The archaeological evidence for such activities comes from a series of kill sites, among them the Agate Basin site in eastern Wyoming, where, judging from the age of the animals, the hunters apparently maneuvered ten to twenty animals into an arroyo bottom in late February or early March (Frison, 1978). The hunters then drove them upstream until they reached a natural trap in the gully where the confused bison could be killed with stone-tipped spears.

The Olsen-Chubbock site in Colorado is an example of a kill site where approximately 200 bison of all ages were stampeded into a deep, narrow arroyo, probably during the summer or fall (Frison, 1978; Wheat, 1972). Because the skeletons of the prehistoric bison faced north, the excavators concluded that the wind was blowing from the south on the day of the hunt. The stampeding herd was driven into a gully and could not catch the scent of the people waiting for them at the arroyo. The hunters' artifacts were scattered around the carcasses of their quarry (Figure 7.5): scraping tools, stone knives, and flakes used for dismembering the bison.

Bison hunting was practiced on the plains right up until the advent of the horse and the repeating rifle, but Paleo-Indian peoples flourished throughout North America. Clovis sites are known from many locations in the east, including Meadowcroft shelter in Pennsylvania, where even earlier signs of human occupation may also be found. Herds of caribou may have provided sustenance in northern sites around the Great Lakes and in the northeast (Dragoo, 1976). Paleo-Indian hunting and gathering economies may have varied a great deal from region to region, some bands specializing in big game, others in fishing or gathering, depending on the resources available in each territory. This variation is reflected in Paleo-Indian archaeological sites that can vary from kill locations to shell middens. That hunting was important in places where large game was abundant seems unquestionable, but this activity diminished rapidly in importance as the big game became extinct at the end of the Pleistocene.

BIG-GAME EXTINCTIONS

In the northern latitudes of both Old World and New at the end of the Pleistocene, many big-game species became extinct, but nowhere were

Figure 7.5 A layer of excavated bison bones from the Olsen-Chubbock site in Colorado, where a band of hunters stampeded a herd of bison into a narrow arroyo.

the extinctions so drastic as in the Americas. Three quarters of the large mammalian genera there abruptly disappeared at the end of the Pleistocene (Martin and Wright, 1967). Extinguished were the mammoth, the mastodon, the Pleistocene camel and horse, to say nothing of several bison species and numerous smaller mammals. Why did the American fauna die off so abruptly? Speculations have been long and lively. One theory that has long held on is that the large mammals were killed off by the Paleo-Indian bands' intensive hunting, as they preyed on large herds of animals that had formerly had relatively few predators to control their populations. This overkill hypothesis is weakened by the fact that many Pleistocene animals disappeared before the heyday of the Paleo-Indians. Besides, the Indians existed in very small numbers, and they had other subsistence activities than the chase. Surely the animals would have adapted to changed conditions and new dangers. Instead, the extinctions accelerated after the hunters had been around for a while; the modern bison, for example, never adapted to mounted hunters.

Overkill

Change in climate gives a second hypothesis for the cause of extinction. Changing environments, spreading aridity, and shrinking habitats for big game may have reduced the mammalian population drastically. Strong objections face this hypothesis too. The very animals that became extinct had already survived enormous fluctuations in Pleistocene climate without harm. If they had once migrated into more hospitable habitats, they could have done so again. Furthermore, the animals that became extinct were not just the browsers; they were selected from all types of habitat. This too-simple hypothesis about climate change is supported by the notion that desiccation leads to mass starvation in game populations, an idea refuted by ecological research on African game populations. What actually happens is that the smaller species and those with lower growth rates adapt to the less favorable conditions, leaving the population changed but not defunct (Olivier, 1982).

Climate change

A third hypothesis cites the great variation in mean temperatures at the end of the Pleistocene as a primary cause. In both New and Old Worlds, the more pronounced seasonal contrasts in temperature climates would have been harder on the young of species that are born in small litters, after long gestation periods, and at fixed times of the year. These traits are characteristic of larger mammals, precisely those which became extinct. The less equable climate at the end of the Pleistocene, then, would have been a major cause of late Pleistocene extinctions in North America.

Seasonal contrasts

All three hypotheses have truth in them. Complex variables must have affected the steps that led to extinction, with intricate feedback among the effects of intensive big-game hunting, changing ecology, and the intolerance of some mammalian species to seasonal contrasts in weather conditions. It may be that the hunters, being there as persistent predators, were the final variable that caused more drastic extinctions among the mammalian fauna than might otherwise have occurred.

LATER HUNTERS AND GATHERERS

As the world climate warmed up at the end of the last glaciation, New World environments changed greatly. The western and southwestern United States became drier, but the East Coast and much of the Midwest grew densely forested. The large Pleistocene mammals of earlier times became extinct, but the bison remained a major source of food. In the warmer Southeast, the more favorable climate brought drier conditions that meant less standing water, markedly seasonal rainfalls, and specialization among humans for fishing or intensive gathering instead of big-game hunting. Many areas had much economic diversity, as we see among the desert gatherer peoples of the Tehuacán Valley in Mexico. They flourished between 10,000 and 7000 B.C., at the same time other hunter-gatherers in the Pacific Northwest were probably taking advantage of seasonal salmon runs in the fast-moving rivers.

Tehuacán
10,000 to 7000 B.C.

Desert Tradition

Economic emphasis shifted in the arid West and Southwest. As big game became scarce, many hunting bands relied more heavily on wild vegetable foods that required much more energy to collect and process than game meat. In the Great Basin, smaller animals such as rabbits, squirrels, and deer became more common prey. At the same time, gathering vegetable foods grew dominant in economic life, combined with some fishing and, in maritime areas, exploitation of shellfish. We are fortunate that arid climates in Utah, Nevada, and elsewhere have preserved many plant and vegetable foods eaten by these early hunter-gatherers. By 7000 B.C., a distinctive desert form of culture had been developed over much of the western United States by small bands camping in caves, rock shelters, and temporary sites.

Desert tradition
??7000 B.C. to modern times

The excavations at later sites like Danger Cave in Utah and at the Gypsum and Lovelock sites in Nevada reveal that the hunters were making nets, mats, and baskets, as well as rope (Figure 7.6) (Irwin-Williams, 1968; Heizer and Berger, 1970; Jennings, 1957, 1975). The Hogup Cave in Utah has yielded one of the world's most complete and longest archaeological culture sequences (Aikens, 1970). The site displays gradual adaptations at one settlement, changing it from a base camp to a short-stay camp that was associated with other base camps or with horticultural villages after people learned how to produce food. At all these sites the inhabitants used digging sticks to uproot edible tubers, and much of their toolkit consisted of grinding stones used in preparing vegetable foods. Most Great Basin peoples were obliged to be constantly on the move, searching for different vegetable foods as they came into season and camping near scanty water supplies. Only a few communities living near relatively permanent food sources or good fishing grounds could afford a more sedentary life.

Danger Cave
Gypsum Cave
Lovelock Cave

Hogup Cave

The deposits at Gatecliff rock shelter near Austin, Nevada, are 40 ft

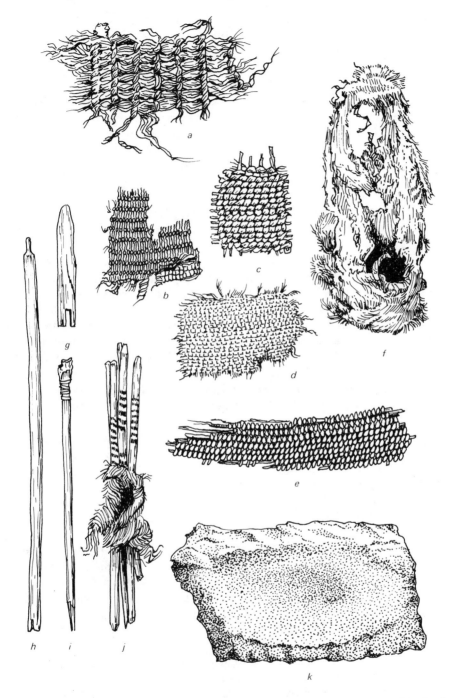

Figure 7.6 Artifacts from Danger Cave, Utah, preserved by the dry climate: (a–b) twined matting; (c) twined basketry; (d) coarse cloth; (e) coiled basketry; (f) hide moccasin; (g) wooden knife handle, 7.4 cm (4.5 in) long; (h) dart shaft, 41 cm (16 in) long; (i) arrow shaft with broken projectile point in place, 84 cm (33 in) long; (j) bundle of gaming sticks, 29 cm (11.5 in) long; (k) milling stone.

deep and span more than 8000 years of human occupation. The inhabitants lived by valleyside streams in the winter, then moved up to the shelter in the summer, gathering pinon nuts on the mountain slopes as well as hunting game, just as Shoshone Indians did in recent times (Thomas, 1973; Thomas and Bettinger, 1983).

Desert life in the United States survived almost without change into the eighteenth and nineteenth centuries A.D., when many hunter-gatherer groups were just about exterminated by expanding Euro-American settlement.

Eastern North America

Archaic tradition
c. 7000 to 2000 B.C.
and modern
times

While the Great Plains are dominated by grasslands, eastern North America, the region from the Mississippi Valley eastward, is covered by deciduous woodlands, and in the southeast by evergreen forest. Superficially, this could be considered a homogeneous natural environment with no sharp geographical barriers to interaction between different human groups, but in fact the area includes an almost bewildering array of microenvironments (Caldwell, 1958; Stoltman, 1978). As a result, it is very difficult to generalize about cultural developments after the end of the Paleo-Indian era in approximately 8000 B.C. The archaeological literature is complicated, mainly focused on chronology and stylistic changes in pottery and other artifacts, and it is very confusing to the nonspecialist. The account that follows here and in Chapter Thirteen emphasizes changes in subsistence and social organization rather than artifacts and chronologies.

Between approximately 8000 and 6000 B.C., the climate became warmer as the northern ice sheets continued to recede. Big-game hunting was of minimal importance, since the people now concentrated their hunting on smaller species such as the white-tailed deer, rabbits, turkeys, and muskrats. Fish, shellfish, and wild vegetable foods were surely important, but exact details of the Indians' diet at this time is still lacking. For 3000 years after 6000 B.C. the climate was warmer than it is today, with a higher preponderance of deciduous trees at the expense of pine forests which yield many more edible foods. Fish and shellfish became a vital part of the diet, especially in the more southerly parts of the east.

Much of the population was concentrated on major river valleys and floodplains. It comprised self-sufficient communities, perhaps best known to us from a remarkable series of excavations in the Illinois River valley of the Midwest between the 1960s and 1980s. The largest excavations have been at the Koster site near Kampsville, Illinois, one of the most remarkable archaeological sites in North America, a chronicle of prehistoric life from as early as approximately 10,000 years B.C. up to as late as A.D. 1200 (Struever and Holton, 1979). The Indians occupied the same location near the Illinois River time and time again, building their villages beneath the sheltered bluffs that overlooked the floodplain.

More than twenty-seven layers of the Koster site show how the local people first lived in small villages, then later abandoned the area and just visited it to mine the abundant chert that outcrops nearby — a wonderful toolmaking material.

By 5000 B.C., the Koster Indians were living in a village of permanent wood and thatch houses covering at least 1.75 acres. A thousand years later, a five-acre, permanent community of between 100 and 150 people thrived at the same location. The people were still relying entirely on game and wild vegetable foods but in new ways that involved very careful scheduling of collecting and the chase. They harvested annual "crops" of fish, duck, hickory nuts, and freshwater shellfish. Sometimes several families would band together to harvest vegetable foods or hunt geese. It was so easy to miss the vital harvest that large groups of several families probably ganged together to collect the seed at exactly the right moment. Both scheduling and cooperation in the food quest enabled the Illinois villages of 3000 B.C. to collect enough food to last through the lean winter months. So successful were the Indians that they collected food yields that compare favorably with those from agricultural production elsewhere in the world.

The same pattern of intensive hunting and gathering was commonplace throughout the eastern United States 5000 years ago. Population densities rose slowly, and permanent settlements became more commonplace. At first these communities were self-sufficient, but by 3000 B.C. dozens of villages were engaged in sporadic long-distance trade. The Indians exchanged seashells from Florida and many exotic materials, among them copper and mica. The Koster people were making beads out of copper obtained from as far away as Lake Superior, then trading these for fine flint minted in southern Illinois and Indiana quarries. The copper trade was particularly widespread, in hammered artifacts such as spearheads, knives, and pins, and even in ingot form (Figure 7.7) (Mason, 1981). The Koster villages demonstrate how the social organization became more intricate as local culture became more complex. The villagers now buried their dead in cemeteries where high-status individuals were laid to rest with prestigious items such as ornaments made of rare materials, seashells, or "bannerstones," specially shaped stones perforated with a hole, once hung around the neck to denote status. Only a small minority of the dead wore exotic ornaments, perhaps important lineage and kin leaders, the people who acted as chieftains and engaged in long-distance trade.

The term *Archaic tradition* has long been used to describe the many regional variants of hunter-gatherer culture under a single archaeological umbrella, although the label is now under attack (Stoltman, 1978; Willey, 1966). The Archaic tradition had many minor variations because of specialized ecological adaptations or particularly successful economic strategies. Much of the Archaic hunting tradition survived until modern times, especially in the northern parts of the eastern United

Figure 7.7 Archaic copper artifacts (approximately one-half actual size).

States and in Canada, where the first explorers found hunters and gatherers living much as the Archaic people had millennia before (Morison, 1971).

Specialized Hunter-Gatherers in Central and South America

The hunter-gatherers of the central and southern portions of the New World enjoyed a wide variety of specialized adaptations after 8000 B.C. Sites of these specialized hunter-gatherer groups have been excavated from Mexico to Tierra del Fuego, at the southern tip of South America. One characteristic adaptation has been identified in the Andes, and another flourished on the uplands of eastern Brazil (Lynch, 1978, 1980; Rick, 1980). As in North America, intensified hunting and gathering concentrated the human population in favored localities such as lake shores and seacoasts, where resources were unusually abundant.

Sophisticated hunting and gathering strategies ensured food at all seasons. Kent Flannery has shown, for instance, that the hunter-gatherers of the Tehuacán Valley in Mexico had a regular, almost scheduled, annual round of hunting and gathering activities that caused the population to gather in large camps during the plentiful season and scatter into small groups during the lean months (Flannery, 1968a). The people obtained a balanced diet by using different food procurement systems that varied in importance with the time of year.

Tehuacán
10,000 B.C.

Some of these specialized hunter-gatherers remained at the simple hunting and collecting level because of limitations in their environment and plentiful natural resources, making economic change unnecessary. However, in some areas of Mesoamerica and on the coasts and highlands of Peru, hunter-gatherer bands began to experiment with the deliberate planting of vegetable foods, perhaps in attempts to expand the areas in which certain favored vegetable foods were found. These experiments became one of the vehicles of dynamic cultural change that resulted from the first development of agriculture in the New World (Chapter Thirteen).

The southernmost extremities of Latin America were inhabited until recent times by scattered bands of hunters and fishermen. The Ona, Yaghan, and Alacaluf peoples are vividly described by early missionaries who settled among them. They lived in small bands, using only the crudest shelters of skins or grass and driftwood, with nothing but skin for body covering during the height of the antarctic winter. Shellfish, some game, fruits, berries, and fish provided a simple diet, and for tools they had none of the more sophisticated weapons made by more northern hunters. Tierra del Fuego, however, was occupied remarkably early, and it is thought that the Fuegian tradition began as early as 4000 B.C., if not earlier. Many roots of these most southerly prehistoric humans lie back in early hunting cultures that elsewhere were replaced thousands of years before by more advanced farming cultures.

Fuegian Indians
4000 B.C. to modern times

ALEUTS AND ESKIMOS

We started the story of the first Americans with Alaska, and now end with a brief return to Arctic latitudes to trace the origins of the Aleuts and Eskimos, whose remarkable hunter-gatherer cultures survived long beyond European contact into recent times. The origins of both the Aleut and the Eskimo go back many thousands of years into prehistory, and their ultimate ancestry may lie both in Asian roots and in local cultural evolution. The differences between them are more cultural than physical and reflect different adaptations to arctic maritime environments. It is logical for us to end this chapter with the Arctic, for the Eskimos were the first native Americans to come into contact with Europeans, in Greenland and in the extreme continental northeast (Dumond, 1977).

As we have seen, there is good reason to suspect that people have been living in Alaska and parts of northern Canada for at least 20,000 years, and perhaps for double that time, but the earliest cultural tradition which makes any archaeological sense at the moment is the Paleoarctic tradition, which was flourishing by 13,000 B.C. and had some connections with contemporary cultures in Siberia. The Paleoarctic people were tundra-dwelling hunter-gatherers, whose culture and language *may* be the ancestor of both Eskimo and Aleut culture and language. It should be noted that both peoples are the most Asian of all indigenous Americans.

Paleoarctic tradition
13,000 to 4000 B.C.

By 7000 B.C., these two peoples had moved south as far as the Alaskan peninsula. Only a millennium later they had settled in the Aleutian Islands.

By 4000 B.C., there was more cultural diversity in the Arctic, as specialized adaptations developed on the coast and in the interior, and some American Indian groups moved northwards into formerly glaciated regions in the interior. On the Pacific Coast, and in the eastern Aleutians, the Aleutian tradition was among those which emerged.

The Aleuts have been in their island homeland twice as long as the Eskimos have been in Greenland (Laughlin and Harper, 1979). They entered their archipelago at a time when the sea level was lower than it is today. The earliest occupation dates to approximately 6700 B.C. at Anangula, about a third of the way along the chain, at the terminus of the Bering Land Bridge. Anangula lies on a cliff 20 m (65.5 ft) above sea level and probably was occupied for at least 500 years, with an estimated population of at least one hundred souls (Aigner, 1970; Laughlin, 1980). The inhabitants lived by fishing, sea mammal hunting (Figure 7.8), and fowling, an ideal strategy for an isolated, stable marine environment. The nearby and later site of Chaluka carries the story of Aleutian occupation up to recent times. Radiocarbon dates from sites at both ends of the Aleutian chain suggest that the eastern and western ends of the archipelago were occupied in approximately 1000 B.C., the people expanding outward from the Anangula area as the population density grew.

Figure 7.8 Aleuts returning from a sea otter hunt, probably in the 1890s. They are wearing eye visors made of wood. Photograph by an unknown government surveyor.

The origins of the Eskimo cultural tradition of modern times lie in the Arctic Small-Tool tradition, a distinctive small-artifact technology that appears in Alaska in approximately 2300 B.C. The Arctic Small-Tool people may have had strong connections with Siberia and are thought to have been nomadic land mammal hunters who preyed on caribou and musk ox (Giddings, 1967). Some settled in Alaska; others of them wandered as far east as Greenland by 2000 B.C., the first people to settle in the eastern Arctic. The eastern Small-Tool tradition eventually evolved into the long-lived Thule tradition, whose people were the first native Americans to come into contact with Europeans (Maxwell, 1976).

Arctic Small-Tool tradition
2300 to 1500 B.C.

The Arctic Small-Tool tradition began to disappear in Alaska in 1500 B.C. or so, to be replaced by cultures based on the intensive hunting of both sea mammals and land animals. This hunting tradition, called the Norton tradition, in turn gave rise to a magnificent Eskimo sea mammal hunting culture, the Thule tradition, that is thought to have originated among whale hunters in the Bering Strait. The Thule tradition first emerged in the first millennium A.D. and developed into a highly distinctive sea mammal hunting culture with all the characteristic Eskimo artifacts so well known from popular publications — among them, the kayak, the umiak (open skin boat), and toggled harpoons, as well as fine ivory work (Figure 7.9). Many of the Eskimo lived by then in larger settlements, especially those who hunted whales. In approximately A.D. 900 the Thule people started to expand to the south, and then to the east. Thule whale hunters appeared in the Arctic islands of the east in approximately A.D. 1000, where their open-water hunting techniques could be used with great effect. By the time the Thule reached northwest Greenland, the Norsemen had been living in the southern parts of the island for some time.

Norton tradition (west)
1500 B.C. to A.D. 500

Thule tradition
A.D. 500 to modern times

A.D. 1200

Eskimo cultural traditions, like those of the Fuegians and other

Figure 7.9 Ornamented ivory object, perhaps a comb, from the Seward Peninsula in Alaska (Northern tradition and style). Length: 26 cm.

hunter-gatherer groups, continued to flourish after European contact, but within a few centuries, traditional lifeways were modified beyond recognition and exotic diseases decimated hunter-gatherer populations. Today, few of America's hunter-gatherers still practice their millennia-old life styles: there are no longer the resources nor the territorial space for them to do so.

GUIDE TO FURTHER READING

Hopkins, David M., Matthews, John V., Schweger, Charles E., and Young, Steven B. (Eds.) *Paleocology of Beringia.* New York: Academic Press, 1982.
A fascinating and highly technical set of essays about the Bering Land Bridge that discusses everything from animal life to sea level changes.

Jennings, Jesse D. *Ancient Native Americans.* 2 vols. New York: W. H. Freeman, 2d ed., 1982.
A comprehensive volume of essays on the archaeology of North, Middle, and South America, each written by an established authority. Up-to-date, highly technical, and crammed with useful information.

Shutler, Richard, Jr. (Ed.). *Early Man in the New World.* Beverly Hills: Sage Publications, 1983.
Authoritative, well-written essays on what we know about the first Americans in the 1980s. Strongly recommended.

Willey, Gordon R. *An Introduction to American Archaeology; North and Middle America,* vol. 1; and *South America,* vol 2. Englewood Cliffs, N.J.: Prentice Hall, 1966, 1971.
The ultimate sources on New World archaeology as of the early 1970s. Willey's unrivaled knowledge is the basis for all more specialized research. Superb illustrations, if a little outdated by the fieldwork of the past decade.

Chronological Table E

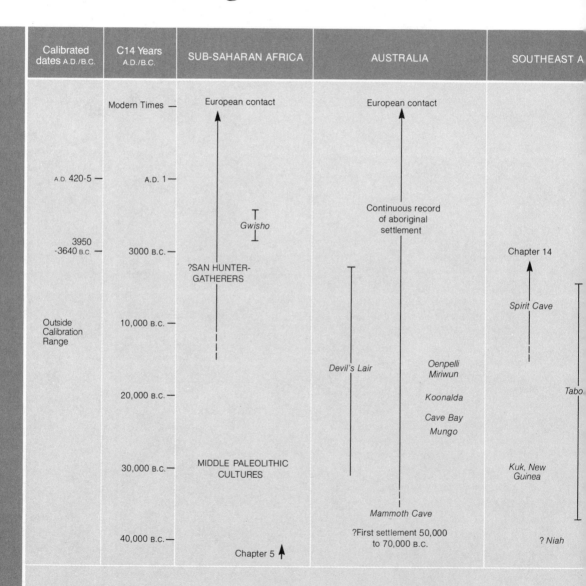

Calibrated dates A.D./B.C.	C14 Years A.D./B.C.	SUB-SAHARAN AFRICA	AUSTRALIA	SOUTHEAST A
	Modern Times —	European contact	European contact	
A.D. 420-5 —	A.D. 1 —			
		Gwisho	Continuous record of aboriginal settlement	
3950 -3640 B.C.	3000 B.C. —			Chapter 14
		?SAN HUNTER-GATHERERS		Spirit Cave
Outside Calibration Range	10,000 B.C. —			
			Devil's Lair	Oenpelli Miriwun
	20,000 B.C. —		Koonalda	Tabo
			Cave Bay Mungo	
	30,000 B.C. —	MIDDLE PALEOLITHIC CULTURES		Kuk, New Guinea
	40,000 B.C. —		Mammoth Cave	? Niah
		Chapter 5	?First settlement 50,000 to 70,000 B.C.	

Chapter Eight

Africans and Australians

PREVIEW

✤ Like hunter-gatherers in northern latitudes, the post-Pleistocene peoples of tropical regions adopted increasingly specialized economies after 8000 B.C. They also made much use of the bow and arrow, and toolkits became smaller and more lightweight as a result.

✤ This chapter concentrates on the San hunter-gatherers and Australian aborigines, whose traditional lifeways originated many thousands of years ago in prehistoric times.

✤ The San of southern Africa flourished in savannah woodland country that was rich in game and vegetable foods. Their lively rock art depicts their hunting and gathering activities. These paintings, and the waterlogged Gwisho sites in central Zambia, have shown that their portable toolkits changed little over the centuries. The San's highly flexible band organization of today doubtless ensured the continued viability of prehistoric hunter-gatherers as well. They also lived at small campsites which were often reoccupied at certain seasons of the year for many generations.

✤ During the Weichsel glaciation, New Guinea and Australia formed a single landmass for much of the time, a landmass called Sahul.

✤ It has been estimated that human settlement of Sahul goes back 50,000 to 70,000 years, although the earliest archaeological sites date to about 32,000 years ago.

✤ The archaeological record shows that the Australian lifeway changed little during its long history, but there were steady, slow changes in tool technology. The Tasmanians were isolated in their homeland as sea levels rose at the end of the Pleistocene and, as a result, did not acquire some of the later mainland tool types, such as the boomerang.

✤ Living archaeology and ethnographic analogy play an important part in our modern interpretation of the prehistory of tropical hunter-gatherers.

The end of the Weichsel glaciation had less profound effects on tropical latitudes than it had on northern latitudes. However, it did result in minor shifts in rainfall patterns, which may have had a significant effect on the distribution of critically important game populations and cereal

Chronological Table E

grasses. The archaeological record for the many hunter-gatherer populations of southern latitudes consists for the most part of thousands of stone implements from dozens of isolated sites (Allchin, 1966). Instead of attempting a detailed chronicle of isolated local cultures, we concentrate on two adaptations of particular interest — those of the San peoples of southern Africa, and those of the Australian aborigines. Both these peoples continue to display a wide range of relatively specialized adaptations that include not only hunting and gathering, but fishing and exploitation of shellfish as well.

The modern hunter-gatherer populations of Africa and Asia are among the very few survivors of the longest-lived and perhaps most viable of all human lifeways. Only 15,000 years ago, probably everyone lived by hunting and gathering. Ethnographer George Peter Murdock has estimated that perhaps fifteen percent of the world's population was still hunting and gathering at the time Columbus landed in the New World (Murdock, 1968). We are fortunate that modern anthropological studies of the San and Australians have given us at least a few insights into traditional lifeways of southern hunter-gatherers.

AFRICAN HUNTER-GATHERERS: PAST AND PRESENT

Until 15,000 years ago or so, many hunter-gatherers in Africa were still making prepared cores and flake tools characteristic of the Middle Paleolithic. These were replaced in part by tools made with blade technology after 13,000 B.C. (J. D. Clark, 1970). By the end of the Pleistocene, savannah woodland groups were beginning to rely heavily on the bow and arrow. Stone technology was modified to produce enormous numbers of tiny, stone arrow barbs that are known to archaeologists as "microliths." These were fitted onto arrow shafts (Figure 8.1). Later stone toolkits were much smaller than earlier ones. The bow has the important advantage that it can be used to dispatch game from a distance, especially if the arrow is smeared with vegetable poison. Thousands of microlithic arrow barbs are found in the caves and rock shelters and open living sites of the woodland cultures. In more densely forested regions, the people relied on heavy stone-headed picks and a variety of woodworking tools to exploit the closed-in environment of dense woodland and rain forest.

In Africa, as elsewhere, we find increasing economic specialization. The peoples of the open savannah lived off the abundant game populations and supplemented their diet with seasonal gathering of the rich vegetable resources of the woodland. Other bands settled on the shores of lakes and on riverbanks and lived by fishing. This valuable and reliable source of protein encouraged more lasting settlement and increased specialization. The rain forest peoples of the Zaire river basin in central Africa were unable to hunt such a wide range of game as their savannah

13,000 B.C.

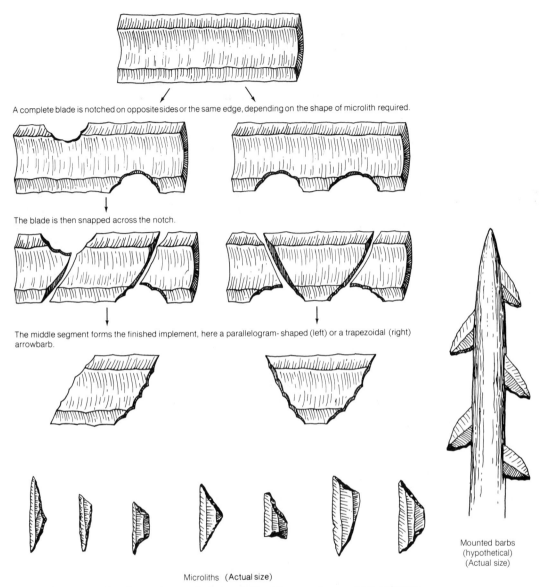

A complete blade is notched on opposite sides or the same edge, depending on the shape of microlith required.

The blade is then snapped across the notch.

The middle segment forms the finished implement, here a parallelogram- shaped (left) or a trapezoidal (right) arrowbarb.

Microliths (Actual size)

Mounted barbs
(hypothetical)
(Actual size)

Figure 8.1 Microliths. Stages in manufacturing a microlith, a small arrow barb or similar implement made by notching a blade and snapping off its base after the implement is formed.

counterparts, and so they relied heavily on vegetable foods and wild roots for much of their livelihood.

The lifeway of the savannah hunter-gatherers of eastern and southern Africa has been immortalized by the people themselves. They lived in open living sites, under convenient rocky overhangs, and in the mouths of deep caves. It was on the walls of these caves and rock shelters that the people painted vivid depictions of the game they hunted, of the chase, and of life in camp (Lewis-Williams, 1981; Vinnecombe, 1976). The San drew running hunters, people fishing from boats, and scenes of gathering honey and vegetable foods (Figures 8.2 and 8.3). The hunters can be seen stalking game in disguise, in hot pursuit of wounded quarry, even raiding cattle herds of their agricultural neighbors of later centuries. This extraordinary artistic tradition is found on the walls of caves that were occupied as early as 6000 B.C., perhaps earlier. The San returned to the same sites year after year, occupying some of them until very recent times. Their lifeway changed but little over the millennia and is well documented from cave paintings and from remarkable discoveries at waterlogged living sites in Zambia, where bands of San camped regularly more than 2000 years ago.

Gwisho
1500 B.C.

The Gwisho hot springs in central Zambia were a favored location for San bands for thousands of years (Fagan and Van Noten, 1971). Because the lower levels of the campsites there are waterlogged, some artifacts were preserved by the water and give us unique insights into the peoples who used them. The economy and material culture of these peoples show a striking resemblance to those of modern San peoples in the Kalahari, although, of course, there are environmental differences (R. B. Lee, 1979; R. B. Lee and DeVore, 1976; Yellen, 1977). The Gwisho people hunted many species of antelope and caught fish in shallow pools of the nearby Kafue river. The waterlogged levels contained more than 10,000 plant remains, which came from only eight species, all of which were apparently collected to the exclusion of many other edible species. Nearby lay some fine arrowheads and some of the wooden artifacts made by the inhabitants, including some simple digging sticks used for uprooting tubers. These tools were identical to those used by Kalahari San today.

Figure 8.2 A running San hunter from Ho Khotso, Lesotho, southern Africa, from a late Stone Age painting colored purple-red. The figure is 21 cm (approximately 8 in) high.

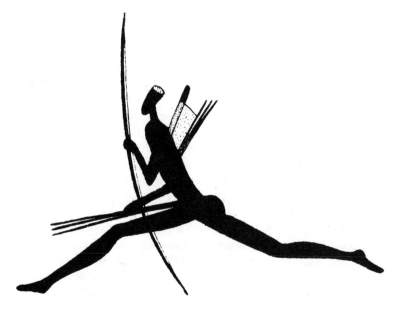

HUNTER-GATHERERS

There were traces of a grass and stick shelter, of hearths, and of layers of grass that may have served as bedding. Thirty-five burials were deposited in the soil of the campsites. The deposits were littered with hundreds of stone arrow barbs and tiny scraping tools that lay alongside pestles and grinding stones used to process the vegetable foods that were an important part of the Gwisho diet. So little have gathering habits changed in the past 3000 years that a San from the Kalahari was able to identify seeds from the excavations and tell archaeologists what they were used for.

The Gwisho hot springs are informative, for they confirm ethnographic observations made about the present-day San of the Kalahari. Like that of their modern successors, the toolkit of the Gwisho people was highly portable and much of it was disposable. Except for bows and arrows, the Kalahari San improvise many of their tools from the bush as they need them, making snares from vegetable fibers and clubs from convenient branches. The women use digging sticks like the Gwisho artifacts for digging tubers and a softened antelope hide, or kaross, as a garment and carrying bag. Their only other artifacts are a pair of pounding stones for breaking up nuts. The Gwisho site contains both the digging sticks and pounders. We know from cave paintings that the San used karosses for thousands of years, and we can assume they were used at Gwisho and elsewhere.

Gwisho **1500 B.C.**

Like those of the San, the Gwisho home bases were little more than small clusters of brush shelters. The average present-day !Kung San camp holds approximately ten to thirty people. The small population of !Kung territory leads to a constant turnover of the composition of camp populations. This constantly changing composition is a reality reflected in the !Kung's highly flexible kinship system. Every member of a band has not only close family ties but also kin connections with a much wider number of people living all over !Kung territory. The !Kung kinship system is based on an elaborate network of commonly possessed personal names which are transmitted from grandparent to grandchild. People with similar names share kin ties even if they live at some distance from one another. This network of personal names and kin ties is such that individuals can move to a new camp and find a family with which they have kin ties to accept them. The resulting flexibility of movement prevents total social chaos. Presumably, the prehistoric San had a similar pragmatic and flexible social organization to aid survival.

A.D. 1
Prehistoric hunter-gatherers enjoyed the savannah woodlands of eastern and southern Africa undisturbed until approximately 2000 years ago, when the first farming peoples (other African folk) settled by the banks of the Zambezi and Limpopo rivers (Phillipson, 1984). The San placed second in the resulting competition for land: the farmers wanted grazing grass and prime land for cultivating, so they drove off the bands of San hunter-gatherers who had to retreat into less favored areas. Some took up the new economies and married into farming communities. White settlement in South Africa increased the isolation of the San still further. As A.D. 1800 the pressure on their hunting grounds increased, the San moved into mountainous areas and into desert regions. Even there they were harassed and hunted. Some of the white settlers even went shooting them on Sunday afternoons. The doomed San of South Africa calmly continued to paint scenes of cattle raids and of European ships and wagons. They even depicted red-coated English soldiers on their expeditions into the mountains. By the end of the nineteenth century, there were no artists still painting in South Africa and the art of stone toolmaking had all but died out. The last stoneworkers made use of glass bottle fragments to make A.D. 1890 their sharp arrowheads. They found this unusually pure "stone" vastly preferable to their usual quartz pebbles (Peringuey, 1911; Schapera, 1930).

PREHISTORY OF THE AUSTRALIANS

The Australian aborigines encountered by Captain Cook and other early explorers were still living in the Stone Age; they were all hunter-gatherers and used a technology that could have stepped right out of prehistory (Figure 8.4). Their ancestry has excited the interest of anthropological archaeologists ever since: Where did the Australians come from, and how long ago did people first settle on this remote continent? (Mulvaney, 1975; J. White and O'Connell, 1982).

The natural area in which to look for Australian origins is, of course, southeastern Asia. When sea levels were at their lowest during the height of the Weichsel glaciation, perhaps 50,000 years ago, only a relatively short open water passage separated Australia from the islands that lie off

Figure 8.4. An Australian aborigine with his lightweight hunting kit. This somewhat romanticized portrait was drawn by François Peron, a naturalist attached to the Baudin Expedition of 1802.

Asia and the mainland (Allen, Golson, and Jones, 1977). Unfortunately, archaeological research in southeastern Asia has been too sparse to demonstrate close connections between the toolkits of the earliest Australians and those of their Asian contemporaries. No one, however, challenges the accepted hypothesis that Australian origins lie in the north.

We do know that the stone technologies of southeastern Asia were startlingly conservative for long periods of time, and at both Niah Cave in Borneo and at Tabon Cave on the island of Palawan the same crude flake and chopper stone technology remained in use almost unchanged from 38,000 to 5000 B.C. (Harrisson, 1957). The same long-term conservatism

Niah
38,000 B.C.

is found in Australia, where the simplest of stone technologies proved effective for tens of thousands of years.

The constant fluctuations of sea level during the Weichsel glaciation had profound effects on the geography of Australia. For at least 80 percent of the time humans have lived on the continent, New Guinea and Australia were joined by a continental shelf, now submerged by higher, post-Ice Age water. This single landmass is known as Sahul. For about the first 40,000 years of their history the peoples of Sahul shared a common history. Then at the end of the Weichsel sea levels rose and separated the two countries.

Throughout this long 40,000-year period, the climate fluctuated constantly. About 20,000 to 15,000 years ago, Tasmania was part of the Australian mainland, present coastlines were far inland, and much of the region was considerably drier. The first traces of human settlement in Australia may date to as early as 50,000 years ago, but no traces of such occupation have yet come to light. This is hardly surprising, since most archaeological sites are the remains of short-term, outdoor encampments that contain little more than hearths and stone tools.

The earliest dated sites are from dry Lake Mungo in western New South Wales. A series of carbon patches appear to be hearths, associated with simple stone artifacts and some heavily encrusted human bones. The hearths contained fish bones, some birds, shellfish, and a few mammal fragments. A series of radiocarbon dates place this occupation in the range 31,000 to 22,000 B.C. (White and O'Connell, 1982). The skeletal remains are entirely of modern people, who may have reached Australia during a period of low sea level, perhaps as early as 50,000 years ago (Bowler, Allen, and Thorne, 1970).

As in the Americas, there are precious few sites dating to earlier than 10,000 years ago. The Devil's Lair Cave in the southwestern part of western Australia contains occupation levels that date from earlier than 27,000 B.C. — perhaps much earlier (Dortch and Merrilees, 1973). Nearby Mammoth Cave was excavated early in this century without good stratigraphic control, but many bones from extinct marsupials (pouched animals) were found. There is a possibility that this site may be as much as 40,000 years old, although the evidence is inconclusive (White and O'Connell, 1982).

The only other piece of archaeological evidence contemporary with Lake Mungo comes from Kuk in highland New Guinea, where fire-cracked and humanly transported rocks have been dated to about 30,000 years ago (White and O'Connell, 1982). It is probable that Sahul was settled between 70,000 and 50,000 years ago, during times of low sea level, but this is a mere guesstimate.

How did the actual settlement occur? Almost certainly as a result of accidental voyages. At no time was the Southeast Asian mainland joined to Sahul, not even during the periods of lowest sea level. Many of the islands off the mainland are less than 6 mi (10 km) apart. These islands could have been easily reached intentionally on simple rafts, or even floating logs, but not the more distant islands, which were probably colonized by accident, when people drifted offshore. It is interesting to note that almost no Asian animals colonized the islands, so the settlement of Sahul was probably an accident, and even if the shortest sea routes were used, the trip would have involved at least one open water crossing of over 50 mi. Therefore, the human settlement of Sahul was probably a very slow process, with no return voyages, a process that may have started way back in the Ice Age, since human settlement on the mainland took place at least a million years ago.

At present, it is impossible to go far beyond speculation. Few archaeologists have worked in any part of Sahul, many of the early sites are on the ocean floor, and initial human settlement was very sparse indeed.

Once settlement was established, on a continent that at the time was three times its present size, one can assume that humans spread slowly through the entire region. By 20,000 years ago, people were certainly living around the modern coasts and on the fringes of the desert. By 10,000 years ago, they had settled in all the major environmental zones. And by that time the island of Tasmania was separated from the mainland by the rising waters of the Bass Strait. How did this process of colonization take place? Some argue that it was a relatively rapid process, a matter of pursuing big game, or of the population doubling every twenty years or so, a natural rate of increase that would give rise to the modern density of indigenous Australians in about 2000 years. But there are too many variables for this model to be truly convincing, among them such factors as birth spacing and physiology. Another hypothesis holds that the first settlers were coastal peoples, who later moved into the interior. While many of the first colonizers may have been coastal peoples, it seems more likely that the interior would have been settled at the same time as the coast, and, in any case, the notion that the earliest sites were coastal ones is as yet unproven (for detailed arguments, see White and O'Connell, 1982). White and O'Connell have compared the Australian situation to that in America, where some people (Martin, 1973) believe that rapid colonization by big game hunters led to a very rapid settlement as far south as Patagonia. They believe that it would take hunter-gatherers a considerable period of time to adapt to the many different environments between the Plains and Tierra del Fuego, that this process took many millennia, and that the settlement of both America and Australia was a very slow process. The main barriers to rapid human settlement were not the environments, it was peoples' ability to learn how to exploit them. Generations of field work are needed to underpin any of these hypotheses.

Between 25,000 and 10,000 years ago, the population of Australia may have reached approximately modern levels, an estimated 300,000 people. Sites in this time bracket have been found throughout Australia, at Oenpelli and Miriwun in the north, the latter shelter dating to nearly 18,000 years ago (Dortch, 1977). Another famous location is Koonalda in southern Australia, a cave on a treeless plain where hearths and flint nod-

Miriwun
16,000 B.C.

ules were discovered at a mining site and date to between 15,000 and 23,000 years ago. Some wavy patterns made by human hands have been found on the soft limestone walls and may be of high antiquity (R. Wright, 1971).

The same traditions of stoneworking and bone technology found in these early sites survived almost unchanged for thousands of years (R. Wright, 1977). For instance, flakes showing wear patterns characteristic of adze blades made by modern aborigines date back as far as 20,000 B.C., and the same bone points used to fasten skin clothes in historic times have been found deep in the prehistoric levels of Devil's Lair as well. The Australian aborigines were famous for their artistic traditions and elaborate ceremonial life. Abundant traces of ritual belief have been found in Australian sites. The Devil's Lair site yielded stone plaques, a deep pit, and human incisor teeth that had been knocked out with a sharp blow: such evulsion of teeth was a long-lived Australian tradition. If the Koonalda engravings are as old as claimed, then some Australian art is as ancient as European Upper Paleolithic artistic traditions.

Despite the essential conservatism of Australian stoneworking practices, some regional variations in stone technology did appear over the millennia. Steep-edged scrapers which were probably used as woodworking tools were made over a wide area of Australia during much of the Late Pleistocene. These, and crude flake tools, remained in use until recent times; they were joined after 4000 B.C. in some areas by stone points set on shafts and other microliths. There is good reason to believe that Australian aboriginal technology developed within Australia over a long period of time in response to local needs, and without the benefit of cultural innovation from outside (Figure 8.5).

Some idea of the simple level of early Australian life can be obtained from the saga of the Tasmanians (Plumley, 1969). When the first European voyagers visited Tasmania in 1642, they found bands of huntergatherers living on the island, separated from the mainland by the stormy Bass Straits. The Tasmanians lasted precisely eighty years after European settlement in 1802. They had no shafted tools (that is, tools composed of stone heads or points with wooden shafts or handles) and relied instead on scrapers and choppers somewhat like those used by early huntergatherers on the mainland; they lacked the boomerangs, spear throwers, shields, axes, adzes, and lightweight stone tools the Australians of the mainland had when they first entered written history. Tasmania was settled when it was attached to the mainland during the Weichsel glaciation, but many of the earliest sites are probably buried under the sea.

Cave Bay
19,000 B.C.

The earliest archaeological record of occupation is from a cave at Cave Bay on Hunter Island, now isolated from Tasmania by the higher sea level that cut Tasmania away from Australia as well. The cave was used by occasional visitors who left sparse occupation levels behind them dating from 21,000 B.C. (Bowdler, 1982). The result of Tasmania's isolation was that its populations, although forming part of the Australian cultural

Figure 8.5. Australian aborigines making stone tools.

group, never received the later cultural innovations that spread through Australia after the sea levels rose.

Fortunately for archaeology, at least some investigations of aboriginal culture have been made that have important bearing on the interpretation of the archaeological record. Richard Gould spent many months among the Ngatatjara people of the Western Desert carrying out ethnographic investigations that had objectives somewhat similar to those of Richard Lee among the San in Africa: he was interested in their cultural ecology and in the ways in which ethnographic observations could be used to interpret the archaeological record (Gould, 1977). His aboriginal informants took him to Puntutjarpa rock shelter, a site that they still visited regularly. Gould excavated the occupation levels in the shelter and found that people had lived there for more than 6800 years. The later stone implements at the site were almost indistinguishable from modern Ngatatjara tools, to the extent that Gould was able to compare the wear patterns on both ancient and modern artifacts and decide which 5000-year-old tools had been mounted on shafts and which had not. He also compared modern living surfaces with equivalent features found in the rock shelter (Figure 8.6).

Puntutjarpa
5000 B.C.

The study of living aborigine bands shows just how conservative Australian lifeways have been. There were few major technological innovations during Australian prehistory. Indeed, it was possible for the

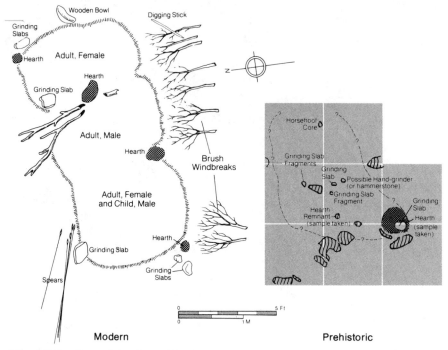

Figure 8.6. Comparison of a prehistoric campsite at Puntutjarpa rock shelter, Australia, with a modern aboriginal campsite in the same area. Note that the modern encampment can be subdivided into living areas by using informants' data and anthropological observation, while the archaeological site is devoid of such information, consisting merely of artifact patterns.

prehistoric Australians to maintain a thoroughly viable lifeway with minimal technology and but the simplest of artifacts. The Tasmanians, for instance, used only two dozen or so tools to hunt and forage. The great elaboration of Australian and Tasmanian culture was in social and ritual life, neither of which can readily be recovered by archaeological investigation. That much of this activity was designed to maintain the delicate balance between the aborigines and their available resources in their environment was no coincidence (J. White and O'Connell, 1982). A belief in such balance lay at the very core of Australian life.

GUIDE TO FURTHER READING

Clark, J. Desmond. *The Prehistory of Southern Africa*. Baltimore: Pelican Books, 1959.
  The relevant chapters are those on the Late Stone Age. Clark's description of the San lifeway using rock art is a classic.

Clark, J. Desmond. *The Prehistory of Africa*. London: Thames and Hudson, 1970.
  A synthesis of African prehistory with emphasis on the Stone Age. This book is best combined with the first text listed here.

Gould, Richard. *Living Archaeology*. London: Cambridge University Press, 1980.
A definitive primer on ethnoarchaeology that covers most major field research conducted thus far. Excellent on basic principles.

Lee, Richard B. *The !Kung San*. London: Cambridge University Press, 1979.
If there is one classic ethnographic study of hunter-gatherers, Lee's account of the Kalahari San and their complex ecology is it. Strongly recommended to give the reader a clear understanding of hunter-gatherer lifeways.

White, J. Peter, and O'Connell, James. *A Prehistory of Australia, New Guinea, and Sahul*. New York: Academic Press, 1982.
The definitive, analytical synthesis of the prehistory of Australia. A superb, even masterly account.

PART FOUR

FARMERS

(c. 10,000 B.C. to Modern Times)

"Agriculture is not to be looked on as a difficult or
out-of-the-way invention, for the rudest savage, skilled as he
is in the habits of the food-plants he gathers, must know
well enough that if seeds or roots are put in a proper place
in the ground they will grow."
– Sir Edward Tylor, 1883

The beginning of food production — of agriculture and animal domestication
— was one of the catalytic events of human prehistory. Part Four not only
describes the sequence of farming cultures in all parts of the world but also
analyzes some of the recent theories about the origins of farming. We will start
with the theoretical background first and then study farming in geographical
areas. With the beginnings of food production we find the first signs of rapidly
accelerating cultural evolution, of processes that are still operating at a record
pace today. However, our understanding of the early millennia of farming is
incomplete. The archaeological evidence outlined here is extremely sketchy and
often stretched to the limit to produce a coherent narrative. Future research is
certain to modify drastically the story set forth in the chapters of Part Four.

Chapter Nine

Plenteous Harvest: The Origins

PREVIEW

✤ The domestication of plants and animals was one of the momentous developments in world prehistory because the new economic strategies resulted in increased and stabilized food supplies, but generally at a higher energy cost.

✤ Food production proved dramatically successful. Ten thousand years ago almost everyone in the world was hunting and gathering. By 2000 years ago hunter-gatherers were in a minority.

✤ The advent of food production brought more sedentary settlements, improved storage facilities, and new toolkits designed for agriculture and food storage. Population increases appear to have preceded, and followed, the beginnings of food production.

✤ The first theories for the origins of food production were formulated in terms of a single genius who invented agriculture. Others hypothesized that increased desiccation at the end of the Pleistocene concentrated plants, humans, and animals in a close symbiosis, which resulted in domestication. V. Gordon Childe refined this theory and postulated a Neolithic Revolution.

✤ Modern theories have moved away from a Neolithic Revolution toward ecological explanations, which suggest that a variety of factors interacted to cause humankind to experiment with the deliberate cultivation of cereal and root crops. According to this ecology-based account, food production was developed in several areas of the world more or less at the same time.

✤ Braidwood with his nuclear zones, Binford with theories of demographic stress, and Flannery with a systems approach to agricultural origins all argued that the development of food production was a gradual process, one in which hunter-gatherers moved from scheduled gathering activities to experimentation with food crops at the edge of areas where potential domesticates were abundant.

✤ Recently, Mark Cohen has suggested that population pressure was a major factor in the development of food production. He argues that the only significant puzzle is why people turned from hunting and gathering, a relatively low-risk activity, to agriculture, which, at least initially, was a high-risk and much more arduous venture. It could be that the changeover occurred when environmental imbalance caused people to fall back on less desirable foods and therefore to try to grow food for themselves. This would be, after all, a logical step for people familiar with the germination of plants.

✣ We end by looking at some of the genetic changes in plants and animals that resulted from domestication and at the technological changes that followed in the train of domestication.

It is difficult for us, buying our food from supermarkets, to appreciate how awesome were the consequences to human history of agriculture and the domestication of animals. For more than 99 percent of our existence as humans, we were hunter-gatherers, tied to the seasons of vegetable foods or movements of game. However, with economies based on the production of food, people could influence their environment and sometimes control its ecological balance, with drastic consequences for their descendants (Watson and Watson, 1969).

CONSEQUENCES OF FOOD PRODUCTION

The new food-producing economies proved dramatically successful. Ten thousand years ago virtually everybody in the world lived by hunting and gathering. By 2000 years ago most people were farmers or herders and only a minority still were hunter-gatherers. The spread of food production throughout the world took only about 8000 years. The problem for anthropologists is not only to account for why people took up agriculture, but also to explain why so many populations adopted this new, and initially risky, economic transition in such a short time. Food production spread to all corners of the world except where an environment with extreme aridity or heat or cold rendered agriculture or herding impossible or where people chose to remain hunters and gatherers. In some places, food production was the economic base for urbanization and literate civilization; but most human societies did not go further than subsistence-level food production until the industrial power of nineteenth- and twentieth-century Europe led them into the Machine Age.

Food production resulted, ultimately, in much higher population densities in many locations, for the domestication of plants and animals can result in an economic strategy that increases and stabilizes available food supplies, although at the expense of more energy used to produce it. Farmers use concentrated tracts of territory for agriculture and for grazing cattle and small stock, if they practice mixed farming. Their territory is much smaller than that of hunter-gatherers (although pastoralists need huge areas of grazing land for seasonal pasture). Within a smaller area of farming land, property lines are carefully delineated, as individual ownership of land and problems of inheritance of property arise. Shortages of land can lead to disputes and to the founding of new village settlements on previously uncultivated soil (Childe, 1936; Struever, 1971).

More enduring settlements brought other changes. The portable and lightweight material possessions of many hunter-gatherers were replaced by heavier toolkits and more lasting houses (Figure 9.1). Grind-stones and ground-edged axes were even more essential to farming culture than they were to gathering societies. Hoes and other implements of tillage were vital for the planting and harvesting of crops. New social units came into being as more lasting home bases were developed; these social links reflected ownership and inheritance of land and led to much larger settlements that brought hitherto scattered populations into closer and more regular contact.

Food production led to changed attitudes toward the environment. Cereal crops were such that people could store their food for use in winter (Figure 9.1). The hunter-gatherers exploited game, fish, and vegetable foods, but the farmers did more; they *altered* the environment by the very nature of the exploitation. Expansion of agriculture meant felling trees and burning vegetation to clear the ground for planting. The same fields then were abandoned after a few years to lie fallow, and more woodland was cleared. The original vegetation began to regenerate, but it might be cleared again before reaching its original state. This shifting pattern of farming is called slash-and-burn agriculture. Voracious domesticated animals stripped pastures of their grass cover, then heavy rainfalls denuded the hills of valuable soil, and the pastures were never the same again. However elementary the agricultural technology, the farmer changed the environment, if only with fires lit to clear scrub from gardens and to fertilize the soil with wood ashes. Hunter-gatherers had deliberately set fires to encourage the growth of new grass for their grazing

Figure 9.1 A pole-and-mud hut typical of the Middle Zambezi Valley, Africa (left). Such dwellings, often occupied fifteen years or longer, are more lasting than the windbreak or tent of the hunter-gatherer. At right is a grain bin from an African village, used for cereal crops. Storing food is a critical part of a food-producing economy.

prey. In a sense, shifting, slash-and-burn agriculture is merely an extension of the age-old use of fire to encourage regeneration of vegetation.

Food production resulted in high population densities; but growth was controlled by disease, available food supplies, water supplies, and particularly famine. Many peoples controlled their populations by deliberately spacing births. Early agricultural methods depended heavily on careful selection of the soil. The technology of the first farmers was hardly potent enough for extensive clearing of the dense woodland under which many good soils lay, and so the potentially cultivable land could only be that which was accessible in the first place. Gardens probably were scattered over a much wider territory than is necessary today with modern plowing and other advanced techniques. One authority on African agriculture estimates that, even with advanced shifting agriculture, only forty percent of moderately fertile soil in Africa is available for such cultivation (Allan, 1965). This figure must have been lower in the early days of agriculture, with its simpler stone tools and fewer crops.

In regions of seasonal rainfall such as the Near East, sub-Saharan Africa, and parts of Asia, periods of prolonged drought are common. Famine probably was a real possibility as population densities rose. Many early agriculturalists must have worriedly watched the sky and must have had frequent crop failures in times of drought. Their small stores of grain from the previous season would not have carried them through another year, especially if they had been careless with their surplus. Farmers were forced to shift their economic strategy in times of famine. We can assume that the earliest farmers availed themselves of game and vegetable foods to supplement their agriculture, just as even today some farmers are obliged to rely heavily on wild vegetable foods and hunting to survive in bad years (Scudder, 1962, 1971). Many hunter-gatherer bands collect intensively just a few species of edible plants in their large territories. Aware of many other edible vegetables, they fall back on those only in times of stress; these less favored foods can carry a comparatively small population through to the next rains. A larger agricultural population is not so flexible and quickly exhausts wild vegetables and game in the much smaller territory used for farming and grazing. If the drought lasts for years, famine, death, and reduced population can follow.

THEORIES ABOUT THE ORIGINS OF FOOD PRODUCTION

Why did people choose to grow their own crops? What caused food production to be adopted in thousands of human societies and with such rapidity?

Speculations about the origins of agriculture go back for more than a century. The first theories envisaged a solitary genius who suddenly had the brilliant idea of planting seed (Roth, 1887). Others argued for a severe drought at the end of the Pleistocene which concentrated animals, plants, and humans in oases with permanent water supplies where people tamed the flora and fauna for their own purposes. No one still looks for a single genius or for the earliest maize cob. Rather, modern theory concentrates on the complex processes that caused gradual changes in human subsistence patterns (G. Wright, 1971).

Childe: Neolithic Revolution

One of the first scholars to work with excavated data was V. Gordon Childe, who proposed a major economic revolution in prehistory — the Neolithic Revolution (Childe, 1936, 1952). His Neolithic Revolution took place during a period of severe drought, a climatic crisis that caused a symbiotic relationship to be forged between the humans and animals in fertile oases. The new economies ensured a richer and more reliable food source for people on the edge of starvation.

Childe's revolution hypothesis was a refinement of the oasis theory and was widely accepted, but no one has yet found convincing traces of drier climate at the end of the Pleistocene. Other early scholars began to examine the hilly regions above the lowlands of Mesopotamia to see if they might have been the cradle of early food production, for it was there that fossils of potentially domesticable animals and wild cereals were found (Peake and Fleure, 1927).

Braidwood: nuclear zones

Systematic field work into the origins of food production began only in the late 1940s. Robert J. Braidwood of the University of Chicago mounted an expedition to the Kurdish foothills of Iran to test Childe's theories. Geologists and zoologists on the expedition produced field evidence causing Braidwood to reject the notion of catastrophic climatic change at the end of the Pleistocene, despite minor shifts in rainfall distribution. Nothing in the environment, Braidwood argued, could have necessitated the radical shift in human adaptation proposed by Childe (Braidwood and Braidwood, 1983). Braidwood felt the economic change came from the "ever increasing cultural differentiation and specialization of human communities." Thus, he argued, the people were culturally receptive to innovation and experimentation with cultivation of wild grasses. People had begun to understand and manipulate the plants and animals around them in "nuclear zones," that is to say, areas where potentially domesticable cereals and animals flourished in the wild. One of these zones was the hilly flanks of the Zagros Mountains in Iraq and the upland areas overlooking the Mesopotamian lowlands. Braidwood was convinced that the human capacity and enthusiasm for experimentation made it possible for people to domesticate animals and grow crops. However, his hypothesis does not explain *why* food production was adopted.

Sauer: ecology

In 1952, Carl O. Sauer published a remarkable essay on agricultural origins, in which he analyzed the ecology of food production (Sauer, 1952). He saw the origins of food production as a change in the way in which culture and environment interacted. Sauer proposed Southeast Asia as a major center of domestication, where root crops were grown by semisedentary fishing folk. Few scholars were prepared to accept Sauer's theory that the idea of domestication diffused from Southeast Asia to the Near East. Yet Sauer has proved remarkably prophetic on the importance of root crops and the antiquity of food production in Southeast Asia, for evidence of possible early root cultivation may date to as early as 9000 B.C. in Spirit Cave, Thailand (Solheim, 1971). He insisted on the importance of continuous adaptation to the origin of food production. Sauer's was a pioneer interpretation of how food production began.

Lewis Binford rejected Braidwood's contention that human nature brought about agriculture and argued that demographic stress favored food production (Binford, 1968). At the end of the Pleistocene, he hypothesized, population flowed from some of the world's seacoasts into less populated areas because of rising sea levels as the world's glaciers retreated. These movements led to demographic stress where potentially domesticable plants and animals were to be found; consequently the development of agriculture was adaptively advantageous for the inhabitants of these regions. Like Braidwood's, Binford's theory has several weaknesses, not least among them being the repeated fluctuations of sea levels in earlier interglacials. Why did they not lead to similar demographic stress and culture change?

Kent Flannery has argued that the transition from hunting and gathering to food production was a gradual process (Flannery, 1968). In a classic paper that examined the mechanisms by which Mesoamericans took up agriculture (Chapter Two), he maintained that the preagricultural peoples of Mesoamerica who later became agriculturalists adapted not to a given environment but to a few plant and animal genera whose range cut across several environments. Using pollen and animal bone analyses from preagricultural sites, Flannery listed the animals and plants upon which these people depended — among them were century plant leaves, cactus fruits, deer, rabbits, wild waterfowl, and wild grasses, including corn. Foods such as the century plant were available all year. Others, such as mesquite pods and deer, were exploited during the dry season, but cacti were eaten only during the rains.

To obtain these foods the people had to be in the right place at the right season, and the time depended on the plants, not the people: foragers had to plan around the seasons. In other words, their system for procuring food was scheduled. A minor change in any part of the system was reflected in the group's scheduling and might preclude their exploiting foods whose season conflicted with the new schedule.

Genetic changes in two food plants, corn and beans, eventually made these plants increasingly important to the people who used them. Both plants became slightly more productive, and so they tended to become more important in the diet. Gradually more and more time was spent on beans and corn, and the groups had to reschedule their activities to accommodate this change. Because a group could not be in two places at once, foods that were procured at times when corn and beans had to be planted or harvested would necessarily be neglected.

In another paper Flannery considered the problems of Near Eastern food production (Flannery, 1965). He stressed that it was not the planting of seeds or the herding of animals that was important but the fact that

Binford: demographic stress

Flannery: mechanisms

people moved out to niches to which they were not adapted and removed pressures of natural selection, which now allowed more deviants to survive and eventually be selected for characteristics not beneficial under natural conditions. According to Flannery and his colleague Frank Hole (Hole, Flannery, and Neely, 1969), approximately 20,000 years ago people began to shift from a hunting and gathering way of life to a more specialized economy, including the use of both storage pits and ground stone tools used to crush pigments and tough grass seeds. Seasonal use of the environment was typical of many parts of the Near East and Mesoamerica, with different wild foods scheduled for separate seasons. What upset this equilibrium between culture and environment?

Flannery took Binford's demographic model, in which population growth in some areas of southwestern Asia was greatest in the optimum habitats of the seasonal hunters and gatherers of the hilly flanks and the Palestine woodlands. The population increases caused new groups to split off into more marginal areas where the inhabitants tried to produce artificially, around the *margins* of the optimum zone, stands of cereals as dense as those in the heart of the zone.

There are several implications of this hypothesis. First, the hunter-gatherer populations in the optimum areas increased before food producing began. This can be tested in the archaeological record by searching for evidence of dense settlement in the optimum areas and large kill sites and other signs of a culture that hunted and collected food intensively to support its large numbers. Second, the earliest evidence of food production will appear on the margins of the hilly flanks and the woodland areas of Palestine in sites where the material culture is strikingly similar to that of the hunter-gatherers in the best areas. Finally, there will be more than one center of domestication for both plants and animals. The advantage of Flannery's hypothesis is that it can be tested in the field, although the testing is likely to be arduous and time-consuming. Measuring population increases before food production started will be particularly difficult, if indeed such increases took place.

Now that we can look at world prehistory on a far wider canvas than the pioneers could, we know that agriculture appeared in widely distributed parts of the world at approximately the same time — in the Near East, China, southeastern Asia, and the Americas. An increasing preoccupation with population has caused those following up on Flannery's work to look more closely at prehistoric demography. Mark Cohen has argued recently that population pressure on a global scale caused many widely separated hunter-gatherer cultures to abandon gathering because their traditional economy could not sustain their growing populations, which had reached the limit that their food resources could support (Cohen, 1977). This point, argues Cohen, was reached at or near the same time on all the major landmasses except Australia. Cohen assumes that early agriculture was a logical development of existing gathering and plant conservation techniques and that agriculture was neither easier nor a more secure subsistence base than hunting and gathering. All that

Cohen: population growth

can be said for it is that it does yield more calories per acre of land. He went on to assume that hunter-gatherer populations had mechanisms for controlling excessive local population growth but that population densities rose steadily throughout early prehistory, so that the same pressures arose all over the world at approximately the same time. Thus, he concludes, a single explanation for the appearance of agriculture can be invoked for the entire world — population pressure.

Cohen's tantalizing hypothesis is difficult to support from archaeological evidence because some variables such as population size, age-sex structures in society, and many demographic factors are very difficult to recover from archaeological research. The crux of his hypothesis is that early agriculture offered only one major advantage — increased food yield. In the short term, the per capita workload increased and quality of the diet probably declined. An agriculturalist's life is far more arduous than that of a hunter-gatherer. The only circumstances under which people would experiment with a new food procurement system would be those which held a serious ecological imbalance; such an imbalance can be accounted for only by population growth that upsets the efficiency of hunting and gathering for small populations. Once less palatable wild foods were being consumed, the only possible recourse for a growing population would be to start producing its own food. This, after all, is a logical step for people familiar with the germination of plants and used to manipulating vegetable foods for their use.

No one denies that food production led to higher population densities and indeed ignited a population explosion (Lewin, 1984) (Figure 9.2). But there is no evidence for very high population densities in the Near East or Mesoamerica during the millennia when agriculture was taking

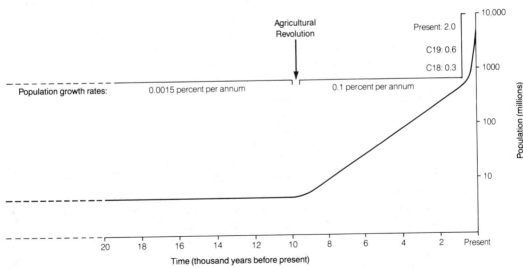

Figure 9.2 World population changes since the beginnings of food production. There has been an explosion in population densities in the past 10,000 years.

hold, certainly not for the sort of densities that cause chronic food shortages. British archaeologist Barbara Bender has taken Braidwood's hypothesis a stage further. She argues that hunter-gatherer societies were becoming more complex, with far more elaborate, hierarchical social organizations. She points to the increasing abundance of trade objects and the appearance of richly decorated burials before food production began. Perhaps, she hypothesizes, an expansion of trade, also of political alliances between neighboring groups, created new social and economic pressures to produce more and more surplus goods, not only foodstuffs but other objects as well. This in turn led to more sedentary lifeways. We know that trade indeed became very important in the millennia following the beginnings of agriculture. Was this, in fact, the continuation and expansion of economic activities that had begun millennia earlier and one of the reasons why people adopted more sedentary economies? As yet we do not know.

Harris: local models

Whatever the general explanation for the beginnings of food production, one still has to account for local variations in the time it took for people to adopt the new economies. David Harris has gone beyond Flannery's work in Mesoamerica. He argues that the more complex the distribution of plant species in an area, the more likely it is that people will settle down in permanent home bases and experiment with cultivation (D. R. Harris, 1978). Conversely, when hunter-gatherers concentrate on one or two plant species to the exclusion of others, in an environment where there are relatively few food resources, they are obliged to move frequently as they exhaust available vegetable staples. This type of rather mobile situation, Harris believes, is not conducive to the emergence of agriculture. Furthermore, he argues, the most likely places for experimentation with food crops are on the edges of major ecosystems. In such areas, maximum local and seasonal variation in vegetable foods is possible (see also D. R. Harris, 1980).

Harris (1980) also argues that hunter-gatherers in subtropical zones like the Near East and highland Mesoamerica were beginning to manipulate potential domesticates among wild grasses and root species at the end of the Ice Age. The dependence on such foods probably came earlier in these regions, where there were only a few foragable species. Such dependence was essential to long-term survival. In contrast, populations in more humid tropical regions like the African and Amazonian rain forests probably did little more than manipulate a few wild species to minimize risk in lean years — as a corollary, many African agricultural peoples turn to hunting and gathering in lean years to this day. The archaeological record shows that agriculture was established considerably earlier in the subtropical Near East, Middle and South America, Southeast Asia, and India than it was in humid, tropical zones, undoubtedly because that environment was very rich in game and wild vegetable foods. Furthermore, domesticated crops and animals were more susceptible to irregular rainfall, locusts and other insect attacks, and endemic stock diseases. A strong and sustained incentive to obtain food must have been a prerequisite for a lasting shift from foraging to agriculture. Some possible incentives may have been increased population, demands for tribute, or the desire to join long-distance trade networks, but such incentives were rarely sustained for long enough to trigger a changeover.

These people were well aware of what agriculture involved. They had been manipulating wild plants for millennia. On the fringes of the tropical rain forests, and within them, they had combined wild food procurement with limited tending of such preferred plants as the wild yam and other tubers. The dry season was short, and wild foods were plentiful for most of the year. It was only with the advent of cereal crops like sorghum and the millets, rice, or maize that they shifted to full dependence on agriculture. And this changeover may have taken place not as a result of indigenous initiative but because agricultural peoples living in neighboring areas with much longer dry seasons were forced to migrate into more tropical zones due to insufficient rainfall.

Harris points out that many variables have to be understood before we can reconstruct the conditions under which agriculture was first regarded as profitable activity. We are searching for a set of conditions in which population pressure, distribution of plants, the rate at which the environment is changing, even techniques of harvesting wild grasses, all played their part in making agriculture work. Then there are variations among the potentially domesticable plants and animals, some of which resist domestication because of their long life span or because parts of their lives take place outside human control. The seasonal distribution of wild vegetable foods or game could also have prevented experiments in domestication, when the seasons during which these wild foods were exploited coincided with the times of year when it was important that the experimenting farmers stay near their growing crops. Under these circumstances, people would tend to pursue their traditional food-getting strategies rather than risk their lives for an uncertain outcome.

As is obvious, research into the origins of food production has shifted its emphasis from a hunt for origins into a study of conditions under which agriculture and domestication became profitable. Unfortunately, many of the studies which throw light on these conditions involve intangibles such as productivity, caloric intake, and other variables that can only be recovered by scientific use of data from living populations. Unfortunately, too, we have no means of knowing if our projections from living populations into the past are reliable. Kent Flannery, for example, has calculated some productivity figures for maize in Mexico that can be applied to early farming sites in the Tehuacán Valley (Flannery, 1968). Perhaps similar figures can be generated for other plants, but even if they are, there are numerous intangible factors that could affect the reliability of both historic and prehistoric figures. The new hypotheses on early food production are beginning to change our thinking about culture change. Previously, people had thought that cultural systems remained in equilibrium unless jogged into changing by environmental or other changes. In fact, human culture may have been changing all the time, with our developing technology acting as a means by which humanity tried to retain the status quo as we occupied more and more diverse environments and were forced to eat more and more unpalatable foods. As Cohen points out, people in prehistory concentrated on big game, then increasingly specialized in vegetable foods, fish, shellfish, and other foods which were not eaten in earlier times. Agriculture was another way of adjusting to changed circumstances; the technology developed to practice it was one of many continual adjustments to the growing population and the increasingly higher costs for food in humanpower terms. Today, humanity is facing the prospect of synthetic foods, another adjustment to the need to feed more and more people. Like other cultural adaptations in human history, this one probably will take place without major disruptions, for people tend to choose the easiest way to preserve the status quo that they have enjoyed in their own and earlier generations.

Was food production a real improvement in human lifeways? For generations archaeologists have argued that human health improved dramatically as a result of agriculture as people worked less and lived on more reliable food supplies (Childe, 1952; Butzer, 1982). In recent years, economist Ester Boserup (1965) and others have argued that in fact agriculture brought diminishing returns in relation to labor expended in the new systems that were adopted to feed many more people. Richard Lee's studies of the !Kung San of the Kalahari desert tended to support her views. They showed that these hunter-gatherers, and presumably others, had abundant leisure and worked less than farmers. Some nutritionists pointed out that foragers may have had better balanced diets than many farmers who relied heavily on root or cereal crops. Not only that, farmers, with their sedentary settlements and higher population densities, were much more vulnerable to famine than their hunter-gatherer predecessors. They would also be more vulnerable to gastrointestinal infections and epidemics (Cohen and Armelagos, 1984).

While the theoretical controversies swirl, actual empirical data is still hard to come by. Some pioneer nutrition studies based on the skeletons of early farmers suggest some incidence of anemia and slow growth resulting from malnutrition. Signs of physical stress are even harder to come by. But ten regional studies of prehistoric populations have suggested a *decline* in mean age expectancy in agricultural populations, which contradicts the commonly held perception that farmers lived longer. Taken as a whole, such paleopathological studies as have been published suggest a general decline in the quality, and perhaps the length, of human life with the advent of food production. It should be pointed out, however, that there are many unknowns involved, among them changes in fertility and population growth rates, that caused the world's population to grow even if general health standards and life expectancy fell. (For details, consult Cohen and Armelagos, 1984).

What impact these studies will have on population pressure theories about the origins of agriculture is still uncertain. Certainly, any shift to food production caused by increasing population pressure could be reflected in a decline in overall health and nutrition displayed by prehistoric skeletons. It is likely that the next generation of theories about early agriculture will be based on researches into the paleopathology of pioneer farming populations.

In the final analysis, people probably turned to food production only when other alternatives were no longer practicable. The classic example is the aborigines of extreme northern Australia, who were well aware that the neighbors in New Guinea were engaged in intensive agriculture. They, too, knew how to plant the top of the wild yam so that it regerminated, but they never adopted food production, simply because they had no need to become dependent on a lifeway that would reduce their leisure time and produce more food than they needed.

HERDS: DOMESTICATION OF ANIMALS

Potentially tamable species like the wild ox, goat, sheep, and dog were widely distributed in the Old World during the late Pleistocene. New World farmers domesticated only such animals as the llama, the guinea pig, and the turkey, and then only under special conditions and within narrow geographic limits. It is possible that the domesticated dog crossed into the New World with the first Americans before 25,000 B.C. or that it was domesticated elsewhere in the Americas, but the evidence is uncertain.

Having one's own herds of domesticated mammals ensured a regular meat supply. The advantages to having a major source of meat under one's own control are obvious. Later, domesticated animals provided byproducts, such as milk, cheese, and butter, as well as skins for clothes and tent coverings and materials for leather shields and armor. In later millennia, people learned how to breed animals for specialized tasks such as plowing, transportation, and traction (Clutton-Brock, 1981).

Domestication implies a genetic selection emphasizing special features of continuing use to the domesticator (Ucko and Dimbleby, 1969). Wild sheep have no wool, wild cows produce milk only for their offspring, and undomesticated chickens do not produce surplus eggs. Changes in wool-bearing, lactation, or egg production could be achieved by isolating wild populations for selective breeding under human care. Isolating species from a larger gene pool produced domestic sheep with thick, woolly coats and domestic goats providing regular supplies of milk, which formed a staple in the diet of many human populations.

No one knows exactly how domestication of animals began. During the Upper Pleistocene, people already were beginning to concentrate heavily on some species of large mammals for their diet. The Magdalenians of southwestern France arranged much of their life toward pursuing reindeer. At the end of the Pleistocene, hunters in the Near East were concentrating on gazelles and other steppe animals. Wild sheep and goats were intensively hunted on the southern shores of the Caspian Sea.

Gregarious animals are those most easily domesticated; they follow the lead of a dominant herd member or all move together.

Hunters often fed off the same herd for a long time, sometimes deliberately sparing young females and immature beasts to keep the source of food alive. Young animals captured alive in the chase might be taken back to the camp and become dependent on those who caged them, thus becoming partially tamed. A hunter could grasp the possibility of gaining control of the movements of a few key members of a herd, who would be followed by the others. Once the experience of pets or of restricting game movements had suggested a new way of life, people might experiment with different species (Flannery, 1969; Higgs and Jarman, 1969). As part of domestication, animals and humans increased their mutual interdependence.

The archaeological evidence for early domestication is so fragile that nothing survives except the bones of the animals kept by the early farmers, and differences between wild and domestic animal bones are often so small initially that it is difficult to distinguish them unless very large collections are found. In the earliest centuries of domestication, corralled animals were nearly indistinguishable from wild species.

One way of distinguishing between domestic and wild beasts is to age a fossil find by its dentition — the number, kind, and arrangement of its teeth. Hunters normally kill animals of all ages but strongly prefer adolescent beasts, which have the best meat. For breeding, however, herd owners slaughter younger sheep and goats for meat, especially surplus males, but keep females until they are no longer productive as breeding animals. In some early farming sites such as Zawi Chemi in the Zagros Mountains in the Near East, the only way domestic sheep could be identified was by the early age at which they were slaughtered or by bone crystal analysis (Perkins, 1964).

The process of animal domestication undoubtedly was prolonged, developing in several areas of the Near East at approximately the same time. Although animal bones are scarce and often unsatisfactory as evidence of early domestication, most authorities now agree that the first species to be domesticated in the Near East was the sheep in 8500 B.C. or so. Sheep are small animals living in herds, whose carcasses yield much meat for their size. They can readily be penned and isolated to develop a symbiotic relationship with people.

Cattle are much more formidable to domesticate, for their prototype was *Bos primigenius*, the wild ox much hunted by Stone Age people (Figure 9.3). Perhaps cattle were first domesticated from wild animals that were penned for food, ritual, and sacrifice. They may have been captured from wild herds grazing in the gardens.

It should be noted that some animals, such as sea mammals, resist domestication because much of their lives is spent out of range of human influence. As mentioned, most early successes with domestication took place with gregarious animals. Kent Flannery has pointed out that

Figure 9.3 *Bos primigenius,* the aurochs or wild ox, as depicted by S. von Herbenstain in 1549. It became extinct in Europe in 1627, although recent breeding experiments have reconstructed this formidable beast.

penned, gregarious animals can, in a sense, be regarded as a "bank" of food protected and maintained against hard times (Flannery, 1969).

CROPS: DOMESTICATION OF PLANTS

An astonishing range of wild vegetable foods has been domesticated over the millennia (J. Renfrew, 1973). In the Old World, wheat, barley, and other cereals that grow wild over much of Asia and Europe became cultivated. In the New World, a different set of crops was tamed. These included Indian corn *(zea mays),* the only important wild grass to be domesticated. Root crops such as manioc and sweet potatoes, chili peppers, tobacco, and several types of beans were all grown. Common to both Old and New Worlds are gourds, cotton, and two or three other minor crops.

Carl Sauer pointed out that seed crops such as maize were first grown in Mesoamerica, and root crops such as manioc and potatoes were grown more commonly in South America (Sauer, 1952). This fundamental distinction between root and seed crops also applies in the Old World, where tropical regions had many potential domesticates such as the yam and gourds. In southeastern Asia and tropical Africa, a long period of intensive gathering and experimenting with the deliberate planting of wild root crops probably preceded the beginnings of formal agriculture. Perhaps, however, the transition from gathering to cultivation of root crops was almost unconscious, for many tubers are easy to grow deliberately. The African yam, for example, can be germinated simply by cutting off its top and burying it in the ground. The hunter-gatherer bands who were familiar with this easy means of conserving their food supplies may simply have intensified their planting efforts to supplement shortages caused by changed circumstances. As with animals, however, certain heavily exploited species tended to resist domestication; among them were the long-lived trees like the oak and plants whose life spans were so long that they inhibited human selection. They also tended to cross-pollinate, a process that undoubtedly discouraged human efforts to trigger or control genetic variation.

In the Old World, the qualities of wild wheat, barley, and similar crops are quite different from those of their domestic equivalents. In the wild, they occur in dense stands (J. G. D. Clark, 1970). The grasses can be harvested easily by simply tapping the stem and gathering the seeds in a basket as they fall off. This technique is effective because the wild grain is attached to the stem by a brittle joint, or *rachis*. When the grass is tapped, the weak rachis breaks and the grass falls into the basket.

The conversion of wild grass to domestic strains must have involved some selection of desirable properties in the wild grasses (Figure 9.4) (Harlan et al., 1976). To cultivate cereal crops extensively, the yield of an acre of grass has to be increased significantly before the work is worth it. If the yield remains low, it is easier to gather wild seeds and save the labor of cultivation. A tougher rachis must be developed to prevent the seed from falling on the ground and regerminating. By toughening the rachis, people could control propagation of the grass, sowing it when and where they liked and harvesting it with a knife blade or sickle (Harland, 1967). Certain patterns of grass harvesting, such as the hand and sickle methods

Figure 9.4 (a) The wild ancestor of a primitive wheat *(Triticum boeoticum)* contrasted with (b) its cultivated form *(T. monococcum).* (Both two-thirds actual size.)

used in the Near East even today, tended to select for useful mutants like the touch rachis, thereby reinforcing the trend toward control of the grasses by humans. The mutations that did take place helped already adaptable wild grasses to grow outside their normal wild habitats (Vavilov, 1951; Zohary, 1969). Early farmers seem to have grown cereals with remarkable success but probably succeeded only after long experimenting in different places.

TECHNOLOGY AND DOMESTICATION

The technological consequences of food production were, in their way, as important as the new economies. A more settled way of life and some decline in hunting and gathering slowly led to long-term residences, lasting agricultural styles, and more substantial housing. As they had done for millennia, people built their permanent homes with the raw materials most abundant in their environment. The early farmers of the Near East worked and dried mud into small houses with flat roofs; these were cool in summer and warm in winter. At night during the hot season they slept on the flat roofs. Some less substantial houses had reed roofs. In the more temperate zones of Europe, with wetter climates, timber was used to build thatched-roof houses of various shapes and sizes. Early African farmers often built huts of grass, sticks, and anthill clay. Nomadic pastoralists of the northern steppes had no concern with a permanent and durable home, yet they, too, took advantage of the related benefits of having a domestic food supply: they made clothing from the skins as well as tents to shelter them during the icy winters.

Agriculture is a seasonal activity, with long periods of the year when the fields are lying fallow or are supporting growing crops. Any farmer is confronted with the problem of storing food in ways the hunter-gatherer never has to ponder. A new technology of storage came into being. Grain storage bins, jars, or clay-lined pits became an essential part of the agricultural economy for stockpiling food for the lean months and against periods of famine. The bins (Figure 9.1, p. 210) might be made of wattle and daub, clay, or timber. Basket-lined silos protected valuable grain against rodents.

The hunter-gatherer uses skins, wood containers, gut pouches, and sometimes baskets for carrying vegetable foods back from the bush. The farmer faces far more formidable transport problems: he must carry his harvest back to the village, keep ready-for-use supplies of foods in the house as opposed to storage bins, and store water. Early farmers began to use gourds as water carriers, and to make clay vessels that were both waterproof and capable of being used to carry and cook food (Figure 9.5). They made pots by coiling rolls of clay or building up the walls of vessels from a lump and firing them in simple hearths. Clay vessels were much more durable than skin or leather receptacles. Some pots were used for several decades before being broken and abandoned. Pottery did not ap-

Figure 9.5 Pottery manufacture. A common method of potmaking was to build up the walls from coils of clay (top). The pot was then smoothed and decorated (left), and fired, either in an open hearth (right) or a kiln. These pictures illustrate Pueblo Indian pottery-manufacturing techniques from the southwestern United States, and are, of course, not necessarily typical of all potters.

pear simultaneously with the appearance of agriculture. It came into use at different times in many widely separated places. For example, the Jomon hunter-gatherers of Japan were making simple clay pots at least 10,500 years ago. They lived a more or less sedentary life by their shell middens, using clay vessels long before agriculture became part of their way of life (Aikens and Higuchi, 1981). In the Near East, however, pottery was first used by farmers in approximately 6000 B.C. (Mellaart, 1975).

For tens of thousands of years, people dug up wild, edible roots with simple wooden digging sticks, sometimes made more effective with the aid of a stone weight. The first farmers continued to use the digging stick to plant crops a few inches below the surface, probably on readily cultivable soils. They also used wooden or clay-bladed hoes (and, much later, iron) to break up the soft soil. These they fitted with short or long handles, depending on cultural preference. European and Near Eastern farmers made use of the ox-drawn plow in later millennia, at first with a wooden-tipped blade, then bronze, and later iron (Chapter Fifteen). The plow was an important innovation, for it enabled people to turn the soil over to a much greater depth than ever before. Every farmer has to clear wild vegetation and weeds from the fields, and it is hardly surprising to find a new emphasis on the ax and the adze. The simple axes of pioneer farmers were replaced by more elaborate forms in metal by 3500 B.C. in the Near East. Present-day experiments in Denmark and New Guinea have shown that the ground and polished edges of stone axes are remarkably effective in clearing woodland and felling trees (Figure 9.6) (Cranstone, 1972). In later millennia, the alloying of copper and bronze, and even later, the development of iron cutting edges, made forest clearance even easier.

New tools meant new technologies to produce tougher working edges. At first the farmers used ground and polished stone, placing a high premium on suitable rocks, which were traded from quarry sites over enormous distances. Perhaps the most famous ax quarries are in western Europe, where ax blanks were traded the length of the British Isles, and Grand Pressigny flint from France was prized over thousands of square miles. In the Near East and Mexico, one valuable toolmaking material was obsidian, a volcanic rock prized for its easy working properties, and for its ornamental appearance. Early obsidian trade routes carried tools and ornaments hundreds of miles from their places of origin. By using spectrographic techniques, scientists have been able to trace obsidian over long distances to such places of origin as Lipari Island off Italy and Lake Van in Turkey (C. Renfrew, Dixon, and Cann, 1966).

All these developments in technology made people more and more dependent on exotic raw materials, many of which were unobtainable in their own territory. We see the beginnings of widespread long-distance trading networks that were to burgeon even more rapidly with the emergence of the first urban civilizations.

We still know tantalizingly little about the ways in which humankind began to exercise control over food resources. We know that in the Near

Figure 9.6 Using a stone adze to fell a tree. A Tefalmin farmer at work in 1966, in New Guinea.

East there was a dramatic shift in human subsistence patterns 10,000 years ago, in northern China about 7000 years ago, and in Mesoamerica some 5000 years ago. But some fascinating clues suggest that people were exercising some sort of control over their food supplies very much earlier. Perhaps Upper Paleolithic people who specialized in hunting reindeer or mountain goat made some attempts to manage the prey herds. Conceivably, too, hunter-gatherers living on the fringes of tropical rain forests could have engaged in deliberate opportunistic horticulture, planting yams and other food plants that could be regenerated for future use. And it seems possible that East Africans had domesticated cattle as early as 13,000 years ago. The beginnings of the agricultural revolution may have taken hold many thousands of years before the explosion came. After all, we should never forget that humans have always been opportunistic, and the planting of food crops and the first taming of animals may have simply resulted from such opportunism.

GUIDE TO FURTHER READING

Childe, V. G. *Man Makes Himself*. London: Watts, 1936.
   Classic Childe arguments for a Neolithic Revolution that summarize all the evidence in favor of a revolutionary change in prehistory when food production began.

Cohen, Mark. *The Food Crisis in Prehistory*. New Haven: Yale University Press, 1977.
   An original and thought-provoking essay on the origins of agriculture that advocates population as a major factor in the origins of food production.

Cohen, Mark, and Armelagos, George J. (Eds.). *Paleopathology at the Origins of Agriculture*. New York: Academic Press, 1984.
   A volume of essays that test basic hypotheses about the origins of food production. Technical but fascinating.

Renfrew, Jane. *Palaeoethnobotany*. London: Methuen, 1973.
   An admirable synthesis of the archaeology of plant remains in the Old World. Much valuable material on basic methodology.

Sauer, Carl O. *Agricultural Origins and Dispersals*. New York: American Geographical Society, 1952.
   Sauer's short essay is full of original ideas about root as well as cereal crops, although the archaeological evidence is much outdated.

Struever, Stuart (Ed.). *Prehistoric Agriculture*. Garden City, N.Y.: Natural History Press, 1971.
   An anthology of articles that brings together the major theories about early agriculture into a single volume.

Chronological Table F

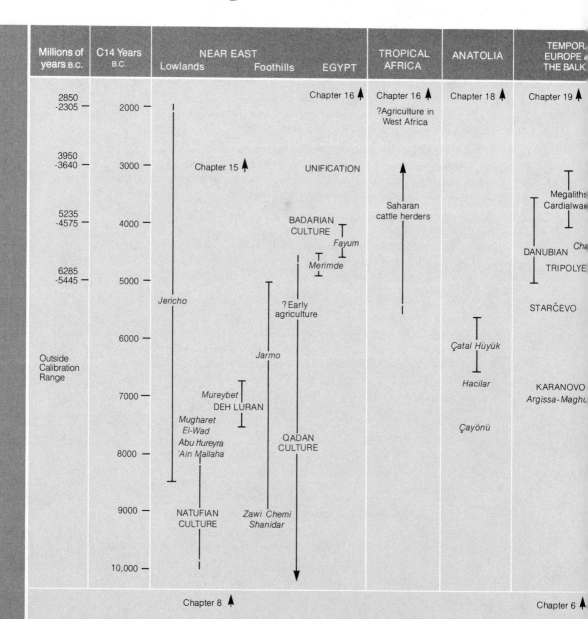

Millions of years B.C.	C14 Years B.C.	NEAR EAST			TROPICAL AFRICA	ANATOLIA	TEMPOR. EUROPE THE BALK
		Lowlands	Foothills	EGYPT			
2850 -2305	2000			Chapter 16 ↑	Chapter 16 ↑ ?Agriculture in West Africa	Chapter 18 ↑	Chapter 19 ↑
3950 -3640	3000	Chapter 15 ↑		UNIFICATION			Megaliths Cardialwa
5235 -4575	4000			BADARIAN CULTURE Fayum	Saharan cattle herders		DANUBIAN Cha TRIPOLYE
6285 -5445	5000	Jericho	Merimde				STARČEVO
	6000		?Early agriculture			Çatal Hüyük	
Outside Calibration Range			Jarmo				
	7000		Mureybet DEH LURAN			Hacilar	KARANOVO Argissa-Maghu
	8000	Mugharet El-Wad Abu Hureyra 'Ain Mallaha		QADAN CULTURE		Çayönü	
	9000	NATUFIAN CULTURE	Zawi Chemi Shanidar				
	10,000						

Chapter 8 ↑   Chapter 6 ↑

Chapter 10

Origins of Food Production: Europe and The Near East

PREVIEW

✤ The Natufian culture of the Jordan Valley flourished as early as 10,000 B.C. and lasted to at least 8000 B.C. The Natufians were intensive gatherers and their settlement at Jericho formed the nucleus of a more lasting settlement with massive defense walls. These Jericho people engaged in extensive trading in obsidian and other commodities.

✤ The hilly flanks of the Near East were occupied by seasonal hunter-gatherers in approximately 9000 B.C. By 7000 B.C., the people were living in more permanent settlements and were on their way to food production. By 5500 B.C., a village farming economy was widespread in the Near East, fostered by extensive intervillage trading networks. One well-known site is Jarmo in the Zagros foothills, a cluster of mud houses that yielded abundant evidences of cereal agriculture.

✤ The agricultural towns of Hacilar and Çatal Hüyük in Turkey provide evidence both of agriculture and of extensive trading in Anatolia by 7000 B.C. Çatal Hüyük was a substantial trading settlement with shrines and a distinctive artistic tradition.

✤ European agriculture is thought to have developed from Balkan roots at least as early as 6500 B.C. The Starčevo culture flourished for a considerable period, while the Danubian people settled the fertile soils of Central Europe and the Low Countries, probably by 5000 B.C. Western Europe was settled by farming peoples by 4500 B.C.

✤ Megalithic tombs are found over a wide area of western Europe and the Mediterranean dating to approximately 4000 B.C. The origins and inspiration of these monumental sculptures and the rituals associated with them are a mystery.

✤ Scandinavia was settled by farming peoples by 3500 B.C.; farming settlements in Britain appeared by 4300 B.C. Hunter-gatherers continued to flourish in arctic latitudes where agriculture was impractical.

Much of the theorizing about early food production has stemmed from archaeological research in the Near East, where many early farming settlements are found (G. Wright, 1971) (see Figure 10.1).

JERICHO AND THE LOWLANDS

At the end of the Pleistocene, both highlands and coastal plains in the Near East were inhabited by hunter-gatherers who hunted wild sheep, goats, gazelles, and other mammals, as well as relying heavily on wild vegetable foods (Braidwood and Howe, 1960). Their microlithic toolkits

13,000 to 9000 B.C. included many grindstones used for processing cereal grasses. One such culture was the so-called Natufian, named after a valley in Israel, which

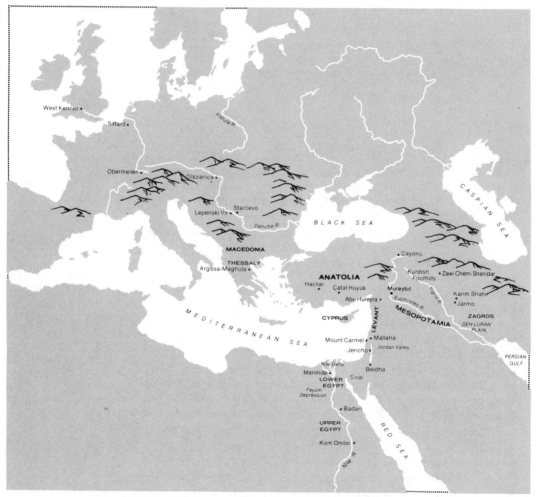

Figure 10.1 Early farming sites in the Near East, Europe, and the Nile Valley.

FARMERS

flourished over much of the coastal strip from southern Turkey to the fringes of the Nile Valley.

The Natufians hunted gazelle (perhaps even semidomesticated them), but obtained much of their food from stands of wild cereal grasses (Garrod, 1957; Mellaart, 1975). Their toolkits included flint sickle blades, of which the cutting edges bear a characteristic gloss that was achieved by friction against grass stalks; the kits also contained bone handles in which the blades were mounted (Figure 10.2).

Natufian
10,000 to 8000 B.C.

Natufians began to live in fairly permanent settlements. 'Ain Mallaha in northern Israel, for example, covers at least half an acre, with circular houses on stone foundations. Storage chambers were an integral part of the houses, a clear sign of increasing sedentariness. Stone bowls, mortars, and paved floors are also common, and many burials reflect greater social differentiation by their varying amounts of adornment. This increasing social complexity logically precedes the more elaborate class structure of later, urban life, but other Natufians were still living in rock shelters and caves like Mugharet el-Wad at Mt. Carmel. A relative abundance of trade objects, such as seashells, seems to indicate expanded bartering in both house communities and rock-shelter communities. Trading was an activity destined to spread greatly in future millennia.

'Ain Mallaha
8000 B.C.

Mugharet el-Wad

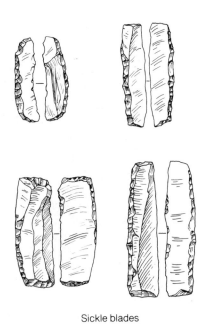

Sickle blades

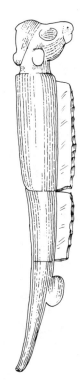

Sickle handle

Figure 10.2 Natufian sickle blades and a bone handle for such blades. This handle (approximately one-half actual size) bears a deer's head.

By 8500 B.C., a temporary Natufian settlement at the bubbling Jericho spring had formed the locus of later farming villages (Kenyon, 1961; Mellaart, 1975), but the Natufians were soon succeeded by more lasting farming settlements that clustered around the spring. Soon these people, whose technology did not include clay vessels, were building massive defense walls around their town. A rock-cut ditch more than 2.7 m (3 yd) deep and 3.2 m (10 ft) wide was bordered by a finely built stone wall complete with towers (Figure 10.3). The beehive-shaped huts of Jericho were clustered within the defenses. The communal labor of wall building required both political and economic resources on a scale unheard of a few thousand years earlier. Why walls were needed remains a mystery, but they must have been for defense, resulting from group competition for scarce resources.

The Jericho people engaged in extensive trading activities, which brought to their town bitumen, salt, obsidian, and shells from the Mediterranean and Dead seas. They also kept large flocks of goats and sheep. Another site, Beidha, has produced many specimens of wild barley, which must have been either gathered in enormous quantities from natural stands or sown deliberately. The emmer wheat (goat grass) seeds from Beidha show a wide range in size, as if domestication had only recently begun. Several other minor crops were either grown or gathered. Large numbers of young goats were also found; their ages imply selective slaughtering, strongly suggesting domestication rather than hunting (Kirkbride, 1968).

Abu Hureyra

Some clues about how farming began come from further north, in Syria. A northern Syrian *tell* known as Abu Hureyra has yielded traces of a small village settlement of pit dwellings with simple reed roofs supported by wooden uprights (Moore, 1979). Using fine screens and flotation equipment, the excavators recovered thousands of wild vegetable foods including wild einkorn, rye, and barley. Abu Hureyra lies outside the present-day range of these wild cereals. However, in the late tenth and early ninth millennia B.C., when the site was first occupied, the climate was somewhat warmer and damper than it is today. As a result, the village lay in a well-wooded steppe area where animals and plants, perhaps even wild cereals, were abundant. At any rate, some hunter-gatherer groups such as the Hureyra people settled down in more permanent settlements and may have started to plant and harvest wild cereals as a deliberate subsistence strategy. Botanist Gordon Hillman experimented with modern stands of wild einkorn in eastern Turkey and concluded that the Abu Hureyra people could have cultivated wild cereals with simple techniques without changing the morphology of einkorn for a very long time. It would take centuries, he argued, for mutations from the wild to the domestic state to appear. There can be little doubt that culti-

Figure 10.3 Excavated remains of the great tower in early Jericho.

vation was practiced, for seeds of modern farming weeds such as mustard were recovered in the excavators' flotation machines.

Abu Hureyra was by no means unique; other contemporary sites near the Euphrates are known to lie near arable lands, unlike earlier settlements. It seems that food production began throughout much of the Near East among hunter-gatherer communities that began to combine simple cultivation with their age-old subsistence patterns, perhaps thousands of years before agriculture became the dominant feature of the Near Eastern economy.

HILLY FLANKS IN THE NEAR EAST

As we pointed out in Chapter Nine, the hilly flanks of the Near East, which are inland from the Mediterranean Sea and at a higher elevation, witnessed a long and complex transition from hunting and gathering to food production. In approximately 9000 B.C., wild goats were a primary quarry for the hunters and gatherers exploiting the resources of the foothills. An adaptive trend such as that of the Natufian is found in this region. Open seasonal sites such as Zawi Chemi Shanidar were occupied by people living in round, semisubterranean houses. The people killed many immature wild sheep, as if they had either fenced in the grazing grounds, penned herds, or even so tamed the sheep that they could control the age at which they would be killed (Perkins, 1964).

Zawi Chemi Shanidar **9000 B.C.**

In approximately 7000 B.C., the inhabitants of Mureybet in northern Syria were gathering wild wheat as well as barley (Oates and Oates, 1976). Conceivably they were cultivating these wild grasses, but there is no certain evidence for farming at the village, which covered approximately a hectare (2.5 acres). Mureybet lies outside the wild distribution of einkorn today, for its habitat is cooler and wetter than the Euphrates Valley. Either the climate was different when the village was occupied or the people were experimenting with cultivation of einkorn outside its natural habitat.

Mureybet **7000 B.C.**

Experimentation was certainly complete by 6000 B.C., when village life became more widespread. A fairly intensive agricultural economy was widely distributed over southwest Asia by 5500 B.C., fostered by extensive trade networks distributing obsidian, much prized for ornaments and sickle blades. Farming villages dating to this time flourished at Jericho and along the Syrian and Palestinian coasts.

One of the best-known early villages is Jarmo, in the Zagros foothills southeast of Zawi Chemi Shanidar, mainly dated to approximately 5000 B.C. (Braidwood and Braidwood, 1983). Jarmo was little more than a cluster of twenty-five houses built of baked mud, forming an irregular huddle separated by small alleyways and courtyards. Storage bins and clay ovens were an integral part of the structures. The Jarmo deposits yielded abundant traces of agriculture: seeds of barley, emmer wheat, and minor crops were found with the bones of sheep and goats. Hunting had declined in importance — only a few wild animal bones testify to such activity — but the toolkit still included Stone Age-type tools together with sickle blades, grinding stones, and other implements of tillage.

Jarmo **9000 to 5000 B.C.**

The lowlands to the southwest of the Kurdish foothills are a vast alluvial delta watered by the Tigris and the Euphrates rivers. As early as 7500 to 6750 B.C., goat herds were wandering over the Deh Luran plain east of the Tigris River (Hole, Flannery, and Neely, 1969). In the late winter and spring they harvested wheat, but nine-tenths of their vegetable diet came from wild plants.

Deh Luran **7500 to 6750 B.C.**

ANATOLIA

By 7500 B.C., scattered farming villages began to appear in the headwaters of the Tigris River and to the west of Anatolia. At Çayönü in southern Turkey, a small community of food producers roughly contemporary with Jarmo used tools resembling those from the Levant and Zagros regions. Obsidian was plentiful and native copper was hammered into simple ornaments. Domestic pigs and sheep were in use, and flax was domesticated. (L. S. Braidwood, 1982; R. J. Braidwood and Cambel, 1980). Çayönü **7500 B.C.**

The first evidence of food production on the Anatolian plateau to the west extends back to approximately 5000 B.C., but farming could have flourished even earlier in the rolling highlands of Turkey. British archaeologist James Mellaart excavated a remarkable early farming village at Hacilar in southwestern Anatolia, which was founded in approximately 6700 B.C. (Mellaart, 1975). Seven phases of village occupation took place at Hacilar before its inhabitants moved. They lived in small rectangular houses with courtyards, hearths, ovens, and plastered walls. Hacilar **6700 B.C.**

No pottery was used at Hacilar, but basketry and leather containers probably were. Barley and emmer wheat were cultivated, and some wild grass seeds were also eaten. The bones of sheep or goats and cattle and deer were present, but there was no evidence for the domestication of any animal except the dog. Hacilar was a simple and unsophisticated settlement, probably typical of many communities in the Near East in the early millennia of farming.

The simplicity of Hacilar contrasts dramatically with the Çatal Hüyük mound, 200 mi (322 km) to the east (Mellaart, 1967). Çatal Hüyük covers 13 hectares (32 acres); it was a town of numerous small houses built of sun-dried brick, which were designed to back onto one another, occasionally separated by small courtyards. Roofs were flat, and the outside walls of the houses provided a convenient defense wall (Figure 10.4). The town was rebuilt at least twelve times after approximately 6000 B.C., presumably when the houses began to crumble or the population swelled. Çatal Hüyük **6000 to 5600 B.C.**

A most remarkable feature of Çatal Hüyük was its artistic tradition, preserved in paintings on carefully plastered walls and in sculptures, some of them parts of shrines (Figure 10.5). Most depicted women or bulls. Some paintings show women giving birth to bulls. Many art themes were about fertility and the regeneration of life, and figurines of women in childbirth have been found.

Much of Çatal Hüyük's prosperity resulted from its monopoly of the obsidian trade from quarries in nearby mountains. Seashells came to Çatal Hüyük from the Mediterranean for conversion into ornaments. In later millennia, trade in raw materials and ornaments between Anatolia and southwestern Asia continued to flourish, as metallurgy and other attributes of urban life took firmer hold in the Near East. Just how important the obsidian trade was in the area has been shown by spectrographic

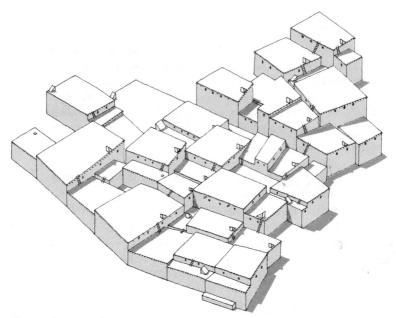

Figure 10.4 Schematic reconstruction of houses and shrines from Level VI at Çatal Hüyük, Anatolia, showing their flat-roof architecture and roof entrances.

analyses of fragments of the volcanic glass in hundreds of sites between Turkey and Mesopotamia. The trace elements in obsidian are so distinctive that it is possible to identify the natural source of the glass by this analysis and to reconstruct the distribution of obsidian from dozens of different localities. Colin Renfrew and others were able to identify no fewer than twelve early farming villages that had obtained obsidian from the Ciftlik area of central Turkey (C. Renfrew, Dixon, and Cann, 1966). The study showed that 80 percent of the chipped stone in villages within 186 mi (300 km) of Ciftlik was obsidian. Outside this "supply zone," the percentages of obsidian dropped away sharply with distance, to 5 percent in a Syrian village, and one-tenth of a percent in the Jordan Valley. Renfrew and his colleagues argued that regularly spaced villages were passing approximately half the obsidian they received to their more distant neighbors. Much early farming trade probably was a form of "down-the-line" bartering that passed various commodities from one village to the next.

EUROPEAN FARMERS

Radiocarbon Chronology

For years, European archaeologists like V. Gordon Childe believed that agriculture, metallurgy, and most significant technological developments had spread into temperate Europe from the Near East (Childe,

Figure 10.5 Reconstruction of the east and south walls of Shrine VI.14 at Çatal Hüyük, Anatolia, with sculptured ox heads, horns, benches, and relief models of bulls and rams. The shrine was entered by the ladder at right.

1925). Today, people no longer think in terms of vast hordes of farmers and metallurgists flooding into temperate latitudes from the innovative East. Radiocarbon chronologies have radically altered our view of European prehistory.

Childe and other pioneers worked before radiocarbon dates were available. All chronologies of epochs before approximately 3000 B.C., when civilization emerged in the Near East, were based on artifact typologies and inspired guesswork. The first radiocarbon dates showed that European agriculture and metallurgy had begun much later than in the Near East and there seemed nothing wrong with the traditional hypotheses.

When people started to calibrate radiocarbon dates against tree-ring chronologies, they found that European time scales between 1500 and 5000 B.C. had to be corrected several centuries backward (Fagan, 1985; C. Renfrew, 1970; Klein et al., 1982; Suess, 1965). Egyptian historical (that is, from the written record) chronology from 3000 B.C. now agrees more closely with calibrated C14 dates, rather than being several centuries too recent, as they were before.

British archaeologist Colin Renfrew has now moved the dates for temperate Europe back far enough to rupture the traditional diffusionist links between the Near East and Europe (Figure 10.6) (C. Renfrew, 1971): that is, it is now apparent that events in Europe were contemporary with those in the Near East and not a later result of the spread of Near East culture, as was once thought. Using historical dates for the Mediterranean has thrown what Renfrew aptly calls a "fault line" across the Medi-

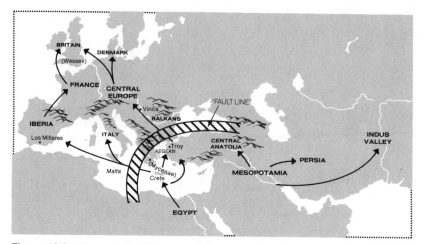

Figure 10.6 Chronology of Europe and calibration of C14 chronology. With the uncalibrated chronology, the traditional view of European prehistory had agriculture and other innovations spreading northwestward from the Near East and eastern Mediterranean into continental Europe. The calibrated chronology has hardly affected the dates after 3000 B.C. for the eastern Mediterranean and sites to the southeast of the fault line marked on the map. The calibrated dates after 3000 B.C. for sites to the west and northwest of the fault line have been pushed back several centuries by calibration, so that the old notion of innovation from the east is replaced by new theories postulating less eastern influence (Renfrew, 1973).

terranean and southern Europe. This fault line marks a chronological boundary, to the west of which radiocarbon (C14) dates after 3000 B.C. have been pushed back by calibration, making them older than the accurate, historically attested dates for the eastern Mediterranean and the Balkans, which are east of the fault. Of course, this fault line is a methodological boundary, but it serves to show that, with the new calibrated chronologies, prehistoric Europeans were much less affected by cultural developments in the Near East than Childe had suggested. They adopted metallurgy and other innovations on their own, just as early as many such inventions were brought into use in the Near East (C. Renfrew, 1973).

Unfortunately, there is still inadequate information on the rate at which farming spread into Europe. In an interesting and highly provocative study, two geneticists plotted the distribution of fifty-three European early farming sites with radiocarbon dates and plotted their distance from a number of supposed centers of domestication in the Near East (Ammerman and Cavilli-Sforza, 1973). The distances between the European sites and the Near Eastern centers were then computed as great circle routes, the shortest distances between the two points allowing for the curvature of the earth. There were very high statistical correlations when the data was tested to see if a constant rate of spread had been achieved over time and space. The authors interpreted their results as what they called "a wave of advance" model, with farming populations on the frontiers of cultivated land increasing fast and pushing forward at a rate of approximately 11 mi (180 km) every generation of twenty-five years or so. Given this rate of advance, Europe would have been settled by agricultural populations by 3800 B.C. The study was rather crude in the sense that it took no account of environmental differences or of detailed archaeological evidence, but it is certainly intriguing, especially when combined with synthetic maps of gene frequencies in Europeans which strongly suggest that population movement and not cultural diffusion was responsible for the spread of agriculture to Europe (Menozzi, Piazza, and Cavalli-Sforza, 1978).

GREECE AND THE BALKANS

The temperate zones north and west of Greece and the Balkans provided environments contrasting to the seasonal rainfall areas in the Near East. Timber and thatch replace the mud brick used effectively for houses in Near Eastern villages (Milisauskas, 1978). Agricultural techniques had to reflect the European climate (Dennel, 1983). The initial development of agriculture in Europe coincided with a warm, moist phase. Midsummer temperatures were at least 2°C warmer than they are now (Butzer, 1974). The forest cover was mainly mixed oak woodland, shadier tree cover that reduced the grazing resources of larger game animals such as deer and wild cattle. As a result, hunter-gatherer populations may have shifted to coastal and lakeside settlements where fish, waterfowl, and sea mammals were readily available (Waterbolk, 1968).

The earliest evidence of food production in Europe comes from the Argissa-Maghula village mound in Greek Thessaly (Figure 10.7). The inhabitants cultivated emmer wheat and barley. Domestic cattle, sheep, and pig bones in the lower levels of the site date to approximately 7000 B.C. The Franchthi Cave in southern Greece was occupied for many thousands of years by farmers who had contacts with the Aegean islands (Dennell, 1983; Jacobson, 1981). The early dates for cattle and pig domestication argue strongly for independent domestication of animals in southeastern Europe (for a recent summary, see Evans and Rasson, 1984).

Argissa-Maghula
7000 B.C.

The earliest agricultural people of the Balkans settled in compact villages of one-room dwellings built of baked mud plastered on poles and wicker (Tringham et al., 1980). These Karanovo culture settlements were occupied over long periods. Farming villages were built on brown forest soils and alluvial river plains, and the economy was based on cultivated wheat and barley and domesticated sheep and goats. Ruth Tringham argues that cereal agriculture reached this area from the Near East, claiming a lack of continuity between earlier hunting artifacts and the new farming cultures (Tringham, 1971). A number of culture traits, including *Spondylus* shells (a characteristic Mediterranean mussel much valued because it could be used for ornamentation), clay seals and figurines, and reaping knives, show continuing connections with the Mediterranean world. The Starčevo site near Belgrade gives a vivid picture of

Karanovo culture

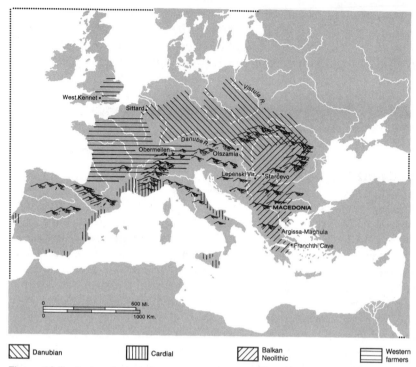

Figure 10.7 Archaeological sites in temperate Europe and the distribution of Linear (Danubian) pottery, Cardial ware, and western Neolithic.

the economic life and pottery styles of this widespread culture. This is an area with great environmental variability and ranges in temperature. For example, there are fertile plains and spring areas where the soils are permanently moist. It was here that many farming communities settled at the same location for centuries, just as Near Eastern and Anatolian farmers had done. The largest mounds are found where good arable soils are most widespread. It was in this area that metallurgy developed in approximately 3000 B.C. (see Chapter Nineteen).

Danubian (Linear Pottery) Culture

Farther north, the European climate is even more temperate. It nurtured quite different European farming traditions, among them a distinctive one centered on the Middle Danube, extending as far west as southern Holland and eastward to the Vistula River and the Upper Dneister. These people were the *Danubians* (Linear pottery culture group), known to generations of European archaeologists because of their characteristic pottery (Champion et al., 1984; Phillips, 1980; Piggott, 1965). The Danubians made round-based vessels with lines (Figure 10.8), spirals, and meanders carefully incised on the clay. They cultivated barley, einkorn, emmer wheat, and minor crops including flax. These

Danubian 5320 to
?4200 b.c.

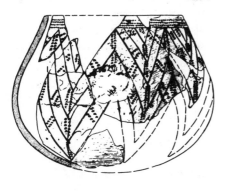
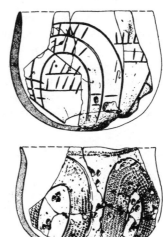
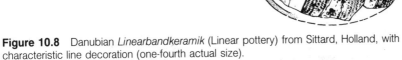

Figure 10.8 Danubian *Linearbandkeramik* (Linear pottery) from Sittard, Holland, with characteristic line decoration (one-fourth actual size).

they planted on the fertile loess soils (rich, fine, wind-deposited soils) of central Europe using a simple form of shifting agriculture that involved careful soil selection and use of lighter soils. The Danubians rapidly settled the loess zones from the Danube to the Low Countries. Cattle, goats, sheep, and dogs were domesticated, and domestic herds were important in the Danubian diet.

The Danubians were living in southern Holland by 4800 b.c. and introduced food production to northwestern Europe much later than it appeared in areas to the southeast. By 5000 b.c., Danubian villages contained rectangular houses from 20 to 50 m (18 to 46 yds) long, which were made of timber and thatch; presumably these houses sheltered stock as well as several families (Figure 10.9) (Champion et al, 1984; P. Phillips, 1980).

Originally the Danubians practiced their shifting agricultural techniques on the loess, but growing populations forced some of them to move onto heavier and poorer soils. In these densely cultivated areas, the Danubians relied heavily on their cattle, sheep, and pigs. When prime grazing land became scarce, they may have moved their herds onto the northern European plain for part of the year. The Brzesc Kujawski site in Poland may have been a seasonal camp about 7300 years ago, occupied by summer cattle herders, who also gathered wild vegetable foods and caught perch in northern streams (Bogucki and Grygiel, 1983). Eventually farmers settled on heavier soils. We find regional variations of Danubian culture in many parts of central Europe. Some farmers had to rely more on hunting and gathering because the soils of their gardens did not yield enough food to support their families. Defensive earthworks appeared later, as if vigorous competition for land had caused intertribal stress.

4800 b.c

While the Danubians were settling in central Europe, other peoples were moving onto the Russian plains in the east. People somewhat similar to the Danubians occupied farming settlements in the Ukraine and around the Dnieper River. Like the Danubians, they lived in rectangular houses. They reached the height of their prosperity during the period of the Tripolye culture, a period when many villages were laid out with houses in a circle (Figure 10.10).

Tripolye culture **4800 B.C.**

Mediterranean and Swiss Lake Cultures

As the Danubians were cultivating the plains of western and central Europe, new farming economies were becoming established around the shores of the Mediterranean. Extensive bartering networks from one end of the Mediterranean to the other exchanged seashells, obsidian, exotic

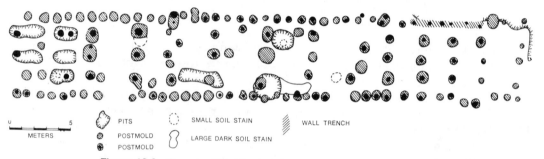

0	5		

METERS

⬡ PITS   ◌ SMALL SOIL STAIN   ⫽ WALL TRENCH

⊘ POSTMOLD   ∞ LARGE DARK SOIL STAIN

⊛ POSTMOLD

Figure 10.9 Plan of a Danubian long house from Olszanica, Poland, with wall trenches, postholes, pits, and other features.

Figure 10.10 A Tripolye culture village.

stones, and, later, copper ore. A characteristic type of pottery decorated with the distinctive imprint of the *Cardium* (scallop) shell is widely distributed on the northeastern shores of the Mediterranean, on Adriatic coasts, and as far west as Malta, Sardinia, southern France, North Africa, and eastern Spain (Figure 10.11) (Trump, 1980). Cardium-decorated wares spread widely because of trading. The new economies were flourishing in the western Mediterranean and in France and Switzerland by the fifth millennium B.C. This constant trading led to considerable cultural uniformity over wide areas of southern France, which was reflected in the Chasseen culture. The Chasseens were cereal and bean farmers who opened up thousands of acres of hitherto unexploited territory to agriculture.

Cardium-decorated wares **4500 b.c.**

A series of farming villages were thriving on the shores of the Swiss lakes at about this time, communities with close links to the Chasseen (Lee, 1866; Muller-Beck, 1961). They were occupied by cattle and sheep farmers who cultivated barley and wheat as well as many minor crops, including cider apples and flax (used for textiles) (Figure 10.12). Their houses were built on the damp ground between the lake reed beds and the scrub brush of the valley behind. The first dwellings were small rectangular huts, but they eventually gave way to larger, two-room houses. Some villages grew to include between twenty-four and seventy-five houses clustered on the lakeshore, a density of population much the same as modern Swiss villages that have approximately thirty households.

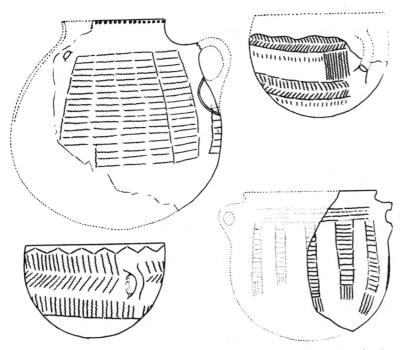

Figure 10.11 Cardium-shell-impressed pottery from southern France (one-fourth actual size).

ORIGINS OF FOOD PRODUCTION   243

Figure 10.12 Sample prehistoric stone axes mounted in deer antler handles from the Swiss lake dwellings, typical of those used by early farmers in Europe.

WESTERN EUROPE: THE MEGALITHS

Agriculture was well established in central and northern France by the early fifth millennium B.C. As early as 4000 B.C., some French farmers were building large communal stone tombs, known to archaeologists as *megaliths* ("large stone" in Greek). Megaliths are found as far north as Scandinavia, in Britain, Ireland, France, Spain, the western Mediterranean, Corsica, and Malta. For years, scholars thought that megaliths had originated in the eastern Mediterranean in approximately 2500 B.C. and spread westward into Spain with colonists from the Aegean, who had carried a custom of collective burial and their religion with them. Megalithic tombs were believed to have then been built in western Europe, witnesses to a lost faith perhaps spread by pilgrims, missionaries, or merchants. With their massive stones and large burial chambers, megaliths remained one of the mysteries of European prehistory (Figure 10.13) (Daniel, 1973; C. Renfrew, 1967, 1973).

This popular and widely accepted hypothesis was badly weakened by C14 dates from France that turned out to be earlier than others from western Europe. Furthermore, new calibrated dates have dated Spanish megalithic sites and their associated culture to as early as approximately 4000 B.C., much earlier than their alleged prototypes in the Aegean. Thus,

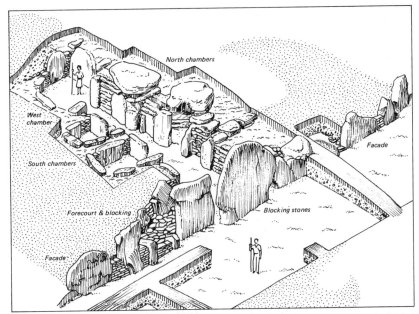

Figure 10.13 Interior of a megalithic chamber tomb at West Kennett, England, C14 dated to approximately 5500 B.C. (Piggott, 1965).

megaliths were being built in western Europe at least a millennium before massive funerary architecture became fashionable in the eastern Mediterranean. This remarkable freestanding architecture is a unique, local European creation (P. Phillips, 1980).

What exactly were megaliths? Were they the surviving remains of a powerful religious cult that swept western Europe, or did they symbolize the emergence of new, more sophisticated political and social structures in the West? Colin Renfrew (1983) has argued that the tradition of communal burial developed in very early west European farming societies, and that it is manifested by the famous long barrows of southern Britain (Figure 10.13), many of which had stone boulder, megalithic, interiors. The long barrows were fairly small structures, requiring not more than about 5000 to 10,000 man-hours to build (a figure equivalent to twenty men taking fifty days). Between 4000 to 3500 b.c., these barrows were associated with more elaborate monuments, among them enclosed earthworks (often called "causewayed camps"), which are known to have been protected by timber palisades. Recent excavations have shown that these camps were littered with human bones, many of them skeletons from which the flesh had weathered in the open. Perhaps these camps were places where the dead were exposed for months before their bones were deposited in nearby communal burials.

As time went on, the argument goes, these burial ceremonies revolved around even larger monuments, the so-called "henges," stone and wood-built circles of which Stonehenge in southern Britain is the most famous (Figure 19.6, p. 416). In this sense, megaliths of all types formed a kind of settlement hierarchy on the prehistoric landscape, a hierarchy that may have reflected profound changes in European society.

Renfrew and others have called megaliths the "tombs of the living," lasting humanly made symbols of continuity of human life, as well as symbols of the continuity of ownership of land from one generation to the next. The annual round of religious rituals at places like Stonehenge reinforced this continuity, and, at a time when population densities were rising sharply, the megaliths associated with them became important symbols of political and social continuity. They also reinforced the political, economic, and spiritual power of those who supervised the building and worship at such places as Stonehenge. That such supervision was necessary is certain, for it has been estimated that Stonehenge required at least 30,000 man-hours to complete. So the appearance of megaliths and the hierarchy of more elaborate stone and wooden monuments associated with them may have foreshadowed profound social changes in prehistoric Europe that came with the increasing use of bronze and other metals.

3500 b.c.

Agriculture and domestic stock were in use in southern Scandinavia and on the north European plains by 3500 b.c. A vigorous hunting and gathering cultural tradition had flourished on the shores of the Baltic for thousands of years (J. G. D. Clark, 1975). Then it seems that some hunters adopted the new economy from the Danubian farmers on their southern boundaries; pollen diagrams from Scandinavian bogs show a striking disturbance in the natural forest cover at this time. The forest, especially elm trees, diminishes in the diagrams; cereal grasses and the pollen of typical cultivation weeds appear for the first time. Layers of charcoal fragments testify to forests being cleared by burning. The drop in elm cover is thought to mean that this tree was used for cattle fodder, or possibly these trees died because of elm disease.

General features of this early farming activity are familiar — growing of cereal crops and grazing of stock, sizable settlements of rectangular houses, and forests cleared with polished stone axes. The farmers began building sizable family tombs. They developed a characteristic clay beaker with a flared neck, later widely distributed over central and northwestern Europe.

4300 b.c.

The British Isles stand at the extreme northwest corner of Europe, the receiving end of culture traits from many peoples. Before 4300 b.c., farming communities were established in southern Britain. Communal burial chambers and large cattle camps with extensive earthworks came into use. British sites reflect cultural influences from both western France and Scandinavia. Flourishing barter networks carried stone blades, and the material to make them, throughout England. Similar exploitation of flint and other stone outcrops is persistent in early European farming.

By 4000 b.c. or thereabouts, stone-using peasant farmers were well established over most of temperate Europe. Many Stone Age hunters had adopted the new economies; still others lived by hunting and gathering alongside the farmers. Both subsistence patterns survived side by side for many centuries. In Scandinavia fishermen and fowlers of the Ertebølle culture absorbed some new economic practices without making major changes in their traditional way of life. They traded fish for grain products grown by their neighbors and lived on the outskirts of cleared farmlands.

GUIDE TO FURTHER READING

Champion, T. G., Gamble, C. S., Shennan, S. J., and Whittle, A. W. R. *Prehistoric Europe*. New York: Academic Press, 1984.
An up-to-date summary of European prehistory, with a major emphasis on trade, subsistence, and social organization.

Clark, J. G. D. *Prehistoric Europe: The Economic Basis*. Palo Alto: Stanford University Press, 1952.
The classic essay on prehistoric European economic life that is still of immense value to the general reader.

Dennell, R. C. *European Economic Prehistory: A New Approach*. New York: Academic Press, 1983.
A thoroughly up-to-date, provocative book of fundamental value to economic archaeology.

Phillips, Patricia. *The Prehistory of Europe*. Bloomington: Indiana University Press, 1980.
A synthesis of Old World prehistory that is a fundamental source on a key area of the world. Technical but clearly written account for the informed reader.

Piggott, Stuart. *Ancient Europe*, Chicago: Aldine, 1965.
Piggott's elegant essay on European prehistory is somewhat outdated but a clear exposition of the major issues of European prehistory. Superb illustrations.

Renfrew, Colin. *Before Civilization*. New York: Knopf, 1973.
A well-written essay on recent advances in European prehistory that concentrates on the calibration of radiocarbon dating. Essential reading for any more-than-casual student of Old World archaeology.

Trump, David. *The Prehistory of the Mediterranean*. New Haven: Yale University Press, 1980.
Another synthesis of Old World prehistory that, like the Phillips text, is a fundamental source on a key area of the world. For the informed reader.

Chapter Eleven

Early Farmers of Africa

PREVIEW

❖ There are no signs of extensive agricultural settlement in Egypt before 4500 B.C., although evidence of earlier farming may someday be found. Opinion is divided over whether the Egyptians developed food production on their own or with the aid of cereals or animals from the Near East or the west.

❖ The earliest Egyptian farmers probably had little need for irrigation agriculture, the appearance of which appears to coincide with the political unification of Egypt in approximately 3000 B.C.

❖ The Sahara was sufficiently well watered to support cattle-herding peoples from approximately 5500 to 3000 B.C. With the desiccation of the desert, Saharan peoples moved southward into sub-Saharan Africa, where they domesticated summer rainfall crops like sorghum and millet.

❖ Cattle-herding people were living in East Africa by 1000 B.C., and cattle may have been domesticated much earlier. But agriculture and domesticated animals did not spread to tropical Africa as a whole until the advent of ironworking approximately 2000 years ago.

Chronological Table F
p. 228

The Nile Valley was a rich environment for human settlement in the late Pleistocene times (Figure 11.1) (Aldred, 1961; Fedden, 1977). The Nile 14,000 years ago already flowed through desert, although intervals of higher rainfall did occur, the last between approximately 13,000 and 9000 B.C. At that time the Nile Valley was occupied by hunting and gathering populations, making much use of wild grains and seeds as well as large game animals, fish, and birds (J. D. Clark, 1971).

HUNTER-GATHERERS ON THE NILE

Qadan culture
12,500 to 4550 B.C.

One such culture of hunter-gatherers, named the *Qadan*, flourished between approximately 12,500 and 4550 B.C. It is best known from micro-

Figure 11.1 The Nile, close to the First Cataract.

lithic tools found on riverside campsites near the Nile. In the earlier stages of the Qadan, fishing and big-game hunting were important, but large numbers of grindstones and grinding equipment came from a few localities, which seems to show that gathering wild grains was significant to at least part of the economy. Some Qadan settlements were probably large and occupied for long periods. The dead were buried in cemeteries in shallow pits covered with stone slabs. Some pits held two bodies. In six instances, small stone tools were embedded in the bones of these Qadan people, who must have met a violent end (Wendorf, 1968).

Other distinct cultural traditions are known to have prospered in the Nile Valley at this time. Around Kom Ombo, upstream of Qadan country, Stone Age hunter-gatherers lived on the banks of lagoons and flood channels of the Nile, seeking game in the riverside woodlands and on the plains overlooking the valley. They fished for catfish and perch in the swamps. Here, too, wild grasses were important in the hunter-gatherer economy from approximately 12,000 B.C. (Wendorf and Schild, 1980).

The valley is unusual in that its water supply depends on the seasonal floods from Ethiopia, not on rainfall. Its boundaries are severely constricted by the desert, confining humans to the Nile banks. This highly favorable environment was being exploited by hunters with a bow and arrow toolkit superior to that of earlier millennia, so that population densities inevitably rose, increasing competition for a habitat that was the only means of survival for the people of the valley. They could not move away from the river, for the arid deserts would not support them. The logical solution was more specialized exploitation of natural resources — or agriculture.

For years, people assumed that cereal crops and animal domestication spread into the Nile Valley from Southwest Asia sometime after 8000 B.C. (Childe, 1952), but there is no evidence to support this view. Whatever the beginnings of food production on the Nile, it seems clear that the shift toward agriculture was slow and undramatic; it was no sudden revolution in human behavior. However, around 10,000 B.C. there are signs of larger settlements near Esna and elsewhere that average as much as 1000 m (3500 sq yd) in area. By 5000 B.C., the Nile Valley supported thousands of villages large and small. Some, such as a transitory settlement found on the shores of a former lake in the Fayum Depression to the west of the Nile Valley, were little more than temporary camps of crude matting or reed shelters (Caton-Thompson and Gardner, 1934). The inhabitants lived at a simple subsistence level by fishing and hunting both crocodiles and hippopotamuses. They cultivated wheat and barley and kept both sheep and goats. The floodplain settlements were more like the village of Merimde near the Nile Delta. There a cluster of oval houses and shelters were built half underground and roofed with mud and sticks (Hoffman, 1979). An occupation mound 2 m (7 ft) high accumulated over 600 years from approximately 4130 B.C. Simple pottery, stone axes, flint arrowheads, and knives were in use. Agriculture and the cultivation of cereal crops is evidenced by grains stored in clay pots, baskets, and pits. Dogs, cattle, sheep or goats, and pigs were kept. Farming at a subsistence level was characteristic of large areas of the Nile floodplain for thousands of years (Hoffman, 1979).

Other farmers who flourished in the Upper Nile are known to us mainly from cemetery burials. Like their northern neighbors, they used bows and arrows in the chase, many of them tipped with finely flaked arrowheads. Emmer wheat and barley were cultivated, and cattle and small stock provided much of their meat. Settlements here were typified by mud-brick and transient architecture. The dead, however, were buried with some ceremony — in linen shrouds, and the bodies were covered with skins. The women wore ivory combs and plaited their hair. This culture, named the *Badarian* after a village where the first settlements were found, is thought to be broadly contemporary with Merimde (Butzer, 1976; Hays, 1984; Hoffman, 1979).

The early farming communities of the Nile continued to use the forested river banks for settlement (Butzer, 1976; Trigger, 1968). Animals grazed in the flat grasslands of the plain for most of the year and crops were planted on wet basin soils as the waters receded. Game was still abundant in the Nile Valley 6000 years ago; even so, the people ventured to the edge of the deserts in search of gazelle and other small animals.

They buried their dead in huge cemeteries overlooking the Nile, where the graves would not take up valuable agricultural land.

The unification of Egypt into a single state took place in approximately 3100 B.C. Agriculture was practiced for at least 2000 years before this event. The density of population was probably low enough that the people had no need of either government or government-regulated irrigation canals. They made use of natural floods and drainage basins to grow their crops. One authority has estimated that an average Nile flood would have allowed early Egyptian farmers to harvest grain over perhaps two-thirds of the floodplain of the Nile (Hamden, 1961). The first appearance of irrigation seems to coincide with the unification of Egypt and is described in Chapter Sixteen.

THE SAHARA

Many people think of the Sahara as a vast sand sea, one of the most desolate places on earth. But in fact the Sahara is a highly diverse, albeit dry, region that has undergone major climatic changes during the past 12,000 years (Wilkins, 1984). Before 6000 B.C. there were shallow lakes in the central and southern Sahara that supported hippopotamuses and many species of fish. Many prehistoric hunting camps have been found on these long dry lakes (A. Smith, 1984). Similar hunter-gatherer groups flourished along the Nile in the Sudan.

After a short drying period around 5000 B.C. climatic conditions in the central and southern Sahara improved (Rognon, 1981). The lakes expanded and filled again. This time cattle herders camped by their shores. The earliest cattle bones come from a cave in southwest Libya dated to about 4000 B.C., but they may date to as early as 5000 B.C. Pastoralists were widespread in the central and southern Sahara during the fourth millennium B.C. and it seems certain that they were making use of wild cereal grasses and perhaps cultivating such tropical crops as sorghum. Opinions vary as to how domestic animals reached the Sahara. The most common hypothesis has goats and sheep being introduced to North Africa about 6000 B.C., with cattle domestication about a millennium later. It is thought that wild cattle in the Sahara were the source of local domestication.

The cattle herders had but the simplest of possessions, unsophisticated, round-based pots and flaked and polished adzes. They also hunted with the bow and arrow. The Saharan people left a remarkable record of their lives on the walls of caves deep in the desert. Wild animals, cattle, goats, humans, and scenes of daily life are preserved in a complicated jumble of artistic endeavor extending back perhaps to 5000 B.C. (Lhote, 1959). The widespread distribution of pastoral sites of this period suggests that the Saharans were ranging their herds over widely separated summer and winter grazing grounds.

About 3500 B.C., climatic conditions deteriorated. The Sahara became slowly drier and lakes vanished. Rainfall rose in the interior of West Africa and the northern limit of the tsetse fly belt moved south (this insect is endemic to much of tropical Africa and is fatal to cattle). So the herders shifted south, following the major river systems into savannah regions. By this time, the Saharan people were probably using domestic crops, experimenting with such summer rainfall crops as sorghum and millet as they moved southward out of areas where they could grow wheat, barley, and other Mediterranean crops (for a full discussion, see J. D. Clark, 1984).

SUB-SAHARAN AFRICA

At the end of Pleistocene times, the indigenous inhabitants of sub-Saharan Africa were already adapted to many kinds of specialized environment. Some lived by intensive fishing, others by gathering or hunting, depending on their environment. In a primitive way the techniques of food production may have already been used on the fringes of the rain forests of western and central Africa, where the common use of such root plants as the African yam led people to recognize the advantages of growing their own food (J. D. Clark, 1984; M. Harris, 1968). Certainly the yam can easily be germinated by replanting the tops. This primitive form of "vegeculture" may have been the economic tradition onto which the cultivation of summer rainfall cereal crops was grafted as it came into use south of the grassland areas on the Sahara's southern borders (Harlan, DeWet, and Stemler, 1976; McIntosh and McIntosh, 1981).

Vegeculture (plant manipulation)

The East African highlands are ideal cattle country, and the home of such famous cattle-herding peoples as the Masai today. They were inhabited by scattered bands of hunter-gatherers living around mountains near the plains until about 3300 years ago, when the first cattle herders appeared. Their emergence may be connected with shifts in climatic zones that opened up the highlands to pastoral peoples for the first time (Ambrose, 1984). These cattle people may have moved between fixed settlements during the wet and dry seasons, living off hunting in the dry months and their own livestock and agriculture during the rains (Bower, 1984).

Stone Age cattle herds appeared in other parts of sub-Saharan Africa as well, in the grasslands south of the Sahara in West Africa and even at the extreme southern tip of Africa. These Khoikhoi people were still flourishing when Portuguese explorer Bartolemew Diaz rounded the Cape of Good Hope in A.D. 1488. The explorers who had dealings with them commented on their simple material culture and constantly nomadic lifeway, which was finely attuned to the seasonal Cape environment. They are known to have lived at the Cape for at least 2000 years (Elphick, 1977; R. Klein, 1984). It is not known how they reached their Cape homeland. The Khoikhoi did not long survive European settlement in the seventeenth century, and their lifeway is extinct today.

Approximately 2000 years ago, with the arrival of ironworking, the practices of food production and keeping domestic animals spread throughout the African continent (Phillipson, 1977). For thousands of years after the Near East had started to enjoy literate civilization, San hunter-gatherers continued to flourish on the rich savannah woodlands of east and southern Africa. Their environment was so rich that they had no incentive to take up the new economies, even if they were aware of them. Agriculture finally came to the savannah when widespread forest clearance was made easier by iron tools and tougher working edges, from approximately 2000 years ago.

A.D. 100

GUIDE TO FURTHER READING

Butzer, Karl. *Early Hydraulic Civilization in Egypt.* Chicago: University of Chicago Press, 1976.
A fundamental source on Ancient Egyptian irrigation that has great relevance to this chapter.

Clark, J. Desmond, and Brandt, Steven A. (Eds.). *From Hunters to Farmers.* Berkeley: University of California Press, 1984.
A set of scholarly essays summarizing recent evidence for early agriculture in Africa. Excellent for specialists, but definitive.

Hoffman, Michael A. *Egypt Before the Pharaohs.* New York: Knopf, 1979.
A fascinating account of prehistoric Egypt that recounts not only key discoveries, but also recalls the archaeologists who made them. The first detailed account of this subject for many years, written for the general reader.

Oliver, Roland, and Fagan, Brian M. *Africa in the Iron Age.* London: Cambridge University Press, 1975.
A general history of Africa from approximately 500 B.C. that covers much of the material in this chapter in a wider historical context.

Chronological Table G

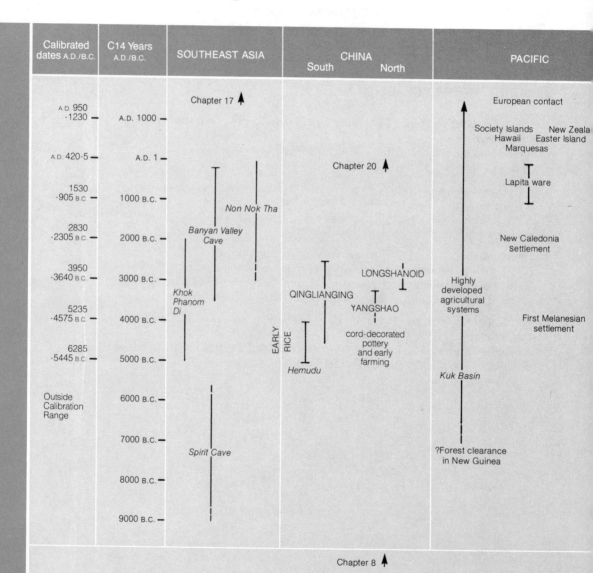

Calibrated dates A.D./B.C.	C14 Years A.D./B.C.	SOUTHEAST ASIA	CHINA South North	PACIFIC

A.D. 950 -1230 — ... A.D. 1000 — ... Chapter 17 ↑ ... European contact

Society Islands   New Zeala
Hawaii   Easter Island
Marquesas

A.D. 420-5 — ... A.D. 1 — ... Chapter 20 ↑

Lapita ware

1530 -905 B.C. — ... 1000 B.C. — ... *Non Nok Tha*

2830 -2305 B.C. — ... 2000 B.C. — ... *Banyan Valley Cave* ... New Caledonia Settlement

3950 -3640 B.C. — ... 3000 B.C. — ... LONGSHANOID

5235 -4575 B.C. — ... 4000 B.C. — ... *Khok Phanom Di* ... QINGLIANGING ... YANGSHAO ... Highly developed agricultural systems ... First Melanesian settlement

6285 -5445 B.C. — ... 5000 B.C. — ... EARLY RICE ... cord-decorated pottery and early farming

Hemudu

Outside Calibration Range ... 6000 B.C. — ... *Kuk Basin*

7000 B.C. — ... *Spirit Cave* ... ?Forest clearance in New Guinea

8000 B.C. —

9000 B.C. —

Chapter 8 ↑

Chapter Twelve

Asia: Rice, Roots, and Ocean Voyagers

PREVIEW

✤ Southeast Asia is widely believed to be an early center of root crop domestication. The archaeological evidence from Spirit Cave, Thailand, and other sites is still insufficient to establish whether people were hunting and gathering a broad spectrum of animal and vegetable foods 11,000 years ago or were deliberately planting some individual species.

✤ Distinctive farming cultures were flourishing in northern and southern China by at least 8000 B.C. The first agriculturalists had a wide range of potential domesticates to choose from.

✤ Rice was, and still is, a key cereal crop in Asia. Its origins are still not certain. Rice cultivation appears at Khok Phanon Di in Thailand approximately 5000 B.C. The date of the earliest rice cultivation in China is unknown, but may be as early. The widespread dispersal of rice cultivation in China is thought to be associated with the Longshanoid cultures, after 3000 B.C.

✤ The human settlement of the Pacific was dependent on Asian root crops and the development of deepwater canoes. The Kuk Basin in New Guinea has yielded traces of forest clearance and drainage as early as 7000 B.C., with the cultivation of taro and yams probably beginning as early as 4000 B.C.

✤ The first settlement of Melanesia is believed to be associated with the development of trading networks, which later were elaborated into ceremonial trade routes. First settlement may have occurred as early as 4000 B.C., with the widespread Lapita pottery tradition flourishing about 2000 years ago and being used as far east as Samoa.

✤ Polynesia was settled within the last 2500 years: the Marquesas were colonized approximately A.D. 400, Hawaii some 1350 years ago, and Easter Island approximately A.D. 500. The Polynesians were technologically in the Stone Age, but they developed powerful chiefdoms that were at the height of their power when the first Europeans arrived in the eighteenth century.

✤ New Zealand was first colonized by Polynesians in A.D. 900 or so, but the introduction of the sweet potato led to rapid population buildup that coincides with the emergence of Maori culture approximately 600 years ago. The Maori developed a warlike society with constant competition for prime agricultural land and for prestige that reached its peak approximately 300 years ago.

Fifteen thousand years ago much of Southeast Asia was inhabited by hunter-gatherers whose stone toolkits reveal remarkable uniformity over large areas of the mainland and islands (Sauer, 1952). These stone assemblages do not necessarily reflect a stagnation of cultural innovation or a simple lifeway. Rather, it seems certain that these people were exploiting a broad range of game and vegetable foods (Glover, 1977).

13,000 B.C.

Very few scientific excavations have been made on sites that cover the period 13,000 to 6000 B.C., the period when food production may have begun in this region (Gorman, 1969, 1971). The controversies about early food production in Southeast Asia surround two questions:

When did people first start to cultivate root crops?

What are the origins of rice cultivation (rice being the vital staple cereal crop in much of Asia throughout later prehistory)?

EARLY FOOD PRODUCTION IN THAILAND

As Carl Sauer points out (1952), the domestication of root crops is difficult to identify in the archaeological record at the best of times. The only way that one can deduce cultivation is by examination of vegetable remains found in excavations, comparing these finds with the modern flora, and extrapolating modern uses of the flora into the past, on the assumption that use patterns have not changed.

Spirit Cave
9000 to 7000 B.C.

Chester Gorman's excavations at Spirit Cave in northeastern Thailand took him to a limestone cave overlooking a small stream (see Figure 12.1). He found that the lowest levels of the site were formed more than 11,000 years ago. What he called Hoabhinian tools, including small flakes and choppers, came from these horizons and it was clear that such tools were used for a long time. Gorman was able to identify quantities of seeds from the Hoabhinian levels. When botanists examined these finds, they found that the people had eaten almonds, betel nuts, broad beans, gourds, water chestnuts, peppers, and cucumbers. D. E. Yen of the Bishop Museum in Honolulu visited the area and collected modern floral specimens for comparative purposes (Yen, 1977). He even ate some of the wild foods himself. He noted that there were at least eight wild species of yam in the area and that the seeds found in the Spirit Cave were from plants that can be collected in the wild and have a variety of dietary, medicinal, and other uses. The botanists had great difficulty in establishing whether the Spirit Cave seeds were domesticated or wild and in fact have produced no definite grounds for calling them deliberately planted.

The Spirit Cave finds provide no firm evidence for domestication of plants as early as 9000 B.C., but despite the uncertainty of the botanical evidence, Wilhelm Solheim and others have claimed that Southeast Asia was a major center of early plant and animal domestication (Solheim, 1971). There is certainly insufficient evidence from the few excavations

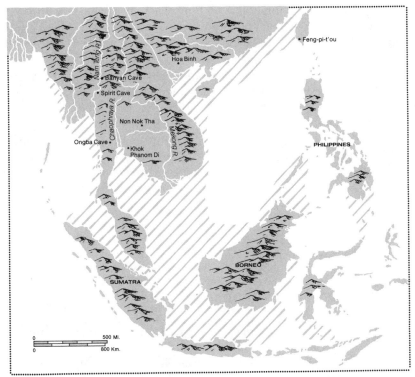

Figure 12.1 Southeast Asian sites mentioned in this chapter. Shaded areas show extent of low sea levels during the Weichsel glaciation.

in the area to make such a claim. However, there are indications of the following:

There was a wide variety of yams and other potential domesticates in Thailand and elsewhere; these were exploited by hunter-gatherers at the end of the Pleistocene.

In the case of the yams, there were enough species present for people under demographic or other stress to experiment with hybridization if they wished.

In view of these two factors, there is no reason to doubt that food production could have begun in this area quite independently from other regions.

As we have pointed out before, yam planting is very simple, and hunter-gatherers are well aware that deliberate cultivation is possible. The problem is to identify the factors that led people to deliberate experimentation with various plants. In the absence of firm archaeological evidence, we can speculate that primitive shifting agriculture, with a combination of diverse crops and some animal herding, may have had its roots in a broad spectrum of hunting and gathering, as it did in other regions of the world. In the final analysis, all that is needed for a culture to make the transition are some clearings at the edge of the forest and a simple digging stick, already used for gathering, to plant the crop (Yen, 1977).

Charles Higham, who studied the animal bones from Spirit Cave and other localities in northern Thailand, argued that the large range of species found in the sites indicated a broadly based hunting economy that focused on deer, pigs, and arboreal creatures such as monkeys (Highan, 1972). Perhaps the caves reflected only the hunting aspect of an otherwise agricultural economy; in any case, there was no sign of domestic animals in the collections. Chester Gorman believed that this broadly based hunting was a preadaptation to early animal domestication (Gorman, 1969, 1977).

The case for indigenous development of agriculture and animal domestication in Southeast Asia is still unproven, although there is no reason to believe that it did not take place.

RICE CULTIVATION IN SOUTHEAST ASIA

Spirit Cave
7000 to 5000 B.C.

The material culture of the Spirit Cave people shows a distinct change after 7000 B.C. From then until approximately 5600 B.C. the inhabitants began to use adzes, pottery, and slate knives. These last strongly resemble later artifacts used for rice cultivation in parts of Indonesia and may suggest that cereal was cultivated near the site.

6500 B.C.

In approximately 6500 B.C., people were moving from the hills onto river plains and into lowland areas. River plains were the best place for the intensive cultivation and simple irrigation needed for rice agriculture. Crop yields, far superior to those from small highland root crop gardens, were ample and easily obtained. While everyone agrees that rice was domesticated in an Asian lowland area, there is little agreement about where or when it was cultivated, partly because there is no archaeological evidence bearing on the problem. In all probability, the wild ancestor of rice was a perennial grass that grew wild in lowland areas from India to southern China, and in the Pacific islands. Perhaps rice was first encountered as a weed in taro gardens; if so, it would have been transplanted, then harvested with a knife. In any case, it seems probable that rice was first cultivated by root crop farmers.

Khok Phanom Di
5000 to 2000 B.C.

Charles Higham (1984) has excavated an early rice farming community at Khok Phanom Di in Thailand, a settlement that was close to coastal mangrove swamps between 5000 and 2000 B.C., but is now over 12 mi from the seashore. The site covers 5 hectares and is 12 m (39 ft) deep and contains rice specimens and other evidence of agriculture. Higham hypothesizes that the inhabitants of the coastal plains took up wild rice cultivation as sea levels rose, inundating the game and woodland resources of the fertile shoreline. Other rice specimens come from Banyan Valley Cave in northern Thailand and Non Nok Tha, a low mound on a Mekong river tributary in the same general area (Bayard, 1970, 1972). Gorman found rice husks in Banyan levels dating to between 5500 B.C. and A.D. 800, none of which the botanical experts could positively identify as being fully domesticated. Experiments with milling stones were carried out which showed that the husks had been ground by a quite different method from that used by modern rice farmers in the area. Yen, whose studies of the rice can surely be described as comprehensive, speculates that the Banyan finds were the result of a form of gathering plus selective cultivation of wild rice — a stage in the gradual domestication of the cereal. There are many wild species in the region, several of which were possible candidates for cultivation.

Non Nok Tha may have been occupied before 3000 to 2000 B.C., but it was abandoned at some time before 2000 years ago. (The chronology is controversial.) The excavators found traces of rice in the form of grain impressions on clay pots in the lowest levels. They pointed out that the site dates to the time when the lowlands were already settled and argued that this means that the rice was probably cultivated, not wild. The bones of domesticated cattle came from the same site. The inhabitants were sedentary farmers depending on rice and cattle for most of their diet. Hunting and gathering were less important than in earlier millennia when highland sites were occupied all year.

Non Nok Tha
3000 B.C. to A.D. 1

Rice cultivation has become the major cereal crop agriculture of the world, but its origins are still uncertain. Southeast Asia did not suffer from the drastic climatic changes of northern latitudes. No prolonged droughts or major vegetational changes altered the pattern of human settlement. Only dramatic rises in low sea levels altered the geography and environment of Southeast Asia, creating islands from dry land, and reducing the amount of coastal floodplain available to hunters and gatherers. Conceivably, these major changes in coastline and available land surface were among many factors that moved the inhabitants of Southeast Asia to experiment with plants and domestic animals.

EARLY FARMING IN CHINA

"In the wealth of its species and in the extent of the genus and species potential of its cultivated plants, China is conspicuous among other centers of origin of plant forms." Thus wrote the great Russian botanist N. I. Vavilov more than thirty years ago (Vavilov, 1951). Like the archaeology of early agriculture in Southeast Asia, that of China is still in its infancy, but agriculture seems to have appeared separately in three major areas of China: the southern coastal, the north, and the eastern coastal areas.

Agriculture in Southern and Eastern China

No one knows when agriculture first began in southern China, but Chang (1977) hypothesizes that it may have begun as early as 12,000 years ago with the cultivation of roots and tubers. It is possible that the same broad spectrum of exploiting wild vegetable foods in Southeast Asia may have been practiced in southern China too.

The earliest farming settlement so far discovered in southern China is at Hemudu in the low-lying northern Zhejiang province, close to the southern part of the Yangtze River. Four cultural layers have been radiocarbon-dated to between the late sixth and early fifth millennium B.C., all of them from wooden pile dwellings on the damp shores of a lake. This remarkable site has yielded beautifully mortise-and-tenon-joined building planks, as well as bone hoes and coarse, black pots decorated with cord impressions. This area is ideal rice-growing country, and it is hardly surprising to find abundant rice on the site, as well as the remains of bottle gourds and numerous wild vegetable foods. The Hemudu people were skilled hunters, who kept water buffalo, pigs, and dogs. Hemudu is roughly contemporary with Khok Phanom Di in Thailand, and the cord-decorated pottery made by the Hemudu people is widespread in southern China, as well as in Taiwan. However, it seems that cord-decorated pottery appeared even earlier in Thailand and Japan.

The fifth millennium saw the emergence of several distinct farming traditions in the south, among them the Qinglianging, itself followed in the fourth millennium by even more sophisticated agriculture on the Yangtze River (Chang, 1981). The archaeology of these traditions is known primarily from cemetery excavations that show slow changes in the grave goods deposited with the dead (Pearson, 1981). The earliest graves indicate few social differentiations, but later sepulchers show not only a much wider variety of artifacts — pottery, bone and stone tools, jade objects, and other ornaments — but an increase in the number of elaborately adorned burials. Richard Pearson, who has analyzed several cemeteries, argues that they demonstrate an increase in concentration of wealth, a trend toward ranked societies, and a shift in the relative importance of males at the expense of females; the latter trend may be associated with the development of more intensive agriculture, an activity in which males are valued for their major roles in cultivation and production of food and in which manual labor is carried out by women, when land is plentiful and shifting cultivation is the rule of the day.

Northern China

If it is true that root crops were developed in Southeast Asia and southern China very early, that course of history would lead us to ask: What was the relationship between early agriculture in the south and the first farming in the north? Did agriculture spread from the south, or did food production develop quite independently in both regions?

North Chinese agriculture has one great contrast with the south: It is based heavily on cereals and seeded plants. The first northern agricultural communities were sited in the central regions of the Yellow River Valley (Figure 12.2). The area is a small basin, forming a border between

Hemudu
c. 5000 B.C. to
c. 4000 B.C.

Qinglianging tradition
c. 5000 to 3000 B.C.

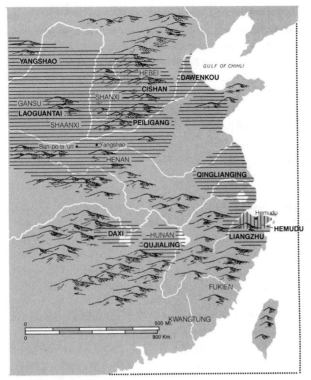

Figure 12.2 Early Chinese farming cultures, with names of three major local variants shown. Yangshao sites occur both within the northern shaded area and outside it. Southern sites of corded pottery are found in Kwangtung, Fukien and Taiwan areas.

the wooded western highlands and the swampy lowlands to the east. Pollen analysis has provided evidence for a prolonged period of warmer climate from approximately 8000 to 4000 years ago, when favorable rainfall patterns and greater warmth made this nuclear area a fine place for agriculture (Ho, 1969).

During the glaciations of the Pleistocene, loess soils were formed over a wide area of the north. The fine, soft-textured earth was both homogeneous and porous and could be tilled by simple digging sticks. Because of the concentrated summer rainfall, cereal crops, the key to agriculture in this region, could be grown successfully. The indigenous plants available for domestication included the wild ancestors of foxtail millet, broomcorn millet, sorghum, hemp, and the mulberry. Ancient Chinese farmers developed their own cultivation techniques, which persisted for thousands of years before irrigation was developed. Although irrigation gradually became the basis of the agricultural economies of Egypt, the Indus Valley, and Mesopotamia, it was not important in northern China until much later (Ho, 1969).

The earliest millennia of northern Chinese agriculture are still a blank on the archaeological map. Two hypotheses are possible. We can assume that the inhabitants of the Yellow River region passed through a long phase of experimental cultivation and intensive exploitation of the indigenous flora before developing their own distinctive agricultural techniques, or we can assume that food production was developed farther south in China and adopted later in the north. Neither hypothesis can be tested with the available evidence. It is known that early farming villages are associated with coarse, cord-marked pottery found on the banks of the Yellow River in western Henan province. Perhaps these cord-marked vessels are related to the cord-decorated pottery traditions of southern China, Southeast Asia, and Taiwan.

Early farming
6th millennium B.C.

Three early agricultural traditions have been identified in northern and central China, each of them dating to the late sixth millennium B.C.: the Cishan, Peiligang, and Laoguantai (Figure 12.2) (Chang, 1981). They share certain common features: the keeping of dogs and pigs and the cultivation of foxtail millet. The villagers built semisubterranean houses, dug large storage pits, and relied on hunting and gathering as well as cultivation.

Yangshao
4000 to 3200 B.C.

The middle reaches of the Yellow River have yielded the Yangshao culture, which dates between 4000 and 3200 B.C. (Chang, 1977, 1981). Similar villages have been found over much of the Yellow River basin, an area as large as the early centers of agriculture in Egypt and Mesopotamia.

Many Yangshao villages were undefended settlements built on ridges overlooking the floodplains, situated to avoid flooding or to allow maximal use of floodplain soils. The villagers lived in fairly substantial round or oblong houses partly sunk into the ground. Yangshao houses had mud-plastered walls, timber frames, and steep roofs (Figure 12.3). Usually there were cemeteries outside the villages. Sometimes the vil-

Figure 12.3 Reconstruction of Yangshao huts from Ban-p'o-ts'un, China.

lages had a special area for pottery kilns where the characteristic Yang-shao painted funerary vessels favored by the householders were manufactured.

Some Yangshao people moved their settlements regularly, but returned to the same sites again and again. Using hoes and digging sticks, they cultivated foxtail millet as a staple crop. Simple dry-land slash-and-burn farming probably supplemented riverside gardens. Irrigation may have been practiced as early as the fifth millennium B.C., however. Dogs and pigs were fully domesticated. Cattle, sheep, and goats were less common. Hunting and gathering were still significant, as was fishing, for which hooks and spears were employed.

Each Yangshao village was a self-contained community, thousands of which flourished in the river valleys of northern China. The Yangshao farmers were distributed over a comparatively limited part of northern China from eastern Gansu in the west to the Yellow River and northwestern Henan in the east. There were other local variants such as Dawenkou and Qinglianging (Figure 12.2) (Chang, 1981). By 4000 B.C. the features of a characteristic, and thoroughly Chinese, culture were already clear. The earliest Chinese farmers already had developed a distinctive naturalistic art style (Figure 12.4). The unique Chinese style of cooking with steam is attested by the discovery of cooking pots identical to later specialized

Figure 12.4 Yangshao pottery from Ban-Po, China (approximately one-fourth actual size). In the photographs, the fish motifs often used to decorate Yangshao pottery are clearly seen (other motifs are drawn separately below).

cooking vessels. Jade was worked; hemp was used for making fabrics; skilled basketry was practiced; even the Chinese language may have roots in Yangshao. There can be little doubt of the indigenous origins of Chinese cereal agriculture, although, theoretically, long-established trade routes to the West could have brought new ideas to the Far East, including some crops, especially in later millennia.

The Yangshao culture itself had a relatively restricted distribution in northern China, centered on the Yellow River Valley. The expansion of the Yangshao was largely confined to gradual taking up of land by villages that split off from larger settlements and needed new gardens. Still, the success of the agricultural adaptation led in part to population increases and greater elaboration of material culture, resulting in the evolution of more complex farming cultures, some concentration of wealth in privileged hands, and more intensive food production. Inevitably, too, farming peoples in both the north and the south spread into hitherto uncultivated areas, taking up new lands. (Figure 12.5) Soon many regional variations of peasant farming culture were flourishing throughout China. The village settlements follow a pattern of river valleys and seacoasts, each regional variant connected to others by a network of waterways. The development of food production in China was a long process

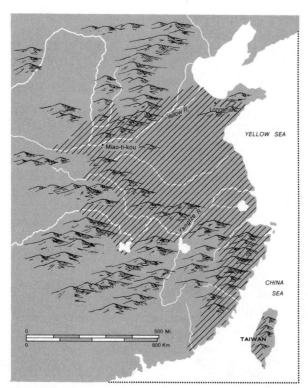

Figure 12.5 Approximate distribution of later farming cultures in China (shaded area).

that occurred at much the same time throughout the land, with people adapting their crops and farming techniques to local conditions.

The typical later farming settlement — insofar as it is possible to generalize — was larger than that of the Yangshao. The settled, permanent villages were often protected by earthen walls. Millet seems to have been a staple crop in the north, while domestic cattle, sheep, and goats, and perhaps the horse were added to the economy. Hunting and gathering as well as fishing were locally important. The economy changed but little from earlier times, except for increased productivity, some evidence for better organization of village life (witness the communally built walls), and the addition of rice to the crops grown. Remains of rice grains have been found in later northern villages, which gives reason to believe that rice cultivation spread into northern China from the south, where fertile floodplains with their lush water meadows provided an effective environment for rice growing. The introduction of rice to the north would have reduced dependence on dry agriculture, and, presumably, led to the use of irrigation and the modification of agricultural technology.

These farmers are thought to have been one of the groups responsible for the rapid spread of rice cultivation not only through the mainland but on the offshore islands of Southeast Asia and far into the Pacific. Certainly, their more intensive agriculture, substantial settlements, and more elaborate material culture were among the roots of Chinese civilization (Figure 12.6).

JOMON AND EARLY AGRICULTURE IN JAPAN

As we learned in Chapter Six, the Jomon people of Japan were using pottery as early as 10,500 B.C., living near coasts and lakeshores, and exploiting a wide range of game, vegetable foods, and shellfish (Ikawa-Smith, 1980). More than 10,000 Jomon sites are known, most of

Jomon tradition
11,000 to 300 B.C.

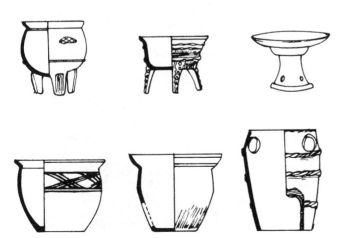

Figure 12.6 Some typical Longshanoid vessels used for cooking and other purposes, from Miao-ti-kou, China (scale not recorded).

them from Honshu in central Japan. All are linked by a common cultural tradition that lasted for thousands of years, but there were probably different ethnic groups that perhaps spoke different languages and adapted to diverse environments. The Jomon people hunted deer and other game with bows and arrows, collected thousands of shellfish, mainly in the spring, and fished much of the year. At first they caught all types of fish, but as time went on they concentrated on a few carefully selected species, both inshore and lake fish as well as deepwater forms such as the bonito and tuna. Above all their diet depended heavily on wild vegetable foods such as acorns, nuts, and edible seeds. They lived in relatively sedentary settlements, perhaps because of carefully scheduled seasonal hunting, gathering, and fishing activities. Others believe that they supplemented these activities with cultivation of root crops, cereals, or simply by careful management of nut trees. The evidence for agriculture is still sketchy, but it seems possible that the Jomon people flourished by virtue of developing an elaborate technology for processing and storing huge stocks of nuts, an activity they may have combined with cultivation of milletlike plants.

The Jomon tradition lasted from as early as 11,000 B.C. until as late as 300 B.C. During this period, the focus of settlement shifted from the coasts to central Honshu and to the northern shores of Japan. By 5000 B.C., the inhabitants of Honshu were enjoying an elaborate material culture, including finely made ritual clay pots adorned with intricate decorations (Figure 12.7). The people often lived not in the caves and simple pit houses of earlier times, but in large clusters of wooden houses with elaborate hearths. After 3000 B.C., the climate began to cool down, overpopulation may have strained the carrying capacity of arable land, and

Figure 12.7 Jomon gray-bodied molded jar, of conical form with loop handles and decorated with combwork.

clearance of natural vegetation affected hunting activities. Hence, the population declined and the major centers of Jomon occupation moved toward the coasts. In the south, the inhabitants of Kyushu took up rice and barley cultivation after 1000 B.C. (for a lengthy discussion, see Akazawa, 1982).

The basis for what was to become traditional Japanese society was formed during the Yayoi period, which began after 300 B.C. when new crops and technologies spread through the islands. Japan was unified into a single state in approximately A.D. 600, by which time complex, stratified societies were commonplace throughout the archipelago.

Yayoi
300 B.C.
Unification
A.D. 600

FOOD PRODUCTION IN NEW GUINEA

A potential center of great importance to the Pacific Islands is New Guinea, where both taro and yams are important crops. Taro is grown in naturally rich soils or as a first crop in newly cleared forest gardens. The older New Guinea crops, which include both taro and yams, flourish at higher elevations. Today, they are combined with the sweet potato, an American cultigen introduced only relatively recently which allows agriculture at lower altitudes and with far greater crop yield.

Jack Golson, Peter White, and others have studied early agriculture in the New Guinea highlands using both pollen analysis and the study of old irrigation channels to amplify the archaeological record (Allen, 1969; Golson, 1977). There are traces, at approximately 7000 B.C., of deliberate diversion of river water in the Kuk basin, which have been interpreted to mean that the people were cultivating taro or yams at a very early date. The evidence is still uncertain, although signs of increased erosion in the area may be the result of forest clearance for taro or yam gardens, or, possibly, for the deliberate growing of indigenous New Guinea plants (White and O'Connell, 1982).

Kuk
7000 B.C.

By 4000 to 3500 B.C., much more organized agricultural works are found in the Kuk basin. There is pollen evidence for quite extensive forest clearance in the general area. These more organized works may have been created for yam and taro crops, while indigenous plants were grown on the better drained soils between the channel banks. After 2000 B.C., the first highly developed drainage systems occurred in the area, a sign that a much more intensive agriculture was expanding. After 500 B.C., the people depended more and more heavily on dry and wet agriculture, for the forest resources they had relied on were replaced by an environment which had been altered permanently by human activity. A slow population growth would have resulted eventually in the taking up of uncleared land. Then, after that was exhausted, the only option was to shorten the fallow periods on cleared gardens — something which, if taro was the crop, would result in lower crop yields.

4000 B.C.

2000 B.C.

500 B.C.

The archaeological and pollen analysis investigations of Golson and others have produced firm evidence for sedentism, forest clearance, agricultural stone tools, and water-control techniques in the New Guinea highlands by 5000 to 6000 years ago. What is uncertain, however, is the means by which food production began in New Guinea. Was it developed locally with introduced plants after the local hunter-gatherers had manipulated local indigenous plants for centuries? Or did the people manipulate local plants as a result of adopting a few introduced crops first? Whatever the answer to these questions, it appears that the New Guinea highlands were an area where people created an artificial garden environment as a result of a long period of experimentation, in which they were raising plants *within* their natural environment. By exploiting a wide range of tropical animals and plants, the people may have become more sedentary, and later might have started to plant small plots of root crops; ultimately, they would have intensified their food production until they modified their environment beyond recognition. This hypothetical model for early agriculture in New Guinea may serve as a possible model for other tropical areas in Asia as well.

AGRICULTURE IN THE PACIFIC ISLANDS

The origins of the peoples of the Pacific islands have fascinated scientists since the eighteenth century (Figure 12.8) (Moorehead, 1966), but most authorities now look to Southeast Asia for the origins of the Melanesians and Polynesians. They point out that settlement of the offshore islands depended on the successful cultivation of root crops such as taro and the yam, as well as breadfruit, coconuts, and sugar cane. Chickens, dogs, and pigs were also valued as food and were domesticated in Asia before being introduced to the Pacific. Why did these foods have to be established in the diets and farming repertoires of the island settlers? Small animals such as pigs and chickens could readily have been carried from island to island in canoes, as could easily germinating root plants such as the yam. Both food sources allowed a sizable population to spread to many hundreds of small islands separated by miles of open water.

The Pacific islanders show no features attributable to American Indian stock. Their physical attributes had probably stabilized before any cultivators left the Asian mainland. Their languages are similar to Thai and other Southeast Asian dialects and bear no resemblance to native American speech. Artifacts such as ground and polished axes and adzes, shell fishhooks, and canoes can be paralleled generally on the western shores of the Pacific.

The first settlement of the Pacific islands is closely connected with the early cultivation of yams, and especially of taro. As we pointed out earlier in this chapter, taro and yams were probably domesticated in Southeast Asia before the development of rice cultivation, but exactly when and where they were first grown is unknown. In all probability, there were several centers of early domestication within Southeast Asia.

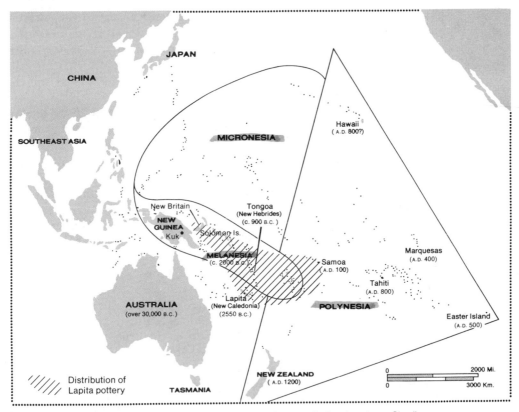

Figure 12.8 Map of Pacific sites and early farming settlements in the Americas. Shading shows distribution of Lapita pottery.

HOW WAS THE PACIFIC SETTLED?

Today, the Pacific island groups are divided culturally into three major areas: Polynesia, Micronesia, and Melanesia (Figure 12.8). These cultural divisions are entirely valid in the twentieth century but gradually lose their validity as we move back into the more remote past (Kirch, 1982). People have tended to think that the Pacific was settled in a series of fast-moving, dramatic migrations that took adventurous canoers into the farthest recesses of the ocean in a few short centuries. Thus, they argue, the cultural differences between the islands have been present since the earliest times. However, archaeological excavations have painted a very different picture, a picture of a gradual and very complex process of settlement from east to west. This process began soon after the end of the Ice Age and continued right into the present millennium. As immigrants moved ever farther out into the Pacific, they settled islands that were more and more isolated, and sometimes biotically more impoverished, so they had to adapt to new conditions, often quite different from those in their homelands. It would appear, then, that the diverse cultural patterns of the Pacific islanders developed over many centuries of adaptation to isolated environments and over a longer period of time than originally thought.

Why were the Pacific islands settled at all? Here archaeologists and anthropologists have indulged in an orgy of speculation.

Current archaeological research in lowland and island Melanesia points to maritime trade as a major factor in the settlement of the hundreds of islands of the western Pacific. The social and economic complexities of Melanesian trading systems have long excited anthropologists, starting with Bronislaw Malinowski, whose immortal work on Trobriand island trading still forms part of the basic training of all anthropologists (Malinowski, 1922). It is now known that related trading systems link all parts of coastal New Guinea and much of Melanesia. Although Malinowski concentrated on the ceremonial aspects of the trade, these networks carried an enormous diversity of different everyday and exotic goods and commodities ranging from foodstuffs to manufactured goods. The anthropologists have shown that these trade networks circulated commodities in huge rings that were reciprocal and self-perpetuating. Concerned as they are with material culture and technology, archaeologists have begun to look closely at this trade and the objects carried by it as a means for interpreting the archaeological record of early settlement on the island (Allen, 1977).

Most long-distance trade was conducted by middlemen or specialist merchants who traveled in sea-going canoes. They made their living by trading food surpluses for manufactured goods. The navigational abilities of the Pacific islanders have long been the subject of vigorous academic controversy, much of which, however, has now been dispelled by some compelling studies of indigenous navigational techniques; these studies were done by anthropologists and practical small-boat seamen like David Lewis. One school of thought argued that long-distance voyages by early islanders were one-way accidental trips, when canoes were blown out to sea (Sharp, 1957). Early navigators were helpless, this school argued, to counteract ocean currents. Their views have been sharply challenged by those who have studied the well-developed maritime technology of the Polynesians (Vadya, 1959). They point out that nearly all the long trips attributed to the Polynesians were from north to south, which involved simple dead-reckoning calculations and a simple way of measuring latitude from the stars. Anthropologist Ben Finney made detailed studies of Polynesian canoes and navigational techniques; his findings support a notion of deliberate one-way voyages, sparked as much by necessity — drought or warfare — as by restless adventure (Finney, 1967). Evidence for the carrying of women, animals of both sexes, and plants for propagation, however, shows that colonization was the deliberate aim.

Amateur seaman David Lewis completed a remarkable study of Polynesian navigation, voyaging under prehistoric conditions and accumulating navigators' lore from surviving practitioners of the art (Lewis, 1972). He found that navigators were a respected and close-knit group. Young apprentices learned their skills over many years of making passages and from orally transmitted knowledge about the stars and the oceans accumulated by generations of navigators. The navigational techniques used the angles of rising and setting stars, the trend of ocean swells, and the myriad inconspicuous phenomena that indicated the general direction and distance of small islands. The navigators were perfectly capable of voyaging over long stretches of open water, and their geographic knowledge was astonishing. They had no need for the compass or other modern aids and their landfalls were accurate. Lewis's findings confirm those of Finney and others who believe that deliberate voyages colonized even remote islands.

By looking at oral traditions, archaeological excavations, and some linguistic data, A. Pawley and R. C. Green have dated the expansion of farming peoples into island Melanesia to approximately 4000 B.C. and as far as New Caledonia to at least 4000 years ago (Green, 1979; Jennings, 1979). These settlers are thought to have introduced agriculture, domesticated animals, and pottery to Melanesia. A later manifestation of this maritime expansion is associated with a characteristic pottery style known as Lapita (Groube, 1971; Jennings, 1979). This is seen as a specialized invention that spread widely through the islands at a time when the double-hulled canoe came into use. This canoe was part of the evolution, we are told, of efficient trading networks that were maintained by regular two-way voyages over distances up to 372 mi (600 km). Obsidian trade was conducted down these networks and has been identified by using trace elements in the raw material to trace rocks from the eastern Solomon islands to a source in New Britain (Bellwood, 1978, 1979). Some people believe that the makers of Lapita pottery were traders and seafarers, but so little is known about them that this is probably a premature hypothesis. Certainly, trade played an important role in the colonization of Melanesia.

Lapita pottery itself was decorated with impressed designs and made of clay tempered with shell (Figure 12.9). It is found from the Santa Cruz islands as far east as the New Hebrides, Fiji, Tonga, and Samoa. It is generally dated to the last thousand years before Christ, but seems to have gone out of fashion approximately 1800 years ago (Kirch, 1982).

From Melanesia canoes voyaged to Polynesia, taking the plants and domestic animals of their home islands with them. The antiquity of human settlement in Polynesia is approximately 2000 years (Jennings, 1979; Kirch, 1982). It is thought that the Polynesians originated in the Fiji area before the great elaboration of Melanesian culture after A.D. 1. After a lengthy period of adaptation in western Polynesia, small groups began to settle the more remote islands. The Marquesas were settled by A.D. 400, and the Society Islands and Tahiti by A.D. 800 (Oliver, 1977). The first canoes arrived at Hawaii some 1350 years ago, and at Easter Island by A.D. 500 (Emory, 1972; Emory et al., 1959). The human settlement of Po-

Melanesia
4000 B.C. to 2000 B.C.

Lapita ware
1600 B.C. to A.D. 1

Polynesia
150 B.C. to A.D. 800

Figure 12.9 Lapita pottery from Melanesia.

lynesia seems to have taken approximately 2500 years from its very first beginnings, in the hands of people who were still, technologically speaking, in the Stone Age. They relied heavily on stone axes and adzes (Figure 12.10) and an elaborate array of bone and shell fishhooks. The crops the people planted varied from island to island, but breadfruit, taro, coconut, yams, and bananas were the staple crops. The food surpluses generated on the larger islands were used as a form of wealth (for a valuable discussion of colonization process, see Kirch, 1982).

When the French and British visited Tahiti in the eighteenth century, they chanced upon the center of a vigorous eastern Polynesian society (Oliver, 1977). The islands were ruled by a powerful hierarchy of chiefs and nobles, many of them descendants of original canoe crews who had settled the archipelago. The chiefs acquired prestige by controlling and redistributing wealth and food supplies. Their formidable religious and social powers led them to warfare and to the undertaking of elaborate agricultural projects and the erection of monumental shrines and temples of stone: the famous *maraes* of Tahiti are typical examples (Figure 12.11). On remote Easter Island the people erected vast statues, as much as 19 m (62 ft) high. No one knows what they signify.

The full diversity of Polynesian culture is still imperfectly understood,

Figure 12.10 Bone and stone fishhooks from Polynesia.

for archaeological research has hardly begun in the South Seas, but it is certain that the Polynesians were making ocean voyages on a large scale at a time when the Greeks and Romans were little more than coastal navigators.

Settlement of New Zealand

New Zealand is the largest and among the most remote of all the Pacific islands; it is actually two large islands. It has a temperate climate, not the tropical warmth enjoyed by most Polynesians. Despite this ecological difference, New Zealand was first settled by Polynesians who voyaged southward in comparatively recent times and settled on the North Island. Maori legends tell of a migration from Polynesia in the mid-fourteenth century A.D. Settlers may have arrived 400 years before, including Toi Ete'hutai who came to New Zealand in search of two grandsons blown away from Tahiti during a canoe race. The earliest C14 dates for New Zealand archaeological sites are a matter of controversy but are within the present millennium (Bellwood, 1978; W. Shawcross, 1969).

Figure 12.11 A *marae* from Tahiti.

First settlement
? A.D. 1000

The temperate climate of the North Island formed a southern frontier for most of the basic food plants of Polynesia. The yam and gourd can be grown only there, but the sweet potato could be cultivated in the northern part of the South Island, if adequate winter storage pits were used. The Polynesian coconut never grew in New Zealand. The earliest settlers relied heavily on hunting, fishing, and gathering. Even later, though some peoples specialized in food production, others did not, especially in the South Island, where many settlements were on the coasts close to abundant ocean resources (Prickett, 1983).

The first settlers found great flocks of flightless Moa birds, cumbersome and helpless in the face of systematic hunting. They hunted the Moa into extinction within a few centuries. Fish, fern roots, and shellfish were important throughout New Zealand's short prehistory. The introduction of the sweet potato made a dramatic difference to the New Zealanders, for the tubers, if carefully stored from winter cold, could be eaten in the cold months and some could be kept for the next year's planting. Sweet potato has a large crop yield and is thought to have contributed to a rapid population buildup, especially in the North Island. This, in turn, led to competition among different groups for suitable agricultural land to grow the new staple (W. Shawcross, 1967).

When the Moa became extinct, the Maori had few meat supplies except birds, dogs, and rats. Their only other meat source was human flesh. The archaeological record of Maori culture from approximately A.D. 1400 onward shows not only population growth but an increasing emphasis on warfare, evidenced by the appearance of numerous fortified encampments or *pa's*, protected with earthen banks. The distribution of *pa's* coincides to a large extent with the best sweet potato lands (Bellwood, 1970; Groube, 1970). In the course of a few centuries, warfare became a key element in Maori culture, to the extent that it was institutionalized and an important factor in maintaining cohesion and leadership in Maori society. The booty of war was not only *kumara* (sweet potato), but the flesh of captives, which became a limited part of Maori diet.

Maori warfare, mainly confined to North Island, where more than 5000 *pa's* have been found, was seasonal and closely connected with the planting and harvest of sweet potatoes, when everyone was busy in the gardens. Military campaigns were short and intense, very often launched from the sea in large war canoes up to 24 m (8.8 ft) or more in length (Figure 12.12). These elaborately carved vessels could hold up to 150 men on a short expedition. So formidable was the reputation of the Maori that European ships avoided New Zealand ports for years before permanent white settlement was achieved. The last Maori war ended in

Figure 12.12 Maori war canoe recorded by Captain Cook in the eighteenth century.

1872, by which time the indigenous population had been decimated by disease, warfare, and European contact.

GUIDE TO FURTHER READING

Bellwood, Peter. *Man's Conquest of the Pacific*. Oxford: Oxford University Press, 1978.
A summary of the prehistory of the Pacific that covers every corner of this vast ocean. A book for the advanced reader, but crammed with useful information.

Chang, Kwang-Chih. *The Archaeology of Ancient China* (3rd ed.). New Haven: Yale University Press, 1977.
The definitive account of Chinese prehistory in the English language. Be forewarned that this is a highly technical work truly designed for the advanced student or professional archaeologist.

Jennings, Jesse D. (Ed.) *The Prehistory of Polynesia*. Cambridge: Harvard University Press, 1978.
A series of essays that provide a state-of-the-art summary of Pacific prehistory.

Lewis, David. *We the Navigators*. Honolulu: University of Hawaii Press, 1972.
An account of traditional Polynesian navigational methods based both on local lore and experiments navigating a yacht without a compass and sextant. What makes this book fascinating is that the author is a practical seaman himself.

Chronological Table H

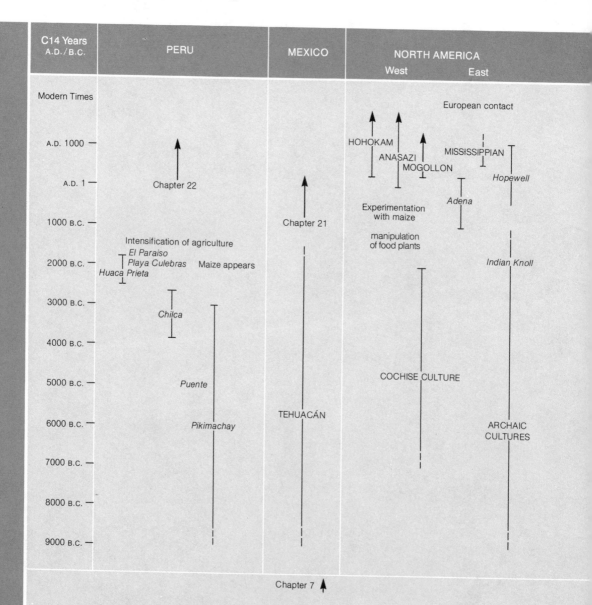

C14 Years A.D./B.C.	PERU	MEXICO	NORTH AMERICA	
			West	East
Modern Times				European contact
A.D. 1000 —			HOHOKAM	MISSISSIPPIAN
	Chapter 22		ANASAZI MOGOLLON	Hopewell
A.D. 1 —				
			Experimentation with maize	Adena
1000 B.C. —		Chapter 21	manipulation of food plants	
	Intensification of agriculture			
	El Paraiso			Indian Knoll
2000 B.C. —	Playa Culebras Maize appears			
	Huaca Prieta			
3000 B.C. —	Chilca			
4000 B.C. —				
5000 B.C. —	Puente		COCHISE CULTURE	
6000 B.C. —	Pikimachay	TEHUACÁN		ARCHAIC CULTURES
7000 B.C. —				
8000 B.C. —				
9000 B.C. —				

Chapter 7 ▲

Chapter Thirteen

New World Agriculture

PREVIEW

❃ New World agriculture was based on crops quite different from those grown in the Old World. The root crops included manioc and sweet potato, while maize was the most important staple cereal. Domesticated animals included the llama, turkey, and guinea pig. The origins of food production in the New World were a shift in ecological adaptation chosen by the peoples living where economic strategies necessitated intensive exploitation of vegetable foods.

❃ The early history of food production and of maize agriculture is best chronicled from excavations in the Tehuacán Valley, Mexico, where food production was well established by 4000 B.C. A long tradition of fishing and gathering in coastal Peru gave way to agriculture in some areas in approximately 3000 B.C. The Ayacucho area of the Andes provides evidence for food production in the highlands of Peru by 3500 B.C.

❃ Maize agriculture reached the American Southwest by approximately 2000 B.C. The Archaic Cochise hunter-gatherer peoples of the area gradually adopted the new economy, experimenting with the cultivation of various hybrid strains of maize. By 300 B.C., sedentary villages and a much greater dependence on farming were characteristic of the Southwest, leading to the emergence of Hohokam, Mogollon, and Anasazi cultural traditions. Hohokam and Anasazi are thought to be ancestral to modern American Indian groups still living in the Southwest.

❃ The Archaic hunter-gatherer cultures of the eastern and midwestern parts of the United States gradually adopted food production after 1000 B.C. A series of powerful chiefdoms emerged in the East and Midwest, peoples amongst whom elaborate burial customs and the building of burial mounds and earthworks were commonplace. The Adena tradition emerged in 700 B.C. or so, and was replaced by the Hopewell in approximately A.D. 200. Both traditions depended on long-distance trade in essential commodities and cult objects for much of their prosperity. A preoccupation with death and status was at the center of Hopewell life, for their burials show extraordinary lavishness. Twelve hundred years ago the center of economic, religious, and political power shifted to the Mississippi Valley with the emergence of the Mississippian tradition, which is thought to owe much to Mexican cosmology. The Mississippian was a state-organized society having powerful religious and secular leaders; it survived in a modified form until European contact in the eighteenth century.

The American Indians domesticated an impressive range of native New World plants, some of which — like maize, potatoes, and tobacco — were rapidly adopted by European farmers after contact.

The most important staple crop was Indian corn, properly called maize, the only important wild grass in the New World to be fully domesticated. It remains the most important food crop in the Americas today, being used in more than 150 varieties as both food and cattle fodder. Root crops formed another important food source, especially in South America, and included manioc, sweet potatoes, and white potatoes. Chili peppers were grown as hot seasoning; amaranth, sunflowers, cacao, peanuts, and several types of bean were also significant crops. Some crops, such as cotton and gourds, are common to both Old and New Worlds but were probably domesticated separately (See Pickersgill, 1972).

In contrast to Old World farmers, the Indians had few domesticated animals, including the llama of the Andes, and alpacas, which provided wool. Dogs appeared in the Americas, and the raucous and unruly turkey and the muscovy duck were domesticated.

Most archaeologists now agree that there were two major centers of plant domestication in the Americas: Mesoamerica for maize, beans, squash, and sweet potato, and the highlands of the central Andes for root crops. There are also four major areas of later cultivation activity: tropical (northern) South America and Peru, Mesoamerica, and eastern North America.

MESOAMERICA: TEHUACÁN AND THE ORIGINS OF AGRICULTURE

Traces of early experimentation with the deliberate cultivation of crops such as maize and squash have come from regions in Mexico, notably from Sierra Madre, Sierra de Tamaulipas, and the Tehuacán Valley (Figure 13.1). One problem in determining the wild ancestor of maize has been that no one has known what to look for. Some botanists believe that there was once a wild corn with a light husk that allowed the seeds to disperse at maturity — something that people sought to prevent by breeding the domestic strain with a tougher husk (Mangelsdorf et al., 1964). This is now extinct, for the wild strain was soon submerged by later, humanly bred forms. George Beadle (1981) and other experts disagree and argue that the wild ancestor of maize is alive and well, a grass known as teosinte that grows over much of Mesoamerica. They point to the close resemblances between the earliest corncobs, which date to approximately 5000 B.C., and teosinte. These early maize cobs show a striking similarity to second generation and later crosses of modern corn and teosinte. There are impressive grounds for considering teosinte the wild ancestor of maize. Experiments have shown it can be "popped" by being placed in a fire, on a hot rock, or on heated sand, just like the popcorn we consume at the movies. Dried teosinte seeds can be cracked with even

Nuclear areas for agriculture   Mogollon   Hohokam   Anasazi   Woodland (Adena and Hopewell)

Mississippian

Figure 13.1 Archaeological sites and culture areas mentioned in this chapter. (After Meggers)

simple grindstones, too, or softened before eating by soaking them in water. The controversy has been heightened in recent years by the discovery of a perennial teosinte in Mexico that has been crossbred with maize. It now seems possible that early maize derived from the heads of wild teosinte evolving in response to major environmental changes sparked by human domestication.

The dry, highland Tehuacán Valley in Mexico has many caves and open sites and is sufficiently arid to preserve seeds and organic finds in archaeological deposits. This was the valley that Richard MacNeish chose as a promising area in which to seek the origins of domesticated maize (MacNeish, 1970, 1978). MacNeish soon found domestic maize cobs dating back to approximately 3000 B.C., but not until he began digging in the small Coxcatlán rock shelter did he find maize that even vaguely resembled what at that time was considered the hypothetical ancestor of maize. Coxcatlán contained twenty-eight occupation levels, the earliest of which dated to approximately 10,000 B.C. MacNeish eventually excavated twelve sites in Tehuacán, which revealed a wealth of information about the inhabitants of the valley through nearly 12,000 years of prehistory.

MacNeish found that the earliest Tehuacán people lived mainly by hunting horses, deer, and other mammals and also by collecting wild vegetable foods (MacNeish, 1978). These hunters used stone-tipped lances in the chase. They also hunted large numbers of jackrabbits, probably in organized drives. MacNeish estimates that 50 to 60 percent of the people's food came from game in 10,000 B.C., and only 30 to 40 percent in 7000 B.C. Hunting seems to have been the major activity all year round (Table 13.1).

10,000 to 7000 B.C.

After 8000 B.C., the game population declined slowly, and the people turned more and more to wild vegetable foods. Instead of hunting all the year round, the Tehuacán bands scheduled their food gathering on a seasonal basis and were able to exploit the vegetable and other foods in their environment very effectively without overtaxing the available resources. In approximately 5000 B.C. the first deliberate planting took place, stemming from a desire to improve the location and abundance of favorite foods. This cultivation resulted in genetic changes, and soon the planted seeds were being laid out in special gardens.

5000 B.C.

The inhabitants of Coxcatlán Cave seem to have continued this trend after 5000 B.C., planting potential domesticates, including some form of maize, in spring or summer. They grew foods that when stored would tide them over lean months: beans, amaranth, and gourds. The people lived in larger and more permanent settlements, grinding their maize with quite well-made grindstones (metates). The maize itself was smaller than modern strains and probably much like teosinte (Figure 13.2). Still, only a tiny proportion of Tehuacán's diet came from domestic sources, compared with the period after 3400 B.C. when up to 30 percent of the diet came from agriculture; much of the produce was maize cobs that were larger than those of earlier centuries, clearly the descendants of earlier wild forms.

Coxcatlán

3400 B.C.

By this time, the scheduled gathering and nomadic settlement patterns of earlier times had been replaced by more sedentary villages; these were small hamlets that moved very rarely and depended on agricultural systems that planted crops in fields. The villages were located near fertile flatlands, and consisted of pit houses with brush roofs. Their ample storage facilities helped the people live through the lean months (Flannery, 1976).

The sequence of events at Tehuacán is by no means unique, for other peoples were also experimenting with cultivation. Different hybrid forms of maize are found in Tehuacán sites; these were not developed locally and can only have been introduced from outside. Dry caves elsewhere in northern Mesoamerica show that other cultures paralleled the

Table 13.1 MacNeish's sequence for Tehuacán summarized.

Years A.D./B.C.	Phase	Characteristics
A.D. 750 to 1531	VENTA SALADA	Spanish contact: A.D. 1531.
100 B.C. to A.D. 750	PALO BLANCO	Village life
800 to 100 B.C.	SANTA MARIA	Village life
1450 to 800	AJALPAN	Establishment of village life. Single season economy with spring and summer agriculture.
2250 to 1450	PURRON	Hamlet villages and appearance of pottery. Agriculture important, but few details known.
3350 to 2250	ABEJAS	Seasonal economy, with hunting important in the winter, collecting in spring, simple agriculture in summer and fall. Some year-round settlements, small food surpluses.
4950 to 3350	COXCATLÁN	Seasonal scheduling of hunting and gathering. Planting of domesticates in spring and summer. Very limited food surpluses. Maize cultivated.
6950 to 4950	EL RIEGO	Seasonally scheduled gathering and hunting. Seed planting appears late in phase during summers. Food storage more important.
9950 to 6950	AJUEREADO	Lance ambushing of game important. Rabbit drives and small game significant. Less gathering than in later phases? Seasonal camps, no food storage.
Before 10,000 B.C.	Hunter-gatherers.	

Note: For full details, see Richard MacNeish, *The Science of Archaeology?* North Scituate, Mass.: Duxbury Press, 1978.

cultural events in Tehuacán. On the other hand, the highland lakes of the Valley of Mexico and elsewhere may well have supported sedentary communities subsisting on fish and wild vegetable foods as well as experimenting with amaranth, corn, and other crops as early as the sixth millennium B.C. (Niederberger, 1979).

Plant domestication in Mesoamerica was not so much an invention in one small area as a shift in ecological adaptation deliberately chosen by peoples living where economic strategies necessitated intensive exploitation of vegetable foods. Kent Flannery has hypothesized as to how this

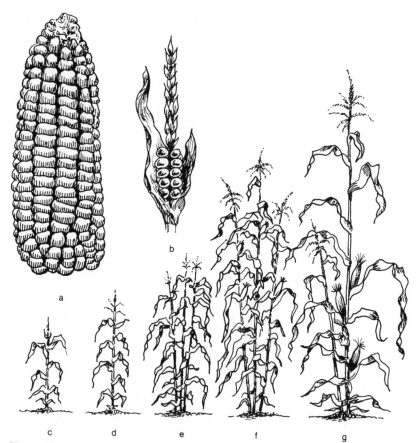

Figure 13.2 Development of maize: (a) a typical ear of modern maize; (b) possible appearance of extinct wild maize; (c–g) evolution of the domesticated maize plant.

shift in adaptation might have occurred in Mesoamerica. In a classic paper on the southern highlands of Mesoamerica, he tried to understand how the human population of this area took up agriculture (Flannery, 1968a). He assumed that the people and their homeland were part of a single, complex system composed of many subsystems — economic, botanical, social, and so on — that interacted with one another. Flannery pointed out that these people had no fewer than five carefully scheduled food-gathering systems that were in use at different seasons of the year. By being able to predict what vegetable foods came into season at different times of the year, the people were able to schedule their harvesting activities. Scheduling and use of seasonal food permitted these and many other Mesoamerican peoples to exploit their environment highly effectively without overtaxing any of the available food sources. Between 8000 and 2000 B.C., the people lived by using these basic procurement systems, but something caused the Mesoamericans to concentrate more heavily on wild grasses: both teosinte and foxtail millet. Between 5000 and 2000 B.C., the cob size of maize increased, and maize was crossed with related forms to produce a hybrid species that was the ancestor of modern maize. Some species of beans became more permeable in water and developed softer pods. Flannery argues that the highland people began experimenting with the planting of maize and other grasses, deliberately increasing the areas where they would grow. After a long time, these deviations in the food procurement system caused the importance of grass collection to increase at the expense of gathering other seasonal foods until the new activity, with its vital planting and harvesting schedules, became the dominant activity, one that was self-perpetuating from one year to the next.

EARLY FOOD PRODUCTION IN PERU

The Peruvian coast forms a narrow shelf at the foot of the Andes, crossed by small river valleys descending from the mountains to the sea. These valleys are oases in the desert plain, with deep, rich soils and blooming vegetation where water is plentiful. For thousands of years Peruvians have cultivated these valley floors, building their settlements, pyramids, and palaces at the edges of their agricultural land. Because conditions for preservation in this arid country are exceptional, the archaeological record often is quite complete. The coast itself forms a series of related microenvironments, such as rocky bays where shellfish are abundant, places where seasonal vegetable foods nourished by damp fogs are common, and the floors or sides of river valleys flowing into the Pacific. One would assume that a combination of these microenvironments would provide a rich and uniform constellation of food resources that could normally be exploited with ease from relatively sedentary base camps (Moseley, 1975a). However, the bountiful maritime environment occasionally is disrupted by a warm countercurrent known as El Niño that can flow for as long as twelve months. El Niño occurs at highly irregular intervals, perhaps every six years and sometimes much longer. It reduces marine upwelling so much that the fish migrate elsewhere, and thus one of the coastal peoples' staple diet sources is greatly reduced. This phenomenon is so unpredictable that the people could not store food against its arrival; they also could not move from the coast and they did not have the offshore vessels needed for deepwater fishing. Their only strategy was to limit their population densities to the lowest levels of available natural resources until such time as they developed alternative food sources, such as maize grown by intensive irrigation agriculture (Raymond, 1981; Yesner, 1980). It was the development of maize agriculture that gave the coastal peoples a major impetus for organizing highly complex societies.

The archaeological evidence for the Peruvian coast is incomplete for the period immediately proceeding early food production. During the dry winter months the inhabitants collected shellfish and other marine

Peruvian coast

resources, and hunting and vegetable foods were more important in the summers. After 5000 B.C., however, more efficient collecting strategies came into use, with greater attention to maximally exploiting natural food sources. Fishing, in particular, became more important. Between approximately 4200 and 2500 B.C., Peruvian coastal peoples depended on marine resources — fish, sea birds, and mollusks — for much of their diet. During the warmest and driest period after the Pleistocene, the coastal people moved closer to the shore, dwelling in larger and more stable settlements. Along with the shift to more lasting coastal dwelling came the development of sophisticated equipment for deep-sea fishing. As early as 5500 B.C., the coastal peoples were manipulating plants for their own purposes. The Paloma site on the central coast was occupied more than 7500 years ago, a settled community with numerous simple huts and grass-lined pits where the inhabitants stored food against the occasional lean year. The people relied heavily on fishing and gathering but also manipulated some plant species, including tuberous begonias, gourds, squashes, peppers, and possibly peanuts. They may also have kept llamas, the same species used by the Incas for load carrying in the Andes (Benfer, 1982).

A later coastal settlement that perpetuates the same subsistence pattern flourished at Chilca, 45 mi. (72 km) south of present-day Lima. Frederic Engel excavated refuse heaps there and C14 dated the earlier Chilca occupation to between 3800 and 2650 B.C. (Engel, 1966). When the site was in use, it probably lay near a reedy marsh, which provided both matting and building materials as well as sites for small gardens. The Chilca people lived on sea mollusks, fish, and sea lions; they apparently hunted few land mammals. They cultivated jack and lima beans, gourds, and squashes, probably relying on river floods as well as rainfall for their simple agriculture.

One remarkable Chilca house was uncovered: a circular structure, it had a domelike frame of canes bound with rope and covered with bundles of grass (Figure 13.3); the interior was braced with bones from stranded whales. Seven burials had been deposited in the house before it was intentionally collapsed on top of them. The skeletons were wrapped in mats and all buried at the same time, perhaps because of an epidemic.

The new emphasis on fish, increased use of flour ground from wild grass seed, and availability of cultivated squashes provided new sources of nutrition for some coastal groups. This may ultimately have set off a sustained period of population growth. Certainly the succeeding millennia of coastal history saw many permanent settlements established near the ocean; the people combined agriculture with fishing and mollusk gathering. Domesticated cotton first appeared in or around 2500 B.C. Squashes, peppers, lima beans, and other crops remained staple foods until recent times. Maize and other basic foods were still unknown. Agriculture remained a secondary activity much later than it did in Mesoamerica.

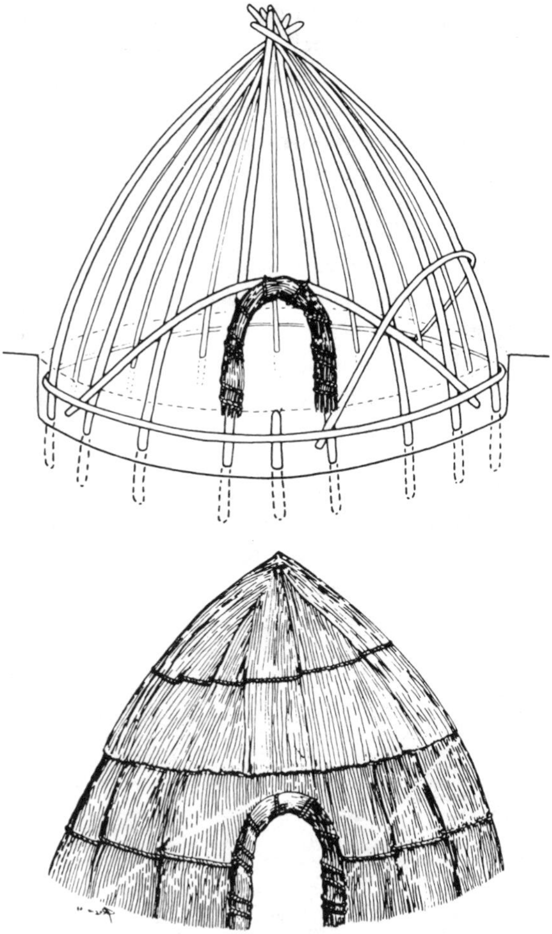

Figure 13.3 Reconstruction of a Chilca house. (After Willey, 1971)

One later site is Huaca Prieta, a sedentary village that housed several hundred people on the north coast of Peru between 2500 and 1800 B.C. (Bankes, 1977). The vast refuse mound here contains small one- or two-room houses built partially into the ground and roofed with timber or whalebone beams. The inhabitants were remarkably skillful cotton weavers who devised a sophisticated art style with animal, human, and geometric designs.

Maize makes its first appearance on the coast at Playa Culebras, another important and contemporary settlement south of Huaca Prieta (Engel, 1957; Willey, 1953). This and other settlements show greater emphasis on permanent architecture not only in domestic buildings but also as large ceremonial structures. A complex of stone and mud mortar platforms lies at El Paraíso on the floodplain of the Chillón Valley, some distance from the sea. At least one mound had complexes of connected

Huaca Prieta **2500 to 1800 B.C.**

Playa Culebras

rooms built in successive stages. Settlements such as El Paraíso obviously depended more on agriculture than earlier sites had. By the time the temple complexes were built there, after 1800 B.C., loom-woven textiles and pottery had come into widespread use (Figure 13.4). All the major food plants that formed the basis of later Peruvian civilization were employed.

Most of our knowledge about the early history of food production in the highlands is from discoveries by MacNeish and others in the Ayacucho region of central Peru (MacNeish, 1978; Moseley, 1978). Food resources in the highland valleys are separated in vertically spaced microenvironments, like layers of a cake. Rarely was it possible for the inhabitants of a valley to exploit all these microenvironments from one locality, nor are they uniformly distributed in all highland valleys. Economic variability between mountain valleys was great, and no one food provided a staple diet. The carrying capacity of the highland valleys depended on the ways in which their populations exploited the resources. On the coast, intensified exploitation of the marine and vegetable resources led to population growth, but the reverse ultimately occurred in the highland valleys. There, deforestation, soil erosion, and temporary

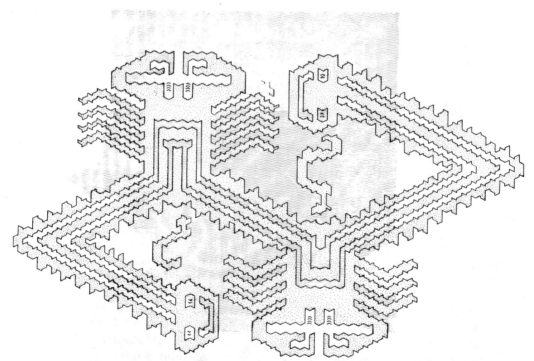

Figure 13.4 A double-headed snakelike figure with appended rock crabs revealed by plotting the warp movements in a preceramic twined cotton fabric from Huaca Prieta, Peru. The original length was approximately 41 cm (16 in). The shaded area indicates the surviving textile. Double-headed motifs have persisted through more than 3000 years of Peruvian art. (Courtesy of Junius Bird)

desiccation partly generated by agriculture reduced carrying capacities after A.D. 500.

Before 9000 B.C.

The early hunter-gatherers of the highland valleys are thought to have exploited only a small portion of the potential resources. According to MacNeish, finds at Pikimachay Cave and elsewhere indicate several subsistence options — hunting various sizes of mammal including the great sloth and varied small creatures, and collecting many species of plant foods. These options were exercised by priority rather than by season, the notion being that one acquired food with the minimum effort. In approximately 9000 B.C., however, the subsistence strategies changed. 9000 B.C. There is reason to believe that seasonal exploitation had replaced other options, with hunting, trapping, and plant collecting at high altitudes important in the dry season. During the wetter months, collecting and possibly penning small game, as well as seed collecting, were dominant activities.

Guitarrero Cave (Figure 13.5) lies 1.5 mi (2.5 km) above sea level on the western slopes of the Andes (Lynch et al., 1980). The site was first occupied about 12,000 years ago. Common beans date from deposits about 10,600 years old, while lima beans occur around 7000 B.C. Wild ancestors of the lima are found in rain forests east of the Andes. It is possible that people living in the forests to the east first domesticated the lima bean and that the domesticated strains later spread to drier areas to the west of the mountains.

Figure 13.5 Guitarrero Cave, looking toward the Andes.

After 5000 to 4500 B.C., the archaeological evidence becomes more abundant. In the Ayacucho-Huanta region twenty-five dry- and wet-season camps have been found that provide signs of continued exploitation of wild vegetables as well as game during the dry season. The Pikimachay Cave levels of this period yielded wet-season living floors. There, wild seeds are abundant along with remains of gourds and seeds of domesticated quinoa and squash. Game remains are very rare, as if a vegetable diet, whether wild or domesticated, was of prime importance during the wet months. Another wet-season locality, Puente Cave, yielded a few bones of tame guinea pigs as well as the remains of many small wild mammals. Grinding stones and other artifacts used for plant collecting, or perhaps incipient agriculture, are also common at Puente. Throughout this period, many wet-season camps became larger and more stable, their use extending over longer periods of the year.

After 4000 B.C., the Ayacucho peoples relied more on food production. The potato was cultivated. Hoes appeared, as well as domesticated corn, squashes, common beans, and other crops. Guinea pigs were certainly tamed, and llama were domesticated in central Peru by at least 3500 B.C. By this time, too, there was more interaction between coast and interior, trade in raw materials, and some interchange of domesticates. MacNeish believes corn spread from the north, ultimately from Mesoamerica, into Ayacucho. Root crop agriculture may have diffused from highland Peru into the lowlands, too.

The Ayacucho sequence is illustrative of the complex adaptive shifts that took place in many parts of South America after 5000 B.C. In both highlands and lowlands, the beginnings of agriculture were a gradual adjustment, with food production gradually supplanting gathering as the major subsistence activity. On the Peruvian coast, the gathering of vegetable foods and fishing were supplemented by irrigation farming as early as 3000 B.C., while the highland peoples were cultivating a variety of crops by the same time, crops that amplified the horizontally stacked natural resources of their mountain homeland. Yet it was the arrival of maize after 2000 B.C. that provided the staple for the large-scale irrigation agriculture which sustained the complex societies that arose on the coast and in the interior in later centuries.

EARLY FARMERS IN SOUTHWESTERN NORTH AMERICA

Eleven thousand years ago the southwestern United States was populated by hunter-gatherers whose culture was adapted to desert living (Cordell, 1984a, b; Lipe, 1978). A distinctive foraging culture, the Cochise, flourished in southeastern Arizona and southwestern New Mexico from about this time. The Cochise people gathered many plant foods including yucca seeds, cacti, and sunflower seeds. They used small milling stones, basketry, cordage, nets, and spear-throwers. Many features of their material culture survived into later times, when cultivated plants were introduced into the Southwest.

We do not know exactly when primitive maize and squash were introduced into the Southwest. But we do know that as early as 3200 B.C., the inhabitants of the area were living in larger and more numerous base camps, using many grindstones and other gathering artifacts. Conceivably, the population rose, partly because of more favorable climatic conditions and partly because of more efficient resource exploitation. The first appearance of primitive maize occurred around 1800 B.C. and a gradual change in the settlement pattern resulted. A fall or winter base camp that brought several bands into one place came into fashion — a place where the people may have lived while they consumed the agricultural surplus and local abundances of wild vegetable foods. This lifeway continued until approximately A.D. 100, after which the gradual evolution of the culture into the later Anasazi tradition can be traced.

3200 B.C.

1800 B.C.

A.D. 100

Cynthia Irwin-Williams and Vance Haynes have suggested that an elementary southwestern culture emerged approximately 3000 B.C., at a time when there was slightly higher rainfall and increased food resources for growing hunter-gatherer populations to feed on (Irwin-Williams and Haynes, 1970). The various bands of the Southwest maintained widespread communication networks which enabled them to share information about new plant foods and other innovations. It seems likely not only that the Archaic peoples were familiar with the germination of seeds, but also that they occasionally manipulated wild plants by careful irrigation and weeding, as Great Basin peoples did in historic times. However, there is a considerable difference between occasionally helping wild foods grow, while not disturbing your annual gathering round, and taking up deliberate cultivation as a priority that competes with your basic lifeway schedule.

How did the changeover occur? One scenario has agricultural peoples from Mexico moving northward into the Southwest. Archaic people may have been absorbed by the newcomers, or may have adopted the new economies on their own account after the initial colonization by newcomers. If one follows Flannery's arguments for Mesoamerica and applies them to the Cochise, then one would see the continued introduction of improved maize strains as new food energy resources that triggered cultural change of the kind Flannery described in Mesoamerica (Flannery, 1968a). Another hypothesis views population growth as a major factor. In this argument, the Southwest received surplus population from hunter-gatherer territories in coastal California (Glassow, 1972). These newcomers tried to adapt to the same favorable location as the indigenous inhabitants but found themselves forced to settle in marginal areas where storage of food and greater dependence on agriculture were essential. Thus, cultural change was stimulated by mechanisms similar to those postulated by Flannery. Even without population growth, increased aridity in the Southwest could have produced a similar effect among people already living in the area.

By 300 B.C., experimentation and new hybrid varieties of maize introduced from the south had led to sedentary villages and much greater dependence on farming. The cultural changes of the period culminated in the great southwestern archaeological traditions: Hohokam, Mogollon, and Anasazi (Cordell, 1984b).

The Hohokam tradition has long been thought to have originated in the Cochise. No one knows exactly when the tradition emerged, but it was probably in the first five centuries of the Christian era. However, Emil Haury, who dug the important Snaketown site in the Gila River Valley, believes that the Hohokam people were immigrants from northern Mexico who brought their pottery and extensive irrigation agriculture with them (Haury, 1976). Under this scenario, the newcomers soon influenced the lifeway of the local people, and a desert adaptation of Hohokam resulted. But recent research tends to discount the migration theory. Reexamination of the Snaketown data and further field work suggest that the Hohokam enjoyed complex trading and ceremonial relationships with peoples living all over the Southwest and northern Mexico. As time went on, this trade expanded, perhaps within the context of a common ceremonial system centered around the ball courts and other ceremonial structures at Snaketown and other centers. In all probability, the Hohokam was an indigenous culture, one that acquired much greater social complexity through time (for a discussion, see Fish and Fish, 1977; Willcox, 1980; 1985).

Hohokam subsistence was based on maize, beans, cucurbits, cotton, and other crops, as well as on gathering. They planted their crops to coincide with the biannual rainfall and flooding patterns. Where they could, they practiced irrigation from flowing streams; otherwise they cultivated floodplains and caught runoff from local storms with dams, terraces, and other devices. Hohokam people occupied much of what is now Arizona. Their cultural heirs are the Pima and Papago Indians of today (Figure 13.6).

Hohokam culture evolved slowly over as much as 2000 years. There are at least five stages of Hohokam culture, culminating in a Classic period from approximately 850 to 500 years ago when large pueblos (communal villages) were built and canal irrigation was especially important. It was at this time and somewhat earlier that Mexican influences are detected in Hohokam culture. These include new varieties of maize, the appearance of platform mounds and ball or dance courts at Snaketown and elsewhere, and imports such as copper bells. Does this mean that Mexican immigrants transformed Hohokam culture, or were there internal factors that caused greater elaboration of local society at the same time as some ideas arrived from Mexico? Archaeologists remain divided on this point.

Originally, anthropologists believed the Mexican influence was transitory and weak, but excavations at a prehistoric town named Casas Grande in northern Chihuahua, Mexico, have changed their minds. [The site should not be confused with Casa Grande, Arizona (Di Peso, et al.,

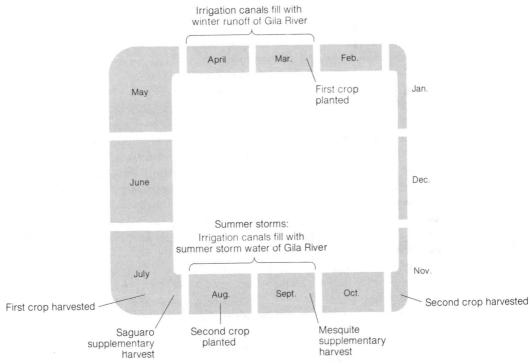

Irrigation canals fill with
winter runoff of Gila River

April

Mar.

Feb.

First crop
planted

May

Jan.

June

Dec.

Summer storms:
Irrigation canals fill with
summer storm water of Gila River

July

Nov.

First crop harvested

Aug.

Sept.

Oct.

Second crop harvested

Saguaro
supplementary
harvest

Second crop
planted

Mesquite
supplementary
harvest

Figure 13.6 This diagram shows how the Pima Indians of the Southwest, descendants of the Hohokam, schedule their plantings and harvests around rainfall seasons. The Hohokam probably relied on a similar annual round. The thickness of the shaded area reflects relative plenty of food resources. (From Jesse D. Jennings, *Ancient Native Americans*, Freeman, San Francisco, 1978, p. 349)

1974).] At the height of its prosperity in the thirteenth century A.D., Casas Grande boasted of approximately 1600 rooms and housed more than 2200 people. The dig showed they exchanged turquoise and painted pottery from the Southwest for marine shells and exotic bird feathers from Mexico. Local traditions connect Casas Grande with a settlement named Paquimé that was more of a Mexican town than an Indian pueblo. The archaeologists argue that Paquimé was founded by Mexican traders from the south, possibly itinerant merchants known to the Aztec as *pochteca*, who often served as spies. Perhaps they used their powerful religious beliefs to strengthen their control of the trade with the north. Perhaps, too, contacts between the Hohokam and Mexican civilization were far more regular than once was suspected.

The Mogollon tradition emerged from Archaic roots between 300 B.C. and A.D. 300 and disappeared as a separate entity between 1100 and 500 years ago, when it became part of Anasazi (Haury, 1936; Lipe, 1978). The Mogollon culture is well known from dry caves in Mew Mexico as an agricultural culture in which hunting and gathering in the highlands were always important. Mogollon agriculture depended on direct rainfall,

Mogollon A.D. 200–300 to A.D. 1100

with only very limited use of irrigation. The people lived in small villages of pit dwellings with timber frames and mat or brush roofs. Their material culture was utilitarian and included milling stones, digging sticks, bows and arrows, fine baskets, and characteristic brown and red pottery.

At least six regional variants of Mogollon are known, and there are five chronological stages, the fifth ending approximately 500 years ago. Early Mogollon villages often were located on high promontories close to more fertile lands. The settlement pattern varied from area to area but with a tendency toward larger sites and increased populations throughout the life of the tradition. By A.D. 1500 pueblos of several hundred rooms had developed in some areas, but by this time Mogollon had become part of the western pueblo Anasazi tradition.

The Anasazi tradition is, in general terms, ancestral to the cultures of the modern Pueblo Indians — the Hopi, Zuni, and others (Judd, 1954, 1964; Zubrow 1971). Its emergence is conventionally dated to 2000 years ago, but this is a purely arbitrary date, for Anasazi's roots lie in Archaic cultures that flourished for a long time before. The Anasazi people made heavy use of wild vegetable foods, even after they took up maize agriculture seriously, after A.D. 400. Most of their farming depended on dry agriculture and seasonal rainfall, although they, like the Hohokam, used irrigation techniques when practicable. They made use of flood areas, where the soil would remain damp for weeks after sudden storms. Moisture in the flooded soil could be used to germinate seed in the spring and to bring ripening crops to fruition after later rains. However, this is a very high-risk type of agriculture, and the Anasazi relied on wild resources to carry them through lean years.

Anasazi chronology is well established thanks to the use of dendrochronology on beams from abandoned pueblos. The tradition is centered in the "Four Corners" area where Utah, Arizona, Colorado, and New Mexico meet. There are at least six Basketmaker and Pueblo subdivisions of Anasazi, each marked a gradual increase in the importance of agriculture and the emergence of some larger sites with *kivas*, ceremonial sweathouses. Pueblos, which are complexes of adjoining rooms, occur more frequently after A.D. 900; the population congregated in fewer, but larger, pueblos after A.D. 1180. These were located in densely populated areas, some of them moved from the open to under cliff overhangs, the so-called cliff-dwellings. Some of the features of these sites, such as turrets and loopholed walls, appear to be defensive. At the same time as people concentrated in larger sites, there was depopulation of many areas of the northern Southwest. The reasons for these changes are imperfectly understood. In some areas, such as Chaco Canyon, New Mexico, the concentrated populations may have enjoyed roads, extensive irrigation systems, and more elaborate social and political organizations as well as trading connections with widespread areas of the Southwest, but most pueblos seem to have been more egalitarian in their organization and relatively self-sufficient in meeting their needs. It may be that the changes generated by the developments in Chaco and elsewhere

Anasazi **Last 2000 years**

caused people to congregate more closely. Alternatively, it has been argued that some climatic and environmental changes, as yet imperfectly understood, may have caused major shifts in the settlement pattern. More likely, a combination of environmental, societal, and adaptive changes set in motion a period of turbulence and culture change.

By approximately A.D. 500, the basic Anasazi settlement pattern had evolved and above-the-ground houses were being substituted for the pit dwellings of earlier centuries. The latter developed into kivas, subterranean ceremonial structures that existed in every large village. Large settlements of contiguous dwellings became the rule after A.D. 800, with clusters of "rooms" serving as homes for separate families or lineages. Large settlements like Pueblo Bonito developed around A.D. 1100; this was a huge D-shaped complex of 800 rooms rising several stories high around the rim of the arc (Figure 13.7). The room complexes surrounded

Figure 13.7   Pueblo Bonito, New Mexico, the first site to be dated by tree-ring chronology to A.D. 919–1130. The round structures are kivas.

courts, with the highest stories at the back. They formed a blank wall; a line of one-story rooms cut off the fourth side. Within the court lay the kivas, always one great kiva and usually several smaller ones. The great kivas were up to 60 ft in diameter with wide masonry benches encircling the interior. The roof was supported by four large pillars near the center, where a raised hearth lay. Two subterranean, masonry-lined rooms were situated on either side of the fireplace. A staircase leading from the floor of the kiva to the large room above it gave access to the sacred precinct.

The period between A.D. 1000 and 1300 was one of consolidation of population into a few, more congested settlements where more elaborate social organizations may have developed. The pueblos were probably communities that were run for the collective good with at least some ranking of society under a chieftain. In modern Hopi society, clan superiority and kinship lineages played an important role in the election of chieftains. Thrust into close intimacy by the nature of pueblo architecture, the people developed well-integrated religious and ceremonial structures to counteract the tensions of close quarters living.

The Anasazi enjoyed a relatively elaborate material culture at the height of their prosperity; at this time they were making distinctive black and white pottery, well-formed baskets, and fine sandals. However, their architecture was neither very sophisticated nor particularly innovative. Baked mud and rocks were formed into boxlike rooms; a roof of mud rested on horizontal timbers. Room after room was added as the need arose, using local materials and a simple architectural style entirely appropriate for its environment.

The southwestern farmer won success by skillfully using limited scarce water resources and by bringing together soil and water by means of dams, floodwater irrigation, and other systems for distributing runoff. Planting techniques were carefully adapted to desert conditions and short water supplies, and myriad tiny gardens supplied food for each family or lineage. This successful adaptation is also reflected in the unique architecture which made full use of local materials.

AGRICULTURAL SOCIETIES IN EASTERN NORTH AMERICA

The Archaic hunter-gatherer traditions of eastern North America enjoyed many regional variations in material culture; these occurred because the people concentrated on different, locally abundant food sources (Jennings, 1978; Muller, 1978). In general, however, the lifeway was similar among them: a seasonal one, based on a very broad spectrum of game and vegetable foods (Brose, 1980). As long as the population density was low, every band could react relatively easily to changes in local conditions. Since many of their favorite vegetable foods were subject to cycles of lean and abundant years, a flexibility in choice and movement was essential. However, as population grew slowly throughout the

Archaic, this flexibility was increasingly restricted and the people tended to specialize on local resources that were available most of the year. They developed better storage techniques and fostered closer contacts with their neighbors through exchange networks that handled foodstuffs and other commodities. The development of these types of responses may have required more complex social organization than the simple band structure of earlier times, and it is no coincidence that burial patterns during the late Archaic, approximately 1700 B.C., reflect greater differentiation in social status.

1700 B.C.

Although the eastern Indians lived in an environment in which cultivation of tropical crops such as maize was possible, agriculture did not take hold for centuries after the people were aware of the potential of the new economies (Stoltman, 1978; Struever and Holton, 1979). The transition to food production seems to have taken place almost imperceptibly. Perhaps some crops, such as the sunflower, were domesticated independently before maize was cultivated, but the first crops to be grown apparently were gourds, used for containers, perhaps as early as 3000 B.C. Between 2300 and 1000 B.C., many eastern groups were turning to agriculture. For three and a half millenia before 1500 B.C., the Koster people relied heavily on nuts and used few grass seeds, but the Salts Cave in Kentucky shows that seeds became much more common after that date, a trend that culminated in the domestication of local wild species and eventually the cultivation of maize and other imported crops. (Watson, 1969; Yarnell, 1974).

3000 B.C.
2000 B.C.

After 2000 B.C., we find increasing signs of preoccupation with burial and with life after death, of a new ideological foundation for local society in the Northeast. These burial cults shared many common practices, among them cremation and the deposition of exotic objects with the dead. Also among these practices was the custom of building burial mounds, which emerged quite independently in the Lower Mississippi Valley between 1700 and 700 B.C. The famous earthworks at Poverty Point, Louisiana, consist of six concentric octagons nested within each other. Each is made up of eight earthen ridges more than 6 ft high. The outermost octagon is more than 1290 m (4300 ft) wide. To the west lies a great mound more than 20 m (66 ft) high and more than 200 m (660 ft) long. A person standing on this mound can sight the vernal and autumnal equinoxes directly across the center of the earthworks to the east. This is the point where the sun rises on the first days of spring and fall, which has prompted some scholars to wonder whether this site has possible Mesoamerican connections (Webb, 1968). There are few other clues from the site itself, except for some small figurines of people found in the earthworks that recall those made by Olmec people on the Gulf Coast of Mexico. Could it be that some influences from Mexican ideology and civilization spread northeast to trigger religious innovations in North America? We cannot be sure. In any event, the Poverty Point culture went into decline in approximately 700 B.C., just as mound building reached new heights in the Ohio Valley to the northeast (Otto, 1980).

Poverty Point
1700 to 700 B.C.

Adena

By 700 B.C., the people of eastern North America enjoyed a tradition of long-distance trading that had flourished for centuries. The trade carried not only prosaic commodities such as stone ax blades but also large quantities of prestigious imports such as conch shells and copper artifacts, most of which were deposited in the graves of their owners. Perhaps the trade reflects the emergence of new chiefdoms in which exotic goods were status symbols, but the evidence is uncertain (Gibson, 1964).

Between 700 B.C. and approximately A.D. 200, the Adena culture flourished in the Ohio Valley, a culture that relied not only on hunting and gathering but also on the cultivation of squash and local weedy plants. Maize agriculture may or may not have been practiced; we do not know. The focus of Adena was the central Ohio Valley with outliers as far northeast as New Brunswick in Canada and deep into the Southeast. There is a temptation to think of Adena as nothing more than burial mounds, when in fact these conspicuous monuments are merely one aspect of a flourishing village culture ruled, it is thought, by chieftains who were powerful kin leaders. The loyalties people felt to their lineages were so strong that the villages commemorated the dead not only with imposing burial mounds, but with extensive earthworks as well.

Adena earthworks follow the contours of flat-topped hills and form circles, squares, and pentagons, enclosing areas perhaps as much as 105 m (350 ft) in diameter. The earth used to make the enclosures came from just inside the walls, giving a false impression of an interior moat. These were probably ceremonial compounds rather than defensive earthworks. The Adena people built large burial mounds, some placed inside enclosures, others standing independently outside. Most are communal rather than individual graves. The most important people lie in log-lined tombs. Their corpses are smeared with red ochre or graphite. Nearby lie ceremonial soapstone pipes and tablets engraved with curving designs or birds of prey. Some prestigious individuals were buried inside round houses, which were burned down as part of the funeral rites. Occasionally, the burial chamber was left open so that additional bodies could be added later. Dozens of people from miles around piled up basketfuls of earth to form an imposing burial mound for a single ruler. More often, the mounds were piled up gradually over the years as layers of bodies were added to the sepulcher. However, the vast majority of less important Adena people were cremated; only their ashes were placed inside the burial mound.

Despite the Adena concern with the afterlife, the basic lifeway of the people remained unchanged from earlier times. They lived in groups of villages and larger settlements that shared communal earthworks and burial mounds. Sometimes they occupied single family dwellings (Figure 13.8), occasionally much bigger communal houses capable of holding as many as forty people. We know from the Koster excavations that the Indians turned to agriculture probably when the population grew to a point

Figure 13.8 Reconstruction of an Adena house from the posthole pattern shown at left.

at which wild food sources were no longer sufficient. The highest densities of game and vegetable were concentrated on very narrow strips of land, mostly in river valleys. The intervening woodlands offered much less to hunters and gatherers. When population densities increased, the people could either move to marginal areas or take up farming, with all the social and economic adjustments that such change implied. At first they shifted their villages away from the river, but by A.D. 200 the Koster Indians had chosen the other option and were growing maize (Struever and Holton, 1979). They added beans approximately 300 years later, just at a time when the Hopewell tradition emerged in the Midwest, a far more complex series of societies which developed the funerary cults of Adena times to a much more elaborate pitch. By A.D. 1000, the Indians were heavily dependent on the crops they planted each year.

A.D. 200

Hopewell

The Hopewell tradition first appeared in Illinois in approximately 200 B.C. Its religious cults were such a success that they spread rapidly from their heartland as far afield as upper Wisconsin and Louisiana and deep into Ohio and New York state. For nearly 1000 years, the Midwest experienced a dramatic flowering of artistic traditions and of long-distance trade that brought copper from the upper Great Lakes region, obsidian from Yellowstone, and mica from the southern Appalachians. Some archaeologists call this the Hopewell Interaction Sphere (Caldwell, 1958). The Hopewell people themselves lived in relatively small farming settle-

Hopewell
c.200 B.C. to
c. A.D. 600

ments and used only the simplest of artifacts to plant maize, hunt game, and fish. They wore leather and woven clothes of pliable fibers. All their wealth and creative skill was lavished on a few individuals and on their life after death. At first glance, the exotic artifacts and ritual traditions of the Hopewell seem completely alien to the indigenous culture of the area, but a closer look reveals the close links between the underlying traditions and the magnificent art created by Hopewell artisans. Their manufactures were traded from hand to hand throughout Hopewell territory in a vast network of gift-giving transactions that linked kin leaders with lasting, important obligations to one another (Brose and Greber, 1980).

The cult objects associated with this trade are found in dozens of Hopewell burial mounds and tell us something of the rank and social role of the people with whom they are buried. Some of the exotic grave goods, such as pipe bowls or axes, were buried as gifts from living clan members to a dead leader. Others were personal possessions, cherished weapons, or sometimes symbols of status or wealth. Hopewell graves contain soapstone pipe bowls in the form of beavers, frogs, birds, bears, and even humans. Skilled smiths fashioned thin copper sheets into head and breast ornaments that bore elaborate repoussé animal motifs (Figure 13.9). There were copper axes and arrowheads, trinkets as well as beads. A few specialists cut mica sheets into striking, lustrous silhouettes of human figures, bird talons, and abstract designs. Most of these artifacts were manufactured by a few craftspeople working near major outcrops or sources of raw materials. They were distributed through the same trade networks that carried foodstuffs and tools throughout Hopewell territory. Most of them show surprisingly little wear, as if they were soon buried with their owners.

Hopewell burial mounds are much more elaborate than their Adena predecessors. For example, Crook's Mound in Louisiana rises 12 m (40 ft) high and is more than 30 m (100 ft) across. Its builders followed the established custom when they buried 168 bodies within an extensive earthen platform. Then they placed a further 214 corpses on the platform before covering the entire sepulcher with a large mound. Another Hopewell burial mound complex in Ohio, appropriately named Mound City, contains no fewer than twenty-four mounds inside an enclosure covering 13 acres.

The decline of the Hopewell culture after A.D. 400 still is imperfectly understood, but it is possible that a rapid and dramatic population increase may have strained the limits of the economic system, causing competition between different trading networks and rupturing long-established economic and political relationships. It is possible, too, that as agriculture became more efficient and spread to other groups, there was an increase in population and in the number of settlements, so much so that there was greater competition for land. This in turn led to the development of local rule by chieftains that could have challenged the overbearing powers of those who controlled the centuries-old burial cults

Figure 13.9 Hopewell artifacts: (a) raven or crow in beaten copper; (b) bird claw in mica; (c) soapstone frog.

(Dragoo, 1976). We do not know why the center of religious and political power had spread southward from the Ohio Valley into the lower Mississippi bottomlands by A.D. 800, but it is certain that the lush floodplain was ideal for cultivating new, higher-yielding strains of maize that came into use during the late first millennium A.D., and also for growing beans, a crop that has not only a high protein value, but also the asset of compensating for the amino-acid deficiencies of corn. Soon the "Mississippian" people were expanding into the tributary valleys of the great river, until they flourished over a large area of the Mississippi drainage between Iowa and northern Louisiana.

Many archaeologists link the Adena and Hopewell cultures into a single "Scioto" tradition, while the term *Woodland* often is used to describe eastern cultures after the introduction of pottery in approximately 600 B.C.

The Mississippian

The Mississippian culture first appeared along the lower Mississippi, then spread along the major floodplain corridors formed by its tributaries. The distribution of the Mississippian is basically restricted to the fertile plains formed by meanders of the great river and its tributaries, which has always been assumed to be because of the availability of easily

Mississippian c. A.D. 800 to European contact

tilled soils. In fact, we know now that this restricted distribution was owing to the complex adaptation that the people developed in an area with well-defined bands of arable soils that were fertilized by spring floods just before planting season. They lived in valleys with many lakes and swamps where fish trapped by receding floods were plentiful and migrating waterfowl paused to rest in spring and fall. The Mississippian people not only grew maize, squash, and beans, but they also relied heavily on seasonal crops of nuts, fruits, berries, and seed-bearing plants. They hunted deer, raccoon, and turkey, and shot thousands of migratory waterfowl in spring and fall. Fish and waterfowl may have comprised up to fifty percent of the diet of the villagers living within the meander zones of the floodplain (Smith, 1975, 1978).

Most of the Mississippian population lived in small, dispersed homesteads or sometimes in compact villages. The larger communities and ceremonial centers that have been the focus of archaeological attention for a century comprise a small minority. In all probability, the villagers visited their local center only for scheduled seasonal ceremonies, major funerals of kin or high-status individuals, for mutual defense in times of war, and to fulfill their labor obligations for building fortifications or mounds. There may have been seasonal changes in settlement patterns. Judging from historical accounts of Indian warfare, isolated families may well have come together in larger defended communities during the summer warfare season, dispersing to their homes in the fall.

By A.D. 900, the larger Mississippian communities housed between 100 and 150 people and were fortified with defensive palisades. The largest Mississippian center was Cahokia on the east bank of the river at Saint Louis (Figure 13.10) (Fowler, 1969, 1978). Cahokia once contained more than one hundred earthen mounds and catered to a population of at least 30,000 to 35,000 people in its heyday. Cahokia was a great ceremonial center; its mounds and plazas dominated the countryside for miles around. Monk's Mound at the center of Cahokia rises 33 m (110 ft) above the floodplain and covers 16 acres (Figure 13.11). This gigantic mound is as tall as a ten-story building and was erected in at least four stages between the ninth and eleventh centuries A.D. Millions of basketloads of soil deposited by thousands of people went into this monumental earthwork. On the summit of the mound stood a thatched temple at the east end of an enormous central plaza. Around the plaza rose other mounds, temples, warehouses, administrative buildings, and the homes of nobles. The entire "downtown" area covered more than 200 acres and was fortified with a log fence with gates and watchtowers. Numerous mounds and lesser communities lay outside the walled inner core of Cahokia, each with their own plazas and burial mounds. The pole and thatch houses of the residential areas extended over 2000 acres, the clusters of houses being separated by several acres of land. There is every reason to believe that Cahokia was planned and controlled by a powerful central authority.

Cahokia was by no means unique. It lay in the north of Mississippian territory, while its southern rival, another great center, was located at

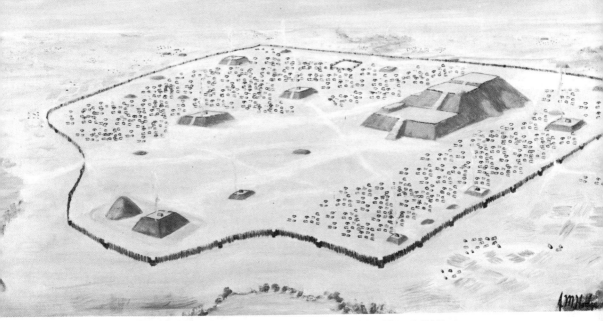

Figure 13.10 A reconstruction of Cahokia during the period A.D. 1200–1500 by A. W. Hodge.

Moundville in Alabama. Dozens of small centers and towns sprang up between the two. More than just sacred places for annual ceremonies of planting and harvest, the centers were markets and focal points of powerful chiefdoms. Cahokia owed some of its importance to the manufacture and trading of local salt and chert, a fine-grained rock used to make axes and other tools. Above all, Cahokia and its neighbors were the places where the Mississippian rulers displayed their political and religious power for all to behold.

We know little about how Mississippian society functioned, but it seems likely that the floodplain was ruled as a series of powerful chiefdoms, by an elite group of priests and rulers who lived a life somewhat separated from the rest of the population. The chieftains probably monopolized most long-distance trade and were the living intermediaries with the ancestors and the gods. As in the Hopewell culture, high-ranking individuals went to the next world in richly decorated graves, with clusters of ritual objects of different styles that betokened different clans and tribes. One small Cahokia burial mound yielded the skeleton of an important man wearing a robe into which had been woven 12,000 shell beads. Six servants lay by his side, together with copper arrowheads and polished stone and mica slabs. No fewer than fifty-three women, perhaps slaves, had been buried in a mass grave nearby.

Was the Mississippian an indigenous cultural development? The debate has raged for more than half a century. It seems likely that the basic cultural traditions evolved in the Mississippi Valley in the late first millennium, for the entire culture depended on a complex adaptation to a highly specialized environment. However, there are signs of Mexican in-

Figure 13.11 Monk's Mound, Cahokia, Illinois, viewed from the southeast during excavation in 1966.

fluence in the layout of plazas and imposing mounds and in the emphasis on public ceremony and display that seems characteristic of the largest ceremonial centers.

Unfortunately, we know almost nothing of the elaborate rituals and beliefs of Mississippian society. The few clues come from surviving examples of Mississippian art, many of them from the Moundville sites. So pervasive are the design motifs — human hands with an eye in the palm, sunbursts, or weeping eyes — that the experts believe that a distinctive "Southern cult" flourished throughout Mississippian country. Southern cult motifs appear on pottery, were embossed on Lake Superior copper, and were incised on imported Gulf conch shells. Perhaps the most famous Mississippian cult objects are the so-called effigy jars, which bear human faces, some with signs of face painting and tattoos. Others are representations of the heads of sacrificial victims, their eyes closed and mouths sewn tightly shut. Often, the effigies are depicted weeping, perhaps denoting a connection between tears, rain, and water in Mississippian cosmology.

The Southern cult appears to be an amalgam of indigenous Indian and Mexican themes. Wind, fire, sun, and human sacrifice are common motifs. One persistent artifact is a small copper mask depicting a long-nosed god, who bears a close resemblance to the god of the merchants found at many Mexican sites. Perhaps it was these *pochteca,* or traders, who introduced Mexican religious beliefs to the Mississippi Valley, but it is only fair to point out that no Mexican artifacts have yet come from Mississippian settlements.

This remarkable society flourished until the sixteenth century. Then, in 1540 to 1542, Spanish conquistador Hernando de Soto encountered Creek Indian chiefs in the South who still lived in fortified towns with temple mounds and plazas. The smallpox he brought with him decimated center after center, weakening Mississippian culture beyond recovery. Nevertheless, when Europeans began to colonize the South in the seventeenth century, they came up against a powerful alliance of fifty large Creek Indian settlements in what is now Alabama and Georgia. To the west lived the Chickasaw and Chocktaw, while the Cherokee to the north numbered more than 60,000 distributed in at least one hundred settlements. The first missionaries who worked among the Cherokee recorded dimly remembered folktales of mound building in earlier centuries.

GUIDE TO FURTHER READING

Jennings, Jesse D. *The Prehistory of North America* (2nd ed.). New York: McGraw-Hill, 1975.
_____(Ed.). *Ancient Native Americans.* 2 vols. New York: Freeman, 1983.
   Two volumes by a leading Americanist that summarize the culture history of the Americas. *Ancient Native Americans* contains essays by various authorities, some with a stronger theoretical background than others.

MacNeish, Richard. *The Science of Archaeology.* North Scituate, Mass.: Duxbury Press, 1978.
   An account of MacNeish's research in Mexico and Peru that summarizes the work and also contains much common-sense advice about contemporary archaeology.

Moseley, Michael. *The Maritime Foundations of Andean Civilization.* Menlo Park, Calif.: Cummings, 1975.
   A clearly written, informative essay on the origins of food production and civilization in Peru that was an important basis for this chapter.

Willey, Gordon R. *An Introduction to American Archeology, North and Middle America,* vol. 1 and *South America,* vol. 2. Englewood Cliffs, N.J.: Prentice-Hall, 1966, 1971.
   The definitive accounts of the culture history of the Americas as of the late 1960s. Strongly recommended for the advanced reader. Somewhat outdated but still one of the ultimate authorities.

OLD WORLD CIVILIZATIONS

(3000 B.C. to Modern Times)

"The great tide of civilization has long since ebbed, leaving
these scattered wrecks on the solitary shore. Are those
waters to flow again, bringing back the seeds of knowledge
and of wealth that they have wafted to the West? We
wanderers were seeking what they had left behind, as children gather up the coloured shells on the deserted sands."

– Austen Henry Layard

As in Part Four, a discussion of the theoretical background and the major
controversies precedes the narrative prehistory. Part Five deals with the beginnings of complex states and urban civilization. These chapters present an
unconventional account of early civilization in that they deal with lesser known
parts of the world such as Africa and Southeast Asia, as well as the Near East.
Research in Africa and Asia has hardly begun; future excavations in these
regions are likely to throw significant new light on such much-debated issues
as the importance of ceremonial centers and long-distance trade in the emergence of complex societies. Once again, the reader is urged to start with the
theoretical background before embarking on the narrative culture history.

Chapter Fourteen

The Development
of Civilization

PREVIEW

✸ V. Gordon Childe's pioneer definition of the Urban Revolution was widely accepted; it
centered around the development of the city, metallurgy, food surpluses, writing, and
a unifying religious force. Unfortunately, his criteria are not universal enough to be
generally applicable.

✸ Evolutionary models of the development of sociopolitical units give us a framework
for looking at the mechanisms that led to the emergence of urban societies.

✸ We summarize various commonly held theories about how complex societies began,
describing the various major potential causes for civilization. These include ecological
stress, population stress, technological change, irrigation agriculture, and the notion
of the hydraulic civilization. Religion, ceremony, and exchange networks have all been
espoused as potential factors in the development of civilization.

✸ Current research stresses a systems approach to the origins of civilization, regarding
the emergence of complex societies as a gradual process caused by many interacting factors. Kent Flannery has argued that complex societies are not susceptible to
simple analysis and that there were many causes of cultural change. He urges us to
look at the processes and mechanisms by which the necessary changes took place.

✸ The ultimate objective is to establish the set of rules by which a complex state could
have come into being. Religious and informational factors seem to be key elements
in the regulation of environmental and economic variables in early civilization.

CIVILIZATION

Civilization

Everyone who has studied the prehistory of human society agrees that
the emergence of civilization in different parts of the world was a major
event in human adaptation. The word *civilization* has a ready, everyday
meaning. It implies "civility," a measure of decency in the behavior of
the individual in a civilization. Such definitions inevitably reflect ethno-
centrism or value judgments because what is "civilized" behavior in one
civilization might be antisocial or baffling in another. These simplistic

definitions are of no use to students of prehistoric civilizations seeking basic definitions and cultural processes.

The generally agreed-upon, special attributes that separate civilizations from other societies can be listed as follows:

Urbanized societies, based on cities, with large, very complex social organizations. The early civilization was invariably based on a specific territory like, say, the Nile Valley, as opposed to smaller areas owned by individual kin groups.

Symbiotic economies based on the centralized accumulation of capital and social status through tribute and taxation. This type of economy allows the support of hundreds, often thousands, of nonfood producers such as smiths and priests. Long-distance trade and the division of labor are often characteristic of early civilizations, as well as craft specialization.

Advances toward record keeping, science and mathematics, and some form of written script.

Impressive public buildings and monumental architecture.

These various attributes are by no means common to all early civilizations, for they take different forms in each civilization (Chard, 1969).

CITIES

Archaeological research into early civilization concentrates on the origin and development of the city. Today the city is the primary human settlement type throughout the world, and it has become so since the Industrial Revolution altered the economic face of the globe. The earliest cities assumed many forms, from the compact, walled settlement of Mesopotamia to the Mesoamerican ceremonial center with a core population in its precincts and a scattered rural population in villages arranged over the surrounding landscape. The cities of the Harappan civilization of the Indus were carefully planned communities with regular streets and assigned quarters for different living groups. The palaces of the Minoans and Mycenaeans functioned as secular economic and trading centers that served as a focus for scattered village populations nearby.

A *city* is best defined by its population, which is generally larger and City denser than that of towns or villages. As we have said, a good and generally used rule of thumb is a lower limit of 5000 people for a city. However, numbers are not a sufficient determinant: many people can congregate in a limited area and still not possess the compact diversity of population which enables the economic and organizational complexity of a city to develop. It is this complexity that distinguishes the city from other settlement types. Most cities have a complexity in both organization and non-agricultural activities which is supported by large food surpluses. The city is not merely complex; it is a functioning part of a complex system of different settlements that rely on its many services and facilities.

AN URBAN REVOLUTION?

Since archaeological research into early civilization has concentrated on excavations into ancient cities and ceremonial centers, it was perhaps inevitable that the first attempts to explain the origins of civilization focused on the city and its implications.

Early scholars who debated the origins of civilization were concerned with the cultural evolution of humankind from a state of savagery toward the full realization of human potential. This, in their eyes, was Victorian civilization. They considered that their civilization had originated in Ancient Egypt and that bold mariners had spread the ideas of civilization all over the globe. These simplistic hypotheses collapsed in the face of new archaeological discoveries in Mesopotamia and the Nile Valley in the early decades of this century. With the discovery of the Sumerians and early Egyptian farming villages, scholars came to realize that early civilization had developed over a wide area and over a considerable period of time.

The first relatively sophisticated theories about the origins of urban civilization were formulated by V. Gordon Childe, of Neolithic Revolution fame (Chapter Two). Childe claimed that his Neolithic Revolution was followed by an Urban Revolution, when the development of metallurgy created a new class of full-time specialists and changed the rules of human social organization (Childe, 1936, 1956). Childe argued that the new full-time specialists were fed by food surpluses raised by the peasant farmers. The products of the craftsworkers had to be distributed, and raw materials had to be obtained from outside sources. Both needs reduced the self-reliance of peasant societies. Agricultural techniques became more sophisticated as an increased yield of food per capita was needed to support the nonagricultural population. Irrigation increased productivity, leading to centralized control of food supplies, production, and distribution. Taxation and tribute led to the accumulation of capital. A new class-stratified society came into being. Writing was essential for keeping records and for developing exact and predictive sciences. Transportation by water and land was part of the new order. A unifying religious force dominated urban life as priest-kings and despots rose to power. Monumental architecture testified to their activities.

The notion of an Urban Revolution dominated archaeological and historical literature for years, but the revolution hypothesis has flaws as an all-embracing definition of civilization and a description of its development. Childe's criteria are far from universal. Some highly effective and lasting civilizations such as those of the Minoans and the Mycenaeans never had cities (Redman, 1979; C. Renfrew, 1973). The Maya built elaborate ceremonial and religious centers with semiurban populations concentrated around them, surrounded by a more scattered rural population clustered for the most part in small villages. Writing is absent from the Inca civilization of Peru. The Mayan and Aztec scripts were used in part for administering an elaborate calendar. Some craft specializa-

Urban Revolution

tion and religious structure is typical of most civilizations, but it cannot be said that these form the basis for an overall definition of civilization.

American archaeologist Robert Adams (1966) stresses the development of social organization and craft specialization during the Urban Revolution. He raises objections to the Childe hypothesis, arguing that the name implies undue emphasis on the city at the expense of social change, the development of social classes and political institutions. Many of Childe's criteria, like the evolution of the exact sciences, have the disadvantage of not being readily preserved in the archaeological record. Furthermore, Childe's Urban Revolution was identified by lists of traits, although the name implies emphasis on the *processes* of cultural change as time passed. Childe believed technological innovations and subsistence patterns were at the core of the Urban Revolution. Adams directed his work toward changes in social organization; he described early Mesopotamia and central Mexico as following "a fundamental course of development in which corporate kin groups, originally preponderating in the control of land, were gradually supplemented by the growth of private estates in the hands of urban elites" (R. M. Adams, 1966). The eventual result was a stratified form of social organization rigidly divided along class lines (Service, 1962, 1975).

Adams: social organization

LATER THEORIES ABOUT THE ORIGINS OF CIVILIZATION

By the time Adams was criticizing Childe's Urban Revolution, people were beginning to investigate the many interacting factors that led to the emergence of complex states. Everyone agreed that complex societies appeared during a period of major economic and social change, but different scholars gave emphasis to different possible factors that contributed to the rise of civilization. These factors included ecology, irrigation, population growth, trade, religious beliefs, and even warfare. In the pages that follow, we examine some of these factors, realizing that no one development led, on its own, to the emergence of cities and civilization.

Ecology

Many have said that the exceptional fertility of the Mesopotamian floodplain and the Nile Valley was a primary reason for the emergence of the cities and states in these regions. The fertility and benign climate led to the food surpluses that were capable of supporting the craftsworkers and the other specialists who formed the complex fabric of civilization (Wheatley, 1971). This notion was the basic foundation of what was known in the 1920s and 1930s as the Fertile Crescent theory.

Reality, of course, is much more complicated. The true surplus is probably one of capacities, a *social surplus*, which is one that consciously reallocates goods or services. A social surplus is created by a society's deliberate action, through some form of governmental force achieving the

Social surplus

reallocations. In a sense this is a taxation authority. This taxation authority is a person or organization that wrests surplus grain or other products from those who grow or produce them. Another problem with the Fertile Crescent theory is that the environments of all the major centers of early civilizations are far too diverse in altitude above sea level, for example, for any assemblage of environmental conditions to be defined and set forth as the requisite conditions which led to civilization's start.

Even on the Mesopotamian floodplain, which superficially appears to be a uniform environment, specialized zones of subsistence vary greatly. Wheat was grown on the Assyrian uplands; barley did better on the margins of swamps and near levees on the plain. Both these winter cereals were staples. Near the permanent watercourses, low-lying orchards ripened in the summers, together with garden crops such as dates. The date crop was a beautiful supplement to the spring cereal harvests, ripening in the fall. Mesopotamian agriculture was combined with cattle herding on cereal stubble and fallow land in the permanently settled areas; many herds were grazed by nomads on the semiarid steppes beyond the limits of settled areas. Fish, too, provided vital protein, taken from the rivers and swamps that also had reeds for building material. Robert Adams argues that these ecological niches, effectively exploited, forged between adjacent segments of society an interdependence that was reflected in increased specialization in subsistence activities, as each segment of Mesopotamian society provided a part of the food supply and, ultimately, social surplus (R. M. Adams, 1966).

Complex subsistence patterns like these were almost certainly active in Mesoamerica and Southeast Asia, to say nothing of Egypt, although the evidence is very incomplete. Even in the best-documented areas, evidence comes from later, well-documented periods, and we can only surmise that complexities were similar in earlier times. The integration of several ecological zones, each producing a different food as a main product, into one sociopolitical unit probably took place as the first ceremonial centers came into being. A localized center of power could control different ecological zones and the products from them, a more deliberate hedge against famine that was indispensable for planning food surpluses. This is not at all the same as saying that favorable ecological conditions caused trade and redistributive mechanisms, and therefore some form of centralized authority, to develop. Rather, ecology was only one component in a close network of the many changes that led to civilization, a subsystem of interactive forces among a great many subsystems in equilibrium.

Population Growth

Malthus and Boserup

Thomas Henry Malthus argued as long ago as 1798 that human reproductive capacity far exceeds the available food supply. Many people have argued that new and more intensive agricultural methods created food surpluses. These in turn led to population growth, more leisure time, and new social, political, and religious institutions, as well as the arts.

Ester Boserup, among others, has criticized this point of view. She feels that population growth provided the incentive for irrigation and intensive agriculture (Spooner, 1972). Her theories have convinced others that social evolution was caused by population growth. No one has explained, though, why the original population should have started to grow. By no means all farming populations, especially those using slash-and-burn cultivation, live at the maximum density that can be supported by the available agricultural land, and population often is artificially regulated. To claim that population growth explains how states were formed necessitates finding out why such decisions would have been made.

Slash-and-burn, or swidden, agriculture with its shifting cultivation is very delicately balanced with the rest of its ecosystem. Populations are dispersed and have relatively little flexibility in movement or growth because the land has low carrying capacity and relatively few ecological niches to carry edible crops (Allan, 1965). More lasting field agriculture is far more intensive and exploits much more of the environment in an ordered and systematic way. The Mesopotamian example shows how effectively a sedentary population can manipulate its diverse food sources. The more specialized ecosystem created by these efforts supports more concentrated populations. It creates conditions in which more settlements per square mile can exist on foods whose annual yields are at least roughly predictable.

Most significant concentrations of settlement that might be called prototypes for urban complexes developed in regions where permanent field agriculture flourished. However, unlike the period immediately after food production began, there is no evidence for a major jump in population immediately before civilization appeared. Also, a dense population does not seem to have been a precondition for a complex society or redistribution centers for trade. We have no reason to believe that a critical population density was a prerequisite for urban life.

Technology

In Mesopotamia, again our best-documented area, agricultural technology did not advance until long after civilization began. The technological innovations that did appear were of more benefit to transportation (the wheel, for example) than to production. Copper and other exotic materials were at first used for small-scale production of cult objects and jewelry. Not until several centuries after civilization started were copper and bronze more abundant, with demand for transportation and military needs burgeoning. Then we see an advance in technology or an increase in craftspeople. Technology did evolve but only in response to developing markets, new demands, and the expanded needs of the elite.

Irrigation

Most scholars now agree that three elements on Childe's list seem to have been of great importance in the growth of all the world's civilizations. The first was the creation of food surpluses, used to support new economic classes whose members were not directly engaged in food production. Agriculture as a way of life immediately necessitates storing crops to support the community during the lean times of the year. A surplus above this level of production was created by both increased agricultural efficiency and social and cultural changes. Specialist craftsworkers, priests, and traders were among the new classes of society that came into being as a result.

Second, agricultural economies may have tended to concentrate on fewer, more productive crops, but they remained diversified so that the ultimate subsistence base still was relatively wide. The ancient Egyptians relied on husbandry, especially in the Nile Delta. The diversity of food resources not only protected the people against the dangers of famine but also stimulated the development of trade and exchange mechanisms for food and other products and the growth of distributive organizations that encouraged centralized authority.

The third significant development was intensive land use, which probably increased agricultural output. Intensive agriculture usually implies irrigation, often hailed as one fundamental reason for a civilization's start. Archaeologists have long debated how significant irrigation was in getting urban life started. Julian Steward and Karl Wittfogel argue that irrigation was connected with development of stratified societies (Steward et al., 1955; Wittfogel, 1966). The state bureaucracy had a monopoly over hydraulic facilities and created the Hydraulic State; in other words, the social requirements of irrigation led to the development of states and urban societies. Robert Adams takes a contrary view (R. M. Adams, 1966). He feels that the introduction of great irrigation works was more a consequence than a cause of dynastic state organizations, however much the requirement of large-scale irrigation subsequently may have influenced the development of bureaucratic organizations.

Adams's view is based on studies of prehistoric irrigation in Mesopotamia, as well as observations of irrigation in smaller societies. Large-scale irrigation had its roots in simpler beginnings, perhaps in simple cooperation between neighboring communities to dam streams and divert water into fields where precious seeds were sown. The floodplain of the Tigris and the Euphrates rivers, with its long, harsh summers, could be cultivated only by irrigation with canals, which had to be dug deep enough to carry water even when the rivers were at their lowest. No means of lifting water was found until Assyrian times, and the earliest inhabitants of the delta were obliged to dig their canals very deep and to keep them that way. Silting, blockage, and flooding were constant dangers, requiring endless manhours to keep the canals working. It paid the earliest delta farmers to live within a limited geographic area where canal digging was kept to a minimum, but even then organizing the digging would have required some centralized authority and certainly more restructuring of social life than the simple intercommunity cooperation typical of many smaller agricultural societies that used irrigation.

Building and maintaining small canals requires neither elaborate social organization nor population resources larger than those of one community or several communities cooperating. Large-scale irrigation requires technical and social resources of a quite different order. Huge labor forces had to be mobilized, organized, and fed. Maintenance and supervision require constant attention, as do water distribution and resolving disputes over water rights. Because those living downstream are at the mercy of those upstream, large irrigation works are viable only as long as those who enjoy them remain within the same political unit. A formal state structure with an administrative elite is essential.

Early irrigation in Mesopotamia was conducted on a small scale (R. M. Adams, 1955, 1981; R. M. Adams and Nissen, 1972). Natural channels were periodically cleaned and straightened; only small artificial feeder canals were built. Maximum use was made of the natural hydrology of the rivers. Most settlement was confined to the immediate vicinity of major watercourses. Irrigation was organized by individual peoples. Large-scale artificial canalization did not take place until long after urban life appeared. The same is true of Ancient Egypt, where construction of large artificial canals seems to have been the culmination of long evolution of intensive agriculture.

Growth of Trade

The origins and evolution of complex societies in human prehistory have long been linked to burgeoning trade in essential raw materials such as copper and iron ore, or in luxuries of all types. However, claiming that a dramatic increase in trading was a primary cause of civilization grossly oversimplifies a complex proceeding. Trade is two things: a helpful indicator of new social developments and a factor in the rise of civilization. Many commodities and goods are preserved in the archaeological record: gold and glass beads, seashells, obsidian mirrors, and many other items. These finds have enabled archaeologists to trace trade routes through the Near East, Europe, and other regions. With the many analytic methods for looking at the sources of obsidian, stone ax blanks, and metals, people now realize that prehistoric trade was much more complex than a few itinerant tradespeople passing objects from village to village (Sabloff and Lamberg-Karlovsky, 1975).

Prehistoric trade frequently is thought of as a variable that developed at the same time that sociopolitical organization was becoming more complex. This notion goes back to the long-established hierarchy of bands, tribes, chiefdoms, and states and to a linear, evolutionary way of looking at civilization's origins. It has been assumed that trade proceeded from simple reciprocal exchange to the more complex redistribution of goods.

Trade and exchange networks

Trade as an institution could have begun when people sought to acquire goods from a distance for prestige and for individual profit. The decision to acquire any commodity from afar depends both on how urgent the need for the goods is and on the difficulties in acquiring and transporting the materials. Much early trade was based on acquiring specific commodities, such as copper ore or salt, that had peculiar and characteristic problems of acquisition and transport. There was no such thing as trading in general. Trade in any one commodity was specific and almost a special branch on its own. Clearly such items as cattle or slaves are more easily transported than tons of iron ore or cakes of salt; the former move on their own, but metals require human or animal carriers or wheeled carts. To ignore these differences is to oversimplify the study of prehistoric trade.

In more complex societies, the ruler and his immediate followers were generally entitled to trade and to initiate the steps leading to acquisition of goods from a distance. The king might employ merchants or traders to do the work for him, but the trade was in his name. The lower-class traders of Mesopotamian society were more menial people, often bound by guilds or castes. These people were carriers, loan administrators, dealers — people who kept the machinery of trade going, with a carefully regulated place in society. Both the royal merchant and the lower-class trader were distinct from trading peoples such as the Phoenicians, who relied on trade as a continuous activity and a major form of livelihood.

Trade before markets were developed can never be looked at as the one cause of civilization or even as a unifying factor. It was far more than just a demand for obsidian or copper, for the causes of trading were infinitely varied and the policing of trade routes was a complex and unending task. It is significant that most early Mesopotamian and Egyptian trade was river-based, where policing was easier. With the great caravan routes opened, the political and military issues — tribute, control of trade routes, and tolls — became paramount. The caravan predates the great empires, a form of organized trading that kept to carefully defined routes set up and armed by state authorities for their specific tasks. The travelers moved along set routes, looking neither left nor right, bent only on delivering and exchanging imports and exports. These caravans were a far cry from the huge economic complex that accompanied Alexander the Great's army across Asia, or the Grand Mogul's annual summer progress from the heat of Delhi in India to the mountains, moving half a million people including the entire Delhi bazaar.

Trade itself has been analyzed intensively by both economists and anthropologists (Polayni, 1975). They distinguish between internal trade between neighboring communities in the same tribal area or state and external trade with other peoples, states, or areas. They examine trade in the form of gifts, such as that probably conducted by the Hopewell people of the Midwest (Chapter Thirteen), which is really barter; and they consider trade by treaty, trading that results from political agreement. Formally administered trade is another important category, normally conducted from a port of trade, a place that can offer military security, commercial and loading facilities, and a safe haven for foreign traders.

There has been much debate about the origins of the market — both a place and a style of trading administration and organization. The market encourages people to develop one place for trading and relatively stable, almost fixed, prices for staple commodities. This does not mean regulated prices. The trade market is a network of market sites (market-places) at which the exchange of commodities from an area where supplies are abundant to one where demand for the same materials is high is regulated to some degree, especially the *mechanisms* of the exchange relationship.

This emphasis on mechanisms had led Johnson, Lamberg-Karlovsky, Rathje (Sabloff and Lamberg-Karlovsky, 1975), and others to study market networks and the mechanisms by which supplies are channeled down well-defined routes, profits are regulated and fed back to the source, providing further incentive for more supplies, and so on. There may or may not be a marketplace; it is the state of affairs surrounding the trade that forms the focus of the trading system and the mechanisms by means of which trade interacts with other parts of the culture. Taking a systems approach to trading activity means regarding archaeological finds as the material expressions of interdependent factors. These include the need for goods, which prompts a search for supplies, themselves the product of production above local needs, created to satisfy external demands. Other variables are the logistics of transportation and the extent of the trading network, as well as the social and political environments. With all these variables, no one aspect of trade is an overriding cause of cultural change or of evolution in trading practices. Hitherto, archaeologists have concentrated on trade in the context of objects or as an abstraction — trade as a cause of civilization — but have had no profound knowledge about even one trading network from which to build more theoretical abstractions.

The reality is that long-distance trade was carefully melded with fluctuating demands and availabilities of supplies. It is not enough to think of trade simply in terms of distribution of exports and imports (Kohl, 1978). Any study of prehistoric trade has to consider not only distribution, but also the production and consumption of the goods involved. Were they essential raw materials or exotic luxuries, finished manufactures or ax blanks that were completed at their destination? Was the trade continuous or seasonal, carried on by specialist traders, only by the wealthy, or by everyone? Changes in the volume and nature of trade can influence and modify not only production in a society, but its social and economic structures as well. For example, we know that the Aztec merchant could purchase the title "Lord," presumably as a measure of his status as a successful trader. There was room for private dealing, specialist merchants, commodities markets, perhaps even smuggling and tax evasion. Ar-

Systems approach

chaeologists cannot understand a trading network without analyzing the social and economic structures of each society participating in the exchange, for, in many cases, they became interdependent, often without realizing that they were. Until there is much more systematic study of the data for early trade, no one will fully understand trade's influence on nascent civilization in Mesopotamia or, for that matter, anywhere.

Warfare

Robert Carneiro (1972) has suggested a "coersive theory" of state origins. Based on the archaeology of Peruvian coastal valleys, it argues that areas like these valleys, where the amount of agricultural land is very limited and circumscribed by desert, are the ones where states may well form through a predictable series of events. Carneiro's scenario begins with dispersed and autonomous farming villages scattered over the valley landscape. As the population grows and as more land is taken up, the various communities start fighting one another and raiding one another's fields as they compete for limited land acreage. Soon some village leaders emerge as successful war lords, become chieftains, and preside over larger tribal politics. But the valley population continues to grow and warfare continues to intensify until the entire region falls under the sway of a single warrior-ruler, who presides over a single state centered within the valley. Then, this ambitious ruler and his successors start raiding neighboring valleys. Eventually a powerful state emerges and rules over several valleys, which creates much larger civilizations.

The Carneiro hypothesis is difficult to test, but an attempt to do so in the Santa Valley, Peru, has produced an interesting picture of changing settlement patterns (see Chapter Twenty-two for a full discussion). Suffice it to say here that there are no signs of the kinds of dispersed, autonomous villages that Carneiro's scenario begins with. The processes that shaped the emergence of state societies in the Santa Valley appear to be much more complex and multifaceted than just tribal warfare. David Wilson points out that the only "coercive" processes came in about A.D. 400, when the Moche people carved out a multivalley state by military conquest of neighboring valleys. Their conquest took place long after complex, irrigation-based societies flourished in the Santa Valley. As with irrigation hypotheses, reality is much more complex than the straightforward scenario Carneiro developed.

There is an attractive simplicity in the idea that the early city was a mighty fortress to which the surrounding tribes would run in times of stress. Thus, goes the argument, they came to depend on one another and their city as a fundamental part of society. However, warfare can be rejected as a primary cause of civilization without much discussion, since large military conflicts appear to have been a result of civilization not a direct cause of it. For one thing, the earliest ceremonial centers apparently were not fortified. For another, in earlier times, the diffuse social organization of village communities had not yet led to the institutional warfare that resulted from the concentration of wealth and power in monopolistic hands. Only when absolute and secular monarchs came into power did warfare become endemic, with raiding and military campaigns designed to gain control of important resources or to solve political questions. This type of warfare is a far cry from the tribal conflict common to many peasant societies. It presupposes authority.

Religion

Religion has been ignored by many writers who favor trade and production as major forces in civilization's beginnings. Yet shrines and sacred places are common in agricultural settlements of great antiquity, such as Jericho, Çatal Hüyük, and Las Haldas (Peru) (Wheatley, 1971). These religious shrines were predecessors of the great ceremonial centers of Mesopotamia and Egypt, Mesoamerica, and Peru. In each part of the world where civilization appeared, ceremonial centers were preceded by inconspicuous prototypes tended by priests or cult leaders. These people must have been among the first to be freed of the burden of having to produce food, supported by the communities they served. In every region the ceremonial center was the initial focus of power and authority, an authority vested in religious symbolism and organized priesthoods.

Priesthoods may have become powerful authorities as people worried more about the cycles of planting and harvest and the soil's continuing fertility. It was no coincidence that the Mesopotamians' earliest recorded gods were those of harvest and fertility, or that in Mexico Tlaloc was the god of rain and life itself. These preoccupations may have become the focus of new and communal belief systems. Those who served the deities of fertility thus became people of authority, the individuals who controlled economic surpluses, offerings, and the redistribution of goods. The temple became a new instrument for organizing fresh political, social, and religious structures.

Priesthoods

As society grew more complex, more sophisticated ethics and beliefs provided a means for sanctioning the society's new goals. The temple was an instrument for disseminating these new beliefs, a means for the new leaders to justify their acts and develop coherent policies. Symbolic statements describing society served as models not only of behavior and belief, but also for the ceremonial centers that perpetuated and formulated them.

The Ceremonial Center

The nucleus of the first cities was some form of temple or ceremonial center, the edifice around which the business of the state, whether secular or religious, went on (Eliade, 1954, 1959). These ceremonial centers were either very compact, like the Mesopotamian *ziggurat*, or dispersed, like Mayan examples. Those of the Mesopotamians and Chinese were relatively compact, with a reasonably dense population around them. Many Mayan centers, such as Tikal in Guatemala, were huge urban complexes, with dense city and rural populations (Hammond, 1982). The priestly elite and rulers who lived at the center were surrounded by retainers and craftsworkers. The rural population in the environs was probably bound to the ceremonial center both economically and by kinship. As a ceremonial center became a focus for a group of independent settlements, it supplied reassurance or what Chinese historian Paul Wheatley calls "cosmic certainty." It was "the sanctified terrain where [the common people were] guaranteed the seasonal renewal of cyclic time, and where the splendor, potency, and wealth of their rulers symbolized the well-being of the whole community" (Wheatley, 1971). The rural population felt no alienation from those who lived at the center; the distinction was between the ruler and the ruled.

Eliade and the
ceremonial center
This classic interpretation of the ceremonial center is long-established, notably in writings by Mircea Eliade (Eliade, 1959). To this school of thought, the ceremonial center was not a prime mover of civilization, but an instrument of "orthogenetic transformation." The religious and moral models of society provided a sacred canon circumscribing economic institutions and laying out the social order. It ensured the continuity of cultural traditions and was recited in temples, where the Word of the Gods rang out in reassuring chants passed from generation to generation. The ceremonial center was a tangible expression of this continuity.

Eventually the ceremonial center became secularized, transformed by the rising secular kings, who were sometimes installed by force. As the kingship's power grew, the ceremonial center's political power declined, although its religious functions were faithfully retained. In Mesopotamia, church and state separated when the power of the temple ruler, or *en*, was restricted to religious matters after 3000 B.C. The *lugal*, or king, assumed the secular and often the militaristic leadership of the state (Kramer, 1963).

We can detect secularization of the ceremonial center in the appearance of the palace, where the secular king resided. The king himself might enthusiastically believe in the state faith, but his functions were almost entirely secular, even if he used religion to justify his actions. He might assume a divine role himself. When the palace appears, we find the royal tombs standing as garish and splendid monuments to the awesome political and social power behind them.

SYSTEMS AND CIVILIZATIONS

Everyone seems to agree that urban life and civilization came into existence gradually, during a period of major social and economic change. The earlier linear explanations invoking irrigation, trade, or religion as a major integrative force are inadequate for our purposes.

Robert Adams has been a pioneer in looking at multiple causes of state formation. Back in 1966 he argued that irrigation agriculture, increased warfare, and "local resource variability" were three factors vital in newly appearing civilization (R. M. Adams, 1966). Each of these affected society and each other with positive feedback, helping them reinforce each other. The creation of food surpluses and the emergence of a stratified society were critical developments. Irrigation agriculture and more intensive horticulture could feed a bigger population. Larger populations and increased sedentariness, as well as trade with regular centers for redistributing goods, were all pressures for greater production and increased surpluses, actively fostered by dominant groups in society. The greatly enlarged surpluses enabled those who controlled them to employ large numbers of craftsworkers and other specialists who did not themselves grow crops.

Adams develops his thesis further by arguing that some societies were better able to transform themselves into states because of the favorable variety of resources on which they were able to draw. Higher production and increased populations led to monopolies over strategic resources. These communities eventually were more powerful than their neighbors, expanding their territories by military campaigns and efficiently exploiting their advantages over other peoples. Such cities became the early centers of religious activities, technological and artistic innovations, and the development of writing (Figure 14.1).

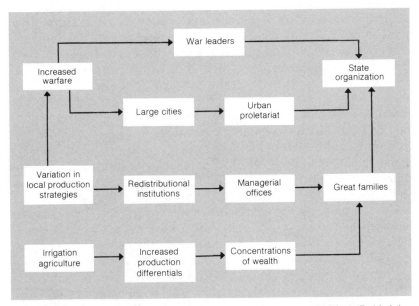

Figure 14.1 Hypothetical model of the state's beginnings, compiled from R. M. Adams, 1966. Compare with Figure 14.2.

Kent V. Flannery has a more complex and somewhat abstract scheme further explaining the state's origins (Flannery, 1972). He and others see the state as a very complicated living system, the complexity of which can theoretically be measured by the internal differentiation and specialization of its subsystems, such as those for agriculture, technology, religious beliefs, and so on. Vital are the ways in which these subsystems are linked, as well as the controls that society imposes on the system as a whole. Archaeologists who think this way make a fundamental distinction between:

> The *processes* of cultural change, the succession of changes by which the early states developed their new complexity.
>
> The *mechanisms,* the actual ways in which the processes of increasing complexity occurred.
>
> The socioenvironmental *stresses* that select for these mechanisms. Socioenvironmental stresses can include food shortages, warfare, and population growth, and are by no means common to all states.

"An explanation of the rise of the state then centers on the ways in which the processes . . . took place," writes Flannery.

A series of subsystems operate in human cultural systems, subsystems that interact with one another, just as the cultural system as a whole interacts with the natural environment. Each subsystem is regulated by a

control apparatus that keeps all the variables in a system within bounds so that the survival of the system as a whole is not threatened. This apparatus of social control is vital, for it balances subsistence needs with religious, political, social, and other ideological values. There is a well-defined hierarchy of regulation and policy, ranging from those under the control of individuals to institutions within society with specialized functions (such as acquiring the information necessary to regulate the system), on up to the basic, highest-order propositions, which are those of societal policy. These abstract standards of values lie at the heart of any society's regulation of its cultural system. It is not only crops and domesticated animals that make up the basis of a civilization; it is all sorts of subtle relationships and regulatory measures as well (see Figure 14.2 for an example from Mesopotamia).

The management and regulation of a state is a far more elaborate and centralized undertaking than that of a hunter-gatherer band or a small chiefdom. Indeed, the most striking difference between states and less complicated societies is the degree of complexity in their ways of reaching decisions and in their hierarchic organizations, not in their subsistence activities. Any living system is subjected to stress when one of the many variables exceeds the range of deviation that the system allows it. The stress may make the system evolve new institutions or policies. Such coping mechanisms may be triggered by warfare, population pressure, trade, environmental change, or other variables. These variables create what Flannery calls an "adaptive milieu" for evolutionary change. His specific mechanisms include "promotion" and "linearization," when an

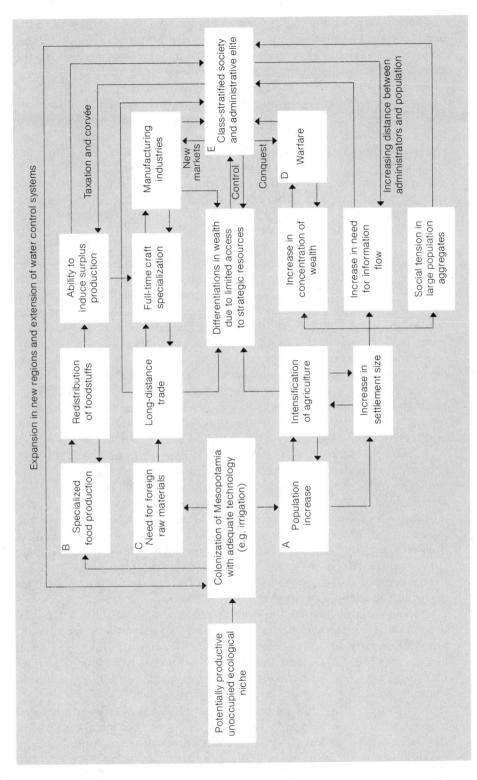

Figure 14.2 A systems diagram developed by Charles Redman, 1979, that shows the interrelationships between cultural and environmental variables that led to increased stratification of class structure in early Mesopotamian urban society.

institution in a society may assume new powers or some aspect of life may become too complex for a few people to administer. Both mechanisms lead to greater centralization, caused by selective pressures on the variables that produced the response (coping) mechanisms.

The ultimate objective of a systems analysis of how a civilization began could be the establishing of rules by which the origins of a complex state could be simulated, but such rules are a goal for the future. Flannery lists fifteen beginning rules that could affect the cultural evolution of a simple human population forming part of a regional ecosystem. The rules can lead to new models for understanding the cultural evolution of civilization. Such models are certain to be most complex. We now have to be specific about the links between subsystems — distinguishing between the mechanisms and processes and the socioenvironmental pressures which are peculiar to each civilization and have, until now, been the means by which we have sought to explain the origins of civilization (Redman, 1979). Religious and informational factors now appear to be key elements in the regulation of environmental and economic variables in early civilizations and, indeed, in any human society. Although Flannery's notions enjoy widespread acceptance, it should be pointed out that he has not defined what either his mechanisms or processes actually were. In other words, his model needs testing in the field.

Testing such a multicausal model is a difficult task. It involves not only developing rigorous methodologies for identifying the variables in the archaeological record but also comparative studies of these variables in regions where civilizations emerged and where they did not. Moreover, one also has to study societies that flourished immediately before the emergence of civilization.

William Sanders and David Webster (1978) point out that Flannery's approach relies heavily on cultural evolution and invokes a variety of universal processes that affected the formation of complex societies (see also Binford, 1983). They argue that it is paradoxical to try to explain variability within human cultures by using universal, evolutionary approaches that are, in themselves, ever-changing. The one component of this scheme that does vary is that of environmental stimuli. In his classic study of the civilizations in the Basin of Mexico, Sanders shows how the Aztecs created and organized great agricultural systems, huge acreages of swamp gardens that spread over the shallow waters of the Basin's lakes. The variability of the Basin environment meant that the Aztecs had to exploit every environmental opportunity afforded them; as a result, the state organized large-scale agriculture. By the time of the Spanish Conquest (1519–1521), their agricultural systems were supporting a population of up to 250,000 people just in the Aztec capital, Tenochtitlán (Sanders et al., 1979).

Karl Butzer (1981) has pointed out that civilizations can be regarded as ecosystems that emerge in response to sets of ecological opportunities. Over time, a variety of social and environmental adjustments are inevitable, some of them successful, leading to population growth, and others unsuccessful, so that the population shrinks. These demographic adjustments are commonly associated with ups and downs of political power. The political structures of, say, Ancient Egyptian civilization are not nearly as durable as the basic adaptive system they purport to control or as the cultural identity of which they were once part. Butzer draws an analogy with the ecological concept of tropic levels among biotic communities, in which organisms with similar feeding habits, such as herbivores and carnivores, define successive tiers interlinked in a vertical chain. Likewise, he hypothesizes, an efficient social hierarchy comprises several trophic levels arranged in what he calls a "low-angle pyramid, supported by a broad base of farmers and linked to the peak of the pyramid by a middle-level bureaucracy. The vertical structures channel food and information through the system, and an efficient energy flow allows each trophic level to flourish in a steady state." In this model, a flatter pyramid with little vertical structure would provide less information flow and limit the potential productivity of the lower levels. Butzer's pyramid would allow growth at the lower levels, with new technologies or organizational devices favoring expanded energy generation at the lower level. A steep, top-heavy pyramid laden with nobles and bureaucrats places excessive burdens on the lowest levels, so much so that external and internal forces can undermine the stability of society.

This model, when applied to the long history of Ancient Egyptian civilization, shows how the Egyptians persisted in adjusting to a floodplain environment for thousands of years. They overcame external and internal crises by reorganizing their state and economic structure. The key variables were the fluctuations of the Nile itself, occasional foreign intervention, the character of the pharaohs' leadership, and a progressively more pathological society of elite nonproducers who persisted in exploiting the common farmer, a process that led to eventual social collapse. However, through all these variables the essential components of the sociopolitical system survived more or less intact, right up to the nineteenth century A.D. Indeed, the visitor to rural Egypt still can see farming villages functioning much as they did in Ancient Egyptian times.

GUIDE TO FURTHER READING

Adams, Robert M. *The Evolution of Urban Society.* Chicago: Aldine, 1966.
    An essay on the origins of civilization that stresses social and economic change, based on the author's fieldwork in Mesopotamia and comparative data from the New World.

Childe, V. G. *Man Makes Himself.* London: Watts, 1936.
    Perhaps the classic exposition of the revolution theory of civilization by a master at eloquent writing. Outdated but seminal.

Flannery, Kent V. "The Cultural Evolution of Civilizations." Palo Alto: *Annual Review of Ecology and Systematics,* 1972. Pp. 326–399.

A masterly summary of the systems approach to early civilization that demonstrates the complexities of explaining the past.

Frankfort, Henri. *The Birth of Civilization in the Near East.* Bloomington: Indiana University Press, 1951.
An often forgotten essay on early civilization that makes the critical point that every complex society has its own distinctive adaptation. Still worth reading for its basic philosophy.

Redman, Charles L. *The Rise of Civilization.* San Francisco: Freeman, 1979.
This book covers all the theories about the origins of civilization and the key sites and concepts for the advanced student. Strongly recommended as a follow-up to this volume.

Sanders, W. T., Parsons, Jeffrey R., and Santley, Robert S. *The Basin of Mexico: Ecological Processes in the Evolution of a Civilization.* New York: Academic Press, 1979.
This is an exemplary area study of highland Mesoamerican civilization that is crammed with wisdoms about the study of complex societies. It is also an unusually thorough archaeological study. Technical, but strongly recommended.

Chronological Table I

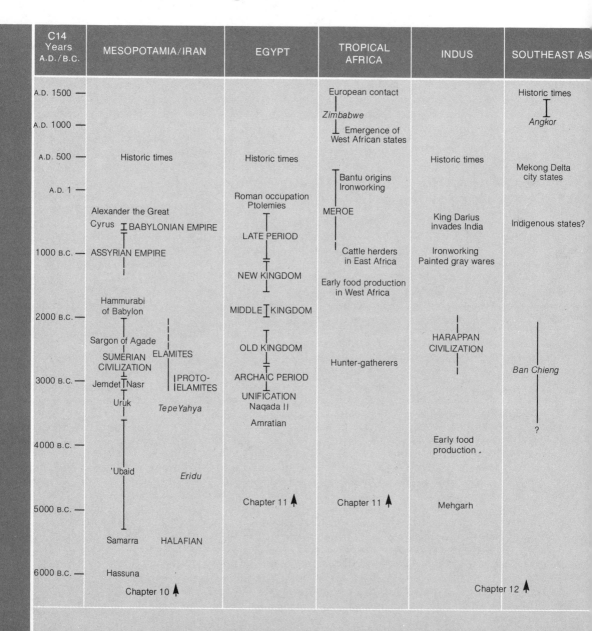

C14 Years A.D./B.C.	MESOPOTAMIA/IRAN	EGYPT	TROPICAL AFRICA	INDUS	SOUTHEAST AS
A.D. 1500 —			European contact		Historic times
A.D. 1000 —			*Zimbabwe* Emergence of West African states		*Angkor*
A.D. 500 —	Historic times	Historic times		Historic times	Mekong Delta city states
A.D. 1 —		Roman occupation Ptolemies	Bantu origins Ironworking		
	Alexander the Great Cyrus BABYLONIAN EMPIRE		MEROE	King Darius invades India	Indigenous states?
1000 B.C. —	ASSYRIAN EMPIRE	LATE PERIOD	Cattle herders in East Africa	Ironworking Painted gray wares	
		NEW KINGDOM	Early food production in West Africa		
2000 B.C. —	Hammurabi of Babylon	MIDDLE KINGDOM		HARAPPAN CIVILIZATION	
	Sargon of Agade SUMERIAN CIVILIZATION ELAMITES	OLD KINGDOM	Hunter-gatherers		
3000 B.C. —	Jemdet Nasr PROTO-IELAMITES Uruk *Tepe Yahya*	ARCHAIC PERIOD UNIFICATION Naqada II Amratian			*Ban Chieng*
4000 B.C. —				Early food production.	?
	'Ubaid *Eridu*				
5000 B.C. —		Chapter 11 ⬆	Chapter 11 ⬆	Mehgarh	
	Samarra HALAFIAN				
6000 B.C. —	Hassuna				
	Chapter 10 ⬆			Chapter 12 ⬆	

Chapter Fifteen

Mesopotamia and the First Cities

PREVIEW

❉ Approximately 6000 B.C. highland peoples began to settle in northern Mesopotamia in areas where agriculture was possible using seasonal rainfall. These Hassuna people lived in close contact with other societies downstream that developed irrigation agriculture.

❉ Approximately 5500 B.C. Halafian painted wares appeared over a wide area of northern Mesopotamia and Anatolia; they are thought to coincide with the emergence of chiefdoms in this area. Two hundred years later the first farmers settled in the Mesopotamian delta.

❉ The Mesopotamian delta, home of the world's first literate civilization, is uncultivable without some form of irrigation agriculture.

❉ A rapid evolution toward urban life ensued — marked by rapid growth of population, the congregation of people in cities, the development of long-distance trade, the prospering of metallurgy, and the establishment of a literature civilization based on the comparatively recent invention of writing.

❉ The Sumerian civilization was in full swing by 2900 B.C. and depended heavily on trading with areas outside Mesopotamia. Its relationships with Proto-Elamites living in Khuzistan to the east were of critical importance. Approximately 3000 B.C. the Proto-Elamites gained some degree of control over major trading centers on the Iranian plateau, centers that supplied obsidian, chlorite vessels, and other commodities and luxuries to Sumer.

❉ Sumerian civilization flourished until approximately 2000 B.C. when it was eclipsed by Babylonian power. In the late second millennium, the city of Assur in the north nurtured the Assyrian Empire, which was extended by vigorous and despotic kings during the first half of the succeeding millennium. The Assyrian Empire at one time stretched from the Mediterranean to the Persian Gulf.

❉ The Assyrian Empire fell in 612 B.C. and the power vacuum was filled by the Babylonians under the rule of Nebuchadnezzar. Babylon fell to Cyrus of Persia in 534 B.C. and Mesopotamia became part of the Persian Empire.

The delta regions and floodplain between the Tigris and Euphrates rivers form a hot, low-lying environment, much of it inhospitable sand, swamp, and dry mud flats. Yet this region, Mesopotamia (Greek for "land between the rivers"), was the cradle of the world's earliest urban civilization (Fagan, 1979; Lloyd, 1980). From north to south, Mesopotamia is approximately 600 mi (965 km) long and 250 mi (402 km) wide. (Figure 15.1 shows its location.) The plains are subject to long, intensely hot summers and harsh, cold winters. Before 5500 B.C. the floodplain was uninhabited except for a few nomadic groups. Dry agriculture, which relied on seasonal rainfall, was totally impracticable, and the plants and animals of the highlands around Mesopotamia were unable to tolerate the climatic extremes of the delta.

There are few permanent water supplies away from the great rivers and their tributaries. However, once watered, the soils of Mesopotamia proved both fertile and potentially highly productive. The agricultural

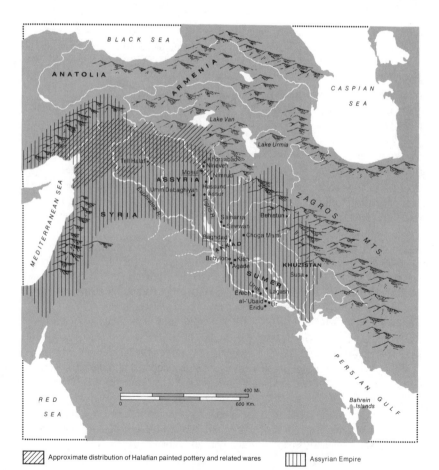

Figure 15.1 Sites and culture distributions mentioned in this chapter. (Tepe Yahya and Shar-i-shokhta lie to the east of the map.)

potential of the areas close to rivers and streams could be realized for the first time. By 5000 B.C. village farmers had settled on the delta and were diverting the waters of the rivers. Within 2000 years the urban civilization of the Sumerians was flourishing in Mesopotamia.

THE FIRST CITIES

With the continued improvement in the effectiveness of agriculture and the development of such technological innovations as pottery, the village communities of the Zagros foothills, east of Mesopotamia, achieved a more efficient subsistence base, which fed a gradually increasing farming population. These technological and economic changes were far from spectacular: sometime in the sixth millennium B.C., the highland people moved out onto the Assyrian plains, at first into areas where they could rely on seasonal rainfall to water their crops; later they settled by the rivers, with animals and crops that could tolerate the climate of the lowlands. There they developed simple irrigation methods to bring water to their crops.

The first farmers to settle in Assyria lived in areas where rainfall would water their crops. They were scattered over the undulating plains in small village settlements like Umm Dabaghiyah (Kirkbride, 1975; Lloyd, 1983; Oates and Oates, 1976; Redman, 1979) that contained a few huts and storage bins made of packed mud. Commonly the houses, which were probably entered from the roof, consisted of two or three rooms with small doors. Ovens and chimneys were an integral part of the houses. The successive occupation layers of these sites are filled with pottery handmade of coarse clay and painted or incised with dots, circles, and other designs (Figure 15.2). Such wares — named Hassunan pottery, after Hassuna, the first village of this type excavated — are found over a wide area of the north, from the upper Tigris Valley to the plains west of the modern city of Mosul.

Hassuna
6000 B.C.

The regions between Mosul in the north and Baghdad in the south were inhabited by irrigation farmers by at least the middle of the sixth millennium B.C. We know this from discoveries of villages in the region of Samarra, on the fringes of the Mesopotamian delta. Samarran culture painted pottery (Figure 15.2), which comes from such sites as Tell es-Sawwan and Choga Mami, reveals early farming villages situated in areas where irrigation agriculture was the only viable means of food production (Oates, 1973). The Samarran sites near Choga Mami are situated along low ridges parallel to nearby hills, located where irrigation could be practiced with the least effort. Traces of canals are found at Choga Mami, as are wheat, barley, and linseed, a crop that can be grown in this area only when irrigation is used. Choga Mami itself lies between two rivers where floodwaters could be diverted across the fields and then drained away to prevent salt buildup. This is a relatively easy form of irrigation, one that was easy to adopt. Presumably, later refinements in

Samarra
5500 B.C.

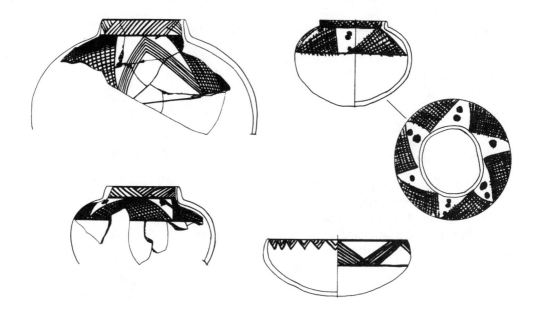

Figure 15.2 Early Mesopotamian painted pottery: above, vessels from Hassuna; below, Samarra-type vessels from Hassuna.

irrigation technology enabled other farming settlements to move away from naturally flooded areas into regions where more extensive irrigation was necessary. There is every indication that the Samarrans were advanced farmers who lived in substantial villages which, in the case of Choga Mami, may have covered up to 6 hectares and housed more than 1000 souls. The other excavated Samarran village, Tell es-Sawwan, was surrounded by a ditch and a wall, as if defense was a major consideration.

The Samarrans occupied relatively low-lying territory between the arid delta of the south and the dry-agriculture areas of the Hassunans to the north. Their newly developed irrigation techniques and heat-tolerant strains of wheat and barley enabled them to settle in areas that were hitherto inaccessible. Their sedentary and permanent settlements and great reliance on agriculture enabled them to forge community and external social and economic bonds that provided a catalyst for more complex societies to develop in future millennia.

Approximately 5500 B.C. many village farmers in the Near East began to make a characteristic style of painted pottery, abandoning the monochrome wares they had made before. The new fashion spread from southwestern Turkey around the shores of Lake Van, famous for its obsidian, and as far east as the Zagros Mountains. The most brilliantly painted pottery was made in northern Iraq by the inhabitants of Tell Halaf (Figure 15.3), whose enormous kilns produced bowls, dishes, and flasks adorned with elaborate, stylized patterns and representations of people and animals. The Halafian cultural tradition flourished in what had once been Hassunan territory, and the people maintained regular contact with the Samarrans to the south (see Figure 15.1).

Halafian
5500 B.C.

The Halafians still lived in much the same way as their predecessors and made no startling agricultural or technological innovations, but they

Figure 15.3 Halafian vessel from Iraq.

developed new, far-flung contacts between villages hundreds of miles apart, trading such commodities as obsidian, semiprecious stones, and other luxury items. Their pottery is remarkably similar from one end of Halafian territory to the other, so much so that continuous and effective interaction over wide areas must have taken place. It has been suggested that this was the result of a major change in social organization, whereby tribal villages of earlier times were now linked under chiefdoms. As with the Hopewell in North America, these new elite groups required greater communication and the sharing of status goods such as painted pottery to reinforce their authority (Redman, 1979).

5300 B.C. Approximately 5300 B.C. the first farmers to settle in the delta of the south moved onto the floodplains. They settled on river banks, where they could obtain water without digging huge ditches or carrying it long distances. At first the farmers do not seem to have done much more than clear out natural, clogged channels, occasionally digging small feeder canals for gardens already sited to take advantage of natural drainage. These simple irrigation works made it possible to grow vegetables in addition to cereal crops. Cattle probably were penned in lush pastures, conceivably on a communal basis. The abundant fish and waterfowl were important dietary supplements. Fruit of the date palm may have been a vital staple.

We do not know anything about how the first inhabitants of the Mesopotamian delta acquired or developed the skills needed to survive in their harsh environment. Mutual interdependence among members of the community was essential, because raw materials suitable for building houses had to be improvised from the plentiful sand, clay, palm trees, and reeds between the rivers. Digging even the smallest canal required at least a little political and social leadership to coordinate the activity. The annual backbreaking task of clearing silt from clogged river courses and canals can have been achieved only by communal effort. As both R. M. Adams (1966) and Flannery (1972) point out, the relationship between developing a stratified society and creating food surpluses was close. Distinctive social changes came from the more efficient systems for producing food that were essential in the delta. As food surpluses developed

**'Ubaid period
5300 to 3600 B.C.** and the specialized agricultural economies of these 'Ubaid villages grew successful, the trend toward sedentary settlement and higher population densities increased. Expanded trade networks and the redistribution of surpluses and trade goods also affected society, with dominant groups of 'Ubaid people becoming more active in producing surpluses, which eventually supported more and more people who were not farmers. The

al-'Ubaid village of al-'Ubaid itself was built on a low mound, and consisted of huts of mud brick and reeds, sometimes with roofs formed from bent sticks (R. M. Adams, 1981; R. M. Adams and Nissen, 1972; Redman, 1979). The al-'Ubaid people relied on hunting and fishing as well as cereal crops, reaping their grain with sickles of clay, sometimes fitted with flint blades. Goats, sheep, and some cattle were herded on the floodplain.

al-'Ubaid and similar small hamlets were clustered in groups, many with their own small ceremonial center. The villages were linked by kinship and clan, with one clan authority overseeing the villagers' affairs and, probably, the irrigation schemes that connected them. In time the small village ceremonial centers grew, as did the one at Eridu (first settled around 4750 B.C., when the Tell Halaf people were still making their painted pottery in the north).

Eridu consisted of a mud-brick temple with fairly substantial mud-brick houses around it, often with a rectangular floor plan. The craftsworkers lived a short distance from the elite clustered around the temple, and still farther away were the dwellings of the farmers who grew the crops that supported everyone. By 3500 B.C. the Eridu temple had grown large, containing altars and offering places and a central room bounded by rows of smaller compartments. It has been estimated that the population of Eridu was as high as 5000 at this time, but exact computations are impossible.

'Ubaid society was fully developed by 4350 B.C.; its institutions and material culture are found all over Mesopotamia. At every sizable 'Ubaid settlement the temple dominated the inhabitants' houses.

As Mesopotamian society grew in complexity, so too did the need for social, political, and religious institutions that would provide an integrative function for everyone. The settlement of Uruk epitomizes cultural developments just before Sumerian civilization began. Anyone approaching Uruk could see the great ziggurat, the stepped temple pyramid, for miles (Figure 15.4). Built with enormous expenditure of work as a community project, the ziggurat and its satellite temples were the center of Uruk life. The temples were not only storehouses and places of worship; they were also redistribution centers for surplus food. Hundreds of craftsworkers labored for the temple as stone masons, copperworkers, weavers, and at dozens of other specialized tasks. None of these people tilled the ground or worked on irrigation; they formed a distinctive class in a well-stratified society (Lloyd, 1978).

The entire life of Uruk and its connections with cities, towns, merchants, and mines hundreds of miles away revolved around the temple. The ruler of Uruk and the keeper of the temple was the *en*, both secular and religious leader of Uruk. His wishes and policies were carried out by his priests and by a complex hierarchy of bureaucrats, wealthy landowners, and merchants. Tradesmen and craftsworkers were a more lowly segment of society, and under them were the thousands of fishers, peasants, sailors, and slaves that formed the bulk of Uruk's burgeoning population.

In its heyday, approximately 2800 B.C., Uruk was far more than a city. Satellite villages extended out for at least 6 mi (10 km), each with its own irrigation system. All provided food for those in the city, whether grain, fish, or meat. Each settlement depended on the others for survival, at first because each provided things essential for a well-balanced existence; later they needed each other for protection from outsiders who would have plundered their goods. The Mesopotamian city had devel-

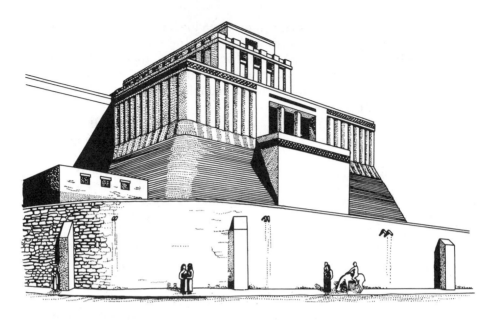

Figure 15.4 Reconstruction of an Uruk temple at Eridu. Notice the great platform supporting the temple and the drainage pipes in the walls. Below is a photograph of the great ziggurat (temple mound) of Ur, built approximately 2100 B.C.

oped an elaborate system of management with a well-defined hierarchy of rulers and priests, landowners and bureaucrats, traders and peasants. This system organized and regulated society, meted out reward and punishment, and made policy decisions for the thousands of people who lived under it.

By 3400 B.C., the Sumerians' commercial transactions were so complex that the possibilities for thievery and accounting mistakes were endless. It was not possible to keep all the details in one's head. Many people used marked clay tokens which they carried around on strings. Eventually some clever officials made small clay tablets and scratched them with incised signs that depicted familiar objects such as pots or animals (Schmandt-Besserat, 1978). From there it was a short step to more simplified, conventionalized, wedge-shaped (cuneiform) signs that were modeled closer and closer to phonetic syllables and spoken language (Figure 15.5). Now trade could expand, unfettered by the limitations of the human memory. At first, specially trained scribes used cuneiform to record inventories and commercial transactions. Soon they began to explore the limitless opportunities afforded by the ability to express oneself in writing. Kings used tablets to trumpet their victories and political triumphs. Fathers chided errant sons, and lawyers recorded complicated land transactions. Sumerian poetry includes love stories, great epics, hymns to the gods, and tragic laments bemoaning the destruction of city after city (Kramer, 1963). Temple records and accounts tell us much not only of economic and social organization, but also of Mesopotamian folklore and religion.

On the plateau to the north, copper tools and ornaments had been in use for centuries, first appearing as early as the fifth or sixth millennium B.C. Copper was intensively used in Iran during the fourth millennium and was imported into the delta areas of Mesopotamia as early as 3500 B.C., probably earlier. It came into widespread use in the Jemdet Nasr period. Although many peasant societies were aware of the properties of native copper, and both the early Egyptians and the American Indians made hammered copper ornaments from it, the softness of the metal limited the uses to which it could be put. Eventually, though, people familiar with kiln firing of pottery developed techniques for smelting copper ore. Copper is fine and lustrous and makes admirable ornaments. Its economic advantages (in terms of sharp cutting edges) were less obvious, until metalsmiths learned to alloy copper with tin or arsenic to produce bronze and other forms of tougher copper. Once alloying was understood, copper assumed a more important place in agriculture and warfare.

Jemdet Nasr period
3100 to 2900 B.C.

By 3000 B.C., copper specialists had begun to work in most Mesopotamian cities, smelting and casting weapons and ornaments of high quality. Some cities attempted to maintain a monopoly on copper weapons and tools by training specialist craftsworkers and controlling trade in ingots and artifacts. The later development of bronze weapons can be linked to the rise of warfare as a method of attaining political ends, for cities such

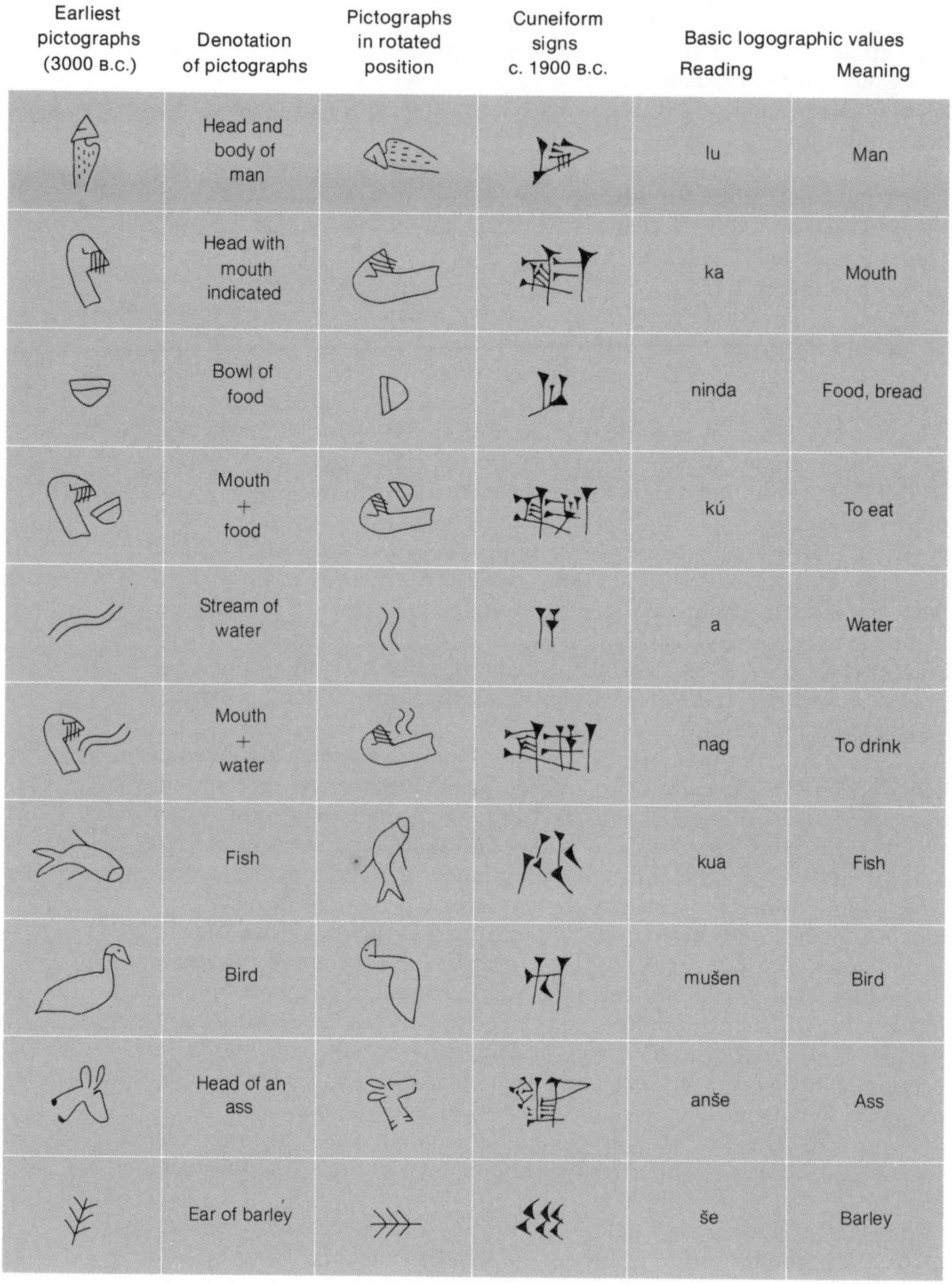

Earliest pictographs (3000 B.C.)	Denotation of pictographs	Pictographs in rotated position	Cuneiform signs c. 1900 B.C.	Basic logographic values	
				Reading	Meaning
	Head and body of man			lu	Man
	Head with mouth indicated			ka	Mouth
	Bowl of food			ninda	Food, bread
	Mouth + food			kú	To eat
	Stream of water			a	Water
	Mouth + water			nag	To drink
	Fish			kua	Fish
	Bird			mušen	Bird
	Head of an ass			anše	Ass
	Ear of barley			še	Barley

Figure 15.5 The development of Sumerian writing, from a pictographic script to a cuneiform script, and then to a phonetic system. The word "cuneiform" is derived from the Latin word *cuneus*, meaning "a wedge," after the characteristic impression of the script.

as Eridu and Uruk were not isolated from other centers. Indeed, they were only too aware of them. Ur of the Chaldees, a city much smaller than Uruk, was only 75 mi (120 km) away. The two were rivals for centuries, constantly bickering, competing in trading, and fighting with each other. Cities soon had walls, a sure sign that they needed protection against marauders. All the elements that made up Sumerian civilization were now in place.

SUMERIAN CIVILIZATION AND TRADE

By 2900 B.C., Sumerian civilization was in full swing in the southern delta. Archaeologically this is reflected in increased wealth (Kramer, 1963). Metal tools became much more common and domestic tools as well as weapons proliferated. Technologically, they were far in advance of earlier tools. Smiths began to alloy copper with tin to produce bronze: Armies and farmers were equipped with wheeled chariots and wagons. With a shift in political power from priests to kings, Mesopotamian rulers became more despotic, concentrating the wealth of the state and controlling subjects by military strength, religious acumen, and taxation, as well as economic incentive.

Sumerian civilization c. 2900 to 2000 B.C.

The cities' power depended in part on intensive agriculture, which irrigation and fertile Mesopotamian soils had so encouraged that rural populations increased sharply. The plow, which depended on draft oxen trained to pull it through the soil for a deeper furrow, was invented and increased agricultural yield. Plows were not used in the New World, where draft animals were not domesticated, and the rice farmers of Asia did not have much use for such a tool either, but it did permit higher yields of cereal crops and supported larger urban and rural populations in the Old World.

Trading was an integral part of Sumerian life, a many-faceted operation absorbing the energies of many people. The redistribution systems of the cities combined many activities, all controlled by the centralized authority that ruled the settlements. Food surpluses were redistributed and raw materials were obtained from far away for the manufacture of ornaments, weapons, and prestigious luxuries. We have every reason to believe that specialist merchants handled commodities such as copper. If later historical records are any guide, there was wholesaling and contracting, loans were floated, and individual profit may have been a prime motivation.

Demands for raw materials appear to have risen steadily, spreading market networks into territories remote from the home state. For these long-distance routes to succeed, political stability at both ends of the route was essential. An intricate system of political, financial, and logistical checks and balances had to be maintained, requiring an efficient and alert administrative oganization to keep the pieces of the puzzle in place.

The raw materials traded by the Sumerians included metals, timber, skins, ivory, and precious stones such as malachite. Many could be found only in the remote highlands to the north and east of Mesopotamia and were traded in bulk from the late third millennium onward. Wheeled vehicles and boats became vital in trade and warfare. Horses, asses, and oxen were put to drawing heavy loads.

Flourishing trade routes expanded along the delta waterways, especially up the placid Euphrates, which was easily navigable for long distances. This great river, whose ancient name *Uruttu* meant "copper," transmitted raw materials from the north and trade goods from the Persian Gulf to the Mediterranean. Well before 3000 B.C., the Euphrates joined together many scattered towns, transmitting to all the products of Sumerian craftsworkers and a modicum of cultural unity.

Mesopotamia lacked the mineral and stone resources that were plentiful on the Iranian plateau to the east and in Anatolia. The Sumerians and their successors obtained them by trading their food surpluses in the form of grain, dried fish, textiles, and other perishable goods for basic raw materials. This capacity to produce surpluses was vital to Mesopotamian trading activities, for on the surpluses depended the viability of long-distance commerce. This dependence on long-distance trading made the Mesopotamians both vulnerable to, and dependent on, the activities of their neighbors and even peoples living at a considerable distance from their own homeland (Kohl, 1978).

THE PROTO-ELAMITES

While early farmers were settling the inhospitable Mesopotamian delta, other peoples were beginning to cultivate the area between the Zagros foothills and the Tigris and Euphrates (Lamberg-Karlovsky, 1978; H. Wright and Johnson, 1975). During the sixth and early fifth millennia B.C., small farming villages flourished in the heart of Khuzistan. The people were irrigation farmers who herded goats, sheep, and cattle as well. So many of their sites are known that it seems certain that areas such as the Deh Luran plain were intensively settled by this time. During the next thousand years or so, Khuzistan was still densely settled and village settlements grew larger and larger. It was about this time that the famous archaeological site of Susa began to achieve special prominence.

The earliest occupation levels at Susa are broadly contemporary with the late 'Ubaid occupation of Mesopotamia. The first village on the site was approximately 25 to30 hectares in area and was inhabited by metal-using farmers. Strong Mesopotamian influence can be detected in slightly later levels at Susa, as if there was at least some colonization of Khuzistan by Uruk people from the delta toward the end of the fourth millennium.

Approximately 3200 B.C., a distinctive cultural tradition known as the *Proto-Elamite* (Elamite is a language) appears at Susa and elsewhere in

6000 B.C.

Susa

Proto-Elamites
3200 B.C.

Khuzistan. The Proto-Elamite state seems to have evolved in what is now southwestern Iran, but within a short time its distinctive tablets, seals, and ceramic types are found on widely scattered sites on the Iranian highlands. Their clay tablets have been found on settlements in every corner of the Iranian plateau, in central Iran, and on the borders of Afghanistan.

The Proto-Elamite expansion took place over a very short time and appears to be connected with a desire of these people to control both key trade routes on the Iranian plateau and access to sources of key materials.

The most thoroughly excavated site on the plateau is Tepe Yahya, which was a prosperous rural community between 3400 and 3200 B.C. (Lamberg-Karlovsky, 1973, 1978). The inhabitants were already importing such raw materials as obsidian and chlorite (steatite). After 3200 B.C. Tepe Yahya grew in size and was engaged in much more intensive trading activities. It is at this period that Proto-Elamite artifacts are found in the site, which seems to have served as a political center that coordinated trade by surrounding settlements. The Tepe Yahya area was a center of chlorite bowl production, for abundant deposits of this raw material are found nearby. The bowls produced at Tepe Yahya and elsewhere were definitely luxury items, so highly prized in Mesopotamia that they may have caused keen competition among those rich enough to be able to afford them (Kohl, 1975). Chlorite tools and ornaments were so popular that they occur over a very wide area of the Iranian plateau as well as on islands in the Persian Gulf, and at Moenjodaro, one of the major cities of the Harappan civilization of the Indus valley (Chapter Sixteen).

The plateau trading networks also extended onto the Susiana Plain, south of the Hindu Kush, where a multitude of river valleys lead south to the Indus floodplain. The village of Shar-i-Shokhta stood by the banks of Lake Helmand in eastern Iran, a small community of mud-brick houses. Traders brought fragments of lapis lazuli embedded in limestone from the distant Hindu Kush to Shar-i-Shokhta. There artisans chipped away the limestone and turned the semiprecious stone into beads. The beads, and lumps of raw lapis, were then traded across the desert to Mesopotamia and also north into southern Turkmenia, probably in exchange for grain, a valued commodity in this dry area (Hammond, 1973).

The chlorite vessels produced near Tepe Yahya were made by local artisans perhaps working part-time or at certain seasons of the year, but the trade itself seems to have been managed by the Proto-Elamites, people who acted as middle agents in the long-distance trade between Mesopotamia and the distant plateau. In a sense the Sumerians controlled the long-distance trade through the laws of supply and demand. Their needs resulted in a degree of economic control of foreign areas without actual political control. The Proto-Elamites, however, seem to have recognized a political and economic opportunity which stemmed from their strategic position between Mesopotamia and Iran, and so they expanded their sphere of interest onto the plateau. Their efforts at controlling trade and raw materials do not seem to have lasted very long. Perhaps their administrative and political system became overtaxed by the new demands made on it. Conceivably the benefits of political control did not justify the effort in terms of trade generated. In any event, Proto-Elamite artifacts vanish from the archaeological record within a few centuries.

Elamites
3000 B.C.

Even if the Proto-Elamites failed in their bid to control trade on the plateau, they certainly continued to flourish in Khuzistan. Susa itself grew into a great city, where the trade routes between Mesopotamia and the East converged. The Elamite state emerged in all its complexity after 3000 B.C. and came under the domination of Akkadian kings from central Mesopotamia for a while, but by 2000 B.C. the Elamites were strong enough to attack and destroy Ur of the Chaldees in Sumer. Their power and importance depended on their geographical position at the center of a network of trade routes that led to the Iranian plateau, to the Persian Gulf, and to most city-states in the lowlands. Elamite history shows us how no great civilization can be considered in isolation, for no complex society flourishes without depending on political and economic factors outside its boundaries. In the case of the Sumerians and Elamites, as well as the many communities living on the Iranian plateau, interdependencies developed that linked lowlands and highlands in lasting ways (Kohl, 1978).

THE WIDENING OF POLITICAL AUTHORITY

2800 B.C.

In the early third millennium B.C., Mesopotamia held several important city-states, each headed by rulers who vied with the others for status and prestige. Political authority was most effective at the city level, with the temple priests as the primary authority for controlling trade, economic life, and political matters. Inevitably, as society became more complex the priests were increasingly concerned with secular matters such as the organization of irrigation systems that expanded as population densities rose and more and more prime agricultural land was taken under cultivation. As the Mesopotamian delta became an increasingly artificial environment controlled by human activities, the people began to concentrate in larger cities under secular leaders, abandoning many smaller towns. The motive for this shift was as much defense as population increase, for both Sumerian inscriptions and the archaeological record tell of warfare and constant quarreling between neighbors. Competition over natural resources intensified as each state raised an army to defend its water rights, trade routes, and city walls. The onerous tasks of defense and military organization passed to despotic secular kings supposedly appointed by the gods. As the wealth and power of the cities increased, so did internecine strife. Such states as Erech, Kish, and Ur of the Chaldees had periods of political strength and prosperity when they dominated their neighbors. Then, just as swiftly, the tide of their fortunes would change and they would sink into obscurity. Then there were the nomadic peoples of the surrounding mountains and deserts, who encroached constantly on settled Sumerian lands. At times, peoples such as the Gutians disrupted city life so completely that any form of travel became an impossibility.

Some Sumerian cities nurtured powerful and wealthy leaders. When Sir Leonard Woolley (1934) excavated a royal cemetery in Sumerian Ur of the Chaldees (Figure 15.6), he found a series of kings and queens who had been buried in huge graves accompanied by their entire retinue of followers. One tomb contained the remains of fifty-nine people who were slaughtered to accompany the king, even courtiers and soldiers, as well as serving women. Each wore his or her official dress and insignia, and had lain down to die in their correct order of precedence, having taken poison. Some archaeologists believe that these are not royal graves but the result of a macabre fertility ceremony (Lloyd, 1978).

The first Sumerian ruler to have ambitions wider than merely controlling a few city-states was Lugalzagesi (approximately 2360–2335 B.C.). Not content with control of Uruk, Ur, Lagash, and several other cities, he boasted of overseeing the entire area from the Persian Gulf to the Mediterranean. The god Enlil, king of the lands, "made the people lie down in peaceful pastures like cattle and supplied Sumer with water bringing joyful abundance" (Kramer, 1963). Sumerian contacts with the outside world should not be judged in terms of conquering armies, but in the context of their constant trading, which was an integral part of their civilization. The people of Sumer traveled far and wide in search of raw materials and luxury imports. Life without trade was impossible. They carried their political and religious ideas with them as far as the shores of the Mediterranean and maintained at least tenuous contacts with dozens of city-states in the Near East. The Sumerians not only developed a civilization, but they also were the first people in human history to record their literature and beliefs in writing. They set down age-old legends of great floods and of warring gods that were to survive through the millennia to become part of the Old Testament and part of the cultural heritage of Western Civilization.

Lugalzagesi
2360 B.C.

THE ASSYRIANS

As Sumerian civilization prospered, urban centers also sprang up in northern Mesopotamia. Soon Assyrian cities began to compete with the delta city-states for trade and prestige. In approximately 2370 B.C., a Semitic-speaking leader, Sargon, founded a ruling dynasty at the town of Agade, south of Babylon. This northern house soon established its rule over Sumer and Assyria by military campaigns and skillful commercial ventures. After a short period of economic prosperity, the new kings were toppled by highland tribes from the north. Mesopotamia entered a

Sargon
2370 B.C.

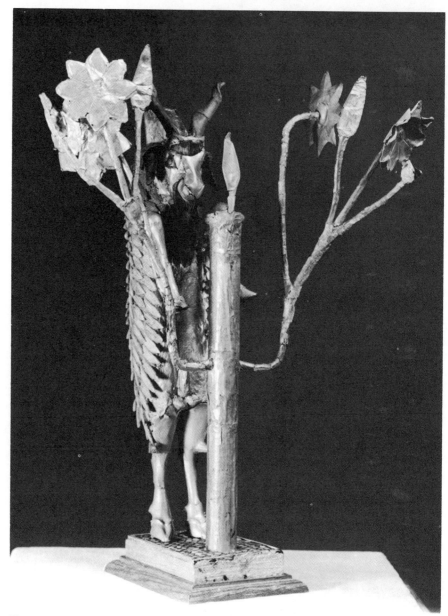

Figure 15.6 A famous ornament from the Royal Cemetery at Ur of the Chaldees, a goat in a tree. The wood figure was covered with gold leaf and lapis lazuli, the belly in silver leaf, and the fleece in shell.

time of political instability, but by 1990 B.C. the ancient city of Babylon was achieving prominence under Semitic rulers, culminating in the reign of the great king Hammurabi in 1790 B.C.

Babylon
1990 B.C.

Hammurabi set up a powerful commercial empire reaching out from Mesopotamia as far as Assyria and the Zagros. The unity of his empire depended on a common official language and a cuneiform writing system for its administration. Small city-states for the first time influenced world culture far more than their geographic territory appears to justify, an influence based on economic and political power maintained by despotic rule and harsh power politics. By this time, Mesopotamian influence was so great that weapon types used by Babylonian armies had spread to Russia, Europe, and the western Mediterranean.

Hammurabi
1790 B.C.

One of the cities of the north that flourished for a long time was Assur on the Tigris, the mounds of which contain the remains of Sumerian temples (Postgate, 1977). The merchants of Assur traded far to the east and west, as well as controlling the trade down the Tigris. Assur came into great prominence during the reign of King Assur-uballit I (1365 to 1330 B.C.), who incorporated the prime cereal-growing lands of northern Assyria into a new empire that his successors extended over a vast territory from the Mediterranean to Egypt, and as far as the Persian Gulf. Great military kings such as Shalmaneser, Assurnasirpal, Sargon, and Tiglath-Pileser were absolute despots, to whom warfare and prestige became veritable obsessions. When Assurnasirpal completed his palace at Nimrud he threw a party for the 16,000 inhabitants of the city, 1500 royal officials, "47,074 men and women from the length of my country," and 5000 foreign envoys (Postgate, 1977). The king fed this throng of more than 69,000 people for ten days, during which time his guests ate 14,000 sheep and consumed more than 10,000 skins of wine.

Assur

Assyrians
c. 1350 to 612 B.C.

The last of the great Assyrian kings was Assurbanipal, who died in approximately 630 B.C. When he died, the Assyrian Empire entered a period of political chaos. The Babylonians achieved independence, and Assyrian power finally was broken in 612 B.C. when Nineveh was sacked by the Persians and Babylonians. For forty-three years, the mighty Babylonian king Nebuchadnezzar ruled over Mesopotamia and turned his capital into one of the showpieces of the ancient world. His double-walled city was adorned with magnificent mud-brick palaces with elaborate hanging gardens, a great processional way, and a huge ziggurat. It was to Babylon that a large contingent of Jews were taken as captives after Nebuchadnezzar's armies sacked Jerusalem, an exile immortalized by the lament: "By the waters of Babylon we sat down and wept" (Psalms 137:1).

The Babylonian Empire did not long survive the death of Nebuchadnezzar in 556 B.C. His successors were weak men who were unable to resist the external forces that now pressed on Mesopotamia. The armies of Cyrus the Great of Persia took Babylon virtually without resistance in 534 B.C., and Mesopotamia became part of an empire even larger than that of the Assyrians. By this time, the effects of constant political in-

Cyrus
534 B.C.

stability and of bad agricultural management were beginning to make themselves felt. The Mesopotamian delta was a totally artificial environment by 2000 B.C., and poor drainage and badly maintained irrigation works in later centuries led to inexorable rises in the salt content of the soil and to drastic falls in crop yields. Nothing could be done to reverse this trend until modern soil science technology and irrigation techniques could be imported to the delta at vast expense.

GUIDE TO FURTHER READING

Fagan, Brian M. *Return to Babylon*. Boston: Little, Brown, 1979.
   A history of archaeological research in Mesopotamia that starts with the first Arab geographers and ends with modern excavations.

Kramer, Samuel. *The Sumerians*. Chicago: University of Chicago Press, 1963.
   The classic account of Sumerian civilization written by one of the foremost experts on Sumerian cuneiform tablets and literature. A model of what such books should be.

Lloyd, Seton. *The Archaeology of Mesopotamia*. London: Thames and Hudson, 2d ed., 1983.
   A synthesis of Iraqi archaeology that concentrates mainly on the early civilizations. Strong on archaeological data, well illustrated, and informative on architecture.

Oates, David, and Oates, Joan. *The Rise of Civilization*. Oxford: Elsevier, 1976.

Postgate, Nicholas. *The First Empires*. Oxford: Elsevier, 1977.
   Two volumes in the "Making of the Past" series that describe for the lay reader the cultures and civilizations discussed in this chapter in more detail than is possible here. Recommended for paper writers.

Chapter Sixteen

Pharaohs and
African Chiefs

PREVIEW

❉ By 3600 B.C., the average Egyptian probably lived much as people do today in some Upper Egyptian villages.

❉ These pre-Dynastic people lived at a time of gradual population growth and enrichment of the native culture, probably as a result of expanded trading contacts. The number of luxury goods increased, metallurgy was introduced from Mesopotamia, and social structure seems to have become more elaborate.

❉ The acquisition of writing by the Egyptians probably was one of the catalytic events that led to the unification of Egypt and the emergence of civilization there. The process of unification culminated under a legendary pharaoh named Menes approximately 3000 B.C.

❉ Ancient Egyptian civilization is divided into four main periods: the Old, Middle, New, and Late kingdoms, the earlier of which were separated by brief intermediate periods of political chaos.

❉ The Old Kingdom is notable for its despotic pharaohs and the frenzy of pyramid construction, an activity that may be connected with pragmatic notions of fostering national unity.

❉ The Middle Kingdom saw a shift of political and religious power to Thebes and Upper Egypt.

❉ New Kingdom pharaohs made Egypt an imperial power with strong interests in Asia and Nubia. These pharaohs were buried in the Valley of Kings near Thebes. The cult of Amun was all-powerful, except for a brief interlude when the heretic pharaoh Akhenaten introduced the worship of the sun god Aten.

❉ Ancient Egyptian civilization began to decline after 1100 B.C., and the Nile eventually came under the rule of the Assyrians, then the Persians, and finally the Greek pharaohs, the Ptolemies.

❉ Egypt had few contacts with sub-Saharan Africa, which was widely settled by tropical farmers approximately 2000 years ago. The spread of farming coincided with both the introduction of ironworking and the spread of the Bantu-speaking peoples from West Africa over much of east, central, and southern Africa.

- Indigenous African states developed on the southern fringes of the Sahara desert at the end of the first millennium A.D., owing their initial prosperity to the gold trade across the desert.

- The later prehistory of Africa is marked by continued contacts between Africans and societies living outside the continent. Complex states like that of the Karanga of southern Africa emerged in the last thousand years, several of them trading actively with foreign merchants and voyagers until Africa came into the purview of written history in recent times.

Chronological
Table I p. 74

By 3600 B.C., the average Egyptian probably lived much as Upper Nile villagers do today (David, 1975; Johnson, 1978; Ruffle, 1977). Wheat and barley were cultivated in riverside gardens and supplemented then by intensive gathering of wild vegetable foods. Cattle, goats, sheep, and pigs were herded. The meat from the herds was supplemented by the rich Nile game population and by fishing. These Amratian (or pre-Dynastic) people were the successors of the Badarians (Chapter Eleven) (Hoffman, 1979; Trigger, 1968). Amratians derive their name from the archaeological site in Upper Egypt, El Amra. Amratian settlements apparently had a material culture somewhat similar to that which flourished in earlier centuries on the same sites of the Nile floodplain (Figure 16.1). The human population of the valley was growing slowly and there was some cultural fusion and increased interaction between more closely spaced settlements. Pottery was still being made, but elegant stone vessels in alabaster and basalt also were used, probably shaped by specialist craftsworkers and traded widely through the valley. Amratian flintworkers created magnificent knives and daggers which also were prized possessions. A gradual enrichment of pre-Dynastic culture can be discerned over the centuries, an enrichment resulting in part from the introduction of copperworking from Asia. Soon metalworkers were making pins, flat axes, and daggers of the new material. The Amratians began to import copper from Sinai, while lead and sliver came from Asia. The proportion of luxury goods to functional goods rose steadily; one of the locally manufactured items was *faience,* a form of glass widely traded in prehistoric times. Amratian settlements slowly became larger, and social structure became more elaborate. The archaeological record contains some signs of social classes, in the form of graves of varying opulence.

Amratian
3600 B.C.

METALLURGY, WRITING, AND UNIFICATION

The increased volume of trade is reflected not only in the importation of copper, but in other exotic items found in pre-Dynastic sites. Many of them are of unmistakable west Asian or Mesopotamian origin. The Naqada site, for instance, yielded a cylinder seal of Mesopotamian form. Some of the late pre-Dynastic pottery is painted with dark red colors on a

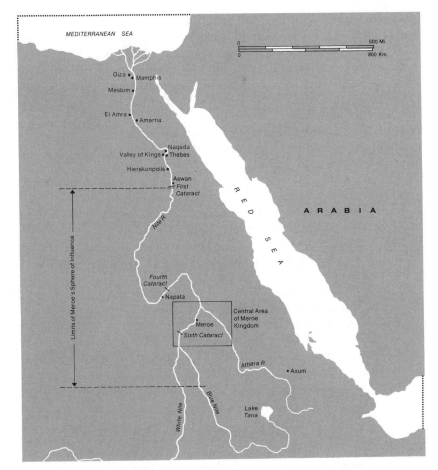

Figure 16.1 The Nile Valley.

buff background, in Asian style. There are depictions of Mesopotamian boat designs and of fabulous animals and creatures with intertwined necks and other motifs that derive from Asia.

The most important innovation of all, however, was the art of writing, which became fully developed in Egypt. Hieroglyphs (Greek for "sacred carving") are commonly thought to be a form of picture writing. In fact, they comprise a combination pictographic (picture) and phonetic (representing vocal sounds) script which was not only written on papyrus but also carved on public buildings or painted on clay or wood. It seems most likely that writing was first developed in Mesopotamia and that Egyptian priests developed their own script which was easier to produce with papyrus reed paper and ink rather than clay. Ultimately they developed a form of cursive (running on) hieroglyphic script that was a form of handwriting, much easier to use on documents and other less formal communications. Only the consonants were written in all forms of hieroglyphs;

the vowel sounds were omitted, although both were pronounced. With practice, reading this form of script is easy enough, and a smpl tst 'f ths srt shld shw ths qt wll (Figure 16.2) (Diringer, 1962; Pope, 1973).

The acquisition of writing, with all its organizational possibilities, probably was one of the main catalysts of the unification of the whole of Egypt into a single political entity. Unity was not imposed on Egypt from Asia, despite the increase in Asian influences in the material culture of the pre-Dynastic cultures. Rather, it was the culmination of local social and political developments that resulted from centuries of gradual change in economic and social life. Pre-Dynastic villages are autonomous units, each with its local deities. During the fourth millennium B.C., the more important villages became the focal points of different territories, which, in Dynastic times, became the *nomes,* or provinces, through which the pharaohs administered Egypt. The nomarchs (provincial leaders) were responsible for the gradual coalescence of Egypt into larger political and social units. Their deeds are recorded on ceremonial palettes that were used for moistening eye powder. Some of these palettes show alliances of local leaders dismantling conquered villages. Others commemorate the administrative skills of leaders who brought their villages through drought years by skillful management. The unification of Egypt was a gradual process of both voluntary and involuntary amalgamation. Voluntary unification resulted from common need and economic advantage. Perhaps it was only in the final stages of unification that military force came into play to bring larger and larger political units under single rulers (Hoffman, 1979).

The actual process of unification is poorly documented, although there is reason to believe that Upper Egypt was unified under Narmer (Menes) at Hierakonpolis in approximately 3100 B.C. In economic terms, the unification of Egypt may have involved some intensification of agriculture as population densities rose; but, as Karl Butzer has pointed out,

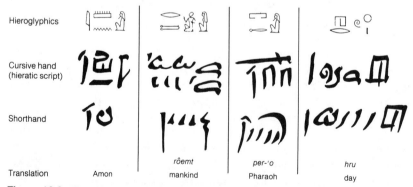

Hieroglyphics				
Cursive hand (hieratic script)				
Shorthand				
Translation	Amon	*rôemt* mankind	*per-'o* Pharaoh	*hru* day

Figure 16.2 Egyptian writing is referred to as hieroglyphs, the familiar symbols that appear on formal inscriptions and on tomb walls. In fact, Egyptian scribes developed cursive hands used in everyday life. These examples show formal hieroglyphic script (top line) and below it both the cursive style and the scribe's shorthand, which was used for rapid writing.

the technology for lifting water was so rudimentary that the early rulers of Egypt were unable to organize any elaborate forms of irrigation (Butzer, 1976). In all probability, most Ancient Egyptian agriculture involved irrigation schemes on a modest scale that merely extended the distribution of seasonal floodwaters from natural food basins. Still, even these efforts must have involved a considerable degree of administrative organization. Also, with a centralized form of administration, the divine leader, the pharaoh himself, was responsible for the success of the harvest. Since the Nile flood fluctuated considerably in cycles of abundant and lean years, and the pharaohs could do little to control the success or failure of irrigation without much more elaborate technology than they possessed, their political position could, theoretically at any rate, be threatened by famine years. If the divine leader could not provide, who could? Perhaps a different leader could. Small wonder that some periods of political instability, which may have coincided with poor flood years, saw rapid successions of ineffective pharaohs.

Karl Butzer (1981) argues that episodes of rapid growth in Ancient Egyptian civilization were made possible by a series of important innovations. One was improved irrigation organization in the Old Kingdom, after 2800 B.C. This made possible the development of the delta regions of Lower Egypt, once the bureaucratic structure to organize the work was in place. During the Middle Kingdom (1991–1786 B.C.), the pharaohs responded to several centuries of repeated low floods by placing closer government controls over food distribution, moving large numbers of people out of the valley into such areas as the Fayum Depression, where they organized huge drainage and irrigation works. The New Kingdom (1567–1085 B.C.) saw the introduction of the *shaduf*, a bucket-and-lever lifting device that raised water a meter or so from wells or ditches to water gardens and estates. One result of this innovation was a shift of population from the narrow valley to the broad delta. The culmination of agricultural productivity came in the last few centuries B.C. when the last pharaohs undertook the complete drainage of the Fayum, introduced summer crops such as sorghum, and encouraged the development of the animal-drawn waterwheel, known as the *saqiya*. The impact of all these innovations was to increase both the productivity of the state and the size of the labor force. It is probable that the population of Ancient Egypt rose from less than a million in 3000 B.C. to approximately 5 million in the second century B.C. These innovations were to continue to support Egyptian agriculture right up to the building of the High Dam at Aswan in the twentieth century A.D. (Fedden, 1977).

PYRAMIDS AND THE OLD KINGDOM:
3100 to 2181 B.C.

Egyptologists conventionally divide Ancient Egyptian civilization into four broad periods, separated by at least two intermediate periods that were intervals of political change and instability (Table 16.1). The most

Archaic and Old Kingdoms
3100 to 2181 B.C.

Table 16.1 A much simplified chronology of Ancient Egyptian civilization.

Years B.C.	Period	Characteristics
30 B.C.	Roman occupation	Egypt an Imperial Province of Rome
332 to 30 B.C.	Ptolemaic Period	The Ptolemies bring Greek influence to Egypt, beginning with conquest of Egypt by Alexander the Great in 332 B.C.
1085 to 332 B.C.	Late Period	Gradual decline in Pharaonic authority culminating in Persian rule (525 to 404 B.C. and 343 to 332 B.C.).
1567 to 1085 B.C.	New Kingdom	Great imperial period of Egyptian history, with pharaohs buried in Valley of Kings. Pharaohs include Rameses II, Seti I, and Tutankhamen, as well as Akhenaten, the heretic ruler.
1786 to 1567 B.C.	Second Intermediate Period	Hyksos rulers in the delta.
1991 to 1786 B.C.	Middle Kingdom	Thebes achieves prominence, also the priesthood of Amun.
c.2181 to 2173 B.C.	First Intermediate Period	Political chaos and disunity
2686 to 2181 B.C.	Old Kingdom	Despotic pharaohs build the pyramids and favor conspicuous funerary monuments. Institutions, economic strategies, and artistic traditions of Ancient Egypt established.
3100 to 2686 B.C.	Archaic Period	Consolidation of state (treated as part of Old Kingdom in this book)
3100 B.C.	Unification of Egypt under Narmer-Menes	

striking feature of Ancient Egyptian civilization is its conservatism. Many of the artistic, religious, and technological features of early Egyptian civilization survived intact right into Roman times. The political and religious powers of the pharaohs changed somewhat through time, as later rulers became more imperialistic in their ambitions or different gods assumed political supremacy, but the essential continuity was there, in the form of a civilization whose life was governed by the unchanging environment of the Nile Valley with its annual floods, narrow floodplain, and surrounding desert.

The Old Kingdom (c. 2700–2181 B.C.) saw four dynasties of pharaohs governing Egypt from a royal capital at Memphis near Cairo. Apparently the country's resources were well organized and controlled by a centralized government. Some of the pharaohs had reputations as cruel despots, notably Cheops and Chephren, who built the pyramids of Giza. The building of pyramids is regarded as the mark of the Old Kingdom pharaohs (Edwards, 1973; Mendelssohn, 1974). The first royal pyramid was built by Djoser approximately 2680 B.C., a six-step pyramid that was surrounded by a veritable town of buildings and shrines. The Step Pyramid is a somewhat hesitant structure, its architectural roots in earlier mastaba tombs, but the great pyramids built over the next century show increasing confidence, culminating in the brilliant assurance of the pyramids of Giza with their perfect pyramid shape (Figure 16.3). The largest of these, the Great Pyramid, covers 13.1 acres and is 146 m (481 ft) high. It dates to the Fourth Dynasty reign of Cheops, approximately 2600 B.C. Just under two centuries later, the pharaohs stopped building huge pyramids and diverted their organizational talents to other public works.

There is something megalomaniacal about the pyramids, built as they were with an enormous expenditure of labor and energy. They reflect the culmination of centuries of gradual evolution of the Egyptian state, during which the complexity of the state and the authority of the bureaucracy grew hand in hand. The pyramids were the houses and tombs for the pharaohs in eternity, symbols of the permanence of Egyptian civilization. They reflect the importance that the Egyptians placed on the life of the pharaoh in the afterworld, and in the notion of resurrection, a central belief in their religion for thousands of years.

Kurt Mendelssohn (1975) has argued that the pyramids were built over a relatively short period of time, during which the architects experimented with the pyramid shape. At least one pyramid collapsed during construction, before the builders mastered the correct 52° angles of the Great Pyramid. Every flood season when agriculture was at a standstill, the pharaohs organized thousands of peasants into construction teams who quarried, transported, and laid the dressed stones of the pyramids. The permanent (year-round) labor force was relatively small, mainly skilled artisans, the fruit of whose work was placed in position on the main structure once a year. As far as is known, the peasants were paid volunteers, fed by the state bureaucracy, whose loyalty to the divine pharaoh provided the motivation for the work. Mendelssohn feels the construction of the pyramids was a practical administrative device designed to organize and institutionalize the state. As construction proceeded from one generation to the next, the villagers became dependent on the central administration for food for three months a year, food obtained from surpluses contributed by the villages themselves in the form of taxation. After a while the pyramids fulfilled their purpose, and the state-directed labor forces could be diverted to other, less conspicuous state works. A new form of state organization had been created, one that both fostered and exploited the interdependence of Egyptian villages.

Figure 16.3 The pyramids of Giza.

The Egyptian State

Egypt was the first state of its size in history. The pharaohs ruled by their own word, following no written laws, unlike the legislators of Mesopotamian city-states. The pharaoh had power over the Nile flood, rainfall, and all people, including foreigners. He was a god in his own right, respected by all people as a divine and tangible god whose being was the personification of *Ma'at,* or "rightness." *Ma'at* was far more than just rightness, it was a "right order," and stood for order and justice. The pharaoh embodied *ma'at* and dispensed justice. *Ma'at* was pharaonic status and eternity itself — the very embodiment of the Egyptian state (Morenz, 1973).

The pharaoh's pronouncements were law, regulated by a massive background of precedent set by earlier pharaohs. Egyptian rulers lived a strictly ordered life. As one Greek writer tells us: "For there was a set time not only for his holding audience or rendering judgment, but even for his taking a walk, bathing, and sleeping with his wife; in short, every act of his life."

A massive, hereditary bureaucracy effectively ruled the kingdom, with rows of officials forming veritable dynasties. Their records tell us that much official energy was devoted to tax collection, harvest yields, and administering irrigation (Figure 16.4). An army of 20,000 men, many of them mercenaries, was maintained at the height of Egypt's prosperity. The Egyptian Empire was a literate one; that is to say, trained scribes who could read and write were an integral part of the state government. Special schools trained writers for careers in the army, the palace, the treasury, and numerous other callings (Aldred, 1961; Johnson, 1978).

Figure 16.4 A tomb painting from the tomb of Menena at Thebes showing the harvesting and measuring of fields near the Nile.

Despite the number of scribes and minor clerics, a vast gulf separated one who could read and write from the uneducated peasant worker. The life of a peasant, given good harvests, was easier than that of a Greek or a Syrian farmer, although the state required occasional bouts of forced labor to clear irrigation canals or to haul stone, both tasks being essential to maintain Egyptian agriculture. Minor craftsworkers and unskilled laborers lived more regimented lives, working on temples and pharaohs' tombs (Steindorff and Steele, 1954). Many were organized in shifts under foremen. There were strikes, and absenteeism was common. A scale of rations and daily work was imposed. Like many early states, however, the Egyptians depended on slave labor for some public works and much domestic service, but foreign serfs and war prisoners could wield much influence in public affairs. They were allowed to rent and cultivate land.

THE FIRST INTERMEDIATE PERIOD AND MIDDLE KINGDOM: 2181 to 1786 B.C.

First Intermediate Period **2181 to 2173 B.C.**

The Old Kingdom ended with the death of Pepi II in approximately 2200 B.C. (Wilson, 1951). By this time the authority of the monarchy had been weakened by constant expenditure on lavish public works and, perhaps, by a cycle of bad harvest years which undermined the people's confidence in the abilities of the rulers to provide for them. A period of political instability now known as the First Intermediate ensued, during which there were Asian incursions into the fertile delta country and Egypt was ruled by the local nomarchs, even though there was nominal allegiance to a central government.

Middle Kingdom **1991 to 1786 B.C.**

In approximately 2133 B.C. the city of Thebes in Upper Egypt became the center of rebel movements that eventually took over the country under pharaoh Mentuhotep II in 2040 B.C. The Middle Kingdom pharaohs who followed were mostly energetic rulers who extended trading contacts throughout the Near East and conquered the desert lands of Nubia south of the First Cataract (see Figure 16.1). The pharaohs became somewhat less despotic and considered themselves more like shepherds of the people, who had some concern for the common welfare. It was during the Middle Kingdom that the city of Thebes came into prominence, especially as a center for the worship of the sun god Amun.

THE SECOND INTERMEDIATE PERIOD: 1786 to 1567 B.C.

Second Intermediate Period **1786 to 1567 B.C.**

The Middle Kingdom lasted until approximately 1786 B.C., when another period of political instability and economic disorder ensued. Disputes over the royal succession at Thebes led to a whole procession of pharaohs who reigned for short periods. Pharaonic control of the Nile Valley as a whole weakened, and Asian intruders managed to penetrate the fertile lands of the delta downstream. Their leaders became known as the Hyksos and formed two dynasties that ruled over much of Egypt between 1675 to 1567 B.C. They probably were nomadic chiefs from the desert, who brought the horse and chariot to Egypt for the first time.

The Hyksos had little control over Upper Egypt, where the pharaohs of Thebes quarreled among themselves. Eventually, though, the Thebans came to realize that they could never control the whole of the country again unless they threw out the Hyksos and paid careful attention to the political realities of Asia. From this point on, the Egyptian pharaohs took an active interest in their Asian neighbors and there was a constant flow of people and ideas with other nations.

THE NEW KINGDOM: 1567 to 1085 B.C.

The New Kingdom began when a series of Theban pharaohs fought and won a war of independence from the Hyksos. It was Ahmose the Liberator who finally overcame the foreigners and established a firm hold on Egypt from the delta to Nubia. He was the first of a series of great rulers whose names have become symbolic of the power of Ancient Egypt: Tutmosis, Amenophis, Seti, and Rameses. Rameses, the greatest of Egypt's pharaohs, who extended the Egyptian Empire into deepest Nubia and far into Palestine. The pharaohs campaigned against the Hittites in Syria and tried to keep their eastern boundary secure against raiding Mesopotamian armies. The spiritual center of the empire was at Thebes, where the great temples of Luxor and Karnak housed the priests of Amun. This priesthood was a formidable political force in New Kingdom Egypt.

New Kingdom 1567 to 1085 B.C.

The New Kingdom pharaohs adopted new burial customs and abandoned conspicuous sepulchers. Their mummies were buried in the desolate Valley of Kings on the west bank of the Nile at Thebes (Romer, 1981). An entire community of workers did nothing else but prepare the rock-cut tombs of the pharaohs, their queens, and privileged nobles. To date, only one undisturbed royal tomb has come to light in the Valley of Kings, that of the pharaoh Tutankhamun, who died in 1346 B.C. (Carter, 1923; Desroches-Noblecourt, 1963). The world was astounded when Howard Carter and Lord Carnarvon discovered and cleared the tomb of the young pharaoh in the 1920s (Figure 16.5). It gives us an impression of the incredible wealth of the New Kingdom pharaohs' courts.

Tutankhamun died in his late teens but was responsible for restoring religious order after a curious interlude of chaos during the reign of Akhenaten (1363–1350 B.C.) (Aldred, 1968). Like many pharaohs before him, Akhenaten had been worried about the overriding power of the priests of Amun at Thebes, and so he espoused the worship of the god Aten, the life-giving disk of the sun. Akhenaten took up the new religion with fanatical zeal, and even founded a new capital downstream of Thebes called Akhetaten, near the modern village of el-Amarna. After his death in 1350 B.C., the regents for Tutankhamun worked hard to restore

Figure 16.5 The antechamber of Tutankhamun's tomb with two wooden figures of the king guarding the sealed entrance to the burial chamber.

the power and prestige of Amun, a move apparently supported by the mass of the people, for Akhenaten had produced no viable alternatives for the established political and religious institutions he had abolished.

THE LATE PERIOD: 1085 to 30 B.C.

Late Period **1085 to 30 B.C.**

With the death of Rameses III in 1085 B.C., Egypt entered on a period of political weakness, when local rulers exercised varying control over the Nile. The pharaohs were threatened by Nubian rulers, who actually ruled over Egypt for a short time in the eighth century B.C. The Assyrians were a constant hazard after 725 B.C. and actually occupied parts of the country and looted Thebes in 665. After the eclipse of Assyria, the Egyptians enjoyed a few centuries of independence before being conquered by the Persians in 343 B.C. and Alexander the Great in 332 B.C. He in turn was succeeded by the Ptolemies, pharaohs of Greek ancestry, who ruled Egypt until Roman times. It was they who brought much of Egyptian lore and learning into the mainstream of emerging Greek civilization and who ensured that the Land of the Pharaohs made a critical contribution to Western civilization.

THE EMERGENCE OF AFRICAN STATES

What were Egypt's relationships with the vast African continent that bordered the Nile? Her influence on southern and Saharan neighbors was surprisingly small, for her ties were closer to the Mediterranean world than to Black Africa. The pharaohs exercised political control only as far south as the First Cataract, near today's Aswan Dam, but the areas to the south were an important source of ivory for ornaments and of slaves for the divine rulers.

Meroe

In approximately 900 B.C., an unknown governor of the southernmost part of Egypt founded his own dynasty and ruled a string of small settlements extending far south into the area that is now the Sudan. His capital at Napata began to decline because the fragile grasslands by the Nile were overgrazed. The inhabitants moved south and founded a town called Meroe on a fertile floodplain between the Nile and Atbara rivers (Figure 16.1). There they built their own thriving urban civilization, which was in contact with peoples living far to the west on the southern edge of the Sahara (Shinnie, 1967). Meroe's inhabitants kept up at least sporadic contacts with the Classical World. They gained prosperity from extensive trading in such items as copper, gold, iron, ivory, and slaves. Some of Meroe's prosperity may have been based on iron-working, for deposits of this vital material were abundant near Napata. Iron artifacts are, however, fairly rare in the city itself.

In the early centuries after Christ, the empire declined, following raids from the kingdom of Axum centered on the Ethiopian highlands (Oliver and Fage, 1963). Meroe was abandoned and the stratified society that had ruled it collapsed. A scattered rural population continued to live along the banks of the Nile. The fertile grasslands that had surrounded Meroe were now overgrazed and the increasingly arid countryside made urban life difficult. A dispersed settlement pattern replaced the centralized city style of Meroe's heydey. Chiefdoms replaced divine kings.

North Africa

The North African coast had long been a staging post for maritime traders from the eastern Mediterranean. During the first millenium B.C., the Phoenicians set up ports (N. K. Sanders, 1977). The colonists came into contact with well-established barter networks that criss-crossed the Sahara (Bovill, 1968). The desert is rich in salt deposits that were controlled by the nomadic peoples who lived there. They came in touch with

900 B.C.

590 B.C.

A.D. 300

Negro tribesmen living to the south of the desert who bartered salt for copper, ivory, gold, and the other raw materials that Africa has traditionally given to the world. Soon, long trading routes connected North Africa with tropical regions, well-trodden highways that provided much of the Greek and Roman wealth during the height of their civilizations.

A.D. 350

Most of the Saharan trade was in the hands of nomadic tribesmen, middlemen between Black Africa and the bustling markets of the Mediterranean. In Roman times the camel was introduced to the Sahara. These "ships of the desert" enabled merchants to organize sizable camel caravans that crossed the Sahara like clockwork, from the North African coast to West Africa; the caravans increased direct contact between the Mediterranean world and West Africa and built a much greater volume of trade.

Ironworking and African States

300 B.C.

Ironworking had reached West Africa by the fourth century B.C., perhaps by the Saharan trade routes (Shaw, 1978). The new metallurgy, unlike that of copper, spread rapidly over sub-Saharan Africa in a few centuries. Its spread was connected in part with the dispersal of Bantu-speaking peoples over much of eastern, central, and southern Africa. Bantu languages are now spoken by many inhabitants of tropical Africa. The original area of Bantu tongues may have been north of the Zaire forest (Oliver and Fagan, 1975).

A.D. 250

This spread of new language coincides with the arrival of negroid (a racial term) peoples both in the Zaire forest and on the savannah woodlands to the east and south of it. Ironworking farmers were living near the great East African lakes by the third century A.D., by the banks of the Zambezi River at approximately the same time, and crossing the Limpopo into South Africa during the first millenium A.D. They introduced farming and domestic animals into wide areas of Africa, absorbing, eliminating, or pushing out the indigenous hunter-gatherers (Phillipson, 1977).

The Bantu farmers used shifting agriculture and careful soil selection to produce a diet of sorghum, millet, and other cereal crops. They kept cattle and sheep or goats, and relied on hunting and gathering for much of their diet. Their architectural styles and pottery have a clear but indirect relationship with those of many present-day rural Black Africans.

West African States

The past 1000 years have seen the proliferation of prosperous African states ruled by leaders whose power was based on religious ability, entrepreneurial skill, and control of vital raw materials (Davidson, 1966; MacIntosh and MacIntosh, 1981). The West African states at the southern edges of the Sahara, such as Ghana, Mali, and Songhay, based their prosperity on the gold trade with North Africa (Figure 16.6). The Saharan

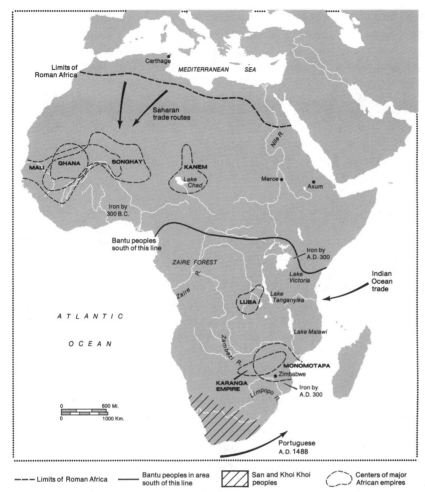

Figure 16.6 Map of later African prehistory, showing extent of Bantu Africa, indigenous states, and distribution of San and Khoi Khoi peoples.

trade passed into Islamic hands at the end of the first millennium A.D., and Arab authors began describing the remarkable African kingdoms flourishing south of the desert. The geographer al-Bakri drew a vivid picture of the kingdom of Ghana, whose gold was well known in northern latitudes by the eleventh century. "It is said," he wrote, "that the king owns a nugget as large as a big stone."

Ghana The Kingdom of Ghana straddled the northern borders of the gold-bearing river valleys of the Upper Niger and Senegal (Levetzion, 1972). No one knows when it first came into being, but the kingdom was described by Arab writers in the eighth century A.D. The Ghanians' prosperity depended on the gold trade and the constant demand for ivory in the north. Kola nuts (used as a stimulant), slaves, and swords also crossed the desert, but gold, ivory, and salt were the foundations of their power. Islam was brought to Ghana sometime in the late first millennium, the religion linking the kingdom more closely to the desert trade. The king of Ghana was a powerful ruler who, wrote al-Bakri, "can put 200,000 men in the field, more than 40,000 of whom are bowmen."

Ghana was a prime target for Islam reform movements, whose desert leaders longingly eyed the power and wealth of their southern neighbor. One such group, the Almoravids, attacked Ghana in approximately A.D. 1062, but it was fourteen years before the invaders captured the Ghanian capital. The power of Ghana was fatally weakened, and the kingdom fell into its tribal parts soon after.

A.D. 1062

Mali The kingdom of Mali appeared two centuries later, after many tribal squabbles (Levetzion, 1973). A group of Kangaba people under the leadership of Sundiata came into prominence in approximately A.D. 1230 and annexed their neighbors' lands. Sundiata built his new capital at Mali on the Niger River. He founded a vast empire that a century later extended over most of sub-Saharan West Africa. The fame of the Malian kings spread all over the Muslim world. Timbuktu became an important center of learning. Malian gold was valued everywhere. When the king of Mali went on a pilgrimage to Mecca in A.D. 1324, the price of gold in Egypt was reduced sharply by the king's liberal spending. Mali appeared on the earliest maps of West Africa as an outside frontier of the literate world, providing gold and other luxuries for Europe and North Africa.

A.D. 1230

A.D. 1324

The key to Mali's prosperity was the unifying effect of Islam. Islamic rulers governed with supreme powers granted by Allah and ruled their conquered provinces through religious appointees or wealthy slaves. Islam provided a reservoir of thoroughly trained, literate administrators, too, who owed allegiance to peace, stability, and good trading practices.

Songhay Approximately A.D. 1325, the greatest of the kings of Mali, Mansa Musa, brought the important trading center of Gao on the Niger under his sway (Hunwick, 1971). Gao was the capital of the Dia kings, who shook off Mali's yoke in approximately A.D. 1340 and founded the kingdom of Songhay. Their state prospered increasingly as Mali's power weakened. The great chieftain Sonni Ali led the Songhay to new conquests between A.D. 1464 and 1492, expanding the frontiers of his empire deep into Mali country and far north into the Sahara. He monopolized much of the Saharan trade, seeking to impose law and order with his vast armies to increase the volume of trade that passed through Songhay hands. Sonni Ali was followed by other competent rulers who further expanded Songhay. Its collapse came in the sixteenth century.

A.D. 1325

A.D. 1464 to 1492

A.D. 1550

Karanga and Zimbabwe

Powerful African kingdoms also developed in central and southern Africa. The Luba kingdom of the Congo and the Karanga empire between the Zambezi and Limpopo rivers were led by skilled priests and ivory traders who also handled such diverse raw materials as copper, gold, seashells, cloth, and porcelain. Their power came from highly centralized political organizations and effective religious powers, which channeled some of their subjects' energies into exploiting raw materials and long-distance trade.

The Karanga peoples lived between the Zambezi and Limpopo where Rhodesia is today, and developed a remarkable kingdom that built its viability on trade in gold, copper, and ivory and on its leaders' religious acumen (Garlake, 1973). The Karanga leaders founded their power on being intermediaries between the people and their ancestral spirits, upon whom the people believed the welfare of the nation depended. Approximately A.D. 1000, the Karanga began to build stone structures, the most famous of which is Zimbabwe, built at the foot of a sacred hill in southeastern Rhodesia. Zimbabwe became an important commercial and religious center. Its chiefs lived in seclusion on the sacred hill, known to archaeologists as "the Acropolis." In the valley below sprawled a complex of homesteads and stone enclosures, which were dominated in later centuries by the high, free-standing stone walls of the Great Enclosure, or Temple (Figure 16.7). A.D. 1000

At least five stages of occupation have been recognized at Zimbabwe, the first of them dating to the fourth century A.D., when a group of farmers camped at the site but built no stone walls. They were followed by later occupants who constructed the Great Enclosure in stages and built retaining walls on the Acropolis. The heyday of Zimbabwe was between A.D. 1350 and 1450, when imported cloth, china, glass, and porcelain were traded to the site. Gold ornaments, copper, ivory, and elaborate iron tools were in common use. A.D. 1350 to 1450

Zimbabwe declined after A.D. 1450, probably because overpopulation impoverished the environment, where agricultural resources were relatively poor anyway.

Foreign Traders

Much of African history is about exploitation of the peoples and raw materials by foreign traders and explorers. The East African coast was visited by Arabs and Indian merchants who used the monsoon winds of the Indian Ocean to sail to Africa and back within twelve months on prosperous trading ventures. The Portuguese skirted Africa's western and southeastern coasts in the fifteenth century and rounded the Cape of Good Hope in 1488, establishing precarious colonies ruled from Portugal to exploit raw materials (Alpers, 1975). Some parts of Africa, however, had no contact with the outside world until Victorian explorers and missionaries met remote and exotic peoples as they strove toward elusive goals, including such prizes as the source of the Nile (see Brodie, 1957). A.D. 1488 A.D. 1850

Figure 16.7 The Zimbabwe ruins, Rhodesia: an important trading and religious center of the Karanga peoples of south-central Africa in the second millennium A.D. Most of the Great Enclosure, or Temple, was built by A.D. 1500.

GUIDE TO FURTHER READING

Aldred, Cyril. *The Egyptians.* New York: Praeger, 1961.
> A superb, short essay on Ancient Egyptian civilization that is especially good on the daily life and society. Exceptional illustrations.

Fagan, Brian M. *The Rape of the Nile.* New York: Scribners, 1975.
> A history of Egyptology, complete with tomb robbers, travelers, and the most flamboyant of archaeologists. Concentrates on Giovanni Belzoni, circus performer and grave robber extraordinaire.

Fedden, Robin. *Egypt.* London: John Murray, 1977.
> The best book ever written on ancient and modern Egypt for the casual tourist. Gives a striking impression of modern Egyptian life and also of Islamic architecture and the Egyptian personality.

Johnson, Paul. *The Civilization of Ancient Egypt.* London: Weidenfeld and Nicholson, 1978.

A comprehensive account of Ancient Egyptian civilization from pre-Dynastic times up to the advent of Roman rule. Especially good on religious and economic life and changing political conditions.

Romer, John. *The Valley of Kings.* New York: Morrow, 1981.

Romer describes centuries of excavations in the royal burial grounds near Thebes in exhaustive detail. Shows very vividly how modern Egyptology is as much a matter of detective work as it is excavation.

Chapter Seventeen

The Harappan Civilization and Southeast Asia

PREVIEW

❉ The Harappan civilization of the Indus Valley (present-day Pakistan) is thought to have developed from indigenous roots sometime in the third millennium B.C.

❉ The Harappans maintained extensive connections with areas to the north, especially Afghanistan, and are thought to have been in sporadic contact with the Iranian plateau and Mesopotamia.

❉ Harappan civilization flourished from approximately 2800 to 1900 B.C. over an enormous area of the Indus Valley. Harappa and Moenjo-daro were the largest cities, each laid out in an inflexible design, which was dominated by a great citadel. It is assumed that the civilization was ruled by priest-kings who controlled both religious and economic life.

❉ After 1900 B.C., Harappan civilization declined, perhaps in part because of declining rainfall and deterioration of the environment. The period between the end of the Harappan culture and the beginnings of ironworking is obscure. Ironworking in India, by comparison, is associated with the period of painted gray wares, when the subcontinent was occupied by the Persian King Darius, in 516 B.C.

❉ Southeast Asian peoples had developed bronzeworking by at least 1500 B.C., possibly very much earlier. The process of local state formation began in the first millennium B.C., but the first historical records of complex states date to the fourth century A.D.

❉ Later Southeast Asian prehistory was dominated by the changing fortunes of various empires ruled by divine kings who espoused a strongly centralized economic system, as secular and religious concerns were molded together in a single type of complex society.

Chronological
Table I

Water has always played an important role in Indian life and thought, for India's great rivers are the perennial gift of the snow-clad Himalayas. The Indus River, on the banks of which Indian civilization began, rises in southern Tibet and then descends 1000 miles through Kashmir before debouching onto the Pakistani plains (Figure 17.1). The Indus floodplain landscape now is almost entirely humanly made, a network of irrigation canals and flood embankments used to control the inundation that reaches the plains between June and September of each year. The people plant their wheat and barley on the fertile alluvial plains as the floods recede, then harvest them the following spring. They use the flood-borne silts as a natural fertilizer. The soils are soft enough to be cultivated without the aid of metal artifacts. Five thousand years ago, the Indus farmers were making use of the same flood cycle to irrigate their fields.

THE ROOTS OF INDIAN CIVILIZATION

As in other parts of the world, it seems that the roots of South Asian farming and later civilization were almost entirely indigenous. Most authorities on South Asian archaeology agree that humped cattle, buffalo, and pig were domesticated there from local wild populations. Perhaps sheep and goats were also. The earliest dates for domesticated animals are in the 4500 to 4000 B.C. range, from sites near Quetta in Baluchistan and Rajastan in northwest India. However, it seems likely that farmers and herders have lived in these areas for much longer, for palynologists have found evidence for recurrent fire in the desert savannah of Rajastan starting approximately 10,000 years ago (Jacobson, 1979). These may signal repeated clearance of sour grass to allow lush grazing for cattle, a practice followed in the area to this day. The farmers eventually domesticated not only indigenous Indian cultigens such as rice and dwarf wheat, but also peas, barley, lentils, and other West Asian species, but the dates of early domestication still are unknown. In the millennia before the emergence of urban civilization in India, dozens of regional variations of farming culture flourished throughout India and Pakistan; these peasant cultures still are little understood (Allchin and Allchin, 1982; Posselh, 1982).

For six years between 1974 and 1980, French and Pakistani archaeologists excavated a series of agricultural settlements at Mehrgarh south of Quetta, 125 miles west of the Indus River (Jarrige and Meadow, 1979). They found traces of farmers who had settled in the area before 6000 B.C. By the fifth millennium, the Mehrgarh people lived in sizable, permanent houses of mud brick, a building material used not only by the Harappan civilization in later times, but also by Indus people to this day. They possessed copper tools and imported turquoise from Iran and shells from the Arabian coast. Living as they did on a direct trade route from the Indus Valley to the Iranian highlands, the Mehrgarh people learned of the unique qualities of a new Indian domesticated crop: cotton. This white, fluffy flower turned out to be a priceless asset, for it could be woven into fine cloth, not only for convenient domestic use in a hot climate, but also for export to people looking for a light, hard-wearing textile. Cotton was to become a staple of Indian trade for the rest of recorded history.

Mehrgarh
c. 6000 to 3000 B.C.

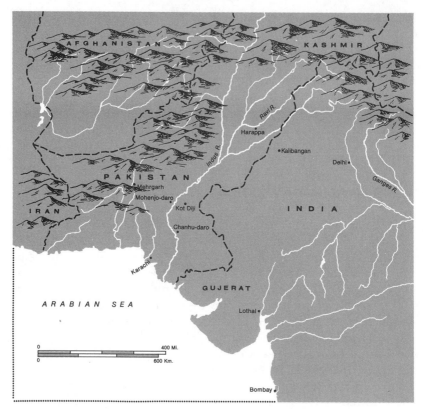

Figure 17.1 The Harappan civilization, showing sites mentioned in this chapter.

Mehrgarh flourished on the cotton and metal trade until the rise of the Harappan civilization in the mid-third millennium. Its workshops manufactured millions of beads and hundreds of clay vessels every year. They were in demand throughout the Indus Valley. The simple technologies used by village artisans in settlements such as Mehrgarh provided all the artifacts needed to create an urban civilization on the Indus floodplains. The ancient trade routes that linked villages all the way from the Indus deep into Afghanistan and Iran became the regular caravan highways monopolized by the Harappans.

The alluvial plains themselves were settled as early as the fourth millenium B.C. Scattered across a vast area of the plains are hundreds of pre-Harappan settlements, many of them boasting fortifications, metallurgy, and planned streets. There are clear signs that many villages and small towns practiced intensive agriculture, many of them built above the highest flood level but as close to the river as possible. Typical of these settlements is Kot Diji on the left bank of the Indus approximately 20 mi (33.3 km) from the river (Jacobson, 1979; Mughal, 1974). As early as 2600 B.C., the inhabitants were forced to pile up boulders to protect themselves against the inundation. They ended up erecting a massive defensive wall

Kot Diji
c. 2600 B.C.

that served both as a flood dike and as a fortress. The stone and mud-brick houses of the village clustered inside the walls. Nevertheless, Kot Diji was attacked and burned at least twice. The same fate must have awaited many other settlements that became involved in quarrels between ambitious local chieftains vying for control of smaller communities and prime agricultural lands. The increased competition is hardly surprising, for between 3000 and 2500 B.C. farming had changed the natural ecology of the Indus Valley beyond all recognition (Agrawal, 1982).

The botanists have chronicled these ecological changes by using the minute pollen grains embedded in the Indus Valley soils. They found that the natural tree and grass cover on the floodplain increased between 2400 and 1000 B.C., perhaps as a result of a period of higher rainfall that lasted at least 2000 years. This thicker tree cover became established just as the farming population was taking advantage of good rains and expanding agricultural production. The pollen counts show not only more trees but dramatic rises in the proportions of cereal grains and cultivated weeds at the expense of the natural vegetation. A complex multiplier effect then linked rapidly rising village populations with corresponding increases in agricultural production, with drastic consequences for the plains environment. As the valley population rose, so did pressure on the land. The farmers cleared and burned off ever more riverine forest and grazed ever-growing herds of goats and sheep on watershed meadows. Acres of forest were burned to bake bricks for the houses of growing villages and newly founded cities. Mile after mile of the plains was denuded of natural vegetation, with disastrous consequences for erosion control and the floodplain environment. Deprived of natural controls, the rising floodwaters swept over the plain, carrying everything with them. Confronted with what may have seemed like the wrath of the gods, the people had but one defense — cooperative flood-works and irrigation agriculture that fed more mouths and provided at least a degree of security against the vagaries of the elements. The obvious leaders of these new communal efforts were the chieftains, priests, and kin leaders who acted as intermediaries between the people and the gods. The religious philosophy and motivation that provided the catalyst for these efforts was a simple one, a pervasive belief that humans were part of an ordered cosmos that could be maintained only by unremitting toil and a subordination of individual ambition to the common good.

This is a hypothetical scenario, but one that seems to fit the few archaeological facts available. It is one that accounts for the remarkable drabness and conservatism of the urban civilization that arose in the changing landscape of the Indus Valley. Like the Sumerian and Egyptian civilizations, the Harappan arose from deeply ingrained indigenous roots with cultural traditions that stressed unquestioned allegiance on the part of everyone, whether priest, merchant, artisan, or farmer. The philosophies of the Indus people would have been entirely alien to the ambitious, individualistic Sumerians or to the balanced, intelligent Egyptians. The Harappans suffered a much grimmer, regimented existence, one in which personal wealth and success counted for little. We can only wonder at the remarkable abilities of the anonymous leaders who blended an austere mix of secular and religious authority to secure the loyalty of not thousands but millions of people for a thousand years.

THE HARAPPAN CIVILIZATION

2700 B.C.

By 2700 B.C., the Indus people had mastered the basic problems of irrigation and flood control, partly by using millions of fired bricks made of river alluvium, baked with firewood cut from the riverine forests. Like the Sumerians, they adopted the city as a means of organizing and controlling their civilization. We know of at least four major Harappan cities: Harappa, after which the civilization is known, Moenjo-daro, Kalibangan, and the recently discovered Dhoraji in Gujerat (Posselh, 1982). Harappa and Moenjo-daro were built on artificial mounds above the floods at the cost of Herculean efforts. Moenjo-daro was rebuilt at least nine times, sometimes as a result of disastrous inundations. Yet on each occasion the builders followed a gridlike street pattern that was set by the first city fathers and followed until the end. Mortimer Wheeler (1962, 1968) characterized both cities as giving an impression of "middle-class prosperity with zealous municipal supervision." Both cities are so similar that they might have been designed by the same architect.

A high citadel lies at the west end of each city, dominating the streets below. Here lived the rulers, protected by great fortifications. Nearby rose the granary, under the careful supervision of the municipal authorities. Harappa's citadel is 414 m (460 yd) long and 194 m (215 yd) wide, surrounded by a forbidding brick wall at least 13.5 m (45 ft) high. Moenjo-daro's towering citadel rises 12 m (40 ft) above the plain and is protected by massive flood embankments and a vast perimeter wall with fortified towers guarding against a surprise attack. The public buildings on the summit include a pillared hall almost 27 m (90 ft) square, perhaps the precinct where the rulers gave audience to petitioners and visiting officials. Everything is utilitarian, efficient, and unostentatious, for there are no spectacular temples or richly adorned shrines. Religious life was centered around a great lustral bath made of bitumen-sealed brickwork and fed by a well. An imposing colonnade surrounded the pool, which was approached by sets of steps at both ends. We cannot be sure of the exact use of the great bath, but perhaps it was the place where the devout carried out their ceremonial bathing rituals.

Moenjo-daro's municipal granary lies on the west side of the citadel. The builders erected twenty-seven rectangular brick supports and then built a huge wooden granary on top so that the air could circulate freely under the stored grain. There is no more eloquent testimony to the tight control the rulers exercised over the city than this heavily fortified and inaccessible granary. The food surpluses it contained were their ultimate, material instrument of social and economic control, for the grain fed or paid thousands of menial laborers and state employees. Harappa's granary lay to the north of the citadel and formed part of an entire grain-processing complex, including both threshing floors and two rows of barracklike buildings for the laborers who toiled there.

The rulers of each city looked down on the north-south street grid laid out in city blocks. The widest east-west thoroughfares at Moenjo-daro were only 9 m (30 ft) wide, the cross streets only half as wide and unpaved (Figure 17.2). Hundreds of drab, standardized houses presented a blind brick facade to the streets and alleys they lined. The more spacious dwellings, perhaps those of the nobility and merchants, were laid out around a central courtyard where guests may have been received, where food was prepared, and where servants probably lounged. Staircases and thick ground walls indicate that some houses had two or even three stories, with wooden balconies overlooking the courtyard rather than the street, as was the case at Sumerian Ur. The larger residences owned a

Figure 17.2 A typical street in Moenjo-daro, Pakistan, uncovered in Sir Mortimer Wheeler's excavations.

well and had bathrooms and toilets that may have been joined to an elaborate system of public drains.

The ever-organizing tentacles of the government extended to every detail of city life. Some areas of Harappa and Moenjo-daro were designated as bazaars, complete with shops (Fairservis, 1976). The archaeologists have inventoried the finds from artisans' quarters where bead makers, coppersmiths, cotton weavers, and other specialists manufactured and sold their wares. The potters' workshops were filled with painted pots decorated with animal figures and everyday plain wheel-made vessels manufactured not only in the cities but also in villages for hundreds of miles around. There were water jars and cooking bowls, storage pots and drinking vessels. Metalworkers cast simple axes in open molds, and manufactured chisels, knives, razors, spears, and fishhooks. Only a few expert artisans made more elaborate objects such as small figurines or a piece as complicated as a canopied cart. They would make a wax model of the cart and encase it in clay which was fired to melt the wax. Then molten copper or bronze was poured into the mold. This "lost-wax" method is still employed by Indian artists today. The technologies used in Harappan cities were developed centuries earlier in small villages and were merely transferred to the cities without change. One of the most developed manufactures was the seal, made from steatite and other soft rocks. Seal workshops have yielded not only finished specimens, hardened in a furnace, but the blocks of steatite from which square seals were cut as intaglios. For hours, the seal makers would crouch over the tiny squares, expertly cutting representations of animals in profile. They reserved some of their best efforts for religious scenes, such as the depictions of Shiva as Lord of the Beasts, that provide us with tantalizing links with modern Indian beliefs. Indian archaeologists working at the Harappan city of Chanhu-daro south of Moenjo-daro found a complete bead maker's shop that gave some idea of the labor needed to produce small ornaments. The bead makers prepared bars of agate and carnelian approximately 3 in. long that were then ground and polished into shorter, perforated cylinders and strung in necklaces. To experience the bead-making process, the archaeologists took a Harappan stone-tipped drill and some abrasive powder from the workshop and attempted to drill through one of the bead blanks. It took them 20 minutes to drill a small pit in the end of the bead. At that rate, it would have taken 24 hours to drill a single bead!

The overall impression of Harappan cities is faintly depressing. Perhaps the most striking memory of many visitors might have been the constant thump of grain pounders wielded by hundreds of menial workers laboring at the public granaries. The city authorities provided row after row of standardized, two-room houses for those who labored on this and the many other routine but essential tasks that kept this labor-intensive civilization running on oiled wheels. With so many unskilled hands and abundant food supplies, there was no incentive for technological innovation, nor, apparently, did the religious philosophies of the time encourage cultural change. The Harappan civilization did not change at all for an entire millennium.

Who Were the Harappans?

Half a century of excavations has revealed a standardized, monotonous civilization that the archaeologists have named the *Harappan,* simply because they did not know what the Harappans called themselves. Their archives, thoughts, and beliefs elude us. We do not even know the names of the rulers who controlled at least five great cities and a civilization that extended over a half million square miles of the Punjab and Sind plains, from Baluchistan to the deserts of Rajastan, and from the Himalayan foothills to near Bombay. The Harappan leaders controlled their own people as well as long-distance trade routes that extended along the Arabian coast, into northern Afghanistan and Turkmenia, and onto the Iranian plateau, through thousands of square miles of mountainous terrain rich in minerals and other natural resources. The cities sent merchants with wheeled carts driven by oxen and water buffalo along regular caravan routes far into the highlands. They exported grain and textiles, carnelian beads, pearls, and sweet-smelling rosewood, and received minerals and other raw materials in exchange. Much of the long-distance trade was conducted by deep-sea vessels coasting the shores of the Indian Ocean into the Persian Gulf. Ever thorough, the authorities controlled even this commerce. During the 1950s and 1960s, Indian archaeologists uncovered a Harappan port at Lothal, a landlocked town on the Gulf of Cambay. The only way to enter the harbor was through a specially dug canal at high tide. Every oceangoing ship had to berth at the official, brick-lined dock surrounded by government warehouses. Probably other similar ports await discovery elsewhere on the Pakistani coastline. We know that Harappan seamen voyaged as far afield as Sumer and Bahrein, for a scatter of Indus seals dating to between 2300 and 2000 B.C. have come from Ur and other Sumerian cities. Perhaps there was a colony of Harappan merchants in Sumer at one time, but we know nothing of its transactions. Few Mesopotamian imports have come from excavations in Indus cities, yet we cannot doubt that there was contact between the two areas, perhaps through such entrepôts as the walled Sumerian trading port of Dilmun on the island of Bahrein in the Persian Gulf.

The anonymity of those Harappan leaders extends even to their appearance. These were no bombastic rulers, boasting of their achievements on grandiose palace walls. They left almost no portraits behind them. One exception is a limestone figure from Moenjo-daro that depicts a thick-lipped, bearded man staring at the world through slitted eyes, perhaps dazzled by the brilliant Indus sunlight. He seems to be withdrawn in meditation, perhaps detached from worldly affairs. The man wears an embroidered robe that was once inlaid with metal. The only clue to his status is that one shoulder is uncovered, a sign of reverence during the Buddha's lifetime more than 1000 years later. Could it be that the same convention applied to Harappan times and that the portrait is that of a priest or a priest-king? (Figure 17.3). Thus far, the evidence of archaeology reveals leadership by rulers who led unostentatious lives marked by a complete lack of priestly pomp or lavish public display. There is nothing of the ardent militarism of the Assyrian kings, nor of the slavish glorification of the pharaohs.

The secular power of this civilization was based almost completely on bountiful agricultural production. Harappan civilization may have revolved around cities, but most people still were village farmers, cultivating irrigated fields of barley and wheat that lapped the city suburbs. The Harappans ate rice, too, a crop first cultivated somewhere between India and Southeast Asia before 5000 B.C. They cultivated cotton and dates and kept cattle and water buffalo. Every farmer turned over a substantial portion of the annual harvest to the state, and indeed the authorities may have controlled the ownership of much of the land. The entire agricultural enterprise was a much larger-scale version of the communal village farming that originally had made colonization of the Indus Valley possible.

Both Harappa and Moenjo-daro housed a comfortable and unpretentious middle class of merchants and petty officials who lived in stolid and standardized brick houses along the city streets. They wore finely woven, decorated cotton robes. Judging from clay figurines, the women wore short skirts and headdresses, and perhaps longer robes. Dozens of shops

Figure 17.3 Bronze figurine of a dancing girl from Moenjo-daro, Pakistan, 11 cm (4.3 in) high.

sold wire neck bangles, necklaces, and pendants, but there is nothing of the elaboration found in Egyptian or Mycenean palaces. The more prosperous city dwellers sometimes owned some ornate, carved rosewood furniture, but the lifestyle was far from lavish. Even the wealthiest and most powerful merchants maintained a low profile in public. The artisans — metalsmiths, potters, weavers, bead makers, seal carvers — formed a distinct class, as did the many petty bureaucrats and priests needed to run the multifarious affairs of government, each with their designated quarters. However, such people were a tiny minority compared with the vast mass of the populace: farmers, laborers, seamen, and menial workers of every type. They lived in servile dwellings and wore but the simplest of cotton loincloths or robes. Their unquestioning hands kept the Harappan civilization in existence, although in their way they were as deadening a cultural influence as were the armies of slaves that sustained Mesopotamian civilization. To judge from modern Indian life, they had an extended family in several generations which provided a network of kinship ties and other benefits such as communal ownership of property. Perhaps, too, the Harappan people were organized in a hierarchy of castes that restricted upward mobility and provided a wider identity outside the confines of the family.

Harappan Beliefs

Like the Sumerians, the Harappans lived in an environment that they modified for their own protection, one in which the annual floods meant a renewal of life and food for the coming year. Like the Mesopotamians, they seem to have believed that they lived in the valley to serve the gods who caused crops to grow and soils to be fertile. The primeval roots of Indian religion may been age-old fertility cults that served the same function as Inanna among the Sumerians and the mother goddess in many other Near Eastern civilizations — an assurance that life would continue. The only clues we have to the origins of Indian religion came from minute seal impressions and small clay figurines from Harappan villages and cities that depict a female deity with conspicuous breasts and sexual organs. We do not know her name, but she probably embodied earth and life-giving nature for the Indus people. A seal from Moenjodaro bears a three-headed figure who sits in the yogic posture and wears a horned headdress. He is surrounded by a tiger, elephant, rhinoceros, water buffalo, and deer. Some archaeologists believe that the seal represents a forerunner of the great god Shiva in his role of Lord of the Beasts. Many Harappan seals depict cattle that may be symbols of Shiva, who was worshipped in several forms. To judge from later beliefs, he may have had a dual role, serving as a fertility god as well as tamer or destroyer of wild beasts (Wolpert, 1977). Shiva gave life by planting the seed but also could destroy any creature, including human beings, at a flick of the finger. In part he may symbolize the unpredictable dangers of flood and famine that could threaten a village or a city without warning. Harappa and Moenjo-daro have yielded dozens of carved phallic symbols and circular stones with round holes that represents his consort Devi's teeming womb. Perhaps these are simple prototypes of the Hindu *lingam* and *yoni* symbols that are found in the temples of Shiva and Devi to this day. If the evidence of figurines and seals is to be believed, the symbolism of early Indus religion bears remarkable similarities to that of modern Hinduism. This similarity highlights the deeply ingrained conservatism of Indian society from the very earliest moments of Harappan civilization.

Writing and Weights

One reason we know so little about the Harappans is that their script still has not been deciphered. Finnish and Russian scholars have used computers to encode and analyze the pictures and signs of the Harappan seals but without success. Almost 400 different pictographic symbols have been identified from their seals, far too many to have meaning but too few to be ideographic. Linguists do not even agree on the language in the script, let alone the ultimate identity of the Harappans. Some authorities believe the seals served not only as religious symbols but also as tags or labels written in Sumerian on bundles of merchandise sent to distant Sumer. Some success has been attained with computer-aided deciphering techniques that have established the script as logo-syllabic; that is to say it is a mixture of sounds and words, just like Egyptian hieroglyphs (Fairservis, 1983). Many scholars believe it is written in a Proto-Dravidian language, for Dravidian exercised a considerable influence on the Sanscrit used widely in India centuries later. Enough of the Indus script has been deciphered to show how many of the short seal inscriptions designate the names of individuals and their ranks. It seems, too, that some describe major figures of the Harappan cosmos and the names of chiefs, as well as identifying scribes and artisan leaders in society. There are certainly close links between the Harappan script and later writings. Many of the Indus symbols are similar to those appearing on Brahmi documents from the Ganges Valley centuries later. Both were written in what is called the *boustrophedon* style. This writing alternates lines going from right to left and then left to right. This contrasts with English, which progresses from left to right, and Arabic, which runs in the opposite direction. Many signs and symbols used on Harappan seals are found on pottery and other objects made as late as the ninth century B.C.

Even more striking evidence for cultural continuity comes from the humble half-ounce weight. No government monopoly can survive without weights and measures, and so the Harappan authorities developed a standard weight that was close to one-half of a modern ounce. Later, Indian societies used a unit known as the *karsa* for the same purpose. This weighed the equivalent of 32 *rattis*, seeds of the Gunja creeper, a measure that could fluctuate slightly from year to year. Four karsas weighed almost exactly the same as the basic Harappan unit of a half ounce. Similar devices could be found in nineteenth-century bazaars.

The Decline of Harappan Civilization

The Harappan civilization reached its peak in approximately 2000 B.C. Moenjo-daro housed at least 40,000 people 4000 years ago, but the city was already in trouble from repeated floods that undercut the citadel's defenses and inundated acres of city streets. The authorities deployed more and more laborers to strengthen the flood-control works and to re-build houses, but there are revealing signs of architectural degeneration after 1900 B.C., as if the constant battle against the Indus was taking its material and psychological toll (Raikes, 1967). At first the serious floods may have resulted from centuries of uncontrolled deforestation and grazing that removed natural barriers for the waters. However, this was not enough to destroy the cities. Approximately 1700 B.C., the Indus changed its course abruptly at both Harappa and Moenjo-daro, perhaps as a result of a series of earthquakes and enormous floods, conceivably inundating the river cities beyond hope of recovery (Dales, 1966; Raikes, 1967).

The effects of the floods were felt throughout the Indus Valley. The great cities of the interior collapsed. Only Lothal and a few coastal centers that were located away from the destructive river continued to flourish as local states, deprived of the authoritative umbrella that had maintained their political and economic stability before. They survived unscathed for two centuries more, until Aryan nomads swept down on the Indus Valley and took over the plains. By that time, the Harappans had passed on a priceless legacy of beliefs and philosophies that formed one of the mainstreams of all subsequent Indian history.

From the archaeological point of view, the period between the break-down of the Harappan cities and the beginning of ironworking is the most obscure in India's later prehistory (Wolpert, 1977). Despite the abandonment of the cities, there were no major disruptions in economy or material culture. Iron tools appear in India in the late second millen-ium B.C. and are associated with painted gray wares, made on a wheel and adorned with simple black painted designs. The advent of iron tools en-abled farmers to break up the hard, calcareous soils of the Ganges plain, an area that was to become the heartland of later empires.

Meanwhile, King Darius of Persia invaded the subcontinent in 516 B.C. and incorporated part of India into the Persian Empire. Two centuries later, Alexander the Great ventured to the Indus River and brought Greek culture to the area. His incursion also provided a stimulus for cultural developments in the Ganges that culminated in a nationalistic revolt headed by the priest Chandragupta. This leader founded an empire which linked the Indus and the Ganges in a single administrative unit that traded as far afield as Malaya and the Near East. The period between

2000 B.C.

1700 B.C.

Painted gray wares
1000 B.C.

516 B.C.

316 B.C.

approximately 200 B.C. and A.D. 300 saw India linked with lands far to the east and west by regular trading links that persisted more or less independently of political developments. By this time, the influence of Indian religion in the form of Buddhism and Hinduism was being felt over enormous areas of Asia.

SOUTHEAST ASIAN CIVILIZATIONS

The emergence of complex states in Southeast Asia probably is closely connected with the spread of rice cultivation and bronze metallurgy. As we saw in Chapter Twelve, the early history of rice cultivation is inadequately documented, but we do know that the spread of rice agriculture throughout Southeast Asia may prove to be connected with southern Chinese farmers. Pottery that shows influence of their widespread traditions has been found in Thailand and possibly Malaya. The genesis of copper and bronze metallurgy in Southeast Asia is even less well documented than the genesis of rice cultivation. The Non Nok Tha cemetery yielded some bronze axes originally dated to about 2100 B.C. (Bayard, 1977). However, the contexts from which the dates came have been a matter of controversy. Some authorities believe they date to no earlier than the second millennium B.C. (Higham, 1984; for more discussion, see Bayard, 1984).

Ban Chiang Date
uncertain

More controversy surrounds the emergence of bronzeworking in southeast Asia. Until recently, the Ban Chiang cemetery in northern Thailand was claimed as evidence for very early bronzeworking in the area, with burials dating to a long period between about 3600 B.C. and A.D. 300, and bronze artifacts to at least 2500 B.C. (White, 1982) (Figure 17.4). But the radiocarbon dates from the burial pits have been questioned by archaeologists digging three other sites nearby (Higham, 1984). At Ban Nadi, fourteen mi (22 km) south-west of Ban Chiang, securely dated occupation levels with bronze equivalent to those at the cemetery dated on average to about 1350 B.C., fully a thousand years later. These later dates are confirmed by excavations elsewhere. A vigorous debate surrounds claims for early bronzeworking in Thailand (see Bayard, 1984; Higham, 1984). Only future excavations and further radiocarbon dates can resolve the chronological conundrum.

1500 B.C.

Higham's shorter controversy receives important support from excavations in Viet Nam's lower Red River Valley. There, bronze appears by about 1500 B.C. in sites of the late Phung Nguyen culture (Huyen, 1984). Unfortunately, only isolated radiocarbon dates are available, so the chronology is still loosely anchored. Bronze metallurgy was also well established on the Vietnamese coast during the late second millennium B.C. One site near Ho Chi Minh City has yielded sandstone moulds and bronze artifacts identical to those found in northeast Thailand (Higham, 1984).

There are two possible interpretations of this dating evidence. The long time scale means that the Ban Chiang people worked bronze at least

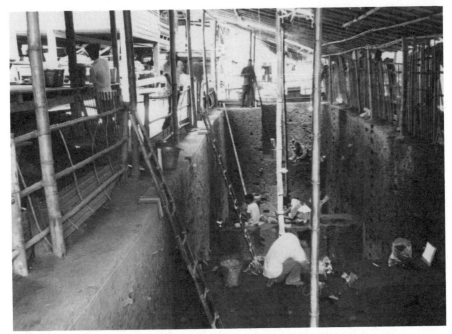

Figure 17.4 Excavation at Ban Chiang, Thailand, 1975.

1500 years earlier than people elsewhere in southeast Asia. Proponents of the shorter chronology say that bronzeworking was present in coastal Viet Nam and the Mekong Valley by 1500 B.C., and that the Ban Chiang metal objects are imports dating to between 300 and 500 B.C. (Higham, 1984).

Viet Nam's Dong Son culture represents the culmination of early bronze- and ironworking in prehistoric times. Co Loa, near Hanoi, comprises three sets of ramparts, with moats supplied with water by a tributary of the Red River. At its greatest extent, the fortifications enclosed about 600 hectares. By this time, rice cultivation was sufficiently productive to support a considerable population density, combined as it was with plow cultivation, double cropping, and water control. According to Chinese records, local chieftains named Lac Lords, keepers of the drums, controlled the rights to rice land. The area was incorporated as a Chinese protectorate in 111 B.C., by which time the Dong Son rulers were in regular contact with Han China (Wheatley, 1979).

Dong Son Culture
300 B.C.

Foreign Influences

Although archaeological evidence still is largely lacking, it seems likely that state forms of society were evolving in Southeast Asia from the second millennium B.C. (Higham, 1984). What is uncertain is the extent to which foreign influences played a part in the dissemination of more complex state organizations. Much of our information on early Southeast Asian states comes from Chinese and Indian sources (Wheatley, 1975; Hall, 1985)

Trading systems established For centuries Southeast Asia was dominated, at least tangentially, by two foreign presences. To the north the Chinese imposed their political will on the Lăc peoples on the Tong-king lowlands and extended their tribute systems into the Red River Valley. This was an arbitrary imposition of an entirely different economic system onto trading systems based on reciprocity. It was quite different from the cultural changes going on in the southerly parts of Southeast Asia.

A.D. 1
Approximately 2000 years ago, the busy sea-trading networks of Southeast Asia were being incorporated into the vast, oceanic trade routes stretching from China in the east to the shores of the Red Sea and the east coast of Africa in the west. No one people controlled the whole of this vast trade. Most of the Indian Ocean commerce was in the hands of traders, who used monsoon winds to traverse the long sea lanes from India to Africa and from Arabia to both continents. The trade carried raw materials and luxury goods such as glass beads and cloth. During the heyday of the Roman Empire, the Greeks and Egyptians of Alexandria took some interest in the Indian Ocean trade but rarely ventured farther than the Red Sea.

Beyond India, the trade was held by Indian merchants who penetrated deep into the numerous islands and channels of Southeast Asia. The traders themselves were an entirely maritime people, called *Mwani* or *barbarians* by the Chinese of the time. They spoke a polyglot of tongues and were of many lands, some Malays, some Indians, true wanderers who ventured as far east as the South China Sea. The Gulf of Tonkin and South China were served by *Jiwet*, Chinese mariners who brought luxuries to the coast, whence they were transported overland to the Chinese capital.

Indian merchants certainly were active on Southeast Asian coasts by the early centuries of the Christian era. They were actively trading with the tribal societies of both mainland and islands. Voyaging was now accelerated by changing circumstances. First came larger cargo vessels with a more efficient rig that enabled them to sail closer to the wind. No one knows how large these vessels were, but they must have been substantial. The Chinese are known to have transported horses by sea to Indonesia in the third century A.D., and the monk Fa Hsien recorded his sailing trip from Ceylon to China with 200 other passengers in A.D. 414.

Another factor influencing trade was a new demand for gold and other metals. The Roman Emperor Vespasian had prohibited exporting metals from the Roman Empire in approximately A.D. 70, a move that turned the Indian merchants' eye to the southeast, particularly because the Siberian gold mines had been closed to them by nomadic raids on Asian caravans. Metals were not the only attraction; spices could be obtained in abundance. Trade was expanded entirely for commercial profit.

Imported religions Buddhism had made great strides in India since it appeared in the fourth century B.C. The older religion, Brahmanism, had placed severe and authoritarian restraints on foreign voyages, but Buddhism and Jainism, a form of Hinduism, rejected the notion of racial purity espoused by the predecessor religion. Travel was encouraged; the merchant became a respected part of Buddhist belief. As voyaging increased, especially from southern India to Southeast Asia, a strong cultural influence emanated from the former to the latter. The tribal societies of Southeast Asia were introduced to many alien products and some of the foreigners' philosophical, social, and religious beliefs. In a few centuries, kingdoms appeared with governments run according to Hindu or Buddhist ideas of social order.

Chieftains become divine kings The initial but regular contacts between merchants and tribal societies were seasonal, dictated by the monsoon winds. The chieftains who represented the people of the tribes would have acted as intermediaries between the foreigners and the indigenous people. All exchanges and transactions having to do with the trade were channeled through them. Inevitably, argues Sinologist Paul Wheatley (1975), the chieftains would learn a new way of seeing society and the world, perhaps organizing the collection of commodities for trade, acquiring new organizational skills alien to their own societies. As principal beneficiaries of the trade, they would acquire status, many more possessions, and strong interest in seeing the trade maintained. However, the authority and powers needed to expand and maintain the commerce were not part of the kin-linked society in which the chieftains had lived all their lives. In time, they might come to feel closer sympathy with their visitors, the people who gave them their power and prestige. Philosophically they would come to feel closer to Indian models of authority and leadership. They would become familiar with the Brahman and Buddhist conceptions of divine kingship. There was even a brahmanic rite by which chieftains could be inducted into the ruling class, a group whose authority was vested in an assumption of divine kingship. Wheatley hypothesizes that regular trading contacts, combined with changes in beliefs about the legitimizing of authority, led to the birth of states in Southeast Asia.

Divine kingship was a cultural borrowing from India that revolutionized social and political organization in Southeast Asia. Numerous city-states arose in strategic parts of this huge region. Many were served by Brahman priests, who, among other functions, consecrated divine kings as they started their reigns. Some of these states became very powerful, with extensive trading connections and large Brahman communities. As early as the third century A.D., Chinese envoys to Southeast Asia reported on a state in the northern part of the Malay peninsula that enjoyed regular trading contacts with Parthia and India as well as with southern China.

The Chinese visited many small Southeast Asian kingdoms that modified Indian civilization to their own purposes, but the most famous was
Funan, a mercantile empire that extended along the Mekong delta in
Vietnam and some distance inland into Kampuchea (Briggs, 1951).
Funan appears in Chinese histories from approximately the third to seventh centuries A.D., but probably came into being in approximately A.D.
100. Most accounts of Funan extol its "port of a thousand rivers" and its
rich trade in gold, silver, bronze, and spices. They tell of the Funan people who built a drainage and irrigation system that rapidly transformed
much of the delta from barren swamps into rich agricultural land. The
development of these fields took the communal efforts of hundreds of
people living off the fish that teemed in the bayous of the delta. Most
Funans lived in large lake cities fortified with great earthworks and
moats swarming with crocodiles. Each major settlement was a port connected to the ocean and its neighbors by a network of artificial canals.

Funan
c. A.D. 100 to 546

Funan prospered greatly from the third to sixth centuries. The ports
handled goods from all over the east, even horses brought by sea from
central Asia. Large numbers of Chinese merchants and Indian artisans
settled in the cities and worked with bronze, ivory, silver, gold, even
coral. They brought new skills with them that the local people copied, for
they were not creative folk. In the sixth century many more Indian Brah-
mans arrived in Funan. They brought the cult of Shiva with them, the god
who was to become the focus of all subsequent Southeast Asian civilization. He appeared in the temples in the form of a *linga*, a phallic emblem.
The royal linga stood in a temple on the hill that symbolized the center of
every capital. Shiva's omnipresent emblem soon was the focus of all
Kampuchean civilization, surviving the fall of Funan in the sixth century.

The Rise of the God-Kings

Funan was succeeded by the state of Chenla, the economic hub of
which lay around the Great Lake in the central basin of Kampuchea
(Briggs, 1951). Most of the year the lake is a shallow series of muddy
pools some 40 mi (66.6 km) long, drained by the Tonle Sap River that
runs into the Mekong. However, so much water floods into the Mekong
delta downstream from July to January that the Tonle Sap's course is re-
versed and the pools become a vast lake, 80 to 100 mi (133–167 km) long,
15 to 30 mi (25–50 km) wide, and up to 50 ft (15.5 m) deep. Late in October the water starts receding, trapping millions of fish in the muddy
bayous. The Great Lake provided such favorable opportunities for rice
cultivation and fishing that its shores supported a far higher population
density than even the irrigated delta downstream. This unique environment enabled the Chenla kings not only to embark on ambitious conquests but also to develop a new political concept of divine kingship that
united their far-flung domains together in a common purpose — the glorification of the god-king on earth. The earlier Khmer kings were unable

Chenla
A.D. 611 to 802

Khmer
A.D. 802 to 1218

to hold the kingdom together, until a dynamic monarch named Jayavarman II was crowned king in A.D. 802. He had spent some years in Java, where he had studied a new cult, the worship of the god-king. This *Devaraja* cult taught that the king did not rule by divine authority alone but that he was a god himself to be worshipped and obeyed without question. Jayavarman II adopted the teachings of this powerful cult to consolidate his vast kingdom. His subjects were taught to worship him as a god. All resources were devoted to the preservation of the cult of the god-king. Everyone, whether noble, high priest, or commoner, was expected to subordinate his or her own ambitions to the need to perpetuate the existence of the king on earth and his identity with the god in this life and the next. The symbol of the king's authority was the royal *linga*, the representation of masculine creative power (Briggs, 1951). Jayavarman II's new strategy was brilliantly successful. He reigned for forty-five years, founded a dynasty that prospered for 600 years, and united the Khmer kingdoms into a colorful spectacular empire that reached the height of its prosperity between A.D. 900 and 1200 shortly after his death.

Previous monarchs had encouraged the worship of Shiva in the form of this phallic image, but now Jayavarman II presented himself as the reincarnation of Shiva on earth. He was the *varman*, the protector, and his priests were the instruments of practical political power. The high priests were invariably energetic imposing nobles, who presided over a highly disciplined hierarchy of religious functionaries. They supervised every aspect of Khmer life, from agriculture to warfare and the rituals of the state religion. The custom of building a new majestic and holy temple to house the royal linga of each new king was the most important of all the religious rituals. As a result, most of the thirty monarchs who followed Jayavarman II left massive religious edifices to commemorate their reigns. These they built on temple mountains or artificial mounds in the center of their capitals, the hub of the Khmer universe.

Jayavarman II's new policies, based on the assumption that he had no living superior on earth, were brilliantly successful, but only after several decades of brutal suppression and cruelty. The king played one prince off against another, planted spies everywhere, and executed everyone who stood in his way. His propaganda machine successfully convinced the masses that their individual welfare as well as that of the kingdom depended on the success of the new cult. For the next three centuries, each Khmer king ruled as "great master, king of kings." Inevitably, the despotism overwhelmed them. They surrounded themselves with a brilliant and powerful court that upheld their desire for supreme power, so much so that the kings lost touch with their subjects. Soon they were completely obsessed with life after death and their memorials on earth. Thousands of their subjects toiled to build fabulous temples and palaces such as Angkor Wat purely for the king's pleasure. When the people were admitted, they prostrated themselves not before the gods but before the god-king. The Khmer's unique form of divine kingship produced, instead of an austere civilization like that of the Indus, a society with a blind faith in powerful kings who carried the cult of wealth, luxury, and self-aggrandizement to amazing lengths.

Angkor Wat

Angkor Wat
A.D. 1200 to 1432

The Khmer kings who followed Jayavarman II indulged two passions: warfare and temple building. They surrounded themselves with artists, poets, and sculptors whose sole task it was to embellish and adorn their magnificent capitals. Most of these capitals were built in a fertile area teeming with fish near the Tonle Sap, an area known as *Angkor*. Of all the edifices there, the most famous is Angkor Wat (Figure 17.5). This extraordinary shrine is a spectacle of beauty, wonder, and magnificence, the largest religious building in the world, greater even than Vatican City, 1500 m (5000 ft) by 1200 m (4000 ft) across. The central block measures 215 m (717 ft) by 186 m (620 ft) and rises more than 60 m (200 ft) above the forest. It dwarfs even the largest Sumerian ziggurat and makes Moenjo-daro's citadel look like a village shrine. Angkor Wat took forty years to build and finally was abandoned in 1432.

Angkor Wat is approached through an entrance gallery with a tower by a paved causeway 150 m (500 ft) long that is flanked with balustrades adorned with mythical multiheaded snakes. It opens onto a cruciform terrace in front of a rectangular temple that rises in three imposing tiers to a central cluster of five towers. Each tower bears a lofty pinnacle that, from afar, looks like a giant lotus bud. The causeway leads across a huge moat 180 m (600 ft) wide enclosed in masonry walls 4 mi in circumfer-

Figure 17.5 The temple at Angkor Wat.

ence. The engineers built the walls with a total error of less than an inch! The moat still is a beautiful sight, with floating water lilies, wild orchids, and other shimmering blooms. Angkor Wat is built in three great rising squares (Giteau, 1966). A central group of chambers and then long open galleries extend all around each square, with a double square of columns on their outer face. Each terrace is surrounded by a gallery interspersed with corner towers, pavilions, stairways, and other structures. On the highest terrace, the central tower is tied to axial pavilions by galleries supported by pillars that divide it into four paved courts. The towers themselves are without interior windows or staircases and are finished with superb lotus-bud cones.

Every detail of this extraordinary building reproduced part of the heavenly world in a terrestrial mode. The Khmer believed that the world consisted of a central continent known as *Jambudvipa* with the cosmic mountain *Meru* rising from its center. The gods lived at the summit of Meru, represented at Angkor Wat by the highest tower of all. The remaining four towers depicted Meru's lesser peaks; the enclosure wall, the mountain at the edge of the world; and the surrounding moat, the ocean beyond. Angkor Wat was the culminating attempt of the Khmer to reproduce a monument to the Hindu gods: Shiva, the creator, Vishnu, the preserver of the universe, and Brahma, who raised the earth. Everything about Angkor Wat is on a massive and lavish scale, as if expense, time, and slave labor were of little importance.

The galleries of Angkor Wat are adorned with more than 1212 m (4000 ft) of polished sandstone bas-reliefs, each approximately 2.42 m (8 ft) high (Giteau, 1966). Some 2000 temple dancers wearing ropes of pearls dance in graceful, acrobatic poses along the galleries, walls, and pillars. These lovely, smiling, and often seductive creatures soften the dark gray edifice, stretching naked to the waist for hundreds of feet over the walls of the second and third terraces. Most of the bas-reliefs depict religious scenes, popular legends, and wars. Hundreds of soldiers mounted on elephants ride victorious over opposing armies, warriors fight from chariots, and fleets sail to battle. There even are armies of monkeys and men, and victory marches with bands and banners. The sculptures invoke the Hindu Trinity, gods, goddesses, and guardian deities. The god-king rides on a royal elephant surrounded by slaves and soldiers. He is depicted setting forth to fight Angkor's enemies with the blessings of his priests, and is seen administering his domains and enjoying the triumphs of his reign.

Angkor Wat taxed the resources of the kingdom so severely that civil war ensued. Undeterred, the rulers used thousands of prisoners of war to erect a huge new capital at Angkor Thom nearby. The sheer size of Angkor Thom is overwhelming. A dark and forbidding 8-mile wall surrounds the capital. The five gateways rise 18 m (60 ft) high and the crocodile-filled moat is 162 m (540 ft) across. When visitors walked into the capital, they entered a symbolic Hindu world with the king's funerary temple at the center. Great triple-headed elephants guard the flanks of the gates, and four great Buddha faces adorn the towers above the massive doorways. The Grand Plaza of Angkor Thom was the scene of ceremonies and contests, of vast military reviews and massed bands. Long bas-reliefs of animals and kings walking in procession above seas of snakes and fish lead to the Plaza and look down on its wide spaces. It is said that a million people once lived in or near Angkor Thom. The architectural and artistic legacy they left behind them is mind-boggling, one so large that a single frieze of marching elephants extends over 360 m (1200 ft) of sculpted wall! The task of building the city beggared the state. The temple of the king's father contained no fewer than 430 images, with more than 20,000 in gold, silver, bronze, and stone in the wider precincts. Another inscription in the same temple records that 306,372 people from 13,500 villages worked for the shrine, consuming 38,000 tons of rice a year. An inscription in the nearby temple of Ta Prohm inventories a staff of 18 senior priests, 2740 minor functionaries, 615 female dancers, and a total of 66,625 "men and women who perform the service of the gods." The same temple owned gold and silver dishes, thousands of pearls, 876 Chinese veils, and 2387 sets of clothing for its statues. The result of the ruler's megalomaniacal orgy was a totally centripetal and macabre religious utopia in which every product, every person's labor, and every thought was directed to embellishing the hub of the universe and the men who enjoyed it (Wheatley, 1975).

After A.D. 1218 an exhausted nation built no more stone temples. The seemingly endless pool of prisoners of war dried up once the economy faltered, and there were no longer the resources to support the army or maintain the great irrigation works of Tonle Sap. The only way the Khmer could maintain their strange utopia was by oppression, promiscuous use of slave labor, and through the blind obedience of their own subjects. Once the image of the divine king was challenged and the slaves ceased to serve, the empire was doomed. Angkor Thom fell to alien armies in approximately 1430 and the divine kings and their works soon were soon just a shadowy memory.

GUIDE TO FURTHER READING

Allchin, Bridget, and Allchin, Raymond. *The Rise of Civilization in India and Pakistan.* Cambridge: Cambridge University Press, 1982.
A summary account of the roots of the Indus civilization that is readable and well argued.

Fairservis, Walter A. *The Roots of Ancient India* (2d ed.). New York: Macmillan, 1975.
A popular account of the Harappan that contains an excellent description of the cities.

Wheeler, Sir Mortimer. *The Indus Civilization.* Cambridge: Cambridge University Press, 1962.
Wheeler's classic account is based on his Indus Valley excavations in the late 1940s. Somewhat outdated, but it reads well.

White, Joyce. *Ban Chiang: Discovery of a Lost Bronze Age.* Philadelphia: University of Pennsylvania Press, 1982.
A brief but clearly written account of this remarkable site written to accompany a museum exhibition. Gives a useful insight into Southeast Asian bronzeworking.

Wolpert, Stanley A. *A New History of India.* London: Oxford University Press, 1977.
By far the most lucid account of Indian history for the beginner. A good synthesis of archaeology, legend, and documentary sources.

Southeast Asia is difficult to study in any depth, for books on Khmer civilization are few and far between. However, the following are suggested:

Briggs, L. Cabot. "The Ancient Khmer Empire." *Transactions of the American Philosophical Society* 41, 1951.
Perhaps the standard archaeological and historical source for specialists and lay readers alike. Highly technical, but crammed with useful information, much of it from very obscure sources.

Giteau, M. *Khmer Sculpture and the Angkor Civilization.* London: Thames and Hudson, 1966.
A wonderful lay reader's guide to the elaborate artistry and architecture of the Khmer. Lavishly illustrated.

Chronological Table J

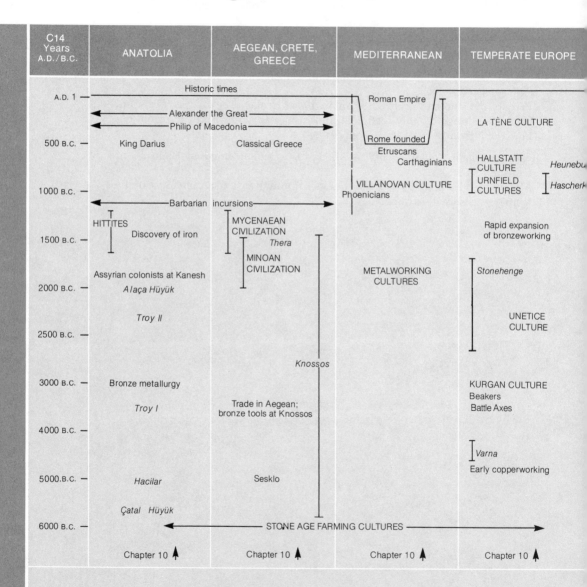

C14 Years A.D./B.C.	ANATOLIA	AEGEAN, CRETE, GREECE	MEDITERRANEAN	TEMPERATE EUROPE
	Historic times			
A.D. 1 —			Roman Empire	
	←————— Alexander the Great —————→			LA TÈNE CULTURE
	←————— Philip of Macedonia —————→			
500 B.C. —	King Darius	Classical Greece	Rome founded	
			Etruscans	HALLSTATT CULTURE	*Heunebu*
			Carthaginians	URNFIELD CULTURES	*Hascherk*
1000 B.C. —			VILLANOVAN CULTURE	
	←————— Barbarian incursions —————→		Phoenicians	
	HITTITES	MYCENAEAN CIVILIZATION		Rapid expansion of bronzeworking
1500 B.C. —	Discovery of iron	*Thera*		
		MINOAN CIVILIZATION		
	Assyrian colonists at Kanesh		METALWORKING CULTURES	*Stonehenge*
2000 B.C. —	*Alaça Hüyük*			
	Troy II			UNETICE CULTURE
2500 B.C. —				
		Knossos		
3000 B.C. —	Bronze metallurgy			KURGAN CULTURE
	Troy I	Trade in Aegean; bronze tools at Knossos		Beakers Battle Axes
4000 B.C. —				
				Varna
				Early copperworking
5000 B.C. —	*Hacilar*	Sesklo		
	Çatal Hüyük			
6000 B.C. —	←————— STONE AGE FARMING CULTURES —————→			
	Chapter 10 ↑	Chapter 10 ↑	Chapter 10 ↑	Chapter 10 ↑

Chapter Eighteen

Anatolia, Greece, and Italy

PREVIEW

❊ Anatolia was a major locale for the development of early farming villages, one of which, Çatal Hüyük, became a small town in the sixth millennium B.C. Strangely, however, Çatal Hüyük failed to develop the necessary administrative and social mechanisms to cope with the increased complexity of the settlement and its trading activities. The town failed, and Anatolians of the fifth millennium reverted to village life.

❊ Small fortified villages, such as the one preserved in the later levels of Hacilar, flourished in the fourth millennium. One of them, Troy I, dates to just after 3500 B.C. Troy II, founded in approximately 2300 B.C., was a fortified town with more elaborate architecture and fine gold and bronze metallurgy. By this time the Anatolians were trading widely over the highlands and into the Aegean, and chieftaincies were scattered over mineral-rich areas. In 1900 B.C., the Assyrians set up a trading colony at Kanesh in central Anatolia that was similar to those set up by the Mesopotamians elsewhere.

❊ The Hittites were a small group of leaders who originated in the north and assumed power in Anatolia approximately 1650 B.C. They held a vital place in contemporary history, for they played the Assyrians off against the Egyptians. Hittite power was based on diplomatic and trading skills and lasted until approximately 1200 B.C. They are associated with the discovery of iron smelting.

❊ The Aegean and the Greek mainlands were settled by sedentary farming villages well before 5000 B.C. Painted pottery styles came into widespread use near that time.

❊ There were radical changes after 3500 B.C., when the cultivation of the olive and the vine became widespread, and trading of minerals, stone wares, and other products expanded rapidly. Numerous small towns were flourishing throughout the Aegean and eastern Greece by 2500 B.C., linked by regular trading routes.

❊ The Minoan civilization of Crete developed as a result of these cultural routes approximately 2000 B.C. and lasted until approximately 1400 B.C. The development of this civilization is known from the ruins of the Palace of Knossos. The Minoans traded as far afield as Egypt and the eastern Mediterranean and were expert metalworkers and potters, with a lively artistic tradition.

❊ Minoan power apparently was weakened by the great explosion of its satellite island, Thera, in 1500 B.C. The center of civilization passed to the mainland, where the

Mycenaeans flourished until 1150 B.C. The Mycenaeans were able to develop some trading connections with temperate Europe as well as continue many Minoan trade routes. They were overthrown by Phrygian peoples at the end of the second millennium.

✿ Trading activities continued to expand in the Aegean after the decline of Mycenae. Small city-states flourished, unifying only in the face of a common danger such as the Persian invasions of the fifth century B.C. The Athenians enjoyed a long period of supremacy among city-states, the period of Classical Greek civilization in the fifth century B.C.

✿ Alexander the Great built an enormous empire across the Near East, of which Greece was part, in the late fourth century B.C. The Roman Empire which followed marks the entry of the entire Mediterranean area into historic times. Developed from Villanovan and Etruscan roots in Italy, the Roman Imperial power was based on the ruins of Alexander's empire.

This chapter begins with a disclaimer: the prehistory of Anatolia, Europe, and the Mediterranean Basin is so complicated, and our knowledge so spotty, that we can touch only the highlights here (Trump, 1980). Interested readers should consult the references included in the Bibliography of Archaeology for more information on these areas.

ANATOLIA

Çatal Hüyük
5600 B.C.

During the height of its prosperity in the sixth millennium B.C., the town of Çatal Hüyük controlled trade over huge areas of central Anatolia (Figure 18.1), so much so that it was the focus for villages hundreds of miles around (Mellaart, 1967). This complex settlement was oganized by creating ritual and other mechanisms that attempted to retain the close kinship ties of village life while adapting to the new complexities of long-distance trading and growing population. Unlike Mesopotamia, where new mechanisms and organizations evolved to handle social change, the system at Çatal Hüyük broke down. Anatolia's first and largest town was abandoned and people went back to living in small villages (Mellaart, 1975; Redman, 1978).

The entire plateau of Anatolia seems to have experienced a subsequent, gradual population increase during the fifth millennium B.C., as long-distance trading with Mesopotamia in minerals and other materials increased. The evidence for the concentration of power and wealth in major Anatolian settlements is found after 3000 B.C. in the walled fortresses of Hissarlik (Troy) and Kultepe (ancient Kanesh) (Blegan, 1971).

Troy I (Hissarlik)
3500 B.C.

Hissarlik was first occupied approximately 3500 B.C., when a small fortress was built on bedrock. Its foundations show it contained a rectangular hall of a basic design that had been in use for centuries. The structure was to become the standard palace design of later centuries and perhaps a prototype for the Classical Greek temple. Approximately 2300

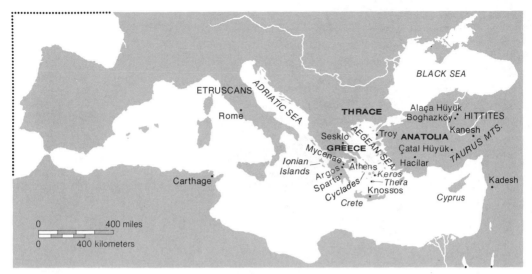

Figure 18.1   Sites and cultures mentioned in this chapter.

B.C., a new settlement known to archaeologists as Troy II flourished at Hissarlik. This fortified town boasted of more elaborate buildings and yielded valuable hoards of gold and bronze ornaments — a clear sign that the rulers of the settlement were supporting skilled craftspeople who designed and executed fine ornaments of rank.

Troy II
2300 B.C.

Thirteen royal tombs were found at the site of the town of Alaça Hüyük in central Anatolia, dating to the end of the third millennium B.C. The tombs contain the bodies of men and their wives accompanied by domestic vessels, weapons, and many metal items (Piggott, 1965). The ornaments include copper figurines with gold breasts and finely wrought cast bronze stags inlaid with silver which were perhaps mounted on the ends of poles (Figure 18.2).

Alaça Hüyük
2000 B.C.

Both the Alaça Hüyük and Hissarlik finds testify to widespread trade in gold, copper, tin, and other raw materials by 2000 B.C. Major centers like these maintained long-distance trading contacts throughout the Near East. These, along with trading offshore to Cyprus and the Aegean islands, could well have influenced social and political developments.

Toward the end of the third millennium, Indo-European-speaking peoples seem to have infiltrated Anatolia from the northwest, causing considerable political unrest. By this time, central Anatolia was coming into much closer contact with Mesopotamia. By 1900 B.C., there was a sizable Assyrian merchant colony outside the city of Kanesh, one of several important trading centers or *karums* that were staging posts for long-distance commerce in minerals and other commodities (Lloyd, 1967). The karums served as marketplaces and termini for caravans, neutral entrepôts (commercial centers, sometimes warehouses) where prices for goods were regulated. Local rulers levied taxes on the caravans, which

Kanesh
1900 B.C.

Figure 18.2 Bronze stag from Alaça Hüyük, inlaid with silver (left), and miniature gold figure of a Hittite king.

brought important Assyrian ideas to Anatolia and reinforced the political and economic power of Anatolian kings.

THE HITTITES

Hittites
1650 to 1200 B.C.

The Hittites appear to have been a group of able Indo-European people from the vast steppes north of Anatolia, who infiltrated the plateau and seized power from the leaders of Kanesh and other cities, probably just before the seventeenth century B.C. (Gurney, 1961; Lehmann, 1977).

No historian would be taken in by the Hittites' own extravagant claims for their glorious history. The Hittites seem, in practice, to have been a foreign minority who rose to political power by judiciously melding conquest and astute political maneuvering. The minority soon became acculturated into its new milieu, even though it seemed to have preserved its traditional values and outlook on life.

The Hittites were a down-to-earth people, with a talent for political and military administration. They were not intellectuals, but religion was important to them. The king was not deified until after his death, if then. His duties were well defined: to ensure the state's welfare, wage war, and act as high priest under clearly defined circumstances. A hierarchy of officials supported the king. One unusual institution was the *pan-*

kush, a form of assembly that may have had a restricted membership, perhaps open only to those of pure Hittite stock. However, we see no sign that this institution, with its undertones of racial superiority, ever wielded much power.

The Hittites exercised enormous political influence in the Near East from their vast capital at Boghazköy with its 4 mi (6.4 km) of city walls. They used their wealth and diplomatic skill to play Assyria and Egypt against one another. They were hardened warriors as well, who campaigned as far south as Babylon and fought Rameses II on the outskirts of Kadesh. Their objectives were simple enough: to acquire new spheres of political influence and to control trade routes. Boghazköy

One major achievement of the Hittites was the systematic use of iron, thought to have been smelted first in the middle of the second millennium B.C., in the highlands immediately south of the Black Sea. The military advantages of this metal lay in its relative abundance in a natural state, even if it was harder to smelt. The Hittites seem to have guarded the secrets of ironworking for some time, but eventually foreign mercenaries in their armies carried the new techniques to their homelands. Iron tools soon became commonplace over a wide area of Europe and the Near East, although it was some time before domestic artifacts such as axes and hoes were invariably made of the new metal (Wertime and Muhly, 1980). Ironworking

Hittite rule did not last long in Anatolia. Approximately 1200 B.C., repeated migrations of foreigners flowed into Anatolia from the northwest, whence the Hittites had come only four centuries earlier. These population movements came to a head when the Phrygian peoples from Thrace (see Figure 18.1) ravaged the plateau as far as the Taurus mountains. Anatolia became the homeland of dozens of small city-states, each striving to maintain its independence. Only a few Hittite communities survived, in small states in northern Syria that lasted until they were engulfed in the vast Persian Empire. Phrygians
1200 B.C.

THE AEGEAN AND GREECE

Parts of mainland Greece and the Aegean were settled by farming peoples as early as 6500 B.C., but more intensive settlement of western Greece, the islands, and Crete did not occur until much later. **6500 B.C.**

The Sesklo village in Thessaly, northern Greece, was occupied approximately 5000 B.C. and is typical of northern Greek sites of the time (Warren, 1975). The people lived in stone and mud houses connected by courtyards and passages. Their mixed farming economy depended heavily on cereal cultivation. Somewhat similar villages are found on Crete where farming settlement dates back to at least 5500 B.C. Sesklo
5000 B.C.

There were radical changes in the settlement pattern after 3500 B.C. when villages were established in the Cyclades, throughout Crete, and on the Ionian islands of the west. In contrast, northern Greece seems to **3500 B.C.**

have lagged behind. The reason may have been agriculture, for southern Greece and the islands are ideal environments for the cultivation of olives and vines, with cereal crops interspersed between them (C. Renfrew, 1972). There was a veritable explosion in village crafts as well, in the manufacture of fine painted pottery, marble vessels, and magnificent stone axes. Stone vases and fine seals were made by Cretan workers (Figure 18.3); the seals were used to mark ownership of prized possessions or pots full of oil or other commodities. By 3500 B.C., the peoples of the Aegean and Greece were smelting copper and making bronze artifacts as well as ornaments in gold and silver. These included exquisite gold and silver drinking cups and the elaborate ornaments found at Troy II, which included more than 8700 gold beads, wire ornaments, chain links, and objects of fine gold sheet. The achievements of the Aegean metallurgists were in part owing to the rapid expansion of trading throughout the Aegean, far into Anatolia, and to Cyprus, with its rich copper outcrops (see C. Renfrew and Wagstaff, 1982).

2500 B.C. The Aegean is well endowed with comfortable ports and alternative trading routes that provided easy communication from island to island for most of the year. Even relatively primitive vessels could coast from one end of the Aegean to the other in easy stages. Sailing vessels are depicted on Cretan seals dating to approximately 2000 B.C. The Aegean trade flourished on olive oil and wine, metal tools and ores, marble vessels and figurines, and pottery. The success of the trade led to a constant infusion of new products and ideas to Greece and the Aegean. By 2500

Figure 18.3 Harpist in marble, executed by a craftsworker on the island of Keros in the Aegean.

B.C., numerous small towns housed farmers, traders, and skilled crafts-workers on the mainland and the islands.

The beginnings of town life created considerable cultural diversity in the Aegean, a diversity fostered by constant trading connections and increased complexity in social and political organization. Nowhere is this better documented than in Crete, where a brilliant civilization flourished at towns and palaces throughout the island. In contrast, mainland Greece lagged somewhat behind, its many small towns having only occasional contact with the Aegean islands and Crete.

THE MINOANS

The development of the Minoan civilization of Crete was almost certainly the result of many local factors, among them the intensive cultivation of the olive and the vine. Its development is best documented at the famous Palace of Knossos near Heraklion in northern Crete (Figure 18.4) (Hood, 1973; Warren, 1975).

The first prehistoric inhabitants of Knossos settled there in approximately 6100 B.C. No fewer than 7 m (23 ft) of early farming occupation underlie the Minoan civilization. The first Knossos settlement was founded at approximately the same time that Çatal Hüyük was first occupied in Anatolia. The Knossos farmers lived in sun-dried mud and brick

Knossos
6100 to 1400 B.C.

Figure 18.4 General view of the Palace of Minos at Knossos.

huts of a rectangular ground plan that provided for storage bins and sleeping platforms. By 3730 B.C., signs of long-distance trading increase in the form of exotic imports such as stone bowls. The first palace at Knossos was built in approximately 1930 B.C., a large building with many rooms grouped around a rectangular central court.

At least nine periods of Minoan civilization have been distinguished by pottery styles found in the later levels of the Knossos site. Even during the earlier periods of the civilization, the Minoans were trading regularly with Egypt, for their pottery and metal objects have been found in burials there. In 1700 B.C. the earlier palaces were destroyed by an earthquake.

The high point of Minoan civilization followed that destruction, occurring between 1700 and 1450 B.C., when the Palace of Knossos reached its greatest size. This remarkable structure was made mainly of mud brick and timber beams with occasional limestone blocks and wood columns. Some buildings had two stories; the plaster walls and floors were decorated, initially with geometric designs, and after 1700 B.C. with vivid scenes or individual pictures of varying size. Sometimes the decorations were executed in relief; in other cases, colors were applied to the damp plaster (Figure 18.5).

Figure 18.5 Reconstruction of the throne room at Knossos, Crete. The wall paintings are modern reconstructions from fragments found at the site; details may be inaccurate.

Artistic themes included formal landscapes, dolphins and other sea creatures, and scenes of Minoan life. The most remarkable art depicted dances and religious ceremonies, including acrobats leaping vigorously along the backs of bulls (Figure 18.6). Writer Mary Renault has vividly reconstructed Cretan life at Knossos in novels that bring Minoan culture to life (Renault, 1963).

At the height of its prosperity, Crete was self-supporting in food and basic raw materials, exporting foodstuffs, cloth, and painted pottery all over the eastern Mediterranean. The Cretans were renowned mariners. Their large ships transported gold, silver, obsidian, ivory, and ornaments from central Europe, the Aegean, and the Near East, and ostrich eggs probably were traded from North Africa.

We know very little of Minoan religious beliefs, except for some chilling finds made by Peter Warren in a house on the north side of Knossos. This fine building had collapsed in the great earthquake of 1450 B.C. The first-floor ceiling fell into the basement, taking a magnificent set of ritual vessels with it. The basement fill also contained the scattered bones of two children in perfect health. A microscopic examination of the limb bones showed that knives had been used to remove flesh from the bone. Warren believes that this may be evidence not only of human sacrifice but, perhaps, of ritual cannibalism as well, and, possibly, this related to a fertility rite associated with the Cretan Zeus and the Earth Mother (Warren, 1984).

In 1473 B.C., a volcano on the island of Thera, a Minoan outpost 70 mi (113 km) from Crete, exploded with such violence that it probably caused catastrophic destruction on the north coast of the Minoan kingdom. This event is equated by some people with the eternal legend of Atlantis, the mysterious continent said to have sunk to the ocean bottom after a holocaust thousands of years ago (Luce, 1973). The Thera eruption may have accelerated the decline of Minoan civilization, which was already showing signs of weakness. Fifty years later many Minoan sites were destroyed and abandoned. Warrior farmers, perhaps from mainland Greece, established sway over the empire and decorated the walls of Knossos with military scenes. Seventy-five years later the palace finally was destroyed by fire, thought to have been the work of Mycenaeans who razed it. By this time the center of the Aegean world had shifted to the Greek mainland, where Mycenae reached the height of its power.

The dramatic flowering of Minoan civilization stemmed from the intensified trading contacts and the impact of olive and vine cultivation on hundreds of Greek and Aegean villages. As agricultural economies became more diversified and local food surpluses could be exchanged both locally and over longer distances, a far-reaching economic interdependence resulted. Eventually this led to redistribution systems for luxuries and basic commodities, systems that were organized and controlled by Minoan palaces and elsewhere in the Aegean where there were major centers of olive production.

Thera
1473 B.C.

?1400 B.C.

1375 to 1350 B.C.

Figure 18.6 A Minoan bull and dancers, as painted on the walls of the Palace of Knossos. The bull, a domesticated form, has a piebald coat. This very fragmentary scene has been reconstructed from rather inadequate original pieces and is somewhat controversial. (After Evans, 1921)

The redistribution networks carried metal objects and other luxury products the length and breadth of the Aegean as the self-sufficiency of earlier farming communities was replaced by mutual interdependence. Interest in long-distance trading brought about some cultural homogeneity from trade, gift exchange, and perhaps piracy. The skills of specialist craftsworkers were highly valued in village and palace alike. Specialized artisans practiced their crafts in the major palaces; they lived well, in stone buildings with well-designed drainage systems, and had wooden furniture.

Colin Renfrew describes both Minoan society and that of its successors, the Mycenaeans of the Greek mainland, as civilizations (C. Renfrew, 1973). He points to their sophisticated art and metalwork, to the complex palaces organized around specialized craftsworkers, and to their developed redistribution networks for foods. The Minoans and Mycenaeans did not build vast temples like those at Tikal in Guatemala (Chapter Twenty-One) or those in Egypt. They also did not live in cities. Palaces and elaborate tombs were the major monuments. Renfrew looks for the origins of Minoan and Mycenaean civilization within Greece and the Aegean, and considers them to be the result of local social change and material progress, not external population movements. His theory sharply differs from earlier hypotheses that claimed migration of new peoples into Greece from the north or diffusion of new culture traits from Anatolia or the eastern Mediterranean were responsible (Childe, 1956).

THE MYCENAEANS

Mycenaeans
1600 to 1200 B.C.

The Mycenaean civilization, centered on the fertile plain of Argos on the Greek mainland, began to flourish during the sixteenth century B.C. (Taylour, 1969). The chieftains who ruled over the walled fortress of Mycenae (Figure 18.7) were buried in spectacular shaft graves that con-

Figure 18.7 The Lion Gate at Mycenae.

tained weapons adorned with copper and gold, as well as fine gold face masks modeled in the likeness of their owners (Figure 18.8). Their wealth and economic power came from far-flung trading contacts as well as from their warrior skills (Figure 18.9). The kings were skilled charioteers and horsemen, whose material culture and lifeway are immortalized in the Homeric epics. These epics, however, were written many centuries after the Mycenaeans themselves had become folk memories (Rieu, 1945).

Mycenaean commerce took over where Minoan left off. Much of the rulers' prestige was based on their contacts in the metal trade. Minerals were in constant demand in the central and eastern Mediterranean, especially tin for alloying copper to make bronze. Both copper and tin were abundant in central Cyprus and Anatolia, and the Mycenaeans developed the necessary contacts to obtain regular supplies.

The Mycenaeans also prized Baltic amber, a yellow-brown fossil resin that when rubbed seems to be "electric." Occasional pieces of this precious substance reached Mycenae, and amber is found in the royal graves there (Piggott, 1965). Just how extensive the Mycenaeans' European

Figure 18.8 Gold mask of a bearded man, from Shaft Grave V at Mycenae, Greece, sixteenth century B.C.

trading activities were has been much debated. They may well have been minimal (for a discussion, see Harding, 1984).

So complex did Mycenaean trading transactions become that the Mycenaeans found it necessary to establish a writing system. They refined one that had first been developed by the Minoans. The Mycenaeans used a form of script written in the Greek language, known now as Linear B (Chadwick, 1958; Diringer, 1962). Eighty-nine characters make up Linear B, forty-eight of which can be traced back to Minoan writing, Linear

Figure 18.9 Impression of a warrior fighting an enemy with a dagger, from an engraved gold ring, shaft graves, Mycenae, Greece.

A. Linear A probably originated in the simple pictographic script of the earliest Minoans (Figure 18.10). The terms Linear A and Linear B were coined by Sir Arthur Evans when he first studied Minoan writing. Linear B was in more widespread use than A, partly because the Mycenaeans exerted greater political and economic power than their Cretan neighbors.

Mycenae continued to dominate eastern Mediterranean trade until the twelfth century B.C., when its power was destroyed by warrior peoples from the north. In the same century, other northern barbarians destroyed the Hittite kingdom in Anatolia. These incursions into the Mediterranean world were caused by unsettled political conditions in Europe, at least partly the result of population pressures and tribal warfare. (Chapter Nineteen).

1150 B.C.

THE MEDITERRANEAN AFTER MYCENAE

After Mycenae fell in 1200 B.C., small-town merchants on the Greek mainland continued to trade as their Mycenaean predecessors had, monopolizing commerce in the Aegean and the Black seas. By the seventh and eighth centuries B.C., small colonies of Greek settlers lived on the northern and western shores of the Black Sea and along the north coast of Anatolia, and developed trade in gold, copper, iron, salt, and other commodities. Other Greeks voyaged westward and settled in

1200 B.C.

700 to 600 B.C.

Figure 18.10 Early forms of writing: (a) Cretan pictographic script; (b) Linear A signs.

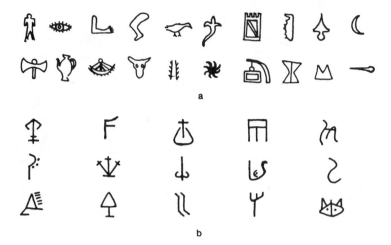

a

b

southern France; they soon made a brisk trade in wine and other commodities with central Europe.

The Greek City-States

In Greece many fertile agricultural areas are separated by ranges of mountains. Traders and seamen of the Aegean islands and the Greek mainland therefore formed a network of small city-states that competed with each other for trade and political power. Athens was one of the larger and more prosperous states. The island of Sifnos in the Aegean was another, famous for its gold and silver. Paros marble was known all over the eastern Mediterranean, while Milos provided obsidian for many centuries.

Greek states unified only in times of grave political stress, as when the Persian King Xerxes sought to add Greece to his possessions. Xerxes' defeats at Marathon (490 B.C.) and ten years later in a naval battle at Salamis ensured the security of Greece and made Classical Greek civilization possible. Athens was foremost among the Greek states (Kinley, 1963; Kitto, 1958), becoming head of a league of maritime cities, which was soon turned into an empire. This was the Athens that attracted wealthy immigrants, built the Parthenon, and boasted of Aeschylus, Sophocles, and other mighty playwrights. Classical Greek civilization flourished for fifty glorious years.

However, throughout the brilliant decades of Athenian supremacy, bickering rivalry with the city of Sparta in Peloponnesus never abated. A deep animosity between the two cities had its roots in radically different social systems. Sparta's government was based on military discipline and a rigid class structure. Athenians enjoyed a more mobile society and democratic government.

The long rivalry culminated in the disastrous Peloponnesian War from 431 to 404 B.C. that left Sparta a dominant political force on the main-

490 B.C.

Athens

450 B.C.

431 B.C.

land. The contemporary historian Thucydides documented the war, which was followed by disarray (Livingston, 1943). Greece soon fell under the sway of Philip of Macedonia, whose rule between 359 and 336 B.C. began to develop political unity. His son Alexander the Great then embarked on a campaign of imperial conquest that took him from Macedonia into Persia and then to Mesopotamia. Alexander was welcomed as a hero and a god in Egypt, where he paused long enough to sacrifice to local deities and have himself proclaimed pharaoh. His continued quests took him as far east as the Indus Valley and back to Babylon, where he died of fever in 323 B.C. By the time of his death, Alexander had united an enormous area of the ancient world under at least nominal Greek rule. His extraordinary empire fell apart within a generation, but his conquests paved the way for the uniform government of Imperial Rome.

359 B.C.

323 B.C.

The Phoenicians

While the Greeks were developing their trading endeavors in the Aegean and Black seas, other maritime peoples, too, had turned into vigorous traders. The Phoenicians of Lebanon first rose to prosperity by acting as middlemen in the growing trade in raw materials and manufactured products (Harden, 1962; N. Sanders, 1977). Phoenician ships carried Lebanese cedarwood and dye to Cyprus and the Aegean area as well as to Egypt. After Mycenae declined, they took over much of the copper and iron ore trade of the Mediterranean. Their trading networks later extended far to the west, as they ventured to Spain in search of copper, tin, and the purple dye extracted from seashells and much used for expensive fabrics. By 800 B.C., Phoenician merchants were everywhere. They were using a fully alphabetical script by the tenth century B.C.

Phoenicians

1200 B.C.

800 B.C.

Phoenicians not only traded widely but also set up small colonies that served as their vassals and were marketplaces for the hinterland of Spain and North Africa. Some settlements won independence from home rule. The greatest was the North African city Carthage, which challenged the power of the Roman Empire.

The Etruscans

The Greeks and Phoenicians were expanding maritime activities at the same time as skilled bronze workers and copper miners in northern Italy were developing a distinctive but short-lived urban civilization.

In approximately 1000 B.C., some Urnfield peoples from central Europe (Chapter Nineteen) had settled south of the Alps in the Po Valley (Wells, 1981). They developed a skilled bronzeworking tradition, in which products were traded far into central Europe and throughout Italy. This people evolved into the Villanovan culture, which appeared in the ninth century B.C. and was soon in touch with Greek colonies in southern Italy and perhaps with the Phoenicians (Piggott, 1965). Ironworking was introduced to the Villanovans in approximately the ninth

1000 B.C.

Villanovan culture
850 B.C.

century. Iron tools and extensive trading contacts won the Villanovans political control over much of northern and western Italy. They established colonies on the islands of Elba and Corsica. Several centuries of trade and other contacts culminated in a literate Etruscan civilization.

Etruscans
650 to 450 B.C.

Like Classical Greece, Etruscan civilization was more a unity of cultural tradition and trade than a political reality (Pallotino, 1977). The Etruscans traded widely in the central Mediterranean and with warrior peoples in central Europe. Etruscan culture was derived from the Villanovan, but it owed much to eastern immigrants and trading contacts that brought oriental influence to Italian towns.

Etruscan territory was settled by city-states with much independence, each with substantial public buildings and fortifications. Their decentralized political organization made them vulnerable to foreign raiders. Warrior bands from central Europe overran some Etruscan cities in the centuries after 450 B.C., at which time Etruscan prosperity began to crumble.

450 B.C.

By the time of Etruscan decline, however, the Mediterranean was a civilized lake. Phoenician colonists had founded Carthage and other cities in North Africa and Spain and controlled the western Mediterranean. The rulers of Greece and Egypt and later Philip of Macedonia controlled the east, and the Etruscans were in control of most of Italy and many central European trade routes.

The Romans

The Etruscans had been the first people to fortify the seven famed hills of Rome. In 509 B.C., a foreign dynasty of rulers was evicted by these native Romans, who began to develop their own distinctive city-state. The next few centuries saw the emergence of Rome from a cluster of simple villages by the Tiber River to the leadership of the Mediterranean and far beyond. The Romans inherited the mantle of Classical Greece and added their own distinctive culture to this foundation. They then carried Greco-Roman civilization to many parts of the world that were still inhabited by preliterate peasant societies. Roman legions campaigned not only in Egypt and Mesopotamia and as far as India, but also in central and western Europe and in Britain. If it were not for the Romans, the administrative and linguistic face of Europe would be very different today (Grant, 1960; Selincourt, 1966; Vickers, 1977).

Romans
509 B.C.

295 B.C.

By 295 B.C., the power of Rome dominated the whole of Italy. At this time Rome was a form of democracy, governed by a delicate balance of aristocratic and popular authority. This type of governance was appropriate for a large city-state but was helplessly inadequate for the complexities of governing a huge empire. Eventually, civil strife led to autocratic rule of the empire under the emperors, the first of whom was Julius Caesar, familiar to every student of Roman history for his epic conquest of Gaul (France). (His great-nephew Augustus was the first ruler to actually claim the title of emperor.)

After two vicious wars with their rich rival, Carthage, the Romans achieved mastery over the western Mediterranean by 200 B.C., and by 133 B.C. much of Asia was under uneasy Roman domination. Unfortunately, the Romans lacked the mechanisms to administer their empire successfully until the Emperor Augustus reorganized the civil service and established the Pax Romana over his vast domains. There ensued a period of great material prosperity and political stability, at the price of political freedom of speech.

The stresses that led to the collapse of the Roman Empire first began to appear on the European frontiers in the second and third centuries A.D. Roman power began to decline as ambition and sophistication grew among the Iron Age tribes living on the fringes of Roman territory. The "barbarians" on the fringes of the Empire were mainly peasant farmers who had obtained iron by trading and intermarriage with La Tène peoples (Chapter Nineteen). Many served as mercenaries in the Roman armies, acquiring wealth and sophistication, and perhaps most important of all, an insight into Roman military tactics.

Shortage of farming land and increasing disrespect for Rome caused many Germanic tribes to raid Rome's European provinces. The raids were so successful that the imperial armies were constantly campaigning in the north. In A.D. 395, after Emperor Theodosius died, the Roman Empire was split into eastern and western divisions. Large barbarian invasions from northern Europe ensued. Fifteen years later, a horde of Germanic tribesmen from central Europe sacked Rome itself; then the European provinces were completely overrun by warrior peoples. Other Germanic hordes disturbed North Africa and crossed much of Asia Minor, but left little lasting mark on history there.

What was the legacy of Rome? Its material legacy can be seen in the road system, which still provides a basis for many of Europe's and the Near East's communications, and in the towns, like London, which are still flourishing modern cities. In cultural terms, its principal legacy was the legal system, which lies at the core of most western law codes. Roman literature and art dominated European culture for centuries after the Renaissance. Their spoken and written language, Latin, survived for centuries as the language of the educated person and as the principal means of business communication between nations. Latin lies at the base of many modern European languages and was only recently abandoned as the liturgical language of the Roman Catholic Church. The Romans and their culture lie at the foundations of our own Western Civilization.

GUIDE TO FURTHER READING

Gurney, O. R. *The Hittites*. Baltimore: Pelican Books, 1961.
    Probably the classic source on this remarkable civilization, written from both archaeological and documentary sources.

Hood, Sinclair. *The Minoans*. London: Thames and Hudson, 1973.
An excellent summary of the origins, history, and decline of the Minoan civilization for the informed lay person. Excellent illustrations.

Luce, J. V. *Atlantis*. New York: McGraw-Hill, 1973.
A convincing account of the Atlantis legend and a possible explanation for it in the eruption and explosion at Santorini (Thera) in the Aegean.

Renfrew, Colin. *The Emergence of Civilization*. London: Methuen, 1972.
Renfrew's study contains a mass of information about Aegean civilization and trade, and adopts a systems approach. Technical, but invaluable to the general reader.

Taylour, Lord William. *The Mycenaeans*. London: Thames and Hudson, 1969.
Mycenaean civilization described by a leading authority, a companion volume to Hood on the Minoans. Lavishly illustrated.

Warren, Peter. *The Aegean Civilizations*. Oxford: Elsevier Phaidon, 1975.
An up-to-date synthesis of Bronze Age Greece and its antecedents for the beginner. Excellent illustrations and thoughtful text.

Chapter Nineteen

Temperate Europe Before the Romans

PREVIEW

�֍ In contrast to earlier hypotheses, archaeologists now believe that copperworking was developed independently in southeastern Europe in the fifth millennium. The Varna cemetery in Bulgaria shows just how elaborate the gold and copper metallurgy of the area became. The industry flourished because of a demand for fine metal ornaments. Copperworking also developed early in southern Spain and northern Italy.

✖ Copperworking developed in several areas of Europe and was a logical development from earlier stone and ceramic technologies. Its more widespread use coincides with the spread of Beaker and Battle Ax artifacts throughout much of Europe.

✖ Bronzeworking began at an unknown date but was widespread in what is now Czechoslovakia by 2500 B.C., as part of the Unetice culture. The trading networks of earlier times expanded to meet increased indigenous demand for metal artifacts during a period of rapid technological change after 1700 B.C. Some rich chieftaincies developed in the temperate zones, among them the Wessex culture of southern Britain.

✖ The Urnfield peoples of central Europe began to expand from their homeland in approximately 800 B.C. Armed with new slashing swords, they settled all over Europe, bringing their new and more effective agricultural techniques with them. Their economic organization probably included specialist smiths and traders.

✖ After 1000 B.C., ironworking techniques diffused into temperate Europe and spread through the Hallstatt and La Tène cultural traditions during the first millennium B.C. The La Tène people were the Celtic-speaking warriors encountered by Julius Caesar and his Roman legionnaires in the first century B.C.

✖ After the Roman conquest of central and western Europe, much of the temperate zone became at least superficially Romanized. The ultimate downfall of the Roman Empire was owing not only to internal weaknesses in the system but to the independence of the subjugated European peasants. Living on the frontiers of the Empire, they were able to use their military skills finally to overthrow Roman rule in the West.

The fundamental question about the emergence of complex societies in temperate Europe is simple: did they emerge as a result of indigenous cultural evolution, or because of diffusion of people and ideas from the Near East?

V. Gordon Childe, Stuart Piggott, and others have argued that the constant demands by Near Eastern societies for copper, tin, and other metals led to cultural development in the backwater that was temperate Europe (Childe, 1956; Piggott, 1965). However, this traditional viewpoint has been challenged by the new calibrated radiocarbon chronologies that place the appearance of copperworking in the Balkans earlier than in Greece or the Aegean. Many people now believe that Europeans were just as innovative as their eastern neighbors (Champion et al., 1984; Milisauskas, 1978).

EARLY COPPERWORKING

Colin Renfrew and Ruth Tringham have argued that the farmers of southeastern Europe developed copper smelting independently, partly because they already used improved pottery firing techniques that were very suitable for copper smelting (Figure 19.1) (C. Renfrew, 1978;

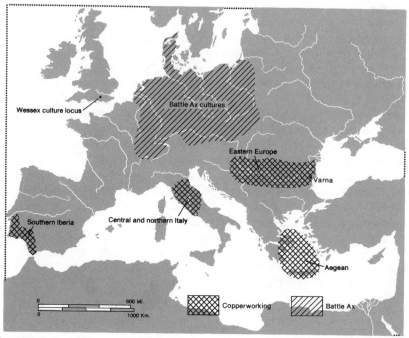

Figure 19.1 Major centers of early metallurgy in temperate Europe and the distribution of Battle Ax cultures.

Tringham, 1971). They cite as proof of the early development the finds at the Varna cemetery near the Black Sea in Bulgaria.

The Varna Cemetery

At the Varna cemetery, more than 130 richly decorated graves have yielded dozens of fine copper and gold tools and ornaments. Colin Renfrew has described the Varna finds as "the earliest major assemblage of gold artifacts to be unearthed anywhere in the world," for they date to approximately 4600 to 4200 B.C. (C. Renfrew, 1978). Both the copper and the gold are of Balkan origin; indeed both metals were being worked here earlier than they were in the Near East. (Such a statement reflects findings thus far; it does not preclude future discoveries of earlier metals in the Near East.) The Balkan copper industry was quite sophisticated and was organized to serve trading networks over a wide area. At Rudna Glava in Yugoslavia deep fissures mark the places where early miners followed ore veins deep into the ground. One mine in Bulgaria has ancient shafts more than 10 m (32 ft) deep. These copper mines are the earliest so far discovered in the world and show that metallurgy developed rapidly into a considerable industry in the Balkans during the fifth millennium B.C. (Jovanovic, 1980).

The Varna burials provide striking evidence for differential wealth, for some of the graves are richly decorated with gold ornaments while others contain few artifacts. Unfortunately, the settlement associated with the Varna cemetery has yet to be found, but Renfrew (1978) has suggested that the users of the burial ground were part of a chiefdom in which the leaders used gold and copper ornaments to fulfill the social need for conspicuous display. As he points out, the problem with explaining the rise of metallurgy is not a technical but a social one — defining the social conditions under which metal objects first came into widespread use. The earliest copper artifacts had few practical advantages over stone axes. Both copper and gold were used mainly for ornamental purposes (Figure 19.2). Perhaps it was no coincidence that the first metallurgists in temperate Europe developed a wide range of ornaments, luxury items widely traded through exchange networks that accelerated the spread of copperworking to other parts of temperate Europe.

BATTLE AXES AND BEAKERS

The technology of copperworking is really an outgrowth of that used for pottery manufacture, and probably arose after many experiments with fire, clay, and stone. The beginnings of copper metallurgy in temperate Europe were probably almost imperceptible, since a handful of simple, hammered copper artifacts date to as early as 3500 B.C. At least two possible areas of indigenous copperworking have been identified in southern

Varna
4680 to 4200 B.C.

3500 B.C.

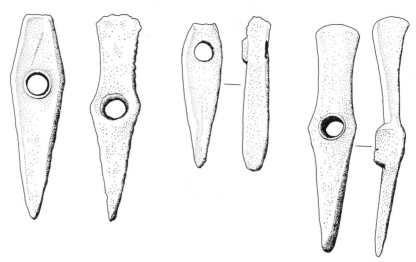

Figure 19.2 Copper ax heads from Czechoslovakia (one-third actual size).

Europe, both near copper outcrops. One is in southern Spain (Iberia), the other in northern Italy (Figure 19.1). In both regions, the copper workers started smelting in approximately the first half of the third millennium B.C. Britain is also rich in copper ores, and the metal was exploited early there too. Wherever it developed, copper smithing was probably a seasonal, or at best a part-time occupation, and it was not until much later that tougher, bronze artifacts came into daily, utilitarian use in the field and the chase.

The archaeological record of the period between 3500 and 2000 B.C. is incredibly complicated, but we can discern two broad groupings of societies, the so-called Battle-Ax and Beaker peoples, groups that ultimately mingled.

In eastern Europe, settled farming societies had lived on the edge of the huge Russian steppe for hundreds of years. Like the peoples of Anatolia and Greece, they had sporadic contacts with the nomads who roamed the plains to the east; about these we know little. In the southern Russian region, a widespread population of copper-using agriculturalists lived in rectangular, thatched huts, cultivated many crops, and also tamed domestic animals, possibly including the horse. This loosely defined Kurgan culture was remarkable for its burial customs, depositing each corpse under a small mound (Piggott, 1965). The Kurgans used wheeled vehicles and made the copper or stone battle ax a very important part of their armory. The wheeled cart and the battle ax had spread widely over central and parts of northern Europe by 3000 B.C. The globular pots associated with these characteristic artifacts, many of them bearing characteristic cord-impressed decorations, have been found at hundreds of sites. The same artifacts have often been found in megalithic tombs. These new cultural traits were absorbed into the millennia-old European

Kurgan culture
3000 B.C.

cultural tradition, and many experts feel that Indo-European language spread into Europe at about this time. (Indo-European speech is thought to have originated in the region between the Carpathian and Caucasus mountains.)

It was at about this time that new house forms appeared in temperate zones. Smaller, timber dwellings just large enough to house a single family replaced the Danubian longhouse of earlier times. You also find warriors buried with their battle axes under small mounds, a reflection of new cultural traditions that were to persist in Europe for thousands of years. The warrior leaders who descended from Bronze Age chieftains were the German tribesmen that the Romans encountered on the frontiers of their European empire.

Between 2700 and 2000 B.C., a series of highly characteristic artifacts came into fashion over a large region of Western Europe: coastal Spain, southern France, Sardinia, northern Italy, eastern and central Europe, the Low Countries, and Britain (Harrison, 1980) (Figure 19.3). These include finely made bell-shaped beakers found in hundreds of graves and burial mounds. Archaeologists like Gordon Childe thought in terms of tribes of "Beaker Folk," who spread the length and breadth of Europe

Beakers 2700 to 2000 B.C.

Figure 19.3 Beaker vessels and other artifacts, including arrowheads, from various localities in south-central Britain.

bringing a new culture, and copperworking with them. But it seems more likely that these vessels spread widely not as a result of itinerant merchants or great population movements but simply because beakers, as well as other trinkets like metal brooches, became prized status symbols throughout Europe. Perhaps they became valued heirlooms, priceless grave furniture, and artifacts exchanged as bride wealth or displayed at tribal gatherings. Beakers were but one of several innovations that were changing the face of European society. Another was the plow, which came into widespread use about 2200 B.C., thus opening up the way for the cultivation of heavier soils and much larger acreages.

Plowing **2200 B.C.**

THE BRONZE AGE

In the Aegean, there was steady development from this early threshold of metalworking toward complex state organizations, but Europe remained settled by small village societies. The temperate zones were densely occupied and exploited and vast acreages of forest had been cleared and brought under cultivation by 2000 B.C. The villagers managed woodland carefully, engaged in hunting to supplement their diet, and mined both hard ax stone and soft copper ore. They also panned for gold. Communal burials and individual internments were part of tribal tradition. Should ambitious community works be needed, the basic metal technologies were known, and both boats and wheeled transport were available, as well as the manpower and resources. European village society was stable and self-sufficient, with thousands of communities connected to one another by ties of kin and family, and by long-established paths that led from valley to valley along well-drained ridges. Above all, European society enjoyed assured and reliable food supplies that helped bind these thousands of communities together.

The European Bronze Age began not as a result of dramatic events and military conquest, nor because of some startling invention (Coles, 1982; Coles and Harding, 1979). It was merely a gradual, and inevitable, quickening of responses to a number of new opportunities. Many of these changes were in material culture and in settlement patterns. A series of landscape surveys in southern Britain, for example, have revealed vast networks of fields and land boundaries joining river valleys, ridges, and watersheds into a managed landscape, in which different communities now owned closely defined agricultural land. One Dorsetshire Bronze Age agricultural system encompassed 200 hectares, with settlements of four to five huts linked to enclosures with sunken herd paths. There were fields, hoe plots, stock corrals, and homesteads, all linked into single, managed agricultural units. By 900 B.C., Bronze Age food production was sophisticated. It relied heavily on plow agriculture and field fallowing, as well as manuring, and it was based on the rotation of many different cereal and root crops.

From early in the second millenium B.C., metallurgy was a growth industry throughout temperate Europe. A series of local bronze industries
developed in different parts of Europe, bringing with them a whole range
of related activities: trading of ores and finished artifacts from major
mining centers and the barter of both prosaic and prestigious artifacts
and ornaments over considerable distances. For the first time, a major
European industry was practiced in areas where supplies of raw materials were scarce. For instance, Bronze Age communities in Scandinavia,
which had no metals, went to considerable trouble to acquire metal ore
and finished tools both from Britain tribes and from central European
sources. European smiths produced some of the finest bronze artifacts
ever made in the ancient world: axes and adzes, battle axes, daggers,
swords, spearheads, shields, and an enormous range of brooches, pins,
and other ornaments. They also made delicate, prestigious gold ornaments that were highly prized and buried with important chieftains.

For all these metallurgical changes, the basic tenor of agricultural life
remained unchanged, except for gradual changes in the structure of European society — the emergence of social ranking. Just what form this
ranking took is a matter of lively controversy (Coles, 1982), since it is reflected only in a differentiation of grave goods between a few individuals
and the rest of society. In Denmark, for example, excavations on the island of Fyn have revealed rich Bronze Age burials and a nearby settlement with a wealth of gold and bronze. This is clear evidence that there
was a powerful community there, a community with extensive trading
connections with metal-rich regions to the south. The evidence from
Bronze Age graves across the length and breadth of Europe shows that
the rich and the poor were buried side by side, the former with substantial quantities of valuable metal artifacts that were thus lost to the people
burying them. This can only mean that some members of society, perhaps
important traders, more probably influential kin leaders, were aggran-
dized at the expense of others and became a new elite in European society (Coles and Harding, 1979).

Although the first occurrence of bronze may one day be shown to date
to the fourth millennium in southeast Europe, the earliest widespread
use of tin-copper alloys was approximately 2500 B.C. in what is now
Czechoslovakia (Coles and Harding, 1979). The new bronze implements
with tougher working edges (Figure 19.4) were initially in short supply,
but their use spread gradually as new trade routes were opened across
central and western Europe. The earliest bronzeworking was centered
around Unetice, an industry manufacturing axes, knife blades, halberds,
and many types of ornament (Piggott, 1965). The bronzeworkers themselves obviously belong to cultural traditions long established in the
area, for their burial customs are identical to those of earlier centuries.
Some believe that the art of alloying tin with copper, as well as casting
techniques, came to Europe from Syria. Most people now argue, however, that bronzeworking developed independently in Europe, for the

Unetice culture
2400 B.C.

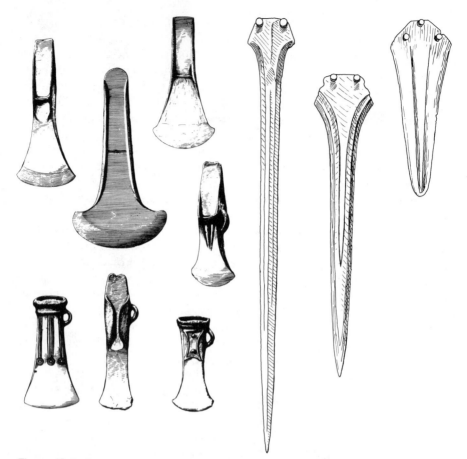

Figure 19.4 Copper and bronze implements from Britain: simple flat axes and flanged and socketed axes (left, one-third actual size); a dagger and sword blades (right, one-fourth actual size).

calibrated C14 dates for the Unetice industry are earlier than those for the Near Eastern prototypes from which the other school of thought assumes Unetice to have evolved.

Bronzeworking soon appeared in southern Germany and Switzerland as well, where deposits of copper and tin were to be found. Other places with copper outcrops were soon using the new methods, including Brittany, the British Isles, and northern Italy, all more remote from the initial centers of bronzeworking. The period between approximately 1700 and 1300 B.C. was one of rapid technological progress and considerable social change, generated in large part by the reinforcing effects on the local centers of bronzeworking of persistent demand for critical raw materials and finished tools.

1700 to 1300 B.C.

By this time, European trading networks carried far more than bronze artifacts and metal ores. The amber trade went from the shores of the Baltic to the Mediterranean, following well-established routes (Figure 19.5) (P. Phillips, 1980). Seashells, perhaps faience (glass) beads, and

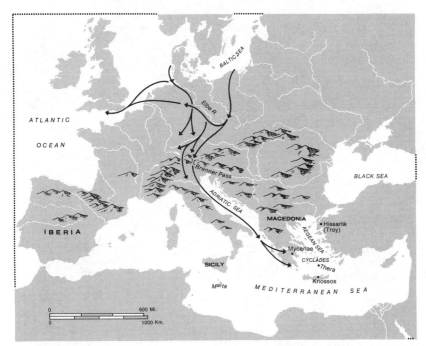

Figure 19.5 Amber trade routes in Europe and to Mycenae. The northern coastlines were the primary sources of Baltic amber, a yellow-brown fossil resin that when rubbed seems to be "electric." Amber was being passed southward to the Mediterranean by the time the Mycenaeans came to power.

other exotic luxuries were dispersed northward into the temperate zones in exchange for raw materials. Some centers of bronze production became major places for redistributing other goods as well. The salt mines of Austria also were very active in the long-distance trade.

By 1300 B.C., even societies remote from metal outcrops were engaged in metallurgy, but the archaeological record tells little of increased specialization, although many richly adorned burials testify that the trade was concentrated among wealthy chieftains. The surplus food and energy were not devoted to generating additional surpluses and extra production, but, in some societies, were channeled into erecting majestic religious monuments, of which Stonehenge in southern Britain probably is the most celebrated (Figure 19.6).

1300 B.C.

Shrouded in fantasy and speculation, associated by many people with the ancient Druids' cult, Stonehenge is in fact a fantastically old religious temple (Atkinson, 1960; Hawkins, 1965; Thom, 1974). It began as a simple circle of ritual pits in approximately 2700 B.C. and went through vigorous reconstructions, reaching the zenith of its expansion in the late second millennium B.C. That Stonehenge was associated with some form of astronomical activity seems unquestionable, although the details are much debated.

Stonehenge

The inhabitants of southern Britain also erected enormous earthwork

Figure 19.6 Stonehenge as seen from the air.

enclosures and huge circles of timber uprights known as *henges* (see Chapter Ten and C. Renfrew, 1983). Doubtless special priests were needed to maintain these spectacular monuments and to perform the rituals in their precincts. Religious activity was supported by the food surplus, not the increased productivity that generated spectacular social evolution in the Near East. Thus, during the third and part of the second millennia B.C., little social evolution went on in Europe; political power and wealth belonged to the chieftains and warriors rather than to divine kings and a hierarchic society.

BRONZE AGE WARRIORS

European societies became more socially ranked as time went on. As trade intensified, so local monopolies over salt and other supplies became concentrated in the hands of comparatively few individuals. Population growth and perhaps some climatic deterioration put new pressure on agricultural land (Phillips, 1980; Piggott, 1965). All of this may have led to considerable political instability in Europe, to alliances of small tribes under the rule of powerful and ambitious chieftains, themselves once minor village leaders. Some warrior groups even began to strike at the fringes of the Mediterranean world, destroying Mycenae and the Hittite empire.

As time went on, many more copper and bronze artifacts became available for domestic consumption. Some new tool forms were introduced by central European smiths, including socketed axes, varied woodworking tools, and the *ard* (a scraping plow drawn by oxen). The ard was a particularly important innovation, for it allowed deeper plowing, more advanced agricultural methods, and higher productivity. The new farming techniques were vital to feed the many new mouths, and prime farming land was harder to find than ever before.

Between 1200 and 800 B.C., the population movements associated with central European peoples introduced a more consolidated system of agriculture to much of Europe, which allowed exploitation of much heavier soils, as well as stock breeding (J. G. D. Clark, 1952). For the first time, stock were fully integrated into the food-producing economy, and cattle were used for meat, milk, and draft work, though sheep were bred as much for wool as for their flesh. Improved technology for new implements of tillage was fully exploited to achieve a truly effective economic symbiosis between flora and fauna, carefully balancing forest clearance with cultivation and pasturage.

One powerful group of warrior tribes in western Hungary is known to archaeologists as the Urnfield people because of their burial customs: their dead were cremated and their ashes deposited in urns; huge cemeteries of urn burials are associated with fortified villages, sometimes built near lakes. Urnfield people began to make full use of horse-drawn vehicles and new weaponry. Skilled bronzesmiths produced sheet-metal helmets and shields. The Urnfield people also used the slashing sword, a devastating weapon far more effective than the cutting swords of earlier times.

Urnfield culture
?1000 B.C.

Approximately 800 B.C., the Urnfield people began to expand from their Hungarian homelands. Within a couple of centuries, characteristic slashing swords and other central European tools had been deposited in sites in Italy, the Balkans, and the Aegean. By 750 B.C., Urnfield peoples had settled in southern France and moved from there into Spain (Figure 19.7). Soon Urnfield miners were exploiting the rich copper mines of the Tyrol in Austria. Bands of miners used bronze-tipped picks to dig deep in the ground for copper ore. Their efforts increased the supplies of copper and tin available to central Europeans (J. G. D. Clark, 1952).

800 B.C.

750 B.C.

The Scythians and Other Steppe Peoples

The vast rolling grasslands and steppes from China to the Ukraine were not settled by farming peoples until they had a culture enabling

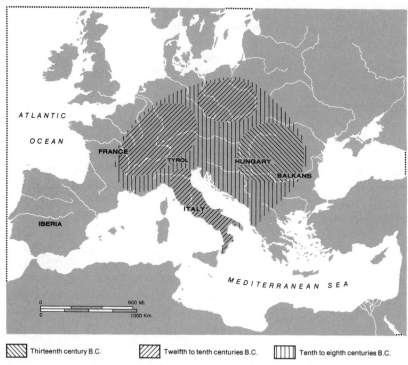

Thirteenth century B.C.   Twelfth to tenth centuries B.C.   Tenth to eighth centuries B.C.

Figure 19.7   Approximate distribution of Urnfield cultures in Europe.

them to survive in an environment with extreme contrasts of climate and relatively infertile soils. The carrying capacity of the land is such that only a vast territory can support herds of domestic stock. The prehistory of this huge area is obscure until the first millennium B.C., when the Scythians (from Scythia, an area in southeastern Europe) and other steppe peoples first appear in the historical record. No one should doubt, however, the importance of nomads in the prehistory of Europe in earlier millennia (E. D. Phillips, 1972). The Kurgan people and other possible Indo-European speakers were familiar with the vast open spaces of the steppes, where domestication of the horse ultimately made the nomadic life a potent force in frontier politics. For centuries before the Scythians came out of history's shadows, people had roamed the steppes, relying on the horse and wagon for mobility, living in stout felt tents, and subsisting mostly on horse's milk and cheese, as well as on food from hunting and fishing. The nomadic life, though, leaves few traces in the archaeological record, except when permafrost has preserved burials in a refrigerated state.

We are fortunate in having extensive data about the vigorous society of nomad peoples from the spectacular frozen tombs of Siberia. Russian archaeologist Sergei Rudenko has excavated several nomad burial mounds at Pazyryk in northeastern Siberia (Rudenko, 1970). The chiefs

Scythians **c. 500 B.C.**

400 B.C.

of Pazyryk were elaborately tattooed, wore woollen and leather clothes, and employed skillful artists to adorn their horse trappings and harnesses with exuberant, elaborate, stylized animal art. A powerful chief was accompanied to the next world by his wife and servants, horses and chariots, and many of his smaller possessions. The Pazyryk burials contain fragments of woven rugs, the earliest examples of such art in the world.

The steppe peoples lived to the north of the well-traveled trade routes of Greek merchants, but their territory was constantly being explored and sometimes colonized by farmers whose lands were becoming overpopulated or overgrazed. Enormous areas of steppe were needed to support even a small band of horsemen, for just a slight increase in population could drastically affect the food supplies of the original inhabitants. The result was constant displacement of populations as the nomads sought to expand their shrinking territory to accommodate their own population pressures. The nomads menaced the northern frontiers of the Mediterranean world throughout Classical and more recent times.

The Eurasian nomad populations flourished during the closing millennia of prehistory. The Pazyryk finds let us see into a prehistoric way of life that in some areas survived unchanged right into historic times.

THE EMERGENCE OF IRONWORKING

The Urnfield people were effective agriculturalists as well as traders and metallurgists, capable of exploiting Europe's forested environment far more efficiently than their predecessors could. They lived amid a complicated network of trade that carried not only metals but also salt, grain, gold, pottery, and many other commodities. Their economic organization probably included community smiths, specialists supported by the community, but still no centralized state system of the Near Eastern type.

The secrets of ironworking, guarded carefully by Hittite kings, were slow to reach Europe, but sometime after 1000 B.C., ironworking techniques were introduced into temperate Europe, presumably down existing trade routes. Ironworking is much more difficult than bronzeworking, for the technology is harder to acquire and takes much longer, but once it is learned, the advantages of the new metal are obvious. Because the ore is found in many more places, the metal is much cheaper and could be used for weapons and for utilitarian artifacts as well. These would, of course, include both axes and hoes, as well as plowshares, all of which contributed much to agricultural efficiency, higher crop yields, and greater food surpluses. The population increases and intensified trading activities of the centuries immediately preceding the Roman Empire are partly attributed to the success of iron technology in changing European agriculture and craftsmanship. As iron technology spread into the country north of the Alps, new societies arose whose leaders exploited the new metal's artistic and economic potentials. The tribal

Ironworking **1000 B.C.**

Figure 19.8 Bronze ritual cart from a Hallstatt grave in Austria, approximately .3 m (1 ft) long.

chieftaincy was the structure of government; the most coherent broader political unit was a loose confederacy of tribes formed in time of war or temporarily under the aegis of a charismatic chieftain. Despite the on-slaught of Roman colonization and exploitation, European culture beyond the frontiers retained its essentially European cast, an indigenous slant to cultural traditions that began when farming did (Wells, 1981).

For all the technological changes, farming life continued much as before. Peter Wells has excavated an Iron Age farming community near Hascherkeller in lower Bavaria, Germany, where he found three enclosed farmsteads (Wells, 1984). The farmstead complexes included dwellings, barns, sheds, and workshops, with between fifteen and thirty people living in each settlement. Occupied between 1000 and 800 B.C., they were self-sufficient communities without iron tools that traded food stuffs for such items as imported bronze scraps, beads, and graphite, which were used for pottery decoration. Hascherkeller was apparently

Hascherkeller **1,000 to 800 B.C.**

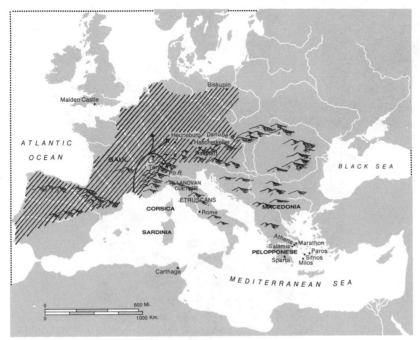

Figure 19.9 Distribution of Hallstatt Iron Age cultures (shaded area) in Europe during the seventh to fifth centuries B.C. The trade routes in southern France and the Mediterranean sites mentioned in this chapter are also shown, but Pazyryk is not on the map.

without iron, which was still a new metal. But it was occupied at a time when the first towns were emerging in central Europe, communities like the Heuneburg, a significant cluster of timber houses occupied between 800 and 400 B.C. by about 200 people. The Heuneburg was a market town, one of many such local centers that were the forerunners of much later medieval communities of the same type.

Heuneburg **800 to 400 B.C.**

The Hallstatt Culture

One strong culture was the Hallstatt, named after a site near Salzburg, Austria (Rowlett, 1967; Wells, 1981). Hallstatt culture began in the seventh and sixth centuries B.C. and owed much to Urnfield practices, for the skillful bronzeworking of earlier times was still practiced, although some immigrants from the east may have achieved political dominance over earlier inhabitants. Bronze, however, was still the dominant metal for horse trappings, weapons, and ornaments. Chiefs were buried in large mounds within wooden chambers, some in wagons (Figure 19.8).

Hallstatt **730 B.C.**

The Hallstatt people and their culture spread through former Urnfield territories as far north as Belgium and the Netherlands and into France and parts of Spain (Figure 19.9). Many Hallstatt sites are particularly notable for their fortifications. The Hallstatt people traded with the Medi-

Figure 19.10 Iron Age helmet from the bed of the River Thames in London, 20.5 cm (8.07 in) at base.

terraneans, along well-traveled routes up the Rhone River and through the Alps into central Europe. A significant import was the serving vessel for wine; containers of Mediterranean wine were carried far into central Europe, as Hallstatt chieftains discovered the joys of wine drinking.

The La Tène People

La Tène **450 B.C.**

By the last quarter of the fifth century B.C., a new and highly distinctive technology, La Tène, had developed in the Rhine and Danube valleys (Jacobsthal, 1944; Megaw, 1970). An aristocratic clique of chieftains in the Danube Valley enjoyed implements and weapons elaborately worked in bronze and gold. Much of their sophisticated art had roots in Classical Greek and Mediterranean traditions, for La Tène craftsworkers were quick to adopt new motifs and ideas from the centers of higher civilization to the south (Figure 19.10). The La Tène people spoke Celtic, a language that spread widely through Europe from perhaps as early as the ninth century B.C. Greek and Roman writers referred to these people as Celts, a term that has survived in their linguistic label.

350 B.C.

La Tène technology was a specific adaptation of ironworking to woodland Europe. The culture extended north into the Low Countries and

Britain in the fourth century. La Tène art is justly famous, and the hill forts and defensive settlements of this Iron Age culture are widespread in western Europe. The superior military tactics of the La Tène people introduced the Romans to the short sword, for La Tène peoples survived long after France and southern Britain had been conquered by Rome (Cunliffe, 1974). Much territory in the temperate zones came under Roman domination, an uneasy frontier province that eventually crumbled before the inexorable pressure of the warlike tribes on its boundaries. The illiterate peoples who eventually sacked Rome and ravaged its provinces were the descendants of prehistoric Europeans whose cultural traditions had been evolving ever since the first farming cultures developed north of the Mediterranean basin.

Roman conquest
55 B.C.

GUIDE TO FURTHER READING

Champion, T. G., Gamble, C. S., Shennan, S. J., and Whittle, A. W. R. *Prehistoric Europe*. New York: Academic Press, 1984.
A textbook on European prehistory that goes from the earliest times up to the expansion of the Roman empire. A major emphasis on subsistence, trade, and social organization.

Coles, J. M., and Harding, A. F. *The Bronze Age in Europe*. London: Methuen, 1979.
An authoritative account of the complexities of the European Bronze Age that covers the topic far more fully than we can in this book.

Cunliffe, Barry. *Iron Age Communities in Britain*. London: Routledge and Kegan Paul, 1974.
The literature on the European Iron Age is scattered and is published in many different languages. Cunliffe's account of Iron Age hill forts and other settlements in Britain will give you a general impression of the archaeology of the period.

Phillips, Patricia. *The Prehistory of Europe*. Bloomington: Indiana University Press, 1980.
A detailed synthesis of western European prehistory from the earliest times. Particularly good on the later periods.

Piggott, Stuart, *Ancient Europe*. Chicago: Aldine, 1965.
Somewhat outdated, this account of prehistoric Europe is closer to Childe than to current evolutionary thinking, but it is still authoritative, with excellent illustrations.

Chronological Table K

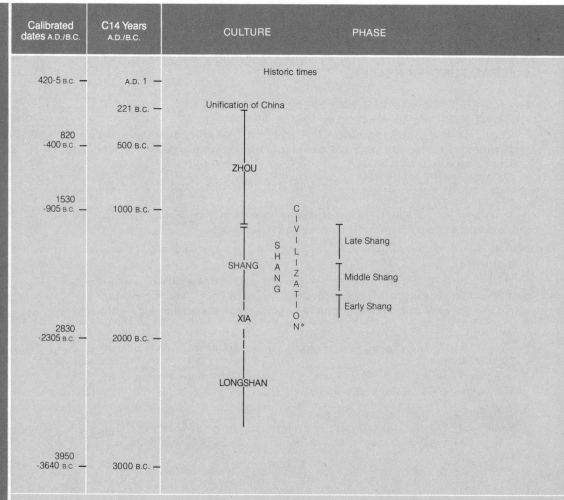

Calibrated dates A.D./B.C.	C14 Years A.D./B.C.	CULTURE	PHASE
		Historic times	
420-5 B.C.	A.D. 1		
	221 B.C.	Unification of China	
820 -400 B.C.	500 B.C.	ZHOU	
1530 -905 B.C.	1000 B.C.		Late Shang
		SHANG	Middle Shang
			Early Shang
2830 -2305 B.C.	2000 B.C.	XIA	
		LONGSHAN	
3950 -3640 B.C.	3000 B.C.		

SHANG CIVILIZATION*

Chapter 12 ▲

*SHANG CIVILIZATION refers to a civilization that survived the changing of ruling dynasties.

Chapter Twenty

Shang Civilization in East Asia

PREVIEW

❊ Early Chinese civilization, which emerged somewhat later than urban civilization in the Near East, generally is agreed to have developed independently of similar developments in the West.

❊ The roots of Chinese civilization lie in the Longshan culture, which is associated with the spread of rice cultivation throughout much of China, after 3200 B.C.

❊ The Shang civilization of the Yellow Valley is the best-known early Chinese state, flourishing from approximately 1766 to 1122 B.C. It probably was the dominant state among several that flourished throughout northern China. Shang origins are partly from Longshan roots and partly from influences that came to the Shang from the east.

❊ There are at least three stages of Shang civilization, associated with distinctive writing and bronze metallurgy. Shang society was organized along class lines, with the rulers and nobles living in segregated precincts while the mass of the people were scattered in townships and villages in the surrounding countryside.

❊ Shang civilization ended with the overthrow of the Shang dynasty by Zhou rulers, who reigned over a wide area of northern China from 1122 to 221 B.C.

The origins of Chinese civilization were known only from legend until Chronological Table K the late 1920s, when Tung Tso-pin and, later, Li Chi began digging in the Anyang area of Henan province in northern China. Their excavations resulted in the discovery of the Shang civilization that flourished in the Yellow Valley more then 3500 years ago (Chang, 1977, 1980).

THE EMERGENCE OF CHINESE CIVILIZATION

By 2500 B.C., agriculture had taken such hold in China that population 2500 B.C. densities rose throughout the country. The farmers took more and more land into cultivation until there was little new acreage available for planting. Some pollen analyses from northern villages show how the trees that once surrounded many settlements were felled as the fields lapped right up to the houses (Chang, 1977). This population growth also coincided with an expansion of rice farming in lowland areas, on moist floodplains, and in lush water meadows where irrigation was easy (Figure 20.1). Those villages fortunate enough to possess lands that could be irrigated, especially in the Yellow and Yangtze valleys, soon turned into much more permanent settlements, often protected with earthen walls to guard against floods and marauding neighbors. Even these larger communities were part of a self-regulating folk society in which kinship loyalties and the extended family were all-important, and age was deeply revered. The family ancestors were the conduit to the gods who controlled the harmony of the world.

However, there are signs that a new order existed, for some settlements of 3000 B.C. contain elaborate burials adorned with jade ornaments and ceremonial weapons. Village artisans created fine clay vessels exclusively for the use of these privileged people. These were important leaders who are known to have raided their neighbors, for the corpses of their enemies have been found buried in village wells. Both in the north

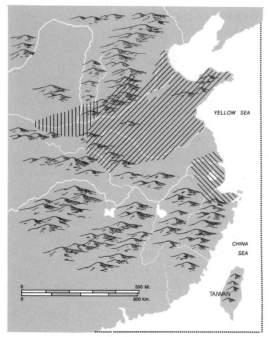
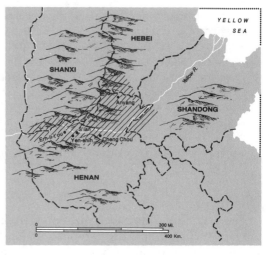

Figure 20.1 (Left) Distribution of farming cultures that immediately preceded Shang civilization in China (commonly called Longshan). Each shaded area represents a different regional variant of Longshan (not discussed in detail in the text). Compare with the second map (right), which shows the approximate distribution of Shang culture in about 1400 B.C. (Xiao-tun and other royal sites are close to Anyang.)

and south, a few peasant villages became important centers ruled by new generations of kin leaders who became the nobles of new, more sophisticated societies. They probably were expert warriors and certainly were people of great spiritual authority, who were experts at predicting the future and communicating with the ancestors.

These developments would never have been possible without the unswerving conservatism of the country farmer. The village crops might change from rice to cereals, the fertility of the soils depend on radically different rainfall patterns, and building materials alter from brick and tile to bamboo, but what never varied was the unquestioning acceptance by the peasants of an emerging social order that imposed an almost alien, wealthy privileged society. The viability of this aristocratic civilization depended on simple loyalties that persisted from the earliest centuries of farming life right into modern times. Every Chinese noble, however unimportant, cashed in on this loyalty.

Shoulder Blades and Oracles

When archaeologists dug into a village named Longshan on the Yellow River in Shando province in 1930 to 1931, they found not only the remains of a farming village, but also dozens of cracked ox shoulder blades that they identified as oracle bones used in divination ceremonies (Keightley, 1983) (Figure 20.2). The cracks were made by applying hot metal to the bone and then were interpreted as messages from the ancestors. None of the Longshan bones bore written inscriptions, but the hundreds of shoulder blades found in pits near Anyang further upstream are a mine of information about the origins of Chinese civilization, a unique written archive of official deliberations by the very first kings of northern China. One scholar has suggested that Chinese writing may have originated from the need to interpret the cracks on the bones, with the new writing symbols resembling persistent crack patterns found on oracle bones. Clearly some Chinese ideographs originated as pictograms, such as that for the hill, originally shown with three humps and now written as a horizontal line with three vertical strokes (Fitzgerald, 1978).

Perhaps as early as 2500 B.C. divination rituals were a vital part of village government. All official divinations were addressed to the royal ancestors, who acted as intermediaries between the living and the ultimate ancestor and supreme being, the ruler of heaven and the creator, Shang Di. This deity served as the ancestor not only of the royal line, but also of the "multitude of the people." The king was the head of all family lines that radiated from his person to the nobility and then to the common people. These actual and imputed kinship ties were the core of early Chinese civilization, for they obligated the peasants to provide food and labor for their rulers.

In addition to shoulder blades from oxen and water buffalo, the diviners used tortoiseshell for their ceremonies. The term *scapulimancy*,

Longshan
?2700 B.C.

Figure 20.2 Shang oracle bones.

meaning "shoulder blade divination," refers to the bones used most frequently in the ceremonies. The bones and shells were smoothed and cleaned and perhaps soaked in liquid to soften them. Rows of hollows were then produced on the underside to make the substance thinner and the surface more susceptible to being cracked. When a question was posed, the diviner would apply a metal point to the base of the hollow, causing the surface to crack. The response of the ancestors was "read" from the fissures. A skillful diviner could control the extent and direction of his cracks. Thus, divination provided an authoritative leader with a useful and highly effective way of giving advice; a leader could regard disagreement as treason.

Xia and Shang: ?2700 to 1100 B.C.

The obvious starting point in the study of Chinese civilization is Chinese legends, which tell us that the celebrated Yellow Emperor Huang Di founded civilization in the north in approximately 2698 B.C. This great legendary warlord set the tone for centuries of the repressive harsh government that was the hallmark of early Chinese civilization. In 2200 B.C., a Xia ruler named Yu the Great gained power through his military prowess and his knowledge of flood control, by which he could protect the valley people from catastrophic inundations.

Xia and Shang dynasties
?2700 to 1100 B.C.

What exactly do these legends mean? Who were the Xia and the Shang? In all probability the Xia and Shang were dynasties of local rulers who achieved lasting prominence among their many neighbors after generations of bitter strife (Chang, 1980). Every chieftain lived in a walled town and enjoyed much the same level of material prosperity; but each ruler came from a different lineage and was related to his competitors by intricate and closely woven allegiances and kin ties. Each dynasty assumed political dominance in the north in turn, but, for all these political changes, Shang civilization itself continued more or less untouched, a loosely unified confederacy of competing small kingdoms that quarreled and warred incessantly.

The archaeological record reveals that Shang-type remains are found stratified on top of Longshan occupation levels at many places in northern China, and they represent a dramatic increase in the complexity of material culture and social organization (Chang, 1977). The same trends toward increasing complexity are thought to have occurred elsewhere in China at approximately the same time, for literate states may have emerged from a Longshan base not only in the north but in the south and east as well. In form they probably resembled the Shang closely, but few details of the others are known. It seems likely that the Shang dynasty was dominant from approximately 1766 to 1122 B.C., but that other states continued to grow at the same time. The larger area of Chinese civilization ultimately extended from the north into the middle and lower courses of the Yellow and Yangtze rivers. In this account, we concentrate on northern Chinese civilization, simply because more is known about the archaeology of the Shang than any other early Chinese state.

Shang
1766 to 1122 B.C.

Capitals and Sepulchers

The oracle bones and other historical sources provide but a sketchy outline of the early dynasties and the ways in which the Shang kings went about their business. The bones inform us that they lived in at least seven capitals, situated near the middle reaches of the Yellow River in the modern provinces of Henan, Shandong, and Anhui. The sites of all these towns

Early Shang
?1750 to 1650 B.C.

are still uncertain, but in approximately 1557 B.C. the Shang kings moved their capital to a place named Ao, which archaeologists have found under the modern industrial city of Zhengzhou, some 95 mi south of Anyang close to the Yellow River (Wheatley, 1971). Unfortunately, the royal compound lies underneath the modern downtown area, and so only limited excavations have been possible. However, the diggers have found traces of a vast precinct surrounded by an earthen wall more than 9.9 m (33 ft) high enclosing an area of 2 sq mi. It would have taken 10,000 workers laboring 330 days a year for no fewer than eighteen years to erect the fortifications alone. This walled compound housed the rulers, the temples, and the nobles. Some foundations of their large houses and ancestral altars have come from excavations inside the compound. The residential quarters and craft workshops lay outside the Shang walls. These include two bronze factories, one of them covering more than an acre. The metalworkers lived in substantial houses near their furnaces. There were bone workshops, too, places where animal and human bones were fashioned into arrowheads, pins, and awls. Zhengzhou's potters lived in a satellite village close to the kilns where they fired hundreds of fine vessels. The excavations revealed dozens of unfired and incomplete vessels.

The capital moved to the Anyang area in approximately 1400 B.C. (the beginning of the Late Shang phase), where it remained until the fall of the Shang more than 250 years later. This new royal domain was known as *Yin* and may in fact have encompassed a network of compounds, palaces, villages, and cemeteries extending over an area some 120 sq mi on the northern bank of the Yellow River. The core of this "capital" was near the hamlet of Xiao-tun, 1.5 mi northwest of the modern city of Anyang. Years of excavations at Xiao-tun have revealed fifty-three rectangular foundations of stamped earth up to 36 m (120 ft) long, 19.5 m (65 ft) wide, and as much as 1.5 m (5 ft) high, many of them associated with sacrificial burials of both animals and humans (Chang, 1980). One group of fifteen foundations on the north side of the excavated area supported timber houses with mud and stick walls, devoid of sacrificial victims. These are believed to be the royal residences that housed extended families of nobles living in large halls and smaller rooms closed off with doors (Figure 20.3). Twenty-one massive foundations on an elevated area in the

Figure 20.3 Reconstruction of a structure from the ceremonial area at Xiao-tun, Anyang in Henan province, China.

center of the excavations formed two rows of temples associated with a series of five ceremonial gates. The builders buried animals, humans, and even chariots in this vicinity, perhaps to dedicate the temples. Nearby lay semi-subterranean houses where the royal servants and artisans lived. The service areas included bronze foundries, workshops, and pottery kilns.

The Shang Royal Burials

The Shang rulers at first buried their dead among the compound houses but later moved their cemetery to a new location just more than a mile northeast. Eleven royal graves from this cemetery were excavated during the 1930s (Chang, 1977). They were furnished on a lavish scale and date to between the twelfth and fourteenth centuries B.C. The best-known grave is in the shape of a crosslike pit approximately 9.9 m (33 ft) deep with slightly sloping walls. Four ramps lead from the surface to each side of the pit (Te-k'un, 1960). The coffin of the ruler, which was placed inside a wooden chamber erected in the burial pit, was accompanied by superb bronze vessels and shell, bone, and stone ornaments. One ceremonial halberd has an engraved jade blade set in a bronze shaft adorned with dragons and inlaid with malachite. The rulers were accompanied in death by slaves and sacrificial victims buried both in the chamber itself and on the approach ramps. Many were decapitated, and so their bodies were found in one piece and their heads in another.

The Shang kings surrounded their sepulchers with hundreds of lesser burials. No fewer than 1221 small graves have been dug up nearby, many of them multiple burials of between two and eleven people in a single tomb. Some of the skeletons are associated with pottery, weapons, or bronze vessels, but most of them are devoid of all adornment. In 1976 the archaeologists uncovered nearly 200 of these graves. Most of them contained decapitated, dismembered, or mutilated bodies. Some of the victims had been bound before death. These can only be sacrificial offerings consecrated when the kings and their relatives died.

The Bronzesmiths

The Shang people are justly famous for their bronzework, best known to us from ceremonial artifacts found in royal tombs. The prestigious metal was not gold, which was in short supply, but bronze. Most Shang bronzes are food or drinking vessels, some are weapons, a few are musical instruments, and many are chariot and horse fittings. Bronzeworking was the guarded monopoly of the rulers, a complex art that the Chinese developed quite independently from the west before 2000 B.C. Their smiths produced some of the most sophisticated and elegant bronze objects ever crafted (Figure 20.4).

The Shang people discovered bronzeworking on their own, perhaps as a result of their long experience with kiln-fired pottery baked at high

Figure 20.4 Shang ceremonial bronze vessels, from approximately the twelfth century B.C.

temperatures (Barnard, 1961). The smaller objects, such as spear- and arrowheads and halberds were made by pouring a mixture of copper and tin into a single or two-piece mold. Much more complex procedures had to be employed to manufacture large ceremonial vessels. These elaborate display pieces were copies of clay prototypes carefully sculpted around a baked clay core and encased in an outer segmented mold. Once the clay version was completed, the baked outer mold was removed, the model broken away from the core, and the two parts reassembled to receive the molten bronze. This complex technique remained in use for at least five centuries. An alternative would have been the "lost-wax" method, in which a single-piece mold encases a wax mold that was heated and then poured out to be replaced with metal.

THE WARLORDS: 1100 to 221 B.C.

Every early Chinese ruler stayed in power by virtue of a strong army which backed him. Shang society was organized on what might be called military lines, so that the royal standing army could be supplemented with thousands of conscripts at very short notice. The kings frequently were at war, protecting their frontiers, suppressing rebellious rivals, or raiding for as many as 30,000 sacrificial victims at one time. In a sense, every early Chinese state was an armed garrison that could call on armies of more than 10,000 men. The secret was a sophisticated, permanent military establishment and a kin organization through which people were obligated to serve the king when called upon. The same basic organization persisted long after the fall of the Shang dynasty in 1100 B.C.

The Anyang graves reveal that every foot soldier carried a set of weapons: a bow and arrows, a halberd, shield, small knife, and a sharpening stone. The bows were made of horn and ox sinew and were approximately a man's height. They propelled stone-, bone-, or bronze-tipped arrows equipped with feathers (Kiernan and Fairbank, 1974). The Shang soldiers used a small leather or basketry shield for chariot warfare and a longer one on foot, both painted with tiger designs. Most surviving Shang weapons come from sacrificial chariot burials, such as the one excavated near Anyang in 1973. The archaeologists did not uncover the wooden chariot itself but a cast of the wooden parts preserved in the soil (Figure 20.5). They brushed away the surrounding soil with great care

Figure 20.5 Chariot burial from the royal Shang tombs. The wooden parts of the chariot were excavated by following discolorations made by the decaying wood in the ground.

until they reached the hardened particles of fine sand that had replaced the wooden structure of the buried chariot. They were able to photograph not only the "ghost" of the chariot, but also the skeletons of the two horses. The charioteer had been killed at the funeral and his body placed behind the vehicle. The yokes of the chariot rested on the horses' necks. Even the reins were marked by lines of bronze roundels in the grave. The charioteer rode on a wicker and leather car measuring between 0.9 and 1.2 m (3 and 4 ft) across and borne on a stout axle and two spoked wheels with large hubs adorned with bronze caps. In all probability, the nailless chariot was held together with sinew lashings, adorned with bronze and torquoise ornaments, and perhaps painted in bright colors.

The Shang dynasty fell in 1100 B.C. at the hands of the neighboring Zhou. The conquerors did not create a new civilization; rather, they took over the existing network of towns and officials and incorporated them into their own state organization, thus shifting the focus of political and economic power to the south and west, away from Anyang into the fertile Wei valley near the modern city of S'ian. By this time, the influence of what may loosely be called Shang civilization extended far beyond the north, into the rice-growing areas of the south and along the eastern coasts. The Zhou divided their domains into various almost independent provinces, which warred with one another for centuries (Fitzgerald, 1978). It was not until 221 B.C. that the great emperor Xuang Ti unified China into a single empire. By Roman times, Chinese civilization had been flourishing for more than 2000 years, a distinctive and highly nationalistic culture that differed sharply from its Western contemporaries in its ability to assimilate conquerors and the conquered into its own traditions. In contrast, the Roman Empire was built on the groaning backs of slaves and collapsed into the Dark Ages when attacked by barbarian nomads. The ability of the Chinese people to simply assimilate these same nomadic conquerors explains why the essential fabric of their civilization survives to this day.

GUIDE TO FURTHER READING

Chang, Kwang-Chih. *The Archaeology of Ancient China* (3rd ed.). New Haven: Yale University Press, 1977.
 The fundamental account of prehistoric China for all serious students, with the priceless advantage that it is regularly updated. Lavishly illustrated. Major emphasis on chronology and artifacts.

————. *The Shang Civilization*. New Haven: Yale University Press, 1980.
 Chang's detailed reconstruction of Shang civilization is derived not only from archaeological data but also from a complicated palimpsest of legends, oracle bone inscriptions, and documentary records. An impressive, meticulous book that is an ultimate source on this remarkable society.

Fitzgerald, Patrick. *Ancient China*. Oxford: Elsevier Phaidon, 1978.
 A well-illustrated history (and prehistory) of China for the lay reader which

concentrates on the period after the Shang dynasty. Clearly written and a good starting point.

Keightley, David. *The Origins of Chinese Civilization*. Berkeley: University of California Press, 1983.
An up-to-date and authoritative description of early Chinese civilization, with a strong historical emphasis. Useful to read in conjunction with Chang's works.

Wheatley, Paul. *The Pivot of the Four Quarters*. Chicago: Aldine, 1971.
Wheatley concentrates on the early Chinese city in a learned book that will daunt many casual readers, but it is a crucial source for understanding early Chinese civilization.

PART SIX

NEW WORLD CIVILIZATIONS

(1550 B.C. to A.D. 1530)

"What, then, must have been the emotions of the Spaniards, when, after working their toilsome way into the open air, the cloudy tabernacle parted before their eyes, and they beheld these fair scenes in all their pristine magnificence and beauty. It was like the spectacle which greeted the eyes of Moses from the summit of Pisgah, and, in the warm glow of their feelings, they cried out, 'It is the promised land!' "
– W. H. Prescott, *The Conquest of Mexico,* 1843

Part Six contains descriptions of the great and complex states of the New World. The theoretical literature surrounding the emergence of states in Mesoamerica and Peru is enormous, and interested readers are referred to Chapter Fourteen for some of the principal arguments surrounding the subject.

Chronological Table L

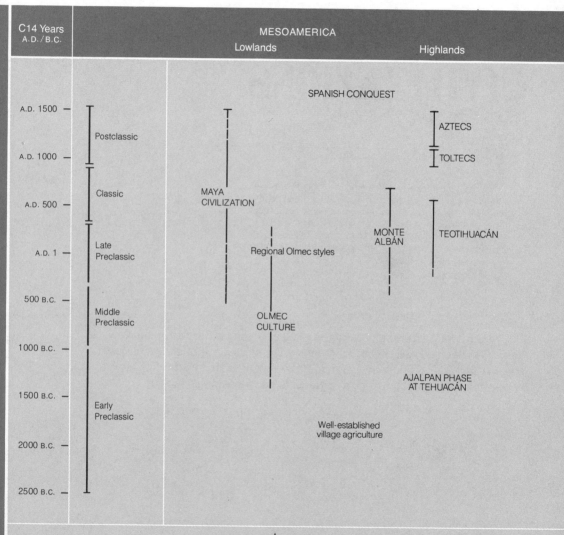

C14 Years A.D./B.C.		MESOAMERICA Lowlands	Highlands

SPANISH CONQUEST

A.D. 1500 —

Postclassic

A.D. 1000 —

Classic

A.D. 500 —

MAYA CIVILIZATION

Late Preclassic

A.D. 1 —

Regional Olmec styles

MONTE ALBÁN TEOTIHUACÁN

AZTECS

TOLTECS

500 B.C. —

Middle Preclassic

OLMEC CULTURE

1000 B.C. —

1500 B.C. —

Early Preclassic

AJALPAN PHASE AT TEHUACÁN

Well-established village agriculture

2000 B.C. —

2500 B.C. —

Chapter 13 ▲

Chapter Twenty-One

Mesoamerican Civilizations

PREVIEW

❋ The Preclassic period of Mesoamerican prehistory lasted from approximately 2500 B.C. to A.D. 300, a period of major cultural change in both lowlands and highlands. Sedentary villages traded with each other in raw materials and exotic objects. These exchange networks became increasingly complex and eventually came under the monopolistic control of larger villages. Increasing social complexity went hand in hand with the appearance of the first public buildings and evidence of social stratification.

❋ These developments are well chronicled in the Valley of Oaxaca and in the Olmec culture of the lowlands, which flourished from approximately 1500 to 500 B.C. Olmec art styles and religious beliefs were among those that spread widely over lowlands and highlands during the late Preclassic period.

❋ The Preclassic cultural developments culminated on the highlands in a number of great cities, among them Monte Albán and Teotihuacán. The latter housed more than 120,000 people and covered more than 8 sq mi at the height of its prosperity. Teotihuacán collapsed approximately A.D. 700, probably as a result of warfare with other, rival states in the highlands.

❋ Maya civilization rose in the lowlands where trading activities may have been of prime importance in the development of a complex society. Classic Maya civilization flourished from A.D. 250 to 900, and was remarkable for its sophisticated trade networks, great ceremonial centers, and elaborate ceremonies, known through sculptures and hieroglyphs. Maya civilization was far from uniform and was unified more by religious doctrine than by political and economic interests.

❋ Maya civilization collapsed suddenly in the Yucatán after A.D. 900; the reasons for the collapse are still uncertain, but pressure on the labor force and food shortages doubtless were among them.

❋ Teotihuacán's collapse on the highlands resulted in a political vacuum for some centuries which eventually was filled by the Toltecs and then the Aztecs, whose bloodthirsty civilization was dominant in the Valley of Mexico at the time of the Spanish conquest in A.D. 1519.

❋ Aztec civilization was unable to resist the Spanish and collapsed suddenly, partly as a result of serious internal stresses and rebellion by subject tribes.

Few topics are surrounded by more fantasy, myth, and archaeological lunacy than the origins of pre-Columbian civilization in the Americas. Ever since Columbus first set foot in the Bahamas, scholars and others have speculated about the origins of the American Indians. The discovery of the Aztec and Inca civilizations fueled speculation and mythmaking to new and even more frenzied heights. The Ten Lost Tribes of Israel, the Canaanites, and all manner of other strange candidates have been invoked as the first civilized peoples to settle in the Americas. The survivors of the Lost Continents of Atlantis and Mu have been prime candidates for generations (Wauchope, 1962). Nineteenth-century readers were entranced by stories of a great Mound Builder Civilization that flourished in the Midwest, only to perish under attack from savage hordes (Silverberg, 1968). Today, we are treated to sagas about ancient astronauts who colonized the Americas from space and then left, leaving the roots of civilization behind them (von Däniken, 1970).

In the latest attack of incredible speculation, a respected Harvard zoologist tells us that America was settled by colonists from Europe and North Africa in the first millennium B.C., long before the Vikings or Columbus (Fell, 1976, 1980). His evidence consists of a comparison of alleged ancient American inscriptions and "timeworn" ruins in the lands from which the "Colonists" came. According to Fell's theories, the settled civilizations of America, which were founded by Old World colonists, were subjected to upheaval and disaster in approximately A.D. 1000, just as the Vikings arrived. Hundreds of people have written to him, he claims, some of them American Indians trying to relate his fables to their own cultural traditions of people who arrived across the water centuries before. In other words, the inspiration for pre-Columbian civilization came from the Old World, perhaps only 3000 years ago.

What are we to make of these centuries of fantasy? Why is American archaeology so surrounded with crazy myth with no basis in scientific reality? One obvious explanation is peoples' appetite for a good adventure story, for epic heroes and transoceanic voyages. Another is that stories such as Fell's or von Däniken's are based on a haphazard collection of facts that are strung together into a convincing pattern without the rigor of systematic scientific analysis: This makes an adventure story easy to compile and to enjoy. Thirdly, unlike Europeans, most Americans, because they are immigrants, feel no cultural identity with the Indians or their history. They feel more comfortable believing stories of age-old colonization by familiar peoples from the world of Egypt and the Near East. For many people, history is a faith, too, something to cling to and to believe against all scientific odds. Most of the strange works that purport to describe early civilization in the Americas play on such faith. They invite the reader to join in the group who knows the "truth," and either attack scientists as frauds or simply ignore their work. It is significant, for example, that Fell (1980) cites no works of archaeological scholarship in his *Saga America* except some descriptions of American Indian rock art. One can conclude only that scientific archaeological research is irrelevant to his tale, or that he is unfamiliar with it, or that it challenges the "faith."

The account of early American civilization that follows is based on scientific archaeological excavations and surveys by which evidence has been accumulating for the indigenous origins of New World civilization for more than a century. The cumulative scientific evidence is overwhelming and impressive in its consistency. No one can dismantle a sincerely held faith, and so I shall make no attempt to destroy the illusions of those who believe that American was settled by Atlanteans, Ancient Egyptians, or anyone else: to do so is a waste of time. The irony is that the unfolding story of New World civilization revealed by science is far more fascinating and intellectually stimulating than any outer space adventure story, however well conceived or well marketed. (For more serious accounts of transoceanic voyaging, see Carter, 1981; Davies, 1979; Jett, 1978.)

PRECLASSIC PEOPLES IN MESOAMERICA

By 2000 B.C., sedentary farming villages were common in most of Mesoamerica (R. E. W. Adams, 1977a; W. T. Sanders and Price, 1968; Weaver, 1981). In their agriculture, people relied on many plant species, and slash-and-burn farming methods were in wide use in the lowlands. With such methods people could clear small gardens in the forest by cutting tree trunks and brush, carefully burning branches to fertilize the soil with a layer of wood ash. Then, using pointed digging sticks, they planted maize and other crops. A few seasons later they abandoned the land, planting less important crops on older plots or leaving them to the forest. The search for new lands was constant, even when slash-and-burn was combined with irrigation or riverside agriculture.

Preclassic
2500 B.C. to A.D. 300

Early Preclassic

Many centuries elapsed between the beginnings of village life and that of Mesoamerican civilization. Mesoamericans began to live in larger settlements and to build elaborate ceremonial centers at the beginning of an era named the *Preclassic* or *Formative* period, approximately 2500 B.C. to A.D. 300. The earliest centuries of the Preclassic witnessed the appearance of pottery and the first ceremonial centers. One such site is Cuello in lowland northern Belize, which is radiocarbon dated to between c. 2000 B.C. to A.D. 300 (Hammond, 1980, 1982). The inhabitants of this site were cultivating maize and probably relied heavily on wild swamp plants for their diet (Figure 21.1). The Middle Preclassic period is known for the Olmec culture, appearing from 1200 to 300 B.C. The Late Preclassic period has various regional centers, some with Olmec-like artistic and cultural characteristics (Willey, 1966).

Cuello
c. 2000 B.C. to A.D. 300

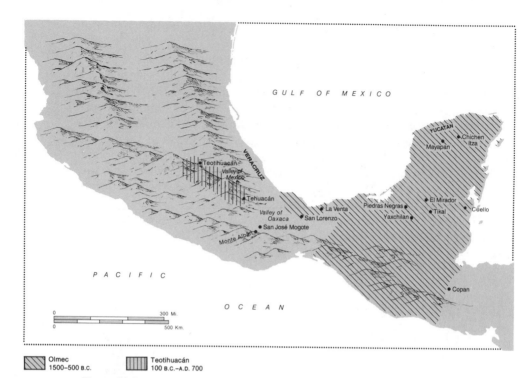

Figure 21.1 Mesoamerican archaeological sites mentioned in this chapter. Approximate distributions of various traditions are shown.

Middle Preclassic: the Olmecs

The first major ceremonial centers appear in the Middle Preclassic period, marking the transformation of village society into a wider social order with more complex social and economic organizations (Coe, 1962). Signs of social stratification begin to appear at the time when food surpluses were achieved; the extra food was used to support certain individuals, probably religious leaders, whose contribution to the society was to organize the production and distribution of food on a new scale. The first ceremonial centers probably developed as a response to population increase and the desire to maintain and symbolize kinship and religious unity. These revered centers became the foci of political and religious power, as their new priest-leaders engaged in trading, employed increasing numbers of specialized craftspeople, and manipulated labor forces and food surpluses.

Olmec
1500 to 500 B.C.

The best-known Preclassic culture is that of the Olmec, centered in the lowland regions of southern Veracruz and western Tabasco (Bernal, 1969; Coe, 1965, 1968; Coe and Diehl, 1980). There, ceremonial centers achieved remarkable complexity at an early date. *Olmec* means "rubber people," and the region was long important for rubber production. Although the Olmec homeland is low-lying, tropical, and humid, its soil is fertile, and the swamps, lakes, and rivers are rich in fish, birds, and other animals. Olmec societies prospered in this region for 1000 years from approximately 1500 B.C. and created a highly distinctive art style.

San Lorenzo The earliest traces of Olmec occupation are best documented at San Lorenzo, where Olmec people lived on a platform in the midst of frequently inundated woodland plains. They erected ridges and mounds around their platform, upon which they built pyramids and possibly ball courts and placed elaborate monumental carvings overlooking the site. The earliest occupation of San Lorenzo shows few Olmec features, but by 1250 B.C., the inhabitants were beginning to build some raised fields, a task that required enormous organized labor forces. By that time, too, distinctive Olmec sculpture began to appear. A century later, magnificent monumental carvings adorned San Lorenzo (Figure 21.2), distinctive and often mutilated by the Olmec themselves (Coe and Diehl, 1980).

San Lorenzo
1250 B.C.

One archaeologist has estimated the population of San Lorenzo at 2500. The inhabitants enjoyed extensive trade, especially in obsidian and other semiprecious materials obtained from many parts of Mesoamerica. San Lorenzo fell into decline after 900 B.C. and was surpassed in im-

Figure 21.2 Giant stone head from San Lorenzo made from basalt, approximately 2.4 m (8 ft) high. Michael Coe (1965) has suggested that these heads are portraits of rulers, while David Grove (1973) has identified what he thinks are name glyphs on the "helmets" of the heads.

portance by La Venta, the most famous Olmec site, nearer the Gulf of Mexico.

La Venta
800 to 400 B.C.

La Venta The La Venta ceremonial center was built on a small island in the middle of a swamp (Drucker, 1959). A rectangular earth mound, 120 m long by 70 m wide and 32 m high (393 ft by 229 ft and 105 ft high), dominates the island. Long low mounds surround a rectangular plaza in front of the large mound, faced by walls and terraced mounds at the other end of the plaza (Figure 21.3). Vast monumental stone sculptures litter the site, including some Olmec heads bearing expressions of contempt and savagery. Caches of jade objects, figurines, and a dull green rock (serpentine) are common, too (Figure 21.4). Every stone for sculptures and temples had to be brought from at least 60 mi (96 km) away, a vast undertaking, for some sculptured blocks weigh more than 40 tons. La Venta flourished for approximately 400 years from 800 B.C. After approximately 400 B.C., the site probably was destroyed, which we deduce from signs that many of its finest monuments were intentionally defaced.

La Venta is perhaps most renowned for its distinctive Olmec art style, executed both as sculptured objects and in relief. Olmec sculpture concentrated on natural and supernatural beings and its dominant motif, the "were-jaguar," or humanlike jaguar. Many jaguars were given infantile faces, drooping lips, and large swollen eyes, a style also applied to human figures; some have almost negroid faces; others resemble snarling demons in their ferocity. The Olmec contribution to Mesoamerican art and religion was enormously significant. Elements of their art style and imagery were diffused widely during the first millennium B.C. southward to Guatemala and San Salvador and northward into the Valley of Mexico.

Late Preclassic

Late Preclassic
300 B.C. to A.D. 300

We believe that the spread of the Olmec art style and the beginning of the Late Preclassic period in approximately 500 to 300 B.C. signals the period during which a common religious system and ideology began to unify large areas of Mesoamerica. A powerful priesthood congregated in spectacular ceremonial centers, commemorating potent and widely rec-

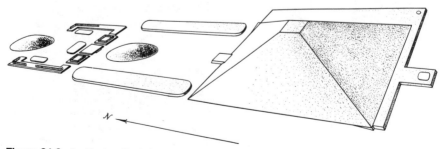

Figure 21.3 La Venta, site 4: layout of the major structures.

Figure 21.4 An Olmec altar or throne sculpture from La Venta. The sculpture is 2 m (approximately 6 ft) high. At least one of these thrones shows the ruler in front connected to his parents on the side by umbilical cords.

ognized deities. Distinctive art and architecture went with the new religion, the practice of which required precise measurements of calendar years and of longer cycles of time. Writing and mathematical calculations were developed to affirm religious practices, a unifying political force in the sense that they welded scattered village communities into larger political units. By the time the Classic Mesoamerican civilizations arose, dynasties of priests and aristocrats had been ruling parts of Mesoamerica along well-established lines for nearly 1000 years.

THE RISE OF COMPLEX SOCIETY IN OAXACA: MONTE ALBÁN

The Preclassic cultures of the Valley of Oaxaca have been studied intensively by Kent Flannery and his students, using highly sophisticated systems approaches to document changing settlement patterns and economic and demographic trends (Flannery, 1976). Something like ninety percent of the Preclassic Oaxaca villages were little more than small hamlets of fifty to sixty people, while the remainder were much larger settlements of 1000 to 1200 souls, with populations of priests and craftspeople.

The evolution of larger settlements in Oaxaca and elsewhere was closely connected with the development of long-distance trade in obsidian and other luxuries such as seashells and stingray spines from the Gulf of Mexico. The simple barter networks for obsidian of earlier times evolved into sophisticated regional trading organizations where village leaders controlled monopolies over sources of obsidian and its distribution. Magnetite mirrors, seashells, feathers, and ceramics all were traded on the highlands, and from the highlands to the lowlands as well. Olmec pottery and other ritual objects began to appear in highland settlements between 1150 and 650 B.C., many of them bearing the distinctive were-jaguar motif of the lowlands, which had an important place in Olmec cosmology.

Public buildings began to appear in villages such as San José Mogote between 1400 and 1150 B.C., many of them oriented eight degrees west of north; they were built on adobe and earth platforms. Conch shell trumpets and turtle shell drums from the Gulf of Mexico are associated with these buildings, as are clay figurines of dancers wearing costumes and masks (Figure 21.5). There were marine fish spines, too, probably used in personal bloodletting ceremonies that were still practiced even in Aztec times. [The Spanish described how Aztec nobles would gash themselves with knives or with the spines of fish or stingray in acts of mutilation before the gods, penances required of the devout (Valliant, 1941).] It has been suggested that the diffusion of the Olmec art style through Mesoamerica resulted both from an increased need for religious rituals to

Figure 21.5 Four clay figurines shaped and posed deliberately to form a scene, buried beneath an Early Preclassic house at San José Mogote, Oaxaca, Mexico.

bring the various elements of society together, and because the Oaxacan elite, aspiring to the status of their Olmec neighbors, took to the new beliefs in slavish conformity (Flannery, 1976). This diffusion took place after long-distance trading had been in existence for centuries, and probably signaled an increase in larger villages such as San José Mogote.

Monte Albán

By 400 B.C., there were at least seven small states in the Valley of Oaxaca, of which the one centered on Monte Albán soon became dominant in the area. Although massive population increases and increased economic power were among the interacting factors that aided in the rise of Monte Albán, the special terrain of Monte Albán may have been of vital importance in its ascendancy (Blanton, 1978). Richard Blanton has surveyed more than 2000 terraces on the slopes of Monte Albán, terraces used for agriculture and housing areas. Monte Albán commanded the best terrain in the valley, sloping land that was organized for agriculture and dense settlement by a population of several thousand people, far larger than that of most major settlements in Mesoamerica at the time. Even as early as 400 B.C., some of the terraces already were in use by a highly organized population whose leaders resided in a ceremonial and civic center built on the summit of the Monte Albán ridge. Although the large-scale buildings of later times have contoured the summit of Monte Albán beyond recognition, it is clear that the first leaders to live there undertook major public works, many of them wood and thatch buildings, which had incised sculptures of what may be dead and tortured enemies set into the walls.

Monte Albán went on to develop into a vast ceremonial center with splendid public architecture; its settlement area included public buildings, terraces, and housing zones that extended over approximately 15 sq mi (40 sq km) (Figure 21.6). The more than 2000 terraces all held one or two houses, while small ravines were dammed to pond valuable water supplies. Blanton suggests that between 30,000 and 50,000 people lived at Monte Albán between A.D. 200 and 700. Many very large villages and smaller hamlets lay within easy distance of the city. The enormous platforms on the ridge of Monte Albán supported complex layouts of temples and pyramid-temples, palaces, patios, and tombs. A hereditary elite seems to have ruled Monte Albán, the leaders of a state that had emerged in the Valley of Oaxaca by A.D. 200. Their religious power was based on ancestor worship, a pantheon of at least thirty-nine gods, grouped around major themes of ritual life. The rain-god and lightning were associated with the jaguar motif; another group of deities is linked with the maize god Pitao Cozabi. Nearly all these gods were still worshiped at the time of Spanish contact, although Monte Albán itself was abandoned after A.D. 700, at approximately the same time as another great ceremonial center, Teotihuacán, in the Valley of Mexico, began to eclipse.

Figure 21.6 Monte Albán, Valley of Oaxaca — Zapotec ruins, 1951.

MESOAMERICAN STATES ARE SHAPED
BY AGRICULTURAL TECHNIQUES

Everyone agrees that the emergence of unifying artistic traditions (such as the Olmec), religious ideologies, ritual organization, and extensive trading networks were key factors in the development of Mesoamerican civilization (Hammond, 1982). But it is only in recent years that people have begun to study early Mesoamerican agriculture in an attempt to understand how the Maya and other peoples were able to support the enormous urban populations that built and organized the ceremonial centers of both highland and lowland Mesoamerica (R. E. W. Adams, 1977b).

There are sharp contrasts in subsistence patterns between lowlands and highlands. The former is a much more uniform environment where there is far less diversity of soils and resources than on the highlands. The traditional views of early Mesoamerican agriculture have been highly colored by hypotheses about lowland practices which do not apply to the highlands at all.

Long-held views of Mesoamerican agriculture, specifically those concerning the Maya, always have assumed that the populations lived in dispersed villages and used only slash-and-burn agriculture, which, as we have seen, cannot support a high population density (R. E. W. Adams, 1977a). This viewpoint is now discarded, for it has been shown that raised fields and terracing were important in lowland cultivation not only of maize, but of other subsistence crops as well. Dennis Puleston believed the lowland Maya relied heavily on tree culture, notably that of the ramon tree *(Brosimum alicastrum)*, a species that produces a highly nutritious nut that can be stored up to eighteen months and requires little care (Puleston, 1971). As valuable as maize as a protein source, the ramon may have permitted much higher carrying capacities in the lowlands, of up to 400 to 600 people per square kilometer (R. E. W. Adams, Brown, and Culbert, 1981). Some fascinating experiments involving scanning the Maya lowlands from the air with imaging radar have shown that areas of wet season swamp near known Maya sites often have irregular grids of grey lines in them, multitudes of ladder, lattice, and curvilinear patterns. These have been compared to known ancient canal systems and are thought to represent long-forgotten large-scale swamp irrigation schemes (R. E. W. Adams, Brown, and Culbert, 1981). The investigators believe that nearly all the swamp edges in the Petén, the rain-forest lowlands of northern Guatemala, once were extensively canalized for agriculture and communication purposes. Thus, the swamps became assets rather than liabilities, artificial environments wherein one could grow large food surpluses and also readily transport goods by canoe. The location of such large Maya centers as Tikal, that may have housed as many as 50,000 people, can be explained as a result of the successful exploitation of the fertile swamps nearby. The radar imagery research still is in its preliminary stages, but the initial results at least help to explain why the Maya could support such an elaborate civilization.

The lowland forest environment tends to be a uniform one, but those of the highlands are much more diverse, as we have seen in the case of Tehuacán (Chapter Thirteen). The earliest farming villages in Oaxaca are concentrated in the valley floors, in areas where water is available within easy reach of the surface. Modern farmers choose similar villages for simple "pot" irrigation, where they plant their maize and other crops near small shallow wells. They simply water the plants by dipping pots into the wells and watering surrounding plants from the shallow water table before moving on to the next well. Flannery has argued that the Oaxacans used the same technique in prehistoric times (Flannery, 1968b).

Pot irrigation does not require large numbers of people or complex social organization to support it. From approximately 1300 B.C. to 350 B.C., Oaxaca was inhabited by widely spaced larger villages with small villages dependent on them. The changing settlement pattern was accompanied by population growth that led to the taking up of less desirable agricultural land on slopes and the development of new agricultural techniques to work this land. The Oaxaca environment was so diverse that the people were able to build on their simple and highly effective original techniques, which still remained part of their repertoire. They expanded to the slopes, and then even cultivated the arid lands as populations grew. Eventually the economic power generated by these rising populations gave highland areas such as Oaxaca a decided edge in cultural evolution.

Similar diversity of agricultural techniques is found in the Valley of

Pot irrigation

Agriculture on the slopes

Mexico, where slash-and-burn methods, dry farming, and irrigation agriculture all were in use. Irrigation used both floodwaters and canals to bring water to dry gardens. The most famous of all irrigation techniques, however, is the *chinampa* or floating garden technique, a highly intensive and productive agricultural system based on the reclaiming of swamps. The farmers made use of standing water and built up marshy areas by piling up natural vegetation and lake mud to form huge grids of naturally irrigated gardens. The chinampas were used very systematically to grow a variety of crops, so timed that different crops came into harvest throughout the year (Sanders et al., 1970). This system is amazingly productive and is estimated to have supported approximately 100,000 people from 25,000 acres in 1519, at the time of Spanish contact. However, each chinampa produced large food surpluses that could be used to support thousands of nonagricultural workers and specialists. Sanders has argued that the 25,000 acres of chinampas referred to previously actually could have supported approximately 180,000 people. That this highly effective agricultural system was the basis of early civilization and urban life in the Valley of Mexico is beyond question.

The agricultural system of the Valley of Mexico may seem complicated, but it supported and was part of a far more elaborate system of food marketing, which provided not only tribute for taxes, but also opportunities for the trading of specialist foodstuffs from one area of the highlands to another. The highland peoples relied on elaborate markets that were strictly regulated by the state and conducted on a barter system. The Valley of Mexico was an economic unit before Teotihuacán made it a political one as well. It was the great agricultural productivity of the Valley and the sophisticated market economy of the emerging city that made the prodigious social and religious, as well as material, developments of later centuries possible. This economic system fostered the development of specialist crafts that were sold in the markets of the cities and exported over wide areas.

The sequence of events in the highlands may have begun with the buildup of agricultural populations in diverse environments such as the Valley of Oaxaca in the first and second millennia B.C. This population buildup led to the development of more intensive agricultural methods, including both irrigation and chinampa systems. At the same time, different areas were linked by increasingly sophisticated trading networks and by an emerging market economy, with, perhaps, some specialized merchants.

Religious activity was stimulated by the introduction of religious beliefs and sacred objects from the lowlands. Trade in exotic luxuries increased as ceremonial centers and stratified societies were founded. By 200 B.C., the effects of increased religious activity, intensified trading, and the production of huge food surpluses from the diverse environment had led to the founding of at least two major cities in the Valley of Mexico. One of these, Teotihuacán, reached an enormous size and enjoyed vast political, economic, and religious power in the centuries that followed.

In the Valley of Oaxaca, Monte Albán achieved a similar dominance. The two great states probably enjoyed an uneasy alliance.

Teotihuacán

Teotihuacán lies northeast of Mexico City and is now one of the great archaeological tourist attractions of the world. It was one of the dominant political and cultural centers of all Mesoamerica in approximately A.D. 500, the culmination of centuries of vigorous cultural development in the Valley of Mexico (Millon, Drewitt, and Cowgill, 1974).

The first buildings appear at Teotihuacán in approximately 200 B.C., comprising a handful of villages, at least one of which may have specialized in obsidian manufacture. By 100 B.C., Teotihuacán had begun to expand rapidly, and the scattered villages became a settlement covering more than 3.5 sq mi. Much of this early settlement is covered by the vast structures of later times. It is estimated that 600 people inhabited this early town. There were several public buildings.

Teotihuacán
200 B.C. to A.D. 700

René Millon, who carried out a systematic survey of Teotihuacán, found that by A.D. 150 the city extended over 5 sq mi and housed more than 20,000 people. Obsidian trade and manufacture were expanding fast (Parsons and Price, 1971). There were two major religious complexes for which, among other structures, the Pyramids of the Sun and Moon were first built at this time.

Between A.D. 150 and 750, Teotihuacán exploded in size. Anyone passing through the Valley of Mexico had to pass through the city with its diverse population of priests, merchants, craftspeople, and other specialists. The rulers of the city erected hundreds of standardized apartment complexes and continued a master plan that laid out the city on a north-south axis, centered on the Avenue of the Dead (Figure 21.7), with another great avenue oriented east-west. The 8 square miles of Teotihuacán consisted of avenues and plazas, markets, temples, palaces, apartment buildings, and complex drainage and agricultural works. The entire city was dominated by the Pyramid of the Sun (an Aztec name), a vast structure of earth, adobe, and piled rubble. The pyramid, faced with stone, is 64 m (210 ft) high and 198 m (650 ft) square. A wooden temple probably sat on the summit of the terraced pyramid. The long Avenue of the Dead passes the west face of the pyramid, leading to the Pyramid of the Moon, the second largest structure at the site (Figure 21.7). The avenue is lined with civic, palace, and religious buildings, and the side streets lead to residential areas. A large palace and temple complex dedicated to the Plumed Serpent (Quetzalcóatl), with platform and stairways around the central court, lies south of the middle of Teotihuacán, across from a central marketplace.

City layout

The Avenue of the Dead and the pyramids lie amid a sprawling mass of small houses. Priests and craftsworkers lived in dwellings around small courtyards; the less privileged lived in large compounds of rooms connected by narrow alleyways and patios. By any standard, Teotihuacán

Figure 21.7 Aerial view of the ceremonial precincts at Teotihuacán, Mexico, with the Pyramid of the Moon in the foreground. At left in the background (to the left of the Avenue of the Dead) is the Pyramid of the Sun.

was a city, and once housed up to 120,000 people. Although some farmers probably lived within the city, we know that rural villages flourished nearby. These villages were compact, expertly planned, and administered by city rulers.

The comprehensive settlement pattern data from the Millon survey enables us to say something about the structure of Teotihuacán society. The food surpluses to support the city were produced by farmers who lived both in the city and in satellite villages nearby. Tribute from neighboring states also helped feed the city, and control of large areas of the plateau ensured that adequate food supplies came to Teotihuacán's huge market. Most of the people lived in the city. It is not known how important chinampa agriculture was for Teotihuacán, but irrigation farming was a key element in subsistence. Craftspeople accounted for perhaps 25 percent of the urban population, people who lived in compounds of apartments near the more than 500 workshops that produced everything from obsidian tools to clay vessels. Merchants probably were an important class in the city, as were civil servants who carried out the routine administration of Teotihuacán. There were even foreign quarters, one of

Agriculture

which housed Oaxacans. The elite included priests, warriors, and secular leaders, who controlled the vast city and its many dealings through a strictly class society. Religious beliefs continued the rituals of earlier times, but it appears that cannibalism and human sacrifice became increasingly important in later centuries, as the leaders of the city became more and more militaristic in their outlook, a trend that was to continue into Aztec times.

Teotihuacán ruled the Valley of Mexico and parts of Puebla, but its influence through alliance, tribute, and warfare, as well as trading, extended over a far larger area of Meosamerica. As in later times, the rulers of Teotihuacán probably controlled some highly strategic and economically important zones, but there were large areas where their influence was minimal. The final analysis is this: Teotihuacán probably was a huge city-state bound to other city-states by uneasy alliances and tribute exchanges.

By A.D. 600, Teotihuacán probably was ruled by a secular ruler who was looked upon as a divine king of some kind — a person with formidable military powers. A class of nobles controlled the kinship groups that organized the bulk of the city's huge population. In approximately A.D. 650, Teotihuacán was deliberately burned down. Only fifty years later its urban population was scattered in a few villages. Much of the former urban population settled in neighboring regions, which thereby reaped the benefit of Teotihuacán's misfortunes. No one knows exactly why this great city collapsed so suddenly. The rapid development of the city may have resulted in serious internal weaknesses which made Teotihuacán vulnerable to easy overthrow. Conceivably, a drought may also have weakened the city and provided an opportunity for jealous rivals to attempt an attack.

The very success of Teotihuacán may have accelerated its downfall. The new orders of society and politics spawned by the city may have been copied by other leaders, perhaps more aggressive and less tradition-bound than the mother city. Teotihuacán was not the only sophisticated city-state in the highlands between A.D. 500 and 700. Sanders has argued that Teotihuacán was overthrown by a coalition of city-states that included Tula to the northwest, Xochicalco in the southwest, and Cholula to the southeast (W. Sanders, 1965). All these states expanded after the downfall of Teotihuacán, and all had been powerful regional states at the time of the former's collapse. Whatever the causes of Teotihuacán's downfall, its end resulted in a dispersal of specialist craftsworkers, priests, and other functionaries throughout Mesoamerica, as a period of political and military competition among rival states ensued.

THE CLASSIC PERIOD IN FULL FLOWER: THE MAYA

The Maya civilization probably is the best known of all early American civilizations, one that has excited the imagination of scholars for more than a century. Maya civilization took shape slowly. It was centered on lowland rain-forest areas that provided a relatively uniform environment in which people grew both maize and other crops, as well as relying heavily on the harvesting of trees such as the ramon. Traces of primordial Maya culture are discernible in the Yucatán and Belize many centuries before the brilliant Maya civilization flourished in the lowlands. Norman Hammond has found platforms and other structures at Cuello in Belize that date to the second millennium B.C. (Hammond, 1978, 1980; Henderson, 1981). The associated pottery styles can be traced through the first millennium B.C. and appear to be ancestral to Classic Maya ceramics.

In the early second millennium B.C., the farmers of northern Belize were growing at least three kinds of maize, probably in small forest gardens. By the late second millennium, pollen analyses at Cuello show that the forest cover was considerably reduced, with a corresponding increase in grassland, probably as a result of more forest clearance and possibly also owing to a decrease in the length of time fields lay fallow. The trend toward more forest clearance appears to have continued until the late first millennium B.C., when there was a massive increase in the lowland population. Preliminary investigations at Cuello reveal that maize was still the staple crop, together with a range of as yet unidentified root crops. Norman Hammond points out (Hammond and Miksicek, 1981) that large numbers of an edible snail called *Pomacea* come from these particular Cuello layers. This species flourishes in shallow water and swampland, and strongly suggests that raised fields and irrigated swamps were then in use near the settlement (see also Turner and Harrison, 1981). At the same time the Maya may have grown tree crops, carefully tended fruit trees nurtured in house gardens and mulched with domestic waste. This new reliance on swamp agriculture and tree crops was essential to support the larger populations of Classic Maya times.

Although the roots of Maya culture go back far into the Preclassic period, considerable debate surrounds the origins of Maya civilization, partly because until recently virtually nothing was known about their subsistence patterns (R. E. W. Adams, 1977a; Hammond, 1982). Perhaps the initial Maya settlement pattern was a dispersed one, with villages scattered through the rain forest, in situations that seemed to militate against political or economic unity. They flourished in a fundamentally empty landscape, where there was plenty of room for slash-and-burn agriculture and little incentive for cooperation between neighboring communities.

Debate about the origins of the Maya civilization centers around the dramatic population growth that occurred in the mid-first millennium B.C. and the changes in subsistence and settlement patterns that led the dispersed Maya villages into closer economic and social cooperation, and eventually to the concentration of tens of thousands of people into huge urban centers. William Rathje has provided one possible explanation. He suggests that the Maya environment was very deficient in many vital resources, including stone for grinding maize, salt (always vital for agriculturalists), obsidian for knives and weapons, and many luxury materials (Rathje, 1972). All these could be obtained from the highlands in the north, from the Valley of Mexico as well as from Guatemala and other regions, if the necessary long-distance trading networks and mechanisms could be set up. Such connections, and the trading expeditions to maintain them, could not be organized by individual villages alone. The Maya lived in a uniform environment where the rain forest provided similarly deficient resources for every settlement. Long networks therefore were developed through the authority of the ceremonial centers and their leaders. The integrative organization needed must have been considerable, for communications in the rain forest, especially in areas remote from the highlands, were extremely difficult to maintain.

Rathje carries his arguments a stage further. Obviously, peoples living on the border between the lowlands and the highlands had the best opportunities for trade. Those who lived farther away, such as the Maya, were at a disadvantage. They offered the same agricultural commodities and craft exports as their more fortunate border neighbors but were farther from markets. They had one competitive advantage, however — a complex and properly functioning state organization and the knowledge to keep it going. This knowledge itself was very exportable. Along with pottery, feathers, specialized stone materials, and lime plaster, they exported their political and social organization, as well as their religious beliefs.

The Rathje hypothesis probably explains part of the complex processes of state formation during the early Classic period (Rathje, 1971). Long trading networks did connect the lowlands and the highlands. A well-defined cosmology with roots in Olmec beliefs, a strongly centralized economic and religious system based on ceremonial centers, and sophisticated and highly competitive commercial opportunities all contributed to a complex system that caused the dramatic rise of Classic Mesoamerican civilization. It should be pointed out, however, that Rathje's hypothesis suffers from the objection that suitable alternative raw materials for metates (grindstones) and other imported objects do exist in the lowlands. It could be, too, that warfare became a competitive response to population growth and the increasing scarcity of prime agricultural land.

Recent excavations in Guatemala's Petén promise to throw new light on the development of Maya civilization. The late Preclassic city of El Mirador flourished long before the great later Classic Maya cities of A.D. 600 to 850. Most of El Mirador's public buildings were built in the Late Preclassic, between 150 B.C. and A.D. 50. The city covered about 10 square mi., lying in low undulating land; parts of the area flooded during the rainy season. Archaeologists from Brigham Young University have uncovered more than 200 buildings; among them are great complexes of pyramids, plazas, causeways, and buildings.

El Mirador
300 B.C. to A.D. 600

The Danta pyramid at the east end of the site dominates El Mirador. It rises from a natural hill more than 210 feet (70 m.) high. The western face of the hill is sculpted into large platforms that are surmounted with buildings and temples. Two km. west rises the Tigre complex, a pyramid 182 feet (55 m.) high surrounded by a plaza, a small temple, and several smaller buildings. The Tigre complex covers an area of about 58,000 sq. m.—an area a little larger than the base of Teotihuacan's Pyramid of the Sun. Three buildings, with the largest in the center, are found on a truncated landing on the pyramid. This "triad" theme is also found at later sites such as Tikal.

El Mirador is unique because it was only occupied during the Preclassic. As excavations proceed, it should be possible to compare Preclassic with Classic occupation, and to study the evolution of Maya architecture, city planning, and social and political organization. El Mirador is yielding some of the earliest examples of Maya writing. It appears on an inscribed potsherd and some symbols are inscribed on the Tigre sculpture. El Mirador itself was an elaborate city and was probably controlled by a highly organized elite. They built a magnificent city using artisans, priests, architects, and engineers, as well as traders and thousands of unskilled villagers. This magnificent city, together with some other Preclassic centers, flourished successfully for centuries before it suddenly collapsed in the early Christian era. It was to be centuries before Maya civili-

Figure 21.8 Archaeologists at work on the east stucco mask on the Tigre temple, El Mirador. The building and mask date to the late Preclassic. *Inset:* El Mirador, Petén, Guatemala: Reconstruction of the Tigre complex of buildings and platforms. The entire complex dates to the late Preclassic period, ca. 100 B.C. to A.D. 50.

zation recovered, only to collapse again in the eighth century A.D. And the Classic Maya collapse (see p. 461) may have been a replay of the unknown forces that had destroyed El Mirador centuries earlier.

Classic Maya civilization had been in existence for centuries when such centers as Copán and Tikal were founded in the fourth century A.D. (for Tikal, see Coe and Haviland, 1982). Their rubble-filled pyramids were topped with temples ornamented with sculptured stucco (Figure 21.9) (Coe, 1984). The pyramids were faced with cemented stone blocks and covered with a high-quality plaster to protect against the rains. The large temples on top had small, dark rooms because the builders did not know how to construct arches and were forced to corbel their roofs, supporting them with external braces. Tikal was an important trade center and, like others, attracted specialized craftsworkers who served the priests and the gods.

Maya rulers constantly sought to appease their numerous gods (some benevolent, some evil) at the correct moments in the elaborate sacred

Figure 21.9   Temple I at Tikal, Guatemala, which dates to about A.D. 700.

calendar. Each sacred year, as well as each cycle of years, had its destiny controlled by a different deity. The state's continued survival was ensured by pleasing the gods with sacrificial offerings, some of them human.

Astronomy

The Maya were remarkable astronomers who predicted most astronomical events, including eclipses of the sun and moon (Figure 21.10). Religious events were regulated according to a sacred year *(tzolkin)* with thirteen months of twenty days each. The 260 days of the sacred year were unrelated to any astronomical phenomenon, being closely tied to ritual and divination. The length of the sacred year was arbitrary and probably established by long tradition. Tzolkins were, however, closely intermeshed with a secular year *(haab)* of 365 days, an astronomical calendar based on the solar cycle. The *haab* was used to regulate state affairs, but the connections between sacred and secular years were of great importance in Mayan life. Every fifty-two years a complete cycle of all the variations of the day and month names of the two calendars occurred, an occasion for intense religious activity.

The Maya developed a hieroglyphic script used for calculating calendars and regulating religious observances (Coe, 1984; Jones, 1984; Thompson, 1950). The script was much used for recording genealogies, king lists, conquests, and dynastic histories. Partly because of the Spanish bishop Diego de Landa, who recorded Maya dialects surviving in the mid-sixteenth century, scholars have been able to decipher part of the script that was written on temple walls and modeled in stucco. The symbols are fantastically grotesque, consisting mostly of humans, monsters, or gods' heads (Figure 21.10).

Copán

Copán, founded in the fifth century A.D., was one of the major astronomical centers of Mesoameria. Its pyramids, temples, and pillars are a remarkable monument to Maya skill. Copán, like Tikal, preserves the essential architectural features of Maya ceremonial centers. These include platforms, pyramids, and causeways, grouped around open concourses and plazas presumably for religious effect and also to handle the large numbers of spectators who flocked to the religious ceremonies.

Ball courts were built at some late centers. They were used for an elaborate ceremonial contest, perhaps connected with the fertility of crops, between competing teams using a solid rubber ball. The details of the game remain obscure, but it is known that the players hit the balls so as to strike stone markers shaped like parrot heads.

Maya civilization was far from uniform; each major center kept its political identity and ruled a network of lesser religious complexes and small villages (Marcus, 1973). The calendar and hieroglyphic script were common to all, essential in regulating religious life and worshiping Maya gods. Architectural and artistic styles in ceramics and small artifacts varied from center to center as each developed its own characteristics and cultural traditions (Coe, 1984). The Maya were unified more by religious doctrine than by political or economic interests, in much the same

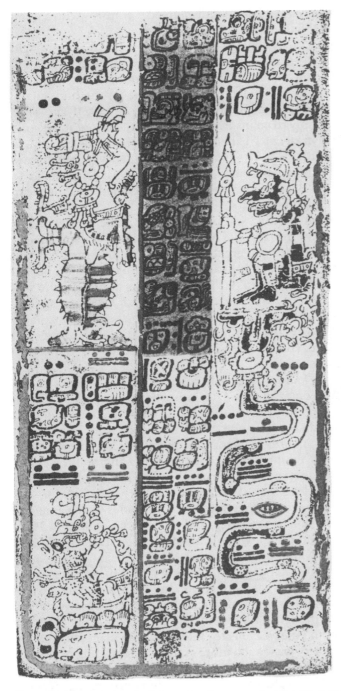

Figure 21.10 Only three certain, and perhaps one doubtful, Maya codices (books of picture writing) are known to have survived destruction by the Spanish. Here is a page from the so-called Dresden Codex, which records astronomical calculations, ritual detail, and tables of eclipses.

MESOAMERICAN CIVILIZATIONS   459

way, perhaps, as the spread of Islam unified diverse cultures with a common religious belief (Figure 21.11).

The partial decipherment of Maya hieroglyphs has thrown some light on their society. At Piedras Negras, Mayanist Tatiana Proskouriakoff identified seven successive groups of rulers' monuments, each of them erected on the fifth anniversary of their ascent to the throne (for key references and a summary description, see Hammond, 1982). The Tikal rulers are known not only from inscriptions but from iconographic studies as well. The Sky dynasty at Tikal has been traced from the late fourth to the late eighth century A.D. The first identified ruler was Jaguar Paw, who died in A.D. 376. Three celebrated, but anonymous, rulers, known to Mayanists as Rulers A, B, and C, revitalized and expanded Tikal between A.D. 682 and the late eighth century.

Palenque yielded an exciting discovery in 1952, when Alberto Ruz cleared a stairway below the pyramid of the inscriptions. The stairs led to a rock-cut chamber containing a great sarcophagus with a finely carved lid. The inscriptions on the coffin revealed that the elderly man buried within was named Pacal ("Shield"). The hieroglyphs tell us that he was born on March 24, A.D. 603, ascended to the throne of Palenque on July 27, A.D. 615, and died on September 29, A.D. 684 at age eighty-one. Pacal commissioned texts to record the history of the rulers who preceded him, and his successors continued to keep up the records on wall panels until around A.D. 799.

In 1983, the burial of an Early Classic ruler dating to A.D. 450 came to light at the 500-acre center at Rio Azul in northern Guatemala, 50 mi north of Tikal. The body was buried in a shroud atop a wooden bier. The remains of a jade necklace lay among the bones, which were surrounded with fine clay vessels, including tripod jars and a unique, screw-topped container, made by dovetailing clay spirals in the lid and on the neck of the pot. The walls of the rock-cut burial chamber are decorated with hieroglyphs that should tell experts much about Early Classic life.

The Maya inscriptions reveal that many local dynasties were passed on from father to son for many centuries, and the rulers of different Maya centers were in constant touch with one another. The Tikal Sky dynasty extended their influence not only by long-distance trade but also by judicious political marriages that gave neighboring rulers maternal-kin ties to the great city. Unfortunately, we still know almost nothing of the extent of the many political and military alliances contracted by Maya rulers.

Originally, people thought of Maya society as a civilization ruled by priests, who interpreted the heavens for thousands of village farmers. In fact, Classic Maya society was much more complex, consisting of a series of social layers, one's position within society being determined by birth. The ruling elite were an exclusive, self-perpetuating group. Below them were various specialists — administrators who supervised public works projects and ran the complex affairs of state, priests, architects, artisans like potters and stoneworkers, and also performers, laborers, and common farmers (Figure 21.12). This type of social organization is typical of

Figure 21.11 A richly clad Maya ruler wears the mask of the long-nosed god. His name is Bird-Jaquar. Three people, probably prisoners about to be sacrificed, kneel before him. From Yaxchilán, c. A.D. 750. (From J. Eric S. Thompson, *The Rise and Fall of Maya Civilization.* Copyright 1954, 1966, by the University of Oklahoma Press)

many early civilizations, among them the Sumerians and Ancient Egyptians. Like the ens and pharoahs of the Near East, the Maya ruler extracted labor and food from those they ruled, but the means by which they did so are still unknown (Hammond, 1982).

The Maya civilization flourished until about A.D. 900, when it suddenly, and inexplicably, collapsed.

THE COLLAPSE OF CLASSIC MAYA CIVILIZATION

Maya civilization reached its peak after A.D. 600. Then, at the end of the eighth century, the great ceremonial centers of the Petén and the southern lowlands were abandoned, the calendar was discontinued, and the structure of religious life and the state decayed. No one has been able to explain this sudden and dramatic collapse of Maya civilization, the subject of a prolonged debate in American archaeology (Culbert, 1973).

The Classic Maya collapse has fostered varied traditional explanations, most of them unilinear and monocausal. They have included catas-

Figure 21.12 A portion of the famous Bonampak murals at Chiapas, Mexico. This segment is in Room 4.

trophes, such as earthquakes, hurricanes, and disease. Ecological theories mention exhausted soils, water loss, and erosion. Internal social revolt might have led the peasants to rebel against cruel rule by their elitist overlords. Each of these hypotheses has been rejected because either the evidence is insufficient or the explanations are oversimplified. Another popular hypothesis is that there was a disruptive invasion of Maya territory by peoples from the highlands. Certainly evidence reports Toltec instrusions into the lowlands, although it is hard to say how broad the effects of the invasions were or what damage they did to the fabric of Maya society.

Invasion and the limited evidence for population stress and ecological stress do not by themselves provide an explanation for the Classic Maya collapse. Most people now agree that invasion, ecological stress, and social disruption had something to do with the collapse, but how do we interpret the evidence, and how widely can we extrapolate over Maya country the parts of the archaeological picture?

A multifactor approach now is universally accepted as the only valid avenue of inquiry. Important studies of the problem have been published in book form (Culbert, 1973). The interested reader is urged to consult this volume, for only a summary of the multivariate model for the Maya collapse is possible here. In this model, the collapse of Teotihuacán placed the Maya in a position to enlarge their managerial functions in Mesoamerican trade. Competition between ceremonial centers was intensified as the elite became increasingly involved in warfare, trade and competition between regions, and prestige activities, many of them secular. This competition for prestige and wealth grew during the Late Classic period. The result was a frenzy of prestige-building projects and increased pressure on the labor force that resulted in lower agricultural productivity. Malnutrition and disease increased during the Late Classic Maya. Disease may have reached endemic or pandemic proportions under circumstances of warfare or crop failure. Population loss may have been so severe that recovery was impossible and productivity reduced to grossly inadequate levels. If the elite failed to make social or economic adjustments to the drastically changed situation, then collapse of the system was inevitable, for they recruited their numbers from a very small segment of the population.

The Maya were but a small part of the Mesoamerican scene. The highland peoples from central Mexico encroached on the Maya lowlands more and more during the Late Classic, but the effect of this still is uncertain. However, trade networks to the west must have gone through some disruption. This trade was critical to the prestige and survival of the Maya elite. Because of all these internal and external stresses and strains, the Maya society in the lowlands, at least 5 million souls, partly urbanized and living with much sociocultural integration, was no longer structurally viable. At some time between A.D. 771 and 790, these pressures came together and quickly collapsed the sociocultural system over much of the lowlands. The system could not recover from the shock.

The model has many gaps, of course, especially in not showing how the collapse affected the lowland population and why the Maya did not simply adopt several useful technological devices known to them that could have dramatically enhanced agricultural productivity, but we can be fairly sure that varied, interacting pressures helped overthrow the Maya civilization. To test all the hypotheses in this comprehensive model will require much new field data and many new excavations.

The collapse was by no means universal, for the Maya elite continued to flourish on a reduced scale in northern Yucatán (Sabloff and Friedel, 1984). We do not know how much of the population from the collapsed area moved north to this region.

THE TOLTECS

Although by A.D. 900 the Classic period had ended, Maya religious and social orders continued in northern Yucatán (Figure 21.13). The continuity of the ancient Mesoamerican tradition survived unscathed. Basic economic patterns and technological traditions were retained, although religious and ideological patterns and priorities were disarranged. New ceremonial centers were built, but war and violence became primary as militaristic rulers achieved dominance in Mesoamerica (Davies, 1973, 1977, 1980).

Postclassic
A.D. 900 to 1521

Toltec

Tula
A.D. 900

A.D. 1160

We have mentioned the unsettled Postclassic political conditions caused by population movements and tribal warfare. Many groups of invaders vied for political power in central Mexico until the Toltecs achieved dominance in the tenth century. The oral legends of the Aztec rulers, who followed the Toltecs, describe how the Toltecs came into Mesoamerica from the northwest frontiers beyond the civilized world. They settled at Tula, 37 mi (57 km) north of the Valley of Mexico, where they built a ceremonial center dedicated to their serpent god, Quetzalcóatl (Figure 21.14) (Davies, 1977; Diehl, 1984; Wolfe, 1959). Tula is notable for its animal sculpture and pottery styles, but it did not have a long life, for in approximately A.D. 1160 some newcomers with a less developed religious organization arrived from the north and destroyed the temples.

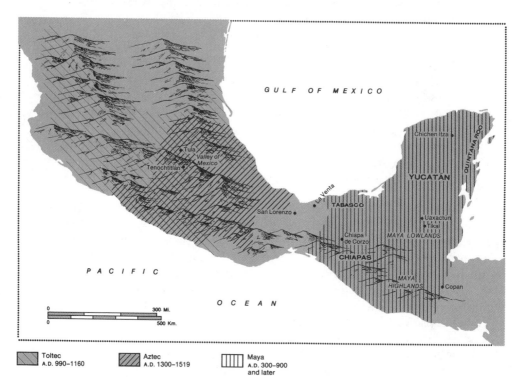

Figure 21.13 Distribution of Classic Maya, Toltec, and Aztec civilizations.

Figure 21.14 Tula: The summit of its pyramid bears statues of richly adorned warriors with elaborate breast plates. These once supported the roof of the temple of the feathered serpent god Quetzalcóatl that once stood there.

Chichén Itzá in northern Yucatán was an important Maya ceremonial center in Postclassic times. In the tenth century A.D., Chichén Itzá came under Toltec influence (Figure 21.15) (Roys, 1972; Weaver, 1981). It may have become a way by which the Toltec controlled the two great resources of the northern Yucatán: a talented, well-organized population, and the massive salt fields along the coast. The Toltecs introduced no new architectural elements to Chichén Itzá but still used Maya hieroglyphs. Chichén Itzá boasted a sacred pool or *cenote* into which numerous sacrificial offerings were thrown. The site was abandoned in the thirteenth century, but the city of Mayapán rose to prominence elsewhere in northern Yucatán, a walled settlement clustered around a ceremonial center. At least 12,000 people lived in this Maya city, which was ruled by the Cocom family. Maya civilization enjoyed a resurgence in this area, although Mayapán declined during the civil wars of the fifteenth century. A century later, the Spanish found Yucatán ruled by numerous petty chiefs.

The militaristic Toltecs were the leading military and political force in

Figure 21.15 Chichén Itzá, Temple of the Warriors.

Mesoamerica for such a short time that their influence evaporated rapidly when Tula was destroyed. Another period of political chaos in the Valley of Mexico ensued, as more barbarians from the north (Chichimecs) maneuvered for political power (Davies, 1980).

THE AZTECS AND THE SPANISH CONQUEST

When the first Spanish conquistadors arrived in highland Mexico in 1519, they were astounded by the rich civilization they found there. The capital city of Tenochtitlán was the headquarters of a series of militaristic Aztec kings, who ruled over a wide area by religious decree, constant human sacrifice, and bloodthirsty campaigning. Within a few years of Spanish contact, Aztec civilization literally ceased to exist. Tenochtitlán was reduced to rubble after a siege that lasted ninety-one days.

The Aztecs were one of several nomadic, Chichimeca, semicivilized groups who settled in the Valley of Mexico after the fall of Tula (Davies, 1973). They arrived during the early twelfth century, a politically weak but aggressive group, who barely retained their own identity. After years of military harassment, the Aztecs fled into the swamps of Lake Texcoco in about 1325. There they founded a small hamlet named Tenochtitlán. Less than two centuries later, this tiny village had become the largest city in pre-Columbian America (Conrad and Demarest, 1984).

At first the Aztecs lived peaceably with their neighbors, and Tenochtit-lán quietly flourished as an important market center. But by judicious diplomacy, discreet military alliance, and well-timed royal marriages, the Aztecs quietly advanced their cause until they were a force to be reckoned with in local politics. Then, in the early fifteenth century, they changed their foreign policy abruptly and embarked on a ruthless cam-paign of long-term military and economic conquest. Soon they con-trolled a loosely connected network of minor states and cities that extended right across Mesoamerica. The real leader behind this change was a counselor and general named Tlacaelel, who was adviser to a series of aggressive Aztec rulers. It was he who encouraged the use of terror and human sacrifice as a means of controlling conquered terri-tory. The rich tribute from conquered states and cities made Tenochtit-lán the center of the Mesoamerican world, the hub of a political and economic confederacy that extended from the Pacific Ocean to the Gulf of Mexico, and from northern Mexico as far south as Guatemala.

Tenochtitlán was a spectacular sight in the sixteenth century, with enormous markets where more than 60,000 people are said to have as-sembled every day (Diaz, 1963; Morris, 1962). The market sold every form of foodstuff and provided every luxury and service. The principal streets of Tenochtitlán were of beaten earth, and there were at least forty pyramids adorned with fine decorated stonework (Moctezuma, 1984). Tenochtitlán certainly was larger, and probably cleaner, than many Eur-opean cities of the time (Figure 21.16).

Large residential areas surrounded the central precincts, while houses with chinampa gardens lay on the outskirts of the city. Six major canals ran through Tenochtitlán, and there were three causeways that con-nected the city with the mainland. At least 200,000 canoes provided con-venient transport for the people of the city, which was divided into sixty or seventy well-organized wards. Tenochtitlán was a magnificent city set in a green swath of country and a clear lake, with a superb backdrop of snow-capped volcanoes (Fagan, 1984a).

Aztec society was moving closer and closer to a rigid aristocratic class system at the time of Spanish contact. No commoner was allowed to enter a waiting room in the palace used by nobles. The king was revered as a semigod and had virtually despotic powers A highly stratified class system supported the king's power. The king was elected from a limited class group of *pipiltin*, or nobles. There were full-time professional mer-chants called *pochteca*, and also a class of warriors whose ranks were determined by the numbers of people they had killed in battle. Groups of lineages called *calpulli* (big house) were the most significant factor in most peoples' religious, social, and political life. Many of them coincided with wards in the city. The great mass of the people were free people or *macehualtin*, while serfs, landless peasants, and slaves made up the bot-tom strata of society.

Much of Aztec society's efforts went toward placating the formidable war and rain gods, Huitzilopochtli and Tlaloc, deities whose benevolence

Figure 21.16 A general view of the excavations and restoration at the Aztec Temple of Huizilopochtli and Tlaloc, the Temple Major, Mexico City.

was assured by constant human sacrifices. These sacrifices reached their peak at the end of each fifty-two-year cycle, like those of the Maya, when the continuity of the world would be secured by bloodthirsty rites.

By the time of the Spanish Conquest in 1519, Aztec society seems to have been functioning in a world of frenetic and bloody terrorism that flourished at the behest of arrogant, imperial rulers. The Aztecs had learned the fine art of terror as a political instrument and regularly staged elaborate public displays in Tenochtitlán to which subject leaders were invited. The Spaniards estimated that at least 20,000 people were sacrificed to the gods throughout the Aztec empire each year. This figure may be an exaggeration, but there is no doubt that a considerable number of prisoners of war and slaves perished by having their hearts ripped out in the presence of the gods. There was also a steady flow of sacrificial victims from the Aztecs' constant military campaigns. Indeed, the finest death for an Aztec warrior was to perish under the sacrificial knife after honorable capture in battle. Such a fate was known as the "flowery death."

The Aztecs have acquired a formidable reputation from historians — and, it must be confessed, from some archaeologists — because of their penchant for human sacrifice and cannibalism. That they were addicted to human sacrifice is certain, the cannibalism less so. There are some who believe that the Aztec nobles ate human flesh to compensate for a lack of meat in their diet, but the beans they ate as a staple were more than sufficient as a source of protein. It seems more likely that the Aztec nobles and priests engaged in occasional ritual cannibalism as part of their intensely symbolic religious beliefs (for a discussion, see Fagan, 1984a).

By the time the Spaniards landed on the Mexican lowlands, Aztec civilization was in danger of being torn apart by divisive forces. Their society was becoming top heavy with nobles, because they were allowed to marry commoners and their children automatically became aristocrats. The demands for tribute both from subject states and from the free people of the city became ever larger and more exacting. There may well have been intense philosophical disagreements between the militant priests and warriors, who increasingly encouraged conquest and human sacrifice, and those more sophisticated and educated Aztecs, who believed in a gentler, less aggressive world. It is fascinating to speculate what would have happened had Cortés not landed in Mexico. Given the past history of Mexico, it seems likely that Aztec civilization would have collapsed suddenly, to be replaced in due time by another society much like it. In truth, Aztec civilization had reached a point of complexity that was beyond the capacity of its rulers to control and administer, a complexity that Old World civilizations had brought under control, and we can be certain that the Aztecs' successors would have eventually done so as well.

The Aztec were one of the most important groups in Mesoamerica when the Spaniards first explored the New World. From coastal villagers in the lowlands they heard stories of the fabled rich kingdoms in the high interior. Soon the conquistadores pressed inland to check on these stories of gold and other marvelous riches. Hernando Cortés was the first Spaniard to come into contact with the Aztec, now ruled by Moctezuma II, a despotic ruler who assassinated most of his predecessor's counselors and had himself deified. Moctezuma's reign was disturbed by constant unfavorable omens of impending doom and predictions that the god Quetzalcóatl would return one day to reclaim his homeland (Anderson and Dibble, 1978). The king was deeply alarmed by the reports of Spanish ships on the coast. There were, then, considerable internal psychological stresses on Moctezuma and his followers before the Spaniards even arrived.

It took Cortés only two years to reduce the Aztec to slaves and their marvelous capital to rubble. A handful of explorers on imported horses, armed with a few muskets, were able to overthrow one of the most powerful tribute states in the history of America. Without question, Cortés's task was made easier by both rebellious subjects of the Aztec and the extraordinary stresses the Aztec had placed on themselves.

In the next 160 years (by 1680), the Indian population of the Aztec heartland was reduced from approximately 1.2 million to some 70,000

— a decimation resulting from war, slavery, disease, overwork and exploitation, famine, and malnutrition. Mesoamerica as a whole lost between 85 and 95 percent of its indigenous population during that 160-year period. Only a few fragments of the fabulous Mesoamerican cultural tradition survived into modern times, as the Indian population faced a new and uncertain chapter in their long history (Gibson, 1964).

GUIDE TO FURTHER READING

Adams, R. E. W. *Prehistoric Mesoamerica*. Boston: Little, Brown, 1977.
A college text that is readable and very thoroughly illustrated. Particularly good on environmental background. Covers all aspects of Mesoamerican prehistory.

Coe, Michael D. *The Maya* (3rd ed.). London: Thames and Hudson, 1984.
This is regarded by many as the definitive account of the Maya civilization, with an emphasis on art styles, chronology, and culture history.

Davies, Nigel. *The Aztecs*. Norman: University of Oklahoma Press, 1973.
A skillfully assembled narrative of the rise of the Aztec, largely compiled from oral histories and codices as well as archaeological evidence. Complicated but authoritative.

Fagan, Brian M. *The Aztecs*. New York: W. H. Freeman, 1984a.
A straightforward description of the Aztecs written for the general public. Strong on description and narrative, little theoretical argument.

Hammond, Norman. *Ancient Maya Civilization*. New Brunswick: Rutgers University Press, 1982.
Authoritative synthesis of the Maya civilization by an expert on the lowlands and on Maya ecology. A good starting point, with an excellent theoretical underpinning.

Weaver, Muriel Porter. *The Aztecs, Maya, and Their Predecessors* (2nd ed.) New York: Academic Press, 1981.
Weaver's culture history has been a standard reference for a decade and the second edition is even more thorough than the first. Strongly recommended for detailed reading. Comprehensive illustrations of sites and artifacts.

Chronological Table M

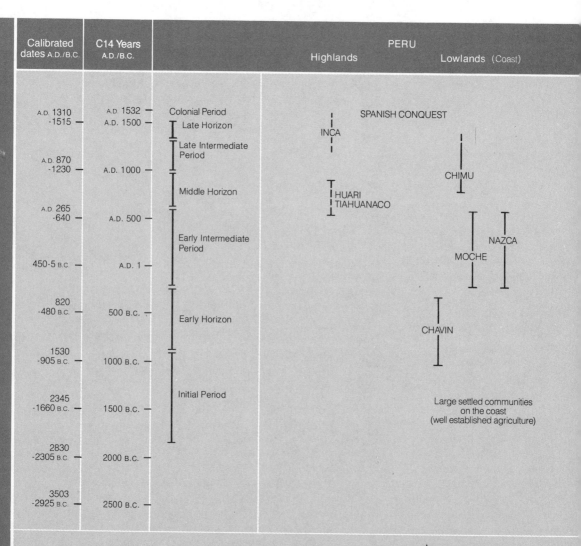

Calibrated dates A.D./B.C.	C14 Years A.D./B.C.		PERU	
			Highlands	Lowlands (Coast)
A.D. 1310 -1515	A.D. 1532 A.D. 1500	Colonial Period / Late Horizon	SPANISH CONQUEST / INCA	
		Late Intermediate Period		CHIMU
A.D. 870 -1230	A.D. 1000	Middle Horizon	HUARI TIAHUANACO	
A.D. 265 -640	A.D. 500	Early Intermediate Period		MOCHE NAZCA
450-5 B.C.	A.D. 1			
820 -480 B.C.	500 B.C.	Early Horizon		
1530 -905 B.C.	1000 B.C.			CHAVIN
2345 -1660 B.C.	1500 B.C.	Initial Period		Large settled communities on the coast (well established agriculture)
2830 -2305 B.C.	2000 B.C.			
3503 -2925 B.C.	2500 B.C.			

Chapter Twenty-Two

Early Civilization in Peru

PREVIEW

�֍ The earliest complex societies of coastal Peru developed as a result of a combination of socioeconomic and socioenvironmental, as well as behavioral, factors. They were based on maize irrigation agriculture. Approximately 2500 B.C. cotton was introduced to the coast, at a time when the first larger sites with public works begin to appear in the archaeological record.

✷ During the so-called Initial Period of Peruvian prehistory, the coastal peoples began to move inland and to practice irrigation in river valleys, but fishing remained important on the coast. The level of material culture throughout Peru continued to be almost startlingly simple, despite the fact that large settled communities enjoyed political autonomy and erected large complexes of public buildings.

✷ New cultural developments came to the coast as the Chavín art style and the religious beliefs associated with it spread widely over Peru between 900 and 200 B.C. Settlements such as Chavín de Huántar became important ceremonial centers, unifying many villages with a common religious belief. Chavín provided a vital basis for the spectacular cultural developments of later centuries.

✷ After the Chavín style disappeared, a series of coastal kingdoms developed, the political and economic influence of which spread beyond their immediate valley homelands. These empires included the Moche, Lima, and Nazca, which were remarkable for their fine pottery styles and expert copper and gold metallurgy. They flourished in the first millennium A.D.

✷ The Middle Horizon lasted from A.D. 600 to 1000 and saw the rise of numerous small states that traded with one another and depended heavily on irrigation agriculture. We describe the highland kingdoms of Huari and Tiahuanaco, in which an acceleration of the process of broader unification took place.

✷ Approximately A.D. 1000, Chimu, with its great capital at Chan Chan on the northern coast, dominated a wide area of the lowlands. Its compounds reflect a stratified state, with many expert craftspeople and a complex material culture.

✷ During the Late Horizon of Peruvian prehistory, there was unification of highlands and lowlands under the Inca empire, which may have emerged as early as A.D. 1200 and lasted until the Spanish conquest in A.D. 1534. The Inca rulers were masters of bureaucracy and military organization and governed a highly structured state — one, however, that was so weakened by civil war that it fell easily to the conquistador Francisco Pizarro and his small army of adventurers.

Chronological Table M The coastal foundations of Peruvian civilization began to develop after 2500 B.C., when the peoples of the coast adopted more sedentary settlement patterns. They took up maize agriculture and developed simple irrigation works, and soon population densities rose rapidly. At first these developments were confined to single valleys, but eventually ambitious, warlike rulers established their hegemony over much wider areas into the first millennium A.D., linking neighboring valleys in large empires. Unfortunately, we still know very little about the early stages of these important developments.

THE RISE OF COMPLEX SOCIETIES ON THE PERUVIAN COAST

The mechanisms by which complex states arose on the coast or in the highlands are little understood, partly because most field research has been selective and concentrated on larger, more spectacular sites (Moseley, 1975a, 1978; Wilson, 1983). Such researches tell us little about the relative size of different communities within a landscape or about population densities, which are critical measures of an evolving state society. A few large-scale valley surveys, like Willey's classic work on the Viru (1953) and Donald Proulx's researches in the Nepeña Valley (1968,1973), have shown that there were changes in site clusterings after 1000 B.C., but many details remain obscure. David Wilson has recently completed a survey in the Santa Valley, between the Nepeña and Viru (1983). This research was designed to test Robert Carneiro's theory of state formation based on the Peruvian coast, the notion that population density, land shortage, and warfare within areas of limited irrigable land led to the emergence of powerful chieftains and complex states (see Chapter Fourteen and Carneiro, 1972). Wilson's survey showed that the Santa Valley was sparsely occupied about 2000 B.C. by scattered fisherfolk, who may have engaged in some horticulture and hunting and gathering. But once irrigation agriculture took hold up-valley about 1000 B.C., population densities exploded, perhaps as much as 600 percent during the next millennium. The upper and middle valley areas were of steeper gradient, which allowed canal construction for the least possible labor expenditure, so it is logical to find the densest population concentrated there. The population continued to rise until the Santa Valley became part of the Moche empire in the first millennium A.D., when it plummeted for reasons that are still not understood. Conceivably, the Moche rulers forced the people to relocate elsewhere, or maybe heavy tribute assessments had an effect on population density.

As the population rose, so did the diversity of different site types. The first inhabitants lived in small hamlets, while the earliest irrigation farmers started living in small villages, with occasional larger settlements interspersed. It seems clear, too, that there was considerable cooperation among different communities, probably both in trading and irrigation agriculture. By the time the Moche people impinged on the Santa Valley in the fifth century A.D., there was at least one regional center with a population of more than 3500 people, and a network of local centers and large villages superimposed on nearly seventy villages and hamlets in the sample survey area alone. The big change seems to have come in the first few centuries A.D., by which time the total valley population may have risen from about 6000 to 8000 people up to 20,000 or more. By this time, too, farmers were settling not only in the upper and middle valley but in the gentler lower reaches as well. In earlier times, village settlements had been more dispersed. Now they were an almost continuous distribution, perhaps as a result of an increase in general public works like long canals, which enabled communities to cooperate more closely than ever before. Wilson believes that there were already chiefdoms in the valley in the second millennium B.C., with much more developed forms of such societies in the centuries before the Moche intervention.

Wilson believes that Carneiro's theory is not supported by the Santa Valley survey, partly because the site distributions show close clustering from the earliest stages of irrigation agriculture, and not the sort of dispersed layout that would foster competition and welfare as people competed for land. He also used maize yield statistics and settlement data to conclude that there was never enough population pressure on agricultural needs to trigger the kind of coercive warfare the Carneiro hypothesis would require. Rather, he argues that the Santa Valley people were locked into a new, irrigation-based form of subsistence after 1000 B.C., one quite different from that of their preceramic predecessors. The valley, unlike its neighbors, had water all year-round, a circumstance that made it a potential target for raiders from outside. That such raids did take place seems certain; there are fortress sites throughout the lower, more exposed areas of the valley. The people may have had to organize many communities to cooperate in their defense, as well as adapt to such times of stress by storing large food surpluses (Figure 22.1). Apart from defense and storage needs, it would be necessary to coordinate the ownership of the valuable agricultural land in the valley, since more people than the local acreage could support lived in the upper valley, with more fields available downstream.

Wilson also believes that a vital socioeconomic stress was the reason for defense against intruders. The Santa Valley may have been a virtual "garrison valley," with the constant external threat becoming a powerful catalyst toward close cooperation and sociocultural complexity. The only time when Carneiro's model might apply is late in the valley's history, when the Moche people created a multivalley state. At this point, the

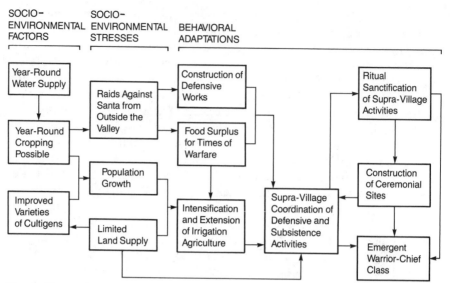

SOCIO-ENVIRONMENTAL FACTORS | SOCIO-ENVIRONMENTAL STRESSES | BEHAVIORAL ADAPTATIONS

Year-Round Water Supply

Year-Round Cropping Possible

Improved Varieties of Cultigens

Raids Against Santa from Outside the Valley

Population Growth

Limited Land Supply

Construction of Defensive Works

Food Surplus for Times of Warfare

Intensification and Extension of Irrigation Agriculture

Supra-Village Coordination of Defensive and Subsistence Activities

Ritual Sanctification of Supra-Village Activities

Construction of Ceremonial Sites

Emergent Warrior-Chief Class

Figure 22.1 Multivariate model of the emergence of prestate societies, Santa Valley, Peru. (After Wilson, 1983)

forces of state formation were much more straightforward than the complex, multivariate developments of earlier times.

With the Wilson hypothesis in mind, let us examine the archaeological evidence from the coast.

COASTAL FOUNDATIONS

The Initial Period: 1900 to 900 B.C.

Sometime between 2500 and 1800 B.C., maize agriculture came to the Peruvian coast and many villages moved inland. By this time the fishing villages were much larger communities with highly organized social structures, as is reflected in the first signs of communal structures, such as a 24 m (80 ft) high temple mound at Salinas de Chao. The people may have cooperated in fishing and food gathering, but the cooperative effort involved in erecting large earthen platforms for temples or other public buildings satisfies entirely different needs and requires explanation. Some of the sites were large platform mounds, flanked by two smaller lateral mounds forming a U-shaped complex. Within this large enclosed courtyard a sunken courtyard is sometimes found. Many of these complexes were oriented toward the northeast (Williams 1978–80). Most of the larger constructions were temple mounds built in multiple stages with shrines on their summits. The most ambitious works of all were erected by the people of El Paraiso, close to the mouth of the Chillon river near Lima (Bankes, 1980; Engel, 1979). They joined forces to erect seven huge square buildings constructed of roughly shaped stone

El Paraiso c. 1500 B.C.

blocks that were cemented with unfired clay. They painted the polished clay-faced outer walls in brilliant hues. Each complex consisted of a square building surrounded by tiers of platforms reached by stone and clay staircases. The largest is more than 250 m (830 ft) long and 50 m (166 ft) wide, standing more than 10 m (30 ft) above the plain. The rooms apparently were covered with matting roofs supported by willow posts. Perhaps as much as 100,000 tons of rock excavated from the nearby hills were needed to build the El Paraiso buildings. There are few signs of occupation around them, though, as if they were shrines and public precincts rather than residential quarters.

What is most surprising is that these huge structures were erected by people from dozens of scattered villages. For reasons not yet understood, they united in a vast communal building project that channeled most of their surplus energies into a very big monumental center, into a place where few people lived but where everyone apparently congregated for major public ceremonies. The people themselves lived a life of seeming simplicity. They owned but the simplest of stone and wooden artifacts and wore cotton clothing decorated with basic geometric patterns and stylized animallike motifs. They buried their dead in several layers of garments, nets, or looped sacks. Why should such an unsophisticated society build such enormous structures, and who were the leaders who organized these massive public works? Some clues are found at an imposing mound of boulders and adobe lying approximately 8 mi inland from El Paraiso, at a site known as Huaca Florida. Built somewhat later, in approximately 1700 B.C., and on an even larger scale, the great platform is more than 252 m (840 ft) long, 54 m (180 ft) wide, and towers 30 m (100 ft) above the valley. A rectangular court lies close to the north side of the platform, but here the landscape is revealing, for Huaca Florida lies in the midst of an artificial environment created by large-scale irrigation agriculture. The focus of human settlement had now moved inland, and the subsistence base changed from fishing to large-scale irrigation agriculture.

Huaca Florida

This was by no means the earliest irrigation in Peru, for even the earliest farmers probably made some limited use of canals to water their riverside gardens. However, the new works were on a far larger scale, spurred along by the availability of large numbers of people to labor in the valleys, an army of workers fed by abundant Pacific fish, and by the presence of gentle, cultivable slopes inland, and the expertise of the local people in farming cotton, gourds, and many lesser crops such as squashes and beans. Huaca Florida's leaders organized the reclamation of the desert by building canals along the steeper areas of the coastal valleys, in places where the gradients made the diversion of river water an easy task. This earliest of irrigation works may seem straightforward, but considerable organization was required to coordinate and develop it, and many people were needed to supervise the digging, to mediate land ownership disputes, and to maintain canals.

At first, each family may have worked together to irrigate its own sloping gardens, but gradually each community grew so much that essential irrigation works could be handled only by cooperative effort. Organized irrigation perhaps began as many minor cooperative works between individual families and neighboring villages. These simple projects eventually evolved into elaborate public works that embraced entire inland valleys, controlled by a corporate authority who held a monopoly over both the water and the land it irrigated. The process of organization, which may have taken centuries, was the result of many complex interacting factors, among them population growth and the emergence of increasing numbers of nonfarming society members such as priests and artisans whose food needs had to be met by other people. By the time El Paraiso and Huaca Florida were built, it is possible that public works such as irrigation canals and temples were constructed using a form of taxation by labor. Perhaps the rulers devised a forerunner of the *mita* tax employed 2000 years later by the Inca, by which people worked a certain number of days per year for the state, either as construction laborers or farmers tilling the soil. When one worked for the state, pay was given in food and shelter, sometimes in the form of a share of the yield from the land allocated to one's kin group.

The shift to agriculture triggered many material changes, among them the development of pottery to store foods and to cook the cereal grains that now formed a much more significant part of the diet. The distribution of the principal corporate centers, though, remained very restricted, along approximately 400 mi of coast between El Paraiso northward to Lambayeque. This was one cradle of Peruvian civilization; the other lay inland, further to the south, in the highland valleys north of Cuzco to as far south as Lake Titicaca (Figure 22.2). Finally, in the fifteenth century A.D., these two centers competed on an imperial scale to produce the unified Inca homeland, Tawantinsuyu, the Land of the Four Quarters.

The Initial Period saw the emergence of distinctive religious and architectural traditions of highlands and coast. From about 2000 to 200 B.C., the small ceremonial center at Huaricoto in the highlands, only 34 mi (55 km) from the famous temple of Chavín de Huántar, described below, was the home of a religious ideology that lasted for more than 1800 years (Burger and Burger, 1980). This "Kotosh Religious Tradition" is known to us with sacrificial hearths in which ceremonial offerings were burnt. These included animal bones and grain. The ritual hearth was sunk into the floor with a ventilator leading to the outside. Once the sacrifice was complete, the hearth was filled in. At first the rituals were performed in the open, but by late Initial Period times the hearths were surrounded by larger superstructures. The rituals may have been performed sporadically at certain times of the year, with the audience watching in the open. The Kotosh Religious Tradition appears to have flourished over an area of at least 155 mi (250 km) north to south in the highlands, in the region where the Chavín cult with its wild and extravagant animal motifs was to

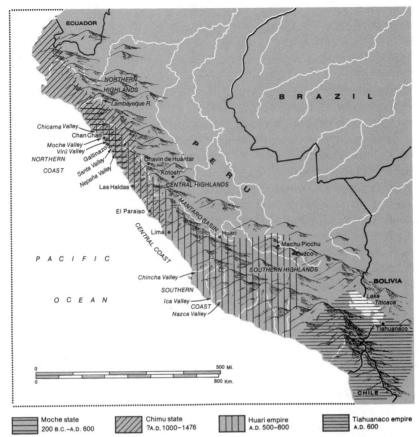

Figure 22.2 Peruvian archaeological sites mentioned in this chapter. Approximate distributions of various traditions are also shown.

Legend:

Moche state 200 B.C.–A.D. 600	Chimu state ?A.D. 1000–1476	Huari empire A.D. 500–800
Tiahuanaco empire A.D. 600		

gain strength after 900 B.C. (see "Early Horizon" below). Still the rituals persisted, and some Chavín ideological innovations were adopted.

THE EARLY HORIZON: CHAVÍN

Most cultural development on the coast came from small societies that achieved more social and political unity over wider areas. Not until approximately 900 B.C. did a semblance of greater cultural unity begin to appear in Peru. At about that time a distinctive art style in stone, ceramics, and precious metals appeared in northern Peru. This Chavín style was recognized by Julio Tello (1943) and later used to define the Early Horizon in Peruvian prehistory. For many years, Peruvianists used the distinctive Chavín sculpture as a way of tracing the rise of complex societies at near and distant sites on the coast and in the highlands, as if

Early Horizon

Chavín **900 to 200 B.C.**

the cult associated with the art was a catalyst of Peruvian civilization. But this perspective is being replaced with a more local interpretation of the art style (for one viewpoint, see Pozorski, 1983).

The Chavín style takes its name from the famous temple of Chavín de Huántar in central Peru. The temple area is terraced, with an impressive truncated pyramid on the uppermost level. The 10 m (32 ft) high pyramid appears solid, but is in fact hollow, a honeycomb of stone passages and rooms. The galleries are ventilated by special rectangular tubes. The temple housed a remarkable carving of a jaguarlike human with hair in the form of serpents (Figure 22.3) (Burger, 1984; Rowe, 1962). Chavín art, like this carving, is dominated by animal and human forms: jaguar motifs predominate; humans, gods, and animals are given jaguar-like fangs or limbs; snakes flow from the bodies of many figures. The art has a grace that is grotesque and slightly sinister. Many figures were carved in stone, others in clay or bone.

With its tangled animal and human motifs, Chavín art has all the flamboyance and exotic touches of tropical forest. The animals depicted — cayman, jaguar, and snakes — are all forest animals. The art may have originated in the tropical forests to the east of the Andes, but the Early Horizon Chavín temple, U-shaped with a sunken plaza in the center, is of an architectural design associated with the coast. Conceivably the Chavín culture is a coalescence of traits and ideas coming from both the coast and the forest that form a new cultural manifestation in the highlands.

But Chavín de Huántar is far more than just a temple. Richard Burger has recently excavated areas outside the well-known ceremonial precincts and established that the site was occupied between about 850 and 200 B.C. At first the population was small, perhaps little more than 100 people. But it seems to have expanded considerably by the fourth century B.C., at which point as many as 2000 to 3000 people may have been living near the temple precincts. Chavín de Huántar was certainly a large center, probably an influential place within its local area, and one of the largest places in Peru at the time of its occupation. It failed to expand into a fully developed urban center, however, and the nascent civilization that worshipped there collapsed, leaving nothing more than a small town and a persistent art style and iconography in its train.

The Chavín art style may have influenced artistic traditions over a wide area of Peru, and it may also be that the religious beliefs behind the motifs was more important than the art itself. Settlements like Chavín de Huántar were important ceremonial centers that unified surrounding farming villages with a common religious belief, but Chavín de Huántar was not unique. There were probably many other such local centers in the first millennium B.C. So far, almost nothing is known about them, which is one reason why Chavín has assumed such importance in Peruvian archaeology.

The Early Horizon is still a little-known period in prehistory, so the picture given here is necessarily incomplete.

Figure 22.3 A Chavín wall insert (approximately 20 cm high) showing feline features, from Chavín de Huántar and a Chavín carving on a pillar in the temple interior at Chavín de Huántar. Stone insets such as these are common on the walls of the Chavín ceremonial buildings.

THE EARLY INTERMEDIATE PERIOD: 200 B.C. to A.D. 600

By 200 B.C., irrigation agriculture had developed on a very large scale on the coast, so much so that some settlements, such as Cerro Arena in the Moche Valley, covered more than a square mile. Excavations during the 1970s revealed more than 2000 separate structures, some with as many as twenty rooms (Bankes, 1977). A small group of twenty-five finely finished houses may have formed the administrative and residential quarters of Cerro Arena. There were considerable variations between the humbler dwellings that surrounded them, as if Cerro Arena society was more complex than that of earlier settlements. This and other large settlements were supported by irrigation systems that required not only organized labor to construct and maintain, but strict water-control restrictions as well. Most of the cultivated land lay along the terraced edges of the valleys where the soils were better drained and easily planted with simple wooden digging sticks, just as they are to this day. Even today the local people divert the seasonal river water into side canals by building a dam of stakes and boulders into the stream. There is no reason to suppose that the same simple but effective technique was not used in antiquity. The ancient irrigation canals wound along the sides of the valleys, series of narrow channels approximately 1.2 m (4 ft) wide, set in loops and S-shaped curves, watering plots approximately 21.3 m (70 ft) square. The surplus flowed off into the Pacific.

Moche

Moche
200 B.C. to A.D. 600

By 200 B.C., the Moche state had begun in northern coastal Peru. It continued to flourish for 800 years. Its origins lay in the Chicama and Moche Valleys, with great ceremonial centers and huge irrigation works (Donnan and McClelland, 1979). Information about the Moche Indians of 2000 years ago comes not only from irrigation systems and spectacular monuments but also from hundreds of finely modeled clay pots and human burials preserved in the dry desert sand of their cemeteries. Unfortunately, their burials are a prime target of commercial grave robbers. Many Moche cemeteries look like pockmarked battlefields after heavy bombardment, for their pots fetch astronomical prices on the international art market. What little we know about Moche society comes from undisturbed burials. They show that Moche society consisted of farmers and fisherfolk, as well as skilled artisans and priests, who are depicted on pots with felinelike fangs set in their mouths and wearing puma-skin headdresses. A few expert craft potters created superb modeled vessels with striking portraits of arrogant handsome men who can only have been the leaders of Moche society (Figure 22.4). The potters modeled warriors, too, soldiers complete with shields and war clubs, with well-

Figure 22.4 Moche portrait vessel approximately 29 cm (11.4 in) high.

padded helmets and colorful cotton uniforms. Moche burials show that some members of society were much richer than others, lying in graves filled with as many as fifty vessels or with weapons or staffs of rank. We do not know exactly how Moche society was organized, but we can assume that the ruler wielded authority over a hierarchical state of warriors, priest-doctors, artisans, and the mass of the agricultural population.

Fortunately, the Moche artists and artisans gave us some more intimate glances at their society than do many civilizations (Figure 22.5). Their paintings show the ruler with fine feather headdress seated on a pyramid, while a line of naked prisoners parades before him. A decapitated sacrifice at the base of the painting reminds us that human sacrifice may have been the fate of some prisoners of war. We see Moche soldiers in battle, charging their opponents with raised clubs. The defenders raise their feather-decked shields in defiance as the battle is fought to the death. The potters modeled maize-beer befuddled drunks being supported by their solicitous friends, women giving birth with the obstetrician in attendance, and wives carrying babies on their backs in shawls

Figure 22.5 Moche vessel depicting an owl-woman healer.

and in wooden cradles suspended by nets. The women carried out all domestic activities, while the men served as warriors, farmers, and fishermen. We see them on a seal hunt, clubbing young seals on the rocky coast as their prey scurries in every direction. A clay llama strains reluctantly under its load, and a mouse eats a maize cob.

The pots depict very vividly what the Moche people wore. The men worked in short loincloths or cotton breeches and a short sleeveless shirt underneath a tunic that ended above the knee, fastened around the waist with a colorful woven belt. More important people wore large mantles and headdresses made from puma heads or feathers from highland jungles. Nearly everyone donned some form of headgear: brightly decorated cotton turbans wound around small caps and held in place with a fabric chin strap were in common use. A small cloth protected the back of the neck from the burning sun. Moche women dressed in loose tunics that reached the knee, and went bareheaded or draped a piece of cloth around the head. Many men painted their lower legs and feet in bright colors and tatooed or daubed their faces with lines and other motifs. They often wore disk or crescent nose ornaments and cylindrical bar earrings sometimes modeled in gold. Their necks bore large collars of stone beads or precious metal, while bracelets covered arms and legs (Figure 22.6). Many people wore fiber sandals to protect their feet against the hot sand.

By this time the coastal people were expert metalworkers (Benson, 1979). They had discovered the properties of gold ore and extracted it by panning in streambeds rather than by mining. Soon they had developed ways of hammering it into fine sheets and had learned how to emboss it to make raised designs. They also had worked out the technique of annealing, making it possible to soften the metal and then hammer it into more elaborate forms, and they joined sheets together with fine solder. However, they did not start to work copper until some centuries after Christ. The smiths used gold as a setting for turquoise and shell ornaments, crafted crowns, circlets, necklaces, pins, and tweezers. Gold was in such short supply in prehistoric times that the metalworkers became expert at depletion gilding, an annealing technique which oxidizes the metal in an alloy of copper and gold to give the finished product a gold-like appearance even when the gold content is as low as 12 percent by weight. Many of the large gold objects such as animals and plate decorations seized from the Inca by Pizarro's soldiers were, in fact, manufactured of an elaborate alloy of some gold, silver, and copper.

Few early societies can rival the textile artistry of the coastal Peruvians. They lived in an environment in which both animal and plant (especially cotton) fibers were plentiful, and had the leisure time to create fine and complex fabrics adorned with colorful intricate patterns (Figure 22.7). The textiles survive remarkably well in the dry coastal environment, in huge cemeteries where the dead were wrapped in fabric burial shrouds. The most spectacular textile finds come from huge cemeteries of mummified Indians on the sandy desolate Paracas peninsula

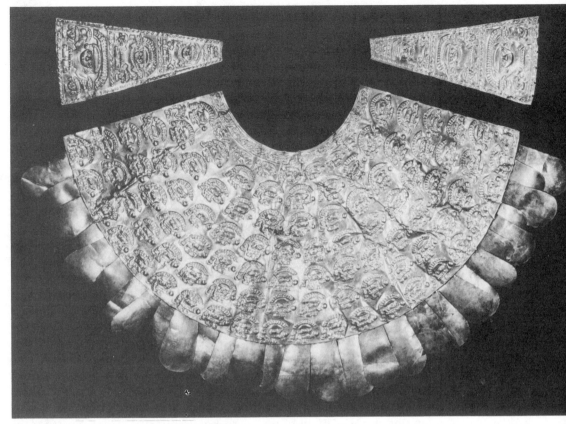

Figure 22.6 Moche hammered gold breast plate.

south of the modern town of Pisco. The (Early Horizon) Paracas people lie in bottle-shaped chambers or stone-lined subterranean vaults with wooden roofs approximately 4.87 m (16 ft) high and 3.90 m (13 ft) across cut through sand into soft rock. The sepulchers were divided into small chambers where dozens of mummy bundles were placed. The Indians did not practice mummification in the formal Ancient Egyptian sense. They simply took advantage of the exceptionally dry climate. Each corpse was disemboweled and then allowed to dry out in the hot sand in a fetal position with the knees at the chin. Eventually, the bodies were wrapped in brightly colored cotton, wool, or both. Sometimes the dead wore decorated mantles, shirts, turbans, or loincloths tailored to the size of the mummy bundle rather than the living person. Occasionally, the mourners attached small gold ornaments to the mummies, or buried tools, food, or even pet monkeys or parrots with the deceased (Figure 22.8).

It is from these mummies that we learn the most minute details of Peruvian textiles, for the wrapping cloths often are almost perfectly preserved. The earliest textiles preserved on the coast date to approximately

Figure 22.7 A border motif from a Paracas mantle showing an anthropomorphic figure wearing a tunic and skirt similar to those found on Paracas mummy bundles.

4500 B.C., soon after cotton was first cultivated. The weavers were expert dyers and used more than 190 hues from plant dyes. The earliest dye in common use was blue, followed by red and then a multitude of bright colors. Decorative motifs included simple checkerboards, filled squares, and stylized depictions of birds, felines, and other animals. The oldest textiles had rather coarse and uneven yarns produced by twisting untreated yarn. After 2000 B.C., however, the weavers began to use delicate wood and thorn spindles mounted in a special pottery, gourd, or wooden cup that minimized vibration. Thus they could produce much finer cloth. Most of the textiles found in coastal tombs were made on backstrap looms just like those still in use in Peru today. Two sticks carry the lengthwise threads, the upper one suspended from a post and the lower tied to a belt around the weaver's back. As the work proceeds, the fabric is unrolled from the upper bar and the finished cloth is rolled onto the lower stick. The yarn is wound with a figure-of-eight motion between the two stakes and is laced fast to the loom sticks so that the edges of the fabric are uniformly finished off. The disadvantage of this type of loom is that the width of the cloth is limited by the span of the weaver's arms. The Indians sometimes combined several backstrap looms together to create wider cloths.

The greatest efforts of the Moche people were devoted not to irrigation systems or elaborate burials, but to the erection of vast monumental platforms and temples on the southern edge of the cultivated land in the

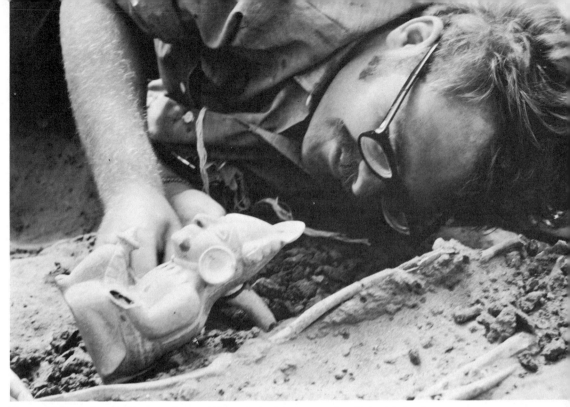

Figure 22.8 Archaeologist excavating an effigy pot of a kneeling warrior at a burial site at the Pyramid of the Sun and the Moon, Chan Chan, Peru.

Moche Valley, approximately 4 mi southeast of the modern town of Tru-jillo. They used tax labor to build a huge adobe temple platform rising 23 m (76 ft) above the plain at the foot of a conical hill named Cerro Blanco. The Spaniards called this complex *Huaca de la Luna,* the Temple of the Moon. *Huaca del Sol* (Temple of the Sun) stands close to the west, a con-fused mass of mud brick that once consisted of a ramp that gave access to five temple platforms, the highest, to the south, towering 41 m (135 ft) above the ground. The sides of the pyramid were steeply terraced and have been badly damaged by erosion and looters. Both platforms once supported courts, corridors, and room complexes, perhaps roofed with matting. Huaca del Sol may have been a palace, for there are deep rub-bish heaps on the summit of the platform. In contrast, Huaca de la Luna is spotlessly clean, its temple buildings painted with brightly colored murals.

The Moche state was a multivalley state that may have consisted of a series of satellite centers that ruled over individual valleys and yet owed allegiance to the great centers of the Moche Valley. At one time the Moche Valley presided over the coast as far south as the Nepeña Valley. Where possible, the Moche extended their ambitious irrigation systems to link several neighboring river valleys, and then constructed lesser copies of their capital as a basis for secure administration of their new domains.

Their traders were in contact with the north and with the Nasca people on the southern coast as well (Proulx, 1983a). The Moche blueprint was eventually followed by the Inca centuries later. Approximately A.D. 600, the Moche people moved their center of administrative activity north to Pampa Grande in the Lamayeque Valley. By this time the southern centers were abandoned, as the political and economic influence of the southern highlands and coast began to rise, while the Moche quietly slipped into relative obscurity.

THE MIDDLE HORIZON: A UNIFICATION PERIOD

A series of brilliant states had flourished on the coast and in the highlands during the Early Intermediate Period — Moche on the north coast, Nasca in the south, and Recuay in the northern highlands (the latter two are not described here owing to space restrictions). The same period also saw the beginnings of monumental building at a highland site that would influence much of the Peruvian world — Tiahuanaco (Proulx, 1983b).

The wealthiest highland districts lay at the southern end of the central Andes, in the high flat country surrounding Lake Titicaca. This was fine llama country. The local people maintained enormous herds of these beasts of burden and grew abundant supplies of maize and other crops. The *altiplano* supported the densest populations in the highlands, and almost inevitably, the Titicaca region became an economic and demographic pole to the prosperous northern coast. By A.D. 200 Tiahuanaco, on the eastern side of the lake, was becoming a major population center, as well as an important economic and religious focus for the region (Browman, 1978). The arid lands on which the site lies were irrigated and supported a population of perhaps 20,000 near the monumental structures near the center of Tiahuanaco. By A.D. 600 Tiahuanaco was acquiring much of its prosperity from trade around the lake's southern shores. Copperworking was especially important and probably developed independently of the well-established copper technology on the northern coast.

Tiahuanaco
**? A.D. 200 to c.
A.D. 1200**

Tiahuanaco was not only an economic force, it was a very important religious one as well. The great enclosure of Kalasasaya is dominated by a large earth platform faced with stones. Nearby, a rectangular enclosure is bounded with a row of upright stones and there is a doorway carved with an anthropomorphic god, believed to be the creator diety, Viracocha (Figure 22.9). Smaller buildings, enclosures, and huge statues are also near the ceremonial structures.

But it is the Tiahuanaco art style that is most striking. Like Chavín, this art tradition probably represents a powerful iconography. Tiahuanaco's art motifs include jaguars and eagles, as well as anthropomorphic gods being attended to by lesser deities or messengers. They occur over much of southern Peru, as well as in Bolivia, the southern Andes, and perhaps as far afield as northwestern Argentina. So powerful was the iconogra-

Figure 22.9 Gateway of the Sun at Tiahuanaco, made from one block of lava. The central figure is known as the Gateway god; notice its jaguar mouth and serpent-ray headdress. The running figures flanking the god often are called messengers.

phy, and, presumably, the political and economic forces behind Tiahuanaco that there was a serious political vacuum in the south after A.D. 1200, when Tiahuanaco inexplicably collapsed into obscurity.

The influence of Tiahuanaco can be seen at Huari in the Mantaro Valley, an important ceremonial center that stands on a hill (Isbell and Schreiber, 1978; Rowe, Collier, and Willey, 1950). It is associated with huge stone walls and many dwellings that cover several square miles. The Huari art styles show some Tiahuanaco influence, especially in anthropomorphic, feline, eagle, and serpent beings depicted both on ceramic vessels and stone carvings. Like their southern neighbors, the Huari people seemed to have revered a Viracocha-like being. By A.D. 800, their domains extended from former Moche country in the Lambayeque Valley on the northern coast into the southern Peruvian Andes. They were expert traders, who probably expanded their domain through religious conversion, warfare, and commercial enterprise. Storehouses and roads

Huari
? A.D. 600 to A.D. 900

probably were maintained by the state. As with the Inca of later centuries, the state controlled food supplies and labor.

Huari itself was abandoned in the ninth century A.D., but its art styles persisted for at least two more centuries. Both Huari and Tiahuanaco were a turning point in Peruvian prehistory, a stage when small, regional states became integrated into much larger political units. This unification may have been achieved by conquest and other coercive means, but the common iconography shared by many coastal and highland Peruvians at the time must have been a powerful catalyst for closer political unity.

These two great polities collapsed toward the end of the first millennium, which created a vast political vacuum of small, competing tribes that was eventually filled by the Inca.

THE LATE INTERMEDIATE PERIOD: LATE COASTAL STATES

Chimu

Chimu
? A.D. 1000 to 1476

The highland states traded regularly with at least four emerging polities on the coast, each of them centered on extensive irrigation systems. Of these, the most famous is the Chimu kingdom, centered on the Moche Valley of the northern coast, the same area inhabited 400 years earlier by the Moche peoples. The Moche Valley had long been densely cultivated, but the Chimu people now embarked on much more ambitious irrigation schemes; they built large storage reservoirs and terraced hundreds of miles of hillside to control the flow of water down steep slopes. One channel extended nearly 20 mi from the Chicama Valley to the capital, Chan Chan, designed to supplement the relatively limited water supplies that came from the nearby Moche Valley (Figure 22.10). Even in periods of extreme drought these canals carried water from the deep-cut river bed to terraces long distances away. Thus, the Chimu created thousands of acres of new fields and used water from long distances away to harvest two or three crops a year from plots where only one crop had been possible before, and that at the time of the annual flood. So effective were these irrigation techniques that the Chimu controlled more than twelve river valleys with at least 125,000 cultivable acres, all of it farmed with hoes or digging sticks. Today, the local Indians water their maize crops approximately every ten days, and this probably was the practice in Chimu times as well (Bankes, 1977).

According to seventeenth-century Spanish chroniclers, the Chimu always maintained that their domains were originally ruled over by petty chiefs, but when the Inca conquered them between 1462 and 1470 they were led by a ruler named Michancaman, who governed through a network of hereditary local nobility. His courtiers held specific ranks, such as "Blower of the Shell Trumpet," "Master of the Litter and Thrones," and "Preparer of the Way," the official who scattered powdered shell dust wherever the ruler was about to walk. An archaeologist working at Chan

Figure 22.10 Chan Chan: oblique air photograph of a walled enclosure or compound.

Chan in 1969 to 1970 found a layer of powdered shell dust on a bench in a forecourt, perhaps evidence that the Preparer of the Way had been at work. The various provinces of the kingdom were ruled by loyal local leaders. They enjoyed not only tribute privileges, but also rights to crops and land and to agricultural labor from commoners. Perhaps the most privileged members of society were the *Oquetlupec*, herb curers paid by the state to look after the sick. This was a hierarchical, highly organized society with strict social classes of nobles and commoners, but one in which women's rights were nearly equal to those of the men. Perhaps to enforce the social hierarchy, the legal system was very strict.

The focus of the Chimu state was Chan Chan, a huge complex of walled compounds lying near the Pacific at the mouth of the Moche Valley. Chan Chan covers nearly 4 sq mi, the central part consisting of ten large enclosures laid out in a sort of broken rectangle. Each enclosure probably functioned as the palace for the current ruler of Chan Chan, who probably built himself a new headquarters near those of his predecessors (Lanning, 1967; Moseley, 1975b; Moseley and Mackey, 1973). The adobe walls of these compounds once stood as high as 9.9 m (33 ft) and covered areas as large as 201 m (670 ft) by 600 m (2000 ft). The walls were not constructed to defend the rulers but to provide privacy and some shelter against the ocean winds. Each enclosure had its own water supply, a burial platform, and lavishly decorated residential rooms roofed with cane frames covered with earth and grass. The same enclosure that served as a palace during life became the ruler's burial place in death. The common people lived in tracts of small adobe and reed-mat houses on the western side of the city. Similar dwellings can be seen on the coast to this day.

Oral traditions tell us that when a Chimu ruler died, his successor inherited the office of supreme leader, but the lands, revenues, and wealth of the deceased went to junior members of the family, who were responsible for venerating the memory of the dead man. Consequently, the new ruler had to build his own palace and raise new revenues to finance his reign. He had only one resource to achieve such goals: control of a huge labor pool. The Chimu rulers employed laborers to expand and maintain irrigation works, in addition to their serving as military levies to acquire new lands and expand the tax base. Rulers soon learned the value of efficient communications, of officially maintained roadways that enabled them to move their armies from one place to the next with rapid dispatch. They constructed roads that connected each valley in their domains with the capital. The rural routes were little more than tracks between low adobe walls or widely spaced posts, mostly following centuries-old paths through the fields. In the densely populated valleys, Chimu roads were between 4.5 and 7.5 m (15 and 25 ft) across. In some places the roadway widened dramatically to 24 m (80 ft) or more. These were the roads that carried gold ornaments and fine hammered vessels to Chan Chan and textiles and fine black painted vessels throughout the empire. The traveler occasionally would encounter heavily laden llamas carrying goods to market, but most loads were carried on people's backs, for the Chimu had never heard of the wheeled cart. All revenues and tribute passed along the official roadways, as did newly conquered peoples being resettled in some area far from their original homeland. This draconian resettlement tactic was so successful that the Inca adopted the same strategy. The ruler then would install his own appointee in the new lands, in a compound-palace that was a smaller version of Chan Chan itself.

The Chimu empire extended far south along the coast, for the main focus of civilization lay on the northern Peruvian littoral, where the soils were more fertile and large-scale irrigation was a practical reality. Chimu armies fought with powerful neighbors to the south, among them the chief of Pachacamac who controlled some narrow valleys south of the modern city of Lima founded by Pizarro. Pachacamac was to become a venerated shrine in Inca times but already boasted of a terraced temple covering an area of two-thirds of an acre. Pachacamac has been a grave robbers' paradise for centuries. Later, the Inca built a vast Temple of the Sun at Pachacamac, an irregular trapezoid erected in a commanding position on a rocky hill.

For all its wide-ranging military activities and material wealth, the Chimu empire was very vulnerable to attack from outside. The massive irrigation works of the northern river valleys were easily disrupted by an aggressive conqueror, for no leader, however powerful, could ever hope to fortify the entire frontiers of the empire. We know little of the defenses, except for Paramonga in the Fortaleza Valley, a massive terraced structure built of rectangular adobes that overlooks the probable southern limits of Chimu territory. The Chimu were vulnerable to prolonged drought, too, for the storage capacity of their great irrigation works was only sufficient to carry them over one or two lean seasons but not a long cycle of dry years. Perhaps, too, the irrigated desert soils may have become too saline for agriculture, so that crop yields fell drastically at a time when population densities were rising sharply. Since the Chimu depended on a highly specialized agricultural system, once that system was disrupted — whether by natural or artificial causes — military conquest and control of the irrigation network was easy, especially for aggressive and skillful conquerors such as the Inca who pounced on the Chimu in the 1460s.

THE LATE HORIZON: THE INCA STATE — A.D. 1200 to 1534

The Late Horizon of Peruvian archaeology is also the shortest, dating Late Horizon from A.D. 1476 to 1534. It is the period of the Inca empire, when those mighty Andean rulers held sway over an enormous area of highland and lowland country (Bankes, 1977; Rowe, 1946).

The Inca were born into an intensely competitive world, their homeland lying to the northwest of the Titicaca basin, in the area around Cuzco (for an extended description, see Conrad and Demarest, 1984). They were a small-scale farming society living in small villages, organized in kin groups known as *ayllu*, groups claiming a common ancestry and also owning land in common. The Inca were a self-sufficient people, and their *ayllu* leaders contributed labor to one another as a means of organizing and distributing labor on a reciprocal basis. The *ayllu* was legitimized in its land ownership and protected by the ancestors. It was small wonder that the Inca always took good care of their ancestral mummies. The bodies of the dead, their tombs, and their fetishes, as well as numerous other sacred places and phenomena, were known as *huaca*.

The later Inca rulers clothed their origins in a glorious panoply of heroic deeds. It is likely, however, that the Inca were a fractious, constantly quarreling petty chiefdom. The chronicles of early conquest reflect the constant bickering of village headmen, and the earliest Inca rulers were probably petty war leaders *(sinchi)*, elected officials whose success was measured by their victories and booty. But to stay in office, they had to be politically and militarily adept so that they could both defeat and appease their many potential rivals. The official Inca histories spoke of at least eight Inca rulers who ruled between 1200 and 1438, but these genealo- Inca
A.D. 1200 to 1533 gies are hardly reliable (Rowe, 1946). They are probably little more than legendary figures. During the fourteenth century, a number of small tribal groups in the southern highlands began to develop a more powerful military confederacy, but the Inca flourished in this competitive atmosphere because their leaders were expert politicians as well as warriors. An Inca leader named Viracocha Inca rose to power at the beginning of the fifteenth century. Unlike his raiding predecessors, however, he turned to permanent conquest and soon presided over a small kingdom centered around Cuzco. Viracocha Inca became the living god, the first in a series of constant religious changes that kept the new kingdom under tight control. At about the same time a new religious cult emerged, that of Inti, a celestial divine ancestor who was part of the sky god. (We say part because Inti was more of a cluster of solar aspects than the sun god).

Around 1438, a brilliant warrior named Cusi Inca Yupanqui was crowned Inca after a memorable victory over the neighboring Chanca tribe. He immediately took the name Pachakuti ("He Who Remakes the World") and set about transforming the Inca state. In particular, he and his henchmen developed a form of royal ancestor cult. This in itself was not especially significant, since Pachakuti simply reworked an age-old Andean tradition of ancestor worship, but the law of split inheritance that went along with it had a lasting and profound significance. A dead ruler was mummified. His palace, servants, and possessions were still considered his property and were maintained by all his male descendents *except* his successor, normally one of his sons. The deceased was not considered dead, however. His mummy attended great ceremonies and would even visit the houses of the living. Those entrusted to look after the king ate and talked with him, just as if his life were still going on. This element of continuity was extremely important, because it made the royal mummies some of the holiest artifacts in the empire. Dead rulers were living sons of Inti, visible links with the gods, the very embodiment of the Inca state and of the fertility of nature. Meanwhile the ascending ruler was rich in prestige but poor in possessions. The new king had to acquire wealth, both so he could live in royal splendor and to provide for his mummy in the future — and the only wealth in the highland kingdom was taxable labor.

Therefore, every adult in Inca country had to render a certain amount of labor to the state each year after providing for the basic subsistence needs of his own *ayllu*. This *mita* system repaired bridges and roads, cultivated state-owned lands, manned the armies, and carried out public works. It was a reciprocal system. The state, or those benefiting from the work, had to feed and entertain those doing it. But the split inheritance of the Inca rulers meant that all taxes levied by their predecessors went to them and not to the newcomer. He had to develop a new tax base and could do this in only two ways: by levying more labor from existing taxpayers or by conquering new lands. Since the Inca rulers needed land to provide food for those who worked for them and the earlier kings owned most of the land near Cuzco, the only way a new ruler could obtain his own royal estates was by expansion and still more expansion into new territory. This expansion could not take the form of temporary raids, however. The conquest had to be permanent, the conquered territory had to be controlled and taxed, and the ruler's subjects had to be convinced of the value of a policy of long-term conquest.

The Inca rulers turned into brilliant propagandists, reminding everyone that they were gods and that the welfare of everyone depended on the prosperity of all rulers, past and present, and on constant military conquest. There were initial economic advantages, too, in the form of better protection against famine. Also, the rulers were careful to award prowess in battle. Nobles were promoted to new posts and awarded insignia that brought their lifestyle ever closer to that of the king, and even a brave commoner could become a member of the secondary nobility. A highly complicated set of benefits, economic incentives, rewards, and justifications fueled and nourished the Inca conquests. Their successful ideology provided them with a crucial advantage over their neighbors, and within a decade of Pachakuti's accession they were masters of the southern highlands. Their army had become an invincible juggernaut, and in less than a century the tiny kingdom taken over by Pachakuti had become a vast empire. Topa Yupanqui (1471–1493) extended the Inca empire into Ecuador, northern Argentina, parts of Bolivia, and Chile. His armies also conquered the Chimu state, the water supplies of which Topa already controlled. The best Chimu craftsworkers were carried off to work for the court of the Incas. Another king, Huanya Capac, ruled for thirty-four years after Topa Inca and pushed the empire deeper into Ecuador.

The Inca rulers developed an efficient administrative system to run their empire, one based firmly on the precedents of earlier societies. *Tawantinsuyu*, "The Land of the Four Quarters," was divided into four large provinces known as *suyu* (quarters), each in turn subdivided into smaller provinces, some of them coinciding with older, conquered kingdoms. The conquered peoples in the Inca empire were usually ruled by a leading member of a local family, known as a *curaca*. These hereditary chiefs were a form of secondary non-Inca nobility who governed a tax-paying population of 100 people or more, but all the really important government posts were held by Inca nobles. The Inca rulers realized, however, that the essence of efficient government in such varied topography was efficient communications from one end of the empire to the other, and so the road builders commandeered a vast network of age-old Indian highways from the states they conquered. They linked them together in a coordinated system with regular rest houses so that they could move armies, trade goods, and messengers from one end of the Inca's kingdom to the other in short order (Hyslop, 1984).

The Incas' passion for organization impinged on everyone's life. Their society was organized into twelve age divisions for the purpose of census and tax assessment, divisions based on both physical change like puberty and on major social events like marriage. The most important stage was adulthood, which lasted as long as one could do a day's work. All the census and other data of the empire were recorded not on tablets but on knotted strings. The *quipu* were a complex and sophisticated record-keeping system that seems to have been so efficient that it more than made up for the lack of writing (Ascher and Ascher, 1981). They also were a powerful instrument for social conformity, codifying laws, and providing data for the inspectors, who regularly visited each household to check that everyone was engaged in productive work and living in sanitary conditions. No one could travel without official permission. Everything about the Inca lifeway stressed conformity, and the need to respect and obey the central government.

At the time of the Spanish Conquest, the Inca controlled the lives of as many as 6 million people, most of them living in small villages dispersed around religious and political centers. It was here that Inca artisans worked, producing major works of art in gold and silver. Bronze was widely used also, mostly for agricultural implements and weapons. Brightly painted Inca pottery is found throughout the empire; it is decorated with black, white, and red geometric designs. Despite the widespread distribution of Inca pots and artifacts, however, regional pottery styles flourished because the village potters, many of whom were conquered subjects rather than Inca, continued the cultural traditions of earlier centuries.

Inca political and religious power was centered on major urban complexes like Cuzco in the Andes, where the ceremonial center was built of carefully fitted stones (Figure 22.11). Such urban centers as Machu Pic-

Cuzco
Machu Picchu

Figure 22.11 Inca masonry from the fortress of Sacshuaman, near Cuzco, Peru.

chu high in the Andes (Figure 22.12), are famous for their fine masonry structures (Gasparini and Margolis, 1980). The Inca himself held court in Cuzco, surrounded by plotting factions and ever changing political tides. The villain was the very institution of split inheritance that fueled Inca military conquest. Every ruler faced more and more complex governance problems as a result. The need for more and more conquests caused great military, economic, and administrative stress. The logistics of long-distance military campaigns was horrendous, and the soldiers had to be fed from state-owned land, not royal estates. Moreover, while their tactics were well adapted to open country, where their armies were invincible, the rulers eventually ran out of open country and had to start fighting in forest country, where they fared badly. Meanwhile the empire had grown so large that communication became a lengthier and lengthier process, compounded by the great diversity of people living within the Inca domain. Also the increasing number of high-ranking nobles devoted to the interests of dead rulers led to chronic factionalism in Cuzco, as the living ruler grappled with the ever-constant nightmare of finding new land, or bringing marginal environments under cultivation through conquest or forced colonization. Under its glittering facade, *Tawantinsuyu* was becoming a rotten apple. In the end, the Inca empire was overthrown not by Peruvians but by a tiny band of foreigners armed with firearms who could exploit the inherent vulnerability of such a hierarchical, conforming society.

THE SPANISH CONQUEST: 1532–1534

This vulnerability of the Inca empire came home to roost in 1532, when a small party of rapacious Spanish conquistadors landed in northern Peru. When Francisco Pizarro arrived, the Inca state was in some political chaos. Inca Huayna Capac had died in an epidemic in A.D. 1525. The empire was plunged into a civil war between his son Huascar and another son, Atahuallpa, half-brother to Huascar. Atahuallpa eventually prevailed, but, as he moved south from Ecuador to consolidate his territory, he learned that Pizarro had landed in Peru.

The Spaniards had vowed to make Peru part of Spain and were bent on plunder and conquest. Pizarro arrived in the guise of a diplomat, captured Atahuallpa by treachery, ransomed him for a huge quantity of gold, and then brutally murdered him. A year later the Spaniards captured the Inca capital with a tiny army. They took over the state bureaucracy and appointed Manco Capac as puppet ruler. Three years later, Manco Capac turned on his masters in a bloody revolt. Its suppression finally destroyed the greatest of the Peruvian empires.

A.D. 1533
A.D. 1536

The Spanish conquest of Mexico and Peru saw the first major confrontation between the forces of an expanding Europe emerging from centuries of feudalism and complex, non-Western societies that were still

Figure 22.12 Machu Picchu. Forgotten for 400 years after the Spanish conquest, it was rediscovered by the American explorer Hiram Bingham in 1911.

living with the full legacy of prehistoric times. The four and a half centuries since the conquest have seen Europeans settle in all corners of the world, the emergence of the industrial state, and the acting out of the last, tragic chapter of human prehistory: the clash between the Western and non-Western worlds (Fagan, 1984b). We Westerners live with this tragic legacy of bitterness and misunderstanding as we face what will probably be the question of questions for the twenty-first century: How do we bridge the great gulf of incomprehension that exists between the Western and non-Western worlds, the rich and the poor? Hopefully, *People of the Earth* has given you some understanding of the compelling biological and cultural forces that produced the complex world we live in.

GUIDE TO FURTHER READING

Bankes, George. *Peru Before Pizarro*. London: Phaidon, 1977.
A useful introduction to Peruvian archaeology that examines different aspects of prehistoric life. Good for the beginner.

Conrad, Geoffrey W. and Demarest, Arthur A. *Religion and Empire: The Dynamics of Aztec and Inca Expansionism*. Cambridge: Cambridge University Press, 1984.
A clear and succinct analysis of two imperial, preindustrial civilizations. A sophisticated, well-argued book. Strongly recommended.

Moseley, Michael. *The Maritime Foundations of Andean Civilization*. Menlo Park, Calif.: Cummings, 1975.
A short essay which argues that the foundations of Peruvian civilization lay on the coast, in subsistence patterns that relied heavily on maritime resources. Controversial but convincing for the most part.

Rowe, John H. *Inca Culture at the Time of the Spanish Conquest. Handbook of South American Indians*, vol. 2. Washington, D.C.: Smithsonian Institution, 1946.
The classic account of Inca culture reconstructed from historical documents and limited archaeological investigations.

Willey, Gordon R. *An Introduction to American Archaeology: South America*, vol. 2, Englewood Cliffs, N.J.: Prentice-Hall, 1971.
Willey's culture history of South America still is the ultimate source for all basic research conducted in Peru up to the 1970s. Especially strong on the coast. Very much a book for the advanced student.

The Calibration of Radiocarbon Dates

IMPORTANT NOTE

It has been apparent for some time that the radiocarbon ages provided by most radiocarbon samples suffer from considerable inaccuracies owing to variations in cosmic ray bombardment of the earth. As is explained in Chapter One, dates from sites to about 7250 years old (about 5300 B.C.) can be calibrated by using tree rings to provide absolutely accurate dates.

These calibrations place me in somewhat of a chronological dilemma. Calibrated radiocarbon dates are used regularly only in a few parts of the world, noticeably in Europe, whereas many American archaeologists ignore them. Should one use calibrated dates in *People of the Earth?*

I have set up the text in such a way that you can use calibrated dates if you wish. Each chronological table has a column giving radiocarbon ages, another giving the calibrated dates as well. You can read off from whichever column you wish.

The dates in the margins are uncalibrated except in the European chapters where such dates are commonly used. You can convert them to C14 ages by referring to the requisite chronological table. The following conventions are used:

> *Radiocarbon ages and dates* established by historical chronologies, tree-ring dating, and other methods are expressed as follows: A.D. 1225 or 3250 B.C., with the A.D./B.C. convention in *Roman* letters.
> *Calibrated dates* are expressed: a.d. 1225 or 3250 b.c., with lower case letters.

This procedure follows common European practice. It should be noted that dates *earlier* than about 5300 B.C. are at present beyond the range of calibration tables and, as such, must be treated as radiocarbon ages.

Until recently, there were several different calibration tables. However, the major laboratories have got together and produced an agreed-upon calibration chart, which is used in this book. The tables can be consulted in Jeffrey Klein, J. C. Lerman, P. E. Damon, and E. K. Ralph, "Calibration of Radiocarbon Dates: Tables Based on the Consensus Data of the Workshop on Calibrating the Radiocarbon Time Scale," *Radiocarbon*, 1982, 24(2):103–149. I urge everyone to use these tables in the future.

CALIBRATION TABLE

The following are the calibrations for 500-year intervals from A.D. 1500 to 5300 B.C.:**

Radiocarbon age A.D./B.C.   Calibrated age range a.d./b.c.

** Calibrated dates are based on an assumed standard deviation of 100 years. Date range varies with standard deviation (see tables).

Radiocarbon age A.D./B.C.	Calibrated age range a.d./b.c.
A.D. 1500	a.d. 1300 to 1515
1000	870 to 1230
500	265 to 640
1	420 to 5 B.C.
500 B.C.	820 to 400
1000	1530 to 905
1500	2345 to 1660
2000	2830 to 2305
2500	3505 to 2925
3000	3950 to 3640
3500	4545 to 3960
4000	5235 to 4575
4500	5705 to 5205
5000	6285 to 5445
5300	6585 to 5595
before 5500	Outside calibration range

Bibliography
of Archaeology

The chapters on the basic methods and theory of archaeology in this book are necessarily sketchy. To supplement these, here is an annotated bibliography of primary sources on aspects of archaeology itself.

WORLD PREHISTORIES

It is fashionable but shamefully wasteful for textbook authors to ignore their competition, for all world prehistories have different things to offer. J. G. D. Clark's *World Prehistory: A New Outline,* Cambridge University Press, London and New York, 1977, is the third edition of a global culture history that is strong on later prehistory and gives little consideration to theoretical controversies. Robert Wenke's *Patterns in Prehistory,* second edition, Oxford University Press, New York, 1984, is an authoritative account, with a strong ecological and evolutionary emphasis. Ronald L. Wallace's *Those Who Have Vanished,* Dorsey Press, Homewood, Illinois, 1983, is a basic college text that covers most major culture areas of the world.

GENERAL BOOKS ON METHOD AND THEORY IN ARCHAEOLOGY

A good starting point is my own *Archaeology: A Brief Introduction,* second edition, Little, Brown, Boston, 1982, or, if you want a more detailed treatment, any of the following: Brian M. Fagan, *In the Beginning,* fifth edition, Little, Brown, Boston, 1984; Frank Hole and Robert F. Heizer, *An Introduction to Prehistoric Archaeology,* third edition, Holt, Rinehart and Winston, New York, 1973; and the same authors' *Prehistoric Archaeology: A Brief Introduction,* Holt, Rinehart and Winston, New York, 1977; and Robert J. Sharer and Wendy Ashmore, *Fundamentals of Archaeology,* Cummings, Menlo Park, California, 1979. All these works will lead the reader to the major controversies in the field.

HISTORY OF ARCHAEOLOGY

Glyn Daniel's *A Short History of Archaeology,* Thames and Hudson, London, 1981, can be amplified with the same author's *A Hundred and Fifty Years of Archaeology,* Duckworth,

London, 1976. Daniel's *The Origins and Growth of Archaeology,* Pelican Books, Harmondsworth, 1967, is an excellent anthology of early archaeological writings. American archaeology is described by Gordon R. Willey and Jeremy A. Sabloff in *A History of American Archaeology,* W. H. Freeman, San Francisco, 1974. The history of archaeological theory has been poorly served by archaeological writers, but Marvin Harris, *The Rise of Anthropological Theory,* Crowell, New York, 1968, is an invaluable if polemical source. W. W. Taylor, *A Study of Archaeology,* American Anthropological Association, Menasha, Wisconsin, 1948, also is a landmark monograph.

TIME

How archaeologists date their finds has been summarized by Joseph W. Michels, *Dating Methods in Archaeology,* Seminar Press, New York, 1973. H. N. Michael and E. K. Ralph, editors, *Dating Techniques for the Archaeologist,* MIT Press, Cambridge, 1971, also is useful. So is Stuart Fleming, *Dating in Archaeology,* St. Martin's Press, London, 1977. Karl Butzer's *Environment and Archaeology,* second edition, Aldine, Chicago, 1972, is the best source on Pleistocene geochronology, to which K. P. Oakley's *Frameworks for Dating Fossil Man,* Aldine, Chicago, 1964, adds some detail. David Q. Bowen's *Quaternary Geology,* Oxford University Press, Oxford, 1978, describes the subject with clear eloquence. V. Gordon Childe's *Piecing Together the Past,* Routledge and Kegan Paul, London, 1956, contains an interesting and cogent section on chronology and dating. Stratigraphy is well summarized by Sir Mortimer Wheeler, *Archaeology from the Earth,* Clarendon Press, Oxford, 1954; and Edward Pydokke, *Stratification for the Archaeologist,* Phoenix, London, 1961, is a useful source.

ARCHAEOLOGICAL SURVEY

A good survey of preservation conditions is to be found in J. G. D. Clark, *Archaeology and Society,* Barnes and Noble, New York, 1965. S. J. de Laet, *Archaeology and Its Problems,* Macmillan, New York, 1957, is also useful. Remote sensing is a burgeoning field. Try Thomas R. Lyons and Thomas Avery, *Remote Sensing: A Handbook for Archaeologists and Cultural Resource Managers,* National Park Service, Washington, D.C., 1972. This volume is updated regularly. Thomas N. Hester, J. Shafer, and R. F. Heizer, *Field Methods in Archaeology,* Mayfield Publishing, Palo Alto, 1985, contains much of value on archaeological survey.

EXCAVATION

Really good excavation manuals are far and few between. I think H. S. Dancey, *Archaeological Field Methods: An Introduction,* Burgess Publishing Company, Minneapolis, 1981, is the best one on American conditions. Martha Joukowsky, *A Complete Manual of Field Archaeology,* Prentice-Hall, Englewood Cliffs, New Jersey, 1981, and Hester, Shafer, and Heizer's *Field Methods,* already mentioned, are widely used. Phillip Barker, *The Techniques of Archaeological Excavation,* second edition, Batsford, London, 1983, gives a more international perspective. On conservation, see Elizabeth A. Dowman, *Conservation in Field Archaeology,* Methuen, London, 1970, and for photography see V. M. Conlon, *Camera Techniques in Archaeology,* John Baker, London, 1973.

Historical archaeology is most ably covered by Ivor Noël Hume, *Historical Archaeology,*

Knopf, New York, 1968, and underwater archaeology is summarized by George Bass, *Archaeology Underwater,* Praeger, New York, 1966. The same author's *A History of Seafaring Based on Underwater Archaeology,* Thames and Hudson, London, 1972, is a beautiful summary of the results of underwater research. Paul L. MacKendrick, *The Greek Stones Speak,* St. Martin's Press, New York, 1962, and *The Mute Stones Speak,* St. Martin's Press, New York, 1961, are two surveys of Classical archaeology. On industrial archaeology, see Kenneth Hudson, *World Industrial Archaeology,* Cambridge University Press, London and New York, 1979. Last, Warwick Bray and David Trump, *A Dictionary of Archaeology,* Penguin Press, London, 1970, is a useful tool.

ENVIRONMENT AND SUBSISTENCE

There is no one comprehensive volume on economic archaeology, but the following are widely used and cited: bones are covered by Richard G. Klein and Kathryn Cruz-Uribe, *The Analysis of Animal Bones from Archaeological Sites,* University of Chicago Press, Chicago, 1984; also R. E. Chaplin, *The Study of Animal Bones from Archaeological Sites,* Seminar Press, New York, 1971. Seeds and vegetal remains are covered by Jane M. Renfrew, *Palaeoethnobotany: The Prehistoric Food Plants of the Near East,* Methuen, London, 1973. Michael Jochim's *Strategies for Survival,* Academic Press, New York, 1981, focuses on the relationship between culture, behavior, and the environment.

TECHNOLOGY

The literature on ancient technology is enormous, but the following are useful introductions. Stone technology is summarized by J. Bordaz, *Tools of the Old and New Stone Age,* American Museum of Natural History, New York, 1971. François Bordes, *The Old Stone Age,* McGraw-Hill, New York, 1968, contains much information on stone tool types. Earl Swanson's edited *Lithic Technology,* Mouton, The Hague, 1975, surveys the techniques. Anna O. Shepard, *Ceramics for the Archaeologist,* Smithsonian Institution, Washington, D.C., 1956, is the definitive work on pottery, and R. F. Tylecote's *Metallurgy in Archaeology,* Edward Arnold, London, 1962, is a useful reference book on metals. David L. Clarke's *Analytical Archaeology,* revised edition, Methuen, London, 1978, Chapters 11–14, has a lengthy analysis of advanced taxonomic methods.

ORDERING AND INTERPRETATION

Gordon R. Willey and Philip Phillips, *Method and Theory in American Archaeology,* University of Chicago Press, Chicago, 1958, contains fundamental reading on archaeological units. V. Gordon Childe, *Piecing Together the Past,* Routledge and Kegan Paul, London, 1956, is another thought-provoking source. The principles of diffusion, migration, and independent invention are well described by Bruce C. Trigger, *Beyond History: The Methods of Prehistory,* Holt, Rinehart and Winston, New York, 1968, and by V. Gordon Childe, *Piecing Together the Past,* Routledge and Kegan Paul, London, 1956. Colin Renfrew has edited a large volume of papers, *The Explanation of Culture Change: Models in Prehistory,* Duckworth, London, 1973, which contain much provocative and theoretical discussion on cultural process. See also W. W. Taylor, *A Study of Archaeology,* American Anthropological Association, Menasha, Wisconsin, 1948; and Fred Plog, *The Study of Prehistoric Change,* Academic Press, New York, 1974. A good volume on typology is Robert Whallon and James A. Brown, *Essays on Archaeological Typology,* Center for American Archaeology, Evanston, Illinois, 1982.

PROCESSUAL ARCHAEOLOGY

Patty J. Watson, Steven LeBlanc, and Charles Redman, *Archeological Explanation,* Academic Press, New York, 1984, is a useful starting point. Then try Lewis R. Binford, *An Archaeological Perspective,* Academic Press, New York, 1972, which has a very personal essay on the development of processual archaeology and reprints Binford's major papers. The same author's *In Pursuit of the Past,* Thames and Hudson, New York, 1983, summarizes his basic viewpoints, while *Working at Archaeology,* Academic Press, New York, 1983, is a collection of his papers. Charles L. Redman, editor, *Research and Theory in Current Archaeology,* John Wiley Interscience, 1984, contains many useful essays on processual archaeology and its problems.

SETTLEMENT ARCHAEOLOGY

K. C. Chang, editor, *Settlement Archaeology,* National Press, Palo Alto, California, 1968, is a fundamental source, as is Kent V. Flannery's edited *The Early Mesoamerican Village,* Academic Press, New York, 1976, which talks more common sense about contemporary archaeology than any other source known to me. For trade in prehistory, see Jeremy A. Sabloff and C. C. Lamberg-Karlovsky, editors, *Early Civilization and Trade,* University of New Mexico Press, Albuquerque, 1975. Perhaps the most comprehensive settlement study to date is William T. Sanders, Jeffrey R. Parsons, and Robert S. Santlay, *The Basin of Mexico: Ecological Processes in the Evolution of a Civilization,* Academic Press, New York, 1979.

ETHNOARCHAEOLOGY (LIVING ARCHAEOLOGY)

This probably is the most fashionable field of archaeology at the moment. Try Richard A. Gould, editor, *Explanations in Ethnoarchaeology,* University of New Mexico Press, Albuquerque, 1978. Also see John E. Yellen, *Archaeological Approaches to the Present,* Academic Press, New York, 1977. Lewis Binford, *Nunamiut Ethnoarchaeology,* Academic Press, New York, 1978, is bound to become a much quoted case study. Another aspect of living archaeology is ably summarized by John Coles, *Archaeology by Experiment,* Hutchinson University Library, London, 1973. Also see D. Ingersoll and colleagues, *Experimental Archeology,* Columbia University Press, New York, 1977.

THE DESTRUCTION OF ARCHAEOLOGICAL SITES

Karl Meyer, *The Plundered Past,* Atheneum Press, New York, 1973, is a fascinating and shocking account of the illegal traffic in antiquities. C. R. McGimsey, *Public Archaeology,* Seminar Press, New York, 1972, is fundamental reading for all American archaeologists. M. Pallotino, *The Meaning of Archaeology,* Thames and Hudson, London, 1968, is a thoughtful analysis of archaeology in the modern world. For the new and expanding field of cultural resource management, I would advise you to start with the chapter on this subject in my *In the Beginning,* fourth edition, Little, Brown, Boston, 1984, simply because it is the only available beginning summary of the complex issues involved.

ATLAS OF ARCHAEOLOGY

Although several atlases of archaeology are on the market, by far the best tool is David and Ruth Whitehouse, *Archaeological Atlas of the World,* Thames and Hudson, London, and W. H. Freeman, San Francisco, 1975. This book belongs on every archaeologist's bookshelf.

Bibliography
of World Prehistory

This Bibliography is not intended as a comprehensive reference guide to world prehistory. Rather, it is a compilation of both the majority of the sources used to compile this book and a cross section of the most important monographs and papers relating to all parts of the world. Readers interested in probing even more deeply into the literature should consult the references given in the text and in the publications listed below.

Adams, R. E. W., ed. 1977a. *The Origins of the Classic Maya.* Albuquerque: University of New Mexico Press.

———. 1977b. *Prehistoric Mesoamerica.* Boston: Little, Brown.

Adams, R. E. W., Brown, W. E., and Culbert, T. Patrick. 1981. "Radar Mapping, Archeology, and Ancient Maya Land Use." *Science* 213 (4515):1457–1462.

Adams, Robert M. 1966. *The Evolution of Urban Society.* Chicago: Aldine.

———. 1981. *Heartland of Cities.* Chicago: University of Chicago Press.

Adams, Robert M., and Nissen, Hans J. 1972. *The Uruk Landscape.* Chicago: University of Chicago Press.

Adovasio, J. M. et al. 1981. *Meadowcroft Rockshelter and the Archaeology of the Cross Creek Drainage.* Pittsburgh: University of Pittsburgh Press.

Agrawal, D. P. 1982. "The Indian Bronze Age Cultures and Their Metal Technology." *Advances in World Archaeology* 1:213–264.

Aigner, Jean S. 1970. "The Unifacial, Core, and Blade Site on Anagula Island, Aleutians." *Arctic Anthropology* 7 (2):59–88.

Aikens, C. Melvin. 1970. *Hogup Cave.* Salt Lake City: University of Utah Press.

Aikens, C. Melvin, and Higuchi, Takayasu. 1981. *Prehistory of Japan.* New York: Academic Press.

Aitken, Martin. 1977. "Thermoluminescence and the Archaeologist." *Antiquity* 51:11–19.

Akazawa, Takeru. 1982. "Cultural Change in Prehistoric Japan." *Advances in World Archaeology* 1:151–212.

Aldred, Cyril. 1968. *Akhenaten.* London: Thames and Hudson.

———. 1984. *The Egyptians.* 2nd ed. New York: Thames and Hudson.

Allan, William. 1965. *The African Husbandman.* Edinburgh: Oliver and Boyd.

Allchin, Bridget. 1966. *The Stone Tipped Arrow.* New York: Barnes and Noble.

Allchin, Raymond, and Allchin, Bridget. 1982. *The Rise of Civilization in India.* Cambridge: Cambridge University Press.

Allen, J. 1969. "The Hunting Neolithic: Adaptations to the Food Quest in Prehistoric Papua

New Guinea." In J. V. S. Megaw, ed., *Hunters, Gatherers, and First Farmers Beyond Europe*. Atlantic Highlands, N.J.: Humanities Press. Pp. 167–188.

———. 1977. "Sea Traffic, Trade and Expanding Horizons." In J. Allen, J. Golson, and Rhys Jones, eds., *Sunda and Sahel*. New York: Academic Press. Pp. 387–414.

Allen, J., Golson, J., and Jones, Rhys, eds. 1977. *Sunda and Sahel: Prehistoric Studies in Southeast Asia, Melanesia, and Australia*. New York: Academic Press.

Alpers, Edward A. 1975. *Ivory and Slaves in East Central Africa*. Berkeley and Los Angeles: University of California Press.

Ambrose, Stanley H. 1984. "The Introduction of Pastoral Adaptations to the Highlands of East Africa." In J. Desmond Clark and Steven A. Brandt, eds., *From Hunters to Farmers*. Berkeley and Los Angeles: University of California Press. Pp. 212–239.

Ammerman, A., and Cavalli-Sforza, L. 1973. "Measuring the Rate of Early Farming in Europe." In Colin Renfrew, ed., *The Explanation of Culture Change*. London: Duckworth. Pp. 343–357.

Anderson, Douglas. 1970. "Akmak." *Acta Arctica* 15:1–25

———. 1979. "Archaeology and the Evidence for the Prehistoric Development of Eskimo Culture." *Arctic Anthropologist* 16 (1):16–26.

Anderson, J. E. 1969. *The Human Skeleton: A Manual for Archaeologists*. Ottawa: National Museum of Canada.

Ascher, Marcia, and Ascher, Robert. 1981. *The Code of the Quipu*. Ann Arbor: University of Michigan Press.

Bada, Jeffrey L., and Helfman, Patricia Masters. 1975. "Amino Acid Racemization Dating of Fossil Bones." *World Archaeology* 7 (2):160–173.

Bailey, G. N., ed. 1983. *Hunter-Gatherer Economy in Prehistory*. Cambridge: Cambridge University Press.

Baillie, M. G. L. 1982. *Tree Ring Dating and Archaeology*. New York: Columbia University Press.

Bankes, George. 1977. *Peru Before Pizarro*. Oxford: Phaidon.

Bannister, Bryant, and Robinson, William J. 1975. "Tree-Ring Dating in Archaeology." *World Archaeology* 7 (2):210–225.

Barker, Phillip. 1983. *Techniques of Archaeological Excavation* (2nd ed.). London: Batsford.

Barnard, Noel. 1961. *Bronze Casting and Bronze Alloys in Ancient China*. Canberra: Australian National University.

Bayard, Donn T. 1970. "Excavations at Non Nok Tha, Northeast Thailand, 1968: An Interim Report." *Asian Perspectives* 13:109–144.

———. 1972. "Early Thai Bronze: Analysis and New Dates." *Science* 176:1411–1421.

———. 1977. "Phu Wiang Pottery and the Prehistory of Northeastern Thailand." In G. Bartstra et al., eds., *Modern Quaternary Research in South East Asia*. Rotterdam: A. A. Balkema. Pp. 57–102.

———, ed. 1984. *The Origins of Agriculture, Metallurgy, and the State in Mainland Southeast Asia*. Dunedin, New Zealand: University of Otago Press.

Beadle, George. 1981. "The Ancestor of Corn." *Scientific American* 242 (1):96–103.

Bellwood, Peter. 1970. "Fortifications and Economy in Prehistoric New Zealand." *Proceedings of the Prehistoric Society* 37 (1):56–95.

———. 1978. *Man's Conquest of the Pacific*. Oxford: Oxford University Press.

———. 1979. *The Polynesians*. London: Thames and Hudson.

Benfer, Robert. 1982. "The Lomas Site of Paloma (5000 to 7500 B.P.), Chilca Valley, Peru." In Ramerio Matos, ed., *Andean Archaeology*.

Benson, Elizabeth, ed. 1971. *Dumbarton Oaks Conference on Chavín*. Washington, D.C.: Dumbarton Oaks.

————. 1979. *Pre-Columbian Metallurgy of South America.* Washington, D.C.: Dumbarton Oaks.

Bernal, Ignacio. 1969. *The Olmec World.* Berkeley and Los Angeles: University of California Press.

Binford, Lewis R. 1964. "A Consideration of Archaeological Research Design." *American Antiquity* 29:425–441.

————. 1968. "Post-Pleistocene Adaptations." In Lewis R. and Sally Binford, eds., *New Perspectives in Archaeology.* New York: Academic Press. Pp. 313–341.

————. 1972. *An Archaeological Perspective.* New York: Academic Press.

————. 1978. *Nunamiut Ethnoarchaeology.* New York: Academic Press.

————. 1981. *Bones.* New York: Academic Press.

————. 1983. *In Pursuit of the Past.* New York: Thames and Hudson.

Binford, Lewis R., and Binford, Sally. 1966. "A Preliminary Analysis of Functional Variability in the Mousterian of Levallois facies." *American Anthropologist* 62 (2):238–295.

Bishop, W. W. 1978. "Pliocene Problems Relating to Human Evolution." In Glynn Isaac and Elizabeth McCown, eds., *Human Origins: Louis Leakey and the East African Evidence.* Menlo Park, Calif.: W. A. Benjamin.

Blanc, Alberto C. 1961. "Some Evidence for the Ideologies of Early Man." In S. L. Washburn, ed., *The Social Life of Early Man.* New York: Viking Fund. Pp. 119–136.

Blanton, Richard E. 1978. *Monte Albán: Settlement Patterns at the Ancient Zapotec Capital.* New York: Academic Press.

Blegen, Carl. 1971. *Troy.* London: Thames and Hudson.

Bogucki, Peter, and Grygiel, Ryszard. 1983. "Early Farmers of the North European Plain." *Scientific American* 248 (4):105–115.

Bordes, François. 1968. *The Old Stone Age.* New York: McGraw-Hill.

Boule, Marcellin, and Vallois, H. 1957. *Fossil Men.* London: Thames and Hudson.

Bovill, E. W. 1968. *The Golden Trade of the Moors.* London: Heinemann.

Bowdler, J. M. 1977. "The Coastal Colonization of Australia." In J. Allen, J. Golson, and Rhys Jones, eds., *Sunda and Sahel.* New York: Academic Press. Pp. 233–248.

Bowdler, J. M., Jones, R., and Thorne, A. G. 1970. "Pleistocene Human Remains from Australia: A Living Site and Human Cremation from Lake Mungo, Western New South Wales." *World Archaeology* 2:39–60.

Bowen, D. Q. 1978. *Quaternary Geology.* Oxford: Oxford University.

Bower, John R. F. 1984. "Settlement Behavior of Pastoral Cultures in East Africa." In J. Desmond Clark and Steven A. Brandt, eds., *From Hunters to Farmers.* Berkeley and Los Angeles: University of California Press. Pp. 252–259.

Braidwood, L. S., ed. 1982. *Prehistoric Village Archaeology in South-Eastern Turkey.* Oxford: British Archaeological Reports, International Series, no. 138.

Braidwood, R. J., and Braidwood, L. S., eds. 1983. *Prehistoric Archaeology Along the Zagros Flanks.* Chicago: Oriental Institute.

————, and Cambel, H. 1980. *Prehistoric Research in Southeastern Anatolia.* Istanbul: Edebiyat Facultesi Basimevi.

Brain, C. K. 1981. *The Hunters or the Hunted: An Introduction to African Cave Taphonomy.* Chicago: University of Chicago Press.

Breuil, Henri. 1908. *La Caverne d'Altamira.* Paris: Payot.

————. 1952. *Four Hundred Centuries of Cave Art.* Montignac: Centre d'Etudes et de Documentation.

Briggs, L. Cabot. 1951. "The Ancient Khmer Empire." *Transactions of the American Philosophical Society* 41.

Brodie, Fawn. 1957. *The Devil Drives.* London: Eyre and Spottiswoode.

Brose, David C. 1980. "A Speculative Model of the Role of Exchange in the Prehistory of the

Eastern Woodlands." In David C. Brose and N'omi Greber, eds., *Hopewellian Archaeology*. Kent, Ohio: Kent State University Press. Pp. 3–8.

Brose, David C., and Greber, N'omi. 1980. *Hopewellian Archaeology*. Kent, Ohio: Kent State University Press.

Brothwell, Don R. 1965. *Digging Up Bones*. London: British Museum.

Browman, David L. 1978. "Toward the Development of the Tiahuanaco (Tiwanaku) State." In David L. Browman, ed., *Advances in Andean Archaeology*. The Hague: Mouton. Pp. 327–349.

Bryan, Alan Lyle. 1983. "South America." In Richard Shutler, Jr., ed., *Early Man in the New World*. Beverly Hills: Sage Publications. Pp. 137–146.

———, ed. 1978. *Early Man in America from a Circum-Pacific Perspective*. Edmonton: University of Alberta.

Bryant, Vaughn. 1974. "Prehistoric Diet in South Texas: The Coprolite Evidence." *American Antiquity* 39:100–109.

Buckley, W., ed. 1968. *Modern Systems Research for the Behavioral Sciences*. Chicago: Aldine.

Bunn, Henry, et al. 1980. "FxJj50: An Early Pleistocene Site in Northern Kenya." *World Archaeology* 12 (2):109–136.

Burch, Ernest S. 1972. "The Caribou/Wild Reindeer as a Human Resource." *American Antiquity* 37 (3):339–368.

Burger, Richard L. 1984. *The Prehistoric Occupation of Chavín de Huántar*. Berkeley and Los Angeles: University of California Press.

Burger, Richard L., and Burger, Lucy Salazar. 1980. "Ritual and Religion at Huaricoto." *Archaeology* 33 (6):26–32.

Butzer, Karl. 1974. *Environment and Archaeology*. 3rd ed. Chicago: Aldine.

———. 1976. *Early Hydraulic Civilization in Egypt*. Chicago: University of Chicago Press.

———. 1981. "Civilizations: Organisms or Systems?" *American Scientist* 68:517–524.

———. 1982. *Archaeology as Human Ecology*. Cambridge: Cambridge University Press.

Butzer, Karl, and Isaac, Glynn Ll., eds. 1976. *After the Australopithecines*. Chicago: Aldine.

Caldwell, Joseph R. 1958. *Trend and Tradition in the Prehistory of the Eastern United States*. Washington, D.C.: American Anthropological Association Memoir 88.

Campbell, Bernard. 1974. *Human Evolution*. 2nd ed. Chicago: Aldine.

———. 1985. *Humankind Emerging*. 3rd ed. Boston: Little, Brown.

Capitan, L., and Peyrony, Denis. 1928. *La Madeleine, son gisement, son industrie, ses oeuvres d'art*. Paris: Librairie Emile Nourry.

Carneiro, Robert L. 1972. "A Theory of the Origin of the State." *Science* 169:733–738.

Carter, George F. 1981. *Earlier Than You Think*. College Station: Texas A & M University Press.

Carter, Howard. 1923. *The Tomb of Tut-ankh-Amun*. London: Macmillan.

Caton-Thompson, G., and Gardner, E. W. 1934. *The Desert Fayum*. 2 vols. London: Royal Anthropological Institute.

Ceram, C. W. 1953. *Gods, Graves and Scholars*. New York: Knopf.

Chadwick, John, 1958. *The Decipherment of Linear B*. Cambridge: Cambridge University Press.

Champion, Timothy, et al. 1984. *Prehistoric Europe*. New York: Academic Press.

Chang, Kwang-Chih. 1977. *The Archaeology of Ancient China*. 3rd ed. New Haven: Yale University Press.

———. 1980. *The Shang Civilization*. New Haven: Yale University Press.

————. 1981. "In Search of China's Beginnings: New Light on an Old Civilization." *American Scientist* 60:148–160.

Chard, Chester S. 1969. *Man in Prehistory.* New York: McGraw-Hill.

————. 1971. *Northeast Asia in Prehistory.* Madison: University of Wisconsin Press.

Childe, V. Gordon. 1925. *The Dawn of European Civilization.* London: Routledge and Kegan Paul.

————. 1936. *Man Makes Himself.* London: Watts.

————. 1942. *What Happened in History.* London: Routledge and Kegan Paul.

————. 1952. *New Light on the Most Ancient East.* London: Routledge and Kegan Paul.

————. 1956. *Piecing Together the Past.* London: Routledge and Kegan Paul.

————. 1958. "Retrospect." *Antiquity* 32:69–74.

Chippendale, Christopher. 1983. *Stonehenge Complete.* Ithaca: Cornell University Press.

Clark, J. Desmond. 1959. *The Prehistory of Southern Africa.* Baltimore: Pelican Books.

————. 1967. "The Problem of Neolithic Culture in Sub-Saharan Africa." In W. W. Bishop and J. Desmond Clark, eds., *Background to Evolution in Africa.* Chicago: University of Chicago Press. Pp. 601–628.

————. 1970. *The Prehistory of Africa.* London: Thames and Hudson.

————. 1971. "A Re-Examination of the Evidence for Agricultural Origins in the Nile Valley." *Proceedings of the Prehistoric Society* 37 (2):34–79.

————. 1984. "Prehistoric Cultural Continuity and Economic Change in the Central Sudan in the Early Holocene." In J. Desmond Clark and Steven A. Brandt, eds., *From Hunters to Farmers.* Berkeley and Los Angeles: University of California Press. Pp. 113–126.

Clark, J. G. D. 1952. *Prehistoric Europe: The Economic Basis.* London: Methuen.

————. 1954. *Star Carr.* Cambridge: Cambridge University Press.

————. 1965. *Archaeology and Society.* New York: Barnes and Noble.

————. 1970. *Aspects of Prehistory.* Berkeley and Los Angeles: University of California Press.

————. 1975. *The Earlier Stone Age Settlement of Scandinavia.* Cambridge: Cambridge University Press.

————. 1977. *World Prehistory: A New Outline.* 3rd ed. Cambridge: Cambridge University Press.

————. 1979. *Mesolithic Prelude.* Edinburgh: Edinburgh University Press.

Clarke, David. 1976. "Mesolithic Europe: The Economic Basis." In G. de Sieveking et al., eds., *Problems in Economic and Social Archaeology.* London: Duckworth. Pp. 449–481.

CLIMAP Project Members. 1976. "The Surface of the Ice Age Earth." *Science* 191:1126–1131.

Clutton-Brock, J. 1981. *Domesticated Animals from Early Times.* Austin: University of Texas Press.

Coe, Michael D. 1962. *Mexico.* New York: Praeger.

————. 1965. *The Jaguar's Children.* New York: Museum of Primitive Art.

————. 1968. *America's First Civilization: Discovering the Olmec.* New York: American Heritage.

————. 1984. *The Maya.* 3rd ed. London: Thames and Hudson.

Coe, Michael D., and Diehl, Richard. 1980. *In the Land of the Olmec.* 2 vols. Austin: University of Texas Press.

Coe, William, and Haviland, William A. 1982. *Introduction to the Archaeology of Tikal, Guatemala.* Philadelphia: University Museum, University of Pennsylvania. (The first of a projected 39 reports on Tikal.)

Cohen, Mark. 1977. *The Food Crisis in Prehistory.* New Haven: Yale University Press.

Cohen, Mark N., and Armelagos, George J., eds. 1984. *Paleopathology and the Origins of Agriculture.* New York: Academic Press.

Coles, J. M. 1962. "European Bronze Age Shields." *Proceedings of the Prehistoric Society* 28:156–190.

———. 1980. *Experimental Archaeology.* New York: Academic Press.

———. 1982. "The Bronze Age in North West Europe: Problems and Advances." *Advances in World Archaeology* 1:266–321.

Coles, J. M., and Harding, A. F. 1979. *The Bronze Age in Europe.* London: Methuen.

Conkey, Margaret W. 1981. "A Century of Palaeolithic Cave Art." *Archaeology* 34 (4):20–28.

Conrad, Geoffrey W., and Demarest, Arthur A. 1984. *Religion and Empire: The Dynamics of Aztec and Inca Expansion.* Cambridge: Cambridge University Press.

Cordell, Linda. 1984a. *The Archaeology of the Southwest.* New York: Academic Press.

———. 1984b. "Southwestern Archaeology." *Annual Review of Anthropology* 13:130–132.

Cotter, John. 1981. "The Upper Paleolithic: However It Got Here, It's Here." *American Antiquity* 46:926–928.

Cotterell, Arthur. 1981. *The First Emperor of China.* New York: Holt, Rinehart and Winston.

Covey, Curt. 1984. "The Earth's Orbit and the Ice Ages." *Scientific American* 280 (2):58–77.

Cranstone, B. A. L. 1972. "The Tifalmin: A Neolithic People in New Guinea." *World Archaeology* 3 (2):132–142.

Crawford, O. G. S. 1953. *Archaeology in the Field.* New York: Praeger.

Culbert, T. Patrick, ed. 1973. *The Classic Maya Collapse.* Albuquerque: University of New Mexico Press.

Cunliffe, Barry. 1974. *Iron Age Communities in Britain.* London: Routledge and Kegan Paul.

Dales, George F. 1966. "The Decline of the Harappans." *Scientific American* May. Pp. 210–216.

Dalrymple, C. Brent, and Lamphere, Mason. 1970. *Potassium Argon Dating: Principles, Techniques and Applications in Geochronology.* San Francisco: Freeman.

Daniel, Glyn E. 1973. *Megaliths in History.* London: Thames and Hudson.

———. 1981. *A Short History of Archaeology.* London: Thames and Hudson.

Dart, Raymond A. 1925. "*Australopithecus africanus:* The Man-Ape of Southern Africa." *Nature* 115:195.

———. 1957. *The Osteodontokeratic Culture of Australopithecus prometheus.* Pretoria: Transvaal Museum.

David, A. Rosalie. 1975. *The Egyptian Kingdoms.* Oxford: Elsevier Phaidon.

Davidson, Basil. 1966. *Africa: History of a Continent.* London: Weidenfeld and Nicholson.

Davies, Nigel. 1973. *The Aztecs.* Norman: University of Oklahoma Press.

———. 1977. *The Toltecs.* Norman: University of Oklahoma Press.

———. 1979. *Voyages to the New World: Fact or Fantasy.* London: Macmillan.

———. 1980. *The Toltec Heritage.* Norman: University of Oklahoma Press.

Deetz, James. 1967. *Invitation to Archaeology.* Garden City, N.Y.: Natural History Press.

de Lumley, Henry. 1969. "A Paleolithic Camp at Nice." *Scientific American* 220:42–50.

Dennell, Robin C. 1983. *European Economic Prehistory: A New Approach.* New York: Academic Press.

de Selincourt, Aubrey, trans. 1966. *Livy's Early History of Rome.* Baltimore: Pelican Books.

Desroches-Noblecourt, G. 1963. *Tutankhamun.* New York: New York Graphic Society.

Diaz, Bernal. 1963. *The True History of the Conquest of New Spain.* Translated by A. P. Maudslay. Baltimore: Pelican Books.

Dibble, Charles E., and Anderson, Arthur J. O. 1978. *Florentine Codex,* vol. 14. Salt Lake City: University of Utah Press.

Diehl, Richard A. 1984. *Tula.* London: Thames and Hudson.

Dillehey, Tom D. 1984. "A Late Ice Age Settlement in Southern Chile." *Scientific American* 254 (4):100–109.

Dincauze, Dena. 1983. "An Archaeo-Logical Evaluation of the Case for Pre-Clovis Occupations." *Advances in World Archaeology* 3:275–324.

Di Peso, C. C., et al. 1974. *Casas Grandes: A Fallen Trading Center of the Gran Chichimeca.* Flagstaff, Ariz.: Amerlnd Foundation.

Diringer, David. 1962. *Writing.* New York: Praeger.

Dolukhanov, Paul H. 1982. "Upper Pleistocene and Holocene Cultures of the Russian Plain and Caucasus." *Advances in World Archaeology* 1:323–358.

Donnan, Christopher B., and McClelland, Donna. 1979. *The Burial Theme in Moche Iconography.* Washington, D.C.: Dumbarton Oaks.

Dortch, Charles. 1977. "Early and Late Stone Industrial Phases in Western Australia." In R. V. S. Wright, ed., *Stone Tools as Cultural Markers.* Canberra: Australian Institute of Aboriginal Studies. Pp. 104–132.

Dortch, Charles, and Merrilees, Duncan. 1973. "Human Occupation of Devil's Lair, Western Australia, During the Pleistocene." *Archaeology and Physical Anthropology in Oceania* 8:89–115.

Dragoo, Don W. 1976. "Some Aspects of Eastern North American Prehistory: A Review 1975." *American Antiquity* 41 (1):3–27.

Drucker, Phillip. 1959. *La Venta, Tabasco: A Study of Olmec Ceramics and Art.* Washington, D.C.: Smithsonian Institution.

Dumond, Don. 1977. *The Eskimos and Aleuts.* London: Thames and Hudson.

Dunnell, Robert C. 1971. *Systematics in Prehistory.* New York: Free Press.

———. 1980. "Evolutionary Theory and Archaeology." *Advances in Archaeological Method and Theory* 3:35–99.

Edwards, I. E. S. 1973. *The Pyramids.* New York: Viking.

Eliade, Mircea. 1954. *The Myth of the Eternal Return.* New York: Pantheon.

———. 1959. *The Sacred and the Profane.* New York: Harcourt, Brace.

Elphick, Richard. 1977. *Kraal and Castle.* New Haven: Yale University Press.

Emory, Kenneth P. 1972. "Easter Island's Position in the Prehistory of Polynesia." *Journal of the Polynesian Society* 81:57–69.

Emory, Kenneth P., Bonk, William J., and Sinoto, Yoshiko H. 1959. *Hawaiian Archaeology: Fishhooks.* Honolulu: Bishop Museum.

Engel, Frederic. 1957. "Early Sites on the Peruvian Coast." *Southwestern Journal of Anthropology* 13:54–68.

———. 1966a. *Geografia Humana Prehistorica y Agricultura Precolumbina de la Quebrada de Chilca.* Lima: Universidad Agraria.

———. 1966b. *Paracas.* Lima: Librería Juan Megia Base.

Evans, Sir Arthur J. 1921. *The Palace of Minos at Knossos.* 4 vols. Oxford: Clarendon Press.

Evans, Robert K., and Rasson, Judith A. 1984. "*Ex Balkanis Lux?* Recent Developments in Neolithic and Chalcolithic Research in Southeastern Europe." *American Antiquity* 49:713–741.

Fagan, Brian M. 1979. *Return to Babylon.* Boston: Little, Brown.

———. 1982. *The Archaeology of the Early Civilizations.* New York: Chanticleer Press.

———. 1983. *Archaeology: A Brief Introduction.* 2nd ed. Boston: Little, Brown.

————. 1984a. *The Aztecs.* New York: Freeman.

————. 1984b. *Clash of Cultures.* New York: Freeman.

————. 1985. *In the Beginning.* Boston: Little, Brown.

Fagan, Brian M., and Van Noten, F. 1971. *The Hunter-Gatherers of Gwisho.* Tervuren: Musée Royal de l'Afrique Centrale.

Fairservis, Walter A. 1976. *The Roots of Ancient India.* 2nd ed. New York: Macmillan.

————. 1983. "The Script of the Indus Valley Civilization," *Scientific American* 243 (3):58–77.

Falk, Dean. 1984. "The Petrified Brain." *Natural History* 93 (9):36–39.

Fedden, Robin. 1977. *Egypt.* London: John Murray.

Fell, Barry. 1976. *America B.C.* New York: Times Books.

————. 1980. *Saga America.* New York: Times Books.

Finney, Ben R. 1967. "New Perspectives on Pacific Voyaging." In Genevieve Highland et al., eds., *Polynesian Culture History.* Honolulu: Bishop Museum. Pp. 141–166.

Fish, P. R., and Fish, S. R. 1977. *Verde Valley Archaeology: Review and Perspective.* Flagstaff: Museum of Northern Arizona.

Fitzgerald, Patrick. 1978. *Ancient China.* Oxford: Elsevier Phaidon.

Flannery, Kent V. 1965. "The Ecology of Early Food Production in Mesopotamia." *Science* 147:1247–1256.

————. 1968a. "Archaeological Systems Theory and Early Mesoamerica." In Betty Meggers, ed., *Anthropological Archaeology in the Americas.* Washington, D.C.: Anthropological Society of Washington. Pp. 67–87.

————. 1968b. "The Olmec and the Valley of Oaxaca: A Model for Interregional Interaction in Formative Times." In Elizabeth Benson, ed., *Dumbarton Oaks Conference on the Olmec.* Washington, D.C.: Dumbarton Oaks. Pp. 79–110.

————. 1969. "Origins and Ecological Effects of Early Domestication in Animals." In Peter J. Ucko and G. W. Dimbleby, eds., *The Domestication of Plants and Animals.* London: Duckworth. Pp. 207–218.

————. 1972. "The Cultural Evolution of Civilizations." Palo Alto, Calif.: *Annual Review of Ecology and Systematics.* Pp. 399–426.

————. 1973. "The Origins of Agriculture." *Annual Review of Anthropology* 2:271–310.

————, ed. 1976. *The Early Mesoamerican Village.* New York: Academic Press.

————, ed. 1982. *Maya Subsistence.* New York: Academic Press.

Fleischer, Robert L. 1975. "Advances in Fission Track Dating." *World Archaeology* 7 (2):136–150.

Flint, R. F. 1965. "The Plio-Pleistocene Boundary." In H. E. Wright and D. G. Frey, eds., *International Studies in the Quaternary.* Washington, D.C.: Geological Society of America. Pp. 497–533.

————. 1971. *Glacial and Quaternary Geology.* New York: Wiley.

Folan, William J., et al. 1983. *Coba: A Classic Maya Metropolis.* New York: Academic Press.

Fowler, Melvin L. 1969. "The Cahokia Site." In Melvin L. Fowler, ed., *Investigations in Cahokia Archaeology.* Urbana: Illinois Archaeological Survey. Pp. 1–14.

————. 1978. "Cahokia and the American Bottom: Settlement Archaeology." In Bruce C. Smith, ed., *Mississippian Settlement Patterns.* New York: Academic Press. Pp. 455–478.

Frison, George C. 1978. *Prehistoric Hunters of the High Plains.* New York: Academic Press.

Gabel, Creighton. 1983. "The Search for Human Origins: Facts and Questions." *Journal of Field Archaeology* 10:193–211.

Gardner, R. Allen, and Gardner, Beatrice A. 1969. "Teaching Sign Language to a Chimpanzee." *Science* 163:664–672.

Garlake, Peter. 1973. *Great Zimbabwe.* New York: McGraw-Hill.

Garrod, D. A. E. 1957. "The Natufian Culture: The Life and Economy of a Mesolithic People in the Near East." *Proceedings of the British Academy* 43:211–237.

Garrod, D. A. E., and Bate, Dorothea. 1937. *The Stone Age of Mount Carmel.* Cambridge: Cambridge University Press.

Gasparini, Graziano, and Margolies, Luise. 1980. *Inca Architecture.* Bloomington: Indiana University Press.

Gerasimov, M. M. 1958. "The Paleolithic Site of Ma'lta (1956–57 Excavations)." *Sovyetskayen Etnografiya* 3:28–52.

Gibson, Charles. 1964. *The Aztecs Under Spanish Rule.* Palo Alto, Calif.: Stanford University Press.

Giddings, J. L. 1967. *Ancient Men of the Arctic.* New York: Knopf.

Giteau, M. 1966. *Khmer Sculpture and the Angkor Civilization.* London: Thames and Hudson.

Glassow, Michael. 1972. "Changes in the Adaptations of Southwestern Basketmakers." In Mark Leone, ed., *Contemporary Archaeology.* Carbondale: Southern Illinois University Press. Pp. 289–302.

Glover, Ian G. 1977. "The Hoabhinian: Hunter-Gatherers or Early Agriculturalists in Southeast Asia?" In J. V. S. Megaw, ed., *Hunters, Gatherers, and First Farmers Beyond Europe.* Atlantic Highlands, N.J.: Humanities Press. Pp. 145–166.

Golson, Jack. 1977. "No Room at the Top: Agricultural Intensification in the New Guinea Highlands." In J. Allen, J. Golson, and Rhys Jones, eds., *Sunda and Sahel.* New York: Academic Press. Pp. 602–638.

Goodall, Jane van Lawick. 1973. *In the Shadow of Man.* Boston: Houghton Mifflin.

Goodman, Jeffrey. 1980. *American Genesis.* New York: Summit Books.

Gorman, Chester A. 1969. "Hoabhinian: A Pebble-Tool Complex with Early Plant Associations in Southeast Asia." *Science* 163:671–673.

———. 1971. "Hoabhinian and After: Subsistence Patterns in Southeast Asia During the Late Pleistocene and Early Recent Periods." *World Archaeology* 2 (3):300–320.

———. 1977. "A Priori Models and Thai Prehistory: A Reconsideration of the Beginnings of Agriculture in Southeast Asia." In Charles A. Reed, ed., *Origins of Agriculture.* The Hague: Mouton. Pp. 321–355.

Gould, Richard A. 1977. *Puntutjarpa Rockshelter and Australian Desert Culture.* New York: American Museum of Natural History.

———. 1980. *Living Archaeology.* Cambridge: Cambridge University Press.

———, ed. 1978. *Explorations in Ethnoarchaeology.* Albuquerque: University of New Mexico Press.

Grant, Michael. 1960. *The Romans.* London: Weidenfeld and Nicholson.

Grasiosi, Paolo. 1960. *Palaeolithic Art.* New York: Abrams.

Grayson, Donald K. 1983. *The Search for Human Antiquity.* New York: Academic Press.

Green, R. C. 1979. "Lapita." In Jesse D. Jennings, ed., *The Prehistory of Polynesia.* Cambridge: Harvard University Press. Pp. 27–60.

Gribben, J., ed. 1978. *Climatic Change.* Cambridge: Cambridge University Press.

Grootes, P. M. 1978. "Carbon-14 Time Scale Extended: Comparison of Chronologies." *Science* 200 (4337):11–15.

Groube, L. M. 1970. "The Origins and Development of Earthwork Fortifications in the Pacific." In R. C. Green and M. Kelly, eds., *Studies in Oceanic Culture History.* Hawaii: Bishop Museum. Pp. 133–164.

———. 1971. "Tonga, Lapita Pottery, and Polynesian Origins." *Journal of the Polynesian Society* 80:278–316.

Grove, David. 1973. "Olmec Altars and Myths." *Archaeology* 26:128–135.

Gurney, O. R. 1961. *The Hittites.* Baltimore: Pelican Books.

Hall, Kenneth R. 1985. *Maritime Trade and State Development in Early Southeast Asia.* Honolulu: University of Hawaii Press.

Hallam, Sylvia. 1975. *Fire and Hearth.* Canberra: Australian Institute of Aboriginal Studies.

Hamden, G. 1961. "The Evolution of Irrigation Agriculture in Egypt." *Arid Zone Research* 17:119–142.

Hammond, Norman. 1974. "Palaeolithic Mammalian Faunas and Parietal Art in Cantabria: A Comment on Freeman." *American Antiquity* 39:618–619.

———. 1978. *Cuello Project 1978: Interim Report.* New Brunswick, N.J.: Archaeological Research Program.

———. 1980a. "Early Maya Ceremonial at Cuello, Belize." *Antiquity* 54:176–190.

———. 1980b. "Prehistoric Human Utilization of the Savanna Environments of Middle and South America." In David R. Harris, ed., *Human Ecology in Savanna Environments.* New York: Academic Press. Pp. 73–106.

———. 1982. *Ancient Maya Civilization.* New Brunswick, N.J.: Rutgers University Press.

———, ed. 1973. *South Asian Archaeology.* London: Duckworth.

Hammond, Norman, and Miksicek, Charles H. 1981. "Ecology and Economy of a Formative Maya Site at Cuello, Belize." *Journal of Field Archaeology* 8:259–269.

Harden, Donald. 1962. *The Phoenicians.* London: Thames and Hudson.

Harding, A. F. 1983. "The Bronze Age in Central and Eastern Europe: Advances and Prospects." *Advances in World Prehistory* 2:1–50

———. 1984. *The Mycenaeans and Europe.* New York: Academic Press.

Harlan, Jack. 1967. "A Wild Wheat Harvest in Turkey." *Archaeology* 197–201.

Harlan, Jack, DeWet, John, and Stemler, Ann, eds. 1976. *Origins of African Plant Domestication.* The Hague: Mouton.

Harris, David R. 1978. "Alternative Pathways Toward Agriculture." In Charles A. Reed, ed., *The Origins of Agriculture.* The Hague: Mouton.

———, ed. 1980. *Human Ecology in Savanna Environments.* New York: Academic Press.

Harris, Marvin. 1968. *The Rise of Anthropological Theory.* New York: Crowell.

Harrison, Richard J. 1980. *The Beaker Folk.* London: Thames and Hudson.

Harrisson, Tom. 1957. "The Great Cave of Neah." *Man* 211:223–224.

Hatch, Elvin. 1973. *Theories of Man and Culture.* New York: Columbia University Press.

Haury, Emil. 1936. *The Mogollon Culture of Southwestern New Mexico.* Globe, Ariz.: Gila Pueblo.

———. 1976. *Hohokam, Desert Farmers and Craftsmen: Excavations at Snaketown.* Tucson: University of Arizona Press.

Haven, Samuel. 1856. *The Archaeology of the United States.* Washington, D.C.: Smithsonian Institution.

Hawkins, Gerald. 1965. *Stonehenge Decoded.* New York: Souvenir Press.

Haynes, C. Vance. 1964. "Fluted Projectile Points: Their Age and Dispersion." *Science* 145:1408–1413.

———. 1982. "Were Clovis Progenitors in Beringia?" In David M. Hopkins et al., eds., *Paleoecology of Beringia.* New York: Academic Press. Pp. 383–398.

Hays, T. R. 1984. "A Reappraisal of the Egyptian Predynastic." In J. Desmond Clark and Steven A. Brandt, eds., *From Hunters to Farmers.* Berkeley and Los Angeles: University of California Press. Pp. 65–73.

Heizer, R. F., and Berger, Rainer. 1970. "Radiocarbon Age of the Gypsum Cave." *Contributions of the University of California Archaeological Research Facility* 7:1–12.

Henderson, John S. 1981. *The World of the Ancient Maya.* Ithaca: Cornell University Press.

Hey, Richard L. 1975. *Geology of the Olduvai Gorge.* Berkeley and Los Angeles: University of California Press.

Higgs, Eric S., and Jarman, P. 1969. "Origins of Agriculture." *Antiquity* 43:31–41.

Higham, Charles F. W. 1972. "Initial Model Formation in Terra Incognita." In David L. Clarke, ed., *Models in Prehistory.* London: Methuen. Pp. 453–476.

———. 1984a. "Prehistoric Rice Cultivation in Southeast Asia." *Scientific American* 84:138–146.

———. 1984b. "The Ban Chiang Culture in Wider Perspective." *Proceedings of the British Academy.* In press.

Ho, Ping-Ti. 1969. "Loess and the Origins of Chinese Agriculture." *American Historical Review* 75:1–36.

Hockett, Charles F., and Ascher, Robert. 1964. "The Human Revolution." *Current Anthropology* 5 (3):135–168.

Hodder, Ian. 1982. *Symbolic and Structural Archaeology.* Cambridge: Cambridge University Press.

Hoffman, Michael A. 1979. *Egypt Before the Pharaohs.* New York: Knopf.

Hole, Frank, Flannery, Kent V., and Neely, J. A. 1969. *The Prehistory and Human Ecology of the Deh Luran Plain.* Ann Arbor, Mich.: Museum of Anthropology.

Hole, Frank, and Heizer, Robert F. 1973. *An Introduction to Prehistoric Archaeology.* 3rd ed. New York: Holt, Rinehart and Winston.

Hood, Sinclair. 1973. *The Minoans.* London: Thames and Hudson.

Hopkins, David M., et al., eds. 1982. *Paleoecology of Beringia.* New York: Academic Press.

Horton, D. R. 1978. "The Extinction of the Australian Megafauna." *Australian Institute of Aboriginal Studies Newsletter* 9:72–75.

Howell, F. Clark. 1957a. "Pleistocene Glacial Ecology and the Evolution of 'Classic' Neanderthal Man." *Southwestern Journal of Anthropology* 8:377–410.

———. 1957b. "The Evolutionary Significance of Variation and Varieties of 'Neanderthal' Man." *Quarterly Review of Biology* 32:330–347.

———. 1966. "Observations on the Earlier Phases of the European Lower Palaeolithic." *American Anthropologist* 68 (2):111–140.

———. 1974. *Early Man.* Chicago: Time-Life Books.

Howell, F. Clark, and Clark, J. Desmond. 1963. "Acheulian Hunter-Gatherers of Sub-Saharan Africa." *Viking Fund Publications in Anthropology* 36:458–533.

Hunwick, John D. 1971. "Songhay, Bornu and Hausaland in the Sixteenth Century." In Jacob F. Ajayi and Michael Crowder, eds., *History of West Africa,* vol. 1. London: Longmans. Pp. 120–157.

Huxley, Thomas H. 1863. *Man's Place in Nature.* London: Macmillan.

Huyen, Pham Minh. 1984. "Various Phases of the Development of Primitive Metallurgy in Viet Nam." In Donn Bayard, ed., *The Origins of Agriculture, Metallurgy, and the State in Mainland Southeast Asia.* Dunedin, New Zealand: University of Otago Press. Pp. 173–182.

Hyslop, John. 1984. *The Inca Road System.* New York: Academic Press.

Ikawa-Smith, Fumio. 1978. "Lithic Assemblages from the Early and Middle Upper Pleistocene Formations in Japan." In Alan Lyle Bryan, ed., *Early Man in America from a Circum-Pacific Perspective.* Edmonton: University of Alberta.

———. 1980. "Current Issues in Japanese Archaeology." *American Scientist* 68 (2):134–145.

Institute of Vertebrate Paleontology and Paleoanthropology, Chinese Academy of Sciences. 1981. *Atlas of Primitive Man in China.* New York: Van Nostrand Reinhold.

Irwin-Williams, Cynthia. 1968. *Early Man in North America.* Portales: Eastern New Mexico University Press.

———. 1973. "The Oshara Tradition: Origins of Anasazi Culture." *University of New Mexico Contributions in Anthropology* 4.

Irwin-Williams, Cynthia, and Haynes, C. Vance. 1970. "Climatic Change and Early Population Dynamics in the Southwestern United States." *Quaternary Research* 1 (1):59–71.

Isaac, Glynn Ll. 1977. *Olorgesaillie*. Chicago: University of Chicago Press.

———. 1978. "The Food-sharing Behavior of Protohuman Hominids." *Scientific American.*

———. 1981. "The Origin of Man." *Quarterly Review of Archaeology* 2:16.

Isaac, Glynn Ll., and Harris, J. W. K. 1978. "Archaeology." In M. D. Leakey and Richard E. Leakey, eds., *The Fossil Hominids and an Introduction to Their Context, 1968–1974.* Vol. 1, Koobi Fora Research Project. Oxford: Clarendon Press.

Isaac, Glynn Ll., and McCown, Elizabeth, eds. 1976. *Human Origins: Louis Leakey and the East African Evidence*. Menlo Park, Calif.: Benjamin.

Isbell, William, and Schreiber, Katherina J. 1978. "Was Huari a State?" *American Antiquity* 43:372–389.

Jacobsen, Thomas W. 1981. "Franchthi Cave and the Beginning of Village Settled Life in Greece." *Hesperia* 50:303–319.

Jacobson, Jerome. 1979. "Recent Developments in South Asian Prehistory and Protohistory." *Annual Review of Anthropology* 8:467–502.

Jacobsthal, P. 1944. *Early Celtic Art*. Oxford: Oxford University Press.

Jarrige, J., and Meadow, R. 1979. "The Antecedents of Civilization in the Indus Valley." *Scientific American* 240 (1):122–133.

Jennings, Jesse D. 1957. *Danger Cave*. Salt Lake City: University of Utah Press.

———. 1975. *The Prehistory of North America*. 2nd ed. New York: McGraw-Hill.

———, ed. 1969. *The Prehistory of Polynesia*. Cambridge: Harvard University Press.

———, ed. 1983. *Ancient Native Americans*. 2nd ed. 2 vols. New York: Freeman.

Jochim, Michael. 1981. *Strategies for Survival: Cultural Behavior in Ecological Context*. New York: Academic Press.

Johanson, Donald C., and Edey, Maitland A. 1981. *Lucy: The Beginnings of Humankind*. New York: Simon and Schuster.

Johanson, Donald C., and White, Tim. 1979. "A Systematic Assessment of Early African Hominids." *Science* 202:321–330.

Johnson, Paul. 1978. *The Civilization of Ancient Egypt*. London: Weidenfeld and Nicholson.

Jolly, Clifford. 1970. "The Seed-Eaters: A New Model of Hominid Differentiation Based on Baboon Analogy." *Man* 5:5–26.

Jones, Christopher. 1984. *Deciphering Maya Hieroglyphs*. Philadelphia: University Museum, University of Pennsylvania.

Jones, Peter R. 1980. "Experimental Butchery with Modern Stone Tools and Its Relevance for Palaeolithic Archaeology." *World Archaeology* 12 (2):153–165.

Joukowsky, Martha. 1981. *A Complete Manual of Field Archaeology*. Englewood Cliffs, N.J.: Prentice-Hall.

Jovanovic, Borislav. 1980. "The Origins of Copper Mining in Europe." *Scientific American* 242 (5):152–168.

Judd, Neil M. 1954. *The Material Culture of Pueblo Bonito*. Washington, D.C.: Smithsonian Institution.

———. 1964. *The Architecture of Pueblo Bonito*. Washington, D.C.: Smithsonian Institution.

Kalb, J. F., et al. 1984. "Early Hominid Habitation in Ethiopia." *American Scientist* 72:168–178.

Kano, Chiaki. 1979. *The Origins of the Chavín Culture*. Washington, D.C.: Dumbarton Oaks.

Keightley, David N. 1978. *Sources of Shang History: The Oracle Bone Inscriptions of Bronze Age China*. Berkeley and Los Angeles: University of California Press.

————. 1983. *The Origins of Chinese Civilization.* Berkeley and Los Angeles: University of California Press.

Kenyon, Kathleen. 1961. *Archaeology in the Holy Land.* London: Edward Benn.

Kidder, A. V. 1927. *An Introduction to the Study of Southwestern Archaeology, with a Preliminary Account of the Excavations at Pecos.* New Haven: Yale University Press.

Kiernan, F. A., and Fairbank, J. K. 1974. *Chinese Ways of Warfare.* Cambridge: Harvard University Press.

Kinley, M. I. 1963. *The Ancient Greeks.* London: Chatto and Windus.

Kirch, Patrick V. 1982. "Advances in Polynesian Prehistory: Three Decades in Review." *Advances in World Archaeology* 2:52–102.

Kirk, Ruth. 1975. *Hunters of the Whale.* New York: Morrow.

Kirkbride, Diana. 1968. "Beidha: Early Neolithic Village Life South of the Dead Sea." *Antiquity* 42:263–274.

————. 1975. "Umm Dabaghiyah 1974: A Fourth Preliminary Report." *Iraq* 37:3–10.

Kirkby, Anne V. T. 1973. *The Use of Land and Water Resources in the Past and Present Valley of Oaxaca.* Ann Arbor, Mich.: Museum of Anthropology.

Kitto, H. D. F. 1958. *The Greeks.* Baltimore: Pelican Books.

Klein, Jeffrey, et al. 1982. "Calibration of Radiocarbon Dates." *Radiocarbon* 24 (2):103–150.

Klein, Richard. 1969. *Man and Culture in the Late Pleistocene.* San Francisco: Chandler.

————. 1971. "The Pleistocene Prehistory of Siberia." *Quaternary Research* 2 (1):131–161.

————. 1979. "Stone Age Exploitation of Animals in Southern Africa." *American Scientist* 67:23–32.

————. 1984. "The Prehistory of Stone Age Herders in South Africa." In J. Desmond Clark and Steven A. Brandt, eds., *From Hunters to Farmers.* Berkeley and Los Angeles: University of California Press. Pp. 281–289.

Klein, Richard, and Cruz-Uribe, Katherine. 1984. *The Analysis of Animal Bones from Archaeological Sites.* Chicago: University of Chicago Press.

Kohl, P. 1975. "Carved Chlorite Vessels: A Trade in Finished Commodities in the Mid-Third Millennium." *Expedition* (Fall): 18–31.

————. 1978. "The Balance of Trade in Southwestern Asia in the Mid-Third Millennium B.C." *Current Anthropology* 19:463–492.

Kornietz, Ninelj L., and Solfer, Olga. 1984. "Mammoth Bone Dwellings on the North Russian Plain." *Scientific American* 251 (5):164–175.

Kramer, Samuel. 1963. *The Sumerians.* Chicago: University of Chicago Press.

Kroeber, A. L., and Kluckhohn, Clyde. 1952. *Culture: A Critical Review of Concepts and Definitions.* Cambridge, Mass.: Peabody Museum.

Kurtén, Björn. 1968. *Pleistocene Mammals of Europe.* Chicago: Aldine.

Kurtén, Björn, and Anderson, E. 1980. *Pleistocene Mammals of North America.* New York: Columbia University Press.

Laitman, Jeffrey T. 1984. "The Anatomy of Human Speech." *Natural History* 93 (9):20–27.

Lamberg-Karlovsky, C. C. 1973. "Urban Interactions on the Iranian Plateau: Excavations at Tepe Yahya 1967–1973." *Proceedings of the British Academy* 59:5–43.

————. 1978. "The Proto-Elamites and the Iranian Plateau." *Antiquity* 52:114–120.

Lancaster, Jane, and Whitten, Phillip. 1980. "Family Matters." *The Sciences* 1:10–15.

Lanning, Eric P. 1967. *Peru Before the Incas.* Englewood Cliffs, N.J.: Prentice-Hall.

Laughlin, William S. 1980. *Aleuts, Survivors of the Bering Land Bridge.* New York: Holt, Rinehart and Winston.

Laughlin, William S., and Marsh, G. H. 1954. "The Lamellar Flake Manufacturing Site on Anangula Island in the Aleutians." *American Antiquity* 20:27–39.

Laughlin, William S., Marsh, G. H., and Harper, A. B., eds. 1979. *The First Americans: Origins, Affinities and Adaptations.* New York: Gustav Fisher.

Laville, Henri, Rigauls, Jean-Philippe, and Sackett, James. 1980. *Rock Shelters of the Perigord.* New York: Academic Press.

Leakey, L. S. B. 1951. *Olduvai Gorge, 1931–1951.* Cambridge: Cambridge University Press.

Leakey, M. D. 1971. *Olduvai Gorge,* vol. 3. Cambridge: Cambridge University Press.

———. 1978. "Pliocene Footprints at Laetoli, Tanzania." *Antiquity* 52:133.

Leakey, M. D., et al. 1976. "Fossil Hominids from the Laetoli Beds." *Nature* 262:460–466.

Leakey, Richard, and Lewin, Roger. 1977. *Origins.* New York: Dutton.

Lee, J. E. 1866. *The Lake Dwellings of Switzerland and Other Parts of Europe.* London: John Murray.

Lee, Richard B. 1979. *The !Kung San.* Cambridge: Cambridge University Press.

Lee, Richard B., and DeVore, Irven, eds. 1976. *Kalahari Hunter-Gatherers.* Cambridge: Harvard University Press.

Lehmann, Johannes. 1977. *The Hittites: People of the Thousand Gods.* London: Collins.

Leroi-Gourhan, H. 1965. *Treasures of Palaeolithic Art.* New York: Abrams.

———. 1984. *The Dawn of European Art: An Introduction to Palaeolithic Cave Painting.* Cambridge: Cambridge University Press.

Levetzion, Nehemiah. 1973. *Ancient Ghana and Mali.* London: Methuen.

Lewin, Roger. 1984. *Human Evolution.* Oxford: Blackwell Scientific Publications.

Lewis, David. 1972. *We the Navigators.* Honolulu: University of Hawaii Press.

Lewis-Williams, David. 1981. *Believing and Seeing: Symbolic Meanings in Southern San Rock Paintings.* New York: Academic Press.

Lhote, Henri. 1959. *The Search for the Tassili Frescoes.* London: Hutchinson University Library.

Lipe, William D. 1978. "The Southwest." In Jesse D. Jennings, ed., *Ancient Native Americans.* San Francisco: Freeman. Pp. 403–454.

Livingstone, Sir R., trans. 1943. *Thucydides' History of the Peloponnesian War.* Cambridge: Oxford University Press.

Lloyd, Seton. 1967. *Early Highland Peoples of Anatolia.* New York: McGraw-Hill.

———. 1978. *The Archaeology of Mesopotamia.* London: Thames and Hudson.

———. 1980. *Foundations in the Dust.* London: Thames and Hudson.

———. 1983. *The Archaeology of Mesopotamia.* 2nd ed. London: Thames and Hudson.

Lovejoy, G. O. 1981. "The Origin of Man." *Science* 211:341–350.

———. 1984. "The Natural Detective." *Natural History* 93 (10):24–28.

Luce, J. V. 1973. *Atlantis.* New York: McGraw-Hill.

Lynch, Thomas F. 1978. "The South American Paleo-Indians." In J. D. Jennings, ed., *Ancient Native Americans.* San Francisco: Freeman. Pp. 455–490.

———, ed. 1980. *Guitarrero Cave.* New York: Academic Press.

Lyons, Thomas R., and Avery, Thomas. 1977. *Remote Sensing: A Handbook for Archaeologists and Cultural Resource Managers.* Washington, D.C.: National Park Service.

MacNeish, Richard, ed. 1970. *The Prehistory of the Tehuacán Valley.* Austin: University of Texas Press.

———. 1971. "Early Man in the Andes." *Scientific American* (4):36–46.

———. 1978. *The Science of Archaeology.* North Scituate, Mass.: Duxbury Press.

———. 1979. "Earliest Man in the New World and Its Implications for Soviet-American Archaeology." *Arctic Anthropology* 16 (1):2–15.

———. 1983. "Mesoamerica." In Richard Shutler, Jr., ed., *Early Man in the New World.* Beverly Hills: Sage Publications. Pp. 125–136.

MacNeish, Richard, et al. 1980. *The Prehistory of the Ayacucho Basin, Peru.* Ann Arbor: University of Michigan Press.

MacNeish, Richard, and Nelhen-Terner, Antoinette. 1983. "The Pre-Ceramic of Mesoamerica." *Journal of Field Archaeology* 10 (1):71–84.

Malinowski, Bronislaw. 1922. *Argonauts of the Western Pacific.* London: Routledge and Kegan Paul.

Malthus, Thomas Henry. 1978. *An Essay on the Principle of Population.* London: J. Johnson.

Mangelsdorf, Paul C., MacNeish, Richard M., and Gallinat, Walton C. 1964. "Domestication of Corn." *Science* 143:538–545.

Marcus, Joyce. 1973. "Territorial Organization of the Lowland Maya." *Science* 180:911–916.

Maringer, J., and Bandi, H. G. 1953. *Art in the Ice Age.* New York: Praeger.

Marks, A. E. 1983. "The Middle to Upper Palaeolithic Transition in the Levant." *Advances in World Prehistory* 2:51–98.

Marquardt, William H. 1978. *Advances in Archaeological Seriation.* Vol. 1, Advances in Archaeological Method and Theory. New York: Academic Press.

Marshack, Alexander. 1972. *The Roots of Civilization.* New York: McGraw-Hill.

———. 1975. "Exploring the Mind of Ice Age Man." *National Geographic* 154:62–89.

Martin, Kay, and Voorhies, Barbara. 1975. *The Female of the Species.* New York: Columbia University Press.

Martin, Paul. 1973. "The Discovery of America." *Science* 179:969–974.

Martin, Paul, and Plog, Fred. 1973. *The Archaeology of Arizona.* Garden City, N.Y.: Natural History Press.

Martin, Paul, and Wright, H. E. 1967. *Pleistocene Extinctions: The Search for a Cause.* New Haven: Yale University Press.

Mason, Ronald J. 1981. *Great Lakes Archaeology.* New York: Academic Press.

Maxwell, Moreau S., ed. 1976. *Eastern Arctic Prehistory: Paleo-Eskimo Problems.* Washington, D.C.: Society for American Archaeology.

McBurney, C. B. M. 1976. *Early Man in the Soviet Union.* London: British Academy.

McIntosh, Susan Keech, and McIntosh, Roderick J. 1981. "West African Prehistory." *American Scientist* 69:602–613.

Meacham, William. 1977. "Continuity and Local Evolution in the Neolithic of South China: A Non-Nuclear Approach." *Current Anthropology* 18:419–440.

Megaw, J. V. S. 1970. *Art of the European Iron Age.* Bath: John Baker.

Meggers, Betty. 1973. *Prehistoric America.* Chicago: Aldine.

Melisauskas, Saraunas. 1978. *European Prehistory.* New York: Academic Press.

Mellaart, James. 1967. *Çatal Hüyük.* New York: McGraw-Hill.

———. 1975. *The Earliest Civilizations of the Near East.* London: Thames and Hudson.

Mellars, Paul. 1973. "The Character of the Middle-Upper Palaeolithic in Southwestern France." In Colin Renfrew, ed., *The Explanation of Culture Change.* London: Duckworth. Pp. 255–276.

Mendelssohn, Kurt. 1974. *The Riddle of the Pyramids.* New York: Praeger.

Menozzi, P., Piazza, A., and Cavalli-Sforza, L. 1978. "Synthetic Maps of Human Gene Frequencies in Europeans." *Science* 201 (4358):786–792.

Michels, Joseph W. 1973. *Dating Methods in Archaeology.* New York: Seminar Press.

Millon, R., Drewitt, R. Bruce, and Cowgill, George. 1974. *Urbanization at Teotihuacán, Mexico.* Austin: University of Texas Press.

Mirambel, Lorena. 1978. "Tlapacoya: A Late Pleistocene Site in Central Mexico." In Alan Lyle Bryan, ed., *Early Man in America from a Circum-Pacific Perspective.* Edmonton:

University of Alberta. Pp. 221–230.

Mochanov, Iuri A. 1978. "Stratigraphy and Chronology of the Paleolithic of Northeast Asia." In Alan Lyle Bryan, ed., *Early Man in America from a Circum-Pacific Perspective*. Pp. 67–68. Edmonton: University of Alberta.

Moctezuma, Eduardo Matos. 1984. "The Great Temple of Tenochtitlan." *Scientific American* 251 (2):80–89.

Moore, Andrew. 1979. "A Pre-Neolithic Farming Village on the Euphrates." *Scientific American* 241 (2):62–70.

Moorehead, Alan. 1966. *The Fatal Impact*. London: Hamish Hamilton.

Morenz, Siegfried. 1973. *Egyptian Religion*. London: Macmillan.

Morison, Samuel Eliot. 1971. *The Northern Voyages*. Vol. 1, The European Discovery of America. New York: Oxford University Press.

Morlan, Richard E. 1983. "Pre-Clovis Occupation North of the Ice Sheets." In Richard Shutler, Jr., ed., *Early Man in the New World*. Beverly Hills: Sage Publications. Pp. 47–66.

Morlan, Richard E., and Cinq-Mars, Jacques. 1982. "Ancient Beringians: Human Occupation in the Late Pleistocene of Alaska and the Yukon Territory." In David M. Hopkins et al., eds., *Paleoecology of Beringia*. New York: Academic Press. Pp. 353–382.

Morris, J. Bayard, ed. 1962. *Five Letters of Cortes to the Emperor, 1519–26*. New York: Norton.

Moseley, Michael. 1975a. *The Maritime Foundations of Andean Civilization*. Menlo Park, Calif.: Cummings.

———. 1975b. "Chan Chan: Andean Alternative to the Preindustrial City." *Science* 187:219–225.

———. 1978. "The Evolution of Andean Civilization." In Jesse D. Jennings, ed., *Ancient Native Americans*. San Francisco: Freeman. Pp. 491–542.

Moseley, Michael, and MacKay, Carol. 1973. "Chan Chan: Peru's Ancient City of Kings." *National Geographic* 152:319–345.

Movius, H. L. 1977. *Excavation of the Abri Pataud, Les Eyziés (Dordogne)*. Cambridge, Mass.: Peabody Museum.

Mueller, James A., ed. 1975. *Sampling in Archaeology*. Tucson: University of Arizona Press.

Mughal, R. M. 1974. "New Evidence of the Early Harappan Culture from Jalipur, Pakistan." *Archaeology* 27 (2):106–113.

Muller, Jon D. 1978. "The Southeast." In Jesse D. Jennings, ed., *Ancient Native Americans*. San Francisco: Freeman. Pp. 222–326.

Muller-Beck, Hansjurgen. 1961. "Prehistoric Lake Dwellings." *Scientific American*

———. 1982. "Late Pleistocene Man in Northern Eurasia and the Mammoth-Steppe Biome." In David M. Hopkins et al., eds., *Paleoecology of Beringia*. New York: Academic Press. Pp. 329–352.

Mulvaney, Derek. 1975. *The Prehistory of Australia*. 2nd ed. Baltimore: Pelican Books.

Murdock, George Peter. 1968. "The Current Status of the World's Hunting and Gathering Peoples." In Richard Lee and Irven DeVore, eds., *Man the Hunter*. Chicago: Aldine. Pp. 13–20.

Murrill, Rupert Ivan. 1981. *Petralona Man*. Springfield, Ill.: Charles Thomas.

Napier, J. R. 1980. *Hands*. Cambridge: Cambridge University Press.

Nelson, Sarah. 1982. "Recent Progress in Korean Archaeology." *Advances in World Archaeology* 1:103–150.

Niederberger, C. 1979. "Early Sedentary Economy in the Basin of Mexico." *Science* 203:131–146.

Oakley, K. P. 1955. "Fire as a Palaeolithic Tool and Weapon." *Proceedings of the Prehistoric Society* 21:36–48.

———. 1964. *Frameworks for Dating Fossil Man.* Chicago: Aldine.

Oates, David, and Oates, Joan. 1976. *The Rise of Civilization.* Oxford: Elsevier Phaidon.

Oates, Joan. 1973. "The Background and Development of Early Farming Communities in Mesopotamia and the Zagros." *Proceedings of the Prehistoric Society* 39:147–181.

O'Brien, Eileen. 1984. "What Was the Acheulian Hand Ax?" *Natural History* 93 (3):23–28.

Ohel, Milla Y. 1979. "The Clactonian: An Independent Complex or an Integral Part of the Acheulian?" *Current Anthropology* 20 (2):685–726.

Oliver, Douglas. 1977. *Ancient Polynesian Society.* Honolulu: University of Hawaii Press.

Oliver, Roland, and Fagan, Brian M. 1975. *Africa in the Iron Age.* Cambridge: Cambridge University Press.

Oliver, Roland, and Fage, John D. 1963. *A Short History of Africa.* Baltimore: Pelican Books.

Olivier, Robert C. D. 1982. "Ecology and Behavior of Living Elephants: Bases for Assumptions Concerning the Extinct Woolly Mammoth." In David M. Hopkins et al., eds., *Paleoecology of Beringia.* New York: Academic Press. Pp. 291–306.

Otto, Martha Potter. 1980. "Hopewell Antecedents in the Adena Heartland." In David C. Brose and N'omi Greber, eds., *Hopewellian Archaeology.* Kent, Ohio: Kent State University Press. Pp. 9–14.

Ovey, C. D., ed. 1964. *The Swanscombe Skull: A Survey of Research on a Pleistocene Site.* London: Royal Anthropological Institute.

Pallotino, Massimo. 1977. *The Etruscans.* Translated by David Ridgeway. Harmondsworth: Alan Lane Press.

Parsons, Lee, and Price, Barbara. 1971. "Mesoamerican Trade and Its Role in the Emergence of Civilization." *Contributions of the University of California Archaeological Research Facility* 11:169–195.

Peake, Harold, and Fleure, Herbert J. 1927. *Peasants and Potters.* Oxford: Oxford University Press.

Pearson, Richard. 1981. "Social Complexity in Chinese Coastal Neolithic Sites." *Science* 213:1078–1088.

Pelto, Peter J. 1966. *The Nature of Anthropology.* Columbus, Ohio: Charles Merrill.

Penck, Albrecht, and Brückner, Edward. 1909. *Die Alpen im Eiszeitalter.* Leipzig: Tauchnitz.

Penniman, T. K. 1965. *A Hundred Years of Anthropology.* New York: Humanities Press.

Peringuey, Louis. 1911. *The Stone Age in South Africa.* Capetown: South African Museum.

Perkins, Dexter. 1964. "The Prehistoric Fauna from Shanidar, Iraq." *Science* 144:1565–1566.

Peyrony, Denis. 1934. "La Ferrassie." *Prehistoire* 3:1–54.

Pfeiffer, John E. 1978. *The Emergence of Man.* 3rd ed. New York: Harper and Row.

———. 1982. *The Creative Explosion.* New York: Harper and Row.

Phillips, E. D. 1972. "The Scythian Domination in Western Asia." *World Archaeology* 4:129–138.

Phillips, Patricia. 1980. *The Prehistory of Europe.* New Haven: Yale University Press.

Phillipson, David. 1977. *The Later Prehistory of Eastern and South Africa.* London: Heinemann.

———. 1984. *African Archaeology.* Cambridge: Cambridge University Press.

Pickersgill, Barbara. 1972. "Cultivated Plants as Evidence for Cultural Contacts." *American Antiquity* 37 (1):97–103.

Piggott, Stuart. 1965. *Ancient Europe.* Chicago: Aldine.

Pilbeam, David. 1980. "Miocene Hominoids and Hominid Origins." *American Journal of Physical Anthropology* 52:268.

————. 1984a. "The Descent of Hominoids and Hominids." *Scientific American* 250 (1):84–97.

————. 1984b. "Bones of Contention." *Natural History* 93 (6):2–4.

Plumley, N. J. B. 1969. *An Annotated Bibliography of the Tasmanian Aborigines*. London: Royal Anthropological Institute.

Polayny, Karl. 1975. "Traders and Trade." In Jeremy A. Sabloff and C. C. Lamberg-Karlovsky, eds., *Ancient Civilization and Trade*. Albuquerque: University of New Mexico Press. Pp. 133–154.

Pope, Michael. 1973. *Decipherment*. London: Thames and Hudson.

Possehl, Gregory L., ed. 1979. *Ancient Cities of the Indus*. Durham: University of North Carolina Press.

————, ed. 1982. *The Harappan Civilisation*. London: Aris & Phillips.

Postgate, Nicholas. 1977. *The First Empires*. Oxford: Elsevier Phaidon.

Potts, Richard. 1984. "Home Bases and Early Hominids." *American Scientist* 72:338–347.

Powers, William R., and Hamilton, Thomas D. 1978. "Dry Creek: A Late Pleistocene Human Occupation in Central Alaska." In Alan Lyle Bryan, ed., *Early Man in America from a Circum-Pacific Perspective*. Edmonton: University of Alberta. Pp. 72–78.

Pozorski, Thomas. 1983. "The Caballo Muerto Complex and Its Place in the Andean Chronological Sequence." *Annals of the Carnegie Museum* 52:1–40.

Premack, Ann James, and Premack, David. 1972. "Teaching Language to an Ape." *Scientific American* 241 (1):92–99.

Prescott, William H. 1847. *History of the Conquest of Peru*. New York: Everyman's.

Prickett, Nigel, ed. 1983. *The First 1000 Years: Regional Perspectives in New Zealand Archaeology*. Palmerston North: New Zealand Archaeological Association.

Proulx, Donald L. 1968. *An Archaeological Survey of the Nepena Valley, Peru*. Amherst: University of Massachusetts, Department of Anthropology Research Reports, no. 2.

————. 1973. *Archaeological Investigations in the Nepena Valley, Peru*. Amherst: University of Massachusetts Press.

————. 1983a. "The Nasca Style." In Lois Katz, ed., *Art of the Andes: Pre-Columbian Sculptured and Painted Ceramics from the Arthur M. Sackler Collections*. Washington, D.C.: Arthur M. Sackler Foundation. Pp. 87–104.

————. 1983b. "Tiahuanaco and Huari." In Lois Katz, ed., *Art of the Andes: Pre-Columbian Sculptured and Painted Ceramics from the Arthur M. Sackler Collection*. Washington, D.C.: Arthur M. Sackler Foundation. Pp. 107–114.

Puleston, Dennis. 1971. "An Experimental Approach to the Function of Maya Chultuns." *American Antiquity* 36:322–335.

Raab, Mark L., and Goodyear, Albert C. 1984. "Middle Range Theory in Archaeology: A Critical Review of Origins and Applications." *American Antiquity* 49:255–268.

Raikes, Robert. 1967. *Water, Weather, and Prehistory*. London: John Baker.

Rak, Yoel. 1983. *The Australopithecine Face*. New York: Academic Press.

Ranov, V. A., and Davis, R. S. 1979. "Toward a New Outline of the Soviet Central Asian Paleolithic." *Current Anthropology* 20 (2):249–270.

Rathje, William L. 1971. "The Origin and Development of Classic Maya Civilization." *American Antiquity* 36:275–285.

————. 1972. "Praise the Gods and Pass the Metates: A Hypothesis of the Development of Lowland and Rainforest Civilizations in Mesoamerica." In Mark P. Leone, ed., *Contemporary Archaeology*. Carbondale: Southern Illinois University Press. Pp. 365–392.

Raymond, J. Scott. 1981. "The Maritime Foundations of Andean Civilization: A Reconsideration of the Evidence." *American Antiquity* 46:806–820.

Redman, Charles L., ed. 1973. *Research and Theory in Current Archaeology.* New York: Wiley Interscience.

———. 1978. *The Rise of Civilization: From Early Farmers to Urban Society in the Ancient Near East.* San Francisco: Freeman.

Renault, Mary. 1963. *The King Must Die.* New York: Random House.

Renfrew, A. C., and Wagstaff, J. M., eds. 1982. *An Island Polity: The Archaeology of Exploitation in Melos.* Cambridge: Cambridge University Press.

Renfrew, Colin. 1967. "Colonialism and Megalithismus." *Antiquity* 41:276–288.

———. 1970. "The Tree-Ring Calibration of Radiocarbon: An Archaeological Evaluation." *Proceedings of the Prehistoric Society* 36:280–311.

———. 1972. *The Emergence of Civilization.* London: Methuen.

———. 1973. *Before Civilization.* New York: Knopf.

———. 1978. "Varna and the Social Context of Early Metallurgy." *Antiquity* 52:199–203.

———. 1983. "The Social Archaeology of Megaliths." *Scientific American* 249:152–163.

———, ed. 1984. *The Megalithic Monuments of Western Europe.* London: Thames and Hudson.

Renfrew, Colin, Dixon, J. E., and Cann, J. R. 1966. "Obsidian and Early Cultural Contact in the Near East." *Proceedings of the Prehistoric Society* 32:1–29.

Renfrew, Jane. 1973. *Palaeoethnobotany: The Prehistoric Food Plants of the Near East.* London: Methuen.

Rick, John W. 1980. *Prehistoric Hunters of the High Andes.* New York: Academic Press.

Rieu, E. V., trans. 1945. *Homer's Iliad.* Baltimore: Pelican Books.

Rodden, Robert J. 1962. "Excavations at the Early Neolithic Site at Nea Nikomedeia, Greek Macedonia (1961 Season)." *Proceedings of the Prehistoric Society* 28:267–288.

Roe, Derek. 1981. *The Lower and Middle Palaeolithic Periods in Britain.* London: Routledge and Kegan Paul.

Rognon, Pierre. 1981. "Interpretation paleoclimatique des changements d'environnements en Afrique du Nord et au Moyen Orient durant les 20 derniers millenaires." *Palaeoecology of Africa* 13:21–44.

Romer, John. 1981. *The Valley of Kings.* New York: Morrow.

Ronen, Avraham, ed. 1982. *The Transition from Lower to Middle Paleolithic and the Origins of Modern Man.* Oxford: British Archaeological Reports, International Series, no. 151.

Roth, H. Ling. 1887. "On the Origins of Agriculture." *Journal of the Royal Anthropological Institute* 16:102–136.

Rowe, John H. 1946. *Inca Culture at the Time of the Spanish Conquest.* Washington, D.C.: Smithsonian Institution.

———. 1962. *Chavín Art: An Inquiry into Its Form and Meaning.* New York: Museum of Primitive Art.

Rowe, John H., Collier, John, and Willey, Gordon R. 1950. "Reconnaissance Notes on the Site of Huari, near Ayacuchu, Peru." *American Antiquity* 16:120–137.

Rowlett, Ralph. 1967. "The Iron Age North of the Alps." *Science* 161:123–134.

Roys, R. 1972. *The Indian Background of Colonial Yucatán.* Norman: University of Oklahoma Press.

Rudenko, Sergei. 1970. *The Frozen Tombs of Siberia: The Pazyryk Burials of Iron Age Horsemen.* Translated by M. W. Thompson. Berkeley and Los Angeles: University of California Press.

Ruffle, John. 1977. *Heritage of the Pharaohs.* Oxford: Phaidon.

Rukang, Wu, and Shenglong, Liu. 1983. "Peking Man." *Scientific American* 248 (6):80–95.

Sabloff, Jeremy A., and Friedel, David A. 1984. *Cozumel: Late Maya Settlement Patterns.* New York: Academic Press.

Sabloff, Jeremy A., and Lamberg-Karlovsky, C. C., eds. 1975. *Ancient Civilization and Trade*. Albuquerque: University of New Mexico Press.

Sahlins, Marshall, and Service, Elman, eds. 1960. *Evolution and Culture*. Ann Arbor: University of Michigan Press.

Salmon, M. 1982. *The Philosophy of Archaeology*. New York: Academic Press.

Sanders, N. K. 1977. *The Sea People*. London: Thames and Hudson.

Sanders, William T. 1965. *The Cultural Ecology of the Tehuacán Valley*. University Park: Pennsylvania State University Press.

Sanders, William T., and Price, Barbara J. 1968. *Mesoamerica: The Evolution of a Civilization*. New York: Random House.

Sanders, William T., et al. 1970. *The Natural Environment: Contemporary Occupation and Sixteenth Century Population of the Valley: Teotihuacán Valley Project Final Report*. University Park: Pennsylvania State University Press.

Sanders, William T., Parsons, Jeffrey R., and Santley, Robert S. 1979. *The Basin of Mexico: Ecological Processes in the Evolution of a Civilization*. New York: Academic Press.

Sanders, William T., and Webster, David. 1978. "Unilinealism, Multilinealism, and the Evolution of Complex Societies." In Charles L. Redman et al., eds., *Social Archaeology*. New York: Academic Press. Pp. 249–302.

Sarich, Vincent. 1971. "A Molecular Approach to the Problem of Human Origins." In Phyllis Dolhinow and Vincent Sarich, eds., *Background for Man*. Boston: Little, Brown. Pp. 60–81.

Sauer, Carl O. 1952. *Agricultural Origins and Dispersals*. New York: American Geographical Society.

Schaller, George B. 1971. *Serengeti: A Kingdom of Predators*. New York: Knopf.

———. 1972. *The Serengeti Lion*. Chicago: University of Chicago Press.

Schapera, Isaac. 1930. *The Khoisan Peoples of South Africa*. New York: Humanities Press.

Schiffer, Michael. 1976. *Behavioral Archaeology*. New York: Academic Press.

———. 1983. "Towards the Identification of Site Formation Processes." *American Antiquity* 48:675–706.

Schiffer, Michael, and House, John. 1977. *The Cache River Archaeological Project*. Fayetteville: Arkansas Archaeological Survey.

Schmandt-Besserat, D. 1978. "The Earliest Precursor of Writing." *Scientific American* 238 (6):50–59.

Scudder, Thayer. 1962. *The Ecology of the Gwembe Tonga*. Manchester, England: Manchester University Press.

———. 1971. *Gathering Among African Woodland Savannah Cultivators*. Lusaka: University of Zambia.

Service, Elman. 1962. *Primitive Social Organization*. New York: Random House.

———. 1975. *The Origins of the State and Civilization*. New York: Norton.

Sharer, Robert J., and Ashmore, Wendy. 1979. *Fundamentals of Archaeology*. Menlo Park, Calif.: Benjamin-Cummings.

Sharp, Andrew. 1957. *Ancient Voyagers in the Pacific*. Baltimore: Pelican Books.

Shaw, Thurstan. 1978. *Nigeria*. London: Thames and Hudson.

Shawcross, Kathleen. 1967. "Fern Root and Eighteenth-Century Maori Food Production in Agricultural Areas." *Journal of the Polynesian Society* 76:330–352.

Shawcross, Wilfred. 1969. "Archaeology with a Short, Isolated Time-Scale: New Zealand." *World Archaeology* 1 (2):184–199.

Shinnie, Peter. 1967. *Meroe*. London: Thames and Hudson.

Shipman, Pat. 1984. "Scavenger Hunt." *Natural History* 93 (4):20–28.

Shutler, Richard, Jr., ed. *Early Man in the New World*. 1983. Beverly Hills: Sage Publications.

Silverberg, Robert. 1968. *The Mound Builders of Ancient America.* New York: New York Graphic Society.

Simons, Elwyn. 1984. "Dawn Ape of the Fayum." *Natural History* 93 (5):18–20.

Singer, Ronald, et al. 1973. "Clacton-on-Sea, Essex: Report on Excavations 1969–1970." *Proceedings of the Prehistoric Society* 39:6–74.

Smith, Andrew B. 1984. "Origins of the Neolithic in the Sahara." In J. Desmond Clark and Steven A. Brandt, eds., *From Hunters to Farmers.* Berkeley and Los Angeles: University of California Press. Pp. 84–92.

Smith, Bruce D. 1975. *Middle Mississippian Exploitation of Animal Populations.* Ann Arbor: Museum of Anthropology.

———. 1978a. "Variations in Mississippian Settlement Patterns." In Bruce D. Smith, ed., *Mississippian Settlement Patterns.* New York: Academic Press. Pp. 479–503.

———, ed. 1978b. *Mississippian Settlement Patterns.* New York: Academic Press.

Solecki, Ralph. 1972. *Shanidar: The Humanity of Neanderthal Man.* Baltimore: Pelican Books.

Solheim, William. 1971. "An Earlier Agricultural Revolution." *Scientific American* 133 (11):34–51.

Sollas, W. J. 1910. *Ancient Hunters.* London: Macmillan.

Spencer, Herbert. 1855. *Social Statistics.* London: Macmillan.

Spooner, Brian, ed. 1972. *Population Growth: An Anthropological Perspective.* Cambridge: MIT Press.

Stanford, Dennis. 1983. "Pre-Clovis Occupation South of the Ice Sheets." In Richard Shutler, Jr., ed., *Early Man in the New World.* Beverly Hills: Sage Publications. Pp. 65–72.

Steindorff, George, and Steele, Keith. 1954. *When Egypt Ruled the East.* Chicago: University of Chicago Press.

Steward, Julian. 1970. *A Theory of Culture Change.* Urbana: University of Illinois Press.

Steward, Julian, et al. 1955. *Irrigation Civilizations: A Comparative Study.* Washington, D.C.: Pan American Union.

Stoltman, James B. 1978. "Temporal Models in Prehistory: An Example from Eastern North America." *Current Anthropology* 19:703–746.

Street, F. Alayne. 1980. "Ice Age Environments." In Andrew Sherratt, ed., *The Cambridge Encyclopaedia of Archaeology.* New York: Cambridge University Press and Crown Publishers. Pp. 52–56.

Struever, Stuart, ed. 1971. *Prehistoric Agriculture.* Garden City, N.Y.: Natural History Press.

Struever, Stuart, and Holton, Felicia Antonelli. 1979. *Koster: Americans in Search of Their Past.* New York: Anchor Press/Doubleday.

Struever, Stuart, and Houart, Gail. 1968. "An Analysis of the Hopewell Interaction Sphere." In Edwin Wilmsen, ed., *Social Exchange and Interaction.* Ann Arbor, Mich.: Museum of Anthropology. Pp. 47–49.

Suess, Hans. 1965. "Secular Variations of the Cosmic-Ray-Produced Carbon 14 in the Atmosphere." *Journal of Geophysical Research* 70:23–31.

Symon, Becky A., and Cybulski, Jerome, eds. 1981. *Homo Erectus.* Toronto: University of Toronto Press.

Tanner, N. M. 1981. *On Becoming Human.* London: Cambridge University Press.

Taylor, R. E., and Meighan, C. W., eds. 1978. *Chronologies in New World Archaeology.* New York: Academic Press.

Taylour, Lord William. 1969. *The Mycenaeans.* London: Thames and Hudson.

Te-k'un, Cheng. 1960. *Shang China.* Vol. 2, Archaeology in China. Cambridge, England: Heffers.

Tello, Julio C. 1943. "Discovery of the Chavín Culture in Peru." *American Antiquity* 9:135–160.

Terrace, H., Petitto, L., Sanders, R., and Bever, T. 1979. "Can an Ape Create a Sentence?" *Science* 206:891–902.

Thom, Alexander. 1974. "Stonehenge." *Journal for the History of Astronomy* 5 (2):71–89.

Thomas, David. 1973. *Archaeology*. New York: Holt, Rinehart and Winston.

———. 1983. *The Archaeology of Monitor Valley 2: Gatecliff Shelter*. New York: American Museum of Natural History.

Thompson, J. E. S. 1950. *Maya Hieroglyphic Writing: Introduction*. Washington, D.C.: Carnegie Institution.

Tobias, Philip V. 1967. *Olduvai Gorge*, vol. 2. Cambridge: Cambridge University Press.

Trigger, Bruce C. 1968. *Beyond History*. New York: Holt, Rinehart and Winston.

———. 1980. *Gordon Childe: Revolutions in Archaeology*. London: Thames and Hudson.

Tringham, Ruth. 1971. *Hunters, Fishers, and Farmers of Eastern Europe: 6000–3000 B.C.* London: Hutchinson University Library.

Tringham, Ruth, et al. 1980. "The Early Agricultural Site of Selevac, Yugoslavia." *Archaeology* 33 (2):24–32.

Trinkhaus, Erik, ed. 1983a. *The Mousterian Legacy*. Oxford: British Archaeological Reports.

———. 1983b. *The Shanidar Neanderthals*. New York: Academic Press.

Trinkhaus, Erik, and Howell, W. W. 1979. "The Neanderthals." *Scientific American* 241:118–133.

Trump, David. 1980. *The Prehistory of the Mediterranean*. New Haven: Yale University Press.

Turekian, K. K., ed. 1971. *Late Cenozoic Glacial Ages*. New Haven: Yale University Press.

Turner, B. L., II, and Harrison, Peter D. 1981. "Prehistoric Raised-Field Agriculture in the Maya Lowlands." *Science* 213 (4506):399–405.

Tuttle, Russell. 1969. "Knuckle-Walking and the Problem of Human Origins." *Science* 166:953.

———, ed. 1972. *The Functional and Evolutionary Biology of Primates*. Chicago: Aldine-Atherton.

Ucko, Peter J., and Dimbleby, G. W., eds. 1969. *The Domestication and Exploitation of Plants and Animals*. London: Duckworth.

Ucko, Peter J., and Rosenfeld, A. 1967. *Prehistoric Art*. London: Thames and Hudson.

Vadya, Andrew P. 1959. "Polynesian Cultural Distribution in New Perspective." *American Anthropologist* 61:817–828.

Valliant, G. C. 1941. *The Aztecs of Mexico*. New York: Doubleday.

Vavilov, N. I. 1951. "Phytogeographic Basis of Plant Breeding." *Chronica Botanica* 13:14–54.

Vickers, Michael. 1977. *The Roman World*. Oxford: Elsevier Phaidon.

Villa, Paola. 1983. *Terra Amata and the Middle Pleistocene Archaeological Record of Southern France*. Berkeley and Los Angeles: University of California Press.

Vinnecombe, Patricia. 1976. *People of the Eland*. Pietermaritzburg: Natal University Press.

von Däniken, Erich. 1970. *Chariots of the Gods*. New York: Bantam.

Warren, Peter. 1975. *The Aegean Civilizations*. Oxford: Elsevier Phaidon.

———. 1984. "Knossos: New Excavations and Discoveries." *Archaeology* 37 (4):48–57.

Washburn, Sherwood. 1967. "Behavior and the Origin of Man." *Proceedings of the Royal Anthropological Institute* 97:21–27.

Washburn, Sherwood, and Moore, Ruth. 1980. *Ape into Man.* Boston: Little, Brown.

Waterbolk, H. T. 1968. "Food Production in Europe." *Science* 162:1093–1102.

Watson, Patty J., ed. 1969. *The Prehistory of Salts Cave, Kentucky.* Springfield: Illinois State Museum.

Watson, Patty J., LeBlanc, Steven, and Redman, Charles L. 1971. *Explanation in Archeology: An Explicit Scientific Approach.* New York: Columbia University Press.

Watson, Patty J., Le Blanc, Steven, and Redman, Charles L. 1984. *Archeological Explanation: The Scientific Method in Archeology.* New York: Columbia University Press.

Watson, Richard A., and Watson, Patty J. 1969. *Man and Nature: An Anthropological Essay in Human Ecology.* New York: Harcourt, Brace and World.

Wauchope, Robert. 1962. *Lost Tribes and Sunken Continents.* Chicago: University of Chicago Press.

Weaver, Muriel Porter. 1981. *The Aztecs, Maya, and Their Predecessors.* 2nd ed. New York: Academic Press.

Webb, Clarence H. 1968. "The Extent and Content of Poverty Point Culture." *American Antiquity* 33:297–331.

Weidenreich, Franz. 1946. *Apes, Giants, and Men.* Chicago: University of Chicago Press.

Weiss, Mark L., and Mann, Alan E. 1985. *Human Biology and Behavior.* 4th ed. Boston: Little, Brown.

Wells, Peter. 1981. *Culture Contact and Culture Change.* Cambridge: Cambridge University Press.

———. 1984. "An Early Iron Age Community in Central Europe. *Scientific American* 249 (6):68–93.

Wendorf, Fred, ed. 1968. *The Prehistory of Nubia.* Dallas: Southern Methodist University Press.

Wendorf, Fred, and Schild, Romuald. 1980. *Prehistory of the Eastern Sahara.* New York: Academic Press.

———. 1981. "The Earliest Food Producers." *Archaeology* 34 (5):30–36.

Wertime, Theodore A., and Muhly, James D., eds. 1980. *The Coming of the Age of Iron.* New Haven: Yale University Press.

Wheat, Joe Ben. 1972. *The Olsen-Chubbock Site.* Washington, D.C.: Society for American Archaeology.

Wheatley, Paul. 1971. *The Pivot of the Four Quarters.* Chicago: Aldine.

———. 1975. "Satyarta in Suvarnadvipa: From Reciprocity to Redistribution in Ancient Southeast Asia." In Jeremy A. Sabloff and C. C. Lamberg-Karlovsky, eds., *Ancient Civilization and Trade.* Albuquerque: University of New Mexico Press. Pp. 227–284.

———. 1979. "Urban Genesis in Mainland Southeast Asia." In R. B. Smith and W. Watson, eds., *Early Southeast Asia.* Oxford: Oxford University Press. Pp. 288–303.

Wheeler, Sir Mortimer. 1954. *Archaeology from the Earth.* Oxford: Clarendon Press.

———. 1962. *The Indus Civilization.* 2nd ed. Cambridge: Cambridge University Press.

———. 1968. *Early India and Pakistan.* New York: Praeger.

White, J. C. 1982. *Ban Chiang: The Discovery of a Lost Bronze Age Civilization.* Philadelphia: University Museum, University of Pennsylvania.

White, J. Peter, and O'Connell, James. 1982. *A Prehistory of Australia, New Guinea, and Sahul.* Sydney: Academic Press.

White, Leslie. 1949. *The Science of Culture.* New York: Grove Press.

Wilcox, David R. 1980. "The Current Status of the Hohokam Concept." In D. E. Doyel and F. T. Plog, eds., *Current Issues in Hohokam Prehistory: Proceedings of a Symposium.* Tempe: Arizona State Museum. Pp. 236–243.

————. 1985. "The Tepiman Connection: A Model of Mesoamerican-Southwestern Interaction." In Randall H. McGuire and Francis Joan Mathier, eds., *Ripples in the Chichimec Sea*. Carbondale: Southern Illinois University Press. In press.

Willey, Gordon R. 1953. *Prehistoric Settlement in the Viru Valley, Peru*. Washington, D.C.: Smithsonian Institution.

————. 1966. *North and Middle America*. Vol. 1, An Introduction to American Archaeology. Englewood Cliffs, N.J.: Prentice-Hall.

————. 1971. *South America*. Vol. 2, An Introduction to American Archaeology. Englewood Cliffs, N.J.: Prentice-Hall.

Willey, Gordon R., and Sabloff, Jeremy A. 1980. *A History of American Archaeology*. 2nd ed. San Francisco: Freeman.

Williams, Leon Carlos. 1978–80. "Complejas de piramides con planta en U." *Revista del Museo Nacional* 44:95–110.

Williams, M. A. J. 1984. "Late Quaternary Prehistoric Environments in the Sahara." In J. D. Clark and Steven A. Brandt, eds., *From Hunters to Farmers*. Berkeley and Los Angeles: University of California Press. Pp. 74–83.

Wilson, David J. 1981. "Of Maize and Men: A Critique of the Maritime Hypothesis of State Origins on the Coast of Peru." *American Anthropologist* 83:931–120.

————. 1983. "The Origins and Development of Complex Prehispanic Society in the Lower Santa Valley, Peru: Implications for Theories of State Origins." *Journal of Anthropological Archaeology* 2:209–276.

Wilson, Edward O. 1980. *Sociobiology: The Abridged Edition*. Cambridge: Harvard University Press.

Wilson, J. A. 1951. *The Burden of Egypt*. Chicago: University of Chicago Press.

Windels, Ferdinand. 1965. *The Lascaux Cave Paintings*. London: Faber and Faber.

Wittfogel, Karl W. 1957. *Oriental Despotism: A Comparative Study of Total Power*. New Haven: Yale University Press.

Wolfe, Eric. 1959. *Sons of the Shaking Earth*. Chicago: University of Chicago Press.

Wolpert, Stanley. 1977. *A New History of India*. London: Oxford University Press.

Woolley, Sir Leonard. 1934. *The Royal Cemetery*. Vol. 2, Ur Excavations. London: British Museum.

Worsaae, J. J. A. 1849. *The Primeval Antiquities of Denmark*. London: John Murray.

Wright, Gary. 1971. "Origins of Food Production in Southwestern Asia: A Survey of Ideas." *Current Anthropology* 12:447–478.

Wright, Henry T., and Johnson, G. 1978. "Population, Exchange, and Early State Formation in Southwestern Iran." *American Anthropologist* 77:267–289.

Wright, R. V. S. 1971. *Archaeology of the Gallus Site, Koonalda Cave*. Canberra: Australian Institute of Aboriginal Studies.

————. 1977. *Stone Tools as Cultural Markers*. Canberra: Australian Institute of Aboriginal Studies.

Yarnell, Richard Asa. 1974. "Plant Food and Cultivation of the Salts Cave." In Patty J. Watson, ed., *Archeology of the Mammoth Cave Area*. New York: Academic Press. Pp. 113–122.

Yellen, John E. 1977. *Archaeological Approaches to the Present*. New York: Academic Press.

Yen, Douglas E. 1977. "Hoabhinian Horticulture: The Evidence and Questions from Northwest Thailand." In J. Allen, J. Golson, and Rhys Jones, eds., *Sunda and Sahel*. New York: Academic Press. Pp. 567–600.

Yesner, D. 1980. "Maritime Hunter-Gatherers: Ecology and Prehistory." *Current Anthropology* 21:727–750.

Zohary, Daniel. 1969. "The Progenitors of Wheat and Barley in Relation to Domestication and Agricultural Dispersal in the Old World." In Peter J. Ucko and G. W. Dimbleby, eds., *The Domestication and Exploitation of Plants and Animals.* London: Duckworth. Pp. 47–66.

Zubrow, Ezra. 1971. "Carrying Capacity and Dynamic Equilibrium in the Prehistoric Southwest." *American Antiquity* 36:127–138.

(Credits continued from page iv)

CHAPTER 2

Figures 2.1, 2.2, and 2.3: From Karl W. Butzer, *Archaeology as Human Ecology* (New York: Cambridge University Press, 1982). *Figure 2.4:* From Richard B. Lee and Irven De Vore (eds.), *Kalahari Hunter-Gatherers* (Cambridge: Harvard University Press, 1976). Reprinted by permission.

CHAPTER 3

Table 3.1: Adapted from *Glacial and Quaternary Geology* by R. F. Flint, © 1971, by permission of John Wiley & Sons, Inc. *Figures 3.1 and 3.2:* Adapted with permission from Karl W. Butzer, *Environment and Archeology*, 2nd ed. (Hawthorn, N.Y.: Aldine Publishing Company, 1971).

CHAPTER 4

Figure 4.1: By permission of Elwyn L. Simons, Center for the Study of Primate Biology and History, Duke University, Durham, North Carolina. *Figure 4.2:* Redrawn with permission of Macmillan Publishing Co., Inc. from *The Ascent of Man* by David Pilbeam. Copyright © 1972 by David Pilbeam. *Figure 4.3:* Photographed by Hugo van Lawick © National Geographic Society. *Figure 4.4:* (a) and (b) Redrawn with permission of Macmillan Publishing Co., Inc. from *The Ascent of Man* by David Pilbeam. Copyright © 1972 by David Pilbeam. (c) Redrawn with permission of Bantam Books, Inc. from *Monkeys and Apes* by Prudence Napier, copyright © 1972. All rights reserved. *Figure 4.6:* D. C. Panagos, Transvaal Museum. *Figure 4.7:* Courtesy of Alan R. Hughes, University of the Witwatersrand. *Figure 4.9:* Photograph by John Reader; courtesy of Mary Leakey and Laetoli Research Project. *Figure 4.10:* From Mark L. Weiss and Alan E. Mann, *Human Biology and Behavior: An Anthropological Perspective*, 2nd ed. Copyright © 1975, 1978 by Little, Brown and Company (Inc.). Reprinted by permission. *Figure 4.11:* Courtesy of the Trustees of the National Museums of Kenya. *Table 4.3:* Adapted by permission from Mark L. Weiss and Alan E. Mann, *Human Biology and Behavior: An Anthropological Perspective*, 2nd ed. Copyright © 1975, 1978 by Little, Brown and Company (Inc.). Reprinted by permission. *Figure 4.12:* Anthro-Photo/K. Cannon. *Figure 4.13:* Henry T. Bunn. *Figure 4.14:* Page 106 and page 107, top: Redrawn from Lowell Hess, *Early Man*, Life Nature Library, © 1965 Time Inc., by permission of the publisher, Time-Life Books Inc. Page 107, bottom: Adapted by permission from *Olduvai Gorge: Excavations in Beds I and II* by M. D. Leakey, © 1971 Cambridge University Press.

CHAPTER 5

Figure 5.1: Courtesy of the Trustees of the National Museums of Kenya. *Figure 5.2:* Cambridge Museum of Archaeology and Anthropology. *Figure 5.4:* Page 120, top: Adapted by permission from *Olduvai Gorge: Excavations in Beds I and II* by M. D. Leakey, © 1971 Cambridge University Press. Page 120, bottom: Adapted by permission of Doubleday and Company, Inc. from *Tools of the Old and New Stone Age* by Jacques Bordaz. Copyright © 1958, 1959 by The American Museum of Natural History. Copyright © 1970 by Jacques Bordaz. Page 121, top: Redrawn from Figure 26, *The Swanscombe Skull: A Survey of Research on a Pleistocene Site* (Occasional Paper No. 20, Royal Anthropological Institute of Great Britain and Ireland), by permission of the Society. Page 121, bottom left: From *The Distribution of Prehistoric Culture in Angola* by J. D. Clark, Companhia de Diamantes de Angola, Africa, 1966. Page 121, bottom right: Adapted from *Prehistory of Africa* by J. D. Clark, Thames and Hudson Ltd., London. *Figure 5.5:* © 1984 Eileen M. O'Brien. *Figure 5.6:* From H. L. Movius, Jr., "The Lower Paleolithic Structures of Southern and Eastern Asia," *Transactions of the American Philosophical Society*, Vol. 38, Pt. 4 (1948). Reprinted by permission of the Society and the author. *Figure 5.7:* Top: From Grahame Clark, *Aspects of Prehistory*. Copyright © 1970 by The Regents of the University of California. Reprinted by permission of the University of California Press. Bottom: Redrawn by permission from Ronald Singer et al., "Excavation of the Clactonian Industry," *Proceedings of the Prehistoric Society*, by permission of the Society. *Figure 5.8:* Courtesy of F. Clark Howell. *Figure 5.9:* By permission of Henry de Lumley, Laboratoire de Paléontologie Humaine et de Préhistoire, Marseilles. *Figures 5.10 and 5.11:* From *Mankind in the Making* by William Howells. Copyright © 1959, 1967 by William Howells. Reprinted by permission of Doubleday & Company, Inc. and Martin Secker & Warburg Ltd. *Figure 5.12:* Adapted by permission from Mark L. Weiss and Alan E. Mann, *Human Biology and Behavior: An Anthropological Perspective*, 2nd ed. Copyright © 1975, 1978 by Little, Brown and Company (Inc.). Reprinted by permission. *Figure 5.13:* Page 134, top: Adapted by permission of Doubleday & Company, Inc. from *Tools of the Old and New Stone Age* by Jacques Bordaz. Copyright © 1958, 1959 by The American Museum of Natural History. Copyright © 1970 by Jacques Bordaz. Page 134, bottom left, and page 135, bottom right: Redrawn from J. M. Coles and E. S. Higgs, *The Archaeology of Early Man* by permission of Faber and Faber Ltd. Page 134, bottom right: Redrawn from *Prehistory* by Derek Roe.

Courtesy the British Museum (Natural History). Page 135, top, middle left and center, and bottom center: Adapted from *The Old Stone Age* by F. Bordes. Copyright © 1968 by McGraw-Hill, Inc. Used by permission of McGraw-Hill Book Company and Weidenfeld & Nicolson Ltd. Page 135, middle right: Redrawn from *The Stone Age of Mt. Carmel* by D. A. E. Garrod and D. M. A. Bate by permission of Oxford University Press. Page 135, bottom left: Adapted from *Prehistory of Africa* by J. D. Clark, Thames and Hudson Ltd., London. *Figure 5.14:* From A. C. Blanc, "Torre in Pietra Saccopastore, Monte Circeo: On the Position of the Mousterian in the Pleistocene Sequence of the Rome Area," in *Hundert Jahre Neanderthaler* (Cologne: Bohlau Verlag, 1958).

CHAPTER 6

Figure 6.2: Anthro-Photo/M. Shostak. *Figure 6.4:* Top and bottom left: Adapted from *The Old Stone Age* by F. Bordes. Copyright © 1968 by McGraw-Hill, Inc. Used with permission of McGraw-Hill Book Company and Weidenfeld & Nicolson Ltd. Top right: Adapted by permission of Doubleday & Company, Inc. from *Tools of the Old and New Stone Age* by Jacques Bordaz. Copyright © 1958, 1959 by The American Museum of Natural History. Copyright © 1970 by Jacques Bordaz. Bottom right: Adapted by permission from *Le paléolithique supérieur en Périgord* by Denise de Sonneville-Bordes, Directeur de recherches au Centre national de la Recherche scientifique, Institut du Quaternaire, Université de Bordeaux. *Table 6.1:* Page 152, bottom, and page 153, bottom left: H. Breuil. Page 153, top and middle left: Adapted by permission from *Le paléolithique supérieur en Périgord* by Denise de Sonneville-Bordes, Directeur de recherches au Centre national de la Recherche scientifique, Institut du Quaternaire, Université de Bordeaux. Middle right: After Lowell Hess, *Early Man*, Life Nature Library, © 1965 Time Inc., by permission of the publisher, Time-Life Books Inc. Bottom right: Adapted from *The Old Stone Age* by F. Bordes. Copyright © 1968 by McGraw-Hill, Inc. Used with permission of McGraw-Hill Book Company and Weidenfeld & Nicolson Ltd. *Figures 6.5, 6.6, and 6.7:* Courtesy of Musée de l'Homme. *Figure 6.8:* © Alexander Marshack 1972. *Figure 6.9:* Top: From Richard G. Klein, *Man and Culture in the Late Pleistocene*. © 1969 by Chandler Publishing Company. By permission of Dun-Donnelley Publishing Corporation. Bottom: From *The Archeology of the USSR* by A. L. Mongait, Mir Publishers, Moscow. *Figure 6.10:* From C. B. M. McBurney, *Early Man in the Soviet Union*, Oxford University Press, 1976. Reprinted by permission of the British Academy. *Figure 6.11:* Reprinted by permission of Faber and Faber Ltd. from J. M. Coles and E. S. Higgs, *The Archeology of Early Man*.

CHAPTER 7

Figure 7.2: Redrawn with permission of the Glencoe Press from *Foundations of Archeology* by Jason W. Smith. Copyright © 1976 by Jason W. Smith. *Figure 7.3:* Redrawn from Gordon R. Willey, *An Introduction to American Archaeology*, Vol. I: North and Middle America, © 1966. Reprinted by permission of the author and Prentice-Hall, Inc., Englewood Cliffs, N.J. *Figure 7.4:* Redrawn from G. H. S. Bushnell, *The First Americans*, Thames and Hudson Ltd., London. *Figure 7.5:* Joe Ben Wheat, University of Colorado Museum. *Figure 7.6:* Redrawn by permission of McGraw-Hill Book Company from *Prehistory of North America* by Jesse D. Jennings. Copyright © 1968 by McGraw-Hill, Inc. *Figure 7.7:* Courtesy Field Museum of Natural History, Chicago. *Figure 7.8:* U.S. Information Agency No. 111-SC-33831 in National Archives Building. *Figure 7.9:* University of Alaska Museum.

CHAPTER 8

Figure 8.1: Top: Redrawn by permission of Doubleday & Company, Inc. from *Tools of the Old and New Stone Age* by Jacques Bordaz. Copyright © 1958, 1959 by The American Museum of Natural History. Copyright © 1970 by Jacques Bordaz. Bottom and right: Adapted from *The Old Stone Age* by F. Bordes. Copyright © 1968 by McGraw-Hill, Inc. Used by permission of McGraw-Hill Book Company and Weidenfeld & Nicolson Ltd. *Figure 8.2: South African Archeological Bulletin* and Professor v. Riet Lowe. *Figure 8.3: South African Archeological Bulletin* and Murray Schoonraal. *Figure 8.4:* F. Peron. *Figure 8.5:* Courtesy Robert Edwards, Aboriginal Arts Board. *Figure 8.6:* Redrawn by permission from Richard A. Gould, "The Archaeologist as Ethnographer," *World Archaeology* 3, 2 (1971), 143–177, Fig. 18.

CHAPTER 9

Figure 9.1: Adapted by permission from *The Material Culture of the Peoples of the Gwembe Valley* by Dr. Barrie Reynolds, published by Manchester University Press for the Livingstone Museum, Zambia. *Figure 9.2:* From Roger Lewin, *Human Evolution* (Oxford: Blackwell Scientific Publications Ltd., 1984). Reprinted by permission. *Figure 9.3:* S. von Heberstain. *Figure 9.4:* From Sonia Coles, *The Neolithic Revolution*, by permission of the Trustees of the British Museum (Natural History). *Figure 9.5:* Top left: Photo by Wyatt Davis, courtesy Museum of New Mexico (Neg. No. 44191). Top right: Photo by Tyler Dingee, courtesy Museum of New Mexico (Neg. No. 73453). Bottom: Photo by Tyler Dingee, courtesy Museum of New Mexico (Neg. No. 73449). *Figure 9.6:* Courtesy of the Trustees of the British Museum.

CHAPTER 10

Figure 10.2: Left: Redrawn from D. A. E. Garrod and D. M. A. Bate, *The Stone Age of M. Carmel* by permission of Oxford University Press. Right: From James Mellaart, *The Earliest Civilizations of the Near East.* Reprinted by permission of Thames and Hudson Ltd., London. *Figure 10.3:* Jericho Excavation Fund. *Figures 10.4 and 10.5:* Redrawn from James Mellaart, *Çatal Hüyük* by permission of Thames and Hudson Ltd., London. *Figure 10.6:* From *Proceedings of the Prehistoric Society* by permission of the Society. *Figure 10.8:* From *Prehistory* by Derek Roe, with permission of the Biologisch-Archaeologisch Institut der Rijksuniversiteit, Groningen, the Netherlands. *Figure 10.9:* From Grahame Clark, *World Prehistory,* 3rd ed., p. 140; © 1977 Cambridge University Press. *Figure 10.11:* From *Prehistory* by Derek Roe, with permission of Presses Universitaires de France. *Figure 10.12:* Neg. No. 39604, Department Library Services, American Museum of Natural History. *Figure 10.13:* Redrawn from *Ancient Europe* by Stuart Piggott, with permission of Edinburgh University Press. Copyright © Stuart Piggott, 1965.

CHAPTER 11

Figure 11.1: Photo Researchers/Carl Frank.

CHAPTER 12

Figures 12.3, 12.4, and 12.6: Reprinted by permission from *The Archeology of Ancient China,* 3rd ed. by Kwang-chih Chang (New Haven: Yale University Press, 1977). *Figure 12.7:* Sotheby Parke-Bernet. *Figure 12.9:* Courtesy Professor R. C. Green. *Figure 12.10:* Courtesy Field Museum of Natural History, Chicago. *Figures 12.11 and 12.12:* Reproduced by courtesy of The British Library.

CHAPTER 13

Figure 13.2: Redrawn from *Prehistory of North America* by Jesse D. Jennings. Copyright © 1968 by McGraw-Hill, Inc. Used with permission of McGraw-Hill Book Company. After P. C. Manglesdorf, R. S. MacNeish, and W. C. Galinat, *Harvard University Botanical Museum Leaflet,* vol. 17, no. 5, and J. Hawkes and L. Woolley, *Prehistory and the Beginnings of Civilization. Figure 13.3:* From Gordon R. Willey, *An Introduction to American Archaeology,* Vol. II: South America, © 1971. Reprinted by permission of Prentice-Hall, Inc., Englewood Cliffs, N.J. *Figure 13.4:* Drawing by Junius Bird. Courtesy of The American Museum of Natural History. *Figure 13.5:* Photograph by Thomas F. Lynch. *Figure 13.7:* Jonathan E. Reyman. *Figure 13.8:* Redrawn by permission of McGraw-Hill Book Company from *Prehistory of North America* by Jesse D. Jennings. Copyright © 1968 by McGraw-Hill, Inc. Used with permission of McGraw-Hill Book Company. After W. S. Webb, *University of Kentucky Reports in Anthropology and Archeology,* vol. 5, no. 2. *Figure 13.9:* (a) and (c) Werner Forman Archive; (b) Courtesy Field Museum of Natural History, Chicago. *Figure 13.10:* Artist's reconstruction by J. W. Hodge. Photograph courtesy of Illinois State Museum. *Figure 13.11:* Photo courtesy of Melvin L. Fowler.

CHAPTER 14

Figure 14.1: Adapted from *Physical Anthropology and Archaeology* by Clifford J. Jolly and Fred Plog. Copyright © 1976 by Alfred A. Knopf, Inc. Reprinted by permission of Alfred A. Knopf, Inc. *Figure 14.2:* From *The Rise of Civilization: From Early Farmers to Urban Society in the Ancient Near East* by Charles Redman. W. H. Freeman and Company. Copyright © 1978. Reprinted by permission.

CHAPTER 15

Figure 15.2: Courtesy of The Oriental Institute, University of Chicago. *Figure 15.3:* Fotoarchiv Hirmer Verlag München. *Figure 15.4:* Top: From *Early Mesopotamia and Iran* by Max E. Mallowan. Thames and Hudson Ltd., London. Bottom: Fotoarchiv Hirmer Verlag München. *Figure 15.5:* From Samuel Noah Kramer, "The Sumerians," *Scientific American,* October 1957. Reprinted with permission of W. H. Freeman and Company. Copyright © 1957 by Scientific American, Inc. All rights reserved. *Figure 15.6:* The University Museum, University of Pennsylvania.

CHAPTER 16

Figure 16.3: Photo Researchers/George Holton. *Figure 16.4:* Michael Holford, London. *Figure 16.5:* Photography by Egyptian Expedition, The Metropolitan Museum of Art. *Figure 16.7:* Courtesy of the Rhodesian National Tourist Board.

CHAPTER 17

Figure 17.2: Roger-Viollet Documentation générale photographique, Paris. *Figure 17.4:* The University Museum, University of Pennsylvania. *Figure 17.5:* Magnum Photos, Inc./M. Riboud.

CHAPTER 18

Figure 18.2: Left: From *Ancient Europe* by Stuart Piggott, with permission of Edinburgh University Press. Copyright © Stuart Piggott, 1965. Right: Courtesy of the Trustees of the British Museum. *Figure 18.3:* Ekdotike Athenon S. A. Athens. *Figure 18.4:* Fotoarchiv Hirmer Verlag München. *Figure 18.5:* Peter Clayton. *Figures 18.7 and 18.8:* Fotoarchiv Hirmer Verlag München. *Figure 18.9:* From *Ancient Europe* by Stuart Piggott, with permission of Edinburgh University Press. Copyright © Stuart Piggott, 1965. *Figure 18.10:* Adapted from *Writing* by David Diringer, with permission of Thames and Hudson Ltd., London. © David Diringer, 1962.

CHAPTER 19

Figures 19.1 and 19.2: From *Ancient Europe* by Stuart Piggott, with permission of Edinburgh University Press. Copyright © Stuart Piggott, 1965. *Figure 19.3:* Courtesy of Ashmolean Museum. *Figure 19.4:* Adapted from R. F. Tylecote, *Metallurgy in Archaeology: A Prehistory of Metallurgy in the British Isles* (London: E. Arnold Ltd., 1962). *Figure 19.6:* Photo Researchers/Georg Gerster. *Figure 19.8:* From *Ancient Europe* by Stuart Piggott, with permission of Edinburgh University Press. Copyright © Stuart Piggott, 1965. *Figure 19.10:* Courtesy of the Trustees of the British Museum.

CHAPTER 20

Figure 20.2: The Peabody Museum of Archaeology and Ethnology, Harvard University. *Figure 20.4:* Courtesy of Smithsonian Institution. *Figure 20.5:* The China Friendship Society; from Grahame Clark, *World Prehistory*, 3rd ed., p. 306; © 1977 Cambridge University Press.

CHAPTER 21

Figure 21.2: Franklin C. Graham. *Figures 21.3 and 21.4:* From Gordon R. Willey, *An Introduction to American Archaeology*, Vol. I: North and Middle America, © 1966. Reprinted by permission of the author and Prentice-Hall, Inc., Englewood Cliffs, N.J. *Figure 21.5:* From Robert D. Drennan, "Contextual Analysis of Ritual Paraphernalia from Formative Oaxaca," in Kent V. Flannery (ed.), *The Early Mesoameri-* *can Village* (Orlando, Fla.: Academic Press, 1976). *Figure 21.6:* Arizona State Museum, The University of Arizona/E. B. Sayles, photographer. *Figure 21.7:* From René Millon, *Urbanization at Teotihuacán, Mexico*, Vol. I: The Teotihuacán Map. Copyright © 1973 by René Millon. By permission of the author. *Figure 21.8:* Photograph copyright © Project El Mirador. Inset: Copyright © Richard Hansen. *Figure 21.9:* Photo Researchers/Carl Frank. *Figure 21.10:* Courtesy of Smithsonian Institution, National Anthropological Archives. *Figure 21.12:* The Peabody Museum of Archaeology and Ethnology, Harvard University. Photograph by Hillel Burger. *Figure 21.13:* Courtesy of Smithsonian Institution. *Figure 21.14:* Lesley Newhart. *Figure 21.15:* Franklin C. Graham. *Figure 21.16:* Lesley Newhart.

CHAPTER 22

Figure 22.1: From David J. Wilson, "The Origins and Development of Complex Prehispanic Society in the Lower Santa Valley, Peru: Implications for Theories of State Origins," *Journal of Anthropological Archeology* 2 (1983), 209–276. *Figure 22.3:* Right: Franklin C. Graham. *Figures 22.4 and 22.5:* The Peabody Museum of Archaeology and Ethnology, Harvard University. *Figure 22.6:* Lee Boltin. *Figure 22.7:* Earthwatch/Anne Paul. *Figure 22.8:* Anthro-Photo/M. Moseley. *Figure 22.9:* The Bettmann Archive Inc. *Figure 22.10:* Anthro-Photo/M. Moseley. *Figure 22.11:* Franklin C. Graham. *Figure 22.12:* Photo Researchers/George Holton.

Index